Arab Detroit

Arab Detroit

From Margin to Mainstream

Edited by

Nabeel Abraham

and

Andrew Shryock

Wayne State University Press Detroit

Great Lakes Books

A complete listing of the books in this series can be found at the back of this volume.

Philip P. Mason, Editor
Department of History, Wayne State University

Dr. Charles K. Hyde, Associate Editor
Department of History, Wayne State University

Manufactured in the United States of America.

04 03 5 4 3 2

Library of Congress Cataloging-in-Publication Data

Arab Detroit : from margin to mainstream / edited by Nabeel Abraham and Andrew Shryock.
p. cm.—(Great Lakes books)
Includes bibliographical references and index.
ISBN 0-8143-2811-3 (alk. paper)—ISBN 0-8143-2812-1 (pbk. : alk. paper)
1. Arab Americans—Michigan—Detroit—Social conditions—Miscellanea. 2. Arab Americans—Michigan—Detroit—Ethnic identity—Miscellanea. 3. Detroit (Mich.)—Ethnic relations—Miscellanea. 4. Arab Americans—Michigan—Detroit—Biography. I. Abraham, Nabeel. II. Shryock, Andrew. III. Series.
F574.D49 A653 2000
305.8927077434—dc21

99-054827

Contents

Acknowledgments

THIS BOOK IS the culmination of five years of research, exhibition, collaboration, and political effort. It began in 1994 as an ambitious National Endowment for the Humanities (NEH) Public Humanities Project, *Creating a New Arab World: A Century in the Life of the Arab Community in Detroit*. The project was sponsored by the Arab Community Center for Economic and Social Services (ACCESS) and directed by Sally Howell and Andrew Shryock. A dozen scholars contributed to the NEH project: Alixa Naff, Ali Jihad Racy, Barbara Aswad, Ann Rasmussen, Janice Terry, Michael Suleiman, Yvonne Haddad, Anton Shammas, Nabeel Abraham, William Lockwood, Yvonne Lockwood, and Andrew Shryock. Much of the research they did in Detroit has found its way onto the pages of this book. The NEH project photographers, Millard Berry and Bruce Harkness, deserve special mention. Their pictures, many of which are now emblematic of Arab Detroit, figure prominently in this volume.

Creating a New Arab World was a political victory for community activists who had been struggling, since the early 1980s, to ensure greater participation of Arab Americans in the public life of metropolitan Detroit. The narratives and images assembled during that project were put to further use by the National Museum of American History (Smithsonian Institution), which in 1995–96 sponsored its own photographic exhibition, *A Community between Two Worlds: Arab Americans in Greater Detroit*. The curators of that exhibit, Richard Ahlborn, Sally Howell, Alixa Naff, and Andrew Shryock, together with Smithsonian project manager, Susan Ostroff, helped create representational frameworks that have surfaced again in this book. Given the complex history of the NEH and Smithsonian programs, thanking everyone involved in them (or even all the key players) would be a hopeless task. Still, we express our deep appreciation to the dozens of scholars, curators, photographers, and public arts programmers who laid groundwork for the project at hand.

Above all, we would like to thank the twenty-seven people who provided material for this book. Some of them are appearing for the first time in print; others are well known in Detroit and beyond; all of them share with us a desire to represent a community that has lived, for too long, at the outer edges of multicultural America. We thank our contributors for helping us create a book as big, as diverse, and (we hope) as fascinating as Arab Detroit itself. We would also like to express our gratitude to Janice Terry, who helped us compile much of the book's content. When we were faced with gaps in coverage, Gary David introduced us to new contributors, as did Sally Howell. Lara Hamza read an early version of the manuscript in its entirety; we thank her for her many editorial interventions. The ACCESS Cultural Arts Program and the Michigan State University Museum kindly allowed us to reproduce photographs from their archives. We thank Melinda Hamilton of the Michigan State University Museum for generating our map of Arab Detroit and Denise Modrynzinski and Henry Morgan for their invaluable computer assistance with the map.

For their willingness to read the book's essays, offer suggestions, and provide necessary information, we thank Sameer Abraham, Leisanne Smeadala, Michael Daher, Norman Finkelstein, Geraldine Grunow, Hassan Jaber, Gary McIlroy, Nancy Nelson, Dawn Ramey, and Mary Sengstock. Two anonymous reviewers at Wayne State University Press gave prudent advice that helped us reconfigure and improve the original manuscript. Our editor at Wayne State University Press, Kristin Harpster, deserves special mention for her meticulous labors and organizational talents; she helped the project move with ease. Our thanks go as well to Vivian Beaty and the entire staff of the Center for Instructional Media at Henry Ford Community College for converting computer files and photographs into a uniform digital format. Finally, we wish to acknowledge the Julian Park Fund of the State University of New York at Buffalo for a generous gift in support of the publication of *Arab Detroit: From Margin to Mainstream.*

Contributors

NABEEL ABRAHAM teaches anthropology at Henry Ford Community College in Dearborn, Michigan, where he also serves as director of the Honors Program. He is coeditor with Sameer Abraham of *Arabs in the New World* (1983).

SALADIN AHMED is completing undergraduate studies at the University of Michigan, Ann Arbor.

SHAMS ALWUJUDE is the pseudonym of a Dearborn resident who is currently pursuing her undergraduate degree.

TALEB M. AZIZ is a Middle East scholar and the author of several studies on Shia politics and political economy.

HAYAN CHARARA edits *Graffiti Rag*, the annual anthology. His work has appeared in numerous publications, and he is the author of *The Alchemist's Diary* (forthcoming, Hanging Loose Press).

GARY C. DAVID worked as a researcher for United Way Community Services in Detroit. He currently teaches sociology at Bentley College in Boston.

JEFFREY GHANNAM was a *Detroit Free Press* staff writer from 1989 to 1999. He has also worked for the *New York Times*, *Time* magazine, and United Press International. He is a candidate for a juris doctor at the University of Detroit Mercy School of Law.

SHARKEY HADDAD is an administrator with the West Bloomfield School District in Michigan and an independent consultant for Education & Ethnic Relations with America 2000, Inc.

LARA HAMZA is studying literature at the University of Michigan, Ann Arbor.

SALLY HOWELL is a graduate student in the program in American Cultures at the University of Michigan, Ann Arbor. She produced the documentary video *Tales from Arab Detroit* (1995).

RICHARD R. JONES is assistant professor of anthropology at Lee University in Cleveland, Tennessee.

LAWRENCE JOSEPH is the author of four acclaimed books: *Lawyerland* (1997), *Before Our Eyes* (1993), *Curriculum Vitae* (1988), and *Shouting at No One* (1983). A native of Detroit and a descendant of Lebanese immigrants, he is professor of law at St. John's University School of Law.

WILLIAM G. LOCKWOOD is professor emeritus of anthropology at the University of Michigan, Ann Arbor. He is the author of *European Moslems: Ethnicity and Economy in Western Bosnia* (1975).

YVONNE R. LOCKWOOD is curator of folklife in the Michigan Traditional Arts Program at Michigan State University Museum, East Lansing, and coeditor with C. Kurt Dewhurst of the *Michigan Folklife Reader* (1988).

ALIXA NAFF is author of *Becoming American: The Early Arab Immigrant Experience* (1985) and *The Arab Americans* (1988). She is also the creator and donor of the Naff Arab American Collection in the National Museum of American History, Smithsonian Institution.

NAOMI SHIHAB NYE is a poet, anthologist, and writer of books for young readers. She recently compiled *The Space between Our Footsteps: Poems and Paintings from the Middle East* (1998).

KEVIN RASHID is a Detroit poet who teaches creative writing and composition at Wayne State University and poetry writing at Southwest Detroit Community Mental Health.

MARILYNN RASHID, a Detroit writer and translator, is a lecturer in Spanish at Wayne State University.

ANNE RASMUSSEN is associate professor of music and ethnomusicology at the College of William and Mary, Williamsburg, Virginia.

KAREN RIGNALL recently completed a master's degree in history at the University of Michigan, Ann Arbor. She worked for ACCESS before joining MADRE, an international women's human rights organization in New York City.

AMIRA SAAD is a teacher in Dearborn.

KIM SCHOPMEYER teaches sociology at Henry Ford Community College in Dearborn, Michigan.

ANDREW SHRYOCK is assistant professor of anthropology at the University of Michigan, Ann Arbor. He is the author of *Nationalism and the Genealogical Imagination: Oral History and Textual Authority in Tribal Jordan* (1997).

DON UNIS is a community activist. He recently retired from the Dearborn Fire Department, where he held the rank of captain.

LINDA S. WALBRIDGE is author of *Without Forgetting the Imam: Shi'ism in an American Community* (1997).

On Margins and Mainstreams

Andrew Shryock and Nabeel Abraham

THIS IS A book about Arabs in Detroit, and like most contemporary attempts to portray immigrant and ethnic communities in America, it is a self-conscious exercise in cultural representation. We realize that Arab Detroit's size (roughly two hundred thousand strong), its age (over a century old), and its economic and cultural prominence (measured in thousands of businesses and hundreds of mosques, churches, and social clubs) all but demand that a book be written about it. Studies of Cubans in Miami (Portes and Stepick 1993), Dominicans in New York (Pessar 1995), and Koreans in Los Angeles (Abelman and Lie 1997) arise from the same imperatives, and their publication can seem just as inevitable. In this respect, the portrait of Arab Detroit we offer here is part of an ongoing, often contentious effort to shape collective perceptions of America's diversity by cataloging its zones of "internal Otherness."

This volume is perhaps unusual among community ethnographies, however, for the wariness with which its many contributors employ themes of celebration and exclusion. These opposed motifs are currently the easiest, most familiar devices for framing the experience of immigrant and ethnic groups (indeed, the experience of all "special," "marked," or "minority" communities) in North America. In simplest terms, the celebration theme says: "Look how far we've come, against great odds. Marvel at our contributions to American society. See what we have accomplished." The theme of exclusion, by contrast, says: "We shall overcome, but we've not yet arrived. Consider the prejudice and adversity we face every day. Recognize all you are doing to keep us down."

Although themes of celebration and exclusion appear in this book, neither manages to capture the mood of Arab Detroit. As editors, we often found ourselves balancing these messages or moving beyond them altogether. Themes of celebration, which dominate the portrayal of "white ethnics" in our popular media, seemed patently wrong to us, since Arabs have not attained the public acceptance (and protection from defamation) that Italian, Irish, Polish, Greek, or Jewish Americans now enjoy. Arabs are still routinely smeared in the national media, and even the most politically correct Americans have trouble thinking of Arabs as a standard "ethnic group." This mental block is evident (outside Detroit at least) in the tendency to exclude Arabs from multicultural school curricula, multiethnic political coalitions, arts festivals, tolerance and diversity workshops, and most other vehicles of mass pluralist conditioning. Just look for Arabs in these settings; you will be surprised by how little you find. At the same time, however, themes of alienation and discontent, so compelling to Americans of color, seemed to us equally inauthentic as representational motifs. Arabs in Detroit have been highly successful in business; they are even influential in municipal and state politics. Mosques and churches are thriving, families are growing, children are going off to college and entering the professions. Is it prudent to accentuate the experience of exclusion when opportunity, upward mobility, and political complacency are no less real for Arabs in Detroit?

In the end, we decided to make use of our own misgivings by framing our portrait of Arab Detroit in relation to taken-for-granted ideas—thus doubly vexed and powerful ideas—about margins and mainstreams. Arab Detroit is peculiar for the extent to which it exists "on the margin" and "in the mainstream" at the same time. It is a place where the administrator at the local high school is involved (they say) in Lebanese militia politics; the college instructor who lectures on feminist literary criticism is having her marriage to an Iraqi immigrant arranged by her parents; the successful businessman and Republican Party activist spends his off-hours crushing, albeit by phone, Yemeni opposition parties; the manager at Taco Bell sends a large check home to Jordan to help cover the "blood money" his family must pay to resolve a dispute with a neighboring tribe. In Arab Detroit, where cases like these are altogether ordinary, it is best to think of margins and mainstreams as overlapping imaginative zones, each with its own relationship to Arab and American things. The people described above enter the American mainstream whenever they represent or think of themselves in relation to a larger, non-Arab society. They enter the American margins whenever they represent or think of themselves in relation to Arab worlds, private or public, that are not generally accessible (or even intelligible) to a larger, non-Arab society. For some Arab Detroiters, life is mostly a mainstream affair. For others, it is a prolonged study in marginality. For those in between, the leap from margin to mainstream (and back again) occurs constantly, as though in the twinkling of an eye.

America/*Amreeka* is the backdrop against which these shifts in perspective take place. Moreover, it is the backdrop against which the essays, memoirs, photographs, and poems that make up this book will make sense to most readers. Though it seems inconsistent with the multicultural rhetoric Americans now use to discuss issues of pluralism and diversity, we have come to the conclusion that Americanization—alongside its occasional twin, resistance to Americanization—is the dominant cultural force in Arab Detroit: it shapes lives, institutions, and, most important of all, it eventually determines what "being Arab" can mean in the realm of ethnic politics and American public culture. This state of play turns Arab Detroit into what poet Hayan Charara calls, rather evocatively, "the center of mystery." In a postmodern age, Americanization is properly viewed as a kind of mystification, often oblivious to itself, supported by no grand narratives, and suffused with false consciousness. Arab immigrants are no longer compelled to jump into the melting pot of assimilation. Like the rest of us, they are nestled snugly in the great American "salad bowl." But beneath the leafy imagery, another message comes through: "You will not fit in here unless you behave appropriately, and this will be possible only if the differences that set you apart from us—your language, your culture, your religion, your attitude—are somehow naturalized, normalized, muted, consigned to another time, or linked to a place and way of life you have left behind."

This message is sent to Arab Detroit as an endlessly repeating signal by the schools, the popular media, the state, and the marketplace. Newly arrived immigrants hear it quite simply for what it is; their American-born and American-educated children internalize it and, more often than not, willingly comply. For them (and for *their* children in turn), a naturalized, normalized, muted, temporally and spatially displaced sense of "Arabness"—comparable in form to other ethnic identities and, in most cases, consciously worked out only during the college years—is all they have left and, usually, all they can handle. This process is perfectly real; nothing is to be gained by pretending it does not happen. Much is lost, however, if we pretend that this version of Americanization is the only one possible. Arab Detroit is a "center of mystery" because something else seems to be happening there. New immigrants are pouring into the city from Yemen, Lebanon, Palestine, and Iraq. Established families are pouring into the American middle class. Margins and mainstreams are differentiating and feeding back into each other at a rapid pace, with sloppy, often inexplicable results. In Detroit, terms like "Arab" and "American" are now up for grabs—who do they describe, exactly?—and there is little agreement on what counts as a "positive" depiction of the Arab American community, not to mention an "accurate" one. Indeed, the idea of a shared Arab American identity has become fashionable in Detroit only in the last thirty years, and for many Arab Detroiters—especially the tens of thousands who have arrived in America only within the last twenty years—Arab American identity is an abstraction, a convenience, a substitute for history, or a political sensibility they do not always endorse or fully understand.

Yet no one who lives in Detroit would deny that new identities are emerging. These identities blend Arab and American content in ways that are strange to the concerns of ethnic politics and threatening to the agendas of cultural purists. As a recognizable place, Arab Detroit is continually pieced together out of the stories and experiences its inhabitants share. Some of these stories are well-rehearsed, public, and easily told; others are intensely personal, concealed from outsiders, and fraught with contradictions. To create a representative portrait of Arab Detroit, we must simultaneously accentuate both ways of talking about it, and this can be done only if we focus on the aspects of Arab Detroit that exist across, between, and in spite of the categories used to determine what is Arab and what is American about the people who live there.

A Map of Sorts: A Quick Survey of Arab Detroit

Greater Detroit is home to the largest, most highly concentrated population of Arabs in North America. There are now roughly two hundred thousand people of Arab descent living in and around the city.[1] Arabs have been coming to Detroit since the late nineteenth century, and they continue to arrive in the thousands each year. The vast majority are from Lebanon, Palestine, Yemen, and Iraq. When asked to explain why so many Arabs have migrated to Detroit, most people in the community will mention the automobile industry. As a kind of historical shorthand, this answer is certainly the best. Arabic-speaking immigrants were a discernible presence in Detroit even before the auto industry began to boom, but it was the romantic allure of their Holy Land origins, not their numerical strength, that made them interesting to other Detroiters. In 1900 the *Detroit Free Press*, February 6, ran a story on "Detroit's Colony of Syrians." The reporter describes a small, exotic community of 75–100 people, most of them Maronite Christians from Lebanon. These early immigrants were peddlers and shopkeepers, not industrial workers. By 1916, however, there were already 555 Syrian men employed in Henry Ford's factories alone, many of them newly arrived Muslims (Schwartz 1974, 256). By 1930, there were nine thousand Arabic-speaking Detroiters: almost six thousand were Syrian, and the rest were a mix of Palestinians, Yemenis, and Iraqi Chaldeans (S. Abraham 1983, 91). The Arab Detroit one sees today evolved out of this core population, most of whose members found their livelihood on production lines, in workshops, and behind the cash registers of stores catering to blue-collar workers.

As Detroit's industrial sector began to wither in the 1970s, the Arab immigrant community continued to grow. Today, most newly arrived Arab immigrants to Detroit are refugees of war (Shia from Lebanon and Iraq) or victims of political oppression, economic hardship, and population displacement (Iraqi Catholics, Palestinians, and Yemenis). They come to Detroit to live among the large networks of kin and fellow villagers that now exist there. Most find jobs in small, family-run shops and stores—in 1994, there were over five thousand Arab-owned businesses in Metropolitan Detroit[2]—or they enter the service sector of the local economy.

Today, Arab Americans are one of Michigan's largest, fastest-growing minority populations. Indeed, certain parts of Greater Detroit have acquired an unmistakably Arab aspect. Barbara Aswad's (1992, 167) description of east Dearborn in 1990 captures the vibrant feel of America's largest Lebanese enclave:

> As one walks along the streets in the Lebanese Muslim community in Dearborn, one feels transplanted back to the Middle East. Fifty or more Lebanese shops line both sides of a six-block stretch of Warren Avenue, where eight years ago there were only eight. Five bakeries and eight restaurants emit the culinary smells of the Middle East. There are also twelve fruit and vegetable markets, two supermarkets, two beauty salons, numerous doctors, dentists, and a pharmacist, a furniture shop, real estate, insurance, and printing office, auto shops, a clothing store, Arabic bookstores, a publishing company, an Arab social service agency, the Islamic Institute for Knowledge, and a Shi'i mosque. Signs are in both Arabic and English. There is much activity on this strip. Men sometimes sit at tables on the sidewalk, women usually cover their heads, and many wear Muslim and village attire. Children are seen rushing to religious and Arabic classes at the Institute.

The area along Warren Avenue, which now has over 117 Arab-owned businesses,[3] is only one of several distinct Arab populations in Metro Detroit (see map, page 62). Highly assimilated middle- and upper-class Christians, whose parents and grandparents came to America from Greater Syria before the fall of the Ottoman Empire, can be found in Detroit's northern and eastern suburbs; Chaldeans, a close-knit community of Iraqi Catholics who own the majority of Detroit's small grocery and liquor stores, live mostly in Southfield, Oak Park, and Bloomfield Hills; Palestinian professionals, mostly Christians from the West Bank village of Ramallah, have settled in Livonia; Palestinians from the Jerusalem suburb of Beit Hanina, and Yemenis, both of peasant backgrounds, live together in Dearborn's Southend, a neighborhood that lies in the shadow of the Ford Rouge Plant and boasts its own mosque and business district.

Portraying Arab Detroit: Internal and External Discourses

This broad range of lifestyles, national backgrounds, and levels of assimilation has made the Detroit Arab community hard to represent, both intellectually and politically. It is not simply an American ethnic community—parts of it make sense only in relation to the Yemeni highlands or the Lebanese countryside—nor is Arab Detroit an integral part of the Arab world. The city is home, for instance, to tens of thousands of Arabs who cannot speak Arabic. It is this persistent in-betweenness that makes Arab Detroit a challenging place for scholars to think and write about. The small body of research that accumulated in the 1970s and 1980s took up the difficult task of determining the size, internal composition, and history of Detroit's major Arab immigrant populations (e.g., Wigle and S. Abraham 1974; Abraham and Abraham 1981; Aswad 1974; Sengstock 1982). The standard work in this genre is still Sameer Abraham and Nabeel Abraham's edited volume, *Arabs in the New World* (1983); the patterns identified in that study have gradually been popularized and woven into the narratives of identity and experience Arab Detroiters tell the outside world.

When the *Detroit News* or *Free Press* do occasional spreads on the Arab community, they use facts, figures, and angles that can be traced back to *Arabs in the New World*. The community is said to be roughly two hundred thousand members strong and one hundred years old. It is divided into four main national groups: Lebanese, Palestinians, Iraqis, and Yemenis. It is divided into two religious communities, Muslim and Christian. It is divided into old-timers and newcomers, who are said to have different attitudes about gender, family, faith, and politics. All of this information is easily packaged for consumption by a mainstream audience. Its underlying message is simple: Arabs in Detroit are people who are now becoming, or have already become, Americans. The details used to flesh out this message are designed to help Americans understand why Arabs are here, what they are like, and what obstacles they face in adapting to life in Detroit.

This way of representing Arab Detroit has been very successful. If it verges on the formulaic, it is because the formula works. Moreover, the formula has been taken up by ACCESS (the Arab Community Center for Economic and Social Services), a social service agency that since the 1980s has sponsored dozens of workshops for journalists, educators, government officials, health care providers, legal and law enforcement professionals, and other representatives of mainstream institutions. At each of these events, the official story of Arab Detroit is told. It is reinforced, visually, by the exhibits in the ACCESS Museum, which decorate this narrative with antique photographs, family heirlooms, and pictures taken by photojournalists in Dearborn and Detroit. This representational package has now gone national. In 1995–96, ACCESS and the Smithsonian Institution presented a photographic exhibition titled "A Community between Two Worlds: The Arab Americans of Greater Detroit." It was seen by roughly five million people. Many more will see this exhibit as it travels the country on a six-city, three-year tour, from 1998–2001. As the audience for Arab Detroit grows, so does the power of the imagery and stories used to represent it, and the fact that all of these ventures are supported by federal funds and corporate grants is essential to any understanding of why they succeed and what they are meant to accomplish.[4]

When people read *Arabs in the New World* or stroll through the ACCESS Museum, few of them realize that the community on display, and this way of representing it, attained their climax forms only in the last fifteen years. They do not correspond neatly to the Arab Detroit Nabeel Abraham grew up in, circa 1960, or the Detroit Alixa Naff grew up in, circa 1940, or the Detroit any real person inhabits today. The Arab Detroit visible in public formats exists only in relation to the larger, non-Arab society that views it. Within the community, other ways of talking about identity prevail. Before any portrait of Arab Detroit goes public, it is filtered through a local identity discourse—a way of talking about being "Arab" and "American" in

Detroit—whose categories are defined by a set of ideal oppositions that separate "immigrant" from "ethnic" Arabs. The oppositions are crude; they seldom apply neatly to real people or actual situations, and they are crosscut by the various national, religious, and village identities that shape Arab Detroit. Still, no discussion of Arab identity in Detroit makes sense without them.

The local identity discourse is summed up, with crystalline precision, by Ismael "Ish" Ahmed, director of ACCESS. When we asked Ish what Arab Detroit looks like from his peculiar vantage as a community leader and spokesman, he noted that the experiences of Lebanese, Iraqi, Palestinian, and Yemeni immigrants are combining to produce a new Arab American identity. This identity, Ish explained, is based on a transition from:

> village politics . . . to . . . multiethnic coalition politics
> living in ethnic neighborhoods . . . to . . . living anywhere
> protective families . . . to . . . open families
> religious conservatism . . . to . . . religious liberalism
> speaking mostly Arabic . . . to . . . speaking mostly English

Ish describes a shift from an insular, Old World culture to a way of life he considers modern, flexible, and recognizably American. The terms of comparison are biased, and with good reason. Ish's great-grandfather came to America from Ottoman Syria three generations ago. Ish does not speak Arabic, he is a nonpracticing Muslim, and his wife is not Arab. Ish identifies strongly as an Arab, but his Arabism is "ethnic" in character. Like many other second- and third-generation Arab Americans, Ish sees his Arabness as a heritage that enriches him. He can embrace the "good parts" of that heritage—the food, the music and dance, the immigrant struggle, the sense of community—and he can leave behind the "bad parts," which he is free to define.[5]

Ish's understanding of identity is based on assimilationist ideas. He assumes, correctly we think, that Arab American identities are better adapted and more responsive to the society that envelops them than homeland identities are. For Ish Ahmed and other community activists, this is most evident in the arena of American politics, where Old World political constituencies—village clubs, church and mosque groups, benevolent associations, and foreign political parties—have proven themselves unable and unwilling to engage effectively in the public life of Detroit. Nabeel Abraham has developed the same theme in slightly different terms, arguing that Arab

American political culture is dominated by "integrationist" and "isolationist" currents (1989). These can be very accurately mapped onto Ish Ahmed's model of "old world" as opposed to "Arab American" identities. The isolationists, according to Abraham, are mostly newly arrived immigrants, socially conservative and religiously devout; they come from village and rural backgrounds and are intent on avoiding assimilation. The integrationists, by contrast, are mostly middle class and professional, ethnically conscious, American-born or American-educated, and eager to reconcile their identity with the dominant culture.

Typologies of this sort are constantly invoked in Arab Detroit, and academics and activists are not the only people invoking them. Mary Darwish, a Lebanese American who was born in Dearborn, introduced us to the term "boater" (i.e., "just off the boat"), a tag she and her friends use to describe immigrants from the home villages of Bint Jubail, Tibneen, and Qaraoun. The boaters, who include Mary's own parents, her husband, and most of the people she socializes with, seem hopelessly old-fashioned to her. They are "stubborn and sexist." They "drive like maniacs." They are socially inbred, unsophisticated, and, in ways Mary never tires of cataloging, they are endearingly, maddeningly "backwards." As the boaters see it, however, Mary belongs to a cultural half-world of kin who are "not really Arabs anymore," who are "Arabs by origin only." Whether they are male or female, Christian or Muslim, Iraqi, Yemeni, Lebanese, or Palestinian, new immigrants dish out the same brand of social critique. Detroit is turning us into a rude lot, they say. The American Arabs let their daughters run wild. Their sons are selfish and disrespectful. They cannot speak Arabic. They neglect their religion, ignore their relatives, are strangers to hospitality, and so on.

Arab Detroiters are not always perturbed by this rhetoric; often it is little more than a joking matter among friends and family. In contexts of explicit cultural representation, however—in newspaper articles on Arab Detroit, in scholarly works, at ethnic festivals, in museum exhibits—the stakes are raised, and the Arab community is left with two faces it must display simultaneously: one is American(izing), one is Arab(izing), and each is potentially a source of embarrassment to the other. Moreover, Arab Detroiters can find themselves trapped beneath the oppressive weight of either representation. A Palestinian girl who was born and raised in Dearborn and barely speaks Arabic seems alien to her newly arrived cousin from Beit Hanina, who was reluctant to marry her because "she has American manners." To a new Iraqi Chaldean immigrant, however, the same girl is a boater because she is Muslim and wears a scarf. To members of the larger society—and to Arabs in other American cities, who know of Detroit's huge immigrant population—all Arab Detroiters are boaters until proven otherwise. This is why a former spokesperson for the Detroit chapter of ADC (the American-Arab Anti-Discrimination Committee), herself an immigrant, urged the national leadership not to send a delegation of journalists for a tour of Dearborn's Arab immigrant neighborhoods.

"We don't want them to see all the people going around with rags on their heads," she told us at the time. "The Arabs in Dearborn are a bunch of stereotypes."

Such commentary is nothing new to Arabs in Detroit, who often internalize it and artfully turn it back on their accusers. Lawrence Joseph's alarming portrayal of himself and his native city, "Sand Nigger" (1988), is sculpted in language that seems ordinary in Detroit's Arab quarters, despite (or perhaps because of) its provocative bluntness.

> . . . I am
> the light-skinned Nigger
> with black eyes and the look
> difficult to figure—a look
> of indifference, a look to kill—
> a Levantine Nigger
> in the city on the strait
> between the great lakes Erie and St. Clair
> which has a reputation for violence, an enthusiastically
> bad-tempered sand Nigger
> who waves his hands, nice enough
> to pass, Lebanese enough
> to be against his brother,
> with his brother against his cousin,
> with cousin and brother
> against the stranger. (27)

Joseph's manifesto, revealed in an intensely personal, poetic idiom, describes the moment at which Arab-as-Other and Arab-as-American converge, scrutinize and assess each other, conceal and appeal to each other, and sometimes look away from each other in shame. It is precisely this moment of recognition that the Americanization process, and the push toward mainstream ethnic identity it entails, is designed to suppress. This book is an attempt to create portraits of Arab Detroit that face down, analyze, and reconstruct the assumptions that make Joseph's imagery so vivid, so intuitively "correct." We will try to deal as explicitly as possible with the ideological frames (and real cultural patterns on the ground) that make Detroit so problematic, and so promising, as a site of Arab American identity formation.

Paths through a Minefield: Comments on Structure and Representational Strategies

The Arab/America Interface

In organizing this book, we have laid out an itinerary that leads the reader through terrain that is sometimes reassuringly familiar, and at other times palpably foreign. We begin, in part 1, "Qualities/Quantities," with Kim Schopmeyer's demographic profile of Arab Detroit. This topic is problematic, since it deals with wildly varying estimates of Arab Detroit's numerical size. Population counts are controversial in all American ethnic communities. They affect the amount of state and federal dollars available to a community, levels of corporate investment in ethnic markets, and the nature of electoral politics at all levels of government. In Detroit, arguments about the size of the Arab population occur wherever that population is connected to the larger society by social service agencies, political action groups, and commercial interests. The numbers generated by and for these interest groups always reflect an agenda, a vision of the community and its potential. The group that has been most effective in generating Arab numbers and visions is ACCESS. Karen Rignall's brief history of this organization doubles as a brief history of Arab Detroit itself. This narrative overlap should be explicitly recognized. ACCESS, more than any other agency, has institutionalized and made official the image of Arab Detroit we explore in this book. To a remarkable extent, the interface between Arab Detroit and the American mainstream is planned, coordinated, administered, evaluated, and represented by ACCESS.

From the Inside Out

The interface with mainstream society is only one point at which Arab identities take shape in Detroit. Much of this book deals with issues whose meaning is located more securely within the Arab community, in realms of experience we have organized under part titles, "Work," "Religion," and "Politics." It is hard to draw clear lines between these categories, and the essays that follow seldom fit neatly into any one of them. For some of our contributors, activist Maya Berry, for instance, politics is a profession, and her brand of politics is largely secular. For Sharkey Haddad, an administrator with the West Bloomfield School District, being Catholic means being Chaldean, and this identity brings with it political as well as religious obligations. For the shop owners described in Gary David's essay, "Behind the Bulletproof Glass," family business is a worldview, a way of life. As the Iraqi merchants he interviewed pursue dreams of financial success, they partake in a common American project: they turn their work into a religion. This conversion to work is sometimes more than figurative. In Nabeel Abraham's poignant account of his father's career as a peddler, "On the Road with Bob," the conditions under which Younis Abraham bought, sold, and socialized with Americans have virtually obscured his identity as a Palestinian Muslim. That all-too-Arab profile was bad for business in New York City, where Younis based most of his trade. When he died in Bellevue Hospital of a perforated ulcer, the chaplain assumed, given his last name, that Younis Abraham was a Jew. It was a rabbi, not an imam, who prayed over his dead body.

Stories like these suggest that some labels are too simple and that even then they are beyond our control. Nonetheless, Arab Americans are quick to set themselves apart from each other in terms of regional, national, religious, sectarian, occupational, class, and urban or rural backgrounds, all of which can be neatly encoded in a person's family name. As editors, we have chosen not to tamper with this need for ready-made labels, even when our contributors use them in ways that seem narrow or even false. We have insisted, however, that contributors to this book avoid using political and religious rhetoric, or job talk for that matter, as public screens that protect the author (or the reader) from self-scrutiny. Those looking for black-and-white commentaries on Arab-Israeli politics, Islamic revivalism, or the relationship between the urban poor and Arab store owners will find little of interest in this book. The political, work-related, and religious sensibilities we explore here are part of much larger, much older, and much more intimate worlds.

In part 3, "Religion," for instance, Sally Howell's interview with Mohsen and Lila Amen, members of a conservative Shia mosque in Dearborn, reveals the complexity of belief and practice in an American Muslim family. For the Amens, Islam is about being different in thought, behavior, and appearance; it is about following the straight path, which, they believe, most Muslims in America do not follow; it is about raising American kids in a morally responsible way, all the while maintaining links to the values that shape Lebanese village life. For members of the Dix mosque in the 1950s and 1960s, whose internal struggles are recounted by Nabeel Abraham, being Muslim meant taking sides on a gamut of hotly debated issues: the role of women in the life of the mosque; the use of ritual space; the selection of religious leaders; defining the difference, if any, between an "Americanized Muslim" and a "good Muslim." For the new wave of Iraqi Shia refugees discussed by Linda Walbridge and Talib Aziz in part 4, "Politics," building a community in Detroit is a matter of survival. The first—and, for the moment, the only—hope of the Iraqi refugees is to return home; "politics," for them, refers to struggles being fought right now in Iraq. U.S. government policy is creating the conditions that bring Iraqi refugees to Detroit, and keep them there, but American identity politics, as well as state, federal, and municipal politics, are of almost no concern to Iraqi Shia. For Egyptian Copts born in the United States, on the other hand, American identity politics is fundamentally reshaping what it means to be Coptic. In the "Religion" section, Richard Jones discusses how "long-distance" versions of Coptic nationalism, unusual, unelaborated, and often disapproved of in Egypt itself, are rapidly evolving in (and perhaps just as quickly dying out of) church-based Coptic communities throughout North America. The degree to which religion, politics, and profession endlessly blend together in Arab Detroit is richly displayed in Alixa Naff's memoir, the centerpiece of part 2, "Work." Although it dwells on what appear to be the sheltered experiences of "an immigrant grocer's daughter," Naff's account reveals a moral imagination that transcends, then and now, the political, religious, and workaday assumptions of the immigrant community in which Alixa came of age in the 1930s and 1940s.

Lives, Images, Voices

As we gathered the poems and memoirs that fill this book, we began to realize that themes of imagination, transcendence, and personal growth are too often missing from the academic literature on Arab Americans. What counts as authoritative knowledge about Arab Americans (in scholarly circles and beyond) is no doubt to blame for this lack. Though we are reluctant to admit it now, we originally thought the memoirs and poetry in this book would serve as adornment for the analytical essays, which would be its "real intellectual substance." We were wrong. The mix of evocative and explanatory genres displayed in this volume actually creates a fuller, livelier image of Arab Detroit, and this expanded representational context has compelled us, as editors, to experiment with modes of commentary and critique that bring new complexity to our work. We are anthropologists, after all, and our training predisposes us to comparisons and composite imagery, tools we will continue to use, but never again with the same confidence. We have acquired a healthy respect for the narrative power of real lives honestly and artfully told.

If the memoirs scattered throughout this volume, especially those included in part 5, "Life Journeys," have representational power, what is the source of that power? At one level, life stories enable their authors to escape, transform, even undermine the labels so easily applied to Arab Americans. They do this by asserting what discussion of Otherness, Us, and Them, is meant to conceal: that behind the Other is an individual, a person who can enter our world, who is already in our world, and was never simply the representative of a group. Memoirs are about selves, even when the selves portrayed are located firmly within contexts that seem collective and radically different. The memoirs we have selected move from highly cohesive, inwardly oriented immigrant households, to settings that, by comparison, are mainstream, outwardly oriented, self-consciously ethnic, and individualistic. In all of these contexts, however, a real person is speaking. An acute awareness of margin and mainstream, a heightened sense of maturation, a grasping for autonomy through perspective: these moods infect the work of all our memoirists.

We should emphasize, however, that narratives of self are not the only or even the best solution to the representational problems posed by American identity politics. In fact, these stories generate the very contradictions they purport to resolve. Americans are devout individualists, our insatiable hunger for peer approval and "community" notwithstanding. The memoir format gives immigrant and ethnic Americans a way of talking to the mainstream in the only language the mainstream can hear, and the feeling of liberation that results comes at a price. Other forms of identity, those based less on images of the heroic self and more on one's immersion in communal identities and kinship ties, are effectively marginalized (even silenced) by individualism and the self-centered narratives it demands. To an extent, this is unavoidable. Learning to speak about and for themselves is how Arab Detroiters, *as individuals,* enter the American mainstream. Some of our prospective contributors could not cross this threshold. They felt stifled by the opinions of their relatives; they thought they had no authority to speak as representatives of their group; they insisted on submitting their testimony to the approval of the priest, the imam, brothers and sisters, parents. In the end, they could not say anything. They have no autonomous voice, and you, as a reader positioned in the American mainstream, have no way of hearing them. They are not quite part of your world; or, in a slightly different sense, there is a part of them they want to keep out of your world.

Ironically, even though the American mainstream compels Arabs to speak as individuals in order to be heard, American political culture insists that Arabs have integrity as a group. Our Lebanese, Yemeni, Palestinian, and Iraqi contributors rarely criticize this assumption. Arab immigrants enter the American mainstream as members of an ethnic category: as Arab Americans. This new identity gives meaning to individual lives even as it circumscribes them within yet another potentially reductive label. Arab American is a new identity that must be learned, and much of this learning takes place in colleges and universities, at the hands of academics and activists, or by reading books like this one. The perceptive reader will notice that the contributors who discuss Arab American identity at any length are those who are the most heavily invested in American academic/intellectual culture, those who are the most solidly middle class, the most closely identified with mainstream institutions, political action groups, and human service agencies, the most assimilated, and the least Arabic-speaking. Being Arab American is a way of surviving in these special contexts; in short, it is a way of entering the American mainstream.

Into the Mainstream

In the final set of essays, part 6, "Ethnic Futures," our contributors explore the ongoing transition from marginal to mainstream consciousness in Arab Detroit. Not surprisingly, this transition is accomplished through the efflorescence of Americanized variants of ethnic identity and their proliferation at the expense of so-called boater or old country identities, languages, attachments, and styles of interaction. The content of Arab American identity is not a random array of survivals from the preimmigrant past. Like other American ethnic groups, Arabs in Detroit have come to rely heavily on music, food, and the traditional folk arts to represent their "culture" in American settings. These three areas of cultural production are succeeding in the marketplace (they can be bought and sold), in the realm of ethnic politics (they can stand for and unify constituencies), and in academic quarters, where they are studied, cataloged, and displayed by museums and community-based organizations as part of a larger, Americanizing project that fosters unity by celebrating diversity.

Anne Rasmussen shows how Arab musicians create and sustain a market for their skills by transforming themselves into "ritual specialists" who know how to make weddings, baptisms, and community events "sound Arab," even when many of the people who attend these events no longer speak Arabic. William and Yvonne Lockwood examine the historical and market forces that conspire to create "Arab food" in Detroit, a public version of Lebanese cuisine that differs markedly from the kinds of food prepared in the privacy of Arab American kitchens, even Lebanese kitchens. Sally Howell's exploration of Arab "traditional arts" in Detroit (embroidery, instrument making, calligraphy, doll making, and the like) follows the channels by which these arts are defined as traditional by government agencies in the United States and are then selected for display in contexts that render them both part of the American cultural heritage and proof of how rapidly the Arab community is moving away from these "endangered" art forms toward more typically American ones.

The most fascinating thing about these Americanizing, mainstreaming processes is the willingness with which most Arabs participate in them. In fact, very few Arab Americans would recognize the growth of ethnic consciousness as a mainstreaming phenomenon at all; they see it as a way of resisting the mainstream, or of establishing a protected zone within it, and this selective vision actually speeds the process onward. The appeal of "mainstreamism" is born in the discomfort "boaters" and "American-borns" come to feel in each other's presence, and this initial sense of difference, contained within the private spaces of the Arab community, evolves gradually into all the diverse, public patterns visible in this book. Andrew Shryock's essay on family life in Arab Detroit roots this evolutionary sequence in the tense interaction between the household culture of immigrant families and the "official," middle-class values young people encounter in American mass media and, more important by far, in the public school system. This interaction is strongly weighted in favor of the public domain—which induces Arab children, by an early age, to stigmatize certain aspects of their home culture—but patterns of resistance, such as marriage between immigrants and ethnics, sending children to the homeland for prolonged visits and arranged marriages, and the establishment of Islamic schools, are evolving in reaction to Americanization.

The outcome of these strategies is hard to predict, but for many Arabs in Detroit the appeal of Arab American identity appears to be closely related to attempts to construct identities and worlds "bigger" than the family, the village, the church or mosque. Sometimes the cultivation of ethnic identity is a substitute for a cohesive family and communal life; sometimes it is a two-way response to the criticism of parents, who say a child is "too American," and of Americans who make the same child feel "too Arab." Whatever the particular case may be, it would seem that, contrary to the popular image of involuted, highly conformist Middle Eastern families, Arabs in Detroit are developing identities quite unlike those of their parents. The cultivation of Arab Americanness is part of this transformation and by no means an attempt to stop it.

Conclusion: Living Beyond and Between

The issues described in this book—changing definitions of self, culturally mixed marriages, lives shaped by repeat migration, higher education as a road to ethnic awareness, the family business as a gateway to the middle class, participation in identity and ethnic politics, folk arts, foodways, and music—are all ways of handling the demands of hegemonic, and often competitive, national identities: Yemeni, Lebanese, Iraqi, Palestinian, Egyptian, Arab, and American. As coping strategies, they are familiar to most immigrant and ethnic Americans, but in Arab Detroit they have a special vitality and appeal. In Detroit, the Arab community is so large, so old, and so diverse, that even the most inclusive definitions of Arab and American identity cannot quite contain it. Even the popular distinction between boaters and American-borns, so pervasive within the community, is inherently negotiable. If the contributors to this book have a single trait in common, it is the need to come to terms with the imaginary hyphen imposed between the words "Arab" and "American" and the sense of marginality this hyphen engenders.

This process of self-definition is a life's work, and it is not easily accomplished. There are many Arab Detroiters for whom marginality is experienced primarily as a form of exclusion from the American mainstream and from other Arab communities. We suspect that the demands of identity politics actually intensify that sense of alienation by compelling Arabs (ethnic and immigrant alike) to represent themselves in linear, assimilationist, "becoming American" narratives that accurately reflect our popular models of national belonging, but do not capture the in-betweenness of places like Arab Detroit. What we try to coax out of this collection is a slightly different but equally important idea: that the unmarked areas that exist between, across, and in spite of sociopolitical boundaries are not simply areas of exclusion; they are also areas of innovation, creativity, and fundamental change. These are exactly the areas in which Detroit, as a new Arab world, is thriving. As immigrants pour in by the thousands each year, and as today's boaters become tomorrow's locals, Arab Detroit will continue to expand across its own borders, and all attempts to make it a stereotypically Arab or American (or even Arab American) place will founder as Arab Detroiters struggle to bring those terms together in their public and private lives.

Readers in search of comparative insights will certainly find them here. Arab Detroit is but one of a growing number of immigrant, ethnic, refugee, expat, migrant, and transnational communities that flourish, and fade away, in North America's (sub)urban spaces. These "remote areas," now undeniably near, are sold to us as ethnic villages, cultivated as political constituencies, mined for cheap labor, developed as points of entry into foreign markets, or cordoned off as crime-ridden slums. The worlds evolving in these zones are not bereft of singularity. One could hardly mistake Arab Detroit for New York's "Little Brazil" (Margolis 1994), Los Angeles's "New Persian Empire" (Naficy 1993), or the myriad Caribbean, Latino, and Asian communities that fill North America's urban landscapes (Basch et al. 1994). Yet the shifting boundaries between Us and Them that turn these immigrant/ethnic communities into distinctive places also cause them to resemble one another in powerful ways. In a recent review of books about American immigrant groups, Nina Glick Schiller (1997, 405) isolates at least a dozen experiences immigrants to the United States share, and we urge our readers to study the list closely, lest they go forward with the romantic illusion that Arab Detroit is a world like no other (the numbered format is imposed by the editors):

1. Immigrants are often shocked and dismayed by what they find in the United States.
2. They are not from the poorest of the poor, and though their actual incomes may increase considerably with migration, many immigrants experience downward social mobility when they arrive in the United States.
3. Some enter the lottery of entrepreneurial activities where a handful realize their dreams of wealth and security and many face grim years of self-exploitation.

4. Gender and family relations go through transformations, but family remains the central mechanism of adaptation and survival.
5. Responses to settlement are structured by gender, age, and class, and so there is not in any immigrant population a unified experience of immigration.
6. The newcomers reconsider and reconstitute their identities in alignment with U.S. concepts of ethnicity and race and in relationship to the political terrain of their homeland.
7. In all cases the identities they adopt are multiple and situational.
8. There is contention among members of each group about how they are to be represented and who should represent them.
9. Finding themselves strangers in a strange land, immigrants reimagine home.
10. Some return home.
11. In the course of several decades of settlement, a section of each immigrant population finds ways to establish ties with "home" and becomes "transmigrant," living their lives across international borders.
12. Past generations of immigrants had strikingly similar experiences, including transnational familial, social, and political connections.

This list serves well as a map of the transitional time-space immigrants must navigate on their way to becoming (or deciding not to become) American. Arab Detroit has been evolving in that time-space for over a hundred years now, and not a single contributor to this book has created a work that falls (even partially) outside the patterns identified by Glick Schiller, even though the contributors are an extremely diverse lot. This century-long congruence suggests the obvious: that immigrant/ethnic communities like Arab Detroit are not the peripheral oddities they appear to be, but instead are inevitable, even necessary features of a national landscape shaped by constant immigration. Each is a place where borders, identities, and selves are created in reaction to the American mainstream and, just as significantly, in reaction to the American margins. The new Americas born of this encounter bear an uncanny resemblance to Arab Detroit.[6] They are unfinished projects, endlessly contested, and bound, by their histories and their own (im)possible futures, to change.

Notes

1. This figure, which debuted in Abraham and Abraham (1983), is probably too high. It is lower, however, than the estimate of 250,000 commonly cited in the press, by social service agencies, and in some academic circles. The latter figure has become a social fact of sorts, but its refusal to change (up or down) during the last fifteen years of steady immigration suggests that 250,000 is a quantitative symbol of Arab Detroit's immense size.
2. This figure was provided by Abe Osta, executive director of the American Arab Chamber of Commerce in Michigan.
3. This figure was provided by Ahmed Chebbani, owner of Omnex, an accounting firm that balances the books for almost all the Lebanese-owned businesses on Warren Avenue.
4. The work of the ACCESS Cultural Arts Program, its content, and larger political context, is discussed in Shryock (1998; n.d.) and Howell (1998).
5. Identities of this sort are often lumped under the category of "symbolic ethnicity." In *Ethnic Options* (1990), Mary Waters elucidates the strategic, pick-and-choose quality of symbolic ethnicity in America. Although her focus is on "white ethnics," much of what she says can be applied to second- and third-generation Arab Americans.
6. For detailed analyses of these "New Americas" and the corporate, political, and class interests underlying American multiculturalism, the reader should consult Rouse (1995) and Dresch (1995).

References

Abelman, Nancy, and John Lie. 1997. *Blue Dreams: Korean Americans and the Los Angeles Riots.* Cambridge: Harvard University Press.

Abraham, Nabeel. 1989. Arab-American Marginality: Mythos and Praxis. In *Arab Americans: Continuity and Change,* edited by Baha Abu-Laban and Michael Suleiman. Belmont, Mass.: Association of Arab-American University Graduates.

Abraham, Sameer. 1983. Detroit's Arab-American Community: A Survey of Diversity and Commonality. In *Arabs in the New World: Studies on Arab-American Communities.* edited by Sameer Abraham and Nabeel Abraham, 84–108.

Abraham, Sameer, and Nabeel Abraham. 1983. *Arabs in the New World.* Detroit: Center for Urban Studies, Wayne State University.

———. 1981. *The Arab World and Arab Americans: Understanding a Neglected Minority.* Detroit: Center for Urban Studies, Wayne State University.

Aswad, Barbara. 1974. *Arabic-Speaking Communities in American Cities.* New York: Center for Migration Studies and the Association of Arab-American University Graduates.

———. 1992. The Lebanese Muslim Community in Dearborn, Michigan. In *The Lebanese in the World: A Century of Emigration,* edited by Albert Hourani and Nadim Shehadi, 167–88. London: I. B. Tauris.

Basch, Linda, Nina Glick Schiller, and C. Szanton Blanc. 1994. *Nations Unbound.* Langhorne, Pa.: Gordon and Breach.

Dresch, Paul. 1995. Race, Culture and ——— What?: Pluralist Certainties in the United States. In *The Pursuit of Certainty: Religious and Cultural Formulations,* edited by Wendy James, 61–91. New York: Routledge.

Glick Schiller, Nina. 1997. U.S. Immigrants and the Global Narrative. *American Anthropologist* 99 (2): 404–8.

Hartman, David, ed. *Immigrants and Migrants: The Detroit Ethnic Experience.* Detroit: New University Thought Publishing.

Howell, Sally. 1998. Picturing Women, Class, and Community in Arab Detroit: The Strange Case of Eva Habeeb. *Visual Anthropology* 10 (2–4): 354–76.

Joseph, Lawrence. 1988. *Curriculum Vitae.* Pittsburgh: University of Pittsburgh Press.

Margolis, Maxine. 1994. *Little Brazil.* Princeton: Princeton University Press.

Naficy, Hamid. 1993. *The Making of Exile Cultures.* Minneapolis: University of Minnesota Press.

Pessar, Patricia. 1995. *A Visa for a Dream: Dominicans in the United States.* New Immigrants Series. Boston: Allyn and Bacon.

Portes, Alejandro, and Alex Stepick. 1993. *City on the Edge: The Transformation of Miami.* Berkeley: University of California Press.

Rouse, Roger. 1995. Thinking through Transnationalism: Notes on the Cultural Politics of Class Relations in the Contemporary United States. *Public Culture* 7:353–402.

Schwartz, Jonathan. 1974. Henry Ford's Melting Pot. In *Immigrants and Migrants: The Detroit Ethnic Experience,* edited by David Hartman, 252–60.

Sengstock, Mary. 1982. *Chaldean Americans: Changing Conceptions of Ethnic Identity.* New York: Center for Migration Studies.

Shryock, Andrew. 1998. Mainstreaming Arabs: Film Making as Image Making in Tales from Arab Detroit. *Visual Anthropology* 10 (2–4): 165–88.

———. n.d. Popular Culture in Arab Detroit: Making Arab/American Identities in a Transnational Domain. In *Mass Mediations: New Approaches to Popular Culture in the Middle East and Beyond,* edited by Walter Armbrust. Berkeley: University of California Press, forthcoming.

Waters, Mary. 1990. *Ethnic Options: Choosing Identities in America.* Berkeley: University of California Press.

Wigle, Laurel, and Sameer Abraham. 1974. Arab Nationalism in America: The Dearborn Arab Community. In *Immigrants and Migrants: The Detroit Ethnic Experience,* edited by David Hartman, 279–302.

Part 1

QUALITIES/QUANTITIES

Fig. 1. Sweet tea, a water pipe, and news of the day. A Dearborn family unwinds, 1995. Photograph by Millard Berry.

Introduction

ARAB DETROIT IS a patchwork of national, religious, and village groups who, in the ordinary run of events, keep very much to themselves. Lebanese Shia in Dearborn have little contact with Palestinian Christians in Livonia: the two groups do not socialize together, they rarely intermarry, and their Arabic dialects are different enough to cause confusion. Yet one could easily find individuals in both groups who believe they belong to an entity called "the Arab American community." We do not endorse the idea, popular at the grassroots level, that Iraqi Shia, Palestinian Christians, and Yemeni Sunnis share an essential "Arabness." Likewise, if these diverse groups can be said to share a "Middle Eastern" culture, then they share much of it with Turks, Iranians, Greeks, Armenians, and Kurds as well.

Arab American identity, as expressed in Detroit today, seldom refers to an ancient regional heritage or even a shared culture. It emerged quite recently as part of a complex (and now largely forgotten) reaction to the 1967 Arab-Israeli War. America's pro-Israel stance in the wake of that conflict increasingly turned "the Arabs" into a problem, both in Detroit and in the Middle East. Arab American identity evolved as one way of dealing with that problematic status. In fact, of the major organizations that represent Arab Americans at the national level, not one predates the 1967 war: the Association of Arab-American University Graduates (AAUG) was established in 1967, the National Association of Arab Americans (NAAA) in 1972, the American-Arab Anti-Discrimination Committee (ADC) in 1980, and the Arab American Institute (AAI) in 1985. These groups spend most of their resources on lobbying, political education, and legal work in support of Arab Americans.

Though opposition to U.S./Israeli policy still animates Arab American identity politics, the pan-Arab, pro-Palestinian activism of the 1960s and 1970s has gradually evolved into an ethnic awakening of a recognizably American sort. Its central concerns—recognition, inclusion, equal treatment under the law—conform nicely to popular American ideals. Because Arabs are viewed negatively by most Americans, attempts to combat this negative image, with or without reference to the geopolitical conflicts that shape it, have become a powerful agenda around which to organize an ethnic community. The image Arab American organizations put forward as a corrective to pervasive anti-Arab stereotypes is upbeat, Americanized, and tailored to the preferences of mainstream culture and its institutions. Writing on behalf of "3 million" Arab Americans (and the Arab American Institute), Casey Kasem notes that:

> Arab Americans are grocers and governors, physicians and farmers, Indy 500 champs and taxicab drivers, financiers and factory workers, bakers and bankers, salesmen and senators, TV stars and TV repairmen, teachers and preachers, Heisman Trophy-winning quarterbacks and neighborhood sandlot heroes. Name it, and an Arab American has probably done it. . . . We Arab Americans and our families are proud of our heritage and proud to be Americans. It's this pride that keeps us all asking, "What can we do for our country?"—the good old U.S.A. (*Arab Americans: Making a Difference,* a promotional flyer distributed by the Arab American Institute, 1997)

But what exactly is the "heritage" to which Kasem refers? Judging from his list of over one hundred famous Arab Americans—everyone from Doug Flutie to Edward Said—the only aspect of the Arab American heritage worth sharing is the (indisputable) fact that Arabs can be "good Americans," as proven by their ability to become celebrities non-Arabs admire. In a world of public relations, role models, and the mass marketing of identities, Kasem's discourse can be highly effective, even uplifting. The sensibility it fosters, however, is ill-equipped to deal with the reality of cultural difference. It implies that, except for a common origin in Arabic-speaking countries, Arab Americans are as much a part of mainstream culture as anyone else. Ironically, this tactical appeal to "sameness" makes ancestry (or blood-based difference) the key element in determining who Arab Americans are. It is all that makes Arab American "loyalty, inventiveness, and courage on behalf of the U.S.A" (Kasem 1997) distinctively Arab.

Its superficiality aside, the ethnic identity Kasem and AAI are promoting is politically useful because it fosters pride in relation to other American racial and ethnic groups, who have their own claims to press, their own accomplishments to celebrate. As a result, "Arab American identity" is invoked today only in a limited array of representational (and usually quite competitive) contexts; government, ethnic business and niche marketing, civil liberties, and public multicultural display account for nearly all of them. Yet even in these particular zones, thousands of Arabic-speaking Detroiters (Iraqi Chaldeans in particular) still adamantly refuse to describe themselves as Arab. A similar reticence is common among the descendants of Arabic-speaking immigrants who came to Detroit before 1918, when Lebanon, Syria, and Palestine were part of the Ottoman Empire. At the other end of the spectrum, many newly arrived immigrants have trouble with the "American" half of the term, which does not yet fit a sense of self shaped in the Arab world.

There is nothing exceptional in all this. The term "Arab American" generates the same patterns of allegiance and ambivalence found among other "special populations" whose names stand for, and must often create, entire communities: Latinos, Asians, African Americans, Native Americans, and now even gays and the disabled. To become a community of this sort, a group must be distinguishable from the mainstream in some ways but essentially like it in others; it must have a definite size and shape (in relation to the national mainstream); it must have a general experience (or at least a memory) of struggle and disadvantage; and, most important, it must possess a history, a collective biography, that it tells the larger society. These attributes of community do not arise naturally out of the populations they describe. Instead, they must be actively produced, distributed, and consumed by individuals who are heavily invested in the community as a resource.

In the essays that follow, Kim Schopmeyer and Karen Rignall explore the qualities and quantities that define Arab Detroit as a community. Their essays are highly specific. Schopmeyer takes on the issue of Arab Detroit's size and internal structure, a topic that requires careful study of U.S. Census figures. Rignall traces the development of ACCESS (Arab Community Center for Economic and Social Services), an influential social service agency in Dearborn. Despite their deceptively narrow scope, both authors manage to reveal the inner workings of identity formation in modern political settings. Numbers and narratives are essential to this process. Arab Detroit would not exist for most Americans if it had no (shared) past worth recounting, no (common) heritage worth preserving. It would hardly count as a commercial zone or a voting bloc if it had no reliable sense of its own size. It could not function as a target of financial investment or government services if its members were unable to state, with bureaucratically useful precision, who belonged to the Arab community and who did not.

The two essays presented in this section, when read together, show just how firmly the agendas motivating Arab community formation are rooted in American political and economic frameworks. The U.S. Census determines how government funds will be distributed. The controversy over the size of Arab Detroit is, at heart, a struggle over money: who gets it and how much. ACCESS, with an annual budget of over five million dollars, most of it from state and federal funding sources, has an obvious stake in deciding how many Arabs live in Michigan, and it continues to generate surveys that support its claims to an Arab Detroit of more than two hundred thousand members. Official government sources, no less interested than ACCESS, insist on numbers less than one hundred thousand. Federal and local population estimates affect levels of corporate investment in Arab Detroit's ethnic niche markets. Similarly, without its large budget, ACCESS could not hope to sustain its success in organizing, mobilizing, and representing Arab Detroit. Rignall's account of the Arab community's history is appropriately framed in relation to the development of ACCESS as a political and cultural force in Detroit. The story Rignall tells originated in the work of social scientists and historians, but it has since been propagated almost entirely by ACCESS in its workshops for teachers in area schools, in interviews with local media, in the exhibit cases of the ACCESS Museum of Arab Culture, in the documentary films ACCESS produces, and in the work of academics who use ACCESS as a point of entry to Arab Detroit. Likewise, Rignall's narrative is in line with ACCESS policy (and at odds with the sensitivities of many assimilated Arab Americans) in its unapologetic admission—indeed, its *insistence*—that large sectors of Arab Detroit are culturally Other, politically disaffected, and desperately in need of government assistance.

The intricacy with which these narratives, numbers, and mainstream interests are tied together in Detroit became evident in April 1997, at a national symposium on Arab Americans organized by the Center for Contemporary Arab Studies at Georgetown University. One of the prominent issues discussed at the symposium was pollster John Zogby's newest demographic survey of Arab America, in which Detroit (at 219,765) was demoted from largest Arab community to second largest, behind Los Angeles (at 283,355). Zogby's figures were immediately seized upon by Beth Krodel, the journalist who covered the event for the *Detroit Free Press,* and her article "Detroit May No Longer Be Top Spot for Arabs" (April 5, 1997) created shock waves in Detroit. Mayor Dennis Archer stepped in to reassure local Arab leaders, announcing for the record that "you'll always be number one in our book, no matter what they say." In a study released by ACCESS in 1998, Zogby arrived at different numbers for Detroit: 206,411 "Arabs," who were a subset of 274,879 "Middle Easterners," a rubric that includes many of Detroit's Arabic-speaking "non-Arabs" and their descendants (Chaldeans and Kurds, some Armenians, Arab/Israeli Jews, and various old-stock Syrian Christians). The results of Zogby's study will be used by ACCESS to influence government and commercial policies in Detroit; in the process, Arabs and "near Arabs" of heterogeneous cultural backgrounds will be offered up to mainstream institutions as a single Arab American constituency with its own internal economy.

In everyday life, however, being Arab American is not the only, or even the most compelling, identity available to Arabs in Detroit. Islam and Christianity foster more inclusive models of self and society. National labels—Palestinian, Lebanese, Yemeni—can be superseded by rhetorical appeals to "Arab unity," but are never far from view. "Middle Eastern" identity, though vague, is appealing to those who wish to avoid the stigma attached to all things Arab in the West. Of course, one can ignore Arabness altogether in most situations, opting instead for affiliations open to anyone: baseball fan, carpenter, book lover, dentist, upstanding member of the Neighborhood Watch or the PTA. Despite all this, "Arab American," with its familiar ethnic overtones, secular credentials, and organizational backing from ACCESS and the local branches of national Arab American organizations, is the communal identity non-Arabs are most likely to see in Detroit, whether these sightings occur at ethnic festivals, cultural diversity workshops, museum exhibits, on public-access cable stations, or on the pages of local newspapers and magazines.

The public nature of Arab American identity is directly related to its dependence on public funding and formats. Activists struggle to incorporate "Arab American interests" in public policy. Entrepreneurs associate Arabness with specific goods and services transacted on the open market. Academics package "Arab society and culture" in forms of knowledge designed to be accessible to the public. This book will gravitate steadily toward forms of Arab identity that are consistently muted, even concealed, in America's public domain; nonetheless, we think it is wise to start by examining the conceptual infrastructure—a blend of numbers and narratives produced by government-funded and community-based institutions—that connects Arab American identity to other ethnic and immigrant identities, and eventually to the American mainstream.

8 Houses from the Birthplace of Henry Ford

Hayan Charara

FOR LAWRENCE JOSEPH

I'm from Detroit. It's French,
the name. And although I've
never met a Frenchman or heard
of one at the factory, it's
obvious this place was theirs
by the names of the dead
and their streets and boulevards
that radiate from the edge
of the water—Cadiuex, Belle Isle,
Rouge, Lafayette, Beaubien.
Utterly ridiculous! Cadillac
rediscovers the great stretch
of blue and his language is
here forever. Forget that,
it's about grammar. How does
the Detroiter pronounce his name?
Meagerly, full of distaste
for the elegant, there's no
accent. My name is Hayan Charara,
from Motor City, and I couldn't
utter the simplest word in French.

Carlin Street, Detroit. 1972.
Arabs, three gypsies, the old

Reprinted from *Forkroads* 1 (winter 1995), 12.

Polish ladies and the black
families that would rise each day
and ride the bus to Miller Road
to build cars they would never
drive. Three blocks and a dead
end. Immigrant houses lodged by
the gravel parking lot and back
wall of an empty warehouse
and the stolen car junkyard.
Wide streets and gray sidewalks
lined on each side with trees
the height of three-story houses
to keep us dark. At the end
of our street there were dandelions
and knotgrass and a brick wall
and a sign that meant the end
of the block not our way of life.
On the other side was the beginning,
Tireman Avenue, the Red Sea Moses
could not part. During the second
riot of '67, Hubbard, Dearborn's
mayor, was greater than God.
Down Tireman any sort of exodus
seemed impossible. Dearborn Police
stood at the edge of the two cities.
Hubbard's orders, plain and simple,
Shoot any nigger that crosses!
Any wonder we stayed in Detroit?

Antoine de la Mothe Cadillac
put an accent to the word
"Detroit" and the first year
of the city began. It was 1701.
And then to the British in 1763
and, twenty years later,
the territory was given up
to another group of frontiersmen
speaking a slightly altered
English, and the neighborhood
beside the strait became American.

And they came. With Henry Ford
and the Model T, they came to
the end of the railroad tracks
out of Alabama and through
a string of empty towns, then
past a bus stop heading through
Toledo. They came for the factory
and five dollars a day, to sleep
beneath the shadow of the Rouge
and break the bread of sacrifice
to thank God for this holy city
where the ashes of their work
would rise each day and night
to the skies and heaven. And that
is the beginning of each story
told about how it was some
grandfather or brother came to be
in this old French town. Before
the riots my father came to
the factory city where the smokestacks
had stopped, and it was only
a matter of time before our family
did as the others who had once
called this great city theirs.
Who remembers my father's name?
Speaks his language?

8 houses from the birthplace
of Henry Ford. That is how far
from Dearborn we lived. It was
in the car maker's hometown,
after my family moved out
of the old neighborhood to
"the largest Arab community
outside an Arab speaking country"
that I was first called
a sand nigger. How could I not
know I was a light-skinned nigger?
After all, I was from the city
on the strait where the citizenry

was prone to acts of violence
and skilled merely at work
with their hands and brutal
and savage. All those years
in Detroit, where I learned about
people and their lives and how
they lived like the seasons,
to rise and work and sleep and die,
I never once heard that word.
I still cannot get the damned
sound of it to leave. 8 houses away
and it was a different place.

Building the Infrastructure of Arab American Identity in Detroit

A Short History of ACCESS and the Community It Serves

Karen Rignall

In April 1997 the Arab Community Center for Economic and Social Services (ACCESS) held its twenty-sixth annual dinner at Cobo Hall in downtown Detroit. In many ways the dinner was like any other fund-raising event for a community organization. There were speeches from prominent figures about the importance of activism, expressions of appreciation from ACCESS leaders for consistent corporate support, and testimonials about the positive impact ACCESS programs have had on the low-income population of southeast Michigan. In other ways, however, the dinner represented a landmark for the Arab community in Detroit: over three thousand people attended, with Michigan senators Carl Levin and Spencer Abraham, Detroit mayor Dennis Archer, representatives of Governor John Engler, and top executives of the "big three" auto companies lending an aura of political prominence to the event. This public recognition of Arab Americans as a regional presence is a hard-won achievement of decades of political activism. From being a largely invisible minority that in the early twentieth century sought to assimilate by Americanizing its names, language, and traditions, Arabs in Detroit have moved toward a more public affirmation of cultural difference as a way of combating the discrimination and economic hardship that have always marked immigration to the United States.

There are an estimated one hundred thousand to three hundred thousand Arabs and Chaldeans (a Christian ethnic group from Iraq) in southeast Michigan. Virtually all nationalities and ethnicities from the Arab Middle East are represented: Lebanese, Yemenis, Syrians, Palestinians, Egyptians, and, since the Gulf War, an increasing number of Iraqi Shia. There has been a steady stream of immigrants to Detroit for over a hundred years, and each wave of arrivals adds another layer to the rich history of this heterogeneous community. Arab immigrants hope Detroit will offer chances of finding work. They also look to Detroit for mosques and churches where they can pray in a familiar manner, stores where they can buy the clothes they prefer and the foods they grew up with; in sum, they know they will find a cultural milieu that can dull the edges of dislocation and adjustment. Traditionally, this heavy concentration of Arabs in southeast Michigan has not translated into political power or a cohesive social community. ACCESS has tried to create a structure in which the Arab population of Detroit can find solidarity and economic security amid the challenges of immigration.

ACCESS offers an entrance to the story of Arab American community formation in Detroit. Here I will set the history of ACCESS against the broader social and historical background of immigrant experience in the United States during a period of backlash against immigrants and the poor. This point of view offers a fuller understanding of the shifting landscape of contemporary immigrant communities in Detroit, Arab and non-Arab alike. Since 1995, major legislative initiatives have drawn national attention to a rising cultural chauvinism that finds expression in increased hostility toward immigrants: Proposition 187 in California, the Omnibus Anti-Terrorism Act of 1996, and the Immigration Reform Law of 1997 are glaring examples of a deepening tendency toward exclusion in American society. The experience of the Arab community in Detroit, and specifically in Dearborn, demonstrates how this increased hostility intersects with exclusionary policies against the poor and disadvantaged in American society as a whole.

Not all Arab immigrants are poor. Nonetheless, considering issues of immigration and poverty together will further our understanding of how social exclusion develops spatially and how cultural nationalism establishes boundaries designed to keep certain ethnic and religious Others from crossing U.S. borders, even as it allows some Others to slip into the American mainstream virtually unnoticed. This selective process of exclusion complements the increasing socioeconomic isolation of low-income Americans. Boundaries that keep immigrants out are reproduced within the urban landscape, cutting off the access of poor people to social services, education, and long-term employment.

Genesis of a Community

Dearborn rests on the southwest edge of Detroit, an industrial zone that once served as the centerpiece of Henry Ford's industrial empire. The Ford Rouge Plant, immortalized in the imposing murals by Diego Rivera at the Detroit Institute of Arts, dominates the landscape of Dearborn's Southend. It is a huge complex; there were once over ninety thousand workers there handling each stage in the production of a car, from the steelworks to the final paint finish. Now only eleven thousand workers remain at the Rouge Plant, though the expansive factory grounds serve as a reminder of an earlier period in the auto industry when production was concentrated in large complexes rather than dispersed all over the country and the world. The Ford Motor Company headquarters is still in Dearborn, but the company itself, like its "big three" competitors, GM and Chrysler, has moved its factories into the suburbs, across the nation, and overseas. With the Rouge Plant dominating the Dearborn landscape, it seems natural to link the growth of the city's Arab population to the rise of the auto industry. In many ways the two are linked, but the history of Arab Detroit extends beyond the history of Ford Motor Company: Arabs began coming to southeast Michigan well before the consolidation of the auto industry.

Arabic-speaking immigrants first arrived in the United States in the 1870s. They were mainly Lebanese, or more precisely, they were from the area of Mount Lebanon in the Ottoman province of Syria that would become Lebanon in 1943. They came in small numbers, looking for work and political stability, the same impetus that sent Lebanese all over the world (Hoogland 1987; Hourani and Shehada 1992). There are large Lebanese populations in West Africa; they served as merchants in the growing trade between African kingdoms, colonies, and nations and the European metropole. Similar communities emerged in Latin America, the Caribbean, and Australia (McKay 1989). In most cases, the Arabic-speaking minorities focused on commerce, enlisting extended families as the labor necessary to set up shops and trading companies. In the United States the Arab experience was a bit different. The first Lebanese were single men who traveled around the Midwest with suitcases of notions, dry goods, and other small commodities, moving from farm to farm, town to town, selling their wares (Naff 1985). Those who succeeded tended to move into metropolitan areas like Detroit and Chicago and sponsor the immigration of others from their villages back in Lebanon. As more and more Lebanese were able to earn enough money to establish general stores, they began to send for their families. This is a familiar immigrant narrative in the United States. It is frequently invoked to explain how an ethnic group became established in a particular city and neighborhood.

Just as the auto industry transformed the economic landscape of Michigan, it restructured Detroit's burgeoning Arab community. Almost all the early immigrant neighborhoods were located near auto plants in Highland Park, Hamtramck, and near the Jefferson Avenue Chrysler plant on Detroit's east side. Because racist hiring policies tended to exclude African Americans from working in the auto plants, the rapid growth of the auto industry meant plentiful jobs for new immigrants from Europe and the Near East. Though Arabs readily found work with Ford, Chrysler, and GM, they suffered the effects of discrimination in the daily operations of the plants. Even today, a disproportionately high percentage of dangerous jobs go to Arab immigrants, especially Yemenis, who lack the support they need from the union or informal factory networks to lobby for better positions on the production line (Abraham 1978; Friedlander 1988).

The development of the auto industry throughout the twentieth century also largely explains the spatial configuration of the Dearborn area. Arabs gradually congregated in the Dearborn row houses constructed by Henry Ford, literally in the shadow of the Rouge Plant. It was not only the Arabs, however, who found economic security in the high salaries paid by Henry Ford: until the 1950s, over fifty languages were spoken in the working-class neighborhoods of south and east Dearborn. Dearborn's Southend still looks like a company town, with many of the same houses standing in carefully laid out grids. But the neighborhood is much smaller than it used to be, and the air of prosperity has given way to visible strains caused by the social and economic problems of Greater Detroit. Now Dearborn's Arab (and non-Arab) communities are spatially separated into those whose foothold in the middle class enabled them to weather the downturn in the Michigan economy of the late 1970s and 1980s and those who are left to navigate the complexities of a segmented labor market and a shrinking social services bureaucracy.

Arabs, like other minority communities in Detroit, have been severely affected by macroeconomic changes. The Arab community in Dearborn, however, long ago assumed a cultural importance independent of the auto industry. With yet more Lebanese arriving with the onset of World War I (1914–18) and the demise of the Ottoman Empire, Dearborn began to emerge as a center for Arab migration, and other Detroit suburbs eventually became immigrant destinations as well. Family histories and genealogies placed Dearborn, Hamtramck, and Southfield alongside Jerusalem, Telkaif, and Sana'a, as the Arabs who followed the initial influx of merchant Lebanese faced the harsh realities of diaspora. Most of the immigrants from the Middle East following World War II (1939–45) fled violent conflicts and severe economic deprivation. Palestinians arrived in greater numbers after the creation of Israel in 1948; Yemeni and Iraqi Chaldean immigration swelled in the late 1960s, as civil wars, military coups, and separatist movements destabilized their homelands; a new surge of Lebanese, mostly Shia from the south of Lebanon, came in the wake of the civil war of the 1970s and the 1978 and 1982 Israeli invasions.

Class and Suburbia in Arab Detroit

The social life of Arab Detroit shifts with the vagaries of Michigan's labor market and with the political and economic transitions now unfolding in places of origin throughout the Middle East. Another important element shaping the character of Arab Detroit is the complex set of sociopolitical rifts that divide this already heterogeneous community. The rifts in question are not age-old Middle Eastern antagonisms—between Catholic and Orthodox Christians, say, or Shia and Sunni Muslims—imported and rewritten in concentrated form on the geography of Detroit. Lebanon has been one of the most troubled sites for religious/sectarian violence in the Arab world, but sectarianism never took hold in southeast Michigan with the same virulence it did in Lebanon during the civil war (1975–90). Relations between Detroit's Arab Christians and Muslims ebbed and flowed with the various stages of the war in Lebanon, but most of the immigrants who escaped the war tried to leave behind the political and communal differences that had caused so much turmoil in their homelands. By far, the more potent sociopolitical divisions in Arab Detroit exist across class lines or reflect degrees of cultural assimilation.

The earliest Arabic-speaking immigrants placed great emphasis on blending into what they perceived to be mainstream American culture. Generally few in number, they tended to establish roots in Anglo-American communities, often through door-to-door sales (Naff 1994). As the community congregated in Greater Detroit, a more cohesive cultural identity began to emerge and more public assertions of Arab heritage were seen in storefronts, social gatherings, and religious practice. Store signs, for instance, displayed Arab names rather than anglicized versions, and families took religious observance from the home into public places of worship. The first mosque in the United States was built in Highland Park in 1919; Detroit's first Maronite Catholic Church was established in 1916; St. George's Orthodox followed in 1918; and the Southend of Dearborn was home to both a Sunni and a Shia mosque by the 1930s. Large weddings and social gatherings perpetuated and remade ritual and religious practice. Gradually, the social stigma many Arab immigrants felt about "being different" gave way, and more public and politicized espousals of a specifically Arab American identity emerged following the 1967 Arab-Israeli War (Suleiman 1994).

As the older Lebanese Christian community became established economically, its members joined the steady stream of Detroit residents who were moving into the suburbs. Dearborn's Arab Muslim neighborhood, by contrast, stayed put and became progressively more important as a staging area where new immigrants from Lebanon, Palestine, and Yemen could learn English, assimilate to an already Arabized American culture, and, if they succeeded, follow their predecessors into the wealthier suburbs. The Seven Mile area in Detroit came to play a similar role for newly arrived Chaldeans from Iraq (Sengstock 1982). Despite an exodus from these ethnic neighborhoods that continues to this day, Seven Mile and Dearborn still provide the backbone for a developing sense of community and shared culture among new immigrants and old residents. In Dearborn, the line between those who remained and those who moved to the suburbs marked a clear class division. Working-class families with two or three generations represented in the auto factories formed the core of Dearborn's Southend. These families have provided a sense of cultural continuity across recent decades, orchestrating a unique kind of assimilation based on an intermediate, generalized Arab/American culture that allows for dialogue across sectarian, ethnic, and national lines (Abraham, Abraham, and Aswad 1983).

This is the Dearborn/Arab culture to which recent Lebanese, Iraqi Shia, Yemeni, and Palestinian immigrants are now assimilating. The cycle of starting out in Dearborn and then moving to the suburbs is happening less and less. The socioeconomic foothold of the most disadvantaged immigrants, the Yemenis and the Iraqi Shia, is so tenuous that it creates virtually insurmountable barriers to long-term, skilled employment. Dearborn's Palestinians, who were mostly from the village of Beit Hanina, have moved en masse to Cleveland, where they now run grocery and convenience stores. Meanwhile, the large number of recent Lebanese immigrants who are finding success in small business are content to live in Dearborn, now the epicenter of Arab Detroit. Their desire to stay (and invest) in the city has triggered an economic boom in east Dearborn, where a new "Middle East Market" business district has been established along Warren Avenue, and where real estate values are soaring as Arab families build new houses and compete to buy old ones from the area's dwindling non-Arab population.

Arab American Political Organization in Detroit

The dominant role Dearborn plays in Arab Detroit today strikes many observers as a sociopolitical and demographic fact of life, but this was not always the case. In the 1970s a challenge to the very existence of the Arab community in Dearborn resulted in the heightened political activism that, over the next three decades, would build the organizational infrastructure of the Arab American constituency in southeast Michigan. This challenge arose out of domestic concerns (the demands of the Ford Motor Company and other industrial interests in Dearborn and the changing spatial politics of Detroit in the aftermath of the 1967 riot) as well as political and economic upheavals in the Middle East (especially the 1967 Arab-Israel War and its fallout in Lebanon).

Throughout the 1960s Dearborn mayor Orville Hubbard, who held office for thirty-five years, enacted numerous "urban renewal" projects that promised to turn Dearborn's Southend into an industrial zone, extending the already expansive perimeter of steel and auto plants into the very neighborhoods that supplied their labor. Over 250 homes were destroyed, along with stores, clubs, and churches, before local activists were able to organize a defense of the community's boundaries. I use the term "community boundaries" pointedly, for this was the kind of challenge that brought a sense of those boundaries into existence, into the consciousness of the Dearborn residents who were being uprooted (Aswad 1974).

The economic situation of most of the affected families was precarious, and they would have few options for affordable housing near their places of work. A court case ensued, and a federal injunction halted the bulldozing and the industrial park project in 1973. The effects were long-lasting, both instilling fears of future neighborhood destruction and compelling stronger political organization to preempt such threats. ACCESS was one outcome of this early struggle. The mobilization that took place around the industrial park project raised awareness among local activists about long-term needs among the newly arrived Arab immigrants. In the absence of social services that met these needs, ACCESS established a storefront community center, offering a few English classes taught by volunteers and simple drop-in services aimed at helping people with tasks essential to establishing a life in Dearborn: filling out social security forms, getting welfare assistance, and settling disputes with employers and landlords. From this modest beginning in 1971, ACCESS grew to become a comprehensive social service agency with a five-million-dollar annual budget, over one hundred employees, and forty-two programs, such as English classes, health care, counseling, employment services, and cultural arts programming (Aswad and Gray 1996).

In contrast to its predecessors in the Arab American community that were organized along lines of religion or nationality, ACCESS offered nonsectarian social services that brought the specific needs of the Arab American population to the forefront of local and regional politics. ACCESS now stands alongside the American-Arab Anti-Discrimination Committee and the Arab American Institute as one of the nation's premier advocacy groups. Moreover, it is the only such group whose funding comes entirely from domestic sources, with most of its operating budget underwritten by state, federal, and (to a lesser extent) corporate grants. Though social service programming at ACCESS is focused exclusively on southeast Michigan, Director Ismael Ahmed and other ACCESS leaders have been heavily involved in lobbying at the national level for immigrant rights and the maintenance of federally funded social programs. Important multiethnic coalitions, linking Detroit's Arab, Latino, Asian, and African American communities, have grown up around these advocacy efforts. These linkages have not erased the many differences that cut across such a heterogeneous population, and no one would assert that they were intended to do so, but they have given Arab Americans a more public political presence. This has helped Dearborn residents begin to challenge the structural problems that affect the most disadvantaged and marginalized sectors of Arab Detroit.

Nonetheless, the forces shaping the economic and social geography of Detroit are often overwhelming. The downturn of the auto industry in the 1980s hit Detroit with a strength far outweighing the resources of a single community organization. This has lent a new gravity to the employment problems that have plagued the Detroit area for years. Currently, with a shift in the demography of recent immigrants, ACCESS faces urgent new challenges from unemployment rates that can run as high as 40 percent in some parts of the Arab community, despite the upturn in the Michigan economy. Today, there are few prospects for job seekers who are largely poor and unskilled, have limited English proficiency, and are often illiterate even in Arabic. Many Arab women are not in the workforce and face acute barriers to entering it. Among the newest wave of immigrants, few women speak English or are able to read or write it, and cultural concerns about the safety and reputation of women who work outside the home rule out many employment options for Arab women in Detroit.

This population of hard-to-employ immigrants, composed of Iraqi refugees with a short history of immigration to the United States and little access to the networks that aided earlier Lebanese immigrants, has become increasingly isolated. Organizations such as ACCESS bring these separate groups together through community-driven social service programs, but this cannot stem the tide of increasing impoverishment when spatial dynamics of the job market place working-class Dearborn on the margins of the regional economy. After national welfare and immigration "reform" programs were announced in 1996, people turned to ACCESS in record numbers. They were worried, understanding only the broad outlines of a complicated set of policies hazy even to lawmakers. Arabic radio shows brought in immigration and social service officials to try to explain, but each individual's case is different, and many are simply overwhelmed by feelings of powerlessness against these hostile moves by a government that has, ironically enough, allowed them to migrate to the United States.

New Challenges

Since the Gulf War in 1991, Greater Detroit has absorbed over three thousand Iraqis a year. Many are Shia from the embattled south of Iraq who have spent the last five years moving from one refugee camp to another, from Saudi Arabia to Jordan to the United States. During this same period, the number of English classes offered at ACCESS has been cut in half. The Iraqis' invitation to settle in the United States is not bringing the relief they were promised, given the elimination of public assistance for many noncitizens and the unlikelihood of finding a job soon after arriving in the area. Promised state and federal funds for job training are not adequate for people with limited mobility, little English, and few employable skills. The

Iraqi-owned groceries and restaurants now appearing in Dearborn are evidence of what can be achieved with minimal public assistance, but these fledgling establishments must compete with Lebanese and Chaldean businesses that are today more numerous and successful than ever before.

Unlike the period of crisis faced by the Arab community in the 1970s, the current situation is marked by some key ironies. As Arab Americans become progressively more vocal in local and state politics, as prominent politicians begin to pay greater attention to this growing constituency, as more Arab Americans in Michigan are elected or appointed to government office, and as Arab-owned businesses spread to every corner of Greater Detroit, the newest and most marginalized additions to Arab Detroit are being further isolated by policies directed primarily by the federal government and by economic trends that have fed the success and financial security of a new class of Arab immigrant entrepreneurs.

References

Abraham, Nabeel. 1978. *National and Local Politics: A Study of Political Conflict in a Yemeni Immigrant Community of Detroit, Michigan.* Ann Arbor, Mich.: University Microfilms.

Abraham, Sameer, Nabeel Abraham, and Barbara Aswad. 1983. The Southend: An Arab Muslim Working-Class Community. In *Arabs in the New World: Studies on Arab-American Communities,* edited by Sameer Abraham and Nabeel Abraham, 164–81. Detroit: Center for Urban Studies, Wayne State University.

Aswad, Barbara. 1974. The Southeast Dearborn Arab Community Struggles for Survival against Urban "Renewal." In *Arabic Speaking Communities in American Cities,* edited by Barbara Aswad. New York: Center for Migration Studies and Association of Arab-American University Graduates.

Aswad, Barbara, and Nancy Adadow Gray. 1996. Challenges to the Arab-American Family and ACCESS. In *Family and Gender among American Muslims: Issues Facing Middle Eastern Immigrants and Their Descendants,* edited by Barbara Aswad and Barbara Bilgé. Philadelphia: Temple University Press. 223–40.

Friedlander, Jonathan, ed. 1988. *Sojourners and Settlers: the Yemeni Immigrant Experience.* Berkeley: University of California Press.

Hoogland, Eric, ed. 1987. *Crossing the Waters: Arabic-Speaking Immigrants to the United States before 1940*. Washington, D.C.: Smithsonian Institution Press.

Hourani, Albert, and Nadim Shehada, eds. 1992. *The Lebanese in the World: A Century of Immigration*. London: I. B. Tauris.

McCarus, Ernest, ed. 1994. *The Development of Arab-American Identity*. Ann Arbor: University of Michigan Press.

McKay, James. 1989. *Phoenician Farewell: Three Generations of Lebanese Christians in Australia*. Melbourne, Australia: Ashwood House Academic.

Naff, Alixa. 1985. *Becoming American: The Early Arab Immigrant Experience*. Carbondale: Southern Illinois University Press.

———. 1994. The Early Arab Immigrant Experience. In *The Development of Arab-American Identity*, edited by Ernest McCarus, 23–36.

Sengstock, Mary. 1982. *The Chaldean Americans: Changing Conceptions of Ethnic Identity*. New York: Center for Migration Studies.

Suleiman, Michael. 1994. Arab-Americans and the Political Process. In *The Development of Arab-American Identity*, edited by Ernest McCarus.

A Demographic Portrait of Arab Detroit

Kim Schopmeyer

Henry Ford and *the auto industry; Barry Gordy and Motown Records; the 1967 riots and "Devil's Night."* Alongside these popular symbols, which have influenced national perceptions of Detroit, is the new image of Detroit as home to the largest concentration of Arabs outside the Middle East. Although this claim may be exaggerated, since the exact number of Arabs in any American city is a matter of uncertainty and speculation, it is clear that the Detroit area—and particularly the suburb of Dearborn—is home to a large, diverse, and vital community of Arab immigrants, children of immigrants, and their descendants.

Many immigrant communities in the United States have been the subject of careful demographic research: Cubans in Miami, Puerto Ricans in New York City, Mexicans in Texas and California. The Arab population of Detroit has not received a proportionate amount of scholarly attention. This oversight can be traced to a number of factors, most of which will go unexplored here. My purpose in this essay is simply to sketch a picture of the Arab population in Metropolitan Detroit by describing its socioeconomic characteristics and general patterns of migration.

Census Data: Strengths and Weaknesses

This exploration of Metro Detroit's Arab American community is based on the analysis of 1990 U.S. census data. The census data have a variety of features that make them the best available source of demographic information on Arab Americans. They contain information on an important range of factors, including national ancestry, age, family structure, education, income, and other basic demographic indicators.

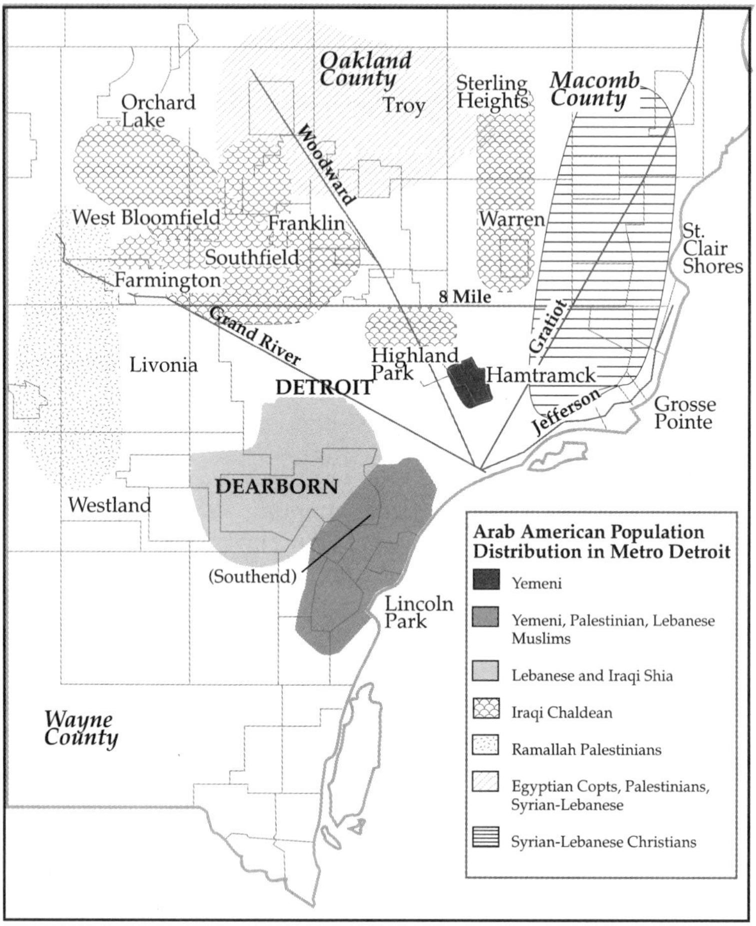

Adapted from Sameer Abraham and Nabeel Abraham, eds. *Arabs in the New World: Studies on Arab-American Communities* (Detroit: Center for Urban Studies, Wayne State University, 1983). Map designed by Melinda Hamilton.

However, the census data also contain serious limitations for a study of this type. The weaknesses of the 1990 census are those of any self-reported mail survey; foremost among these is the problem of nonresponse. Although the Census Bureau took extensive measures to achieve a high response rate and employed various methods to compensate for missing data, the final 1990 enumeration was somewhat disappointing. The estimated undercount nationwide was 1.7 percent, roughly 4.2 million people out of some 248 million. This was larger than in the previous count of 1980, though not as serious as suggested in early reports.[1] The undercount refers to the entire population, however, and is estimated to be much higher in certain areas and among certain groups, such as African American men. One reason for the decline in estimated response rate between the 1980 and 1990 censuses was the larger number of immigrants in the population in 1990. For several reasons, including language barriers and suspicion of government authorities, new immigrants can be difficult to count accurately, a factor of obvious relevance to any discussion of Arab Detroit. Potentially, we can expect a significant undercount among recently arrived immigrants, and we are safe in assuming, therefore, that the Arab American community is larger than census figures report.

Another limitation of the census figures is the difficulty in clearly identifying "Arab Americans" in the data. In 1990 no specific questions were asked about a person's ethnic background, except for one item identifying people of Hispanic origin. However, questions on the "long form" questionnaire, administered to roughly 17 percent of households, probe for the ancestry of each member of the household and allow up to two different ancestries. The data used in this study come from the "long form" samples called public use microdata samples, or PUMS files. These data allow us to identify as "Arab American" any individuals in the tri-county Detroit Metro area who claimed at least one ancestry linking them to any of the following countries or categories: Algerian, Egyptian, Moroccan, Libyan, Iraqi, Jordanian, Kuwaiti, Lebanese, Saudi Arabian, Syrian, Yemeni, Kurdish, Palestinian, or from the broader categories "Arab" or "Middle East" (which includes many non-Arabs).

Because the data are self-reported or reported by one household member for all others in the house, there is room for error. For people with more than two ancestries (for example, German, Irish, and Lebanese), the Arab ancestry may be excluded because only two responses are allowed. Thus, the census tallies of Arab Americans may underestimate people of mixed ancestry, typically descendants of immigrants who married non-Arabs several generations ago. Others choose not to answer the ethnicity question at all, although the Census Bureau tries to contact households to fill in missing data. In spite of the problems generated by nonresponse, we can expect the PUMS data to provide a reasonably accurate estimate of those who choose to identify themselves and their family members as Arab or Arab American in the Detroit area.

Another significant limitation should be noted, however. Because the PUMS data are taken from a 17 percent sample, rather than the complete enumeration of the population, the census data regarding ethnicity are actually *estimates* of the total numbers of Arab Americans. As we focus on particular subgroups of the sample—say, the percentage of Detroit-area Arab Americans who are college graduates or those who live in Macomb County—we are dealing with estimates, not actual population counts.

Estimating Arab Detroit

U.S. census data have been the target of considerable criticism by researchers who study Arab Americans. In a report published by the Arab American Institute, John Zogby (1990) argues that the 1980 census-produced estimates of the Arab American population in the United States were "unacceptably low." Nonetheless, in developing his counteranalysis, Zogby uses the percentage breakdowns derived from the census results. After examining immigration figures from the U.S. Immigration and Naturalization Service (INS), Zogby provides an estimate for the United States, stating that "these 'official' figures alone suggest a population of over 650,000—and that excludes the fact that Arab immigrants tend to have larger household sizes than the national average." This compares to Census Bureau results of about 617,000 Arab Americans for 1980, indicating at least a 5 percent undercount. By contrast, Zogby argues that estimates from various Arab American organizations, religious groups, and unscientific surveys have led to a "consensus figure of approximately two and one-half million Arab Americans," a figure he acknowledges to be unsubstantiated (1990, 40).

The 1990 census identified 62,699 people in Wayne, Oakland, and Macomb Counties as having one or both ancestries from Arab countries. This represents about 82 percent of the 76,773 Arab Americans in Michigan identified in the census. Another 5 percent of the total are found in the adjacent counties of Washtenaw, St. Clair,

Livingston, and Monroe. This means that nearly nine of ten Arab Americans in Michigan live in the southeast corner of the state.

The 1990 census count is much lower than estimates provided by other analysts. In 1983, Sameer Abraham estimated that some 200,000 Arabs and Arab Americans resided in the Detroit area. He based his estimate on a combination of sources and numbers from community leaders. Zogby (1990, 27), as part of his larger report on Arabs in the United States, offered an estimate of 250,000 for Michigan, although he provided no information on how he arrived at this figure. More recently, Zogby (1998) estimated about 206,000 persons of Arab ancestry in Greater Detroit based on a telephone survey conducted in 1997.[2]

Two other studies conducted in the mid-1980s on Detroit-area Arab Americans sought to correct for census undercounts. They suggested the Arab community might have approached 78,000 to 80,000 by 1985 and perhaps 100,000 by 1990 (United Community Services of Metropolitan Detroit 1985; Sands 1986). In any case, the 1990 census figure of 62,699 appears to be quite low, even compared to these more conservative estimates. The 1980 census generated a total of 52,800 Arabs using the ancestry data; thus, the 1990 numbers indicate about a 19 percent increase in Metro Detroit (compared to a 35 percent increase of Arabs *nationwide* between the 1980 and 1990 censuses). While it is impossible to substantiate very high estimates of 200,000 or more, the gap between the census data and higher figures can be traced to the undercounting of Arab immigrants and Arab Americans of mixed ancestry.

Undercounting Immigrants

As noted above, recent immigrants are likely to have higher than average undercounts due to language difficulties, a suspicion of government inquiries, a sense of marginality to the larger society, and little incentive to complete the forms. Local Census Bureau offices attempt to counter these problems by providing language assistance from community representatives, who have a greater understanding of the political and economic advantages of an accurate count. They also work with immigrant community leaders to increase participation. Nonetheless, we must still expect reduced participation from recent immigrants. An examination of immigration figures illustrates this point.

Although most published data from the INS do not provide the geographic detail needed to study the Detroit area, a report

Table 1
Comparison of Estimated Arab Immigrants from Southwest Asia, INS and PUMS, 1983–1990

	Total Arab Immigrants to U.S. (INS)[a]	Percentage of Total Immigrants Going to Detroit	Metro Detroit Immigrants (INS)[b]	Metro Detroit Foreign-Born (PUMS)	Difference (INS – PUMS)
Iraq	12,763	31.1	3,963	1,232	2,731
Jordan	22,981	3.9	916	449	467
Lebanon	30,375	12.8	3,890	4,080	–190
Syria	14,100	4.5	634	312	332
Yemen	4,707	23.1	1,088	180	908
Other Asia	12,019	6.7	805	404	401
Total	96,945	11.7	11,296	6,657	4,639

[a]includes Asians from non-Arab countries
[b]includes other western Asian countries (excluding Iran)

released through the Southeast Michigan Census Council is helpful in exploring immigration to this region (APB Associates 1995). These figures reflect Immigration and Naturalization Service (INS) records of immigrants to the United States based on country of origin and zip code of destination from 1983 to 1992. During this period, an estimated 17,721 immigrants from the Arab countries of southwest Asia identified southeast Michigan zip codes as their destination. (Arabs from Africa may also have been among these immigrants, but the data do not indicate how many.) Table 1 provides estimates of Arab immigrants between 1983 and 1990, allowing us to compare the 1990 PUMS data with the INS figures. The third column provides the estimates of immigrants to the metro area based on the INS figures, while the fourth column uses the census PUMS figures to estimate the number of foreign-born Arabs in Metro Detroit who had entered the country from 1983 to 1990. The comparison shows that, with the exception of Lebanese immigrants, the census data identified fewer Arab immigrants in Metro Detroit during the last seven years of the 1980s than the INS data would lead us to expect. The gap is particularly striking for Yemeni immigrants, among whom less than 20 percent of recent immigrants actually appeared in the census figures. Two-thirds of immigrants from Iraq were also not included in the census figures. By contrast, the census included nearly 5 percent *more* Lebanese immigrants than INS figures would predict (some of which may be due to Lebanese migrants who did not migrate directly from Lebanon or from West Africa). Overall, the estimate of recent immigrants by the INS figures is about 43 percent higher than that suggested by the census data.[3]

While this difference is noteworthy, the result yields a fairly small additional number of Arabs to the total for Metro Detroit, an increase of about 7.3 percent. This would produce a total estimate of about 67,300. In fact, if we assume that the estimate of *all* Arab Americans in the area is 43 percent higher than the census figure shows—a highly unlikely assumption, if we expect that the native-born and long-term immigrants are counted more accurately than recent immigrants—this would still increase the Detroit-area Arab population in 1990 to only about 90,000.

Arabs of Mixed Ancestry

The large estimates of the Detroit-area Arab population—those in the two hundred thousand range or more—are meant to include individuals who *are* being counted in the census but are not being identified as Arab. These large estimates rely on a combination of objective and subjective criteria that are not reflected in the census data. As Nabeel Abraham (1989, 1992, 1994) has shown, the stigmatized status of Arabs and Muslims in America can lead to a reluctance among these groups to openly identify with their ethnic and religious heritage. Others may elect to conceal their connections to the Arab world and Islam altogether. Many of these individuals, though by no means all, are second-, third-, and even fourth-generation descendants of Arab immigrants. Many are of mixed ancestry. Others of mixed ancestry may not view themselves primarily as Arab.

Whether such individuals should be counted as "Arab" is a question that runs to the heart of the sociological issue of ethnicity. As Mary Waters points out in her important analysis of ethnic identification, *Ethnic Options* (1990), most Americans have traditionally thought of ethnicity in *objective* terms, identifying individuals as belonging to groups based on their descent from common ancestors, usually connected to some geographic area. Used in this way, ethnicity has a putative biological component and has often been associated with invidious assumptions about the characteristics of certain national or cultural groups. Sociologists, by contrast, have usually analyzed ethnicity as a *social* and *subjective* phenomenon and relate it to the process by which individuals identify themselves in terms of group membership (Cornell and Hartmann 1998). In this sense, ethnicity is not biological; it is socially created. As Waters notes, ethnic identification involves an element of choice, albeit one that is shaped and constrained by family, community, and cultural practices. The process by which people choose an ethnicity is particularly complicated when generations of intermarriage may provide them with an array of options from which to select. Waters's analysis of ethnic identification among Americans of European descent also shows that ethnicity is unstable and may shift over time—or even in the course of a single conversation (1990, 22–26). This pattern applies to many Arab Americans as well.

In addition, because the census data on ancestry limit individuals to a maximum of two responses, and because research has indicated that relevant ancestral identifications can be missed, the Arab community in Detroit is definitely larger than the census figures show. This conclusion is reinforced by the shifting nature of subjective identities on the part of many assimilated Arab Americans. It is probable that the Arab community in 1990 numbered at least one hundred thousand residents in the tri-county Detroit area. The number could be even larger depending on how ethnicity, or ancestry, is defined. By the year 2000, the Arab American population is likely to have become significantly higher in light of the continued immigration and steady natural increase of the population.[4]

Despite discrepancies in population size, we will confine our analysis to the 1990 population figures provided by the Census Bureau, basing our percentages on the 62,699 individuals in Bureau's data file. These percentages can be considered reasonably descriptive estimates of those who are most likely to identify themselves with Arab ancestries, whether or not they actually appear as Arabs in the 1990 census. In fact, as the exploration of these figures shows, this statistical portrait of the Detroit Arab community is consistent with images most people have. The geographic distribution, the patterns of education and occupation all reinforce accepted views of the metro area's Arab Americans. The figures will still, however, underestimate those—typically the most recent migrants—who chose not to complete the census form, as well as those who elected for one reason or another not to identify themselves as Arab in the 1990 U.S. census.

Metro Detroit's Arab Community as Seen through the 1990 U.S. Census

Detroit's Arab community is predominantly suburban, as is evident in table 2. Ninety-one percent of Arab Americans live in suburban

Table 2
Arab Americans in Metro Detroit, by County, 1990

	Number of Arab Americans	Percentage of Arab Americans	Percentage of Total Population
City of Detroit	5,628	9.0	0.5
Wayne County (excluding Detroit)	28,585	45.6	2.6
Dearborn PUMA[a]	18,118	28.9	8.9
The rest of Wayne County (excluding Detroit)	10,467	16.7	1.2
Macomb	13,447	21.4	1.9
Oakland	15,039	24.0	1.4
Total Detroit Metro area	62,699	100	1.6

[a]Dearborn, Dearborn Heights, and Redford Township

communities, while only about three-fourths of the general population lives outside the Detroit city borders. The largest concentration of Arabs is in the Dearborn PUMA (public use microdata area), where nearly 29 percent of all area Arab Americans reside.[5] Most of them, about fourteen thousand according to other census figures, are in the city of Dearborn. They represent nearly 16 percent of Dearborn's population. Outside the city of Detroit, the Arab community is divided about equally, with some 45 percent in Wayne County and an equal percentage in the northern counties of Macomb and Oakland. As a fraction of the entire population of Metro Detroit, however, the Arab community is relatively small, constituting just 1.6 percent of the total.

Ethnic and National Groups in the Arab Community

In an earlier exploration of Detroit's Arab communities, Sameer Abraham (1983) identified four major ethnic or national groups in the population—Lebanese (Muslims as well as Lebanese/Syrian Christians), Palestinian/Jordanians (Palestinians from the East and West Banks of the River Jordan), Yemenis, and Iraqis (predominantly the Christian Chaldeans)—as well as several smaller groups, such as Egyptians, Kuwaitis, Moroccans, and Jordanians. This analysis will employ the same categories to explore how the census data describe various ethnic and national segments of the population.

Using the census data, however, presents a few challenges, since individuals can be identified by more than one ancestry. We will assume for purposes of investigation that the first ancestry identified represents an individual's primary group affiliation, although in some cases that assumption may not be valid. The Arab population in Metro Detroit identified itself with forty-two different first ancestries, including Belgian, Danish, Welsh, Croatian, Slovak, Mexican, and French Canadian—in addition to twelve Arab ancestries and two broad categories of "Arab" and "Middle East." In most cases, these non-Arab ancestries constitute very small numbers of people, but nearly two thousand "Arabs" identified their first ancestry as German, about 1,300 named Italian, and about 1,400 gave Polish as their first ancestry. More than two hundred "Arabs" reported themselves first as American Indians.

Nonetheless, some 88 percent of the sample cited one of the Arab nationalities or "Arab" as their first ancestry. A key problem in estimating the size of these national groups is that over one-fourth are identified as simply "Arab" (or, in a few cases, "Middle East"). The method here assigns individuals to a national group based on their first identified Arab ancestry. For those with non-Arab first ancestries or unspecified nationalities, the second ancestry is used. This leaves those who have used the general "Arab" or "Middle Eastern" designation. To reduce this still further, place of birth is used. In this case, all those indicating either the People's Democratic Republic of Yemen or the Arab Republic of Yemen are classified as Yemeni and those citing Palestine (not specified), Israel, or the West Bank as Palestinian. This leaves a remaining 10 percent unclassified as "Arab" or "Middle Eastern."

The case of the Iraqis is noteworthy. The Iraqi population in the Detroit area is known to be principally Chaldean, a Christian group from northern Iraq (also sometimes identified as Assyrians), who are more likely to adopt the Chaldean than the Iraqi label (Sengstock 1983). The Census Bureau, however, does not consider Chaldean to be an ancestry and reclassifies such responses as either Assyrian or Iraqi. The sample includes less than 1,000 people identified as Assyrian and about 4,500 Iraqis. However, the group who chose "Arab" as their ancestry includes some 3,100 people who were born in Iraq and whose residences in the Detroit area parallel those regions where Chaldeans are typically concentrated. We have included all those of Iraqi or Assyrian ancestry, together with those citing an unspecified Arab ancestry who also named Iraq as their birthplace, among the Iraqis.

Table 3 provides the detailed national categories and table 4 uses the four major national/ethnic groupings. Leaving aside the

Table 3
Arab Americans in Metro Detroit, by Ancestry Group Identification, 1990

	Detailed Ancestries				
	Identified by First Ancestry	Identified by Second Ancestry[a]	Identified by Place of Birth	Total	Percentage of Total
Algerian	91	53	–	144	0.2
Egyptian	952	84	–	1,036	1.7
Moroccan	171	–	–	171	0.3
Libyan	–	–	–	19	<0.1
Iraqi[b]	4,397	816	3,133	8,453	13.5
Jordanian	1,156	61	824	2,041	3.3
Kuwaiti	19	–	54	73	0.1
Lebanese	26,624	5,019	1,299	32,942	52.5
Saudi Arabian	23	57	368	448	0.7
Syrian	4,263	–	274	4,537	7.2
Yemeni	914	23	750	1,624	2.7
Kurdish	8	–	–	8	<0.1
Palestinian	2,057	–	663	2,720	4.3
Arab (not specified)	–	–	–	8,439	13.5
Total	40,675	7,730	7,302	62,699	100

[a]includes those with non-Arab first ancestry
[b]includes those identified as Assyrian

Table 4
Arab Americans in Metro Detroit, by Major Ancestry Group, 1990

	Number	Percentage
Lebanese-Syrian	37,479	59.7
Iraqi	8,346	13.3
Palestinian-Jordanian	4,761	7.6
Yemeni	1,624	2.7
All others	10,489	16.7
Total	62,699	100

problem of those without specific national identification, it is evident the Arab population in Metro Detroit is principally Lebanese (Muslims) and Syrian (mainly Christians from Lebanon and Syria), with about 60 percent in the latter category. Another 13–14 percent are Iraqi, presumably mostly Chaldean. About 7–8 percent are either Palestinian or Jordanian and about 3 percent are Yemeni. About 17 percent fall into the remaining category of other nationalities or unspecified ancestries.

Geographically, the major ancestry groups are located in various parts of the metro area, as shown in table 5. The primary differences are found between the Iraqis and the other major groups, with the former showing the largest degree of concentration away from the Dearborn area of Wayne County. Two-thirds of Iraqis are located in Oakland County, particularly in the areas of Southfield and Farmington Hills, with significant numbers in the more affluent Bloomfield Hills area and another segment in the vicinity of Oak Park. Another group of Iraqis, principally recent immigrants who entered the country during the 1980s, live in the traditionally Chaldean neighborhoods of northeast Detroit.

The Palestinian-Jordanian population is clustered most heavily in Wayne County, divided between the Dearborn area, adjacent to the city of Detroit, and the more distant suburban communities of Livonia and the Garden City-Wayne-Westland regions. The Lebanese (Muslims) remain concentrated in the Dearborn area, although substantial numbers have located in the northern suburban counties. Syrians (Christians), who are most likely to be native-born rather than immigrant, have moved primarily into Macomb County and, to a lesser degree, Oakland County. By contrast, the Yemenis remain clustered in the traditional neighborhoods of first-generation immigrants in the Dearborn area, especially southeast Dearborn.

Age is another important demographic descriptor. In general, groups with a significant percentage of immigrants are likely to be

Table 5
Major Ancestry Groups, by Location

	Detroit (%)	Wayne County (excluding Detroit) (%)	Macomb County (%)	Oakland County (%)
Lebanese	5	55	23	18
Syrian	4	40	36	20
Palestinian-Jordanian	18	59	12	11
Iraqi	14	21	16	68
Yemeni	13	87	0	0

younger than the general population, since people are most likely to immigrate during their prime working years (Portes and Rumbaut 1996). In addition, many immigrant groups, especially those from traditional societies with less urbanized populations, tend to have higher fertility rates than the host population. This also pulls down the average age.

This pattern is true of the Arab community in Metro Detroit, as table 6 shows. The average age of Arab Americans is twenty-eight, about four years lower than for the area as a whole. While about 12 percent of the Detroit area is sixty-five or over, only 6 percent of the Arab community is in this age group. Over a third of the Arab community are children under eighteen, compared to a quarter of the metro area as a whole. Syrians, with the smallest immigrant population of the major ancestry groups, have the highest average age, with about 9 percent over sixty-five. By contrast, Yemenis—among whom more than three-fourths were foreign-born—report no one age sixty-five and over (a result that may stem more from lack of reporting among elder Yemenis than their actual absence in the population). The Yemeni community, however, has a relatively small percentage under the age of eighteen, most likely reflecting the higher percentage of Yemeni men whose families remain in the Middle East. The Palestinian-Jordanian and the Iraqi communities also have relatively small numbers in the oldest age group. Finally, it is interesting to note that those who have no specified ancestry other than "Arab" are largely children under eighteen born in the United States, thereby pulling down the average age for the Arab population as a whole.

Table 6
Age Distribution by Ancestry Group for Metro Detroit, 1990

	Percentage under 18	Percentage 65 and over	Average Age
Metro Detroit	26	12	32
Total Arab	36	6	28
Lebanese	33	6	29
Syrian	24	9	34
Iraqi	31	5	30
Yemeni	28	0	32
Palestinian-Jordanian	22	3	30
Other Arab and not specified	67	3	18

Migration Patterns

The Arab American community in Metro Detroit is a mixture of recent immigrants and the descendants of immigrants, sometimes several generations removed from the country of origin. The 1990 census data limit our ability to measure how many generations have passed since a family's migration. We can only distinguish the native-born from the immigrants, as well as the approximate year of immigration. As a group, Detroit's Arab community is predominantly native-born, with about 61 percent born in the United States. This figure, however, includes a large number of children who were born in this country, while the older population contains more immigrants—90 percent of Arab Americans under sixteen were native-born, but only 46 percent of those over age twenty-five were born in the United States. Among those identified as householders, just about half were born outside the United States and had immigrated during the two decades before the 1990 census.

There is substantial variation among the major ancestry groups, with the Lebanese-Syrian population most likely to be native-born. In fact, among those self-identified as "Syrian," over 80 percent were native-born. Even two-thirds of those over sixty-five were born in the United States. This largely reflects the fact that earlier immigrants were identified as Syrian before that area was divided into the nations of Lebanon, Jordan, Palestine, and contemporary Syria. Among Arab immigrants who arrived before World War II, the vast majority identified themselves as Syrian (Naff 1994), a tendency that has persisted among their descendants in subsequent generations.

Among the other three major ancestry groups, however, we find a majority immigrant population. Roughly three quarters of the Iraqi, Yemeni, and Palestinian-Jordanian segments of the community were immigrants, the majority of whom had entered the country since 1970. Among those over the age of twenty-five, virtually none in these three groups were born in the United States.

The large numbers of immigrants arriving during the 1970s and 1980s reflect the "third wave" of Arab migration (Orfalea 1988; N. Abraham, 1981), which produced the largest influx of Arabs into the United States during a century-long history of immigration. This wave was triggered by a combination of the relaxation of U.S. laws governing immigration in 1965 and a long period of social, political, and military conflict in the Middle East. The Lebanese civil wars, the Iran-Iraq War, and the ongoing conflicts surrounding Israel have combined to yield as many as 250,000 immigrants to the United States

Table 7
Year of Immigration of Arab Americans in Metro Detroit, by Ancestry Group

	All (%)	Lebanese-Syrian (%)	Iraqi (%)	Palestinian-Jordanian (%)	Yemeni (%)
All Ages					
Born in U.S.	61	64	20	28	23
1980–90	17	16	39	23	22
1970–79	15	16	30	26	40
1960–69	6	2	8	15	15
1950–59	2	1	3	8	0
Before 1950	1	2	0	0	0
Age 25 and over					
Born in U.S.	46	57	1	7	0
1980–90	17	14	69	23	23
1970–79	24	20	43	33	54
1960–69	7	3	13	23	23
1950–59	3	2	5	13	0
Before 1950	2	3	0	1	0

since the late 1960s. By the census figures used here, nearly 22,000 of the Arab Americans in Metro Detroit—about one-third—entered the country between 1965 and 1990. As indicated before, this is quite likely a very low estimate of the total, due both to non-reporting and to the tendency for many migrants to return after a temporary sojourn in the United States or to travel back and forth between the United States and their home countries.

In general, immigrants tend to settle initially in the central city of a metro area, where housing prices are most affordable, then move outward in subsequent generations. This settlement pattern, however, is likely to be influenced by the presence of an established ethnic community, especially if it offers the advantages of an enclave economy. Here family and other community networks will ease the transition into the new society by facilitating employment and housing, as well as mitigating the shock that accompanies adjustment to a different culture. The presence of suburban ethnic enclaves is likely to lead many immigrants to bypass central city "ports of entry" in favor of areas where kin and village networks prevail. The educational background of immigrants also affects settlement patterns. When migrants are highly educated professionals, they are quick to settle in the more affluent suburban areas, although often near to an established ethnic community—especially to the more prosperous and assimilated members of their national group.

These patterns are reflected in table 8. As we saw earlier, the Arab community is well-established in the suburbs and this is clearly strongest among those born in the United States. Among immigrants arriving in the 1980s, about one-fifth reside in the city of Detroit, compared to 7 percent among the native-born. Only about one of ten foreign born have their homes in Macomb County, while more than one-fourth of the native-born live there. Dearborn is home to about two of five foreign-born Arabs, but only about one in five of the native-born reside in or near Dearborn.

Perhaps the most interesting observation is that the proportion of Arabs who live in affluent Oakland County shows little variation with respect to length of residence in the United States. This suggests the impact of established family networks among Iraqi Chaldeans, 68 percent of whom reside in Oakland County. Iraqis arriving during the 1980s appear sharply divided between the majority, who moved directly to Oakland County, most likely uniting with kin, and a smaller group who located in the traditional Chaldean neighborhoods of northeast Detroit.

Family and Household Patterns

Family relationships play an important role in Arab Detroit for a variety of reasons. Traditional Arab society follows patterns similar to

Table 8
Geographic Location, by Time of Entry into United States

	Born in U.S. (%)	Arrived 1970–79 (%)	Arrived 1980–90 (%)	Total Foreign-Born (%)
City of Detroit	7	7	19	12
Wayne County (excluding Detroit)	41	55	48	52
Dearborn PUMA[a]	22	44	41	41
The rest of Wayne County (excluding Detroit)	19	11	7	11
Macomb County	28	12	10	11
Oakland County	24	26	22	24
Total	100	100	100	100

[a]Dearborn, Dearborn Heights, and Redford Township

those found in most preindustrial cultures, where the value system is strongly oriented toward "the primacy of the extended family, collective responsibility for kin, hospitality, respect for status superiors and control of women's sexuality" (Cainkar 1994, 89). Family connections and obligations are central to the organization of everyday life and are highly valued. In addition, family connections are influenced by patterns of settlement within immigrant communities, which are shaped by legal and social factors. U.S. law affects the flow of immigration by favoring applicants who have relatives already established in the country. Accordingly, immigrants are more likely to move into existing family structures in the United States. Not surprisingly, many Arab immigrants to the United States settle in areas like Detroit, New York, or Los Angeles, where existing communities and families are already established. Reliance on kin networks to ease the transition also reinforces the strength of family connections among immigrant populations.

The census data allow us to explore some dimensions of family and household patterns in Detroit's Arab community. The figures in table 9 provide a comparison between types of households among Arabs and the total population in Metro Detroit.

Compared to the general Detroit population, Arab households are more likely to be married-couple families—about two-thirds compared to half in the overall population. Female-headed, single-parent families are also less common among Arab households, as are nonfamily households, although roughly comparable percentages are male-headed, single-parent households.

Table 9
Household Types among Arab and Metro Detroit Households, 1990

	All Households (%)	Arab Households (%)
Married-couple families	51	66
Male-householder families	4	5
Female-householder families	16	10
Nonfamily: male householder alone	N.A.	9
Nonfamily: male householder not alone	N.A.	2
Nonfamily: female householder alone	N.A.	7
Nonfamily: female householder not alone	N.A.	1
Total nonfamily households	30	19

Table 10 indicates the differences in household types among the primary ancestry groups. In all cases, the Arab proportion of married-couple families is higher than that for the metro population, but ranges from about three-fifths among Syrians and Yemenis to about four-fifths in the Iraqi and Palestinian-Jordanian communities. The higher numbers of nonfamily households among the more established and assimilated Syrians is due to more female single householders, especially over age sixty. Among Yemenis, a group with a high percentage of sojourners (immigrants whose stay in the United States is intended to be temporary), it is single male householders who account for more nonfamily households, often men whose families remain in their country of origin (N. Abraham, 1983).

Unfortunately, the data do not allow us to determine the exact composition of households, especially the presence of extended family such as grandparents or other relatives. However, individuals are classified by their relationship to the householder, and these figures suggest that most households fit a traditional nuclear family model. Fully 92 percent of all Arabs in the Detroit area are classified as either householders or the spouses or children of householders. Only about

Table 10
Household Types and Characteristics, by Ancestry Group

	Lebanese (%)	Syrian (%)	Iraqi (%)	Yemeni (%)	Palestinian-Jordanian (%)
Married-couple families	67	60	77	59	79
Male-householder families	5	2	5	19	3
Female-householder families	10	13	5	0	8
Nonfamily: male householder alone	8	8	10	19	9
Nonfamily: male householder not alone	3	4	0	3	0
Nonfamily: female householder alone	7	14	4	0	0
Nonfamily: female householder not alone	1	0	0	0	0
Total nonfamily households	19	26	14	22	9
Age of householder	45	47	44	44	40
Number of persons per household	3.3	2.8	4.3	4.8	3.9

3 percent are identified as either siblings or parents of the householder and another 1 percent are grandchildren of householders. In fact, among those age sixty and over, only one out of ten are living with their children, while 80 percent are either householders or spouses of householders. So, while grandparents may well play an important role in the lives of Arab children, it appears that relatively few of them live in the homes of their grandchildren. The exception to this pattern is the Iraqis, where about one-third of those over age sixty were identified as a parent of the householder.

Households also vary by size and by age of the householder. Overall, households among Arab Americans are larger than typical households in the metro area, due in part to the greater number of family households, particularly married-couple families. Among Arab households, 43 percent have four or more residents, compared to only 27 percent of all metro-area households. Syrian households have the highest average age of householder and smaller household sizes, since fewer dependent children remain in the home. Yemenis have the largest households, with about five occupants each on average. (This average is pulled down by the large number of single male households among Yemenis. If we consider only married-couple families among Yemenis, over half have households with six or seven members.) Lebanese and Iraqi households average about three and four persons, respectively, with four and five persons in married-couple households.

Fertility rates are also important indicators of family patterns. As is common among immigrant populations from more traditional societies, fertility rates tend to be higher among Arab Americans than for Americans as a whole. As table 11 indicates, the average Arab woman in Metro Detroit has had about three children, one more than is typical for women in the United States. But there is considerable variation among the different ancestry groups in the Arab community. As is often found in cross-national comparisons of fertility, differences are closely related to the level of education women receive (Riley 1997). In fact, the correspondence between these two factors is quite striking. For example, Syrian women had the lowest fertility rates and the highest percentage who had education past high school. At the opposite extreme, Yemeni women had much higher fertility rates, with over five children per woman, and no women who reported any education beyond high school. Lebanese and Palestinian-Jordanians had essentially identical rates of fertility and of women's education. Iraqi women were correspondingly

Table 11
Number of Children Born to Women Age Fifteen and over and Percentage of Women Age Twenty-Five and over with Education beyond High School, by Ancestry Group

	Average Number of Children Born to Women Age 15 and over	Women Age 25 and over with Education beyond High School
United States[a]	2.1	45
All Arab in Metro Detroit	3.1	24
Lebanese	3.1	27
Syrian	2.9	33
Iraqi	3.8	18
Yemeni	5.3	0
Palestinian-Jordanian	3.2	26

[a]Source: Data for United States from U.S. Bureau of the Census, *Statistical Abstract of the United States* 1995. (Washington, D.C.), 76, 158.

higher in fertility and lower in the levels of educational attainment among women.

Education within the Arab Community

Education is another factor that illustrates the diversity of the Arab community and an interesting contrast with the larger metro area. As table 12 indicates, the educational attainment of the general population over age twenty-five in Metro Detroit approximates the typical "bell curve," with nearly 60 percent having achieved a high school diploma (or equivalency) or some college, but less than a bachelor's degree. About one-fourth had less than a high school diploma and about one in five had attained at least a bachelor's degree.

The Arab population over age twenty-five does not fit the "bell curve" pattern as neatly, due to a higher percentage who attained less than nine years of schooling. Meanwhile, a percentage comparable to the metro population—about one-fifth—achieved a bachelor's degree or higher. The lower levels of education are more likely to be found among Arab women. About 37 percent of Arab women had less than a high school diploma, compared to 29 percent of the men. On the other end, about one-fourth of Arab men had at least a bachelor's degree, as against only 14 percent of the women.

Considerable differences are also found among the various ancestry groups, as seen in table 13. The Syrians come closest to

Table 12
Educational Attainment of Metro Detroit and Arab Americans

	Metro Detroit (%)	Arab American (%)
Less than 9 years	8	16
9–12 years, no diploma	17	16
High school diploma/GED	30	24
Some college	27	23
Bachelor's degree	12	11
Advanced degree	7	9

Table 13
Educational Attainment, Age Twenty-Five and over, by Ancestry Group

	Lebanese (Muslim) (%)	Syrian-Lebanese (%)	Iraqi (%)	Yemeni (%)	Palestinian-Jordanian (%)
Less than 9 years	14	9	25	56	16
9–12 years, no diploma	15	17	20	25	21
High school diploma/GED	26	24	24	9	19
Some college	26	24	12	6	23
Bachelor's degree	12	13	13	5	7
Advanced degree	8	11	6	0	14

mirroring the metro population, with a slightly higher number of college graduates. Yemenis have a much lower level of educational attainment, by contrast, with more than three-quarters having completed less than a high school diploma. The other ancestry groups fall in between these patterns. The Palestinian-Jordanian community reveals the most unusual pattern: over one-third of them had earned less than a high school diploma, yet they also had the highest percentage of those with advanced degrees. In fact, the majority of college graduates in the Palestinian-Jordanian ancestry group had earned advanced degrees.

In all ancestry groups, men have higher educational attainment, but the gap between men and women varies. Overall, Syrian men and women have the highest educational levels, with 30 percent of men and 21 percent of women earning at least a bachelor's degree. Syrians also have the smallest educational difference between the sexes. Palestinian-Jordanian men have levels of education nearly as high as Syrian men, with 28 percent with a four-year degree or more. But Palestinian-Jordanian women have only a 13 percent rate of college graduation. Lebanese men fall slightly lower, with 26 percent college graduates, and Lebanese women at half that rate, 13 percent. Iraqi men, at 22 percent, are nearly twice as likely as women, at 12 percent, to have earned a four-year college degree. The Yemeni population remains the least educated of the major groups: only 8 percent of Yemeni men reported a bachelor's degree and no Yemeni women had attended college at all. In fact, only 5 percent of Yemeni women were reported in the census to have completed high school.

Occupations

Historically, immigrant groups relocating to the United States have moved into various economic niches, reflecting a variety of factors: education, skills, or trades acquired in the home country, access to capital, networks formed by previous immigrant cohorts, and barriers erected by members of the host society. In addition, U.S. immigration law affects the kinds of occupations entrants will move into. Since 1965 most immigrants have been granted entrance into the United States on the basis of either family reunification or occupational qualifications. Thus, immigrants from countries with fewer established family networks in the United States—particularly Asian and African countries—tend to be more highly educated and move into professional occupations. Immigrants entering on the basis of family reunification are less likely to have higher job qualifications and to move into the professions. Among groups of the latter sort, some migrants have gravitated toward small business ownership, while others have taken up crafts and trades or semiskilled industrial work (Portes and Rumbaut 1996).

The census data allow us to explore the occupations of Detroit-area Arabs using industrial and occupational classifications. In table 14, comparisons between Arab Americans and the larger metro-area workforce indicate that the industrial distributions are fairly similar. Arabs are found in the different industrial sectors in proportions comparable to the larger population. But there are notable exceptions. Arab Americans are less heavily represented in manufacturing and professional services (which include health care, education, and social services) and much more concentrated in the retail trades. This reflects the higher rate of small-business proprietorship among Middle Eastern immigrants. About 22 percent of all employed Arab Americans in Metro Detroit were working in

Table 14
Industry of Employment

	Metro Detroit (%)	Arab American (%)
Agriculture, forestry, and fishing	<1	<1
Mining	<1	<1
Construction	4	4
Manufacturing	24	18
Transportation, communication, and utilities	6	4
Wholesale trade	5	4
Retail trade	18	34
Finance, insurance, and real estate	7	4
Business and repair services	6	5
Personal services	2	2
Entertainment services	1	2
Professional services	23	18
Public administration	4	3

either grocery or food stores, eating and drinking places, liquor stores, or gas and service stations. Among the Iraqis, who have the largest concentration in these areas, about half work in grocery, food, or liquor stores.

Turning to the occupational classifications in table 15, we again find Arab Americans represented in similar proportions to the Metro Detroit workforce in most categories. The exceptions are an underrepresentation in the administrative support and clerical occupations and an overrepresentation in the sales occupations. The larger number in the sales occupations again reflects the concentration in retail-store proprietorship. In the census data, among all Arabs, 9 percent—the largest single occupational category—are classified as supervisors and proprietors in sales establishments, a category that contains fully one-third of all Iraqis and half of Iraqi men. Another 6 percent are identified as cashiers in sales establishments, the majority of whom are in grocery stores, auto service stations, and liquor stores. Beyond the sales occupations, Arabs are distributed widely in all categories, with substantial numbers of physicians, teachers, engineers, secretaries, cooks, auto mechanics, meat cutters, and assemblers in the manufacturing industries.

As educational attainment varies between immigrants and the native-born so do employment patterns. Immigrants are even

Table 15
Occupational Categories

	Metro Detroit (%)	Arab American (%)
Executives, administrators, and managers	12	10
Professional specialty	15	13
Technical	4	4
Sales	12	23
Administrative support, including clerical	18	12
Service	13	13
Farming, forestry, and fishing	1	1
Precision, craft, and repair	11	11
Operators, fabricators, and laborers	15	14

more heavily concentrated in the sales occupations than are Arabs born in the United States, particularly as proprietors and cashiers of grocery and liquor stores and service stations. The native-born are more likely than immigrants to be in professional occupations.

In table 16, the differences among ancestry groups are provided. Overall, there are strong similarities among the Lebanese, Syrians, and Palestinian-Jordanians. About one-fourth are found in managerial and professional occupations and another one-fourth in industrial and construction jobs, either in the skilled trades or in semiskilled functions. By contrast, the Iraqis stand out with a much stronger representation in sales, again largely in family-owned stores, and fewer managers and professionals. The Yemenis are heavily concentrated in industry, predominantly in the lesser-skilled occupations rather than the trades. Yemenis are also overrepresented in service occupations, largely food preparation in eating and drinking establishments.

One final dimension of employment worth exploring is rates of workforce participation. In the case of women, it is typical that employment rates are inversely related to fertility rates, a pattern found within and between societies (Riley 1997). Among Arab women, who tend to have higher fertility rates than women in the United States in general, employment rates are only somewhat lower than those for the country. But, as table 17 indicates, they also vary significantly between ancestry groups. National figures for 1990 document a labor force participation rate of 58 percent among all women and 58 percent

Table 16
Occupational Categories, by Ancestry Group

	Lebanese (%)	Syrian (%)	Iraqi (%)	Yemeni (%)	Palestinian-Jordanian (%)
Executives, administrators, and managers	11	11	9	0	9
Professional specialty	14	15	9	6	15
Technical	4	3	3	0	2
Sales	21	16	46	5	24
Administrative support, including clerical	12	14	8	3	9
Service	12	15	6	24	15
Farming, forestry, and fishing	1	0	0	7	0
Precision, craft, and repair	11	11	11	8	13
Operators, fabricators, and laborers	13	16	10	47	12

Table 17
Percentage of Women in Workforce by Ancestry Group

All U.S.	58
All Arab women in Metro Detroit	52
Lebanese	55
Syrian	70
Iraqi	33
Yemeni	18
Palestinian-Jordanian	33

among married women (U.S. Bureau of Census 1996, 405). Rates for Detroit-area Arab women were 57 percent overall and 52 percent among married women. But these rates are due largely to Lebanese and Syrian women, who are employed at rates higher than among all women in the United States. By contrast, Iraqi and Palestinian-Jordanian women—and particularly Yemeni women—have much lower rates. Less than one-fifth of Yemeni women were in the work-force and only about two-fifths of Iraqi and Palestinian-Jordanian women were employed.

Household Income

Our exploration of the Detroit-area Arab community has shown that, taken as a whole, the Arab population looks fairly similar to the larger metro area in terms of educational attainment and occupational distribution. Internally, however, the Arab community demonstrates considerable diversity. A focus on the economic status of Metro Detroit's Arab households reinforces this perception. The census data provide income figures by household for 1989, the last complete year before the census.

As the figures in table 18 show, the percentage of Arab households in the various income groups very closely matched the figures for the metro area as a whole and the median income of Arab households was only about $1,000 lower. There is a striking contrast, however, between the household incomes of native-born Arabs and those of foreign-born householders and between the native-born and the metro area in general. As a group, the median household income of native-born Arab householders was about one-third higher than that for the area. Also, there were significantly fewer native-born Arab households in the lowest income categories below $20,000.

Foreign-born householders show a very different pattern of household income. About 40 percent of households headed by the foreign-born had incomes below $20,000, compared to about 16 percent of native-born Arabs and about 30 percent of metro-area households. On the other end, less than 10 percent of households

Table 18
Income Distribution and Median Income of Households in Metro Detroit, 1989, by Place of Birth of Householder

	All Metro Detroit (%)	All Arab Households (%)	Householder Born in U.S. (%)	Householder Born Abroad (%)
Less than $10,000	16	16	7	23
$10,000–$19,999	14	15	9	18
$20,000–$29,999	14	15	15	16
$30,000–$39,999	14	14	13	15
$40,000–$49,999	12	12	13	11
$50,000–$74,999	18	16	21	11
$75,000–$99,999	7	6	8	4
$100,000–$149,999	4	4	6	2
$150,000 and over	2	3	5	2
Median income ($)	32,824	31,700	41,674	24,860

headed by immigrants were above $75,000, while nearly 20 percent of U.S.-born householders have incomes above this level.

Interestingly, household income is one area where ancestry group differences are less substantial. While there are variations in income, the gaps are not as large as between the native-born and foreign-born. The median incomes of the lowest-income Yemenis are about 76 percent of those for all Arab households, while the highest-income Syrians had incomes about 9 percent above the median. Some of the equalization of incomes can be traced to the occupational choices of household heads, some of which permit relatively high incomes for those without much formal education. For example, about 11 percent of householders worked in various semiskilled or unskilled jobs in industry or construction with no more than a high school diploma, but reported an average personal (not household) income of more than $30,000 in 1989. Another 7 percent of householders had no post–high school education, but worked as proprietors of small business, earning an average of over $28,000.

Household incomes may also be boosted by more than one household member working to bring in earnings. About 44 percent of women identified as spouses of the householder worked in 1989, and nearly one-quarter of them worked fifty or more weeks in the year. In addition, two-thirds of children over sixteen named as sons or daughters of householders worked in 1989, and one-third worked the full year. With larger families and high rates of workforce participation, families may compensate for somewhat lower earnings by the father and reduce the income gap among the community as a whole.

Table 19
Income Distribution and Median Income of Households, 1989, by Ancestry Group of Householder

	Lebanese (%)	Syrian (%)	Iraqi (%)	Yemeni (%)	Palestinian-Jordanian (%)
$10,000–$19,999	15	15	18	19	14
$20,000–$29,999	14	14	13	28	19
$30,000–$39,999	12	12	20	16	11
$40,000–$49,999	12	12	9	16	7
$50,000–$74,999	17	17	11	0	23
$75,000–$99,999	6	6	4	5	4
$100,000–$149,999	4	7	7	0	0
$150,000 and over	4	4	3	0	2
Median income ($)	33,300	34,550	29,100	24,000	26,040

Conclusions

While the idea of an Arab community in Metro Detroit permits us to capture in summary form an important segment of the population, it also conceals noteworthy variations. The community is, in fact, many communities subdivided along the dimensions of national ancestry, native-born or foreign-born, recent or long- term immigrant, suburban or central city residence, intermixed with non-Arabs or settled within the ethnic enclave, assimilated into the United States or immersed in the culture of the native land. Perhaps one of the most striking observations is that, when examined as a whole, the substantial variations within the Arab population sometimes cancel each other out and produce a demographic portrait that closely mirrors that of the larger metro population.

In terms of residential location, education, occupational distribution, and economic status, Arab Detroit is much like the region that contains it—although important qualifications remain. Like the metro population, Detroit's Arab population is predominantly suburban—although a large fraction remains settled in suburban enclaves, particularly in Dearborn, with its notable concentration of Arab homes and businesses. The percentage of Arab Americans who have completed a bachelor's degree or more is comparable to that in the Greater Detroit area—although an unusually large fraction have less than nine years of schooling. With regard to work, the Arab population is distributed into occupational categories and industries much like the metro workforce—except that a substantially higher number are concentrated in small-business ownership of grocery stores, liquor stores, and auto service stations. Economically, household incomes are similar to the incomes of Detroit-area families—although native-born Arab householders have higher than average, and immigrants have lower than average, incomes. Married Arab women are employed at somewhat lower rates than women in the United States nationwide, but their earnings appear to play an important role in a large percentage of households.

These statistical representations of Arab Detroit help paint a portrait of a diverse group. While there is a measure of unity implied in the concept of community, members of Detroit's Arab population define themselves in ways reflecting their differences. They are "Lebanese" and "Chaldean" and "Palestinian" and other nationalities—including "American" or "Arab American." They are Muslims and Christians, in various forms and to varying degrees of devoutness. They are Dearbornites, Detroiters, and residents of other suburban communities. In their own ways, they reflect the patterns of adaptation and change found among dozens of immigrant populations, both in Detroit and throughout America.

ACKNOWLEDGMENTS: I would like to acknowledge the valuable assistance and advice of Patricia Becker of the Southeast Michigan Census Council. Her extensive knowledge of the methods and procedures of the Census Bureau were indispensable in sorting through the complexities of estimating the Detroit-area Arab community.

NOTES

1. The estimated undercount for 1990 of 1.7 percent compares to a 1.2 percent undercount in 1980. Nevertheless, according to demographer Richard Barrett (1994), the 1990 census still ranks as the second most accurate since 1940, the only censuses that can be reliably compared. The estimated undercount for the city of Detroit was 2.7 percent, roughly 27,700 people. The Census Bureau has not provided undercount estimates for smaller suburban communities or the metro area as a whole.
2. Zogby acknowledges, however, that a large error range for this estimate could mean that Detroit's Arab population could be as high as 450,000 or as low as 100,000.
3. INS figures also have important limitations. Immigrants may resettle in different areas, especially if they have been intentionally dispersed by the INS to avoid a high concentration in particular communities. Many Arabs relocated to Detroit after landing elsewhere in the United States, as indicated recently by the number of Iraqi Shia refugees who moved to Detroit after having been settled elsewhere in the country by U.S. authorities.
4. The deteriorating conditions in Iraq have led to several thousand Iraqi refugees entering the United States and to a notable presence in the Detroit area. Population forecasts from the Southeast Michigan Council of Governments (1996), a regional planning agency, predict population growth in east Dearborn—where the highest concentration of Arab Americans in Metro Detroit resides—of 5 to 7 percent between 1990 and 2000, a figure that likely underestimates the impact of immigration (Schopmeyer 1998). But even assuming a very generous growth estimate for this area applied to the entire Arab American community, the population for 2000 is unlikely to surpass 125,000.

5. While Detroit's Arab community is not uniformly distributed throughout the region, the census data limit our ability to focus on smaller units of geography. As we move below the county level of analysis, we are generally unable to focus on specific cities because the PUMA data are not released for small geographic areas. (This is to preserve the confidentiality of data and reduce the chances that specific households could be identified.) The figures are provided for geographic areas identified by the Census Bureau as PUMAs (public use microdata areas), which contain between one hundred thousand and two hundred thousand people each. The three-county Detroit Metro area is broken into twenty-nine PUMAs. The city of Detroit is divided into eight PUMAs, which can be grouped to produce citywide figures, and a few large suburbs—Livonia, Sterling Heights, and Warren/Centerline—are assigned their own PUMAs. But most metro-area PUMAs contain several communities that are geographically contiguous (with the exception of Hamtramck and Highland Park, which are actually surrounded by Detroit, but here are grouped with the suburbs of Grosse Pointe and Harper Woods).

References

Abraham, Nabeel. 1981. Arabs in America: An Overview. In *The Arab World and Arab Americans: Understanding a Neglected Minority,* edited by Sameer Abraham and Nabeel Abraham, 17–22.

———. 1983. The Yemeni Immigrant Community of Detroit: Background, Emigration and Community Life. In *Arabs in the New World: Studies on Arab-American Communities,* edited by Sameer Abraham and Nabeel Abraham, 109–34.

———. 1989. Arab-American Marginality: Mythos and Praxis. *Arab Studies Quarterly* (Spring/Summer 1989). Reprinted in *Arab Americans: Continuity and Change,* edited by B. Abu-Laban and M. Suleiman, 17–43. Belmont, Mass.: Association of Arab-American University Graduates.

———. 1992. The Gulf Crisis and Anti-Arab Racism in America. In *Collateral Damage: The New World Order at Home and Abroad,* edited by Cynthia Peters, 255–78. Boston: South End Press.

———. 1994. Anti-Arab Racism and Violence in the United States. In *The Development of Arab-American Identity,* edited by Ernest McCarus, 155–214. Ann Arbor: Univ. of Michigan Press.

Abraham, Sameer. 1983. Detroit's Arab-American Community: A Survey of Diversity and Commonality. In *Arabs in the New World: Studies on Arab-American Communities,* edited by Sameer Abraham and Nabeel Abraham, 84–108.

Abraham, Sameer, and Nabeel Abraham, eds. 1981. *The Arab World and Arab Americans.* Detroit: Center for Urban Studies, Wayne State University.

Abraham, Sameer, and Nabeel Abraham, eds. 1983. *Arabs in the New World: Studies on Arab-American Communities.* Detroit: Center for Urban Studies, Wayne State University.

APB Associates. 1995. Immigrants to Southeast Michigan, 1983 to 1992. Detroit: APB Associates. Unpublished.

Barrett, Richard E. 1994. *Using the 1990 Census for Research.* Thousand Oaks: Sage Publications.

Cainkar, Louise. 1994. Palestinian Women in American Society: The Interaction of Social Class, Culture and Politics. In *The Development of Arab-American Identity,* edited by Ernest McCarus, 85–106.

Cornell, Stephen, and Douglas Hartmann. 1998. *Ethnicity and Race.* Thousand Oaks, Calif.: Pine Forge Press.

McCarus, Ernest, ed. 1984. *The Development of Arab-American Identity.* Ann Arbor: University of Michigan Press.

Naff, Alixa. 1994. The Early Arab Immigrant Experience. In *The Development of Arab-American Identity,* edited by Ernest McCarus, 23–36.

Orfalea, Gregory. 1988. *Before the Flames.* Austin: University of Texas Press.

Portes, Alejandro, and Rubén G. Rumbaut. 1996. *Immigrant America: A Portrait.* 2nd edition. Berkeley: University of California Press.

Raymond, James C. 1992. *Population Estimation and Projection.* New York: Quorum Books.

Riley, Nancy. 1997. *Gender, Power and Population Change.* Population Bulletin 52, no. 1. Washington, D.C.: Population Reference Bureau.

Sands, Gary. 1986. An Estimate of the Arab Population of Metropolitan Detroit. *Census Discussion Papers,* no. 6. Detroit: Wayne State University, Michigan Metropolitan Information Center (MIMIC), and Urban and Community Studies (UCS).

Schopmeyer, Kim. 1998. *Changing Demographic Patterns in Wayne County, 1990–2020.* Dearborn, Mich.: Henry Ford Community College.

Sengstock, Mary. 1983. Detroit's Iraqi-Chaldeans: A Conflicting Conception of Identity. In *The Arab World and Arab Americans: Understanding a Neglected Minority,* edited by Sameer Abraham and Nabeel Abraham, 135–46.

Southeast Michigan Council of Governments (SEMCOG). 1996. *2020 Regional Development Forecast: Population, Households and Employment for Cities, Villages, Townships and Detroit Subcommunities.* Detroit: SEMCOG.

United Community Services of Metropolitan Detroit. 1986. A Study of the Middle East Community in the Detroit Metropolitan Area. Unpublished.

U.S. Bureau of the Census. 1996. *Statistical Abstract of the United States 1996.* Washington, D.C.

Waters, Mary. 1990. *Ethnic Options.* Berkeley: University of California Press.

Zogby, John. 1990. *Arab America Today: A Demographic Profile of Arab Americans.* Washington, D.C.: Arab American Institute.
———. 1998. "Detroit Metropolitan Statistical Area Census Report." Washington, D.C.: Zogby International.

Part 2

WORK

Fig. 2. Autoworker Eva Habeeb poses in her factory coveralls, ca. 1925. Courtesy of the ACCESS Museum of Arab Culture.

Fig. 3. Salem Khalil takes a breather at his grocery store, 1957. Courtesy of the ACCESS Museum of Arab Culture.

Introduction

THE INDUSTRIAL BOOM was formative for Arab Detroit and its image. Along with store ownership and peddling, blue-collar work has characterized Arab Detroit through much of its history. A steady stream of immigrants has kept these ethnic specializations alive. Lebanese, Syrian, and Palestinian peddlers graduated into store ownership and were replaced by Chaldean store owners. An earlier generation of Lebanese and Palestinian blue-collar labor was replaced by Yemeni immigrants, who must now compete with Iraqi Shia for Detroit's dwindling supply of unskilled, manual-labor jobs.

Much of what Arab Detroit thinks about itself was formulated on shop floors and behind storefronts. Work, after all, is the nexus (along with school) where margin and mainstream intersect. Being typecast as peddlers, urban grocers, and factory workers—all demanding and dangerous occupations—has long stigmatized the Arabs of Detroit. Within Arab Detroit, however, these specializations carry positive meanings unimagined by the outside world. In "Dumb like a Fox," a story Don Unis has told with relish countless times, the marginality conferred by blue-collar work is turned on its head. The story has acquired the texture of a *Juha* Arab folktale, in which Don's Juha-like stepfather conceals his cunning behind the appearance of a simpleton.

There is a good measure of admiration for the generation of Arab Detroiters who spent their lives working as shopkeepers, peddlers, or factory janitors. In "Fandy" Kevin Rashid is clearly amazed by his father, an intellectually gifted man who earned a law degree but by dint of circumstance spent his life in a liquor store, making deals and dodging bullets. Nabeel Abraham, in "On the Road with Bob," is no less fascinated by his father's work as a peddler, so much so that he wiggles his way into a road trip that allows him to discover his enigmatic father.

When told today, stories like "Dumb like a Fox" enable narrators to turn the tables on marginality, but marginal occupations have already exacted a heavy price and have driven Arab Detroit's American-born generations into mainstreaming, white-collar work. Lawrence Joseph captures the grease and grime of factory labor, and the alienation and loneliness that beset a factory worker's off-hours, in his poems, "You Only Exist Inside Me" and "In the Tenth Year of War." In the latter poem, the laborer's dehumanizing, mechanical servitude is spiritually transformed into an image of hope and redemption. Perhaps. One is not sure what to make of Joseph's concluding line, "I danced before the machine." Who is calling the tune, the worker or the machine?

Lawrence Joseph's ambiguity neatly encapsulates Arab Detroit's dilemma with marginal occupations. Chaldean store owners in Detroit tell sociologist Gary David they feel "imprisoned" by the long hours they spend working behind bulletproof Plexiglas. Not a single store owner wants to see his children enter the business. Alixa Naff's memoir about growing up in the household of a Lebanese peddler-turned-grocer in the 1930s and 1940s highlights the vicissitudes of immigrant store ownership and the demanding array of social obligations that made such a risky lifestyle possible. The Naff family fondly referred to their home as a "hotel," for it was a link in a far-flung network of immigrant settlements that crisscrossed America, bridging new and old worlds.

When Naff's engaging memoir is read in conjunction with Abraham's recollection of the peddling trip he took with his father, two crucial insights emerge that overturn prevalent notions about Arab Detroit's occupational history. The first is that the movement from peddling to store ownership was never a one-way street. Peddlers aspired to store ownership, but in lean times they frequently reverted to peddling, which, as Abraham's story suggests, continued as a way of life for some Arab Detroiters long after it was thought to have ended. The second insight is that the record of store ownership is strewn with hardship and failure. This reality tends to be obscured today by the financial success reputedly enjoyed by Chaldean store owners, who hold a near monopoly on Detroit's (non-chain) food and liquor stores. As these store owners attest in the study by Gary David, their success comes only with great sacrifice, and even then is not assured. Ethnic specializations are marginal with good reason: they exact a heavy social and personal toll by the standards of mainstream America. It is no wonder, then, that the children of peddlers, store owners, and blue-collar workers show little or no desire to take up their parents' work. It is only a matter of time, a generation perhaps, before these ethnic specializations recede to the background, or vanish entirely.

Mainstreaming entails moving into the professions, the government or service sectors, or into businesses that cater to upscale clientele. Despite the appeal of what David calls the "doctor-lawyer-engineer triumvirate," entrepreneurship remains a dominant form of economic livelihood in Arab Detroit today. It assumes many forms: gas stations, auto repair shops, restaurants specializing in "Middle Eastern" or Lebanese food (never "Arabic" food), Middle Eastern pastry shops and bakeries, *halal* meat markets, vegetable markets, Arabic music and video rental stores, Arabic language bookstores, real estate agencies, print shops, Islamic clothing stores, pharmacies, and medical clinics. The list goes on and on. As long as the stream of Arab immigrants continues to flow uninterrupted, enterprises that cater to a predominantly Arab clientele will flourish. Once the stream runs dry, only businesses serving the mainstream will survive.

We have reserved discussion of Arab Detroit's internal economy and the myriad ethnic specializations it now sustains—musicians, wedding videographers, traditional artists, and the booming trade in Lebanese restaurant food—for part 6, "Ethnic Futures." In the present section, we have confined our discussion of work to the traditional specializations of Arab Detroit, which, we believe, still serve as cultural signposts on the road from margin to mainstream.

You Only Exist Inside Me

Lawrence Joseph

Where Dix Highway ends
long boats tug ore
across a green canal.
In a cafe, Yemenites
cheat at dice
and talk about whores.
You drink coffee,
smoke, remember
a room, a table
that held the weight
of your elbows,
the small notebook
in which you wrote
"our labor put the world on wheels";
one day someone
will find it and think
of thick-lipped buckets,
iron pigs growing
into billets.
Alone, I walk this street
of ice, making this up:
you only exist inside me.
A siren blows.
It is 3:30.
I remember how
I punched the clock.
My legs jerked into full stride
toward a room.

Reprinted from *Shouting at No One,* by Lawrence Joseph (Pittsburgh: University of Pittsburgh Press, 1983), 26.

I sat at a table
rubbing my eyes.

I did not feel.
I did not think.

In the Tenth Year of War

Lawrence Joseph

I bend
over the machine. Heat
and oil
tune my inner ear. I'm
not ashamed, I
hang my head in
anticipation. Father,
steel smooth and silver,
make my brain new,
Jesus, the dirt on the walls
is coming from my body,
and love,
the spirit coming from your body—
everywhere you look now,
everything you touch,
it's good.
When,
in the tenth year of war
I prayed for help
and no one came,
I danced before the machine.

Reprinted from *Shouting at No One,* by Lawrence Joseph (Pittsburgh: University of Pittsburgh Press, 1983), 47.

Dumb like a Fox

Don Unis

THIS IS A story about my father.

OK. Let me give a little background leading up to the facts. It wasn't my real dad. It was my stepdad. My [biological] dad had come here in 1917 running from the Ottoman Empire, joined the army, went back to France, fought in World War I, and became an American citizen. By age three, my dad died. I was about three, three and a half. My mother remarried years later, and the man that raised me, his name was Sam Shamey. He worked at the Ford Rotunda.

Now, the Ford Rotunda burned down in 1963. The Ford Rotunda was on Schaefer Road, right across from the old Ford world headquarters, which was a four-story building. The Ford Rotunda had been brought to Dearborn from the world's fair, and it was a round, circular building, and it was the showplace of the Ford Motor Company.

My dad worked there. He was an Arab immigrant. A laborer, who worked maintenance. He worked cleanup. And, of course, what that meant was that he went to work at night, twelve o'clock at night, and he would mop the floors and scrub the toilets and do all those things where thousands of people would go through every day.

One night he was working in the movie theater part of the Rotunda, which was a place where they showed films about the Ford Motor Company and the quality of cars, etc. And as he was cleaning and vacuuming, he noticed a wallet sitting on one of the chairs. Unable to read and write English, he picked up the wallet and opened it, and inside that wallet was fifty one-hundred-dollar bills. Five thousand dollars. Now mind you, this is 1937, 1938, and five thousand dollars would be equivalent to fifty thousand dollars today . . . maybe?

Anyways, not able to read and write English but, of course, he knew the value of fifty one-hundred-dollar bills. He folded the

Recorded by Sally Howell on March 28, 1998, at the Detroit Historical Museum.

wallet back. Went and got one of his very, very good friends. Went to his boss. His boss's name was Paul. And of course he told his friend about the wallet.

He told his boss, "I found this wallet in the movie theater. There's fifty one-hundred-dollar bills in it. Five thousand dollars. Here's the wallet and the money. Give me a receipt that I gave it to you, and here's my witness"—his best friend—"that I gave it to you."

The boss looked at him with his eyes wide open and said, "Well, of course, Sam."

He gave him a receipt that he found a wallet with fifty one-hundred-dollar bills and gave it to him.

So they went back to work.

Next day he comes to work. Now from the Rotunda over to the Ford world headquarters there was a tunnel that went underneath Schaefer Road. I had been through that tunnel many times.

The boss tells my dad, "Sam, go across the street. Mr. Ford wants to see you."

The old man.

"Why?" my dad says.

"Just go ahead. I don't know why," says the boss.

So he goes from the Rotunda. He drops his work. Goes underneath the tunnel. Goes to the fourth floor of the Lincoln Mercury Building, as they called it, that overlooked the Ford Rouge Plant. Goes up to the fourth floor. Goes into Mr. Ford's office, and he had seen Mr. Ford 'cause Mr. Ford, Henry Ford, would walk through the Rotunda occasionally, see what was happening.

His secretary tells him, "Sam, go on right into the office. Mr. Ford is waiting for you."

So. OK. He walks into the office, and as he walks into the office there's this big desk, and there's Mr. Henry Ford, the original Henry Ford, sitting behind the desk, and one guy is sitting next to him. Another man.

Mr. Ford stands up and says, "Sam, how are you?" and he shakes his hand. Says to him, "Sam, you found this wallet?"

He says, "Yes, Mr. Ford."

He said, "And you turned it in?"

He said, "Yes, Mr. Ford."

Mr. Ford turns to the guy next to him and says, "See what honest employees I have?"

Turns back to my dad and says, "Sam, do you know that there are fifty one-hundred-dollar bills in there?"

He said, "Oh, yeah."

He said, "Oh, you know that?"

He said, "Oh, yeah."

He said, "How do you know?"

He said, "I found the wallet. I counted it."

He said, "And you gave it all to your boss?"

He said, "Exactly."

Again Mr. Ford turns to the man next to him and says, "Do you have employees like this?"

He turns back to my dad and says, "Sam, do you know whose wallet this is?"

He says, "No."

He says, "Look. It's right there in the wallet. His name."

He says, "Mr. Ford, I can't read English."

He says, "Well, this wallet belongs to this man. Do you know who this man is?"

He says, "No, sir. I . . . I don't."

He says, "Well, this man makes the tires for my car. His name is Firestone. Harvey Firestone."

My dad, not knowing, said, "Well . . . that's . . . fine. Good."

Mr. Ford looked back at the guy and said, "Do you have employees like this?"

He takes the wallet. He takes five one-hundred-dollar bills from the wallet and reaches over to give it to my dad.

My dad says to him, "Mr. Ford, no. I don't want that."

He said, "You don't want the money? This is half a year's work for God sakes."

He said, "No. That's not the point. The man sat down, it fell out of his pocket. Why should I be rewarded?"

My dad's dumb like a fox, right?

Again, Ford turns to Firestone and says to him, "Do you have employees like this?"

He says, "That's OK, Sam. Fine."

Puts the money back in the wallet and hands it to Harvey Firestone. Calls his secretary in.

He says, "I want you to put in Sam's file that as long as there's a Ford Motor Company, he will always have a job. Is that OK with you, Sam?"

He says, "Yes, sir."

He says, "And let me tell you something, Sam. Anybody ever bothers you in any way, you come see me."

"Yes, sir, Mr. Ford. Thank you very much, Mr. Ford."

And then he leaves.

Now, this story goes untold. I mean, he might have told his buddies, but . . . those were the days when it was very common to see Ford.

Well, years later he'd work midnights and sometimes he'd get home late, or my mother didn't make his lunch, and I'd go to the Rotunda and take him his lunch, two o'clock in the morning on a hot summer night. One summer night I remember, I take his lunch there. Mom made him grape leaves, and they're still nice and hot. I walk in. I see his boss, Paul.

I say, "Paul, where's my dad?"

He points at the auditorium. The movie theater. I come in there. I see my dad. He's got the chairs down. He's got a pillow and a blanket. He's sound asleep. I walk up behind him.

"Ba. Ba. [Dad. Dad.]"

I'm lookin' out for his boss, right?

"Ba!"

"Yeah, yeah. What?"

"Here's your lunch."

"Oh. OK. Put it down."

"But Ba. You know, you can't be sleepin' "

"Tch. Tch. Tch."

In Arabic there's this thing—"Tch. Tch. Tch."—you know, like "never mind." "Shut your mouth." "It's no discussion."

I said, "Ba . . ."

"Never mind! Just go on home."

So I said, "What the . . . , OK."

In the morning, many times, I'd come and pick him up. All the guys, when they'd walk out, they'd have to open up their lunch bucket, to show that they're not taking something home with them. My dad would have his arm full. The boss and the guard would never even question him.

Years later, I found out why. For [refusing to take] that five hundred dollars, he not only bought himself a job for the next thirty years, he also made sure that nobody—boss, foreman, or vice president—would dare say anything to him.

The moral of the story was: this immigrant Arab, who was dumb like a fox, for five hundred bucks, guaranteed his whole future.

And it was based on total honesty.

Growing up in Detroit

An Immigrant Grocer's Daughter

Alixa Naff

DETROIT WAS MY hometown for two decades—from 1930 to 1950. No other city in which I have lived since has so legitimate a claim on my reminiscences. I was not born in it. I was not yet an adolescent when I was sent to live in it with my half sister, Nazha, and her husband, Daher Haney. It was that era in that city where the Naffs matured as a family—where my sister, my three brothers, and I developed as individuals. Although reminiscences tend to confuse and distort memory, of one fact I am certain: the 1930s and 1940s were as critical for the Naff family as for the whole country. Who, old enough to remember, can forget the distress inflicted by the Great Depression? Who of the millions of afflicted did not share in the hope of the New Deal and the anxieties of World War II, or wonder at the seismic social and economic changes of the postwar period?

As I look back through the mist of years, I am awed at how my immigrant parents pulled us through those difficult times. I marvel at their native survival instincts and the strength they drew from their Syrian-Lebanese traditions and customs. I have always taken my parents for granted. Until I published my study on the immigrant experience of Arabic-speaking people in the United States, I self-centeredly failed to comprehend their realities—their fears, failures, frustrations—private as well as familial. Yet, they persevered without my comprehension and because they did, we survived as a family—intact and Americanized, even my mother, in her own way.

Detroit was the city where the Americanization process had its greatest impact on the Naff family, especially its immigrant members, my mother and my seven-year-old sister. Since my father had been naturalized in 1907, we ceased to consider him an immigrant, but he was. My three brothers and I are the American-born generation raised in a thoroughly Syrian-Lebanese household right into our adolescent years, the incipient period of becoming American. Yet, the Americanization process affected the five of us differently according to the chronological sequence of our births and the degree of erosion in the dominance of my parents' native traditions and customs. Except for their indestructible core values, my parents never really resisted the process.

There was nothing in Detroit to impede Americanization except what my parents placed in its path, namely the native traditions they brought with them from Rashayya al-Wadi, their village in the Anti-Lebanon, the western mountain range of what was then Syria. These traditions remained germane to our lives in Spring Valley, Illinois, Fort Wayne, Indiana, and Detroit. As long as the native values dominated in our home, or in the Syrian communities for that matter, there was no room for the Americanization process to flourish. In time, however, away from such communities, native traditions and values tended to lose their force. Correspondingly, the process of becoming American in our family gained ground gradually and unevenly until my mother felt comfortable in her Americanization. Americanization is a very complicated process, as we were to learn.

Detroit was also the city to which my father, enticed by relatives, brought his family in search of a place to fend off the effects of the Depression, which seemed to be plaguing him. I doubt that he was sufficiently informed about the pitfalls in store for a family that had never lived in a large city. Never, or almost never, did so naive a man walk into such a bee's nest of difficulties. He was ill-prepared to cope, yet by the time he decided to move to Detroit, he had no other place to go where he had relatives and friends he could depend on to help him beat back the dragon of the Depression.

Detroit to me now, almost a half-century after we left it, is our house at 57 Tennyson Avenue in Highland Park, a small city completely surrounded by Detroit, whose size and economic power seemed arrogantly to obliterate Highland Park's existence. In my family, we still say we lived in Detroit. It is the image of that house that my memory flashes up to me when I think back, as if there was nothing else worth remembering from those years.

Purchased in the late spring of 1942, about the time the Depression had loosened its disastrous grip, 57 Tennyson was, like most homes on that tree-lined street, reddish brown brick with a front porch that held a large swing with room for several chairs to accommodate guests. In its front yard stood a splendid old maple tree whose leafy branches caressed the second-floor windows. One of them was mine. It was my tree and I loved it.

The house was Mother's idea. She chose it, had it renovated, redecorated it, and equipped it with modern appliances. In a turn of good fortune, Dad paid for it in cash. My parents dreamed it would be the house to which my two older brothers would return from military service, get their college degrees (Mother's plan), and remain in it until they married—preferably to nice Syrian girls Mom and Dad could approve of. It would also be the place where my parents could live out their lives secure and contented, "God willing." But fate had other plans.

The house was my parents' pride and joy. My mother's pride because it elevated the family status from that limbo between lower class and lower middle class to ordinary middle class. As the daughter of a wealthy landowning family, she could reclaim the status she had lost when she left Rashayya. She would not have described her new situation in those terms, for my mother was basically unassuming. That she felt an elevation in her status soon became apparent in her carriage and unfolding self-confidence.

The house was my father's joy because the land on which it sat was large enough for him to garden to his heart's content. With religious conviction, he believed that land was sacred. God meant it to yield nourishment, he would say. From spring until the snow fell, the hours he spent in his garden rivaled those he spent in his store. The wide variety of vegetables and fruit trees were the kind he might have planted in Rashayya. The shelves of our large basement pantry were well stacked with what my mother preserved from the garden: vegetables, fruits, pickles, jams, and jellies; even catsup and relishes she learned to make in America. That garden helped nourish not only the family but many guests year-round.

Mother was a gardener, too. She filled the areas around the sides of the house and along the fences that separated us from our old stock American neighbors with flowers of many kinds and colors. There were also lilac and hollyhock bushes and flower beds that accented the grassy front lawn. She paid as much attention to the appearance of the outside as she did to the inside. The Depression, it seemed, was definitely over for us. In my Detroit fantasy, I am convinced that my parents were never happier than when they lived at 57 Tennyson. In retrospect, however, reality was far different.

It was seven months after Pearl Harbor when we moved into the house. The onset of World War II took my two older brothers away from our house and, at the same time, took away the pleasure of living in it. My sister and my mother's two sisters, who were part of the family, had married and moved away from Detroit before we

Fig. 4. The Naff family, Tennyson Avenue, ca. 1947. *Left to right:* (back row), George, Tom, Nick; (middle row), Nazha Haney, Dad, Mom, Wedad; (front), Alixa. Courtesy of the Naff Arab American Collection, Archives Center, NMAH, Smithsonian Institution.

bought the house. For three years, my parents, my youngest brother, and I lived in a constant state of high anxiety.

Thankfully, my brothers survived the war. George flew navy fighter planes in the Pacific theater. Nick was an officer in the Army's Air Transport Command. In 1945, he was reassigned to San Francisco, a move that would have major significance for the whole family. Like hundreds of other servicemen who breathed the clean, fragrant air of California and were captivated by its way of life, Nick decided that his future in journalism would be brighter in the Golden State. He could not be persuaded to return to Detroit. He launched a campaign to entice our parents to join him out west. He had help. George, Tom, my youngest brother, and I vigorously supported him.

Dad, now seventy-four years old, was the first to acquiesce. "I don't want to go to my grave without having my eldest son close at hand," he announced one day. "It's apparent to me that Nick is not coming home to live, so we will go to him." Mother, on the other hand, was torn. She too yearned to have Nick in their lives, but very strong attachments tugged at her. Her daughter and two of her sisters lived within a day's journey from Detroit; her third and closest sister was only an hour's streetcar ride away. In the end, it was George and Tom who compelled a decision in favor of the move to California. George, with a degree in aeronautical engineering, followed the pied piper of engineering, who summoned new graduates countrywide to join the burgeoning aerospace industry in Los Angeles. Tom then opted to attend college in California. Counterarguments from daughter, sisters, and a host of friends became irrelevant, so we sold the house in late 1949 and made preparations to move. But fate had other plans for the Naff family. It dealt us an untimely and tragic blow as we were almost ready to leave for California. Mother, in the prime of her life, died suddenly and purposelessly. Brokenhearted, Dad and I traveled to Los Angeles alone.

More than a decade later, while visiting Detroit, my brothers and I took a nostalgic trip to Tennyson Avenue. The house was gone, as if it had been singled out from the rest of the houses on the block. A chain-link fence protected a vacant, mowed lawn. It was a shock; it was like another death in the family.

The Naff family's American odyssey began in Spring Valley, Illinois, when on January 1, 1922, my father, his twenty-three-year-old wife, Yamna, and his seven-year-old daughter, Wedad, descended onto the platform of the small, picturesque train station. It was a bitter, cold night and none were dressed for midwinter Illinois temperatures. He led his family toward Main Street to find the bakery and residence of Nazha, his daughter from a previous marriage. They walked back and forth until someone staggered out of a saloon and directed them. Waiting with Nazha was her husband, Daher, and Dad's first cousin, Salimi, who was as close to him as a sister and as beloved. It was a warm reunion for Dad, and a stranger's reception for Mother.

Since the small apartment above the bakery could not accommodate the newcomers, Daher had arranged for us to stay temporarily in a barely furnished and barely heated house. Wedad thinks it was located between the railroad tracks and the river. Nothing at that time could have been further from Dad's mind than Detroit. Here in Spring Valley he was finally home.

Spring Valley was a small rural town in the corn and bituminous coal belt of Illinois, about ninety miles southwest of Chicago. Of its approximately three thousand inhabitants, perhaps twenty families had migrated from Ottoman Syria before 1910. Close to half of them originated in Rashayya. In addition, several other Rashayyan families were scattered in nearby rural towns. The Syrian community was as near a replica of their native village as one could find outside Syria. Dad knew the town well. It had been his home base for several of his peddling years after he migrated to the United States in 1895 as a teenager. He had come there from Fort Wayne, Indiana. Many of his peddling buddies were still there. He also knew many of the rural towns in the northern half of Illinois. It had been a lucrative region in which to peddle before World War I. There could be no doubt about why he decided to return to Spring Valley to settle down with his family: he was planning to go back to peddling. My father, a self-educated man, was a man of limited ambition, more contented by the familiar than challenged by the new.

In 1913 he was summoned to Rashayya to tend to his ninety-year-old ailing mother. By that time he had been widowed for many years. Nazha, eighteen years old at that time, was married and living in Montreal, Quebec, and Dad had resolved never to marry again. His experience with his late wife had been very troubled and unhappy. However, as he wrote in his brief memoir, when Yamna Ghantous served him coffee in her parents' living room, his resolve dissolved before her beauty. When his interest in marrying her reached her parents, they approved and consulted their daughter. At forty, he was tall and strong with a fairly handsome face, a full head of wavy hair flecked with gray, and a mustache. He always looked and moved like a man much younger. That is how I remember him in Detroit. From the perspective of Yamna's parents, he would make a good husband for a daughter who was already sixteen, with no other prospects. The village was practically empty of eligible men. They knew that he was a good man from a good, albeit poor family and that he was devoted to his mother. In addition, he had emigrated to America, which qualified him as a choice pick. From their daughter's perspective, he was too old and a widower who had a daughter two years her elder. Undeterred, Dad enlisted the help of the priest's wife, who had some influence with Yamna. She agreed to help for Yamna's sake, she said, and would discuss the matter during their sewing sessions. Yamna finally agreed, and by prearrangement the priest's wife summoned

Dad. The moment of acceptance is poignantly recorded in Dad's memoir. He was elated that Yamna had agreed to talk to him, he wrote, but there was one matter that required discussion. He explained the unpleasant circumstances of his first marriage, then pleaded with her to accept his proposal only if she was certain that she wanted to marry him. If she agreed, she was to put her hand in his outstretched one. His memoir continues: "She dropped her eyes shyly and put her hand in mine and we walked to her father's house to make arrangements for the wedding."

Were they mismatched? By all conventional Western standards, they were. But Dad's deep, abiding, and unpretentious affection for her and her sterling respect for him sustained their relatively harmonious relationship for thirty-five years. That he was mild-mannered, gentle, easygoing, and affectionate helped. However, he had some strange traits. One was his temper. Although slow to anger, should his sleep be disturbed or his patience be pushed beyond reasonable limits, he exploded like a firecracker and, like a firecracker, when his fire was spent, his anger evaporated. In addition, profanity and cussing in general were repellent to him. Even the innocuous "damn" drew the stern admonition that damning was the prerogative of God; only He has the power to do so.

Fig. 5. Yamna Naff, Spring Valley, Illinois, ca. 1927. Courtesy of the Naff Arab American Collection, Archives Center, NMAH, Smithsonian Institution.

When he returned to Spring Valley in 1922, he simply picked up where he had left off nine years earlier, as if time had stopped in his absence. This time, however, he peddled from a Model T Ford. After a lesson or two, he began to roam from one familiar town to another. It was very fortunate that automobiles on country roads were occasional at best. Otherwise, the couple of accidents he had might have been serious. Frequently, one or two of his peddling friends rode with him. On occasion, he took my growing, restless, and mischievous brothers along. He visited towns with such intriguing names as Delzel, Mendota, Champaign, and Marseilles. The latter, pronounced Marcel by Dad, was named, I was convinced, after the waves he tried to iron into my sister's straight hair. Bartering was common to peddlers whose customers were farmers. In return for items from his suitcases, Dad came home with fresh eggs, corn, as well as fruits and vegetables in season, which Mother preserved. There were even live chickens, squirming river fish, and rabbits on the back seat of his car. Only Mother knew if he brought home any cash.

His peddling day began very early and ended in midafternoon. He would lunch, retire to his bedroom for a short nap, come down to sit in his favorite chair, read his Arabic newspapers and often his Bible, and do Mother's bidding. In season, he gardened until dinnertime.

Dad was pleased with himself in Spring Valley. Peddling was an occupation that suited him. It rewarded his efforts sufficiently to provide for his growing family and build a savings account. Besides, he knew no other trade. What is surprising is that peddling was still lucrative in rural Illinois in the 1920s. Generally speaking, it had been declining as an immigrant occupation since the turn of the century, when Syrian peddlers began moving into family businesses. Dry goods and grocery stores were the most popular. In Spring Valley, many shops on Main Street were Syrian-owned, as they were in other nearby rural towns, a symbol of elevated status for the immigrants.

Perhaps because of his literacy or his bearing, the Rashayyans of Spring Valley treated Dad as they would a village elder. Perhaps it was because he had assumed some of the traditional functions of that role, such as resolving conflicts, inviting out-of-town visitors to dine in his home, and providing lodging for itinerant priests, among others.

From the temporary house near the railroad tracks, we moved for a couple of years to one of the many mining cottages, then to a large frame house with a wraparound front porch, a large front yard, and an even larger backyard, every inch of which Dad planted.

A rococo fresco covered the living room ceiling. Upstairs were four bedrooms and a bathroom with an inside toilet and bathtub, one of the few south of the Silk Stocking district, as the upper-class Irish area located north of Main Street was called.

As for Mother, she arrived in Spring Valley apprehensive and timid. She was young and beautiful, with jet-black hair worn in a bun at the nape of her neck. Sometimes she wound braids around her head like a crown framing her soft features. She was modest, relatively well educated, and well mannered. The older Rashayyan residents were pleased with her. Moreover, they undoubtedly knew that she was the daughter of Mikhail Ghantous, a wealthy landowner, and the sister of Fares, a local political hero and activist against the Ottoman Turks. She was easily absorbed into this transplanted Rashayya with a minimum of culture shock. The women treated her like a daughter. She was nursed and coddled when her six Spring Valley children were born, when any of them became ill, and when two of them died as infants. I remember how profoundly moved I was when I had to memorize Henry Wadsworth Longfellow's poem, "We are Seven." It seemed to describe our family, for we too "are seven" and two of us also "in the churchyard lie."

Actually, we are five. My sister, Wedad, was born in Rashayya. An infant daughter born between her and me died. This made me the third daughter. The older Rashayyan women, pitying my sonless father, insisted that Mother eat the cooked flesh of a black-feathered hen. She did, and it worked: subsequent pregnancies produced three sons. All were welcome, but only the birth of the first, Nick, was celebrated lavishly. Then came George. Another infant died before Mother was thirty, when my youngest brother, Tom, was born in 1929. After that, she wanted no more children and she had no more. Dad obliged.

The patriarchal head of household and theoretical primary authority was Dad, sanctioned by tradition and by Mother, who unwaveringly insisted that none of his children forget it. Actually, it was she who was the disciplinarian—strict but not stern—compared to Dad, who was more inclined to reprimand than punish. She instinctively assumed the responsibility for the molding of our character. Confident in her rightness, strong-willed, energetic, quick-tempered, she was temperamentally best qualified to fulfill that role. She constantly accused Dad of spoiling us. When, however, she could goad him into getting serious about discipline, he could frighten and hurt, as my two older brothers and I can testify. When a spanking proved ineffective, Mother reached for a handy strap hung from a nail near the kitchen sink, which she used effectively as a threat or to sting. If that didn't work, there was always the maximum threat: "Wait until your father gets home." How effective that was is illustrated by an incident Tom likes to tell. When Tom, the family pet, became old enough to warrant serious disciplining, Mother brandished the maximum threat. Then, when Dad arrived home for dinner that evening, she prodded him—no, she nagged him—into punishing Tom. Finally, he rose from his chair angrily and yanked the boy behind closed doors in the living room usually reserved for company only. Tom confessed that he was terrified. Mother, hearing bloodcurdling screams at the sound of flesh on flesh, went to rescue her son from brutality. There were the two of them giggling softly. As Dad clapped his hands, Tom shrieked. At one point, he turned toward the door and saw Mother. She was barely able to conceal a smile between angry protestations. I wonder how Dad mollified her.

If our parents disagreed on the degree of discipline, they were in complete accord on the values we were to learn. They were all drawn from Rashayyan tradition and the Bible: honesty, truthfulness, respect for our elders, and honoring the family name. The virtues of generosity, hospitality, and compassion we learned from example. There was one set of expectations I would list under the heading, "most often defied at some cost to our skins." These were obedience, no fighting, no talking back, and cleanliness. About the latter, Mother was manic.

Every Sunday, the family attended church. Before St. George's Syrian Orthodox Church was dedicated in 1926, my parents didn't have far to go. Liturgy was read in our living room because the itinerant priests lodged at our house. My brothers and I attended Protestant churches: Methodist, Congregational, and Baptist. Even after the Syrian church was dedicated, we were not required to attend it. Our parents thought we would learn the lessons of religion better if we heard them in a language we understood. Although the five of us spoke Arabic as our first language, it was not the classical Arabic of the liturgy.

The Protestant churches are effective Americanizing institutions. We learned much more than religion. We enjoyed the lack of elaborate ritual, which is so much a part of the Orthodox faith, and we loved the singing of hymns. In Sunday school we could win a Bible and participate in biblical pageants in costume. Then there was the exciting celebration of the American Christmas: brightly decorated trees with colorful lights and, above all, gifts. Eastern Orthodoxy celebrated Christmas only by a special liturgy. Easter was the major religious holiday on the Orthodox calendar. Even New Year's Day was more fun than Christmas. In church, as in school, we learned about Thanksgiving, which the Syrians called the chicken holiday, and Halloween, holidays the Syrians learned about only in America. The holiday that mystified my parents the most was Halloween, when all the mischievous instincts of children were released. Halloween in Spring Valley was accurately depicted in the film *Meet Me in St. Louis.* In school we drew the symbols of these holidays: a bearded Santa Claus, turkeys, and pumpkin faces.

Wedad was allowed to attend the Roman Catholic Church with her friends. She was even permitted by my father to take first communion, but he refused adamantly to allow her to be rebaptized. Most of what my brothers and I learned in Protestant churches, Wedad learned in the Catholic Church. When our first Christmas came around, she decided, with me as an accomplice, to "do something for the boys." She talked Dad into giving us money with which we bought a few toys at Woolworth's. The next year we had a Christmas tree and Dad hung our first Christmas stockings.

After our respective churches were out, we joined our parents. We joined the line at the altar to receive a piece of holy bread given to parishioners at the end of the liturgy. We were also present at special rituals and ceremonies. We had the best of all worlds, and it seemed very natural to us. Our sectarian identity, if altered at all, was imperceptible. Most important, we grew up relatively free of religious intolerance.

As each of us came of age, we were enrolled in Lincoln School, the proverbial little red schoolhouse on a hill—eight grades, eight teachers, a principal, and a janitor. Since neither Wedad nor I could speak English when we began school, we learned it the hard way. At home, we were instructed by Mother to speak her language in the house and our language outside. She tried, unsuccessfully, to teach Wedad and me to read and write classical Arabic. Our mother was a traditionalist; Rashayya was a living presence in our house.

Except for her clothes, the Americanization process seemed hardly to touch my mother in Spring Valley. It could not get past Rashayyan traditions, which Mother couldn't have avoided even if she had wanted to. They were everywhere—in the people who surrounded her on Devlin Street and even on Main Street. If she went there to buy our clothes or an odd grocery item, she bought them from friends. If she ventured into Woolworth's for a spool of thread, there was inevitably a Syrian to help her. There was nothing she needed or wanted that wasn't provided by Dad or members of the Syrian community.

Much of life in Spring Valley was communal. Ingredients for Syrian recipes were ordered in large quantities from New York wholesalers who catered to Syrian immigrants. Lambs were butchered to suit Syrian needs by one of the community in his backyard. Their social life was more telling. During the evenings, members of the community exchanged visits. Visitors from out of town were feted by several families. Weddings, births, and baptisms were community affairs. Mourning traditions were observed by all Rashayyans for the requisite first forty days; and the families of the seriously ill were visited by many. In such an ambiance, it is difficult to see how my mother could develop an inclination to become American.

On the whole, she was content in Spring Valley except for her unshakable homesickness. It was somewhat alleviated when Wadia, her younger sister who had traveled with my parents from Rashayya and had been diverted to Canada because of trachoma in her eyes, arrived to live with us. The sisters needed each other. Never more than in 1925, when fate dealt them the first of three tragic blows they would suffer in the next eight years: the murder of their parents.

When the French Mandate government was established in the former Ottoman province of Syria in 1920, it revived the old enmity between Christians and Druze. By 1925, that enmity erupted into revolt. One of the focal points of the rebellion was Rashayya, which was populated almost equally by the two faiths. The western part of Syria as well as the Beqa' Plain and historical Mt. Lebanon were in turmoil. Tensions and mistrust ran high.

With no banks in which to secure his ample earnings and in anticipation of the fighting reaching Rashayya, my grandfather buried his money on his property. When the Druze leaders of the town requested a meeting with him, they had two aims: to seize his money for the purchase of arms and to capture his oldest son, Fares, who was actively petitioning the Christians in villages on the western slope of the Anti-Lebanon mountain range to side with the French. The aim was the incorporation of that region into a larger, semiautonomous national entity of Lebanon. My grandparents were murdered, their fortune stolen, Rashayya was razed, and many lives were lost. Fares escaped to continue his political work from Beirut. He and his wife, Alexandra, became the surrogate parents of six orphaned siblings. They had three very young children of their own.

According to Syrian (and Rashayyan) custom, Mother and Aunt Wadia donned mourning black. Neither could be comforted.

Mother's grief was palpable in the almost constant flow of silent tears and the mournful tunes she hummed whenever she was alone. As in most Mediterranean cultures, death carried with it long-held emotional superstitions and fears as well as social customs closely observed by members of the community. The Rashayyan women of Spring Valley, wearing black, abided by these customs, especially during the initial forty-day period. Mother and Aunt Wadia wore mourning black for seventeen years.

On reflection, it was fortunate that Mother was among people who gave her the kind of comfort and support she would understand. Until we left Spring Valley, Mother's knowledge of the American way of life was formed in the Syrian community, which hardly prepared her for what was to come. Nor did it prepare my father. He continued to peddle, deluded by the uneven and hollow prosperity that deluded all of America in the mid-1920s. In Illinois, toward the end of the decade, coal and farm economies were becoming more uncertain and the prognosis was not promising. I wonder if my father read the warning signals in his Arabic newspapers. Syrian editors and publishers were, at that time, generally diligent in informing and interpreting such developments for their immigrant readers. If he did read the signals, did he understand the full portent of their message, or was it his diminishing income that convinced him to leave Spring Valley?

In any case, by 1929 Dad began to seek advice from Rashayyan relatives and friends in Grand Rapids, Michigan; Fort Wayne, Indiana; and Detroit. Predictably, he gravitated toward the familiar. Fort Wayne was the root of his American experience. That small town was where he arrived and where he learned the peddling trade from members of the relatively large Rashayyan community. He had not returned to Fort Wayne since he was tricked into marrying a woman he disliked. Now, he was willing to gamble on finding a solution to his financial troubles there. His plan was to open a grocery store, alleviate his serious financial concerns, and enjoy once again the companionship and moral support of old friends.

Fort Wayne was a disaster for Dad. While he was trapped in Rashayya because of World War I and his remarriage, Fort Wayne had become a small city whose prosperity over the years had changed the Syrians. Many of his former peddling friends were still there, but they were now owners of profitable businesses. Some were vendors of prestigious Oriental rugs, laces, and linens, others were wholesalers of a variety of products, and still others owned grocery or general dry goods stores. Some had reached the upper levels of the middle class and had become more Americanized and urbanized than the Syrians of tradition-bound Spring Valley. We were rural hicks by comparison. Competition for social status had replaced the warmth and comradery of the old days. Dad anticipated none of these changes.

Thus, my father rented a small, dark, and dingy hole-in-the-wall in the early fall of 1929 and turned it into a grocery store that was patronized more by huge, bold rats than by humans. They terrified my poor sister (and sometimes me) when she opened for business while our father was away buying produce. There was never enough income with which to stock the shelves beyond a facade. This disaster lasted eight or nine months. It was my inexperienced and naive father's first foray into the grocery business. There would be three more.

He rented a house for his family close to the elementary school in which three of us were enrolled. Wedad attended high school in another neighborhood. I don't remember the house or the school, and I remember little else about Fort Wayne because I hated it and because I lived in it for less than three months. I was sent away from my family. It was as if I had fallen asleep and awakened in the home of my half sister, Nazha, on Trowbridge Avenue, an upscale neighborhood in Detroit. I don't remember how I got there or why. Although I was not told, I supposed I was one less mouth to feed.

Nazha's was a handsome house furnished with Oriental rugs, period furniture, and an oil painting or two. We ate on a linen tablecloth with linen napkins. There was a phonograph with an ample collection of Arabic records. The Haneys had become wealthy by selling Oriental rugs, linens, and laces in the resorts of Michigan in the summer and in Florida during the winter. I remained with them for a year or so, and despite their kindness, it was a memorably miserable year. There were no children my age in the neighborhood, and it wasn't the kind of home to which I could bring friends from the public school I attended. Although the Haneys spoke English with no accent, they had no library, nor was there a library in the area. So I spent most of my time reading books I brought home from school, as well as newspapers. I developed a strong appetite for reading and a passion for words, their use, sounds, and meanings. I clipped poetry, pictures of interesting places, drawings of any kind, as well as any words of wit and wisdom that struck a cord, even though many times I did not understand the full significance of what I was clipping. Thus began a lifelong habit curtailed only by Mother's refusal to ship the clippings to California for me in 1949. "I will not ship that box of meaningless papers. What do you plan to do with them anyway?" she asked. Was her refusal because the box resembled a coffin, a dreaded image? I spent three tearful days reducing its contents to a couple of small boxes as she tried to assuage my pain by teasing me. She didn't recognize her budding historian. Neither did I.

When I wasn't reading or clipping in Nazha's house or listening to Arabic music on the phonograph, I daydreamed. My elementary school teachers tried in vain to discipline the habit out of me. I was lonely. I daydreamed about my siblings and my parents and about Spring Valley: its little red schoolhouse on a hill, the terrifying quicksand pond at the bottom of a reddish slag dump on top of which the white-sheeted Ku Klux Klan burned crosses, and the sound of the train as it pulled into the depot and tugged at my imagination. I thought of the itinerant medicine men and minstrel shows, of the boats on the river, and the woods where teachers took us to pick violets in the spring and walnuts in the fall. Detroit had none of this—nothing to stimulate my imagination and warm my heart. I hated it.

One island of joy in this sea of loneliness was the home of my beloved Aunt Wadia. Coincidentally, she and her family left Spring Valley about the same time as we did and moved to the east side of Detroit where her husband, Matt, opened a grocery store. It didn't seem to improve their financial situation much over that of my parents. Infrequently, I was allowed to take the hour-long streetcar ride to Lycaste Avenue to visit her. How I cherished those visits!

It was on these trips that I began to test my comprehension of a new and exciting interest: what we now call "pop psychology." It may have been the *Detroit News* that published a daily question-and-answer column titled "The Psychologist," which asked such questions as "What is an introvert?" or an extrovert, or an inferiority complex, and many others. A whole new world of ideas and questions opened up for me. I would study my fellow streetcar passengers, observing their faces, the expressions in their eyes, the set of their mouths, how they dressed, and the neighborhoods to which they descended. I then tried to add up the observations in terms of the concepts discussed by the psychologist. In this way, the hour passed quickly and my mind was stimulated.

If wearing mourning black was meant to repel death, the custom failed. In the fall of 1930 in Fort Wayne, my mother received the second tragic blow. Fares, her closest brother, her political hero, and the surrogate father of her remaining orphaned siblings, died of pneumonia at the age of thirty-six in Beirut. She was devastated. So was Aunt Wadia. Once again the pall of mourning engulfed our home. The attendant rituals and traditions connected with death were set in motion more intensely than after the death of her parents. Perhaps it just seemed that way because not only did the activity increase, impelled by the untimely death of this revered man, but Mother became more actively involved. Given Fares's status among immigrants from Rashayya and its environs, a steady stream of condoling visitors made its way to our house. Black-bordered condolence letters poured in from numerous communities in the United States, as well as from Canada, South America, and even Australia. The Ghantous sisters took up their positions in the living room and sat there every day and evening as if cast in plaster. Beyond all this, Mother was required to attend liturgies in Fares's honor read in Grand Rapids, Detroit, Spring Valley, and Montreal. It seems that the air of gloom that had for so long framed my mother's beautiful face was becoming a permanent feature.

Soon Mother began to worry about how her sister-in-law and cherished friend, Alexandra, was going to manage the large family left behind. So she and Aunt Wadia scraped together scarce dollars and bundled used and new clothes to send to Beirut. At the same time, Rashayyan clubs were raising money to send Fares's children to school.

Coincidentally, almost a year before his death, Fares and Mother convinced their maternal uncle in Saskatchewan, Canada, to buy fares to America for two of her sisters. Agia and Julia, barely past their teens, were en route when Fares died. On their arrival in Fort Wayne, they were shocked to learn of his death and to find Mother in an appalling state. They became a part of our household that Dad could ill afford. However, he welcomed them into his family, not only as a comfort to Mother, but because Fares was his hero also. During World War I, Dad was Fares's political lieutenant for several years in Lebanon, and on at least two occasions he foiled Fares's capture by the Turks.

Events converged to confer on Mother the unwitting role of head of the Ghantous family here and abroad. Implicit at first, the role would evolve into that of ultimate mother. In America, her sisters, even after they married and left our home, consulted her on matters large and small. Until she died, they relied on her judgement implicitly. On the occasion of births, baptisms, and serious illnesses, she packed her bag, took her youngest son by the hand and traveled to be at their sides. There was no lack of visits from them to our house.

The experience of Rashayya-style mourning and the economic effects of the Depression combined to form an invisible wall that, as in Spring Valley, inhibited my mother from reaching out to become American or to be challenged by the process. Rather, she seemed to withdraw, haunted by the possible death of those most dear to her.

Before the emotional storm over Fares's death subsided, my anxious father decided to leave Fort Wayne for Detroit. A new chapter—a very different chapter in the experience of the Naff family —began in June 1931, when my father turned his gray 1929 Whippet into the Haney's driveway. I had been waiting impatiently on the porch for hours. In reality, I had been waiting for more than a year. For a displaced child, it might as well have been one hundred years. Would my sister and brothers be changed? If so, how and how much? And what of my mother and father? What were my new aunts like? Would Tom, the baby that haunted my thoughts, remember me?

Even before the engine stopped, Nick and George tumbled out of the back seat. Following them, stepping over baggage and limp from heat and exhaustion, came my sister and my two aunts. Mother, carrying eighteen-month-old Tom, was helped out of the front seat. Finally, Dad, flushed with fatigue, anger, and frustration, bounded out, relieved to be free of the steering wheel, the road, the complaints, and the nagging requests to stop. Even now, it is a mystery to me how this man who had rarely driven on a major highway, let alone in a big city, made his way from Fort Wayne to this neighborhood. A trip that should have taken four or five hours lasted for what seemed an eternity. There were no freeways, no rest stops, fast-food restaurants, or restroom conveniences. The alternative was simply to pull over to the side of the road, where passengers and baggage were unloaded. That was where tires had to be repaired also. Often the side of the road was on or near the property of farmers wary of Depression migrants looking for work or food, who helped themselves to whatever was in reach. Once, Mother was soundly scolded by a farmer's wife for plucking two apples for her restless sons. Years later, Wedad would liken this unforgettable experience to that of John Steinbeck's Okies.

There they were, everyone I had ached so long to see. My brothers and I gravitated to each other briefly before they ran off to explore the premises. They hadn't changed very much, but Wedad had. Was she really an adult as she thought she was—more comfortable in the company of my adult aunts than with me? Had a gulf opened between us, and had I lost my best friend? While I was sorting out the rush of confused emotions, I was embraced by my mother and then Dad buried me in his chest with his strong arms. He had such a loving way of embracing. Right then, my world righted itself. When Dad set me down, I saw Mother's tear-worn eyes and pain-drained face. There was a wan smile on her lips and the light in her eyes was gone, extinguished, it seemed to me, by the flood of tears that had flowed from them. She was not the same. My aunts stood by waiting their turn to greet me. Their resemblance to Mother was strong, I thought, especially when they smiled. Despite their mourning attire, they were lovely. Agia was petite and demure, with soft features and a voice to match. Julia, on the other hand, was younger, taller, and charged with energy. Her beauty lay in her flawless olive complexion, strong features, and bright eyes full of mischief. Both had endeared themselves to my brothers, and that was good enough for me.

As it happened, the Haney house was merely a courtesy stop. I watched sadly as my family piled back into the Whippet for the long drive to east Detroit, where Aunt Wadia was anxiously awaiting their arrival. She had endured the shock and pain of Fares's death without the support of Mother and needed to feel connected and comforted. Since Wadia had come to live with us in Spring Valley, she and Mother were inseparable until we all left the town. The reunion of the two families was fortuitous. For the next twenty years we would be as one family, although we lived miles apart.

Dad had been convinced to move to Detroit by the Haneys. I am sure he was told that he could open a grocery store and prosper like the hundreds of Syrians who had grocery stores in that city. Nazha no doubt told him, as she told me in a 1980 interview, that when she and Daher moved to Detroit in 1926 to start their rug and linen business, "There was a small Syrian family grocery store on nearly every corner, and Syrians were delivering and distributing much of the merchandise they sold." Never mind that the competition among them was keen. Hyperbole notwithstanding, this kind of statement probably had some basis in fact. They might have heard such boasting from Louis Shamie, a friend and one of the earliest and leading grocers in the city at the time. He began with a fruit stand around 1906 and by the end of the 1920s, he owned seventeen stores. He would ultimately become a grocery and produce wholesaler as well as the publisher of the *Grocer's Spotlight,* a widely read trade newspaper.

There were incentives to starting a small store in Detroit, according to Mr. Shamie's son. All one needed was a good location and very little capital. Rent for a store and its attached living quarters was usually very cheap. Moreover, bread and milk companies would provide shelves as part of their sales promotion and distributors would provide groceries on credit to the beginners. Mr. Shamie encouraged Syrians to enter the retail grocery business by helping them find good locations and extending credit to them. It is no wonder that so many of the approximately six thousand Syrians in Detroit were grocers. But that was in the booming 1920s. It was now 1931, one of the worst years of the Great Depression. I wonder if, when the Haneys convinced Dad to go into the grocery business, they took that difference into account, because my father seemed to stumble from one failure to the next.

Syrian dominance in the grocery business is not surprising. Syrians were and continue to be innately entrepreneurial. Much of their success was due to the traditional values they brought to their enterprise: a well-developed habit of hard work and frugality as well as strong family unity. The latter meant that all members work to enhance the welfare of the family. When a family enterprise succeeds, one could undoubtedly credit the whole family. Profits and savings depended on this reliable source of unpaid labor. The Naff family didn't have to be taught that lesson. It was instinctive.

In 1931, his cash reserves dwindling fast, Dad set out to find that elusive "good location." In sprawling, depression-ridden Detroit there were hundreds of places to choose from. He finally settled on a barn of a place on the corner of Mt. Elliott and Gratiot Avenues, two commercial thoroughfares. It was equipped with shelves, cash register, sales counters, and walk-in refrigerator. I visited it a couple of times with the Haneys, who drove the ten miles or so from their home to see how our father was doing. In my memory snapshot, it looks grim, shot through a gray filter—gray wooden floors, gray walls, even gray air. Shelves barely stocked, fruit stacked neatly in pyramids in the window and vegetables wilted and unappetizing. In more than two hours not a customer entered the store, and there were few people on the streets transacting any kind of commerce. Those who patronized the store usually bought a few convenience items. Others looked for work or handouts. One day, a desperate man brought a beautiful silver sugar bowl to sell. My sister gave him thirty-five cents, which he eagerly accepted. There was not much more in the cash register. She still recalls with sadness the man's eagerness to accept the paltry change. "We didn't have much," she said, "but we had more than he did."

Wedad, more than any of the Naff children, bore the heaviest burden in the survival of our family during the Depression. She was at Dad's side every morning to open this or the other of his attempts at storekeeping. She returned with him when he closed at midnight. Lamentably, she had to leave high school to be Dad's loyal helper. He trusted her to manage the stores while he bought produce at the Eastern Market. But then, customer traffic was practically nil.

Fig. 6. Wedad Naff in her father's grocery store, Woodward Avenue at Tennyson, in Detroit, ca. 1931. Courtesy of the Naff Arab American Collection, Archives Center, NMAH, Smithsonian Institution.

Unlike many wives of Syrian grocers, mother did not work. Her health was affected by her emotional ordeals and she spoke no English. After I rejoined the family, I spent all of my after-school hours in the store and did my homework with little or no distraction. From the beginning, Nick and George sold newspapers like born entrepreneurs. Each staked out a corner and held it against keen competition from boys of other ethnic groups. They sold both morning and evening editions. At times, they shouted headlines in residential streets. In the first three or four years, they turned all of their earnings over to Mother for household expenses. However, in their early teens, they accumulated enough money to buy bicycles, which enabled them to graduate to the more lucrative paper routes. Later, they would boast that they paid for their clothes, Boy Scout trips, sports gear, and whatever else they could talk my parents into letting them buy. Attempts at wasteful spending were checked by Mother, who was their banker. Later she sent them to open their own bank accounts. This was one of several tiny cracks that began to appear in Mother's Rashayya wall. Nick and George also worked in the store on weekends and after school, stocking shelves and, when prohibition was lifted, stacking beer cases. As soon as Tom was old enough, he followed in their footsteps. Anything his idols did, he was sure to do.

None of us were paid for working in the store, and we expected no payment. Our clothes were purchased by Mother with funds from the cash register, and our meager spending money was available when we asked—if the request was reasonable in our parents' opinion. Sometimes we were allowed to take the ten-cent price of a movie ticket from the register, provided we left a record of it so that accounts balanced at the end of the day. Accountability was demanded.

My family's first residence in Detroit, after three weeks of crowding in Aunt Wadia's house, was a rented one a few doors away. The brick houses in this working-class neighborhood, just a block or so from busy East Jefferson Avenue, which paralleled the Detroit River, were within walking distance of Chrysler Corporation's main plant. They looked alike, with a small porch, and a small front and backyard, the latter extending to an unpaved alley. The neighborhood was within a broad scattered community of Syrian Maronites and Melkites, both affiliates of the Roman Catholic Church. Aunt Wadia had married a devout Catholic and converted to her husband's faith.

Fig. 7. The Naff brothers in their Boy Scout uniforms, Highland Park, 1936. Courtesy of the Naff Arab American Collection, Archives Center, NMAH, Smithsonian Institution.

When I visited my parents' house with Nazha, I was always deeply troubled. I later realized it was the congestion and clutter created by four adults and four children living in such crowded quarters that troubled me. It seemed my aunts were always folding a stack of wash, undoubtedly washed by hand, that had just come off the line. There was no washing machine. Food was cooked and Arabic bread baked on a wood stove. The number of beds was inadequate. Adults slept on beds and sofas and children on the floor. The hope was that when the store succeeded, they would move to a more accommodating house.

However, within six months, it became apparent to Dad that the Mt. Elliott store was a losing enterprise. He began to seek another good location. With the help of the Syrian man who delivered milk, he soon found one. It had been a thriving grocery store with a fresh meat section and a butcher. Dad bought the stock on credit, hired the butcher, and opened for business with much hope and many prayers. Despite his painful experience with the Mt. Elliott store and the general uncertainty that accompanies a new venture, Dad was optimistic.

The store had genuine potential. It was located on Brush Street, in the heart of a middle-class neighborhood just south of Grand Boulevard and two blocks east of Woodward Avenue, which was the city's east-west divide. Customers began to come in and so did the money. Dad was delighted. It seemed fate was finally lifting the dark clouds that had pursued my family for the last two years.

We were now about twelve miles from Lycaste and Aunt Wadia and only a mile or so from Trowbridge Avenue, which put us within the orbit of the Haneys. None of us welcomed this unaccustomed shift in family relationships, but we had no choice. We moved to a more suitable house in a neighborhood near the store, far from any Syrians. I was gratefully returned to the family fold. My brothers and I were enrolled in school, and it seemed we were finally settling down to some kind of normalcy as a family.

During the next three months or so, the store became increasingly successful, proving that "good location," the grocer's mantra, really works. The potential of greater success seemed to lighten the burden of desperation and to dispel the gloom. Even Mother's spirits were lifted. Dad's joy bordered on euphoria. That, plus his naivete, caused his downfall. He allowed himself to be swindled by a man posing as a real estate agent seeking a business investment for a client. After some discussion, he convinced Dad to sign a document. Unable to read English, my innocent small-town father believed he gave the man permission to prepare an appraisal of the store and anxiously awaited the results, which he was certain would confirm his optimism and faith in God.

The next time the man appeared, he was with his "client." They had come to claim their property and to evict my father. The man had purchased the store under false pretenses for a sum less than Dad's investment in it. Dark despair confused the details. Even Dad was unsure of what had happened. What was certain was that he was in debt again due to his own folly. During his peddling days he had learned to speak English passably well but not to read well enough to decipher a legal document. For the rest of the family, there is little that we remember about the Brush Street experience. In retrospect, it seems like a remote shadowy nightmare.

Given his financial situation at the time and his anger at being swindled, Dad did something he might not otherwise have done. He took several boxes of groceries from the shelves before he turned it over. Mother, who had never brought canned foods into her kitchen, fed her family from cans. She learned to use a can opener; I learned about Franco American spaghetti. We ate a lot of it. Here was another chink in the Rashayya wall. Americanization came in unexpected forms.

The Brush Street fiasco was followed by another failure. Heartsick, Dad had to start all over again to find some money and another good location. It was 1932, the worst of the Depression years, when he launched his search. Reluctant to turn to the Haneys again, he and mother took her bridal jewelry, which included several gold bracelets from her parents and Fares, to Rashayyan friends and left them as collateral for a loan of one hundred dollars. A few years later, when Mother went to redeem them, they claimed that the jewelry had been stolen. Too bitter, too devastated, and too tired, my parents bitterly endured the loss. It was imperative that another good location be found as soon as possible. After a long search, Dad decided on a store in another middle-class neighborhood, this time on the west side—on Tireman Avenue near West Grand Boulevard. Without much hope, he opened its doors for business. It looked empty, which it was—almost. He expected to stock it more fully as sales increased. They hardly began. On many days sales did not exceed one dollar. When a customer spent several minutes contemplating the softness of a roll of toilet paper and then rejected it as being the wrong color, Dad reached the end of his tether. He donned his hat and coat, locked the door behind him, and went home. He returned several days later to remove the stock. The future looked bleak. Fear gnawed at him constantly and he hardly slept. What next? Where would it all end? He must have realized that he was one of millions of Americans who asked those same questions that frightful year.

The problems of money and location were pressuring him again. The Haneys, feeling the effects of the Depression themselves, advanced him what they could. By the time 1932 came to an end, he had located a store on Woodward Avenue, less than a block from Tennyson, the southern border of Highland Park. It was located between a Greek family restaurant and a tobacco, candy, and everything else kind of store. Close by was a Kroger's grocery. People were patronizing these stores, and all the streets in all directions were residential. This location seemed to have several qualifications that signaled it as a good location. At least it seemed to have some potential. Was this a considered choice by Dad or the hand of fate? I'll never know.

He had money to rent the store but none to stock it properly. Help came from an unexpected quarter—a Syrian, a stranger from the remnants of an old Syrian community that had developed prior to World War I around Henry Ford's original factory in Highland Park, over a mile north of Tennyson Avenue. It was once a substantial Christian and Muslim neighborhood until Ford transferred his operation to River Rouge in 1916. Most of the community followed their jobs and formed the nucleus of the present Arab American community in Dearborn. The remaining families scattered in residential streets in the vicinity of Davison Avenue. This man, whose name I have forgotten, owned a grocery store on Woodward Avenue near that neighborhood. He was not a Rashayyan, and I am not certain how well Dad knew him, but this savior made a gentleman's agreement with Dad. He would advance Dad money, interest-free, with which to stock the store. Dad was to repay him as he was able to do so. The payment flexibility was as much a blessing as the loan. At first, when Dad offered him payments, this generous man would reject them saying, "When you can better afford to pay." Dad never said that man's name without an accompanying blessing.

Dad opened for business in 1933. Franklin Delano Roosevelt had been elected president. He raised the spirits of the American people and gave them hope. Merchants like Dad were awaiting the repeal of the Prohibition Act and the promised legalization of the sale of light wines and beer. Soon after it took office, the new Administration urged Congress to pass a law, and it did without even a roll call. It was the signal for store owners to register for beer licenses. This reform, one of many that constituted the New Deal, lifted much of the despair in the country and in our family as well.

Several breweries had apparently loaded their trucks in advance and, as if a bell had been struck, they began making deliveries even, it seemed, before the legalizing process was complete. Standing on a box, Nick was cheered by people on the street as he printed the word "beer" in large white letters on the plate glass window. That simple act ushered in a new chapter in our lives. Sales began to mount gradually. Soon Dad repaid his benefactor and began stocking the shelves adequately. Relieved of the recurrent fear of another move—another "good location"—he focused on means to increase sales because survival of the store obviously could not depend entirely on beer sales. Nick began to apply his printing talent to posting weekly specials on the window.

These efforts notwithstanding, the Depression was still very much in evidence, albeit with diminishing effects. There were still many idle hours in the long workday. There were also many idle hours for men who could not find work. A few regulars from the neighborhood used the store to wile away time. Some would call them loiterers; I call them teachers. Collectively, they added an important extracurricular dimension to my education. They were more captivating than any homework assignments. And, like the characters in a novel, each had his peculiar traits and fascinations.

From Johnny Pack, who was obsessed with bodybuilding, I learned about Atlas, the model bodybuilder who is always portrayed carrying the earth on his shoulders, and about lion taming and the circus life he yearned to join. More significantly for me, I learned about modern dance, an incipient and revolutionary form of ballet, which was being developed by the Ruth St. Denis-Ted Shawn School of Dance, where both men and women were trained. Training men in ballet was not only novel, it was revolutionary. Johnny turned me into an ardent devotee of this American art form. There was also the nameless soul who called me his "friend" because I patiently listened to his repeated recitations of state capitals and presidents. I used him as the subject of a prize-winning essay in my composition class at the University of Detroit night school. I learned about the delights of tropical Florida from Maurice, who rode his motorcycle to that "paradise" in the winter to do odd jobs for the rich residents and returned to Detroit in the summer. He took me for thrilling motorcycle rides. He once sent me an unpeeled coconut addressed to Eleanor Roosevelt, Englewood Avenue, Detroit, Michigan, and it reached me. I was thrilled! Apparently, our postman was observant. Gallagher told humorous and entertaining Irish tales and jokes. Fred Logan, whose memory I cherish, deserves special mention. Because he played in one of the Negro baseball leagues, he would vanish for months at a time, but when he returned I eagerly listened to stories of his travels, which he often mixed with black lore. He taught me the soft-shoe dance and introduced me to blues, which he hummed softly. Tall, lean, and graceful, he was my Bojangles and I his Shirley Temple. His memory still clutches at my heart.

Fred was no loiterer. He was kind and helpful, always busying himself with chores in the store lest our white customers question his presence. He refused compensation for his work because, it seemed, Dad had at one time helped him when he was in need. On the day in 1943 when a race riot erupted on Belle Isle, a recreational island in the Detroit River, Fred rushed to the store from downtown to warn me (I was now in charge of the store) that the rioters were marching up Woodward Avenue to connect with rioters from the Davison Avenue neighborhood of blacks. It was midafternoon. He helped close the store and walked me home. As it turned out, the rioters were turned back about a mile before they reached our part of Woodward. With great bravado and curiosity and greater stupidity, I drove to Davison Avenue only to be turned around in terror by flying stones and rotten vegetables. The next day, Fred scolded me about the thoughtlessness of my act and the importance of people knowing their place. I was no better than the rioters in that regard, he pointed out. Fred was not only a protector but a friend. He was always welcome at our table, as a policeman who came to our back door one day discovered. The officer had been summoned by our neighbor, the prototype of the old stock American families who were the predominant homeowners on Tennyson Avenue, who saw Fred knock at our side door.

In the dull, drab days of the Depression, these men added texture to our lives and stirred our imaginations, mine in particular, given my penchant for daydreaming.

We left Bethune Avenue and moved to Englewood, two blocks south of Tennyson Avenue and three blocks east of Woodward. A rented house, it was in a lower-middle-class neighborhood of immigrant families like us. There was an Italian family that made its own wine and a Polish family that made its own sausages. There were two Syrian families other than mine, one of which was Rashayyan, and we even had a synagogue on Englewood. The street was our playground often well past dark. A Greek grandmother, covered in a black shawl from her head to her toes, watched every move we made from her perch on her porch. We could always depend on her to tattle to our parents for some real or imagined mischief. That is how I learned about nationality differences in people. The consensus of the five Naff children is that the nine years we lived on Englewood were growing, developing, learning years, rich with memorable experiences.

The house had the typical porch and the luxury of a swing, enough bedrooms to accommodate all of us—four children and five adults, including my seventeen-year-old sister—and a kitchen large enough to delight Mother. Dad was pleased with the size of the backyard, with its collection of fruit trees. We occupied the house in late spring and he immediately became an urban farmer, an apt characterization because he tended to plant ten or fifteen, maybe even twenty varieties of vegetables.

Mother, influenced by Dad's cautious optimism, began to turn this inelegant but spacious house into a presentable and comfortable home. In addition to furnishings from our smaller residence, she purchased a used sideboard to hold her precious "for company" linens and laces, which included several pieces she had crocheted and embroidered. She also acquired a large used dining-room set with eight chairs. Ours was relegated to the kitchen, where much of our life was carried out.

Mother seemed to be looking ahead now. She had not been able to do so previously. In the Englewood house, life took on an aura of stability. It was the first house since she left Spring Valley in which she was truly the mistress. It was her house. She seemed, too, to sense that significant changes would occur in the Naff household. She probably couldn't put her finger on why she felt that way, but I'm fairly certain that if it was merely hope and prayer in the back of her mind, she was thinking not only of her children's lives but also of her life and Dad's as times improved.

Clues to the changes appeared when our home became what I used to call a "Sunday café." Every Sunday, my parents returned from church leading several friends and relatives they had invited to dine with us. They would spend Saturday evenings and Sunday mornings preparing the meal. It was my responsibility to set the table and clean up the kitchen before company arrived. The custom befitted my father's status as unsolicited traditional "village elder." Mother, it seemed to me, encouraged the revival of that status that had diminished during the worst years of the Depression, which, by extension, were her own worst years.

Our home began spontaneously to take on other roles. It became a haven for several young Syrian men who came to Dad for help in finding work. Their families knew him in the peddling days. One was from Toledo, Ohio, another from Grand Rapids, Michigan, and twins from Manchester, New Hampshire. They stayed with us while they looked for work. The twins found work, the others did not and moved on. When Aunt Salimi's son, Norman, came from Spring Valley, Dad decided to let him start a fresh meat section in the store, an indication of Dad's optimism, or good faith. Both were appropriate in 1936, when Roosevelt was returned to the Oval Office in an overwhelming landslide that included Dad's vote. After a year or so, the meat section was a nominal success, which gave the young man the courage to court Aunt Julia.

It was when Mother took in a couple of indigents that I dubbed our home "vagabond mansion." Mike O'Rourke, a former used-car salesman, slept on a leather couch in the vestibule for several weeks. Sam, an unwashed Italian who reeked of garlic, slept on a mat in the basement next to the furnace for over a year. He had come to the back door begging for food in return for doing odd jobs.

In the last years of the decade our home became a marriage center. Throughout the decade my aunts were courted. Aunt Agia turned down several proposals before she married a wealthy Rashayyan haberdasher from Canada in 1938. It was a lavish wedding paid for by the groom, in which Mother, Wedad, Aunt Julia, and I were given new dresses. A year later Aunt Julia married Norman, and they moved to Grand Rapids, where he opened a store of his own. That same year, Mother's school friend from Rashayya visited her. She was the daughter of a historically wealthy Syrian merchant family and the recent widow of a well-to-do Syrian-Brazilian merchant. The courting traffic was heavy at our house as news of this prize sped along the Rashayyan grapevine. I dubbed her the "merry widow."

We were not in our house but a few weeks when Mother and her three sisters received the third of their blows. Ibrahim, their second brother who had assumed the role of head of household after Fares's death, died of pneumonia in Beirut. He was thirty-three. The news was shocking, the grief was intense, but the mourning rituals were subdued—perhaps because there was no unified Rashayyan community in Detroit in which tradition could thrive. There were only five or six families, and these were scattered within an area of four or five square miles. Englewood was on its southern fringe. A few lived in Windsor, Ontario, across the Detroit River; a few others traveled infrequently from Toledo and Grand Rapids.

Whether it was because we were growing up or because Mother was herself outgrowing them and subtly Americanizing, I can't say, but in some respects Rashayyan traditions (except for the hardcore ones) seemed to be losing much of their effect. In any case,

Mother and her sisters, still wearing black, took their mandatory places in our living room to receive condoling guests. Within a few weeks, life seemed to return to normal in our home, except for the quiet, barely concealed grief that flowed from my mother's eyes.

Nick and George continued their primary school grades at Dwyer School, which I had attended when I lived with the Haneys. I moved up to junior high school, where I made friends of my own for the first time. I had given up trailing my brothers; or, rather, they had given me up. Who wants a sister hanging around? Besides, Mother kept insisting that good girls didn't play with boys.

Living on Englewood offered many more challenges than those encountered in our previous residences. Both on the school yard and on the street, there were new friends to be made, small neighborhood teams to join, turf to compete for, and expanded opportunities for mischief. Nick and George thrived in this environment. On vacant corner lots, they played various ball games season to season. When they acquired newspaper routes, their world began its widening phase, followed almost in tandem by increased earnings, bank accounts, and Scouting. Group trips impelled a burgeoning sense of confidence and maturity. My brothers were growing up. For Tom, who was only four when we moved to Englewood, his brothers were his role models and heroes, and he was their mascot. Where they went, he went, and what they did, he would do in turn. Mother tried to keep up with the changes in her sons that were, in fact, changing her.

In their adolescent years, Nick and George looked like twins and were inseparable. They played on the same teams, sometimes cooperating, sometimes competing seriously. They got into trouble together and took their punishments together, many times unjustly, since Nick was the precocious instigator of most of their punishable mischief. Always the performer, he overshadowed his younger brother and attracted praise and attention. George was in the frustrating position of being the middle son between Nick, the aggressive heir apparent, and Tom, the family pet. However, in his teen years, George began to assert himself. When Nick began to attend the University of Detroit, their paths diverged. The divergence widened when World War II became an American war and both went into military service. That was 1941, the last Englewood year. Yet the bond they had earlier forged withstood all their differences.

George graduated from high school that year, and rather than wait to be drafted, he applied for officer training in the naval air force. He was seventeen and required Dad's signature. It took a long walk and much convincing. When they returned, Dad was downcast and had to contend with Mother's tearful fury. In July, he left for preflight training in Iowa. The family was breaking up, but it was not losing its unity. He became a carrier-based fighter pilot and served in the Pacific theater. When he was discharged and came home, he brought with him the fiancée with "heavenly blue eyes" about whom we had heard so much in his letters. He also had several medals awarded for combat activity he would not discuss, even 'til this day. Mother made certain that the local Arabic press received a photo of him in Navy whites at his citation ceremony.

Several months later, Nick reluctantly enlisted in the Army Reserve Corps because it allowed him to graduate from college before it sent him to officer training class. While in service, he suffered an eye injury. He wasn't assigned to San Francisco until after his recovery and a three-week furlough home. When the international conference that created the United Nations Organization was convened in 1945, Nick sought out the Syrian and Lebanese representatives. When they learned that he was the nephew of Fares Ghantous and that he could communicate with them in Arabic (albeit in the Rashayyan dialect), they prevailed upon him to become the unofficial after-hours interpreter and escort for the full contingent from the Arabic-speaking Middle East, a region that would shortly become known as the Arab World. It was a memorable experience for him. Mother's pride was unbounded when she received a warm note from Fares el-Khoury, the prime minister of the newly independent nation of Syria, who praised her brother, a friend and colleague, and her son. Needless to say, Nick's picture appeared in the local Arabic press.

Nineteen forty-one was the last Englewood year and one of joy and sadness. Wedad married that year. She began dating about 1939, when she joined the Syriads, one of scores of Syrian-American (or Syrian-Lebanese-American or some combination thereof) clubs of young people in the United States. In 1932 these clubs began to coalesce into regional federations and provided greater opportunity for boys and girls to meet. Considering herself too Americanized, Wedad shunned bride hunters who came to our house and instead accepted the proposal of a young Melkite Catholic man she met at the Midwest Federation convention in 1941. A few weeks later he brought his mother from Milwaukee, Wisconsin, to meet her and my parents. All were in agreement and the wedding took place in October. She married into a Syrian family with even stronger ties to tradition than ours, and she was able to accommodate the family ways easily. Her in-laws were very pleased with her.

Wedad's wedding was the first supremely festive event in our family since Nick was born. My parents borrowed money to give her the large, lavish wedding she deserved not only as firstborn, but in genuine gratitude for her dedication to the family and her long years of work in the stores. Wedad enjoyed a special status in our family. She had, from her birth, grown up deep within the orbit of Rashayyan tradition, and she had a very close relationship with our mother. She was a perfect immigrant daughter—uncomplaining, unfailingly obedient, and good natured. She never talked back or got into mischief, and therefore she never got punished. She never strayed from the traditional norm of "good daughter." After mother died, she claimed her maternal mantle by right as firstborn, by conditioning, by inclination, and by desire.

When Wedad left with her husband, I thought the pain in my heart and my tears would never cease. She was more than my sister; she was my best friend. We shared the same room until she married. She was missed by all of her siblings, for whom she made many otherwise impossible things possible by interceding with our parents. She was our "American mother." It took me years to realize that more than her marriage separated us. A gulf had been developing between us for some time. She developed into an adult daughter of Arab immigrants smoothly. I struggled.

I don't know when I started exhibiting the defiance and rebellion I was often accused of by my mother. She might have said, "at birth." Daughters of immigrant parents are not supposed to demonstrate independent mindedness. I did. My faults, I am convinced, stemmed from my conflict with most Rashayyan traditions to which I was expected to conform. I was to be like my sister, to whom I was constantly and unfavorably compared. Try as I might, I could never transform myself into a "good daughter" on Wedad's level. I seemed to lack every basic qualification. I had too much energy that had to be dispelled and too much curiosity that needed to be satisfied. I wanted reasons for what I was asked to do or not do. That seemed reasonable to me but not to my mother or father. From my adolescent years, my eclectic interests failed the traditional good daughter test.

Two of my major habits were daydreaming and reading. The former won me accusations of laziness and shirking my responsibilities. The latter brought admonitions from Mother, who had her eye on my future. "No man will marry a girl if she is smarter than he is," she warned me. Maybe I should have taken her warning to heart. Music was my third passion. Music of any type could make me soar to the highest peaks of reverie. I owe most of these flights to two portable radios purchased by Wedad for the house and store so we could listen to baseball games, to which all five Naff children were addicted. From the age of thirteen, I fell in love with opera on the second floor of our house by listening to broadcasts from the Met every winter Saturday. The NBC Symphony Orchestra under the baton of Leopold Stokowski broadcast its concert from the Shrine Auditorium. Hollywood added spark to my life by featuring big-band swing and jazz programs on radio and in the movies. Fred taught me to love the blues and gospel music.

My contribution to the family furnishings was an unaesthetic upright piano for which I paid fifteen dollars. I insisted that I was going to learn to play it. I never had the opportunity. Still, it provided a great deal of joy. Friends played it as the rest of us jitterbugged on Mother's Oriental rugs in the living room. The "for company only" edict was relaxed. Mother calculated correctly that by allowing us to entertain ourselves at home, she would keep us from frequenting bars. Detroit had a very large assembly-line population, and numerous bars opened to accommodate its tastes. There must have been four or five in proximity to our store. Incidentally, Mother hated the piano.

I loved to dance. At about six, I began by imitating our neighbor's daughter in Spring Valley, who practiced her ballet lessons on their front lawn, and then I imitated what I saw in movies, including classical and modern ballet, until I was very limber. I won dance contests because of that. I have often quipped that I danced about three inches off my stature. I also loved sports of all kinds and participated in most, to the dismay of my mother. "Who would want to marry . . . ?" My love of travel was another point of contention for Mother. I longed to see places I had read and dreamed about. I started traveling during the war. Because of my responsibilities for the store, I could only take short trips on funds so meager that they often ran out (except for the six-cent streetcar fare from the train station) before I returned home. I went to five or six places, hence the nickname "Eleanor Roosevelt." The most special place was New York City. It was even more exciting to experience than it seemed in books and movies. Mother again: "You'll get the reputation of being unstable. Who would want an unstable wife?" None of these proclivities added up to the kind of good daughter pleasing to my Rashayyan parents. Their goal for me was to be a good wife and mother. Like my sister. Their primary concern was to prevent me from going through life with no man to protect me, care for me, and give me social standing. I was not a bad daughter, only a disappointment to my mother.

I desperately wanted to attend college. To my mother, who insisted that her sons go to college, extending that privilege to me was inconceivable. My life seemed to be on indefinite hold. Meanwhile, I went to work at Western Union, which proved to be a blessing and a milestone in my maturing process. I was among a group of young recruits, the first to be hired to take telegrams from the public over the telephone for a generation, judging by the weight, age, and attitude of those we were joining. In high school I was trained, like most girls my age, to be a stenographer. I was sentenced to shorthand and typing classes. I had no inclination or aptitude for a stenographic career. My favorite classes in high school were English literature and composition. My literary illusions were encouraged when the high school paper published my first and last poetic effort. When I attended night classes at the University of Detroit and Wayne State University after the war, my professors tried to convince me to write for slick magazines such as *Cosmopolitan* and *Redbook.* I had in mind *Atlantic Monthly* and *Harper's.*

Western Union saved me, at least temporarily, from stenography and put me in the company of a wonderful group of my peers. They were my passage into the real world. I learned about styles of clothes and makeup and even their trade names, about favorite movie stars, and about popular youthful fads, and much more. In short, I learned what the children of nonimmigrant Americans were like. In their company, I ceased to be just the shy daughter of an immigrant grocer. I developed a personality and some confidence. As it happened, I was working the Sunday Japan bombed Pearl Harbor, on December 7, 1941, but I didn't grasp the gravity of the situation, nor could I relate it to my life.

To the departure of my sister and brothers was added the departure of my boyfriend, whose Marine unit left for duty in the Pacific. As if that was not enough for me to cope with, I had to leave what I had come to consider the most meaningful part of my life. I had to leave Western Union to replace my sister in the store. After his sons left for the military, my father began to age visibly and to work increasingly fewer hours, just as the volume of work in the store tripled, if not quadrupled. In fact, our modest business shared in the nation's growing wartime prosperity. Because of the shortage of numerous consumer products given over to the war effort, the government issued rationing stamps, another problem to contend with. Even the idlers, who had previously made time in the store bearable, came in less frequently. The life that promised so much appeared to collapse in on itself and vanish into a dark hole.

What replaced it was a narrow prison whose formidable bars seemed permanent to me.

Not only did I have to manage the store but my parents as well. However, the burden was not mine alone. Tom, now twelve years old, shared the responsibilities with me. Even as he maintained his paper route and his schoolwork, he spent many hours in the store. For a couple of weeks I wallowed in tearful misery and self-pity, until I realized Tom was as miserable as I was. In fact, he was devastated, lost, and lonely. The two persons around whom his life was tightly bound had gone. This realization jarred me out of myself, and I tried to relieve his sorrow. We soon became close companions and friends. We shared work, play, and concerns about our parents. We kept bad news about the progress of the war secret from our parents, and we read the boys' letters to them with a smile. Our parents were difficult to handle. Nothing seemed to relieve their distress, not even attending church or receiving their regular Sunday visitors who also had sons in the war. They spent much of their free time, each in a bedroom, brooding and weeping. It didn't help to have glum Aunt Wadia and her family visit as frequently as they did. My parents carried the misery factor a bit too far when they decided not to celebrate holidays until the boys returned.

It was about this time, the late summer of 1943, that Lorice, Aunt Wadia's middle daughter, about Tom's age, chose to spend most of her nonschool days and weekends with us. Tom and I adopted her as a sister, helper, source of pleasure, and coconspirator. She was especially helpful in our attempts to placate our parents and defy their edicts. On the Christmas of that year, we broke the holiday rule. We decorated the house and tree, bought and wrapped gifts, invited friends, and with persistence we finally convinced Mother to prepare a festive meal. Aunt Wadia arrived with more food. Christmas carols from the radio filled the house. The boys sent gifts and telephoned. Aside from the fact that we had a merry Christmas, our parents gave up their weeping beds. Subsequently, holidays were relatively happy while the interim days were anxious.

Wartime prosperity gave home-front Americans the mobility denied them by the Depression. When we moved to Tennyson Avenue in 1942, that fact was apparently telegraphed on the Rashayya grapevine. The next three summers were spent receiving guests and giving up our beds for their lodging, justifying the label, "Naff hotel." Looking for someplace to spend a holiday, many Rashayyans chose our house, even though they may not have seen Dad since his early peddling days. Tom and I gave ourselves titles: Dad was the maitre d',

Mother was hostess and chef, Tom was the bell captain, and I was a one-person entertainment committee. I lost count of the number of times I drove guests to see the grand houses in Grosse Pointe, Henry Ford's River Rouge Plant, Belle Isle, and to enjoy ginger ale milkshakes at Vernor's on Woodward Avenue at the river. We scheduled work shifts to accommodate the guests.

When one of the boys came home on furlough, relatives arrived to share Mom and Dad's joy. In the summer of 1944, when Nick came home for three weeks, we entertained family and friends from twenty-seven states and Canada. The floors were littered with sleeping children. All beds, sofas, and chairs were occupied. Young adults slept in shifts on the porch or in the attic, if they slept at all. Mother, her sisters, and other women spent their days in the kitchen or basement preparing meals and gossiping. Thank God for Dad's garden and the store.

Peace arrived like a welcome summer shower after a long drought. But it forced families to face the question, "What happens now?" Many families accepted, even welcomed the often unexpected (but inevitable) changes in their lives. Others, like my parents, anticipated a return to the prewar character of our family. Dad hoped to turn the store over to his sons, but the sons had plans of their own. George was impatient to marry his fiancée and, with Mother's encouragement, attended Wayne State University. Nick, on the other hand, remained in California to pursue his journalism career. Dad was finally forced to acknowledge the impracticality of his dream.

While he was mulling over his dilemma, I did the unthinkable. I sold the store. I took the initiative, and Dad reluctantly signed the papers and committed himself to a necessary but forced retirement. Nothing would have convinced me to remain in the store. I was emotionally and physically exhausted. I had developed an aversion to serving the public—an aversion that persists to this day. Moreover, in addition to the anxieties of the war, the store, and my parents, I had imbibed large drafts of the war sentimentality that was churned out by government agencies and the film industry. Thus, with unwavering dedication, I wrote to "the boys"—twenty-five of them—into the small hours of the night.

The return of the boys from the war precipitated an epidemic of weddings. I too planned my wedding. In 1946 I became engaged to my marine, and we set the wedding date. After the engagement, I began to realize how incompatible we were. We had so little of common interest that conversation between us was strained. We could make no meaningful plans for our future. In fact, I became aware that I was smarter than he was, and I didn't want to marry someone who was less intelligent than I. Mother, after observing my unhappiness for weeks, insisted I discuss my problem with her. She then diplomatically extracted me from my dilemma. After talking with him, she concluded that I was indeed smarter. She also found his manners unappealing and thought that, as she told me, he lacked the capacity to really love. Since my sister's departure, Mother and I had become very close—more like sisters.

The culmination of my emotional and physical exhaustion became manifest in a deep, protracted depression. I dealt with it by concentrating on my night classes. I also went to work as a stenographer. Meanwhile, the campaign to move to California was under way. The thought of California sustained me. I began to feel confined in Detroit and was anxious to leave it. Mother, on the other hand, was anxious to remain. When she arrived in the city in 1930, she was shy and subdued. She had grown comfortable behind her invisible wall, in her mourning black. The depth of her sorrow was understandable, but its duration was unreasonable and incomprehensible. Holding on to her traditional ways held her, in turn, within a narrow frame of reference. If she gave Americanization a thought in Spring Valley, it was subliminal. Life in Detroit had broadened her outlook. First, the setting was urban; second, the relatively few Rashayyans—relatives and friends—were urban and much more Americanized than Mother. That she kept her grieving for Ibrahim within more or less reasonable bounds is telling. Then again, we, her children, were growing up and broadening our frames of reference and bringing our experiences home. Arabic was no longer the only language spoken in the house.

In time, Mother began to understand and speak a few words of English. She even made attempts at forming sentences. However, her inability to speak the language often embarrassed her, so she decided to attend the afternoon classes for immigrants held at Dwyer School in 1934. Since Tom began attending kindergarten that year, both were escorted to school by George. She was proud of her progress and she enjoyed showing it off, as when she wrote notes such as, "don steb on flor," if she had cleaned it. Once during the family's frequent after-dinner conversations, she decided to participate in English. She cleared her throat and began, "Well, under the circumcision . . ." Our laughter shattered her pride. She left the table and Dad followed to soothe her feelings.

With all of us in school, Mother was no longer confined to the house. She had learned to take the streetcar to visit Aunt Wadia or to meet her in the aggregation of department stores that was Detroit's downtown. The two sisters always shopped together, as if one could not purchase an item without the presence of the other. They could usually be found in Hudson's "basemy," where the bargains were.

Mother's diminished contact with Rashayyans and her greater freedom of mobility changed her view of the world and her attitude toward it. These were important changes in her life. But the most significant change came when she shed her black attire. Through the years, Dad and Wedad made futile efforts to persuade her. She only seemed to become more resistant. In time, she was elected president of the St. George's Orthodox Church Ladies Society, which held various functions at which she delivered speeches she had written. Dad used such occasions to point out that her black clothes detracted from her stature. After much arguing and cajoling, she agreed to let Wedad help select an appropriate changeover dress. They returned from downtown with a two-piece dark gray dress with navy blue polka dots on a white top, and a perky hat to go with it. Dad thought he had succeeded, but she soon reverted to her black. His next attempt came when, in the spring of 1942, George was getting ready to leave for naval training school. Mom, Dad, and I accompanied him down the steps of the Englewood house and onto the sidewalk. Between the sad farewells, Dad turned Mother around toward him and looking hard into her face, he said, "Your son is seventeen years old and he has never seen you except in black. Is this the way you want him to remember you when he is on the battlefield?" She turned away from him, but his argument was effective. He liberated her from the worst aspect of the tradition that had become as much a part of her being as her skin.

Besides a new wardrobe, other consequences were evident. She began to exhibit more self-confidence and presence, and her personality became more vibrant. Her ample vanity was concealed by unassuming expressions of gratitude for flattery, which were in keeping with her good breeding. Yet she relished attention. I remember my high school graduation. I had not expected any of my family to attend, least of all my mother. I did not want her to attend. All through my high school years I was ashamed of my immigrant appearance—hand-me-down clothes and long, coarse, black, wavy hair. And Mother, dressed in black from head to toe and unable to speak English, had the stamp of immigrant all over her.

In the hallway where the graduates were assembling, a classmate approached me. "Alixa, do you know that your mother is outside? How can you leave such a beautiful mother waiting?" Mother had come alone and managed to convey that she was looking for me. Pleasant surprise competed with fear of embarrassment, but when I saw her, I was delighted. I took note of her looks, which had elicited such high praise from my classmate. I had never done that before. She stood erect and stately. At thirty-seven and a mother of five, she was relatively slender and shapely. The sun highlighted the shining black braid of hair around her head, a style she wore for special occasions. This day I was proudly her special occasion.

After she converted to colorful attire, men as well as women began to compliment her. One of the wealthy parishioners even invited her to have dinner with him. There wasn't any doubt that she was flattered, as he followed her to where Dad was sitting so she could, she explained to the man, consult her husband. Dad smiled and said that he hoped they would enjoy the evening. The man never asked again. I didn't know that my mother could blush. She did, like a sixteen year old, and she did every time we teased her about the flirtation. I couldn't help but conclude that while she loved Dad, she had never been in love, never enjoyed the youthful passion of first love.

Freed from perpetual housework, Mother began to read newspapers and learned many new things. She seemed to pay particular attention to health and nutritional items. Her vegetable soup, which she served frequently because it was "healthy for us," always contained every kind of vegetable she could get her hands on. In addition, our most common dessert was a large platter heaped with crisp fresh vegetables. Her favorite source for such items was *The Echo of the East,* a local home-published all-purpose magazine that provided its readers with selected news and cultural items as well as a wide range of helpful hints in Arabic and English. Dalal Safadi was its publisher, and she visited with Mother many afternoons. I suspect it was from visits with housewives that she collected items for her newspaper. Once, Mother sent me to buy a particular brand of freckle cream. This was new, and I immediately recognized it as a Safadi tip.

As Mother made new friends, her interests and activities expanded. In 1946, she seemed happier than she had ever been and there was every indication that her happiness would continue indefinitely. That condition was briefly interrupted when George arrived with his fiancée, whom he married shortly thereafter. Del's "heavenly blue eyes" did not impress Mother. In fact, she was devastated. Her plan, dictated by tradition, was to marry her sons to Syrian girls. She had four or five choices in mind. She would not be consoled even when her friends visited our home, where George and his bride now lived, just to see this "Amercaniyyi" who had snagged the navy hero. However, Delphine, with her attractive looks and lively personality, won them over. Mother remained obdurate but coldly friendly. She soon realized, however, that if she persisted in her disapproval, she would lose her son, so she swallowed her pride.

Dad remained on the sidelines. His son's wife was another daughter, and Del, who hadn't known her father, delighted in his affection. Del and I grew as close as sisters and remain so to this day. Within a few weeks, Mother and Delphine became friendlier—even sharing confidences, the kind Mother could not share with me since I was unmarried. When Del presented my parents with a lovely, lively grandson, she could do no wrong. The wrongdoers were her in-laws, who maddeningly interfered with her mothering.

By 1947 the pressure on Nick to come home was intensifying. He countered by inviting his parents to visit him in Los Angeles. It was a brilliant tactic. George drove, and I went along as relief driver and parent-sitter. We left a couple of days after Christmas and the worst snow blizzard in memory. By the time we reached the Rocky Mountain states, some of the verdure and geological formations were reminiscent of Rashayya. The closer we got to Los Angeles, the more excited my parents became. In the environs of the city, we saw citrus, fig, and olive trees as well as vines filled with large clusters of grapes. For my midwestern parents and me, southern California was enticing. That was before freeways, traffic jams, and smog—when the air was fragrant with citrus blossoms, the sky was always blue, and the temperature felt just right. Nick won the campaign. After three delightful months, Mother agreed to move. Back in Detroit, however, she became reticent again, pulled between Dad's determination to move and the life she had made for herself in the last eighteen years. The toughest pull for her was the steel-like attachment to her sisters and Wedad in Milwaukee. When she made her decision, it was wrenching.

George left with his family in the summer of 1949, joined by Tom. That was the signal for Mom, Dad, and me to make our move. We were to take none of our well-used furniture to our new life. Mother packed only the household effects she wanted for Los Angeles and shipped them. The rest she gave to friends, neighbors, and charities. Meanwhile, I advertised the sale of the house, despite threats of damage and destruction from a neighbor, Mr. Phillips.

Mr. Phillips was among the large influx of blacks and whites who had migrated from the South, attracted by jobs and high wages in Detroit's war industry. Relations between the two races were as hostile as ever, as demonstrated by the race riots of 1943. Blacks, whose economic and social status were on the rise, were eager to move out of ghettos and lower-class neighborhoods into middle-class ones like ours, which they could now afford. Mr. Phillips, a former member of the Ku Klux Klan in Tennessee, resented the sale of homes on Tennyson and throughout Highland Park to blacks and was intent on frightening black homeowners into moving by vandalizing their houses and burning their garages. This had the additional advantage of discouraging potential buyers. He committed these crimes with impunity from the city government of Highland Park. Not surprisingly, no white buyers responded to my ads. I became impatient and sold.

Meanwhile, Mother was admitted to the hospital for what we were told was a minor corrective procedure to strengthen her uterus. The evening before she died, Mr. Phillips visited the hospital, and he served her with a subpoena for noncompliance of a restrictive Tennyson Avenue Association covenant. Later, we countersued and won a landmark court case.

On Saturday, April 15, Dad and I drove Mother to Mt. Carmel Hospital to be admitted. The evening before, the three of us had a long talk at her request. She wanted to give us instructions. It was, in fact, her oral will. "In case something should happen to me," she began, "I want you to . . ." Dad and I tried to redirect the conversation to a lighter subject and alleviate her fears. But she persisted. "Everyone in my parents' family died young, and I will too," she continued. "My mother died at fifty, Fares at thirty-six, and Ibrahim at thirty-three." I can no longer remember all of her concerns, with one exception. Dad was to promise that Tom would finish college. What I recall most clearly was her voice. It was sweet and plaintive, and she infected me with her premonition.

Her nonsurgical procedure went well, and we were told she would be released in a couple of days. Dad was with her all day. When I visited her after work, she looked wilted. Her face was almost as white as the pillow on which her head lay; her long black hair was laid loosely over one shoulder. She had refused to eat her meals, and her responses were merely weak sounds. She had not been heavily sedated, and she insisted she was not in pain. She remained unresponsive and uncommunicative for the next four days. Visitors could not arouse her, and they prodded me to do something about it. We could not understand what was happening. Dad was visibly distressed and so was Dr. Cassidy, our family doctor for fifteen years. He called me several times to insist that I make her walk to prevent a possible blood clot. He hoped I would succeed where the nurses and nuns had failed. Three times a day, at her mealtimes, I would sneak up the back stairs of the hospital to her room to feed her, defying my employer, the nurses, and the nuns who tried to stop me. I pleaded, cajoled, demanded, and even tried to force spoonfuls of food into her mouth without success. I tried to lift her head and she resisted me. I had no more success than the nurses who began to feed her intravenously. Dr. Cassidy discharged her in the hope that she might respond better among her family. We were to take her home on Sunday. On Saturday night I made my harshest attempts to get her out of bed. I even tried pulling her. "Leave me, leave me," she cried feebly. "You're going to kill me." These were the last words I heard her say. They are burned into my soul. I gave up, kissed her, and told her I would be outside her room until she slept but would be back to take her home in the morning. Finally, I went home to Aunt Wadia's. After I left, Wedad arrived, unannounced, from Milwaukee, on a dark premonition, to visit her. Mother gave her a cool reception, too.

Sunday morning, Aunt Wadia and Wedad rose early to prepare a welcome-home meal of Mother's favorite dishes. Nazha arrived early to help. The telephone rang and I picked it up. I was being summoned. Mother had taken a turn for the worse. Something in the nun's voice alarmed me, and I sped the fifteen miles to the hospital full of apprehension. Dad and the rest followed. I dashed up the back stairs and past a nun who pleaded with me to wait. I looked into Mother's room and the bed was gone. I didn't have to be told what had happened. I think I realized the worst when the nun didn't scold me for coming up the back stairs. I was caught before I hit the floor. My arms went dead and remained limp and useless for many days. I remember worrying about the impact of her death on my poor aged father. We were told that she had died at breakfast time of a blood clot in her lung. That was April 23, 1950.

She lay in her casket in the church hall as she had lain on the hospital pillow, the same black-and-white contrast, except for the death pallor on her face. Her death drew relatives and friends from several states and Canada. I remember little of it. Like the rest of the family, I was in shock. Aunt Wadia was utterly inconsolable.

Two things, however, are unforgettable. In the front seats of the church hall near the raised casket sat several women in black, many of them Mother's friends, wailing. They wailed for three days. They eulogized her youth, her beauty, her kindness, and her generosity. Others, even men, went up to the casket to add their eulogies. It was blood chilling. When I could no longer bear it, I yelled out to them to stop. "You're killing us!" I screamed. "You're killing my father!" Their response was a scolding, as if I had been irreverent. "Do you want your mother's funeral to be cold? She doesn't deserve a cold funeral." Rashayya is still with us, I lamented. Damn Rashayya! I hadn't given it much thought in a very long time. I was deluded into believing that we were free of its influence. We had all grown up, Mother had new a persona, and Rashayya no longer had a place in our lives. I was wrong.

The second thing I remember was something my father said. In the middle of a particularly torturous spasm of sobbing, I convinced him to step outside. As he rose, he turned to look back at Mother and said between his sobs, "I can't believe I had her for thirty-five years." That was the last time I saw her; I never returned to the hall. We buried her in Woodlawn Cemetery. I have not looked at another dead person since. Two weeks later, Dad and I left to join our family in Los Angeles, while Mother had gone her own way, to join her paternal family. I was furious with her.

In reflecting on the events of Mother's untimely death, my siblings and I concluded that she had willed herself to death, that she unwittingly committed suicide. I cannot, to this day, shake the feeling that, were it not for Rashayya and the traditions and superstitions surrounding the idea of death that engulfed her, my mother might have lived to enjoy the life promised her in California. One might assume that Rashayya was buried with her.

I suspect Dad hoped as much. In any case, he was going to make certain that a culture of mourning would not be repeated in our home. He forbade Wedad and me to wear black. "I know and you know that you loved your mother," he told us. "That's all that matters. You don't have to show the world by wearing black, and I don't want you, Alixa, to stay home. You're young. Go ahead and live your life. Where did seventeen years of mourning get your mother?"

One might rightfully assume that Rashayya was buried with my mother. But despite the individual and diverse lives we, her children, have followed, there remain palpable traces of its traditions and values in each of us.

Fandy

Kevin Rashid

They say a good Lebanese merchant
knows how to get in the way
knows how to get in the middle
  to negotiate between his goods and his customers
  to make them friends
Between his law degree and his liquor store
  Fandy's always dealing—even when he ain't got dealt.
I can hear him, crying over his latest hand of gin rummy
  at Rosenthal's bar on Linwood—
"I got nothing" he says, "not a single thing!"
Two turns and—BOOM—it's Ginney with the light brown
    hair
  and he's laughing like everyone won.

One place Fandy does not act so smooth—
  That is a robbery—a holdup.
I figure Fandy takes the point of a gun
  like an insult to his powers of negotiation.
The gun holds his tongue
  and he doesn't get scared—
  it makes him crazy
So that one day when his brother, Floyd,
  cracks the liquor-store door open after closing
And some kid with a repeater slips in before
  Fandy can scramble to lock the door behind him
And the kid panics and opens up
And, Jesus, there's bullets fly'n
  like wedding rice,
And Floyd, that pit bull of a guy,
  is huddled behind a cooler
  under five-gallon jars of pickles

and pork sausage
panting like he's in labor,
And there is Ballantines and Martel and Nu Grape
bleeding all over . . .
But Fandy, Holy Christ, the guy goes rabid.
He manages to scuttle to a shelf
of his cheapest red wine
Where he lines up and starts firing
bottles at the shooter.
All-of-a-sudden he's a real Koufax, this Fandy,
a real Satchel Paige.
But this is no baseball ballet.
Fandy takes a bullet that time
it tears between
the stomach and liver
and lodges under the hide
of his back.
No, this is no ballet,
But it must have been poetry—
that poor freaked-out kid
and that hellified Leb (And I can call 'em
Lebs, 'cause I've sat at their table,
enjoyed their company,
ate their food.)
It must have been poetry—
the two of them exchanging bullets
for bad red wine
The walls cascading Ripple, Mogan David Red, Bahama
Mama,
smashed glass and hot lead
And there is no lesson to all this,
But that in
and outside of holdups
Fandy deals—
He's gonna come to the table
and show you
what you thought he never had.

Behind the Bulletproof Glass

Iraqi Chaldean Store Ownership in Metropolitan Detroit

Gary C. David

ENTREPRENEURSHIP IS PERHAPS the most important factor in determining whether immigrant groups achieve economic success in industrialized societies, including the United States (Evans 1989). Of course, "success" is not a quality limited to immigrant entrepreneurs, but by taking advantage of cultural resources and structural opportunities to start their own businesses, immigrants often manage to enter the middle and upper classes with amazing speed. Comparisons made within ethnic groups suggest that immigrants who are self-employed enjoy a much higher standard of living than those who are not (Min 1988). Therefore, it is not surprising that entrepreneurship is widespread among immigrants. In fact, immigrant entrepreneurs have always been part of the American urban landscape.

Immigrant entrepreneurs come from many countries and cultures. However, they tend to start businesses of a fairly specific type. A study of sixteen metropolitan regions in the United States found that the most common entrepreneurial niches "were concentrated mainly in low-status traditional retail and service activities such as eating and drinking places, service to dwellings (cleaning and maintenance), grocery stores and other retail establishments, laundry and garment services, beauty shops and child-care homes" (Razin and Light 1998, 345). Troubled relations between immigrant entrepreneurs and the communities in which they work frequently bring media attention to immigrant-owned neighborhood convenience stores and grocery stores.

Because immigrant entrepreneurship is a prominent feature of American economic life, an entire body of scholarship is dedicated to it. The literature on entrepreneurs focuses mainly on the popular question of how and why immigrants become business owners.

Various theories have been applied to studying this process. Often, the principal concern is how the immigrant entrepreneur's presence affects, "positively" or "negatively," the life of the host community. The literature on immigrant entrepreneurs focuses primarily on Koreans, with Cubans and early Jewish immigrants covered to a lesser extent. Middle Eastern entrepreneurs receive little attention, with the exception of works by Sengstock (1974, 1982, 1983a, 1983b), McKay (1985, 1989), and Zenner (1982, 1987), and to a lesser extent El-Badry (1994) and Razin and Light (1998). Moreover, few studies of immigrant entrepreneurs have tried to understand how store ownership is viewed by the people who actually own stores and work in them. To bridge these gaps in the research, this essay will examine the complex world of Chaldean store ownership in Metropolitan Detroit. It will explore the reasons why Chaldeans (a community of Iraqi Catholics) are so attracted to entrepreneurship and will look at life behind the counter, the nature of the relationship between stores and the communities in which they operate, and the process by which individuals and families move out of store ownership.

Middle Eastern Immigrant Entrepreneurship in Metropolitan Detroit

The history of store ownership by Middle Easterners in Detroit can be divided into two phases. The first involved the early-twentieth-century Syrian and Lebanese immigrants, who opened stores near the neighborhoods where they settled. The people who lived in the East Congress and Mt. Elliot communities (named for the streets that ran through them) were the first Arabic-speaking immigrants to own stores in Detroit. According to Naff (1985, 271):

> In Detroit, Syrians began operating (grocery stores) before World War I. At the turn of the century, the Syrian colony, subdivided by sect and scattered in neighborhoods not far from the city center, was initially and primarily a peddling settlement. The Directory (of Syrian businesses) shows that in 1908–9, there were four Syrian dry goods stores, one of which sold groceries, one fruit, one fruit and confectionery shop, four grocers, a "repairing tailor," and two Oriental goods and rug dealers.

The second phase of store ownership began when the Syrian-Lebanese started leaving their mom-and-pop stores for other business opportunities and professional careers. This move created an opening for Chaldean immigrants to enter store ownership en masse (Sengstock 1983b). Chaldeans are Arabic- and Aramaic-speaking Catholics from Iraq. Most of Detroit's Chaldeans come originally from a single Iraqi village, Telkaif. Chaldeans have owned stores in Detroit since 1917 (Sengstock 1982), but only much later did they begin to dominate the market. With a major influx of Chaldeans during the 1970s and 1980s, investment in neighborhood stores and shops boomed. This process was fueled by two events. The first was the dwindling number of Arab and other store owners in Detroit. The second was the departure of chain stores from the city after the 1967 riots and the resulting vacancies. Chaldeans, many of whom already had experience operating businesses in Iraq, were more than willing to enter this very risky economic landscape.

The Chaldeans, like earlier immigrants, pursued a vision of economic opportunity that was thought, at least in immigrant fable, to be easily attained in America. The decision to own a store was driven by an intense desire for success. The concept of success entailed more than financial security, which could be had by working in auto factories. Success meant being one's own boss and controlling one's own business. In an interview conducted by Naff (1985, 279), an early Syrian immigrant said, "You gotta make your own business and prove you are a success, then you are a good American." For the Middle Eastern immigrant, success is a matter of prestige as well as wealth. To be able to say a business is yours is proof you have "arrived" in American society.

Entry into Store Ownership

People living in Metropolitan Detroit commonly ask, "Why do so many Chaldeans own stores?" This is a reasonable question, given the large number of grocery and convenience stores owned by Chaldeans and other Middle Eastern groups. While it is difficult to know exactly how many stores are owned by Chaldeans, informal estimates provided by trade associations suggest that 80–90 percent of Detroit's independently owned grocery and liquor stores are run by Chaldean immigrants and their descendants. Lebanese and Palestinian entrepreneurs, heavily represented in the gas station industry, also form a conspicuous part of Metropolitan Detroit's landscape.

When I discuss entrepreneurship with Arabs and Chaldeans, it is apparent that they entered the field for many of the same reasons other immigrants did: available opportunities, the economic climate, the ability to pool family and group resources, and other cultural factors that predisposed them to store ownership. One advantage held by Chaldeans was the presence of Syrian and Lebanese store owners (Sengstock 1983b), who provided a ready means of support and were willing to sell stores to them. All of these reasons are encapsulated in the following testimony of a Chaldean store owner:

I(NTERVIEWER): How did it come that Chaldeans represent such a large majority of the small store owners?

R(ESPONDENT): Well, it started in the early thirties of this century when a group of Arabs were party-store owners, grocery-store owners, and when I say a group of Arabs, I mean Americans from Arab descent who trace their nationalities to Syria and Lebanon and possibly Jordan and Yemen. Those people were already in the grocery-store business. And I think the reason that they followed that line of work in those years is because of the fact that many Middle Easterners are merchants. Being a merchant in the Middle East goes back thousands of years. That's one of the skills that we are known for, us Middle Eastern people are known for. So maybe that contributed to the fact that they come here and they follow the same line of work.

In my conversations with Chaldean store owners, three primary themes were used to explain the Chaldean presence in the liquor and grocery trades: cultural factors, family/friend networks, and religion. Of course, no one would own a store if it were not profitable. Relying solely on profit as an explanation, however, glosses over other factors that provide a deeper sense of the relationship between the Chaldean community and store ownership. "The store" has meanings that are not directly based on its potential as a moneymaking endeavor. These meanings are an expression of the cultural, communal, and religious values of the entrepreneurial group. In this sense, the desire to own a store goes beyond the logic of the marketplace and into the core areas of social life in the Middle East.

Cultural Factors

Many Detroit store owners believe entrepreneurial activity is a primary component of Middle Eastern history and culture. This theme is clear in the following conversation:

I: So why do you think so many Lebanese and people from the Middle East go into this kind of business. Is it in the blood?

R: You know, I think it is. You notice they're in jewelry stores. Name it. They're entrepreneurial. They are. Something about the Middle East. They're all bargainers [laughs]. You know what I mean? You go there and they're bargaining, you know. Like, guys will tell me they were in Egypt and everybody up and down the street bargains. You know, selling something, and I think it's just the nature of the beast. It's funny, but they're all entrepreneurial people, and I guess you go into what you know the best.

Comments such as "something about the Middle East," "they're all bargainers," "the nature of the beast," and "you go into what you know the best" show the degree to which being Arab or Chaldean is already linked to entrepreneurial activity in the minds of store owners. Entering the liquor and grocery trades in Detroit is seen as a simple extension of cultural practices common in the "old country." Some store owners project this model back to ancient times, citing Phoenician merchants and the silk trade as evidence of the entrepreneurial nature of Middle Eastern culture. It is nearly impossible to determine the causal relationship between economic patterns that have existed for "thousands of years" and entrepreneurial tendencies prevalent today, but the fact that people frequently cite this relationship to explain their own store ownership is important for any understanding of how Middle Eastern immigrants view their business community.

The United States is not the only country to witness Middle Easterners entering store ownership in large numbers. The emigration of Lebanese and Syrians that took place in the late nineteenth and early twentieth centuries resulted in the establishment of Arab entrepreneurial groups throughout the world. This historical process figures prominently in the following conversation with an Arab American brother and sister who work in a store their family has owned for fifty years:

B(ROTHER): Yeah, Arabs have always been merchants and traders. *Always.*

I: Oh yeah.

S(ISTER): From way, way before our grandparents even.

B: Syrian traders, you look back 1400, 1500, 1600. Traveled through the Caribbean in ships.

I: Mm hm.

B: You know. If you ever go throughout the Caribbean. Huge Arab population. Big time. You go to Jamaica. You go to Guadeloupe.

S: South America.

B: South America.

S: Trinidad.

B: Trinidad Tobago. Huge population

S: Mm hm.

Such lore is an important aspect of store ownership; it provides shared narratives of motivation and justification. Many store owners see themselves as part of a long line of entrepreneurial activity rooted in the Middle East. More than an economic enterprise, entrepreneurship is a cultural identity for many Arab and Chaldean Americans. Against this backdrop, it should come as no surprise that immigrants from the Middle East have successfully established themselves in Detroit's retail trade. The store owners are merely pursuing what they believe to be their cultural inclination.

Family/Community Networks

For immigrant entrepreneurs, family is perhaps the most crucial resource contributing to their success. As Aldrich and Waldinger (1990, 128) state, "Families, in addition to providing capital, are often the core work force for small businesses." Along with these kin-based advantages, Chaldean community networks provide mutual support for immigrant store owners (Sengstock 1982, 1983b; Zenner 1982). If a mercantile model of Middle Eastern culture provides the impetus to open a store, then kin and community networks increase the chances of success. A community leader who has watched this process since the early 1950s explains:

R: I don't think I know of anyone that's gone into business that hasn't borrowed large sums of money from their relatives and friends. That money is given to them without any form of collateral, no notes, no interest, and paid back. And the only prerequisite for that is, you know, you work hard. And when they do pay them back, then they're obligated to help others. You know, a lot of nationalities come to me and say, "How come the Chaldeans and Arab people are so successful?" . . . It's because of their work ethics. Because of their family relationships. Because they help each other. I can show you where it's not uncommon for ten, twelve people to loan someone five hundred, a thousand, five thousand dollars. You know, and when they have it they pay it back. And then they help someone else. But that progression started right from day one and it just continued and it's still going on.

The close-knit nature of Arab/Chaldean families has not been lost on outside observers. It has created tension and animosity between store owners and their customers, who notice that very few non-Chaldeans are working in the stores. However, this pattern is not rooted in racial discrimination, as most Americans would understand it, but rather in the structure of Chaldean families. In her description of the traditional Middle Eastern family, Aswad (1993, 13) notes that:

> Its patrilineal nature and extended kinship obligations are quite different from and often opposed to the bilateral, nucleated forms of traditional America, and even more so from the increasingly one-parent households found here. American emphasis on individualism opposes the emphasis upon shared obligations, hierarchies of power and living styles of Middle Easterners. . . . The family, however, also relieves the social and psychological stresses of migration, and is used for economic advancement. The types of kin corporations used by Iraqis in Detroit are seldom understood by the surrounding and often exploited Black population, which has historically been deprived of chances for capital accumulation.

As Aswad indicates, the family as conceptualized in Arab culture is an extensive structure that both contains and transcends American models of the nuclear family. The concept of an extended versus a nuclear family is foreign to most Arabs. The family in its Arab and Chaldean immigrant form is a comparatively large, cohesive group. As such, it is an important resource in starting a business. Repeatedly, store owners express the importance of family in maintaining the business and succeeding economically. A conversation with a Chaldean store owner about whether people in general understand how close Chaldean families are exemplifies this point:

R: My family's very close-tight. I'm still partners with my brothers. Equal partners. You know, if I don't work as many hours as he does, it doesn't mean that I get paid less. Or if he goes on vacation for a week and I cover for him for a whole week, that doesn't mean he's not going to get paid that week, you know. Equal partnership. We get paid the same. We live the same way. We don't live in the same homes or anything. We each have our own life, but we're equal partners. It's close family ties. And that's how we grew up. I'm not saying every Chaldean family's that way. But the majority are.

I: The majority are like that.

R: The majority are.

I: And does that contribute to the success of the family?

R: In business? Sure. Now I have a partner here who's my brother who works with me here. And my other brother works in another place and he's also a partner. If I'm not here and my brother's here, I know he's not ripping me off.

I: Mm hm.

R: He's watching the store very carefully like it's his. And it is his. And he watches it for me, and I watch it for him, and that's why the business is successful.

The ability to use family members as a resource is important in several ways. First, there is the obvious advantage of trust. Family members are not expected to "rip off" one another. Therefore, the store owner has some peace of mind when away from the store. Second, the family provides a labor pool ready to work, often for low or no wages. Hours at the store are long, and store workers often spend six and seven days a week in the store. Relatives are willing to work these hours because they believe it is for the good of the family and that all will benefit.

Family members who own businesses often help newly arriving kin who need start-up funds. Given the difficulties immigrants face in establishing credit or obtaining bank loans, this practice is especially important. It is thought normal for kin to call on family members as a resource, and it is mandatory to help them. To do otherwise would be insulting to the entire family. As one Chaldean interviewee explained, "they feel they are obligated, just like any family from any ethnic group feels obligated to help their own."

Religion

While seen as contributing to business success by creating social networks (Min 1996; Park 1997), religion has not been cited as a primary factor in the tendency for immigrants to become entrepreneurs. Among Chaldeans, however, it is a key component. Chaldeans are Roman Catholic. Islam, the dominant religion of Iraq, forbids the handling and consumption of alcoholic beverages. In Iraq, the consumption of alcohol is technically legal for Muslims, but Muslims do not sell alcohol. This role has been taken up by the Chaldeans (and other Christian sects), who are not constrained by any religious conventions. Thus the selling of alcohol became an ethnic specialization for Chaldeans because of their religion. This is perceived as an advantage by Chaldean store owners, as seen in the following interview:

I: Do you think that had anything to do with going into this business here? I mean over in Iraq you could handle alcohol.

R: And that's why we were in that business by the way. In Baghdad. Because Muslims couldn't have liquor licenses. They couldn't have a license.

I: Right.

R: And we were able to have a license. And that's why my dad went into that business. And my uncles. And all that. We were all in the liquor business

I: Mm hm.

R: So we've been in the beverage business, you know, from the old country.

I: And way back.

R: Yeah. Yeah. I mean, you know, back long time ago in the twenties and thirties. My grandfather was in that business.

Another store owner elaborates on the business advantage of his faith:

R: Because of our Christianity, our Christian faith, we were the only ones allowed to sell alcohol, liquor. The Muslims, who are the majority in Iraq, were not allowed to trade liquor because they were not supposed to consume it in the first place. So Christians were the only ones who were given license to operate liquor stores. I think that was a major factor why they went into the grocery-store business because part of the grocery-store items that they sell was liquor, so that kind of gave them an edge about how to operate a liquor store, and that kind of took off from there.

Nothing in their faith instructs Chaldeans to sell alcohol. The niche occupation of liquor distribution in Iraq was made available because of the absence of any Muslim competition. The liquor business in Iraq is still associated with Chaldeans. Religion and store ownership have thus become connected, and entrepreneurial activity is linked as a cultural trait to religious affiliation.

By seeing entrepreneurial activity as part of culture, family/community, and religion, the store can be understood as more than a business venture and much more than just a building. It becomes a defining element in the community's development and identity in the United States. According to Park (1997, 206), "Small business activities today are a symbol, perhaps the key symbol, of Korean American identity and success." The same could be said of Chaldeans in Detroit.

Behind the Counter

In my discussions with them, Chaldean store owners are eager to describe what life is like behind the counter. While people often recognize that store ownership can be a profitable enterprise, store owners believe that their frustrations are seldom understood. It is difficult to generalize about these frustrations. They are influenced by such factors as location of the store, type of merchandise sold, type of clientele, and length of time in the community. Despite these variables, there is a range of concerns commonly shared among store owners. First, stresses associated with store ownership begin with the investment of savings or the taking of large loans without any guarantee of success. To pay back these sums, store owners (especially convenience-store owners) put in extremely long hours at the store. Second, crime is a source of extreme anxiety for store owners. Third, store owners express dismay at the negative stereotypes they are forced to endure. The segments below, based on conversations with store owners, provide a more detailed account of these frustrations.

Long Work Hours

In order to succeed in any independently owned business, long work hours are a must. When I asked store owners about the biggest drawback of their work, they often complained first about hours spent in the store. The workday may grow shorter over time, but the hours spent at work when a store first opens can be daunting:

I: What's a normal day for you? A normal workday.

R: Now?

I: Yeah, now.

R: Eight hours.

I: Eight hours.

R: Eight to ten hours. Ten hours. And I work about fifty to sixty hours a week.

I: What about five years ago. Was it more?

R: It's been like that for the last seven years because we're established and things are going smooth. But when we first took it over, it was more like an eighty-hour week. A ninety-hour week.

I: And what was it like? What time would you get up in the morning?

R: Get up at eight-thirty in the morning. Take a shower and drive. You know, open up the store nine or nine-thirty and work till eleven, twelve o'clock at night. Day in and day out.

As store owners become established in their business, the hours they spend at the store can decrease. This trend is aided by the presence of family members and fellow Chaldean workers in the store. However, a decrease in the hours worked per day does not necessarily coincide with a decrease in the number of days worked. Five-day workweeks are extremely rare. Most owners work six and sometimes seven days a week.

When asked about their financial success, store owners are quick to mention the long hours they work and how their gains come at a cost. Since they are willing to put in grueling hours, they feel they deserve great rewards. A store owner who works in a suburban area justified the higher prices Chaldeans charge in their inner-city stores by emphasizing the toll taken by working long hours behind bulletproof glass:

R: They're doing a good job of serving the community. If they're charging a little more, by golly they have every right to because they're working their butts off. They're behind the bulletproof glass. They're there fourteen hours a day. And if they want to, they have every right to make more money than me because I'm more comfortable here, let's say.

I: Mm hm.

R: I mean, I'm taking it easy. It's more comfortable for me than being behind the bulletproof glass. So if they're 5 percent, 10 percent higher and risking his life, I think he's selling it too cheap.

Store owners also claim that long work hours can lead to problems between store workers and customers. One owner describes how people do not really understand the work involved in owning a store:

R: Nobody's going to appreciate it unless they see what you do. And we have kind of friction. We got kind of disappreciation. Because we work so many hours. And we suffer so much. And we are so much patient. And the people on the other side, they don't know what's going on in us. And because of the economic situation of the areas we work in, you drive a car [then] they think you have a good car they don't have. If you have a house, they say you have a house and they don't have it. I think everybody who works so many hours, so much effort, who suffer so much is entitled to drive a good car. To have a good house. To have a big family. Whatever it requires. Some people understand it, some people don't. It doesn't matter to me, the people who don't understand it. Black or white. I mean it happens either way.

Another casualty of long hours is the family. Business success is greatly assisted by the family, but, ironically, success often comes at the expense of the family. Because the family is often used as labor, the store limits the time family members can spend together outside the store. Maintaining what would be considered a "normal" family life is nearly impossible for store owners due to long hours. Life basically revolves around the store.

Effects of Store Work on Family

The store has a dual effect on the family. It provides the family with the economic means to become financially secure; the success of the store has been largely responsible for the rapid social mobility of Chaldeans. The ability to pool family resources and use family workers cuts costs and results in a higher profit margin. This also keeps the family together. Many children, especially in their teen years, go directly to work in the store after school. Chaldean children often take their place next to their parents in stores and can be seen running the cash register or lottery machine at a very early age. Chaldeans who grew up working in stores report that this is how they learned the value of work and that a solid work ethic will lead to success:

I: So what was it like working in a store as soon as you came over? Part time, I mean. Was it different?

R: It was different. Yeah, really my responsibility at sixteen was on a Sunday, and I just standed behind the counter, and it wasn't a hard job. You know, at my uncle's. But at my brother's store I had more responsibility. In 1980 I was doing some ordering. I was working weekends. As a matter of fact, I relieved them on Sundays, and I was in there with the employees as a manager at age seventeen years old.

I: Seventeen years old you were managing?

R: Mm hm.

I: Is that uncommon?

R: Not in our community. Maybe now it's uncommon, but back twenty years ago or fifteen we had more responsibility, and I think we had better heads on our shoulders than the kids do now. Well, they're not taught. They're brought up different. So.

I: How were you brought up back then that's different than now?

R: Respect. Responsibility. I mean, uh, work ethics were very important, and I think kids these days are not as responsible.

Even though the store can contribute to family unity, it presents many drawbacks as well. All family and community events must be scheduled with the store in mind. As Sengstock (1982, 36) observes, "Meetings and social affairs are set at times convenient to the retail grocer who closes his store at eight or nine o'clock." One example is the planning of Chaldean weddings. Some community members have told me that it is often more convenient for weddings and receptions to take place on Sundays. Fridays and Saturdays are the busiest days in a store. Saturdays are especially busy, since high-stakes state lotteries are drawn then. It is difficult for owners and their families to get away from the store. The beginning of the month is also especially problematic due to increased customer volume after welfare checks are issued. Because of these patterns, family and social life outside the store must be planned around events inside the store.

The biggest negative effect on the family seems to be the distance long work hours put between parents (mainly the father) and children. Writing about Korean store owners, Park (1997, 83) asserts, "Because many parents . . . are so preoccupied with business, they have limited time, energy, or emotional reserve to give to their children." Due to the fast pace of life in the store, work pressures can make time spent together in the store tense. However, in their conversations with me, people raised in stores do not express resentment over the large amounts of time they spent working for their parents. Both parents and children see the time as a necessary sacrifice for the future:

R: I have three boys. None of them is going to be in the store business, I promise you. I don't want them to be in the store business. They might be in other businesses, but not this type of business we are in because we are from a different generation. We are from a different culture. I got a master's degree, and I've been working eighty hours a week for the last twelve years, and this is a fact. I don't think my kids can work that way because they are Americanized. They are raised different. And I don't want them to be like this. I am suffering for them for their future.

In describing his work in the store as a sacrifice for his children, this speaker reveals another common belief: namely, that children raised outside the store cannot do the arduous work of their parents. Interestingly, the absence of the store from the lives of youth is seen as both good and bad. It is good because the children will not have to work as hard as their parents, and it is bad because the children do not know how to work as hard as their parents.

My discussions with children of store owners suggest that they also see the pros and cons of store ownership. They understand that their parents are making a sacrifice for them, and they appreciate this sacrifice. Still, they wish their parents had more time to spend with them.

I: So what was it like growing up in a store?

S: What was it like growing up?

I: Yeah.

B: Well, my dad worked during the day, and my mom worked at night.

S: Yeah. We never could have dinner together.

B: Never. It was very abnormal.

S: Yep.

B: No weekends off. No family type thing.

S: No.

Later in the same discussion, the brother and sister told of how their parents would close down their store for two weeks so the family could go to Florida together. During this time, responsibility for the store was turned over to a relative. Other store owners thought leaving the store for two weeks was a deviant act:

I: Just close the store down for two weeks?

S: No, my dad had Mom . . .

B: . . . find like a uncle or somebody.

S: Yep, to run it. But we'd get on an airplane and go. Nobody flew then.

B: Right.

S: And my dad would always be told by the Arabs that "how could you leave your business? How could you do that?" My dad said, "Look, it's there when I come back."

I: Mm hm.

S: And that's it. But my father and mother were a rarity when it came to having a business, a seven-day-a-week thing, and getting their whole family on a plane and going, and it was, like, when we got there . . .

B: Only one time a year we'd go to Florida.

S: Right.

That a two week family vacation would be seen as a "rarity" indicates the extent to which owners are chained to their stores. Family time together is an exception rather than the rule. Among store owners, not only is there little time for family vacations, there is little time to spend together outside the store. When children are not involved in the store, children and parents (especially fathers) are in danger of not seeing each other at all:

R: The problem with my father-in-law was my wife didn't see her father for fifteen years. They would open at nine and close at eleven.

I: He was working all the time.

R: Always. Always. She used to go to school. And then she got a job. Never knew her father.

The absence of the father can leave a gap in the family structure that is not easily filled by the mother. Extensive work hours are cited by many Chaldeans as the source of delinquent behavior among their youth. Still, store ownership enables financial gains and economic security of the family (Sengstock 1983b), and children of store owners often view their parents with admiration as opposed to resentment. The situation and its negative consequences are often viewed as an unavoidable aspect of the store business.

Crime and the Bulletproof Glass

The problem of overwork and its effect on the family is generally viewed as tolerable. Crime, on the other hand, is seen not as an inconvenience, or a challenge, but as a mortal threat. Crime is experienced in a variety of ways. Common occurrences such as shoplifting pose no real physical danger to the store owner. Violent crime, however, is a constant source of anxiety. When a violent crime is committed in one store, news of it rolls like a wave through the entire Chaldean community. In a close-knit community, where almost everyone knows everyone else, and most people are actually related, every violent crime hits hard.

The presence of bulletproof glass in some stores is a reminder to both store owner and customer of the hazards associated with the store environment. Bulletproof glass encases the employees behind the counter in a sheath one-inch thick, sometimes more, with only a small circular opening linking one side to the other. People talk through this opening and transactions occur either underneath the glass, via a sunken portion of the counter, or through turntables segmented by glass dividers. Although the width of the glass may be a scant inch, it can effectively cut off interaction between owners and clients. The glass is viewed by store owners as a virtual prison in which they are held captive for eight to twelve hours a day. Neighborhood residents tend to see the bulletproof glass as a symbol of the separation and distance the store owners wish to put between themselves and their customers.

In the transcript below, an African American woman expresses her suspicion of store owners, which is based on her observation that they spend so much time behind the bulletproof glass:

R: I don't know. They just always back there anyway. I mean, it's like the way their store is set up, it's Plexiglased in or bulletproofed in.

I: Right.

R: And the liquor and stuff. I mean, they have certain stuff that is behind the thing. And they're glassed in. And they just normally stay there. They don't normally walk the store. They're always behind there. And they're talking to each other. They're constantly talking. It may not be that they're looking over such-and-such shoulder. But they're just, you know, maybe two of them there, you know, at the store at the time. And they're always constantly talkin'.

Customers understand the need for Plexiglas, given the specter of crime. Nevertheless, that the store owners stay behind the glass can make customers uneasy. The amount of suspicion raised by the glass can be high. One interviewee stated that the round hole in the bulletproof glass, used to communicate with customers, is actually designed so that "store owners can point their guns out of there and shoot you!"

As uncomfortable as customers are with bulletproof glass, store owners are even more so. They never express pleasure at having to stay behind the glass barrier. For the store owner, the glass represents a cell, a sort of confinement.

R: I'd love not having glass. It'd be great. It's like I'm caged in right now. Like I'm in prison.

I: Mm hm.

R: It's sickening, but you gotta have it.

A second owner describes how he views the glass:

I: Tell me about the bulletproof glass. What's it like being behind glass all day?

R: Being in jail. Closed up. If you're working ten hours a day, it would seem like you're there for twenty. It's really, uh, you know, it's not comfortable at all. I don't like it. I never liked it, and that's why I didn't work there much, and when I had to go in there, it was like, "Oh no."

I: What would it be like waking up and knowing you'd be there for ten hours?

R: If you were there . . . and some people are there day and night, and . . . I feel sorry for them, for anybody who works behind the bulletproof glass from nine o'clock in the morning till twelve o'clock at night, day in and day out. And this is happenin' every day.

Clearly, the bulletproof glass takes on different meanings for store owners and patrons. In fact, the glass can be viewed as symptomatic of the general relationship between them. The glass illustrates how a single object can be perceived in radically divergent ways.

The Store/Community Relationship

The issue of intercultural interaction, and multiple interpretations, is especially relevant to Chaldean store owners in Detroit, who find themselves working in predominantly African American communities. Chaldean store ownership increased as Detroit's white population decreased after the 1967 riots. This white flight resulted in a majority African American population. In 1940, 9.1 percent of Detroit residents were black. By 1990 the black population accounted for 75.3 percent of the city's residents. Detroit is now one of the most heavily segregated cities in the United States (Farley and Frey 1994; Jargowsky 1996), and service and retail businesses in African American neighborhoods are typically owned by native whites (Aldrich 1973; Blauner 1969) or immigrants (Aldrich and Waldinger 1990; Min 1996; Sengstock 1983b). As a result, the stores have become a center of interracial and cross-cultural interaction.

Throughout urban America suspicion is often directed against immigrant entrepreneurs because of their alien culture and language and their often rapid financial gains. A report on the relationship between Arab American store owners and African Americans in Cleveland, for instance, found that "for those who have lived for decades in Cleveland's central city, the Arab American community is perceived as the latest wave of immigrants to establish businesses in the area, profit from the community, and then leave without doing anything to empower the residents in the area" (Shadroui and Bahhur 1995).

Rumor and speculation provide commonsense answers to questions about the rapid economic gains of immigrants, as well as immigrant behaviors deemed strange or suspect. Store owners, for their part, try to explain American behaviors that seem unusual to them. In most cases, these are not the same explanations that would be offered by those who enact these behaviors. The examination of individual and group narratives about Others can demonstrate how differing perceptions and expectations can lead to divergent "attributions," or interpretive accounts of Others' motivations and characteristics (Maines 1993; Mullen 1972; Portelli 1991; Turner 1993). The attributions made by Chaldean store owners and their African American customers are a good example of this phenomenon.

Ironically, customers and store owners are often concerned about similar issues. For example, conversations with Chaldean merchants and African Americans reveal that both groups cite disrespect, loitering, graffiti, crime, and parking lot cleanliness as important problems. However, while the two groups share these concerns, they attribute blame differently. In the instance of loitering, community residents tend to place responsibility on store owners for not running off the loiterers. Furthermore, some community members assert that Chaldean store owners encourage loitering, as shown by the comments of an African American woman:

R: . . . if I was an Arab, I would open up a liquor store wherever I think there was more poverty, more problems. People drink when they have problems. And you would think, [imitating an Arab accent] if I go to this area where they're having problems in their homes and drugs, and you just think that I would make money. I mean, I would think like that. That would be me, you know? And I mean that's probably what they do. You think a person . . . and, you know, like there's this one guy, he hang at the store, he has one leg, in a wheelchair. I mean, just sits in front of the store, zero below, beggin'. You would think, he needs his fix. You know what I'm sayin'? It's going to be plenty of people like him who's going to be, you know, sittin' out in a wheelchair in front of my store all day until he get enough money to come in my store and buy some liquor. Because he's a drunk or a whino.

Store owners, on the other hand, place the blame both on the police and the community. They express fear over confronting loiterers and say they need police assistance. When police stop responding to their repeated calls, store owners see themselves as powerless: "There were punks hanging out in front of the street selling crack. In front of the store. We couldn't get rid of them. We called the police. The police would chase them out of there. They'll come right back. And if they know you called the police, they will cause you more problems." Concerning the community's responsibility, store owners expect parents to control the behavior of their children:

I: Do you think that parents or the community starts to blame you for kids hanging around your store?

R: Yeah. I can't do nothing about that. It's their fault. You know the parents should take care of that.

These responses indicate how divergent perceptions can form over the same issue. The woman who described handicapped persons begging in front of stores feels that store owners encourage loitering in order to capitalize on the social ills present in some neighborhoods. Store owners constantly assert that they do not want loitering in front of their stores because it hurts their business. However, they are too fearful to take matters into their own hands. One store owner stated, "I ain't gonna get shot out there. All these teenagers carry guns now."

This pattern of mutual (mis)attribution is repeated across a variety of issues. Concerns about the financial success of the stores and lack of involvement in community development make up another example taken from a group discussion:

R1: I believe that stores on the whole should give back to the community. So without them being involved that makes them, quote-unquote, like my man said, he tried to say, "bloodsuckers." You know [chuckles]. They're bloodsuckers.

R2: Takin' it out and never puttin' it back in.

R1: You know? They takin' it out and never puttin' it back in. You know, they worse than what was characterized as Jews.

R3: What does that leave us?

R1: Yeah, what does that leave us?

R3: Where does that leave us when all the money, you know, is going from . . .

R1: . . . from here back over to wherever.

R3: . . . the store to out there. To wherever. And, you know, we don't have a base, an economic base inside the community. People just comin' in. Takin' money and takin' it back out, you know, not spendin' any money right in the immediate area.

Chaldean store owners feel fully justified in their economic success. When they are challenged about their financial gains, they recount the amount of time and money they have invested. The following segment shows how anti–store owner sentiment is perceived as stemming from envy over the Chaldeans' success.

R: Envy. Jealousy. You know, even in this area. A person walks in and says, "Oh God, another Chaldean store."

I: Is that what they say?

R: Yeah. And that was a couple years after we bought it. A couple months or whatever. The store was for sale before I bought it.

I: Anybody could have bought it.

R: Anybody could have bought it. Their money's as good as mine. So it's not like I came in and *stole* this business. I didn't force the owner with a gun to his head and tell him to sell to me. You know. "Another store." What does that tell me about this person that walks in. That he didn't like us, right?

I: Uh huh.

R: I mean, so he came in and I just charge him five dollars more than my normal price. He said, "What is this?" I said, "Well, it's another Chaldean store. It's a Chaldean price. You want to pay, pay. You don't want to pay, go elsewhere." It *frustrates* you. Why do they generalize Chaldeans? It's envy. You know? If they work as hard as we do, they would get there. You know, in this country you can get *anything* you want. You have more chances to become a millionaire than any other country. You know, one little idea.

I: Mm hm.

R: Will make you a billionaire. Not a millionaire. A billionaire. And there are people in this country that made it from nothing. You know, look at the guy who has Dominos. Look at Mike Illitch. Look at Ross Perot. Look at all these. You know, little ideas. So you work hard, you get something. You don't work, you sit back and relax, and you think these things will come to you working thirty-five, forty hours a week and have holidays off. Have Christmas off. Have Easter off. Have Fourth of July, Labor Day, Memorial Day. We work all these holidays.

Store owners often feel that they are singled out for not contributing to communities, while no one makes the same complaints against larger chain stores. When asked about not putting profits back into the community, one store owner said the following:

R: And the sad thing is that they, you know, say that "here that guy is, a foreigner. He's here. He's coming into our neighborhood. Making the money. And leaving with our money." How come they never say the same thing about every other chain. How come they don't say that about Rite Aid? How come they don't say that about Farmer Jack? How come they don't say that about Kroger? How come they don't say that about Blockbuster? Blockbuster's not even in Michigan. They're in Texas. They not only take it out of the city. They take it out of the state. Farmer Jack is the same thing. They don't take it out of the city. They take it out of the state. I think it goes to Boston for crying out loud. Why don't they say that?

This same person told a story about how his attempts to be part of the community were rebuffed by a neighborhood resident:

R: There was a block club. They said, "Well, we want you to donate money because we want our sidewalks shoveled every year." I said, "Yeah? How much is it to join the block club?" She said, "Oh, joining the block club is just twenty dollars a year." I said, "OK, I want to join the block club twenty dollars a year, plus I'll give you a donation, but I want my driveway shoveled. I want my walk shoveled just like everybody else. All the guy has to do is just continue it on down to the end of the block." And she says, "Why do you have to have something in return? Why can't you just give us the money?" I said, "Well, either you want me to be part of your community or you don't want me to be part of your community. What is it?" A large percentage don't want me to be part of their community. They just want to see what they can take and go on from there.

In this instance, both the community resident and the store owner formulate the same view: the other person is entirely opportunistic.

When store and community concerns are examined, it is done under the assumption that one group's view will be more correct than the other's. Seldom are these concerns approached from the perspective that they might both be correct. Focusing on the correctness of the claims of one group or the other ignores the fact that the same situation can be perceived differently by different people. The practice of extending credit to customers is an example. It is not uncommon for store owners to extend credit to customers. Community members may claim that this is because the store owners are trying to make money off of people who have none, especially when credit is given for the purchase of alcohol or cigarettes. Store owners claim their motivation lies in their concern for their customers. Extending credit is often cited as a type of "community service" by store owners and evidence of their caring. The question then becomes, how can store owners and customers see the same events so differently?

The impact of perception on how groups make attributions about each other is clearly an important consideration. Intergroup conflicts influence the types of judgments people make about each other. Pettigrew (1979) found that when someone from a group committed an act regarded as negative, it was deemed part of the group's disposition by people who did not belong to that group. Conversely, positive acts were explained away as exceptions or the outcome of some set of special circumstances. These results demonstrate how intergroup expectations, when fueled by prejudice and stereotype, form perceptions that confirm previously held negative opinions, or even form new ones.

It would be erroneous to assume, however, that store/community relationships are generally problematic. In my research on this topic I have not found this to be the case. Despite linguistic, class, and cultural barriers, my fieldwork shows an overall congenial relationship. Even though, as Sengstock (1982, 58) states, contacts between store workers and customers tend to be "only a few minutes each day or week," amazingly close relationships form out of these short contacts. It is not uncommon for a store owner to know detailed information about customers' lives, including where they work, how many kids they have (and their names), any recent illness or other problems, and what interests they have. While interactions between store owners and customers can be brief, this does not make them any less meaningful.

Of course, this is not to say that legitimate complaints do not exist on both sides. Some difficulties cannot be explained away as misperceptions. It is hardly a matter of perception when a store is stocked with goods well beyond their expiration date. It is hard to misunderstand the intentions of a store owner who breaks the law by illegally trading in food stamps to make a profit. It is equally hard to misconstrue the fact that a store owner is not respected when his customers berate him with ethnic slurs. However, these conflicts appear to be rare occurrences in the relations between Chaldean stores and local communities in Metropolitan Detroit.

Leaving the Store

The reasons Chaldeans become entrepreneurs, which I discussed earlier, centered on their position as immigrants in America and the influence of their homeland culture. The question then arises as to whether their offspring, born or raised in Detroit, will follow in their footsteps. If they have grown up in the United States, these younger Chaldeans do not experience the same language and cultural barriers their parents faced. Furthermore, as numerous immigrant parents assure me, their children will not be able to suffer through the hardships associated with store ownership. Americanized Chaldeans are beginning to disregard store ownership as a potential career. As they spend more time in Detroit, Chaldeans become part of the economic mainstream, and they begin to work in every kind of profession. Earlier Arab immigrants have already gone through this process. The Chaldean community is likewise beginning to enter this stage.

Sengstock (1983b, 12), in her research on the Chaldean community, reports that "Chaldean respondents who have had an interest in other fields, such as engineering, medicine, law, mechanics, have found that their relatives and friends often pressure them into opening a grocery store, or assisting a relative who owns a store." On this point, my newer findings run contrary to those of Sengstock. While Chaldean store owners do bring their children to the store as a lesson in developing a work ethic, they have told me that they do not actively encourage their children to enter the family business. One reason for this is that store owners see the growth potential of the business declining. The increasing presence of chain stores, along with the changing buying habits of American consumers, threatens to reduce profits, especially for grocery stores. Convenience stores are faced with a saturated market and increased competition (Sengstock 1982), a problem plaguing all immigrant entrepreneurs involved in that business (Min 1996; Yoon 1991). This is compounded by a declining customer base due to the shrinking population of Detroit. The following store owner's comment addresses all these factors:

R: There are a lot of stores and there's less people and there is a lot of competition. The chain stores are coming back. Arbor [drug store] just opened down here. The gas stations are opening all over. They are competing with the stores. They are selling almost everything we are selling in the store. And there is less population. If you come to my direct area in here, when I moved in 1985, I lost 20 to 25 percent of the houses.

I: Oh really?

R: But none of the stores around you are closed. The same stores. As a matter of fact two gas stations opened. An Arbor [drug store] opened down here. So competition is so severe I mean you have to be innovative. You have to be smart. You have to be a survivor to live this way.

Many Chaldeans who have been in the business a long time question whether their children will be able to tackle the challenges of grocery- and convenience-store ownership. They do not question the abilities of their children, but rather their capacity to endure the hardships associated with the business. An Arab American store owner makes the following observation about the American-born generations:

R: See, [Chaldeans] still have what we lost. Know what I mean? But they're going to lose it, too. Believe me, they're going to lose it as their kids become more Americanized and affluent. Know what I mean?

I: Mm hm.

R: College. They're all going to college.

I: Right.

R: Who's not going to college today?

I: Right.

R: You lose it. See what I'm saying?

Fifteen years ago, Sengstock (1983b, 24) observed that Chaldeans did not place a high premium on higher education, "Chaldeans . . . have attained success through entrepreneurial activities, and have not needed much education to attain their success." However, my findings suggest this pattern is changing. The growing entry of Chaldean youth into college shows the emphasis now being placed on professional occupations as opposed to store ownership. Three occupational fields tend to be predominant: medicine (including pharmacy), law, and engineering. In my conversations with Chaldeans, the phrase "doctor, lawyer, or engineer" is recited as a sort of holy trinity or triumvirate.

I: Do you think the store is going to continue to play the important role in the Chaldean community as it has? Because the Chaldean community is very close and the stores [have played a part in that].

R: Over the next probably thirty, forty years I don't see much change. Maybe I'm going too far. For the next twenty years things will remain the same. But after that, who knows. 'Cause my kids probably would not choose to be in this business, and I don't want them to be in this business. I want them to be in the professional life. You know, doctor, attorney, engineer, whatever it takes.

Beyond becoming a doctor, lawyer, or engineer, other fields are being opened for Chaldean youth. A promotional flyer for the 1997 career day, sponsored by three Chaldean organizations, proclaimed "Come Speak to Chaldean American Professionals and Business Entrepreneurs from All Walks of Life." At this event, no fewer than twenty-five different professions were represented, including journalists, computer programmers, law enforcement, stockbrokers, and interior designers.

As Chaldeans move away from store ownership, they are simultaneously moving away from a career that is linked to their ethnic identity. Working in and owning a store is an integral aspect of being Chaldean in the United States (Sengstock 1982). The departure from grocery and convenience stores may have the unintended result of weakening the Chaldean community as an ethnic group.

In the face of what appears to be an inevitable process, attempts to stay in the store business may prove futile, and attempts to stem the flow away from this lifestyle are not necessarily positive. An interesting perspective on this problem is provided by a brother and sister, descendants of a much earlier wave of Arab immigrants, who continue to own and work in their parents' store, long after others of their generation left the business:

B: People who owned stores? Working fools.

S: Yep. And see, because him and I stayed in that business, I made damned sure—and this is the God's truth, and I had daughters—my kids could not come home and tell me, "I think I'm in love." I didn't want them to get married till they were *done* with college

I: Hmm.

S: And, I mean, that's 'cause I never wanted this for them.

B: Never wanted our kids in the liquor business.

S: Granted, it supported us a life, you know. A good life.

B: Remember what I was telling ya? People were all doctors and lawyers.

S: Yeah, they are. Which is smart, because you see you've got to push your kids to go. Because you want them to have a good life. Not that we lacked anything. We didn't. It gave us work ethics. We're certainly not lazy. But we're tired.

B: We're a generation behind from the rest of the people who owned stores.

S: Yeah.

B: Yeah, they're all out, and their kids . . . they sent their kids off. Doctor, lawyer, I mean you're talking older people. I'm talking people sixty years old, they'll tell ya, "Well, my parents owned a store."

S: Right.

The speakers feel out-of-step with the rest of their generation because they stayed in the store business. The practice of store ownership that dominated the Syrian and Lebanese community at the beginning of the century has decreased dramatically; to be a member of this older community and still own a store is the exception rather than the rule.

In comments made to me by Chaldeans, a similar trend is apparent. While Chaldean immigrants still enter the store business, second and third generation Chaldeans are increasingly opting out of the store. The effect this will have on the community is unclear, since the store has played a major role in the Chaldean community's cohesion (Sengstock 1974, 1982, 1983b). Store owners, along with Chaldeans in other professions, continue to be cautiously optimistic about maintaining their strong ethnic identity and community ties.

References

Aldrich, Howard E. 1973. Employment Opportunities for Blacks in the Black Ghetto: The Role of White-Owned Businesses. *American Journal of Sociology* 78:1403–25.

Aldrich, Howard E., and Roger Waldinger. 1990. Ethnicity and Entrepreneurship. *Annual Review of Sociology* 16:111–35.

Aswad, Barbara. 1993. Arab Americans: Those Who Followed Columbus. *Middle Eastern Studies Association Bulletin* 27:5–22.

Blauner, Robert. 1969. Internal Colonialism and Ghetto Revolt. *Social Problems* 16:393–408.

El-Badry, Samia. 1994. The Arab-American Market. *American Demographics*, January, 22–31.

Evans, M. D. R. 1989. Immigrant Entrepreneurship: Effects of Ethnic Market Size and Isolated Labor Pool. *American Sociological Review* 54:950–62.

Farley, Reynolds, and William H. Frey. 1994. Changes in the Segregation of Whites from Blacks during the 1980s: Small Steps toward a More Integrated Society. *American Sociological Review* 59:23–45.

Jargowsky, Paul A. 1996. Take the Money and Run: Economic Segregation in U.S. Metropolitan Areas. *American Sociological Review* 61:984–98.

Maines, David. 1993. Narrative's Moment and Sociology's Phenomena: Toward a Narrative Sociology. *Sociological Quarterly* 34:17–38.

Mckay, James. 1985. Religious Diversity and Ethnic Cohesion: A Three Generational Analysis of Syrian-Lebanese Christians in Sydney. *International Migration Review* 19:318–34.

———. 1989. *Phoenician Farewell: Three Generations of Lebanese Christians in Australia.* Melbourne, Australia: Ashwood House Academic.

Min, Pyong Gap. 1988. *Ethnic Business Enterprise: Korean Small Business in Atlanta.* New York: Center for Migration Studies.

———. 1996. *Caught in the Middle: Korean Communities in New York and Los Angeles.* Berkeley: University of California Press.

Mullen, Patrick B. 1972. Modern Legend and Rumor Theory. *Journal of Folklore Institute* 9:95–109.

Naff, Alixa. 1985. *Becoming American: The Early Arab Immigrant Experience.* Carbondale: Southern Illinois University Press.

Park, Kyeyong. 1997. *The Korean American Dream: Immigrants and Small Business in New York City.* Ithaca, N.Y.: Cornell University Press.

Pettigrew, Thomas. 1979. The Ultimate Attribution Error: Extending Allport's Cognitive Analysis of Prejudice. *Personality and Social Psychology Bulletin* 5:461–76.

Portelli, A. 1991. *The Death of Luigi Trastulli and Other Studies: Form and Meaning in Oral History.* Albany: State University of New York Press.

Razin, Eran, and Ivan Light. 1998. Ethnic Entrepreneurs in America's Largest Metropolitan Areas. *Urban Affairs Review* 33:332–60.

Sengstock, Mary. 1974. Iraqi Christians in Detroit: An Analysis of an Ethnic Occupation. In *Arabic Speaking Communities in American Cities*, edited by Barbara Aswad, 21–38. New York: Center for Migration Studies.

———. 1982. *The Chaldean Americans: Changing Conceptions of Ethnic Identity.* New York: Center for Migration Studies.

———. 1983a. Detroit's Iraqi-Chaldeans: A Conflicting Conception of Identity. In *Arabs in the New World: Studies on Arab- American Communities,* edited by Sameer Abraham and Nabeel Abraham, 136–46. Detroit: Center for Urban Studies, Wayne State University.

———. 1983b. Functions and Dysfunctions of Ethnic Self-Employment: Detroit Chaldeans as a Case Study. Paper presented at the annual meeting of the American Sociological Association. Detroit, Michigan. September.

Shadroui, George, and Riad Bahhur. 1995. *Arab American Merchants and the Crisis of the Inner City: Cleveland—A Case Study.* Washington, D.C.: Arab American Institute.

Turner, Patricia. 1993. *I Heard It through the Grapevine: Rumor in African-American Culture.* Berkeley: University of California Press.

Yoon, In-Jin. 1991. The Changing Significance of Ethnic and Class Resources in Immigrant Businesses: The Case of Korean Immigrant Businesses in Chicago. *International Migration Review* 25:303–32.

Zenner, Walter P. 1982. Arabic-Speaking Immigrants in North America as Middleman Minorities. *Ethnic and Racial Studies* 5:457–77.

———. 1987. Middleman Minorities in the Syrian Mosaic: Trade, Conflict, and Image Management. *Sociological Perspectives* 30:400–421.

There I Am Again

Lawrence Joseph

I see it again, at dusk, half darkness in its brown light,
large tenements with pillars on Hendrie beside it,

the gas station and garage on John R beside it,
sounds of acappella from a window somewhere, pure, nearby it

pouring through the smell of fried pork to welcome
whoever enters it to do business.

Today, again, in the second year of the fifth recession
my father holds pickled feets, stomachs and hearts,

I lift crates of okra and cabbages,
let down crates of buttermilk and beer,

bring live carp to the scale and come, at last, to respect
the intelligence of roaches in barrels of bottles,

I sell the blood on the wooden floor after the robbery,
salt pork and mustard greens and Silver Satin wine,

but only if you pay, down, on the counter
money you swear you'll never hand over, only if,

for collateral, you don't forget you too may have to kill.
Today, again, in the third year of unlimited prosperity,

the Sunday night the city burns
I hear sirens, I hear broken glass, I believe

Reprinted from *Curriculum Vitae*, by Lawrence Joseph (Pittsburgh: University of Pittsburgh Press, 1988), 56–57.

the shadow of my father's hand that touches my hair,
my cousin loading a carbine, my uncle losing his mind

today in a place the length of a pig's snout
in a time the depth of a cow's brain

in Joseph's Market on the corner of John R and Hendrie
there I am again: always, everywhere

apron on, alone behind the cash register, the grocer's son
angry, ashamed, and proud as the poor with whom he deals.

On the Road with Bob

Peddling in the Early Sixties

Nabeel Abraham

THE BLUE AND white 1959 Ford Galaxy had been cruising on the Ohio Turnpike for less than thirty minutes when Bob unexpectedly pulled off at a service area. As the car slowed to a stop, Bob clutched his abdomen, moaning in Arabic "Ahh . . . ach, it's burning."

"What's burning?" I asked, restraining my alarm.

"It's my stomach. The heartburn is killing me, *wa'lek*," he murmured through a pained grimace.

Bob was in the habit of calling his sons by the impolite term "*wa'lek*" ("boy" in Arabic). It was his way of maintaining a respectful distance from me and my four brothers. In a subconscious twist, we acknowledged the emotional gap separating us from our father by referring to him as "Bob" (short for *baba*, or "daddy," in Arabic).

The rush of traffic seemed distant against the sound of Bob's breathing. Traces of white chalk from the anti-acid tablets he was chewing accented the corners of his mouth. How would we get back if he became too ill to drive? I thought about the Oriental rugs and the boxes of Irish and Portuguese linens packed snugly into the car. In place of the back seat, an old blanket disguised several expensive rugs. If we had to leave the car behind, thieves would surely break in and take the goods.

These worries emboldened me to make a barely audible offer: "I can try to drive if you can't manage." Before I could reassure him that a thirteen-year-old boy could handle the wheel of a car, he cut me off with "*tik*" followed by a slight nod of the head that Palestinians make when they want to say "no" with a minimum of effort.

"You're just a kid," he said, still gripping his abdomen. A long silence fell over the car. Then, without warning, Bob turned the ignition key, put the car into drive, and wheeled back onto the turnpike.

This was my first trip out of Detroit since Bob had moved the family from Erie, Pennsylvania, in 1955, some eight years earlier. This was also my first and last peddling trip. Going on *al-Bay'aa* was a way of life for people from Bob's native Beit Hanina, a small Arab village lying just north of Jerusalem on the road to Ramallah. Peddling often took precedence over school for the adolescents and young adults from Beit Hanina. That's why Mother declared peddling unsuitable for her sons. It wasn't so much that she objected to our working and earning spending money. On the contrary, she encouraged us to deliver newspapers, mow lawns, shovel snow off sidewalks, and even sell Christmas cards and boxed candies on consignment door-to-door. What Mother feared about peddling was the social milieu—the potential for gambling, sex, and other delinquencies. Going on *al-Bay'aa* with the boys from Beit Hanina was, in Mother's opinion, to fall in with the wrong crowd.

My brothers and I never aspired to be peddlers. We were too pro-education; and, anyway, going door-to-door peddling tapestries, towels, watches, and trinkets held absolutely no appeal for us. Peddling was what our cousins from Beit Hanina did, and we weren't interested in emulating them. The episodic sales of Christmas cards and boxed candies, which we sold in the neighborhood one year, were viewed as a quick way to earn money with which to buy Christmas presents and clothes of our own choosing. Curiously, when Bob learned of our neighborhood peddling forays, he didn't appear pleased, and he told Mother his children weren't in need of the money. But since he was away so much of the time and had relegated our upbringing to Mother, his opinion in this matter, as in many others, held little sway.

I had fought to get on this peddling trip with Bob not from any desire to learn the ropes but out of an unremitting curiosity about my father's work, the places he visited, and the people he met. Besides, school was out, and I wasn't interested in spending another frustrating summer confined to the streets of southwest Detroit. After a year or so of idle promises, Bob, in a weak moment, agreed to let me come along for the ride. Then in a moment of anger at Mother, and then at me, he tried to wriggle out of it. Ironically, Mother lobbied on my behalf. She had her own reasons for wanting me on the trip and the ever-suspicious Bob knew it. My presence would be a constraint on him and his meanderings to the gambling tables in the back-alley coffeehouses he frequented. As I would discover, it was a tough assignment.

The belief in our house was that Bob's relatives thought Mother a bit too uppity and unconventional. She had cut them off from Bob's largess, which they had grown accustomed to ever since his brother died in a factory-fire several decades earlier. She saw her role as protector of her family and didn't care much about what they thought. She was aided by her class attitude—she was from an upper-class Jerusalemite family; they were country people. Adhering to deeply rooted Palestinian social cleavages, she wasn't reluctant to let them know that city people were better than country people.

My family was unconventional in other ways as well. Bob was twenty-five years older than Mother. Yet he became angry when strangers mistook him for our grandfather and Mother for his daughter. He was fifty-four years old when I was born and sixty-one when my fourth and youngest brother arrived. Bob immigrated before World War I, which placed him among the early Arabic-speaking immigrants to the United States and certainly among the pioneers from Beit Hanina.

Peddling was in his blood. When a fellow peddler from Beit Hanina, Abdel Hamid Shouman, invited him to return to Palestine and be his partner in a banking venture, Father responded by asking, "What do you know of banking?" Shouman went on to found the Arab Bank Ltd., one of the largest banks in the Middle East. Bob loved to boast that he had passed through every state of the Union except Alaska and Hawaii. He was also the consummate salesman. I learned late in life to wonder about some of his boasts, yet he taught me to be leery of free offers and other sales gimmicks.

Bob had long since made the transition from peddling to store ownership. He liked to say that he had to pay protection money to the mob during Prohibition to protect his Madison Avenue store in Manhattan. He also owned stores in Charlotte, North Carolina, where I was born; Erie, Pennsylvania, where three of my brothers were born; and Detroit, Michigan, where the youngest was born. He owned other stores in and around New York City, Yonkers, and White Plains. When a store went bust or he decided to move on, peddling was his fall-back position. After he closed his Detroit store, thanks in part to the unpaid bills his relatives had piled up, he officially "retired" and returned to peddling in Pennsylvania, New York, and North Carolina. He loved to say that he never worried about money; even during the Great Depression he made money. When money ran out, he would take to the road. Although he was socially conservative, when it came to money he was an inveterate gambler; money flowed through his fingers like water, with little thought to tomorrow.

Fig. 8. Younis Abraham, "Bob," in a rare moment without his trademark gray fedora. Courtesy of Nabeel Abraham.

Tall, slender, and dressed in expensive gray business suits with a matching gray fedora, Bob cut the figure of a "high-class" peddler. He remained a New Yorker to the end in the way he comported himself, in his preference for suits tailored in New York, in his slight New York accent. He took pride in selling new and antique Oriental rugs and fine linens to America's wealthy classes. His Palestinian countrymen, in contrast, never shook off their Old Country ways and habits. They sold sundry "dry goods," inexpensive scarfs, linens, watches, and throw rugs decorated with garish prints, which they peddled door-to-door in working-class neighborhoods. We lived in such a neighborhood, and one day a Palestinian peddler from Ramallah unwittingly knocked on our door, throw rug slung over his arm. Insistent on showing me his wares, he moved on only after I explained it would be futile to peddle to a peddler's family. As recently as the early 1990s, some boys from Beit Hanina could be found peddling cue sticks in Detroit's bars and pool halls.

Bob drove straight through Ohio, reaching Union City, Pennsylvania, at nightfall, where we took a room in an old hotel. The next day, we traveled in an arc through Titusville, Oil City, and Meadville before circling back to Union City and on to our final destination, Erie. We drove with the aid of a tattered map. In the span of a day, Bob made a handful of stops to call on established customers. To my disappointment, I was ordered to stay in the car, missing the chance to see the inside of the old stately houses and meet their owners. Occasionally, a customer would invite him in and he would disappear for a half-hour or so. He would reappear suddenly and, without saying a word, drive off to the house of another customer. On one stop, the elderly matron who answered the door noticed me sitting alone in the car and instructed Bob to fetch me so she could offer me a cold drink. On the way in, Bob instructed me to keep my mouth shut. Happy to be invited inside, I eagerly nodded in agreement. Once in the house, I listened as the matron talked about how much she loved the Oriental rug Bob sold her on a previous trip. He, in turn, discoursed on the Persian rug's design and workmanship, while lamenting the migration of the rug weavers to Iran's oil industry. She wondered if he could find her a similar carpet for another room, which they went off to see, leaving me behind to sip my drink and admire the spacious living room and its antique furnishings. Bob assured her he would look for a rug the size and type she wanted the next time he was in New York City, where the wholesalers were located.

I had come on the trip hoping to be of some assistance to Bob. But it was becoming painfully obvious to me that Bob preferred to work alone. He took great care to cultivate his relationship to his valued customers and wasn't going to let a parvenu like me muck things up for him. There is an old family chestnut that indicates the depth of Bob's desire to please his customers. The story involves an incident during my brother Nazeeh's trip with Bob the following year. Ever since Nazeeh was a toddler, Bob loved to kid him about his lips, which he referred to using the colloquial Palestinian term, "*jalagheem.*" On one stop, the woman who owned the house remarked to Bob, "Oh, what a handsome boy you have, Mr. Abraham!" As they entered the house, Bob whispered to Nazeeh in Arabic, "tuck in your *jalagheem* boy, the lady thinks you're good-looking."

As we drove down the scenic two-lane roads of northwestern Pennsylvania, its undulating hills a relief from the monotony of Michigan's flatness, I half-heartedly hoped Bob would tell me something about the places we were passing through. He wasn't accommodating. Sometimes though, when he abandoned his usual reticence, he would burst out singing a few lines from the old Palestinian folk song "*Ala del'ouna.*" Just as often, he would launch into a diatribe against Mother. "Your mother . . . ," he would begin, "accuses me of frittering away my earnings. Do you see me spending on anything but food and gas?" he would ask plaintively.

Bob startled me during one diatribe by asking rhetorically, "Are we spending any money on women?" Before I could grasp what he had in mind, he volunteered an answer: "You're too young and I'm too old for women." I nodded in agreement at the glibness of his observation, even though I felt like protesting the part about my being too young.

During a quiet stretch of two-lane road, a lime green station wagon carrying six nuns suddenly appeared and then disappeared as it headed around a bend going in the other direction. The image of the car and its passengers in their black habits was still fresh in my mind when Bob jolted me by saying, "Hey, boy, make like this . . . like this." Unable to follow what he was saying, I tried to catch a glimpse of his eyes, but he was watching the road.

"Look here, make like this," he repeated. This time I caught sight of his eyes glancing downward momentarily, where I noticed something rather queer. With his right hand Bob made a tickling motion near the crotch of his pants.

"What's that for?" I asked with a mixture of disgust and curiosity.

"Nuns bring bad luck. You should always scratch your balls when you see a nun," he explained.

His advice ran counter to everything I had been taught in school about respecting other creeds.

"Oh, I don't believe that," I said, looking away in embarrassment. "And, anyway, it's not nice to make fun of other religions," I added.

"It's bad luck, I'm telling you," he persisted. Convincing myself that it was better to placate him than to put up with his jabs at my indignation, I feigned a quick tickle. The drone of the car's engine filled the space between us again as I quietly ruminated the wisdom of coming on the trip.

Erie

When we reached Erie, Bob headed straight for his regular haunt, the Richmond Hotel. The luster of its grandeur long-faded, the Richmond offered Bob easy rates. He and I would share a double bed in a cramped room lit by a wall lamp at the foot of the bed. There was a sink and a mirror under the lamp, but the toilet and shower were located at the end of a dark, musty corridor. I didn't allow the state of the hotel to quell my excitement at being back in Erie, the town where my parents settled when I was an infant and the place we left when I was five years old. We dropped off our bags and left as quickly as we had arrived.

Bob drove by his old store on French Street and past the park that we used to stroll in. We got out of the car and walked to the large marble fountain in the park. Sharing a box of popcorn, we reminisced about the evenings the family watched the fountain's multicolor light display. From there we paid a visit to the Akabe'ya family, one of two families from Beit Hanina living in Erie. I had a vague recollection of them. They gave us an enthusiastic welcome, insisting we stay for dinner. The head of the household, Abu Mahmoud, was wearing a pair of overalls, which made him seem like an Arab version of the TV character "Mr. Green Jeans." Abu Mahmoud ran a dry goods store in the Italian part of town. He sold tapestries, towels, and linens on consignment to peddlers from Beit Hanina who drifted through Erie.

I was surprised to hear him say he had recently gone to the movies to see *Lawrence of Arabia.* "This is the first time the Arabs appear in the cinema; it's an accurate story," he said excitedly. His wife added that Abu Mahmoud was so taken by the film that he sat through the credits—every last one. Everyone laughed because it was obvious even to me that Abu Mahmoud was barely conversant in English. Later that week, Bob and I caught sight of him in a movie theater as the lights came on at the end of *Lawrence.* Abu Mahmoud was seated several rows in front of us engrossed in the film's credits, just as we were. As we stood to leave, Bob and I felt taller than usual.

The Richmond served as a kind of base camp for us during the two weeks we spent in Erie. After breakfast, Bob would place some calls on the hotel pay phone and then decide the day's itinerary. Often this included a foray to one of the small towns near Erie. We usually returned by late afternoon or evening. The rest of the day was spent whiling away the hours in an Italian American coffeehouse where Bob would play game after game of pinochle or gin rummy. The coffeehouse was noticeably cleaner and airier than the Arabic coffeehouses my father frequented back in Detroit. Still, I preferred to see the sights than remain confined to a place were a bunch of men sat around gambling, smoking, and bantering in foul language. One night I convinced Bob to let me go to the movies alone. Most of the time, however, I was stuck in the coffeehouse sipping soft drinks and watching my father play cards, as I looked for ways to nudge him into leaving. Once, a denizen of the coffeehouse took pity on me as midnight approached and prodded Bob to take me back to the hotel. Without looking up from the game, Bob mumbled, as he always did when prodded to leave, "We'll go when I finish this hand." If I were lucky, "this hand" would stretch *only* another hour or so.

Forever etched in my mind is the image of Bob seated at a card game. He is dressed in a gray suit, white shirt, and tie. Deep in concentration, he holds his cards guardedly in his left hand, while he alternatively tugs and flicks the corners of the cards with his right hand. A Chesterfield King hangs precariously from his lower lip, its gray ash snaking delicately upward. Unlike the movies, Bob and the other gamblers never leave money on the table. The year before he died, after leaving a card game in Erie, Bob was mugged. He had won big that night. He wouldn't say exactly how much, but it was over a thousand dollars. The mugger struck him on the forehead with the butt of a gun. Mother said that he got his comeuppance.

Dining Out

Back in Erie after a day on the road, Bob suggested that we dine on salami and cheese sandwiches. I had shared Bob's yen for salami ever since he introduced Best's Kosher Salami to our kitchen table as far back as I could remember. Dusk stretched over the town as we headed to a Jewish delicatessen he knew. He pulled up next to a building with a Star of David painted on the storefront. The place appeared closed. But seeing a light in back, Bob knocked anyway. A man wearing a soiled apron appeared behind a partially opened door. Bob convinced him to sell us some salami, bread, and cheese even though the deli man insisted he was already closed for the night. As the man took his place behind the counter, Bob peered through the glass case on the other side. I stood just inside the door, marveling at the strange shapes and colors among the shadows of the cramped, dimly lit store. Bob turned and told me to wait in the car.

What seemed like an eternity passed. Hunger gripped me. I began to wonder if something terrible had happened inside the store. I was still deliberating about going back to the store when Bob appeared. As he slid behind the wheel, I noticed he was empty-handed. "Let's go somewhere else," he murmured.

"What happened?" I asked with gnawing hunger. Bob explained that the deli owner was willing to sell him the salami but wouldn't slice it.

"Why not?" I asked somewhat astonished.

"It's after sundown on the Jewish Sabbath," Bob said.

"But today is Friday; isn't the Jewish day on Saturday?" I stammered, still confused. Bob appeared frustrated and in no mood to talk. It was only in adulthood that I discovered that Jews and Middle Easterners calculate the beginning of a new day from sundown the previous day.

"So, why did you take so long?" I asked, hoping he wouldn't become upset with my persistent questioning.

"The deli man told me he had some sliced chicken in the basement. I agreed out of desperation. But he took so long to come back I began to grow suspicious," Bob explained.

"Suspicious?"

Bob hesitated momentarily before elaborating, "Who knows what he brought back? Maybe it was cat meat."

"Cat meat? How could that be?" No one would knowingly sell cat meat, I thought to myself. That is too far-fetched. A grin suddenly came over Bob's face.

"How about a steak dinner at the Richmond Hotel?" he asked. I eagerly accepted.

Seated behind a table draped in white linen, I fingered the assortment of forks, knives, and spoons arrayed before me, contemplating my good fortune. Here I was on my first trip out of Detroit and I had already tasted shrimp (beer-battered) and eaten a "genuine" spaghetti dinner, both at the Aurora restaurant in the Italian section of town. And now another first—dining on a New York strip steak in a "fancy" hotel restaurant. Bob startled me by vigorously rubbing the flatware with his napkin, instructing me to do likewise.

"Aren't they clean?" I asked.

He responded with *"tik"* and a nod of the head, adding in Arabic, "You can never be sure."

As I rubbed the flatware on my side of the table, Bob pointed out the soup spoon and the salad fork. When the waitress arrived, he ordered a strip steak dinner for himself and a children's steak dinner for me. Fortunately for my sake, the waitress convinced him that the children's portion would be insufficient for a boy my age. In the end, I got the full steak dinner along with the uneasy feeling that perhaps Bob couldn't afford it.

Hoping to convince Bob that my presence on the trip was helping to further my education, I marveled at the large crystal chandelier hanging from the ceiling and the images of the linen-draped tables reflected in the full-length mirrors along the wall. Saying nothing, Bob pulled an envelope from his suit jacket and handed it to me along with the pen he borrowed from the waitress. In a hushed tone he asked me to write his name on the back of the envelope. Confused, I asked for clarification. He repeated his instructions. Thinking he might be interested in seeing how I might spell his name, I printed it in block letters.

After briefly scrutinizing what I had written, he said, "Is this how you *sign* my name?"

Incredulous, I asked, "You want me to *sign your* name?" He nodded in the affirmative. I tried not to imitate his signature, even though I knew how, because I feared he might accuse me of having forged his signature on some document. I handed him the envelope, which he held up to the light and scrutinized intensely. He then asked for the pen. Placing the envelope on the table, he slowly copied the signature, comparing his with mine. He did this twice before the waitress returned, at which point he tucked the envelope back into his jacket and returned the pen.

Puzzled, I asked what was going on. Bob said he wanted to refine his signature. I felt sad, for at age thirteen I had more years of schooling behind me than he had at age sixty-seven. "After a lifetime in business, you certainly know how to sign your name," I reassured him. "And, even though you haven't had much education, you read American and Arabic newspapers. That's more than what most people can do." I pointed out that he was probably the only person in our entire neighborhood who read the *New York Times.* In a final, and self-deprecating, attempt to make him feel better, I reminded him that he was a whiz with numbers and would chuckle when I had to pull out pencil and paper to multiply double-digit numbers. "Look Bob, the fact that you can do the calculations in your head tells me you're smarter than most people," I concluded. Bob listened stone-faced.

Long after he died, Mother revealed that Bob had learned to read and write during a stint in prison. This chapter in his life occurred well before he married Mother, probably when he lived in New York City. Mother told the story about it, which she had heard from Bob. My father had a policy to help new immigrants from Beit Hanina when they first arrived in the country. One day a man from the village arrived at his doorstep with a stranger in tow. The man asked Bob to reimburse the stranger for helping him. Bob was later arrested and tried for smuggling an alien into the country. He served a four-year sentence behind bars, losing his business in the process.

Lake Chautauqua

One morning Bob returned from his round of phone calls to say we were going to New York. I cloaked my excitement lest Bob think I was turning the *Bay'aa* trip into a kid's vacation. I desperately wanted to set foot in New York City, America's premier city and the town Bob had spent much of his life in. Bob, however, had a different New York in mind—Lake Chautauqua, New York—a short drive from Erie.

The air around Lake Chautauqua contrasted favorably with the smoke-filled coffeehouse and the musty hotel back in Erie. Bob was hoping to break his no-win streak at Chautauqua. His mood had picked up, and he was back to rolling the syllables of town names around his tongue. He would toss sounds back and forth like a cat playing with its food: "La-ka-wa-na." On the way to Erie, his syllabic toy word was "Astabula."

Bob parked in front of a sprawling ranch house tucked away in a corner of the countryside around Lake Chautauqua. As usual, I sat in the car as Bob made his call. After exchanging a few pleasantries, he returned and instructed me to help him pull a rug out of the car. At last, I thought, I would be able to justify my keep. We wrestled a big Kirman into the living room of the house. By morning's end, two more Orientals would be unrolled in succession, one laid on top of the other. Each time, Bob paid close attention to how it sat in the room—busying himself laying the rug just so—a tug here, a flap of a corner there, until it harmonized with its surroundings.

He then reestablished eye contact with the couple, zeroing in on the wife, who, he knew from experience, would have to like the rug if the hoped-for sale was to materialize. Bob discussed each rug's design, while attempting to educate the couple, who were relatively young, on the investment value of the rugs. The couple's attractive daughter entered the room briefly. I looked in her direction, hoping not to arouse her parents' suspicion. Bob would never forgive me, I thought, if he lost a sale because of my flirtatious glances. My eyes shifted back to Bob and the couple.

The couple seemed unsure of themselves. Three new Kirmans, not costly antiques, lay before them. Questions and answers went back and forth while Bob expounded on the merits of Orientals over wall-to-wall carpet. Watching him work convinced me that peddling Oriental rugs was not in my blood. The idea of entering people's homes to sell them something they weren't certain they needed or wanted didn't sit well with me. Too many unknowns, too many possibilities for rejection, too nerve-wracking. It was too much like gambling.

In the end, the pretty daughter disappeared, and so did the possibility of a sale. One by one, we rolled up the rugs and carried them back to the car. Bob's assessment: the couple was too young to appreciate Oriental rugs and too taken in by the fashion of the day—wall-to-wall carpeting. He also thought the couple had found the price too steep. The fifteen hundred dollars he was asking for one of the rugs was equivalent to a fifth of the average income at the time.

Detroit

My brothers jumped with excitement when they saw Bob and me entering the house. We were like warriors returning from a battlefield. Mother gave me a big kiss, and my brothers wanted to know what it was like going out on *al-Bay'aa*. I told them about the shrimp at the Aurora, the steak at the Richmond, the vineyards on the way to Lake Chautauqua, the rolling hills of Pennsylvania, and I whispered about the incident with the nuns. I knew the questions my brothers would ask because I once had them too. I had voyaged to the world of *al-Bay'aa*, a world that was as much a part of our consciousness as the West is part of the American consciousness.

Road's End

Six years after Bob and I returned from *al-Bay'aa*, we set off on separate journeys: I on my first trip to the Middle East, he on his last *al-Bay'aa*. The year was 1969. On the eve of my departure, Bob handed me some fatherly advice, "I hear refugee women make good wives," he said.

"Bob, I'm not interested in finding a wife," I replied indignantly with a hint of embarrassment. "I'm going to see the Palestinian revolution."

It was around Labor Day when I returned to Detroit. On the drive home from the airport I regaled my brothers with stories of what I had seen during my summer trip to Lebanon, Jordan, Syria, and Turkey. It was a heady time filled with foreign lands, revolutionary politics, unintelligible languages, new customs, and exotic foods.

As the car wheeled into the garage behind Casper Street, it dawned on me that we had been riding in my father's holly green 1966 Ford Galaxy. No one mentioned that Bob was back from *al-Bay'aa*. "Hey, this is Bob's car. So he's home," I said knowingly.

My brothers' momentary silence was broken by Sameer who responded, "He's not here." Too weary from the trip, I didn't probe as I headed indoors to see my mother and younger brothers. They let me fall asleep without bringing up the subject of Bob's whereabouts.

The next morning Mother broke the news to me in the only way she knew how. "Your father," she said in simple Arabic that I could understand, "died." Years of experience attuned me to the nuances of my mother's voice. Her steady, somber cadence amplified the seriousness of her message. "He died in New York. Sameer and I went there to retrieve his body. We buried him here. Hundreds attended the funeral. Your stepbrother Richard was there, and so were all the people from Beit Hanina."

Mother remained impassive as she spoke, even though I now know that she would have preferred to throw her arms around me.

But my family always leaned toward restraint. We grew up never expressing the deepest emotions between parent and child. "I could have sent word to you to come back, but decided against it because I knew how much this trip meant to you," she added. I was too stunned to take umbrage at her decision.

After Mother broke the news I sat in the bathtub and sobbed quietly to myself. That was the extent of my mourning for my father. I never really buried Bob, and to this day I haven't mustered up the emotional strength to visit his grave site. I dammed a reservoir of emotions that I still refuse to let out for fear of their enormous power. So there they remain—tucked away in my subconscious safely out of reach.

A perforated stomach ulcer fells my father as he plays cards in New York City one summer night. The coffeehouse owner calls Mother. She and Sameer fly to his bedside at Bellevue Hospital. He survives the initial surgery, but it fails to stop the hemorrhaging. Father is unable to speak through the oxygen mask as he is told that he must undergo a second operation. For the first time, Sameer notices fear on Father's face.

Barely eighteen years old, Sameer is sent to Erie to pick up Bob's belongings from the Richmond, where, as usual, he left his things while he went on a quick buying trip to New York. Sameer drives Father's car, laden with unsold rugs and linens, back to Detroit. Mother waits in New York. Sameer flies back to New York City and goes to Bellevue, where he discerns the news on a nurse's face. Father died on the operating table.

At nineteen, I hardly knew the man we called Bob, for he was as emotionally distant as he was physically absent in our lives. Although he had married at least three women in his seventy or so years (we never knew his real age), he seemed to prefer the solitary life of the peddler to the sedate life of father and husband. It was in his blood, and he wasn't about to change even after my four brothers and I came along.

Father died the way he had lived: on the road. He was the consummate peddler—a loner who preferred to meet everyone in his life on his terms, whether they were customers, family, or fellow gamblers. He preferred to roam unhindered and unencumbered by familial obligations, yet he was exceedingly generous to his relatives and covillagers, and he loved and took pride in his six sons. Anomalies were his stock in trade. For most of the seventeen years he spent with his first wife, Grace, he lived in New York City, leaving her to raise their son in Scranton, Pennsylvania. Father was an urban cowboy. He rode into town, swaggered into the local coffeehouse and gambled the night away. When he was out of money, he rode away, looking for opportunity on the trail. He was good at his trade, and it rewarded him in untold ways. To his credit, my father never gave a second thought to the road not taken.

Part 3

RELIGION

Fig. 9. Men pray, meditate, and read the Quran at the Dix mosque, 1979. Photograph by Millard Berry.

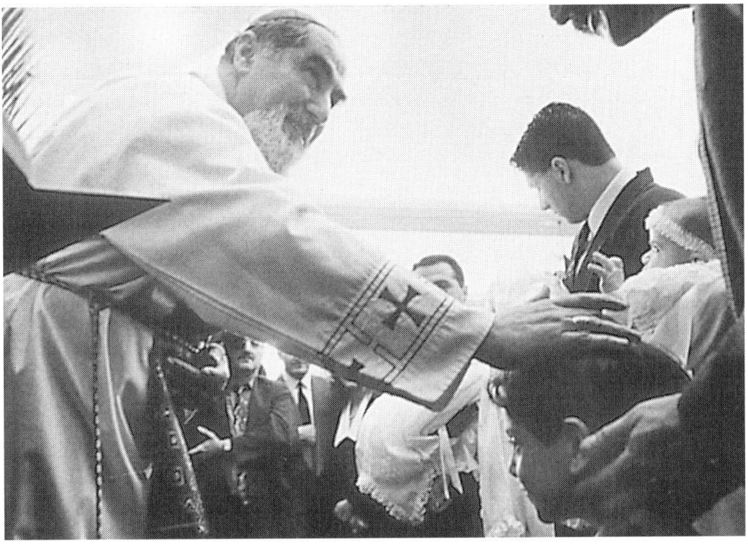

Fig. 10. A first son is baptized at the Mother of God Chaldean Rite Catholic Church in Southfield, Michigan, 1995. Photograph by Millard Berry.

Introduction

In Arab Detroit, the imagery of "margin and mainstream" is nowhere more apt, or more complicated, than in its application to religious life. At the most obvious level, Arab Detroit is composed of faiths and sects that are considered alien in America at large. Islam of any sort is marginalized in a country that defines itself, with careless disregard for millions of its own citizens, as Judeo-Christian. Shia Islam, more suspect still, is repeatedly associated with terrorism and violent political movements. Chaldean Catholics and Egyptian Copts, though Christian, often appear no less peculiar, with their ancient liturgical languages and ritual variations, and with their bilingual congregations made up almost entirely of immigrants and their children. Yet one of the great ironies of this seemingly exotic terrain is that Christian churches and Muslim sects that were minorities in the Arab world are majorities in Arab Detroit. Christians, barely 5 percent of the Arabic-speaking world, make up at least half of Arab Detroit. Chaldean Catholics, a minority within the Arab Christian minority, are arguably the largest group of Arabic-speaking Christians in Detroit. Shii Muslims, who have sizable Arabic-speaking communities only in south Lebanon, Iraq, and parts of the Arabian Peninsula, make up the majority of Muslims in Detroit. With over forty mosques and churches, Arab Detroit is a religiously inverted version of the Arab world, and this upside-down quality has generated a range of unexpected consequences.

Foremost among these consequences is the emergence of religion-based ethnicities where, in the homeland, an overarching Arab identity, with a specific national focus, has typically been the ideal, if not the rule. Sharkey Haddad's memoir shows how completely his personal identity and public career are built on the Chaldean community in Detroit. He freely admits, however, that he grew up in Iraq thinking of himself as an Iraqi and a member of the Arab nation. The fact that he was a Christian did not stand in the way of these identifications. Only in Detroit did he learn about his Chaldean heritage as such; only there did he come to see the advantage in placing a strategic distance between Arab and Chaldean identity. The same themes surface in Richard Jones' essay on Detroit's Coptic Christians. In Egypt, Copts are citizens of an Arab/Muslim state, and their identity (as a minority) must be defined in relation to that state. Clearly, this is not the case in Detroit. As a result, Coptic-American identity can acquire separatist, ethnic, and even national dimensions that would make little sense, and would be altogether dangerous, in Egypt. The same process is discernible among Lebanese Shia, who are now in a position to represent Islam in Detroit not as a minority sect but as the majority of Arab believers. Shiism in Dearborn is remarkable for the extent to which it is local (organized along village and clan lines particular to south Lebanon) and universal (with links to a world community of Shia whose political and spiritual centers are in Iran and Iraq). Islam itself, detached from Lebanon as a place, or Arabism as an ideology, or Iraq as a state, is quickly becoming a total identity for many of Detroit's Muslims. For Arabs, however, this identity has ethnic and political dimensions that link it more to Lebanon, Iraq, Palestine, and Yemen than to, say, Pakistan or the Black Muslim community in Detroit.

As religious minorities who were once contained (and even suppressed) within Arab/Sunni/Muslim nation-states become religious majorities in Arab Detroit, they must contend not only with new political freedoms but with intimidating cultural possibilities. Indeed, the distinction between "culture" and "religion" is the battleground on which immigrants fight to define what is Muslim, what is Christian, and what is Arab. This conflict emerges plainly in all the essays that follow. It is especially pronounced, however, in Nabeel Abraham's study of the Dix mosque in Dearborn and Sally Howell's interview with Lila and Mohsen Amen. In both, the relationship between "Old World" and "Americanized" approaches to Islam prompts individual Muslims, and entire mosques, to ponder what in their way of life is based on eternal, divine truths and what is "merely" cultural and therefore open to change.

A social scientist would immediately insist that hard dichotomies between religion and culture are false: religion is always cultural, and culture has everyday routines and rituals that are observed as religiously as the Feast of Pentecost or the Fast of Ramadan. Still, most devout Arab Christians and Muslims do not see things this way. A common way of dealing with assimilation issues in Detroit—

especially those pertaining to women and what they cannot do—is to cast these issues against a religious backdrop, thus turning them into matters of sin and salvation. The reader should remain alert to the ways in which Copts, Shia, Chaldeans, and competing clerics at the Dix mosque use religious identity as a way of shaping and controlling sexuality, mate choice, and power relations between men and women. Note also how Americanized Muslims and Christians, in hopes of changing these patterns, try to develop alternative readings of their own traditions, or agree simply to ignore or de-emphasize what their parents and newly arrived cousins deem essential to a proper exercise of the faith.

For the most part, the contributors to this book address Christianity and Islam in their social dimensions, as communal frameworks. This slant is not meant to imply that Shia in Dearborn or Chaldeans in Bloomfield Hills are without a devotional, pietistic, intensely individual relationship to their own faith. Many do have a spiritual sense of exactly this sort. We think it important, however, to distinguish between the kind of religiosity prevalent among Arab immigrants in Detroit and the sensibilities commonly thought to prevail among evangelical and fundamentalist Christians in North America, with whom devout Muslims are frequently compared. In assembling the materials for this section, we noticed that few of our contributors wanted to discuss the dogma, the belief content, of their faith. Such talk, they thought, was the province of imams and priests. Some feared they would get the details wrong. Others intimated that the priests and imams would feel slighted if laypeople spoke in their place. Sharkey Haddad, for instance, describes himself as a Chaldean Catholic—not as an Arab or an Iraqi—yet he says nothing of the religious rites and church teachings that make a specifically Chaldean identity possible.

This is reflective of the patriarchal, authoritarian nature of religious leadership in the community—a quality most Arab Detroiters freely acknowledge—but it also says something about what, in practice, is the bedrock of religious life in Arab Detroit: its communal nature and its deep roots in regional, village, and clan loyalties. The conversion narratives offered by Lila and Mohsen Amen are testament to all this; moreover, they reveal the gaps between Mohsen's immigrant, communal, imam-centered approach to Islam and Lila's Americanized, do-it-yourself, individualistic approach. Mohsen and Lila have bridged these gaps within the context of their own marriage. The same differences, though, when they arise within mosques and churches, typically result in dissolution, the establishment of new, breakaway institutions or the increasingly common mosque-within-a-mosque (or church-within-a-church) designed to serve the interests of the congregation's English or Arabic-speaking members.

If immigration from the Arab world to Detroit continues, it is likely that churches and mosques will go on forming, splitting, and dissolving along lines that, beneath all the doctrinal argumentation, are blatantly cultural. Chaldeans, Copts, and Shia and Sunni Muslims are developing new identities akin to American ethnic ones, but modern ethnicity is ultimately a way of confronting the inclusive and exclusive potential of national identities. The relationship of ethnicity to religion, especially universal religions like Islam and Christianity, has always been vexed. Arabs in Detroit can easily use the term "boater" to distinguish the more American from the less American. However, it is another thing entirely to use such terms to determine who is more properly a Muslim. Nonetheless, such determinations are constantly being made in Detroit. The conflict Nabeel Abraham traces in his essay was essentially a struggle between "boaters" and "American-borns." The fact that the "boaters" managed to remove the "American-borns" from the Dix mosque does not mean the Americanized faction were not proper Muslims. It means simply that they were Muslims of a different, locally adapted kind.

Americanized Arabs continue to identify with the Arab immigrant community. It is usually the Americanized Arabs who mobilize immigrants, provide them with social services, and connect them to the political mainstream. Hyphenated, ethnic Arabs continue, in similar fashion, to identify with Islam or Chaldean Catholicism or the Syrian Orthodox Church. They are married, baptized, preached to, and buried in these communities long after the rituals and creeds cease to compel them, or compel them in unforeseen ways. Hayan Charara's reflection on his mother's Muslim funeral service, a rite from which he felt greatly estranged, shows the lingering power of faith. Charara knew that his mother did not look favorably on all aspects of her Islamic upbringing and that she might not have approved of the ritual forms used to lay her to rest. Yet on the fortieth day after her death, the last day of mourning, Charara felt compelled to mark his mother's passing. He did so not with a prayer, or a recitation from the Quran, but by writing a poem. His decision to remember her in this way, on a day set aside for religious observance, was no less an act of worship.

What They Did

Hayan Charara

You died. And because your father
and mother were Muslims,
the next door neighbor, a hajji,
washed your corpse and prayed
over your body. When they
brought you to the mosque
on Joy Road and Greenfield
you were wrapped in green,
veiled so that only your face
shown. As was the custom
you hated, women sat to your left
and men to the right, a sheik
knowing you were a teacher
said that you were not a teacher,
but a school. Everyone cried,
even the father of a boy you taught
and fed once because the boy
was hungry and forgot his lunch,
the father cried although
he never met you. Forty times
the mourners read the Fatihah
to help you out of the streets
into that place beyond prayer.
At the cemetery they lifted
your casket in the wind and
chanted God is Great, the lid
blew open and silenced the crowd.
Dirt was poured over your eyes
and placed in each palm

Reprinted from *Mudfish* 10 (1997), 136–37.

while workers dug a grave
in the March earth. A woman
noticed your grave beside her
sister's and she was relieved
her sister would have company.
Even in the ground, your husband
and daughter did not believe,
your son stared at the space
in front of him, under a widening spell.
For forty days people met secretly
to pray for your soul. And
the day the angels were to take
you away, everyone rejoiced,
in their own way. Your sisters
cried, your husband waited
for a tree to burst forth,
your schoolchildren sat quietly
after the morning bells, your
parents welcomed another daughter
at the airport, and after the first
gentle dream in weeks, your son
woke and sat down at his desk
to write you a poem.

The American Journey of a Chaldean from Iraq

Sharkey Haddad

MY FATHER DISAPPEARED for three days when I was fifteen years old and living in Baghdad, Iraq, with my parents and my three younger brothers. We didn't know whether or not he was alive or what horrible things were being done to him. We could not inquire about where he was or report him to the police as missing for fear that we would be arrested. At the end of the third day of his disappearance, he returned home exhausted, unbathed, and unfed. We wanted to ask him a hundred questions, but all he said to my mother was, "Pack our things. Sell the house. We're getting out of this country as soon as possible. Call your brother in Michigan and see if he can get started on the immigration papers to get us in the United States."

I was the first son of Elias and Amira Haddad, born in Baghdad, Iraq, in 1961. My father was offered a job with the Chrysler Corporation in 1967 and we moved to Jedda, Saudi Arabia. In 1970 we moved to the capital of Saudi Arabia, Riyadh, because my father was promoted to another position within Chrysler. In 1974 my parents made the decision to return to our homeland for good, and we returned to Baghdad.

At that time, Ahmad Hasan al-Bakr was in office as the first Baathist president of Iraq. We had been back in Iraq for two years when my father's disappearance occurred. After he had rested and eaten a meal, he told us that he had been pulled over by the government's "secret police" and taken in for questioning. First he was asked why he drove an American car (Iraq stopped importing American goods after the Arab-Israeli War in 1967). When he told them he worked for Chrysler, the police checked his passport and questioned him at length regarding the time he spent in Saudi Arabia. After further investigation they discovered that he had participated in a prodemocracy movement in Baghdad when he was eighteen years old. That was enough to hold him for more investigation until they were satisfied that he was not a threat. We were fortunate that my father was even allowed to return home; several people who were arrested or taken in for questioning at this time never returned. This incident convinced my father that he did not want to raise his family in a country where his children could "disappear," get arrested, or be drafted during a major war at any time. This turned out to be a wise decision because a year after we left Iraq, the Iran-Iraq War began. Many young people were drafted in the army; many died.

After my father decided that we should leave Iraq and move to the United States, he immediately left for Saudi Arabia and stayed with friends. We were afraid he would be picked up again by the secret police and that the results would be much worse. My mother, my brothers, and I stayed in Iraq to sell our house, while my uncle Najib Jamil in Michigan started processing the necessary paperwork for us to come to the United States. At this time, in the late 1970s, it was relatively easy for a U.S. citizen to get approval within six months for immediate family members to come to the United States, especially if the immigrating family members brought over one hundred thousand dollars to invest.

It took about four months for our paperwork to be approved. Those four months were filled with mixed emotions. We were afraid that the government would figure out that we were planning to leave and arrest us (Iraq's law forbade its citizens to leave the country permanently or to visit the United States or Israel). We were also excited about the thought of going to the United States, a "dream world" where everyone wanted to live. My brothers and I were occupied almost constantly with wondering what life would be like there and what the kids our age were like. My parents must have been very nervous about taking their life savings and everything they owned to a country where they didn't know anything about its culture, people, or language.

On a grander scale, we held an image of the United States as a country where everyone was appreciative of their guaranteed human rights and their democratic government. We could hardly imagine a country where there was no civil war and where it was illegal to discriminate based on race, religion, sex, or age. We naively pictured a country where everyone respected and welcomed all ethnic and religious groups. Once we had our papers to go to the United States, we joined my father in Saudi Arabia and left together from there.

I remember one particular incident that made me realize this country was not as ideal as I had thought. As soon as we got to the United States, my cousin took me for a drive to show me around.

A black person driving another car cut him off, and he said, "You f—— n——!" I didn't know any English at this time, so I asked him what it meant. He said that is what everyone calls black people in the United States. I asked him if it was a bad name, and he said that it was. I asked him why he called black people bad names over here, since we had many black friends in Iraq and we never called them names. He just said, "I don't know. Everyone does it here." We had relocated often and what he said made me remember all the names that followed me to every foreign country or neighborhood ("foreigner," "Christian," "infidel"). I made the decision right there to never use that word, or any other word that would insult another person. I guess my commitment was so strong that I currently work on such issues for a living in the West Bloomfield School District.

Most of the Chaldean immigrants who come here usually settle in Detroit first (in the Seven Mile Road and Woodward Avenue area) and then move to other areas on the outskirts of Detroit. My father, however, wanted to live in an area with newer housing, and he had my uncle find us a house in the suburbs of Detroit, in an area where there was a good school system. Without us ever seeing it, my uncle purchased a house in the Thirteen Mile and Evergreen Road area of Southfield, Michigan (about twenty-five miles north of downtown Detroit), which was located within the Birmingham School District. He chose this area because Birmingham was known as one of the best school districts in Michigan. My father would teach me in many ways that education was to be considered a top priority, but this was one of the first examples.

Attending Groves High School in Birmingham had a big impact on the direction of my academic life. Most Chaldean students who come to the United States attend a school where there is a high concentration of first-generation Chaldean immigrants. I was in an area where there were very few first- or second-generation Chaldean immigrants. As one of only five or six Chaldeans in the entire high school, I was forced to learn to speak, read, and write English very quickly. At first, when I was in the classroom I would only understand one or two words of each sentence the teacher spoke. I was enrolled by my counselor in difficult classes such as American history and American government. I became frustrated and lost and was very tempted to drop out of school and work full-time to help my family get established. At the time it seemed like I could accomplish more by doing that. Now I realize that it would have been the easier thing to do. But, with the encouragement of a Chaldean bilingual teacher at Groves High School, Josephine Sarafa, I stayed in school. Mrs. Sarafa kept telling me not to give up, that I would pick up the language in just a few months, and that I could graduate from high school. She was one of the first important role models to really shape my life when I came to the United States.

A language barrier tends to make members of one ethnic group congregate. Chaldean students who did not even know each other would often just go up and introduce themselves to the group. Within that group they didn't have to be afraid that they would be laughed at if they made a mistake while speaking. Also, these students were given the same rules by their parents, and they didn't have to be embarrassed if they were not allowed to date or go to high school football games or school dances. Congregating with your own ethnic group in a situation where you are the minority relieved a lot of pressure on students, and also encouraged the students to look out for each other. For Chaldeans, looking out for other Chaldeans is sort of a cultural tradition from Iraq, where people were always on the lookout for invaders coming to the Chaldean villages.

On top of the language barrier, it was challenging to adapt to the culture in the United States. My father felt that it was important for my brothers and me to assimilate to American culture very quickly. He encouraged us to socialize with other kids of all ethnic backgrounds so that we would be able to relate to as many different types of people as possible. I remember him telling us, "Your Chaldean family and relatives will always be there for you. What you need to do is become as Americanized as possible and then you can always return to your Chaldean community. If you don't learn the American way of life, you will always be limited." I still think that this advice from my father is what motivated me over and over again to continue the struggle with my educational and professional goals.

Although my parents wanted my brothers and me to "take the good and leave the bad" of American culture, they still wanted us to maintain our Chaldean cultural traditions. When I started dating, I brought an American girl over to meet my parents. My father managed an obviously forced politeness, while my mother was outwardly cold to her. This was because I was still expected to marry a Chaldean, and bringing a girl home to meet the parents was, in Chaldean culture, an indication that you might end up marrying her. I was sort of caught in the middle of two cultures; I wanted to please my parents, but I also wanted to adopt the American customs of my new friends. It was difficult to figure out what was acceptable and what was not. At the same time, I was adjusting to the new experience of attending a coed school. Until that time, I had always attended an all-boys school, and dating in most Islamic countries was not permitted.

Another new challenge that I faced in American culture was confronting individuals who were using drugs. Coming from a culture where drugs were almost nonexistent, I didn't know how to deal with it or the peer pressure associated with it. Fortunately, I was one of the decent soccer players on the high school team, so I decided to use that as an excuse for not wanting to touch drugs. I had also used soccer as an excuse for not wanting to smoke cigarettes with my friends in Iraq.

Participating in school athletics was not common among Chaldean immigrants. My parents allowed me to because I expressed a strong interest in playing soccer. Most Chaldean immigrants need their children to help with a family business or work at a job after school to help the family get established. Chaldean parents are also very leery of activities that involve schedules and customs they know nothing about. Few schools in Iraq had organized sporting events with practice schedules and sports banquets. The children just have "pick up" games in empty fields near their neighborhood. Student and parent participation in school athletics is a foreign concept to new immigrants, but, fortunately, my parents accepted this facet of American life very quickly and playing soccer became one of the main reasons why I wanted to stay in school and stay away from smoking and drugs. Years later, I decided to coach a soccer team and was able to convince many Chaldean parents that participating in sports was a healthy thing for their children to do. The parents trusted me because I was Chaldean and I could tell them that playing soccer was a positive experience for me when I came here.

I have many examples of the challenges I faced while I was trying to learn to understand the American way of life. I remember when my American friends laughed at me because I worked, without being paid, about forty hours a week after school and on the weekends to help my father establish his business. They told me that I should quit working for my father and get a job somewhere else where I could make money for myself. What they didn't understand was that in the Chaldean culture whatever benefits the family as a whole comes first. This is partially because most extended Chaldean families live together, and I was expected to live indefinitely in my father's home for free. It made sense, then, that I would work for the family business for free. In American culture, I learned, the emphasis is on independence. Young Americans often work for their own benefit and are expected to move out on their own at a relatively young age.

At the age of twenty-five, I became one of the first Chaldeans in my community to move out of his parents' house and buy my own home before getting married. In the Chaldean community, people are expected to live with their parents until they are married, no matter how old they are. I decided that I was going to do things the American way and live independently. My parents felt that this was an insult, as if I didn't think their home was good enough for me. But they grew to understand that I was simply becoming more and more Americanized, which is what my father always encouraged my brothers and me to do.

Even though my parents eventually understood why I wanted to move, I still remember that they were ashamed and scared of what other Chaldean families might say about us. The shame factor in the Chaldean community is a very powerful force. Of the approximately seventy-five thousand Chaldeans in the Metropolitan Detroit area, the majority of them are related by either blood or marriage. This is because most of them trace their roots to the same ten villages in northern Iraq, and most of them marry within their faith. Any news of a death, a birth, a marriage, or a divorce spreads very quickly. It is common for this type of news to become common knowledge in the community within twenty-four hours. Because of this there is a lot of pressure to do what is considered the right thing by the community as a whole; the community becomes a makeshift system of checks and balances.

Another challenge I faced when I came to the United States was accepting my identity as a Chaldean. Since I had lived in the capital city of Baghdad and in Saudi Arabia, and most Chaldeans lived in the northern villages of Iraq, the schools that I attended taught neither Chaldean history nor Christianity. In fact, I had to read and interpret the Quran instead of the Bible. In Iraq, I was taught that everyone was Arab, no matter what dialect they spoke or what religion they were. When I came to the United States, I still wasn't sure if I should think of myself as a Chaldean or an Arab or an American. I found that there were many stereotypes of Chaldeans and Arabs here, and throughout high school and college I often let my peers believe that I was Italian or Greek.

It wasn't until I was eighteen and attended a social event held in the basement of the Southfield Mother of God Chaldean Church that I began to be curious about my heritage. Father Sarhad Jammo came up and put his arm around my shoulder and asked, "Do you speak Chaldean?" When I told him that I did not, he asked, "Why not? What language did your grandfather speak?" I told him honestly that I did not know and he became the first person to ever raise my curiosity and teach me about Chaldean history and how to be proud of it. Father Jammo was the second role model I had in the United States. He played a key role in shaping my life.

I decided that after I graduated from high school, I wanted to go to college. I was accepted at the University of Michigan in Ann Arbor, but I had to sacrifice going there to work for the family business. Also, as the oldest child in the family, I was expected to keep an eye on my three younger brothers to make sure they didn't start getting into trouble or picking up bad habits. I started working full time for my father during the day and taking classes at Oakland Community College at night. I received a little encouragement from my father but not in the traditional sense. As his way of getting me back on "the right track," he would criticize my lifestyle. He would tell me things like, "You'll never graduate from college. Why are you wasting your time and money?" I think he knew that this only made me more determined to stick with it and graduate, no matter how difficult it was. It's too bad that my father's methods didn't have the same effect on my brothers, whom I had hoped would follow in my footsteps and be driven by our father's negative remarks.

I had virtually no social life at this point because I worked all day, went to school at night, and studied in any spare time that was left. My Chaldean friends and relatives used to question why I was so determined. They didn't understand why I didn't drop out of high school like they did and become a successful business owner. Today, I smile when those same friends envy me for completing a college degree and for working as a professional with a lot of time on weekends to spend with my family. I had to spend about three times as many hours studying as other students because I was still working on my English vocabulary. I used to carry a giant dictionary with me at all times so that I could look up words during lectures or while I was reading. Other students used to think that I was a prelaw or premedical student because of the books I carried.

There was one particular time when I was tempted to drop out of college. Because my vocabulary was still limited and because I relied so heavily on the information presented in lectures and assigned reading, I had a difficult time in one class. On an exam a professor asked us to write an essay describing the mood in the United States during the 1960s. I went up to him and pointed out that this information wasn't in the text or lectures. His response was that he was aware of this, but that everyone living in America knows what the mood of the 1960s was. I said, "Everyone doesn't know that. If you were born here you would most likely know what the mood was, but neither my parents nor I went to school in the United States." He would not change his mind, and he graded my essay just like everyone else's. I was very angry with him, but in the end I became even more determined to graduate from college. I completed an associate's degree in liberal arts at Oakland Community College, then transferred to Oakland University and completed a bachelor's degree in political science.

My intention at this time was to continue my education and get a law degree. I took the LSAT and scored well enough to be accepted into law school, but I made the mistake of taking a year off from school. After that I wasn't motivated enough to go back. Today, many of my friends continue to think that I would make a good lawyer and encourage me to go back to school.

While Chaldeans as a group are considered highly educated in Iraq, they have acquired a stereotype in America of caring very little about education. There are several reasons why this stereotype exists. The first reason is that because Chaldean students come here knowing very little of the language, they start to feel lost and they see very little progress. Second, the schools here are very different from those in Iraq. There, if a parent goes to the school and questions his child's progress, it is considered a huge insult to the teacher. It implies that the parent feels the teacher is not doing his or her job. This is a drastic contrast to the educational philosophy in America, where teachers are begging for more parent involvement. Because of the language barrier, not only is it impossible for Chaldean immigrants to read a progress report or help their children with homework, parents feel very uncomfortable going to the school to see how their children are doing or if there is anything they can do to help their children succeed. On top of all that, add the fact that while Chaldean students see very little progress in their education, they see a great amount of progress when they make money in business. Too often this is enough to make Chaldean immigrants give up on academic pursuits. However, this situation is improving due to the efforts of support organizations like the Chaldean Federation of America. Each year, the Federation has a special mass at one of the Chaldean churches to honor all the high school and college graduates and award twenty thousand dollars in scholarship money. Events such as this are slowly teaching Chaldean families the importance of completing an education in America.

After I graduated from college, I was working in my father's grocery store when I received a phone call from a friend. He said that the city of Southfield's community relations department was looking for an individual who was bilingual to educate the Chaldean residents about its programs. I applied for the job and started working part time for the Southfield city hall. After six months, I was promoted to a full-time position as a building inspector, which I did from 1986 to 1992. I was still working with Chaldean residents and business owners in the community, explaining ordinances and zoning regulations to them.

Working in an office environment was a completely new experience for me. The only work environment I had experienced was my father's store, where I worked with him and my brothers. It was very exciting to find a job in the field in which I had studied so soon after graduating, but I did not know how to act in this environment. I remember feeling left out or disinterested whenever there were office social functions such as a Christmas party or someone's birthday because to me these were family occasions, not work events. One positive thing that came out of working in that office was that my coworkers often asked about my ethnic background. I would always take the time to answer their questions and try to build more understanding of the Chaldean culture.

During this time, I made sure that I stayed active in volunteer organizations, both for the Chaldean community and for the non-Chaldean community. Volunteerism is not a common activity in the Chaldean community. People are so busy working and raising their families that they don't have time to volunteer or don't choose to spend their free time volunteering. Also, at this time, there were no social programs for Chaldeans that might ask for volunteers, but there are some now. I think I became involved in volunteer organizations because going to college made me more aware of social problems that I could help with, and because I was influenced by friends outside of my ethnic group who were doing volunteer work. Even today, many Chaldeans don't understand why I do so much work that I don't get paid for, and I try to explain that I do it to help fellow human beings, and because it is part of the American culture.

In 1992 I made a big change in my career. I was contacted by the Chaldean Federation of America, a blanket association of five Chaldean churches and seven other Chaldean organizations. I had participated in many of their fund-raising events and was asked to be their first director. I accepted the offer and took a fifteen thousand dollar reduction in pay, hoping this was a decision where one step backward would get me two steps forward. This turned out to be the case because the position allowed me to work with many elected officials, business owners, health care facilities, and educational institutions. Through the Federation I was able to provide services for the Chaldean community and start educating the non-Chaldean community about how to relate better to Chaldeans. I was responsible for reacting to the media during the attack on Iraq and explaining the position of the Chaldeans in the Metro Detroit area. Luckily, I gave the media the appropriate answers, and thankfully, I look older than I am, which probably led the public and the media to think I was a veteran when I was really only thirty years old. Once a week I gave a presentation on Chaldean history and culture to a group, whether it was a health care institution, a school district, or a business organization. This was very rewarding for me, especially when I could begin to see the bridges of understanding that were forming as a result of my work.

After I had worked for the Federation for two years, West Bloomfield High School contacted me to request my assistance. A tragic incident occurred when two male students, one Chaldean and one African American, were fighting. The African American struck the Chaldean and caused him to fall backward and hit his head on the pavement, which put him in a coma. The media escalated the event and turned it into a racially motivated fight, which pressured the West Bloomfield School District to act quickly to halt rumors and any ripple effect that might take place. I contacted my friends at the leadership of the NAACP (National Association for the Advancement of Colored People), and together with the school, we managed to calm students and parents and evoke more rational thought among the members of the entire community.

Because of the success we had in handling this situation, I was asked to join the administrative team of the West Bloomfield School District. I decided to accept the offer because I remembered that the most difficult time of my life was when I was a student, and I wish there had been someone who understood my frustrations and who could have given me direction and encouragement. The percentage of first-generation Chaldean immigrants who drop out of high school is very high. It gets lower with each generation as language and cultural barriers become less of an issue. But students still need role models they can relate to like I could with Josephine Sarafa at Groves High School. Since 1994 I have worked as a community liaison for the school district, helping all students who speak English as a second language become assimilated and involved in activities and manage their frustrations.

As I continued to move on to bigger challenges, I always made time to be involved in politics. I've been interested in politics ever since my mother yelled at me for buying a newspaper that was thought to oppose the Baathist Party in Iraq; she feared that we might be watched by members of the government. Because I was one of the few Chaldeans who was politically active, many elected officials gave me a lot of attention.

In 1992 I was encouraged to run for public office after I resigned from my position with the city of Southfield. But I didn't feel that I would have the time necessary to devote to a campaign. My position as director of the Federation was very demanding, well outside of the nine-to-five range. In 1995, however, I decided to run for a position on the city council in Southfield. I had lived there for twenty years, ever since my family came here from Iraq, and I wanted to remain involved in local politics. Most Chaldeans are not involved in politics—maybe because in Iraq there is no respect for human rights; in fact, there are no human rights. I thought it was important for Chaldeans to see that once they come here, not only is it OK to become politically involved, it is necessary. I always support Chaldeans who run for public office so that the next generation will have more visible role models. That was one of the reasons why I decided it was the right time for me to run for public office. Many of my friends were not surprised by my decision and they all rallied behind my campaign. I was known throughout the election as the only candidate who had the support of the African American, Jewish, Asian, and Hispanic communities as well as my own Chaldean community. It was a great feeling to be accepted and respected by people who were different from me, which is something I never had while I was growing up. Despite coming in fourth out of thirteen candidates in the primary election (there were four seats up for election), I was not elected in the general election. Many of my friends believe that my chances of winning were greatly reduced when the mayor of Southfield encouraged another Chaldean, who had different opinions on many issues than mine, to run for the same office. The way I look at it, it was a great learning experience, and there is always the next time.

Around the time of my campaign I decided to ask my girlfriend of seven years to marry me. This was another case where my decision was very untraditional in the Chaldean community. While my girlfriend, Hilda, was Chaldean, she was divorced and had a daughter from her first marriage. In the Catholic Chaldean community, divorce is very rare and strongly looked down upon, and marrying a divorced person is even rarer. It may seem unusual to Americans that the fact that someone is divorced would keep you from marrying that person if you love her, but as I mentioned before, the shame factor in the Chaldean community is a very powerful force.

Throughout the Middle East, when a couple is divorced it is assumed that the wife did not satisfy the husband and that he requested the divorce. It is unheard of for a woman to be the one to request the divorce. Therefore, the thinking is that no one would want to marry a divorced woman because she has already been an inferior wife. Even though this is not the case in the United States, immigrants from the Middle East still think like they did in the old country in regards to divorced women.

When Hilda and I announced our engagement, my parents were very disappointed. They would not acknowledge that I was going to marry a divorced woman, and they did not speak to me for four months. But I expected this reaction and had purposely planned a yearlong engagement to give everyone time to get used to the idea. After four months, emotions cooled down, and my uncle Najib Jamil encouraged my parents to accept the situation. Fortunately, they decided not to remain stubborn with this issue and gave their blessing.

Even after my parents accepted my engagement to Hilda, other members of the Chaldean community pulled me aside and asked if I was sure about my decision. They felt that as a leader in the community I was condoning divorce by marrying a divorced woman. They felt that my actions were a bad example for the youth in the Chaldean community. I found myself in the position of explaining to them that here in the United States it is very likely that the divorce rate among Chaldeans will go up. Here, either person in a marriage may choose to get a divorce, not just the husband. I told them that my decision to marry a divorced woman is not going to be a poor example to the youth; instead, it would show that I am not prejudiced against anyone. If I am a leader among the youth, I want them to see that loving someone is more important than any label society has put on them.

Our wedding was a mixture of Chaldean and American customs. The typical Chaldean wedding has about six hundred guests, but Hilda and I decided to have a smaller wedding of about two hundred. We ended up with around four hundred, and many distant relatives and acquaintances are still mad at us for not being invited to the party. Most Chaldean weddings take place on Sunday because when Chaldeans first came here most of them worked in the grocery or restaurant business, and Sunday was the only day they didn't work. Now some Chaldean weddings are held on Friday or Saturday, but Sunday is still traditional. We had our reception at the Southfield

Manor, a Chaldean-owned catering hall/private club. The Southfield Manor is the pride of the Chaldean community because it is one of the most elegant banquet halls in Oakland County. Around two hundred Chaldean families raised the capital to build it, and around six hundred families are now members. This same group also owns the Shenandoah Golf Club in West Bloomfield Township, where, by 2005, a Chaldean cultural and recreational center is going to be built.

A year after Hilda and I were married, our daughter Tess was born, and on June 13, 1999, our son, Blake Michael, was born. If I knew before how happy having a family would make me, I would have done it much sooner. I was always determined to live the single life, having my freedom and happiness, but I am much happier now. My goals now revolve around raising my three children, Sindel, Tess, and Blake, to be happy and successful, like most parents presumably do.

Sometimes I think about what would have happened to me if my father hadn't decided to come to America. I wonder what my life would have been like, what other country I might be living in, or if I would have been killed in one of the two Iraqi wars. I don't know what would have become of me, but I do know that I am very lucky to have been able to come here, become an American citizen, and experience the American dream. . . . God bless America!

Egyptian Copts in Detroit

Ethnic Community and Long-Distance Nationalism

Richard R. Jones

> In an anthropological spirit, then, I propose the following definition of the nation: it is an imagined political community—and imagined as both inherently limited and sovereign.
>
> BENEDICT ANDERSON, 1991

> Not least as a result of the ethnicization of political life in the wealthy, postindustrial states, what one can call long-distance nationalism is visibly emerging.
>
> BENEDICT ANDERSON, 1994

MODERN EGYPT IS a nation in the sense meant by Anderson (1991, 6–7). It is imagined because in a country of over sixty-three million people, most citizens are really strangers to each other. It is limited because it is finite in size and geographically defined. It is sovereign because of modern Enlightenment beliefs that pose freedom and national autonomy as political ideals. And finally, Egypt is a community because members of this nation believe they are somehow connected to each other. Regardless of religious, socioeconomic, educational, and linguistic differences (particularly between the dialects of the north and south), Egyptians share the belief that they are *masri* (Egyptian) and that all *masris,* at a fundamental level, are somehow the same.

This is not to say that there is perfect political harmony in Egypt. Quite the contrary. Political tensions between the two largest religious groups in Egypt—the Copts, who are Christian, and the Sunni Muslims—have existed since the Islamic conquest in the seventh century. Until the middle part of the twentieth century, these two communities had little choice except to live close to each other in Egypt. It was not until the 1950s and 1960s that certain political and economic factors, coupled with the availability of affordable, long-distance transportation, brought about the exodus of large numbers of Copts from Egypt to Europe, the United States, Canada, and Australia.

The Copts are only one of a growing number of ethnic migrations; their case is characteristic of an emerging global phenomenon. "Recent ethnic movements," Appadurai writes, "often involve thousands, sometimes millions, of people who are spread across vast territories and often separated by vast distances . . . the new ethnonationalisms are complex, large-scale, highly coordinated acts of mobilization, reliant on news, logistical flows, and propaganda across state borders" (1993, 416). The immigration of Copts to North America has resulted in the formation of spatially dispersed communities centered around approximately eighty U.S. and Canadian churches. These churches are linked to each other and to the Coptic Orthodox Church in Egypt by personal contacts, publications, telephone lines, fax machines, and e-mail. The political situation of the Copts in Egypt is closely monitored by the North American Coptic community. Annual trips back to Egypt by clergy and church members are not uncommon. Return trips tend to reinforce the ties and community identity of expatriate Copts with family and friends in Egypt. This first generation of North American Copts has not fully assimilated to mainstream culture in North America. Instead, they emphasize, perhaps even exaggerate, their Egyptian nationalism in many ways.

What follows is a brief ethnographic account of the Copts in North America and, more specifically, of the members of St. Mark Coptic Church in Troy, Michigan. I will draw out the differences between first-generation Coptic immigrants and later generations in matters of religious practice, nationalism, and ethnic identity. First, I present the more traditional views of the older, first-generation immigrants, then I contrast them to the views of the second generation. Because the Coptic communities I explore in this essay are transnational, I begin by explaining how they achieved their far-flung arrangement in time and space, a task that demands a preliminary return to Egypt.

Background: The Copts in Egypt

The Copts are an Orthodox Christian minority in Egypt and the largest Christian minority in the Middle East.[1] The Copts trace their Christian origins to the first century, when, according to tradition,

St. Mark the Evangelist founded the first church in Alexandria. After persecutions by various Roman emperors in the second and third centuries, Christianity flourished in Egypt from the fourth to the early seventh centuries. In the seventh century, Egypt was conquered by the Arabs, and Islam became the dominant political and religious force.

Egyptian Christianity has made a lasting impact on the development of Christianity as a whole. Monasticism, for example, originated in Egypt in the late third century and was only subsequently adopted by European Christians. Also, the catechetical school of Alexandria, founded by Pantaenus in the third century, profoundly affected the art of biblical interpretation; many hermeneutic principles established there are still taught in Protestant and Catholic seminaries in the West, though many are unaware of the source. In addition, the Copts played a significant role in the formation of the early Christian creeds at the Ecumenical Councils of the fourth and fifth centuries. Finally, the preservation of ancient biblical and other related texts in Egyptian monasteries has challenged modern historians and biblical scholars with a host of new questions concerning the form and development of early Christianity.

Culturally and linguistically, the modern Copts are classified by anthropologists as Arabs, being differentiated from other Egyptians primarily on the basis of their religion. Many Copts, however, do not consider themselves Arab. For them, the term "Arab" signifies a distinct race, and modern Copts are quick to point out that they are descendants of the original Egyptians, and not of the Arabs who conquered Egypt in the seventh century. The exact number of Copts living in Egypt is not known. Population surveys are politically sensitive in Egypt, partly because of the tensions that already exist between Christians and Muslims. Modern estimates put Egypt's population at 63,575,107 (Famighetti 1996, 760). Estimates of the number of Copts in Egypt vary widely, however, depending on the source.

According to a 1976 census by the Egyptian government, there were about 2.3 million Copts in Egypt, a number challenged by the Copts, who claimed, at that time, that their numbers were over 8 million (Pennington 1982, 158). Fegley (1983, 17) says there are over 6 million Copts in Egypt. Famighetti (1996, 760) states that 94 percent of the population are Sunni Muslims; if the remainder were Coptic, they would number about 3.8 million. Hoffmeier (1988, 34) estimates about 7 million Copts in Egypt. The *New York Times* cites a figure of nearly 10 million for Egypt's Christians (Ibrahim 1993). A publication of the American, Canadian, and Australian Coptic Associations called *The Copts: Christians of Egypt* claims 11 million Copts live in Egypt (1993,

13). Which of these figures is most correct is anyone's guess. The figure of 2 million, however, cited by the Egyptian government, is much too low, as is the number 3.8 million derived from Famighetti. An estimate of 8 to 10 million Copts in contemporary Egypt, based on the above figures, seems more reasonable.

Pennington (1982, 159) reports that over 60 percent of all Copts live in Upper Egypt. About 25 percent live in Cairo and 6 percent in Alexandria. The remainder are scattered throughout the delta, various oases, and around the Suez Canal. In Upper Egypt, Copts live in villages with fairly large numbers in and around Asyut and al-Minya. The Cairene Copts are found mostly in Shobra, Abbasia, and al-Daher (Kamil 1993, 44). Most Copts are peasants, but, as a group, the Copts are proportionally overrepresented in the professions. About 80 percent of Egyptian pharmacists, 30–40 percent of Egyptian physicians, and a large number of lawyers and engineers are Copts (Pennington 1982, 159). The Copts have also had some success in national and international diplomacy. For example, the former secretary general of the United Nations, Boutros Boutros Ghali, is a Copt who is well-respected by Copts and Muslims in Egypt.

Despite Coptic achievement in the professions (or perhaps because of it), relations between Copts and Muslims in Egypt today are often strained. In recent elections, held on November 29, 1995, about four hundred seats in the People's Parliament were contested. At public speeches in some districts, I heard Muslim candidates openly criticize Coptic candidates, just for being Copts. I never heard a Coptic candidate offer similar public criticisms of a Muslim. This tendency is no doubt a function of power differentials between the two groups, rather than any graciousness on the part of the Copts. Violence did occasionally erupt at the polls, but how much of that violence could be attributed to ethnic tension is not known.

The Copts in North America

Current books and articles about the Copts—as opposed to Coptic publications intended for Coptic readers—fail to mention the large number of Copts who have left Egypt and settled elsewhere, particularly in the last thirty to forty years (Gaffney 1993, Kamil 1993, Watterson 1988). An exception is Ibrahim (1993), who claims that as many as five hundred thousand Copts, mostly professionals and businesspeople, have left Egypt because of persecution in the last ten years alone. Pennington (1982, 165) also briefly mentions Coptic immigration to the United States, Canada, and Australia.

I personally became aware of the large number of Copts in North America in 1992. Thereafter, I began to pursue my interest in the Copts in general, and North American Copts specifically, because of the lack of reliable information about them available in the West. I completed a preliminary survey of Coptic churches in North America,[2] which is part of a larger, ongoing study that involves fieldwork in Egypt as well as North America. What follows is a summary of the results of part of that study.

A Survey of North American Copts

A survey was mailed in early 1995 to eighty-four Coptic priests in the United States and Canada, who represent nearly as many congregations. Famighetti (1996, 644) reports eighty-five Coptic Orthodox churches in the United States alone, while a list provided by Father Michail, a Detroit-based Coptic priest, claims eighty-four churches for all of North America. Most Coptic churches are found in the major metropolitan areas of the United States and Canada: Detroit, New York, Los Angeles, San Francisco, San Antonio, Houston, Daytona Beach, Tampa, Pittsburgh, St. Louis, Cleveland, Seattle, Atlanta, Toronto, Vancouver, Edmonton, Ottawa, and Montreal. Eighteen priests (21 percent) responded to the survey. The low response rate was due partly to the timing of the mailing, which took place during Lent, a busy time for priests. To a lesser degree, the decision not to reply was probably due to suspicion of my motives, a perfectly understandable concern, given the political situation of Copts in Egypt.

Location, Number of Priests, and Size of Congregation

The 18 churches that responded to the survey are located in California (4), Florida (2), Louisiana (1), Michigan (1), New Jersey (2), New York (1), Ontario (2), Quebec (1), Rhode Island (1), Texas (2), and Wisconsin (1).[3] The only large region of North America not represented in the survey response is the Pacific Northwest, including central and western Canada. Also, to the best of my knowledge, there are no Coptic churches in Mexico. The smallest respondent church, one in San Antonio, Texas, reported 16 families as members. The largest church, one in New Jersey, reported 1,000 families. The remaining churches reported congregation size either as families or as the number of individuals. The reported figures ranged from 18 to 800 families and 117 to 3200 individuals.

Churches with only one priest usually have fewer than six hundred members. Congregations with two priests tend to have more than six hundred members. One church, reporting three priests, has a congregation of eight hundred families and as many as thirty-two hundred members. These numbers provide a rough idea of the ratio of priests to members. The workload for Coptic priests is enormous. In addition to the daily demands of the liturgy (holy communion), priests are engaged in counseling and visiting the sick and in leading special prayers, weddings, and funerals. They are also the chief administrators of their churches, and most are active in their local Christian education programs, which usually involves teaching at least twice a week. The period from Christmas (January 7) to Easter is particularly busy for priests because of the many ritual and social obligations associated with the season.

Founding Dates and Members' Occupations

Of the eighteen respondent churches, eleven said their first members came to North America in the 1960s. The earliest date given was in the 1940s (St. Mary Coptic Orthodox Church, Pompano Beach, Fla.) and the most recent was 1974 (St. Antony and St. Abanoub Coptic Orthodox Church, Corona, Calif.). Note that Nasser ruled Egypt from 1954 until his death in 1970. During the Nasser years, land reform, and the nationalization of businesses in particular, adversely affected many wealthy Coptic families (Pennington 1982, 164). These were undoubtedly the major factors that encouraged their emigration. Indeed, many Copts I have spoken to have cited Nasser's land reform and nationalization programs as their primary reasons for leaving Egypt.

The survey results show that the majority of North American Copts are professionals: physicians, pharmacists, engineers, middle managers, and small-business owners. North America has benefited greatly from this influx of professionals. Egypt, on the other hand, has lost an equal number of talented, educated specialists. Professional skills give Coptic immigrants a number of economic advantages not yet available to other Arab groups who have immigrated to North America, and these economic advantages have important implications for how Coptic communities in North America are now taking shape.

Community among American Copts

Unlike ethnic communities that concentrate spatially in one small area, such as the Arab community in Dearborn, Michigan, the North

American Copts tend to be spread out. Most live farther than a fifteen-minute drive from their church. Nonetheless, the church remains the social center of even the most dispersed Coptic communities. Most social interaction between members occurs there, especially at significant events such as weddings and funerals where attendance involves large numbers of community members. The weekly liturgy in Coptic churches is nearly always well attended. After the liturgy, a large portion of the congregation gathers for a common meal in an area of the church built expressly for that purpose. Most people linger for several hours after the liturgy to visit with each other. At special holidays like Christmas and Easter, there are added opportunities for people to come to church and spend time together. A great deal of social and business networking—though frowned upon by some Copts—is accomplished at these after-church gatherings.

The spatially diffuse nature of Coptic communities in North America is primarily due to the professional status of the immigrants and the economic advantages associated with those abilities. Unlike other Arab groups that have immigrated to Detroit, there has been no need for the Copts to settle near each other for mutual economic support. Neither has there been a need for the Copts to form community organizations, such as the Arab Community Center for Economic and Social Services (ACCESS) in Dearborn. ACCESS was formed in response to stress on Arab families caused, in part, by the fluctuating unemployment rate of the auto industry, in which many Arab immigrants to Detroit were employed (Aswad and Gray 1996, 223). Because most immigrant Copts are professionals, they have not been subject to the economic stresses experienced by Middle Eastern immigrants who own small businesses or belong to the working class. Consequently, Coptic participation in ACCESS (and Detroit's several Arab American business and political associations) is almost nonexistent.

Some Coptic communities have a large number of members who live nearly one hundred miles from the church. At the St. Mark Coptic Orthodox Church in Troy, many members drive in on the weekend from northern Ohio (a two-hour drive) to attend the liturgy. One consequence of belonging to such a diffuse community is that nearly all face-to-face communication with Copts who are not members of one's own household occurs within the context of the church, a pattern that constantly reinforces Coptic ethnic identity. I have as yet met no Copts, even among monolingual English speakers born in the United States, who are not proud of their ethnicity.

Members of a particular Coptic church in North America often come from villages and cities all over Egypt, and the solidarity that binds their congregation is based more on a shared identity as Copts than on any actual kin or village affiliation prior to migration. Importantly, the fact that traditional kinship and communal obligations are radically diminished among Coptic communities in North America has probably contributed significantly to the rapid, though by no means complete, cultural assimilation of second-generation Copts. At least in Detroit, young Copts appear to be entering the American mainstream at a rate (and with an ease) rarely seen among the children of new Lebanese, Iraqi, Palestinian, or Yemeni immigrants. Moreover, although most Copts prefer that their sons and daughters marry other Copts, there are frequent marriages between Coptic immigrants' children and non-Copts. Conversion of the non-Coptic spouse is encouraged, but not always accomplished.

Copts in Greater Detroit: St. Mark Coptic Orthodox Church

In 1992 when I was working as the night manager of a grocery store and attending graduate school by day, I met a customer who, it turned out, was a Copt. At that time, I had not expected to meet a Copt outside Egypt and was unaware of the extensive and ongoing Coptic immigration to North America. This person graciously provided me with the name, address, and phone number of her priest, whom I called and made arrangements to visit the following week. Abouna (literally "Our Father") Roufail Michail met me at the St. Mark Coptic Orthodox Church, where he is the archpriest. From that first encounter until now, Abouna Roufail has always patiently and politely guided me to an understanding of what it means to be a Copt in America. I am personally and professionally indebted to him for much of what I know about Coptic belief and practice. Abouna Roufail is aided in his work by another priest, Abouna Mina Essak, who has also been very kind and helpful to me in my work.

Abouna Roufail's hospitality is typical of most Coptic priests I have met in and out of Egypt. Indeed, such hospitality is typical of most Egyptians. Abouna Roufail is a short man. He has the long grayish white beard characteristic of older priests, wears a traditional black robe, and frequently carries a hand-sized Coptic cross as he goes about his business. For the celebration of the liturgy, he puts on a simple and elegant hooded white robe. His appearance and dress distinguish him from everyone else. No Egyptian would ever mistake him for anything other than what he is: a Coptic priest.

Fig. 11. Abouna Roufail Michail of St. Mark Coptic Orthodox Church in Troy. Courtesy of Richard Jones.

Abouna Roufail and Abouna Mina are much respected and loved in their church. They preside over the social and religious center of the Coptic community in Troy. Without priests, there could be no celebration of the liturgy, no marriage, no baptism, no confirmation, no penance, no unction of the sick, and no holy orders, all of which are sacraments of the church and must be administered by an ordained priest. Priests are crucial to the practice of Coptic religious belief and to the maintenance of the religious community.

The first members of what would become St. Mark Coptic Orthodox Church came to Michigan before 1963, though Abouna Roufail does not know their names. Dr. Samir Ragheb, a physician who immigrated to the United States before Nasser came to power in Egypt, remembers a priest coming from Toronto about once a month to perform the liturgy in people's homes prior to 1967. The first official priest for the congregation was Abouna Mikhail Melika, who served from 1967 to 1977. Abouna Mikhail negotiated the purchase of land and helped in the early planning of church construction. Abouna Roufail came to the Troy congregation in 1977, when Abouna Mikhail returned to Egypt. Construction of the church began on May 1, 1977, when Pope Shenouda III laid the cornerstone, and it was completed in May 1979. Holy communion was celebrated there for the first time on May 8, 1979, on the Feast of St. Mark the Evangelist. Finally, the rite of consecration for the church was performed on June 12–14, 1981, by

Anba Antonious Markos, bishop of African affairs as special envoy of his Holiness Pope Shenouda III.

The church building is located at 3603 Livernois in Troy, an affluent suburb of Detroit. It is laid out in the shape of a cross, with the altar at the eastern end of the church. The church is decorated with several striking stained-glass windows and a number of beautifully executed icons that hang on the iconostasis[4] and that are painted in characteristic Egyptian style. The wooden iconostasis itself is engraved with crosses that fill open spaces around the icons. St. Mark Coptic Orthodox Church is virtually indistinguishable, inside, from many Coptic churches I have visited in Egypt. There are even two ostrich eggs hanging over the central door of the iconostasis.[5] Similar eggs are found in virtually every Coptic church in Egypt and are typical only of Coptic churches.

The church and the priests stand at the symbolic center of the Detroit Coptic community, but they are also located at one end of a continuum of difference between the older and younger generations in North America and at the intersection of a complex set of mediations and representations that shape the Copts as an imagined community. The church and the symbols and behaviors associated with it are raw materials from which the Copts, both first and second generation, construct much of their ethnic identity.

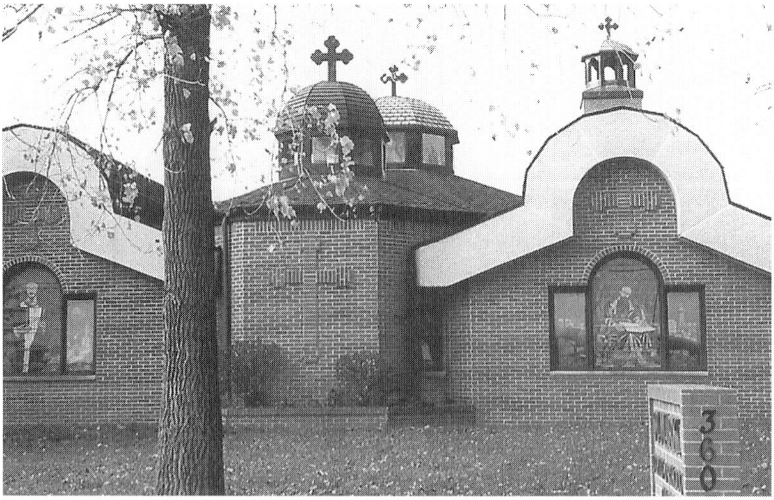

Fig. 12. St. Mark Coptic Orthodox Church. Courtesy of Richard Jones.

Consequently, one might expect that things would be most "Coptic" in the church itself. The reality is otherwise. Just as the Irish in Boston are quite different from the Irish in Belfast, so, too, are Detroit's Copts different from the Copts of Egypt. Nowhere is this distinction seen more clearly than in the liturgy.

The Coptic liturgy as performed in North America is unique in its use of three languages—Coptic, Arabic, and English—with minor borrowings from a fourth language, Greek. The liturgy is a stylized, dynamic discourse between three persons or groups: the priest, the deacons, and the people. The priest officiating at the liturgy sets the pattern of code switching. The deacons and the people must respond in whatever language the priest uses. In Egypt, English is not used in the liturgy. The use of English is a significant adaptation to the developing needs of the Coptic Orthodox Church in North America. It is a necessary change brought about by the increasing number of monolingual English speakers in the congregation. Many traditional hymns and Scripture verses, once sung and chanted only in Arabic, are now sung and chanted in English. The sermon is now also delivered in English.[6]

Other differences between Egypt and North America include how social space is constructed and how people dress. In Egypt, men sit on one side of the church, women on the other. At St. Mark Coptic Orthodox Church, men and women sit together, but communion is still segregated. Men receive communion on the north side of the altar and women on the south side. Also, the churches in North America have nurseries and large parking lots, which churches in Egypt typically lack. Additionally, in contrast to the clothing worn by the priest and deacons, which is essentially the same here and in Egypt, the laypeople dress very differently than do their counterparts in Egypt. Older Coptic women in Egypt frequently wear traditional black garments, while younger women dress modestly in ankle-length skirts and long-sleeved blouses. Both cover their hair in church. At St. Mark's, by contrast, women typically dress in Western fashion, with skirt and sleeve lengths that, although modest by American standards, would seem inappropriate in Egypt. Few women cover their hair, and I have never seen any of the older women at St. Mark's wearing the traditional black dress.

Clearly, the North American Coptic Church is something other than the Egyptian church, but in certain respects it is even more Coptic. Abouna Roufail Michail can be a Coptic priest in Greater Detroit in ways he cannot be a Coptic priest in Egypt. In Troy, he has the freedom to openly display and talk about his ethnicity proudly.

In fact, there is an almost exaggerated sense of being Coptic in the St. Mark Coptic Orthodox Church compared to most Coptic churches I have visited in Egypt. I have noted a similarly exaggerated style of ethnic expression in Egyptian monasteries. Egyptian monks are the quintessential embodiment of Egyptian Christianity and, perhaps, the most Coptic of Copts.

Besides the overt religious significance, the symbols and rituals of the liturgy serve to communicate the solidarity of the group to the individual. The costuming, the ceremonial movements around the altar, the icons, the incense, the colored light, the hypnotic rhythm of the percussion instruments, the hymns, and the chanting are all elaborately coordinated in the Coptic liturgy. Everything works together to instill in the participant a mystical mood that builds slowly and reaches its emotional peak at the time of communion. The ethnic identity of the Copts in St. Mark Coptic Orthodox Church is built around these exported cultural artifacts of symbol, ritual, and belief that are kept alive in the regular performance of the liturgy.

The liturgy itself is divided into twenty-five parts, and communicants stand for most of the three to five hours of its delivery. Some parts of the liturgy have remained essentially unchanged since the fourth century. The Coptic Orthodox liturgy is arguably the most elaborate and most ancient of all the Orthodox Christian liturgies; as a whole, it is an awe-inspiring experience. The St. Mark Coptic Orthodox Church does welcome visitors, and the friendliness of the people and the experience of the liturgy are well worth the visit. Its liturgy should not be seen, however, as an exotic display of historical and religious curiosities. The St. Mark Coptic Orthodox Church is the locus of the cultural patterns that structure Coptic ethnic identity.

Long-Distance Nationalism and First-Generation Immigrants

An appreciation of and desire for the pure traditions of the church, the use of the Coptic and Arabic languages, and the communal interaction centered on the church are of crucial importance to the first generation of North American Copts. The adaptation of some traditions to life in North America and the decreasing use of Coptic and Arabic in the liturgy are viewed with alarm by many. In addition, first-generation Copts in North America have a political interest and awareness of events in Egypt that is exhibited to a lesser degree—or not at all—in the second and third generations. The long-distance nationalism of the first generation manifests itself in various publications and organizations.

In Egypt there are several newspapers and other publications that, in one way or another, promote Coptic nationalism and other Coptic interests. Most notable among them, perhaps, is *al-Watan*. The content of these publications is highly constrained, in a political sense, because the press is controlled by the Egyptian government. Nothing in the native publications even comes close to the nationalism expressed in North American Coptic publications. A periodical called *The Copts: Christians of Egypt* (American, Canadian, and Australian Coptic Associations 1993) contains a number of articles that illustrate the heightened nationalism felt by Copts outside Egypt and that serve as a forum for Coptic political views on human rights and religious issues.[7] An editorial titled "Looking Closely at Human Rights" examines the persecution of Copts in Paris, Lebanon, and the United States and focuses on three Copts imprisoned in Egypt. Another article discusses the rights of non-Muslims in an Islamic state. Still another cites verses from the Quran to support the view that Muslim Scripture encourages discrimination and violence toward religions other than Islam. The publication is highly critical of the Egyptian government and argues for significant political and social reform. The same publication also records a meeting of the Assyrian National Congress, the American Coptic Associations, and the World Lebanese Organization on June 26, 1992, which examined U.S. foreign policy toward the three represented ethnic nationalities and "other repressed non-Arab people in the Middle East" (American, Canadian, and Australian Coptic Associations 1993, 17).

While in Egypt, I observed that Copts and Muslims alike, when asked, uniformly insisted that they were Arabs.[8] It is interesting that in the West at least some members of the Coptic immigrant community are beginning to think of themselves as "non-Arab," yet continue to believe they are Egyptian. The new ethnic and communal identity (American Copt? Coptic American?) formed after immigration is what I believe Appadurai means by a transnation: "For every nation-state that has exported significant numbers of its populations to the United States as refugees, tourists, or students, there is now a delocalized transnation, which retains a special ideological link to a putative place of origin but is otherwise a thoroughly diasporic collectivity" (1993, 424).

Some of the most ardent Copts I know are sons of the immigrants who came to North America in the 1960s and 1970s. Most speak and read little or no Arabic and have only the vaguest notions of what life in Egypt today is really like. In spite of that, they are staunch defenders of an ethnic identity they feel is strongly connected to Egypt. Most are active to some degree in their churches. Though they share the strong nationalism of their parents, they are not culturally connected to Egypt in the same way as their parents. The spirit of their peculiar brand of Coptic long-distance nationalism can be seen in the following passage:

> But act we must! We cannot let our brothers and sisters suffer in isolation while we enjoy our freedom. I am thankful to all of you who responded to my appeal [for the release from prison of three recent converts to Christianity in Egypt]. . . . Thousands of letters were mailed to the Egyptian Embassy. Hundreds wrote to congressmen and senators. The result was an unprecedented success in putting pressure on the Egyptian government to release these three courageous men. You will have other opportunities in this and future issues to help our suffering brethren. (American, Canadian, and Australian Associations 1993, 2)

The recently formulated long-distance nationalism of the Copts in North America is openly hostile (if only in words) toward militant Islamists and the current Egyptian government alike. A full-page ad addressed to Hosni Mubarak, placed in the February 13, 1998 edition of the *New York Times,* condemns Muslim extremists for the recent murders of native Copts and international tourists.[9] The ad says, "Mr. President, this persecution has been happening under your watch," and "Your silence makes you an accomplice to these crimes." Not all expatriate Copts would openly express such dissent or place a significant portion of the blame for Coptic persecution on Hosni Mubarak, though a large number of people in the older generation would. In Egypt, radical sentiments are normally muted by the constant public assurances by both Copt and Muslim leaders that both groups share a common national identity. Coptic-Islamic relations have become politically polarized, however, in the expatriate Coptic community, because the expat community does not have to fear retaliation from the government or other factions in Egypt.

A key historical event that solidified long-distance nationalism and political activism among expatriate Copts was Anwar Sadat's 1981 exile and imprisonment of Pope Shenouda III, patriarch of the Coptic Orthodox Church. The Pope was banished to a monastery in Wadi Natrun and several bishops and priests were arrested (Hirst and Beeson 1981, 334). Pope Shenouda was an outspoken critic of Egyptian government policies toward the Coptic Church, and he often voiced his criticisms in the United States media (Lippman 1989, 239). His arrest came after a number of violent internal conflicts between Copts and Muslims that began much earlier—in November 1972 in Khanka[10]—and led over the next ten years to increasing tensions between the two groups. Pope Shenouda was freed from house arrest by Hosni Mubarak in 1985.

North American Copts old enough to remember these events were outraged. Dr. Ragheb, an early member of the expatriate community in Troy, says that the imprisonment of Pope Shenouda III "brought people together." During that time, Copts in North America organized to put political pressure on the American government to do something about the persecution of the Copts in Egypt. The organizations formed then are still active in trying to influence the American government concerning these issues. Coptic organizations continue to protest the too-frequent murders, imprisonments, and acts of discrimination that mark Coptic life in Egypt today. In short, and as an expression of the long-distance nationalism shared by many Copts in North America, Dr. Ragheb said that, "American-Copts have never lost interest in Egypt."

The transition from a first-generation traditional Coptic immigrant community to a transnational community is also playing itself out in the church. The increasing use of English in worship, new ways of using the church as a space, and other significant cultural shifts have left many of the early immigrants feeling out of place. Dr. Ragheb poignantly expresses this sense of alienation when he notes that "the church is evolving. . . . I feel at home any where I go [in America]. . . . The only place I do not feel at home is in the church."

The Second Generation: A Coptic View

The second generation of Coptic Americans is wrestling with identity issues alien to their parents. Unlike their parents, most of whom came to America already married or promised in marriage, the second generation is confronted with a relatively small pool of potential Copts for marriage and an acute awareness of American values about freedom of marital choice. Second-generation Copts also tend to know little or no Arabic. As children, they interact intensively with people from other ethnic groups, a pattern that contrasts starkly to the childhood experience of their parents. The dissonance created at the interface of the Egyptian and American value systems is causing second-generation Coptic Americans to develop attitudes and beliefs that oppose the convictions of their parents but, at the same time, strongly affirm a Coptic identity.

Stephen Wassef, a young Copt from St. Mark Coptic Orthodox Church, and one of my former students, is typical of this emerging Coptic American identity. His father, a mechanical engineer, and his mother, who works in real estate, came to America from al-Minya in 1968. Stephen is the youngest of three brothers and works as the supervisor of a computer lab. He is conversant in the colloquial Egyptian Arabic spoken in his parent's home. He has been to Egypt, but not for any extended period of time. Stephen explains what it means to him to be a Copt in America: "Well, the advantage that I've had being Coptic is that I'm not the only one. I'm amongst a bunch of people in my church who all have the same exact cultural viewpoint. You have a certain culture you are brought up in . . . we as a group seem to have a standard set of morals and attributes that we all share and we try to reflect them in the community outside the church." But unlike in Egypt, where being a Copt is closely identified with being Egyptian,[11] Stephen's generation extends that view to include an awareness of ethnicity and minority/majority status:

> The Copts are a subset of the Egyptian population. The Egyptian population's mainly composed of Muslims. So, when you say you're Egyptian, people assume you are from the land of the pyramids and a Muslim. So, they're wrong on their assumption, 'cause I'm in the minority. I am a minority amongst a minority. Egyptians in the United States are a minority to begin with, and I am a subset of that. . . . You feel unique, which is kind of nice. And you can be a minority here, as opposed to Egypt.

Stephen also points out that Copts themselves are acutely aware of the generational differences: "The Coptic church is worried, actually, that the new generation is not picking up the old traditions . . . [like] making sure that they all know Coptic. For instance, I don't know Coptic. That's a terrible, terrible thing. I just haven't sat down and learned it. I also don't know Arabic."[12] He is also aware of differences between importance of the church in Egypt as compared to the United States: "In Egypt, your life revolves around the church. As for America, your life revolves around your job and other things. . . . You're not as close to the, at least me personally, I'll say this for myself, I can't say it for everybody, I'm not as tied into the church as I probably would be in Egypt." Another factor contributing to the generational differences is that many Coptic Americans, both male and female, are marrying non-Copts, which, as Stephen relates, poses a problem for the clergy:

> The Bishop . . . Anba Antonius Markos . . . was saying at a convention that I went to, the Midwest Coptic Orthodox Youth Convention, that happens in some of the colleges around here . . . he was frowning upon it. He said we should . . . intramarry, marry within our own culture, to bring up our kids the right way. Obviously, we didn't buy into that because we should be able to marry who we want and bring people into our church, which was brought up in the convention . . . by a guy who brought his American girlfriend. But the Bishop's view, or the way I interpreted it at least, was that we . . . should use our own resources to multiply and make people that are all the same as us so that we don't deviate from the correct path. . . . It would be easier to keep the same traditions and values, if you come from a similar background.

From talking to Stephen Wassef and other young Copts, it seems clear to me that the Coptic experience of the younger generation is markedly different from the experience of their parents. Marriage, as a traditional ethnic boundary, is being crossed more and more frequently, though the preponderance of marriages are still between Copts. The church, so important to the older generation, is less so to many in the second generation. In addition, Arabic has been almost entirely displaced by English in the second generation. Finally, the second generation is, in many ways, bicultural, manifesting a repertoire of behavior that encompasses the norms and values of both traditional Copts and Americans.

As for the future, Stephen Wassef's ideas about how he might raise children underscores the bicultural view held by many second-generation Coptic Americans:

> I'll take them to church. There's no question. . . . I will not make them go to church. I will encourage it, because I think it's a good thing to do from a social standpoint. I will tell them they need some kind of religious background. I will not try to brainwash them and tell them that we are right, we are the only people that are right, and nobody else is right but us, [laughs] and anybody else that tells you anything different is wrong, and you should be totally closed minded, and so forth. No. Keep an open mind. If you have any problems, don't understand something, come to me, you know, and talk about it. . . . It's not a one-way transfer of information. . . . You're supposed to be able to discuss . . . what you feel is right or wrong with the thing [the Coptic Orthodox Church]. You can't

> change it. Don't think that you're going to change it, but we're not going to force-feed you. That's my personal thing, and I was never force-fed.

Surprisingly, the Arabic language is not considered an important part of the cultural tradition:

> I learned it by force. . . . I learned it because my parents told me to get stuff. Get the onions from the garage, for instance. So, I'd get them a tomato. Then, I'd get them a green pepper. I'd finally get an onion. So, I learned onion. . . . I'd pick up the language one word at a time. . . . I apply it by being a translator. . . . [Will you teach your kids Arabic?] Absolutely not. I have no reason to make that a requirement. If they want, they can learn it. . . . I'm not going to use that with my wife, as long as she speaks English—99.99 percent chance she's going to speak English. I want to marry somebody like myself, an American-Egyptian, who was brought up in the same kind of cultural background. . . . That would be my preference. Somebody who has the same experience as I.

For Coptic Americans like Stephen Wassef, group identity is tied to traditions that are spatially, temporally, culturally, and linguistically different from their everyday experience of life in the United States. The culture of Stephen's parents is not quite his own, and the Coptic culture his children will create promises to be something quite different as well. What makes this situation unique—because it is a trivial truth that culture indeed changes through time—is that the construction of cultural identity for the North American Copts in each generation draws upon two cultural sources: Egypt and America. Coptic Americans, to extend Anderson's analogy (1994, 315), are non-Egyptian Egyptians. That is, many are Egyptians who have never been to Egypt, never seen the Nile, do not speak Arabic, and are not citizens of Egypt. Yet in spite of assimilation to and syncretism with American culture, Coptic identity remains linked to the notion of being Egyptian. The long-distance nationalism of the older expatriate Copts, along with the presence of the Coptic Orthodox Church and its links to contemporary Egypt, serves to maintain the idea that Copts in Greater Detroit are both Egyptian and Copt.

Conclusions

The Copts are now a well-established and growing ethnic community in North America. Their immigration has been so successful, in fact, that it has gone virtually unnoticed. Although the number of Copts coming to North America has decreased in the post-Nasser era, migration to North America continues. In addition, the population of the North American Coptic community is increasing naturally, primarily through the birth of children who are baptized into the church as infants, and to a much lesser degree through the conversion of non-Coptic spouses. As their community grows, Copts may soon begin to have a significant impact on official policies related to Egypt (and the treatment of religious minorities in the Middle East generally) as these are formulated in the United States and Canada. Indeed, the North American Coptic community could grow very quickly if political conditions for Copts in Egypt deteriorate in the future, a development that would, without a doubt, bring a new and accelerated wave of immigration.

The long-distance nationalism of the North American Copts, associated mostly with the older generation, is still too new to assess its full implications. It is possible that intermarriage and assimilation by the second generation will totally replace any sense of Egyptian nationalism with the nationalism of the United States or Canada. On the other hand, it is also possible that Coptic nationalism will express itself in militant ways, similar to what we observe among some other immigrant groups, though I personally (and optimistically) do not think this will be the case with the Copts. The political pressure expatriate Copts bring to bear on the Egyptian government, via the international press and by lobbying foreign governments, often results in oppression and reprisals directed at Copts in Egypt. Consequently, long-distance nationalism has politically polarized migrant and native communities alike. I have often heard Copts in Egypt express their desire for politically active Copts living abroad to mind their own business, viewing them largely as meddlers and troublemakers. In general, the view of Egyptian Copts toward foreign Coptic communities is negative, much in the way the Irish in Ireland voice negative opinions about the politically active children of Irish immigrants in the United States.

Whatever the future holds for Copts in Egypt, the members of St. Mark Coptic Orthodox Church in Troy find themselves in the midst of tremendous social change, a predicament they share with Coptic groups throughout North America. At present, the Detroit community is a blend of very traditional Egyptian culture and a new syncretism between Egyptian and American norms and values. Continued immigration serves to balance, to some degree, the traditional with the new. The most significant (and somewhat ambiguous) difference between immigrant parents and their children concerning long-distance nationalism, despite the Coptic-centered identity both generations share, is best summed up by Stephen Wassef's response to my question, "Do you care about what goes on in Egypt?"

He answered, "Not anymore."

ACKNOWLEDGMENTS: Thanks to Abouna Roufail Michail of St. Mark Coptic Orthodox Church in Troy for providing names and addresses of priests in North America and for his inexhaustible patience in answering my questions. Thanks to all the Coptic priests who participated in the survey. Special thanks to Stephen Wassef and Dr. Samir Ragheb for sharing their personal views and concerns. Thanks to the editors of this volume for patient reading and insightful criticism. Finally, thanks to Frances Trix at Wayne State University for her assistance in designing the survey and for her invaluable instruction, help, and constructive criticism of my work. Any errors in the text are solely my own.

NOTES

1. Ethiopia, Sudan, and Eritrea also have large numbers of Orthodox Christians, also referred to as "Coptic," who are historically linked to the Coptic Orthodox Church of Egypt.
2. Abouna Roufail Michail at the St. Mark Coptic Orthodox Church in Troy provided me with the names and addresses of priests and churches in North America and advised me about survey questions. In addition, Frances Trix at Wayne State University helped with the overall research design.
3. Coptic churches are found in the following states, provinces, and islands (the number in parentheses indicates priests in each area): Mass.(1), R.I. (1), Conn. (1), N.J. (8), N.Y. (9), Pa. (2), Va. (1), N.C. (1), Ga. (1), Fla. (5), Ohio (2), Mich. (2), Wis. (1), Minn. (1), Ill. (2), Mo. (1), La. (1), Tex. (5), Calif. (20), Wash. (1), Ontario (11), Quebec (4), Alberta (2), Bermuda (1), and West Indies (1).
4. The iconostasis is a wooden screen that separates the altar from the sanctuary. It is usually decorated with carvings of crosses, and various icons are displayed on it.
5. Ostrich eggs symbolize the watchfulness we should have over our salvation. Just as the ostrich watches over its eggs, so too should we watch carefully over our salvation.

6. At St. Mark Coptic Orthodox Church in Troy, an early liturgy is still performed wholly in Arabic and Coptic. The later liturgy is as described.
7. The articles are printed in both English and Arabic.
8. I was in Egypt from 1995 to 1996 as a Fulbright scholar studying Coptic monasticism. My doctoral dissertation, An Ethnohistory of Coptic Monasticism (1997), was a product of that research.
9. The ad was sponsored by the "Coptic Organizations Worldwide." The phone and fax numbers of Mounir Bishay, Alphonse Kelada, Dr. Helmy Guirguis, and Dr. Selim Naguib are printed at the bottom of the ad.
10. A Coptic place of worship, not yet officially a church, was burned, apparently by Molotov cocktails thrown by Muslims opposed to the site becoming a church. On November 12, about one hundred Coptic clergy and three hundred Coptic laypeople came to the site and celebrated the liturgy in protest of the burning. For details see the extract from *al-Ahram,* translated by Joseph P. O'Kane, in CEMAM Reports.
11. Wakin records that many Copts believe they are the first Egyptians (1963, 3), a sentiment I have also found among many contemporary Copts in and out of Egypt.
12. Stephen Wassef's reference is to the more formal written Arabic and Arabic script. The written dialect, called Modern Standard Arabic, is substantially different from the spoken.

REFERENCES

American, Canadian, and Australian Coptic Associations. 1993. *The Copts: Christians of Egypt* 20 (1–2).

Anderson, Benedict. 1991 *Imagined Communities.* New York: Verso.

———. 1994. Exodus. *Critical Inquiry* 20:314–27.

Appadurai, Arjun. 1993. Patriotism and Its Futures. *Public Culture* 5 (3):411–29.

Aswad, Barbara. 1974. The Southeast Dearborn Arab Community Struggles for Survival against Urban "Renewal." In *Arabic Speaking Communities in American Cities,* edited by Barbara Aswad, 53–83. New York: Center for Migration Studies and the Association of Arab-American University Graduates.

Aswad, Barbara, and Nancy Adadow Gray. 1996. Challenges to the Arab-American family and ACCESS. In *Family and Gender among American Muslims: Issues Facing Middle Eastern Immigrants and Their Descendants,* edited by Barbara Aswad and Barbara Bilgé, 223–40. Philadelphia: Temple University Press.

Center for the Study of the Modern Arab World. 1976. *Tensions in Middle East Society.* CEMAM Reports, vol. 1: 1972–73. Translated by Joseph P. O'Kane. Beirut: Dar el-Mashreq.

Famighetti, Robert, ed. 1996. *The World Almanac and Book of Facts: 1997.* Mahwah, N.J.: K–III Reference Corporation.

Fegley, Randall. 1983. The Plight of the Copts. *Commonweal,* January 14, 17–19.

Gaffney, James. 1993. Among the Copts. *America,* October 9, 15–16.

Hirst, David, and Irene Beeson. 1981. *Sadat.* London: Faber and Faber.

Hoffmeier, J. K., et al. 1988. The Church in Egypt: Confessing Christ in the Heart of Islam. *Christianity Today,* June, 25–39.

Ibrahim, Youssef M. 1993. Muslims' Fury Is Falling on Egypt's Christians. *New York Times,* March 15.

Jones, Richard R. 1997. An Ethnohistory of Coptic Monasticism. Ph.D. diss., Wayne State University.

Kamil, Jill. 1993. *Coptic Egypt: History and Guide.* Cairo: American University of Cairo Press.

Lippman, Thomas W. 1989. *Egypt after Nasser: Sadat, Peace and the Mirage of Prosperity.* Paragon House Publishers.

Pennington, J. D. 1982. The Copts in Modern Egypt. *Middle Eastern Studies* 18 (2):158–79.

Wakin, Edward. 1963. *A Lonely Minority: The Modern Story of Egypt's Copts.* New York: William Morrow.

Watterson, Barbara. 1988. *Coptic Egypt.* Edinburgh: Scottish Academic Press.

Finding the Straight Path

A Conversation with Mohsen and Lila Amen about Faith, Life, and Family in Dearborn

Sally Howell

DEARBORN, MICHIGAN, IS home to roughly twenty-five thousand Lebanese Americans. This population forms the nucleus of what is perhaps North America's largest, most highly concentrated Arab-Muslim community. As of 1998, there were at least eight mosques in the Dearborn area. These mosques are attended by Shia as well as Sunni Muslims, by third-generation Arab Americans as well as recently arrived immigrants. In this interview, Lila and Mohsen Amen discuss the history of one of the most influential Dearborn mosques: the Islamic Institute of Knowledge, a Shia congregation located on Schaefer Road in the heart of the Lebanese business district.

The Islamic Institute was founded by immigrants from the south of Lebanon whose political and religious thought had been shaped by violent upheavals in the Middle East. At the height of the Lebanese civil war, the Iranian revolution of 1979 radicalized a large portion of the Lebanese Shia population. The Israeli invasions of Lebanon in 1978 and 1982, and the continuing Israeli occupation of south Lebanon, forced many Lebanese to flee the countryside. Those who had relatives in America came to Detroit, if they could. This large, newly arrived, and politically brutalized immigrant community built the Islamic Institute in 1984. They continue to establish new mosques and have now begun to build their own private schools as well.

Among Arab Americans nationally, Dearborn's working-class, highly conservative Muslim community has come to stand for Arab Detroit as a whole. Well aware of their reputation among other Arabs in Detroit and beyond, the Amens agreed to speak with me in order to document the social and political thought of the Lebanese Shia community. Rarely are Shia presented in any but the most imagistic and flagrantly politicized terms. In the American (and even the Lebanese) media, Shia wear martyrs' headbands, march in mass demonstrations shouting *Allahu Akbar* (God is Great), wave the flag of the Iranian revolution, and resist the Israeli occupation of south Lebanon with *katushya* rockets and *kalishnikov* rifles. This interview was recorded in hopes of presenting a counterimage.

I interviewed Lila and Mohsen Amen for this volume because I wanted to skirt the official, and always somewhat guarded, pronouncements of the mosque's spiritual leaders. I knew that Lila was heavily involved in the Islamic Institute as a volunteer, teacher, and family activist. Mohsen, likewise, is a board member, cofounder, and youth leader. A discussion with them, I thought, would offer a glimpse of the everyday life of the mosque. We spoke together at the Detroit Historical Museum on March 29, 1998 under circumstances that were less than ideal. We were rushed for time and did not have the opportunity to explore in depth many of the topics we discussed. I was delighted, however, to interview the Amens together. Their different perspectives on the individual, family, and community events that have shaped the last twenty years of their lives represent far more than their own points of view. Lila was born in Dearborn into a well-established Lebanese working-class family. Mohsen was born in the south of Lebanon and came to America in 1970. Their marriage is cross-cultural. It brings together two noticeably different, but intimately related ways of thinking. In this respect, the Amen family is a microcosm of Arab Detroit, where immigrants and the American-born work, organize, worship, and frequently marry among each other. Their differences of opinion are deep and ever-present, but the Amen case is clearly one in which cultural disagreements have strengthened, rather than weakened, individual notions of Islamic faith and practice.

Mohsen and Lila speak in powerful language of their separate conversion experiences. Mohsen's came as a sudden and overwhelming reaffirmation of his rootedness in the Lebanese Shia community. Lila's awakening to Islam was a more gradual reaction to Mohsen's new commitment and an attempt to overcome, with the help of God, a series of personal crises she faced during those years. The Amens discuss the challenge of raising a devout, observant family in contemporary America, a topic that will be familiar to Americans of almost any religious persuasion. They discuss the movement of their "radical" Muslim community toward mainstream social and political engagement. They describe the mundane and extraordinary activities of the Islamic Institute: ongoing fund-raising efforts, plans to build a religious school, the development of youth programs, the details of their religious obligations. They share the story of their courtship, marriage, and family history. Much of this interview will confound commonly held assumptions about the submissive role of women in Arab family life and American working-class homes. But more important than this, our exchange gives Mohsen and Lila a rare chance to present their ideas, and those of their community, directly to Arab and American readers. I have edited the interview only for length and clarity of style; in all other matters, I remain as faithful as possible to the finely articulated voices and dialects of Lila and Mohsen Amen.

SALLY: Why don't you start by telling me who you are and giving me a little bit of your personal history.

LILA: My name is Lila Amen, and I was born and raised in Dearborn, Michigan. I've been married for twenty-three years to Hajj Mohsen al-Amen, and I've got four children, Suehaila, nineteen, Shadia, eighteen, Bilal, sixteen, and Samira, who is going on fifteen. They're a product of the Dearborn public schools, where I'm currently working as a Public School Community Liaison for the Bilingual and Compensatory Education Program.

SALLY: Tell me about your family background. Where is your family from? What neighborhood did you grow up in . . .

LILA: Mom and Dad both came from Lebanon fifty years ago, around 1948. I was raised, in the first years of my life, on Roulo and Amazon Streets in Dearborn's Southend, and later on Evergreen in Detroit. Dad bought a combination house and store in Detroit, which Mom ran while raising us kids. We went to Leslie Elementary School, which is now the Malcolm X Academy. Then we moved back into Dearborn and I graduated from Fordson High School in 1972. My dad worked at Ford Motor, at the Rouge Plant, steel division. He retired after almost thirty-six years. Mom was a housewife. They raised eight children.

SALLY: Would you fill me in a bit on your history as well, Mohsen?

MOHSEN: My name is Mohsen Amen. I came to the United States in 1970 when I was nineteen years old. I came to change my life and work in the factory, just like everybody else.

SALLY: Where did you come from?

MOHSEN: I came from southern Lebanon, from Ayat al Jabal. I brought with me here about thirty-six families so far. It turned out to be a big wave of immigration during the early 1980s. They all came to work in the factories. We lived on Dix in the Southend for a while, and we moved to east Dearborn, and I'm still there.

SALLY: So you came before the war?

MOHSEN: Way before the war. There were no signs at that time.

SALLY: Where is your family from, Lila?

LILA: They're from Rafeet in the Bekaa Valley. Others know it as Rashaya al-Wadi. Mom was first married to Adeeb al-Kadrey, *Allah yarhamu* [God rest his soul], and had three of us kids, Fay, Ikram and myself. She then went through a divorce and remarried her brother-in-law. That was something Jaddu [Lila's grandfather] made her do. Made *him* do, I should say. Because there were three of us children and culturally it's better-liked that a brother-in-law, or someone within the family, should marry a woman if something goes wrong with her marriage. This makes it easier to take care of the children, because the uncle would love the children more than an outsider would.

SALLY: I've heard of this happening in the case of death, but never divorce.

LILA: I am told it happened because my father wasn't aware of some of the things he was doing. He had left the country. But, things went on, and we still met with him and visited with him. He has since passed away. Mom had five other children with Ammi [Lila's uncle], who I call "Dad" since he raised me since I was an infant.

SALLY: Well, tell me about growing up here. I'm especially interested in the religious life of your family. Which mosque were you a part of? How did you mature into the Muslim you are today?

LILA: At first there was the mosque on Dix [in Dearborn's Southend]. It's called the American Moslem Society. We attended that mosque on weekends. They had a weekend school, run by Imam Mohammed Karoub. He taught us kids how to do the Fatihah [the opening verses of the Quran] and how to pray and that sort of thing. We lived a conservative life. It wasn't as if Mom insisted on our wearing *hijab* [Islamic head covering, usually a scarf worn to conceal the hair and neck] or that sort of thing, and she herself never wore it, but it was conservative. It was very promotional, if you will. "This is Islam. These are the things that we do." We fasted at all times. We dressed conservatively. We left the Dix mosque when it changed hands, and Dad started driving us to Canada to attend the Muslim mosque built in Windsor.

Sally: So your parents are Sunni?

[Sunni Muslims are often referred to as Orthodox Muslims. The overwhelming majority of Arab Muslims are Sunni.]

Lila: Sunni Muslim, yes. We attended the Canadian mosque for a couple of years. Then a mosque was built on Joy Road and Greenfield [in Detroit on the border of Dearborn] which is now the Islamic Center of America. It was run by Imam Mohammed Jawad Chirri. We started to attend there because it was closer and more convenient. At that time there was not a Sunni/Shia situation. Obviously, that wasn't the case if Dad was having us attend the mosque at Joy Road and Greenfield, because it was majority Shia.

[Shia Muslims broke off from the Sunni community in the first decades of Islam in a dispute over succession to the Caliphate, the leadership of the spiritual and (then) political community of Muslims. While a highly vocal and politicized minority in Lebanon and the Arab world, the Shia community in Dearborn is numerically in the majority. The everyday practice of the faith differs little between the two communities.]

Sally: I'd like to know how you felt about Islam. Did you feel you had a good knowledge of it when you were growing up? Did you ever feel out of place because you were a Muslim? How much a part of your identity was Islam when you were growing up?

Lila: I think being Arab American was more of an identity for me than being a Muslim. While growing up, there wasn't a big promotion of being a Muslim. People never said, "I am Lebanese. I am Palestinian." It was, "I am Syrian." That was the statement people would make. And, of course, during those years, Lebanon was considered a part of Syria. In some cases it still is today. So as a habit, people would refer to us as Syrians, not as Lebanese. Today it's far different, of course.

Being conservative the way we were, Mom and Dad didn't let us run around in a bikini. We would wear shorts and tops, but nothing like tank tops or things of that sort. Pretty much the whole lifestyle was conservative. It was very Arab American too, because everything we did socially had to do with our own people, whether they were relatives or friends. I spent a lot of time growing up, of course, with Americans. I have to say, whether it was just or not, a lot of the Arabs I had gone to school with actually made me feel annoyed with my own people. I am talking about some of the things the males did growing up. A lot of them even today, the same ones that I grew up with, are either in jail, or on drugs, or things of that sort, which hurts. When I met Mohsen, I used to joke about not being able to stand my own people, aside from the relatives and people that we socialized with. These kids that I'd gone to school with gave a bad name to the community. But it wasn't an Islamic thing at that time, it was an Arab thing. It was a "Syrian" kind of attitude.

SALLY: It was also the neighborhood you grew up in. It was a rough neighborhood back then.

LILA: Yes, it was.

SALLY: How old were you and Mohsen when you met?

LILA: I was nineteen. It was in 1973 that we met. In 1973 he asked me to marry him and in 1975 we got married.

SALLY: How did you meet?

LILA: Blame it on my sister. My sister introduced us to each other in November, and in December he asked me to marry him, and I laughed. I was like, "What? You're kidding!" It was only three weeks after we met. Then we got engaged in July of 1974 and we got married on June 14 of 1975.

SALLY: So tell me about your relationship. Did you date at all?

MOHSEN: Every time I took her out I had to drag her sister along.

LILA: You can consider that sort of a date. But my sister was always with us. Mom and Dad were conservative. Today it's different. When you get engaged, you actually get married in Islam.

[Lila is referring here to the Islamic marriage contract, called a *katib al-kitab.* This ceremony, witnessed by a religious leader, is often conducted in place of (or as part of) a formal engagement because it binds the couple legally and religiously in marriage. The couple are not considered to be married *socially* until they host a public wedding party, consummate their marriage, and set up house together. When Lila and Mohsen were married, the *katib al-kitab* was not undertaken until the day of the wedding party. Today, in Detroit, this practice has changed considerably, and most couples get engaged and married on the same day. Still, they are not expected to consummate the relationship until they are living together, and years might pass before they move into their own house.]

MOHSEN: Culturally, if a woman gets pregnant out of wedlock, that's a big thing. Religiously, it's even bigger. So when the woman is married and she's still in her home, people tend to look at it like . . .

Lila: . . . like *ayb* [disgrace, shame].

Mohsen: They do not understand Islam fully. Now, when they do *katib al-kitab*, they are married. That's it. People understand. Whatever happens, that's his wife. Now they understand more because now they look at it not through culture, but with regard to religion. Now there's more religious people around. They understand.

Sally: I've also heard you talk about when you were dating, before you got married, how Lila wasn't *muhajiba* [did not cover her hair], you used to drink alcohol [which is forbidden in Islam]. At some point you both started to take your religion more seriously. I want to hear about your wilder days and what brought you back into the fold.

Mohsen: I'll start before she starts. I came to America as a young man. I saw. I did. Whatever people did, I went along. I didn't know my religion. I came to this country eager to discover everything. And when you are a young man, you got . . . you know, peer pressure. Your friends, whatever they do you're gonna want to do. You want to show off. So we started on the wrong steps, which the others don't call wrong steps, they call them the "wild years." But to us, now, looking back, we did wrong. But this is part of growing up. We went to the bars. We drank. We did not drink to get drunk. We drank because you have to buy a drink when you go into the bar. And if you want to dance, you have to pay the consequences. So . . . we drank a drink or two and danced. That's about it, really. We did not go overboard.

Sally: This was the two of you?

Lila: No. This was him when he started out in Detroit.

Mohsen: When I met my wife, she was still young. I went to the family and I told them, "I'm happy to see your daughter. I want to settle down. I want to get married." I wanted it to be known as . . . that. They agreed with that, and we read the Fatihah. This made it OK to an extent. She still had to be home at a certain time. If she wanted to go out somewhere, there had to be a third person, so they knew there would be no personal contact.

Lila: So they'd be comfortable with it.

Sally: I understand that.

Mohsen: There's got to be a third person to prevent you from doing the . . . the unmentionable.

[Laughter]

MOHSEN: The taboo. Which is good. It's like we say, "Wherever there's a male and a female [alone together], the Devil is the third."

SALLY: He's right there in the middle.

[Laughter]

MOHSEN: So when there's a third person with you, you know that somebody's gonna stop you. So this is protection for her, and protection for the man.

SALLY: It makes things easier on you.

LILA: Yeah. It does.

MOHSEN: Because if we do something and have a baby, there will be a disaster. What if one of us changes his mind about marriage? The kid will be the one who suffers.

LILA: The kid will be without a name. Well, going back to those days, I never really used to go to nightclubs. I started doing that when I met him. Shame on you.

[Laughter]

LILA: Actually, shame on my sister, because she too used to go to nightclubs at that time! That's when we met, going to the clubs. Yes, we did drink. Yes, we did have a good time. We *dabkeed* [danced the traditional line dance]. We even performed in a *dabkah* troupe for three or four years. I enjoyed that, but it was a folklore *dabkah* troupe, not just where you go to bars. We flew to Washington a couple of times and danced for organizations. It was beautiful. But we drank and we danced and we went places. We were no different than anybody else. Well, not everybody was that way. But we didn't drink to get drunk.

MOHSEN: We did it in a social way.

SALLY: Well, your community was more conservative than the mainstream was back in the 1970s, but it was less conservative than the Arab community is now, in the 1990s. So you were like the majority of people your age?

LILA: Yeah. At that time.

MOHSEN: But they didn't know religion. They thought, this is sociable, so when you go over to somebody's house, you have a beer. Or when you go out, you have to pay for a drink. So you buy the drink.

SALLY: It was no big thing.

Mohsen: It was no big thing.

Lila: You never had beer or things like that in your home. We never did in our home. I remember the only time we did was once we had a New Year's party. People brought their drinks and things like that in my home . . .

Mohsen: We would go to the park and take a six-pack.

Lila: I think things started to change for us when I got pregnant. We were married in 1975, and I had Suehaila in 1979. We waited three-and-a-half years, at least. Mohsen's parents had twenty-one kids together, and Ammi [Lila's father-in-law] just couldn't deal with the fact that his son was not having a child. We put the poor man through some fears and let him think that his son couldn't have children, just so they'd leave us alone. You know the first thing that, I won't say Muslim parents . . .

Mohsen: The parents.

Lila: . . . the Arab parents, say is like, "What's wrong, you're not pregnant yet?" First it's to the woman.

Mohsen: Arab parents, they expect a child in the first year.

Lila: "What's wrong with her? She can't give you children?" So as much as this got on our nerves, we were struggling, paying bills. He was helping his family at that time too, so we weren't able to save for ourselves and get on with our lives. We swore that we would not have children in an apartment. We would wait until we bought a house. Well, the only way to get them off of our backs was to say Mohsen couldn't have any children. His poor father. We never realized how much we'd hurt him.

[General laughter]

Sally: This is cruel.

Lila: We must have hurt him terribly. For months he didn't talk to us.

Sally: So on top of the drinking and the dancing, you were lying.

[More laughter]

Mohsen: They told us to see a doctor. They offered me these tips on the village remedy.

Lila: How you have children . . .

Mohsen: We used to laugh at all that, then we told them that we had to wait, to save some money at least. When we bought our home and we paid our bills and we relaxed, I said "It's time to have a family."

LILA: And we did, right away. We had Suehaila in 1979. Things started to roll in a positive direction. It was about in 1980 when Ammi, *Allah Yarhamu* [God rest his soul], Mohsen's father, started to really fall into the religion. There is a story behind that actually. That's when Sheikh Abd al-Latif came to town and started to introduce Islam on a different basis. And because they were from the same area in the *Janub* [south Lebanon], they went to him.

MOHSEN: Don't forget the revolution in Iran. That changed our perspective.

[This was a specifically Shia, theocratic revolution. Many Lebanese Muslims in Dearborn felt strongly that the Iranian revolution should be supported and, if possible, reproduced in Lebanon.]

LILA: First it was Sheikh Abd al-Latif. He lived over on Riverside and had a place there where everyone would meet. He also took a room at ACCESS [the Arab Community Center for Economic and Social Services; see the essay by Karen Rignall in this collection] and used it for Friday prayers. Then it started to grow, rapidly grow. This was in 1980, 1981. Of course, the Islamic revolution in Iran kicked off in 1979. I believe it was 1981 that Al Sayyed Mohammed Hussein Fadlallah came to town. Then, a whole group of people just woke up. It was very strange. He came to town. He was a very big figure from Lebanon. I'll never forget that they had this event out at a country club in Southfield, the Bonnie Brook. Hundreds of people went there. I think it was more out of curiosity. It was a political time.

MOHSEN: I will tell you a funny story about that. I learned religion when I was young, but it took somebody to shake it out of me and bring it out. One day my father came to me and said, "Hey, we are having a dinner. Do you want to come to it?" And, before, I was away from the religious people, away from them, even in my own family. They used to call me the Americanized person in the family. So I told him, "I'll take two tickets." I took two tickets, not intending to go. It just so happened that on that Sunday, we had nothing whatsoever to do. I looked at my wife and said, "Do you want to go to that dinner?" And she said, "No. You go ahead." For the first time, I just drove myself to the Bonnie Brook. I didn't know where I was going. I just said, "Well I'm gonna go." And I went there and I saw six hundred people, seven hundred people there. Everybody that I knew was there. And I saw Al Sayyed Mohammed Hussein Fadlallah. I knew him since I was a little boy, cause he used to be a sheikh right in my neighborhood. He knew my father. I asked him if he remembered me. He said, "Yes. I do remember you. You are the son of so-and-so." And he reminded me of things I used to do when he was making sermons. For me, that was like I was sleeping and somebody woke me up from a dream. I came back home. I put the Quran in front of me and I started crying. I didn't know what to do. I had forgotten how to pray. I forgot everything. I didn't even know how to read the Fatihah. I forgot all about that. Then I start to read, read. And I start to do my *salah* [prayers], and I cried. My wife saw me. She said, "What the heck is wrong with that man? He goes to a dinner and he comes back like there is something wrong with him."

[Laughter]

MOHSEN: And I took off from there. Like they say, I changed those clothes that I had on before and put on new clothes, with a new vision in front of me.

LILA: He's still a crazy man, though!

MOHSEN: Hey, I'm not a fanatic.

LILA: You don't go into the religion and stop living.

SALLY: You're talking to the daughter of a preacher.

MOHSEN: I'm not a fanatic.

SALLY: I know about being faithful and enjoying life at the same time. God doesn't say you are supposed to sit and pray twenty-four hours a day.

MOHSEN: Exactly. Islam came to save you, not to put you in misery. It came to help you throughout life. And when you understand Islam you will find out that you can have fun. You can live and you can get along with everybody. But . . .

LILA: You have your *wajibs,* obligations.

MOHSEN: You have obligations, like good manners, not making a fool of yourself. You don't have to be a joker to make somebody laugh. And you don't have to laugh out loud to make somebody notice that you are laughing. Everything with manners. Islam comes to teach you a way of life with good sense.

LILA: When Mohsen started to change, it was an annoyance to me. Because it wasn't just a change, a little-by-little, step-by-step thing.

He went from one dinner to the next day. It was, in a way, frightening.

SALLY: Do you remember anything the sheikh said? Did he say anything specific that led you to this sudden change?

MOHSEN: It's not what he said. It's the sight, among all the people that I knew there, of this person who used to teach me when I was young.

LILA: The environment. To see all those people.

MOHSEN: And I looked at myself and said, "Where am I going?" I saw like a dead path with an obstacle, and I said, "Where am I going?" I didn't know where I was going. I go to work. I come home. I take care of the kids. Eat, drink, and go to sleep. And this is it. This is what? God did not make me just for that reason. There has got to be more to it. My subconscious started working. It was like somebody shook me and said, "There is a purpose for you here. You don't work, eat, sleep, and drink and have babies. We are not animals. There is a purpose for you. Go out and find what you can do." That's when Lila started to go through the misery with me because I was hungry to find out what lay ahead of me; the future, the religion, the hereafter . . . Now the kids. How are they going to be when they grow up? I started to look forward to everything. I started to look way ahead of me. I started learning about Islam. I started to inhale knowledge. I started buying books. Whenever there was a visiting imam [a Muslim teacher and scholar], I used to go and listen to what he had to say. A sermon about this, a sermon about that.

[Mohsen was part of a mass conversion, a revitalization movement that influenced the lives of hundreds of Lebanese in Dearborn in the early 1980s. He states specifically that this awakening was, in part, a reaction to political events that were unfolding, rather dramatically, in Lebanon and Iran. Lila's religious awakening, by contrast, was much more gradual and individualistic. It was, from the outset, a careful (and not always enthusiastic) response to Mohsen's new life.]

SALLY: Can I hear your side now, Lila? You said you were frustrated.

LILA: Yes. In the very beginning, when Mohsen started, it was frustrating because we'd already had Suehaila and Shadia at the time, and I found that now this new thing in his life, this Islam, was taking him away from me and the kids. The time we had together on the weekends, he was preoccupied with going to these meetings, listening to sermons. In the evenings it was no longer playing cards until three or four o'clock in the morning, with his cousins—which is what I had problems with prior to that. Now he's going to listen to speeches through all hours of the night, and when they're done they go to his dad's house and have a cup of tea, forty men at a time. So I thought, "I can't deal with this sharing routine." I felt jilted, in a way, because I was working full-time, raising two kids, paying somebody to watch them while I worked to help him keep up with the bills. And on the weekends when we have time to do things together as a family, he doesn't have time for us. He only has time for himself. I began to hate what he was doing, which pulled me away from the religion.

A couple years later, in 1982, I was in a car accident while I was pregnant with my fourth. I had a difficult time, physically and emotionally, wondering if there's going to be something wrong with the child. *Alhamdulillah* [praise be to God] she is healthy! Shortly afterwards, I was told that I either had tuberculosis, sarcoidosis, or lymphoma. Two out of these three are cancerous. This put me in a whole other light on life. "What is going on? What's going to happen next? I've got four children. Who's gonna take care of my kids? I'm gonna die. I know it. Maybe it's because I rejected what Mohsen was trying to teach me." These kinds of things were going on in my mind. It turned out to be sarcoidosis, an inflammation of the lymph nodes, which can shorten your life, but it wasn't as dangerous as lymphoma or tuberculosis. I did the operation. Then my gynecologist came and told me I had to take care of myself from now on. I had my tubes tied. No more kids. It was an agreed thing between us. Mohsen spoke to the sheikh about it, and the sheikh said, "If it's a life or death situation, you need to solve that. Your kids need a mom." So . . . praise God, it worked out.

When I went in for the lymphoma tests, I did a *nidhar* [solemn vow], that if everything turned out OK, I would send Ammi and his wife on the pilgrimage to Mecca. Later, when I came out, and the results were OK, I did. I set aside four thousand dollars from the insurance money from the accident for them. Ammi didn't wind up going for various reasons. He had a heart attack. He had trouble raising the rest of the money he needed. But he gave his wife the permission to use his share from me, and she went.

In February of 1984, Hassan, Mohsen's brother, was killed in a robbery at a gas station in Detroit. That was the most fearful thing we ever dealt with in our lives, and it made me start to think differently. It turns out that it was his own two friends from our community that did it. One is still in jail. But the other was supposedly killed in an air raid in Lebanon, in Mashkara. I always say "supposedly," because at that time it was easy to buy off a name.

It was all of that, then, that woke me up. Mohsen's was seeing his friends make the change. Mine was seeing the things that happened in life.

SALLY: What did the change mean for you? Mohsen started going to the mosque and praying. He became a part of the religious community. What did it mean for your life?

LILA: Well, for me, I started to learn little-by-little. I didn't want to learn in front of him, or with him, because I was still annoyed with the way he had handled things. I started teaching myself, reading books. I started to pray by myself. I never told him I was praying.

SALLY: Before this point in life, did you go to the mosque?

LILA: No. I didn't. Aside from going to Joy Road, but I wasn't involved.

SALLY: How often did you go to Joy Road?

MOHSEN: We didn't go there for religious reasons. We went whenever there was an occasion.

SALLY: When there was a funeral, or a dinner, or something like that? You didn't go every week?

LILA: Yes, for things like that. The kids were too young at that point. There were no programs for them. Now they have classes for children five and older, but it wasn't that way back then. Shortly after that, 1983 or 1984, Sheikh Abd al-Latif started the Islamic Institute of Knowledge on Jonathon and Warren. At that time it was all cinder blocks. They were revamping it, getting it organized, painting it, that kind of thing. I got involved then. I had two kids in school and two kids in strollers. I used to take them and clean the place, or help out during dinners. I handled their purchasing for the first eight or ten years. I was very involved up until last year, when I needed time for myself.

SALLY: You must have been attending for religious events as well. Would you describe for me the religious activities that take place at the mosque?

LILA: Regularly, there will be a Thursday night supplication. On Friday there will be a *salat al juma* [congregational prayer], but that's usually for the men. That isn't something I would stop and go to. Usually on Sunday they have early breakfast, and then lectures in both English and Arabic. We wanted to promote this, because we were trying to attract the younger generation. While they were teaching other kids how to read and write Arabic, I had a class set aside for teenaged girls two days a week, on Saturday and Sunday. The intent was to teach the kids what life is like behind closed doors. That you are a human being. You do have rights in Islam. But your first obligation is to be a good Muslim. And to let them know about some of their rights. A lot of our girls are getting married today having no idea what a right is. "All he has to do is give me a dowry. Give me money for the *mutaqaddim* and the *muta'akhir*." The *muta'akhir* is [a sum of money the groom must set aside] in case anything should happen, they get divorced, they break off the *katib al-kitab*, children or no children. "This is what you get when I am gone." And of course, that's if they both agree to leave each other, or if the man chooses not to keep her anymore. I know that is not a very good choice of words. The *mutaqaddim* is the gift you [as a bride] get in the beginning, the dowry, if you will. Some girls will ask for a Quran. Others will say, "send me to hajj [the pilgrimage to Mecca] some time in the next five or six years or before I have children." This is what some of the girls will ask for. But they don't know their rights. They don't know that they can have a contract; it is not taught to them. So there is a move on among the women to say, "We can't wait anymore for the sheikhs to get together and teach our girls what their rights are before or during marriage."

SALLY: You are speaking in the present tense now. Is this happening now, or was this in the 1980s?

LILA: This happened before, when I was teaching those classes to teenagers.

SALLY: What were you doing at this time at the mosque, Mohsen?

MOHSEN: First, when we opened the Islamic Institute of Knowledge, the name of it was "The Islamic Institute of Knowledge." The purpose was to teach the knowledge of Islam. It is not just a mosque for prayer, no.

LILA: It is a community center.

MOHSEN: It is an institute of knowledge. We are there for you to ask questions. We will provide the answers. That is what we started the place, or program, as. We used to have the supplication on Thursdays, which is for families. We make *salat* [prayer] and ask God for forgiveness. On Friday night, me and the older guys, guys of my generation, used to get together and have educated people talk to us about certain subjects. Now, from those two meetings, we made a program for Saturday night. Each one of us older guys would teach the kids their religion, just a little bit here, a little bit there. We tried to make it fun for them, to let them understand what they are, what Islam is all about, and help them make it a part of their identity. We started bringing our kids, others' kids. We started having a crowd. Each person would prepare a lecture for that night. We ended up with fifty or more teens. Then, when things started rolling along, we started having Sunday breakfast. Instead of everybody having breakfast at home, you come over to the Institute; you have *monaeish* [flat bread with olive oil, oregano, and spices], *labne* [yogurt spread], *zeitun* [olives]. At the same time you listen to the Sheikh. He talks. You ask him questions. He gives you the answers.

Lila was talking about women's rights. You see, I cannot teach you Islam. There is no way I can teach you everything about Islam unless you go to a university where they teach Islam. What the center, and the Sheikh, the imams in the area . . . Whatever you ask them, they are gonna give you the answer. But they are not gonna come to you and tell you about your rights in Islam. Because if they do that, they could never finish with everybody. There are always certain things that you are gonna forget, or you won't teach, or you cannot get to. Even though it is your right, you see. Sometimes you have to give up some of your rights in life to make things go along. So that is why in Islam the imam does not teach you every little thing. You as a Muslim are supposed to look for your rights and understand if I do this am I right or wrong. What happens with this, this, and that. That is what the imam and sheikh are there for. There are books in English, Arabic, Spanish, any language, where you look for your rights.

LILA: You see, this is where he and I disagree. Because if that was the case, then we don't need the sheikh. There are books. There is the Quran. I can read that and I don't need a sheikh to teach me anything. My largest disagreement in the community is that many, many of our girls are getting married at a young age, some by choice and others not. And that means everybody: Lebanese, Palestinian, Yemeni, Jordanian. I don't care what background they come from. They are marrying early, even Chaldeans for that matter. It's not just an Islamic thing. But the sheikhs are there for that purpose, to teach. Not just to teach me the religion of Islam, or to teach our children what being a Muslim is all about, or what they need to do to be a good one, but what their rights are to live a healthy and decent life. And our girls getting married at a young age . . . they are getting set up, literally, in a situation where everything comes to the man. Maybe they find themselves in a situation down the line, maybe in a month or two, where they made the biggest mistake of their life. They can't live with this man. Maybe they don't love him, or vice versa. The man can choose not to divorce her Islamically, and leave her dangling for her life. There is no logic to that. My work is to say to the girls, "Don't sign a paper. Don't agree to a marriage until you have made it clear to that man, or to your parents . . .

MOHSEN: It is a marriage contract.

LILA: . . . whether you do or don't love him, what you wish for in life.

MOHSEN: You sign the marriage contract and that's it.

LILA: Right. You are done. So they need to know that.

SALLY: Can you put a clause in the contract that gives you the right to divorce?

LILA: Yes. Absolutely. They don't know that though. That's why I say it's up to the sheikh to teach them. You know it is written in the holy Quran that a girl has the right to choose or refuse. A forced marriage is forbidden.

MOHSEN: Let me give you an example. There was a program on TV. I think it was *Oprah*. She had people who are married, and they had [prenuptial] contracts. Lights out at eleven o'clock . . . and so on. They are all happy with what is going on. Islam is just like that. I am going to give up some of my rights. You are going to give up some of your rights, and we are going to make a marriage. If I tell you all the woman's rights—she doesn't have to cook, she doesn't have to breast-feed my child, she doesn't have to do anything for me—what is she there for?

LILA: His money is theirs, you know. Her money is hers!

MOHSEN: Just for sex? Hey, wait a minute. The man has rights, too. I don't have to feed you, I don't have to dress you, but buy you one dress a year. I will feed you. Whatever I eat, I will feed you from that. I will let you stay at home. That won't be a marriage. You give up some of your rights. I give up some of my rights. Then we make a go of it.

LILA: A happy medium. My main concern is how the girls are getting hurt. When I saw this happening, this was when my kids were still young . . .

MOHSEN: Now it is changing. The lifestyle is changing.

LILA: My daughters were ten and eleven years old. Now it is changing.

MOHSEN: Those people don't understand their religion, and they hang onto that one thing. "I have the right not to divorce you." But there are other elements, where it leads to a divorce. Even if you go to the imam, he will tell you. When she says, "Well, I don't like him any more, I want to divorce him." Well, in Islam it doesn't work that way.

LILA: The thing is, it's true, sometimes the men hang onto one little thing. "I don't have to divorce her in Islam if I don't want to. Go do what you want to do." Well, hanging onto her in Islam forbids her to marry anybody else or get on with her life. Today, you are starting to see a change in the girls. They are starting to push themselves into a higher educational field. They are starting to really look forward to different careers. We are proud of that.

SALLY: Did you go to college?

LILA: I didn't back then. It wasn't because of a cultural thing. *Baba* [Dad] really couldn't afford it. He had five of his own and he had us three.

SALLY: But you have worked your whole life.

LILA: Yes, I did. Literally. I have been working since I was sixteen. I took a break for about seven years when I had all of the kids. When Samira got into first grade is when I started work at ACCESS. I wanted to study at Henry Ford Community College, because Mohsen said, "Go back to school. Do whatever you want to do during the day. But I want you home by two o'clock P.M." I couldn't get a course during the day that I wanted, so I went to ACCESS. My phone was ringing off the hook with people wanting me to do things for free! I was running myself ragged I figured to no avail. I went there and I had never met Ismael Ahmed [executive director of ACCESS] before in my life. When he heard I was there looking for a part-time job, he came out and he goes, "I know you." I didn't even know he was Ismael. He said, "I know you and I want you here." It was exciting. I remember I came home and I told Mohsen, "You know this man hired me just because of my name? He doesn't even know what I am capable of, or if I can work, or anything."

SALLY: He does now.

LILA: He does now! It excited me so much that this guy hired me because of my name. I realized all my volunteer work in the community had paid off.

[We discuss ACCESS for a few minutes. Lila and I first met each other there in 1990.]

SALLY: What led you to become *muhajiba*?

LILA: I'll tell you how it happened to me. We had a gentleman staying at our house. It was in the Christmas holiday of 1985.

MOHSEN: That is a period I need to tell you about. That is when everything comes into focus. My father had changed his life after the . . . and he wanted to do good.

LILA: After Hassan was killed, actually.

MOHSEN: And every year we used to have an Islamic conference at the Christmas period, when everybody is off school and work. They call it the winter break. We used to have a conference in St. Louis, Oklahoma, Kansas. And after the conference is finished, a couple of days before the New Year, everybody goes back to his home state. And all the imams that come from outside the country, come to the biggest community there is. They come to Dearborn. And where are they coming? To my father's house. Some of them sleep there. Some of them sleep over at my house. Each one of us will take somebody. It just so happened that at that time, Al Sayyed Murtida [a spiritual leader and descendant of the Prophet], I knew him personally. We grew up together. He is even younger than me. He came over and stayed at our house.

LILA: He is from Mohsen's village. Al Sayyed Murtidah. When this man came in, at first I was very paranoid. I thought to myself, "What am I going to do with this man in my house? How am I going to dress? How am I going to act? What can I serve?" And when this guy came in, he was like the guy next door. He was such a riot. He was so funny, so communicative. He spoke English quite well.

SALLY: Who is he? I don't know the name.

LILA: Al Sayyed Murtidah.

SALLY: Is he one of the big imams from Lebanon?

MOHSEN: No. He is from my village, but he is in Africa now. His brother is a higher scholar. He is in history and everybody knows his name. He writes books and stuff like that.

LILA: His brother is Al Sayyed Ja'afar Murtidah.

MOHSEN: He is stationed in Kenya. He lives with poor people and he serves them.

LILA: He opened up a school of his own, an Islamic school of thought.

SALLY: He is a missionary.

MOHSEN: Yes, but he has a school and everything. He just lives there by himself. He is down to earth.

LILA: So when this man came, I was in awe of him. And I could laugh with him. He was cracking jokes. He would take off his, what do you call his turban . . . his *laffi*. He would be funny and take this off. He had long hair, and I thought, "This is a Sayyed?" When I saw that he was so down to earth, he was a friend, I was so comfortable with him that he stayed with us for ten days. After taking him to the airport, everybody came back to our house for a *sahrah* [an evening get together], which is the custom. I was wearing *hijab,* what they call *thiyab al-shari'ah* [Islamic dress], a pair of slacks with a dresslike thing over it that comes to the knee, and a scarf.

SALLY: Did you put this on because he was visiting?

LILA: Yes. Because of him. This is how it all started. When we came back from the airport, I went up to my room and took off these clothes and put my "normal" clothes back on. *My* clothes. I went back downstairs where everybody was having coffee, and I was halfway down the stairs and I felt like something was missing. I thought, "For ten days I was totally covered in front of everybody that entered my house," and now I was going downstairs to be something that I was two weeks ago. I felt funny about it. Then somebody came in the door at the same time I was going down, and he said "*Salaam alaykum* [peace be upon you]. Oh, Oh, I'm sorry!" And he averted his eyes. He made me feel so uneasy, like I had done something wrong!

MOHSEN: You don't know how uneasy it made her feel.

LILA: I was saying to myself, "What did he say that for?" Then it occurred to me that I wasn't wearing *hijab,* and this man thought I was a person who wears *hijab.* When I realized why this man was so up in arms and apologizing, I went back up to the room and put the *hijab* back on. When I went downstairs again, actually, not even Mohsen noticed anything. He had seen me like that for two weeks, and it had become habit to him. The next day, we still hadn't seen my parents, so I said to Mohsen, "You know you haven't even said, 'Lets go see your parents.' You don't even ask about them." I got into him about that. So he said, "*Yallah* [hurry up], come on." So we got up and we went to my parents' house, and I was sitting there waiting for something, for someone to say something. My God, even Mohsen didn't say anything. I was like "Hello! This is me."

And my mother thought (this was before she made the *hajj* herself and started wearing the *hijab*) that young women who wore *hijab* looked like old ladies. She used to think it wasn't a necessity. Well, I always used to argue with her that you shouldn't just wear *hijab* when you're old. You might not ever get old. These are things that you do because you want to follow your obligations appropriately. And when people would say, "Oh, but you look like an old lady!" I would tell them, "That's okay. As long as people like me for who I am, I don't care how old I might be." I would always hear silly things like, "Are you going to be dressed like that when you come over to the house?"

It was that kind of thing I was up against at that time. At any rate, when I took my coat off, Mohsen finally noticed I was wearing *hijab,* the little bugger. He hadn't noticed it for two days. So when I took off my coat and he looked at me, he went like this [Lila raises her eyebrows], and I just went like this [Lila places a finger over her lips]. "Not a word. Don't say a word." Because I knew that had he ever said anything to me like, "What are you doing? What are you wearing? Do you know why you're wearing it?" I would have taken it off forever. I know myself, and I would have. So I told him, "Not a word. Just leave it alone." And he did. He never said a word after that. And from that time on, I wore *hijab.*

But what I was wearing, like I was telling you, is the *thiyab al-shari'ah,* with a dress and a pair of slacks underneath. You can have flowing ones, shiny ones, whatever. They tell you, "Don't wear flashy clothes. It's not nice to attract attention." But I happen to like bright colors. And so does Mohsen, so whenever he would buy me anything, it would be bright. But then I started to slowly, you know, get into skirts and tops, slacks and long shirts. But my long shirts always went to my knees. It was hard to find clothes back then. Today, actually, the stores are catering to the community. They haven't a choice.

MOHSEN: It's not by choice. It so happens that the fashion today is long.

LILA: No. Long skirts are not necessarily "in" anymore, like they used to be; big baggy clothes, baggy shirts with a long flowy skirt. A lot of the girls felt comfortable because they were able to buy *thiyab al-shari'ah* just in a regular store. They didn't have to go to an Islamic boutique. They didn't have to ship clothes from Lebanon, which is what I used to do. I used to have my sister ship me a few boxes of clothes and sell them here at cost, just to help people get clothing.

Little-by-little, as times went on and I started to change my way of dressing back into skirts and tops. Really, because you couldn't find clothes here. And I couldn't keep shipping it from Lebanon. It was too expensive. Now I wear more colorful *hijabs* too, because I find that if you are going to dress Islamically, you don't have to look drab. You will find some people who wear all black, or just a white scarf with maybe a black *abayee* [cloak], or a black scarf, maybe with a long gray outfit. But I don't think that Islam promotes that you have to be unhappy with what you wear. And I believe that how you feel about the way you dress is no different from yourself. If you feel good about how you're dressed, then your whole personality moves with you. And I noticed that change with me.

SALLY: I have a few other questions. The Islamic Institute is mostly an immigrant mosque, right? Lila, you are the exception in that you are one of the long-term . . .

MOHSEN: No. Not necessarily. It's just that the ones who started it were the immigrants. But later on it became . . . because it's a community center. It does not belong to a certain person or to a certain creed of people.

LILA: Well, the people who patronize it are immigrants. You would have to say that. Maybe you are not understanding it, Mohsen. But it's mostly people who immigrated here.

SALLY: Those who came after the civil war [in Lebanon].

LILA: Yes. And their children. You see, Mohsen is thinking about their children, some of whom were born and raised here. But it is mostly those who have immigrated here.

SALLY: And what is the reputation of the Institute? You've said that it was established as a place of learning, and not just as a place you go to pray in or have dinners. Would you say that the types of programs you offer are radically different from what is available, for example, at the Islamic Center? Is the mosque made up of people from the same villages, or extended families? What determines who goes there?

LILA: I think it's both ideological and social.

MOHSEN: You see, Islam, some people give Islam, uh, I don't know how to say it. Some people describe it as "moderate" Islam, "democratic" Islam, "fanatic" Islam. People give us those titles.

LILA: Like reformed or conservative.

MOHSEN: They give those titles. They put labels or titles on people. Now, the Islamic Center of America [on Joy Road] is "Americanized" Islam. The Islamic Mosque of America [on Warren Avenue at Greenfield], tends to have some politics and some Islam and some families. At the Islamic Institute of Knowledge [on Schaefer Road], all the people who go there have beards. They know a beard is part of Islam; every man is supposed to have a beard. And it just so happened that everybody in Iran, all the radicals, have beards. So they called wearing a beard "the Hizballah thing."

[Hizballah is a Lebanese political party that was founded after the Iranian revolution by Shias in south Lebanon. It is committed to armed struggle against Israeli forces occupying Lebanon and to the establishment of an Islamic state in Lebanon.]

MOHSEN: But it's not [a Hizballah thing]. It's just because we are into our religion more than the others and we wear the beard. The other ones will shave it off, or will have just half a beard, or something like that. To us it was a full beard, because we all used to follow Al Sayyed Khouei. Al Sayyed Khouei requires all men to have the full beard. Al Sayyed Khomeini requires all men to have a full beard.

SALLY: But you have never worn a full beard.

MOHSEN: Yes I have. I just wear it smaller now.

LILA: This is to make him look thinner, Sally.

[Laughing]

MOHSEN: This is lately.

SALLY: This is your age, your ego.

MOHSEN: Lately I've had this.

[Laughter]

MOHSEN: So all those other Muslims, they give us the title "radicals" because of the beard.

LILA: Actually, they laugh at the title. They think it's funny.

MOHSEN: Yeah, a friend of mine finished his doctorate and they offered him a job for eighty thousand dollars. But they told him, "You have to shave the beard." He said, " I don't want the job." He refused the job because they told him to shave.

LILA: And he went back home and he's a professor at the American University in Beirut. He is also a principal at *Dar al Muslimun* [a religious school].

MOHSEN: All that just because of shaving the beard. That shows you how strong it is to believe in what you are. That's why they call us radicals. [Laughing] That's the difference between the places [the different mosques in Dearborn], but they are all Islamic. They all teach the same thing. And they all have the same message, which is Islam.

SALLY: So you are saying that the choice of which mosque you attend is an ideological one, not one based on family or village origins?

MOHSEN: Not necessarily, because the same people that come to the *majma'* [the Islamic Institute of Knowledge], their first cousins [might go to another mosque]. Like me and my first cousins, Alan and Ronnie Amen. Ronnie is a board member of the Islamic Center of America. I am a board member of the Islamic Institute of Knowledge.

SALLY: So it is, in part, an ideological decision.

LILA: I know what you are asking. A majority of the people that go to the *majma'*, which is the Islamic Institute of Knowledge, are from [the village of] Tibneen and a bit of [the village of] Bint Jubail. No, not even Bint Jubail. Mostly Tibneen and that area of the south [of Lebanon]. The Islamic Center of America attracts much of Bint Jubail.

MOHSEN: No. Most of it, 90 percent of it, is Tibneen. The whole thing is . . .

LILA: Maybe he knows more about it than I do. That's just how I see it.

MOHSEN: Because I know the families.

LILA: Well maybe, but that's how I see it. Because Sheikh Abd al-Latif is from Tibneen. So you tend to follow your "own." But a lot of what goes on at the Institute . . .

[Participation in specific mosques in Dearborn is often determined by family and village ties, as Lila suggests. It is also influenced by the length of time particular family members have been in America. The Islamic Institute was established in reaction to the Islamic Center of America, whose leadership was largely American-born and English-speaking. The Islamic Center is more closely affiliated with the "less-radical" Lebanese political party, Amal. Mohsen describes this cleavage, quite accurately, as being situated in linguistic and cultural differences. One community concentrates on Arabic language programming, the other on English.]

MOHSEN: They speak more Arabic. Let's put it this way.

SALLY: At your mosque?

LILA: Yes.

MOHSEN: At the Islamic Institute we concentrate more on the Arabic language than the English language. The Islamic Center is the other way around. They concentrate on the English more than the Arabic.

LILA: They do a lot of English, which is good. And now there's the Islamic House of Wisdom. Sheikh Mohammed Ali Elahi came in from Iran. He has promoted—obviously, because he speaks Farsi not Arabic—he has promoted a lot of English. And much of the younger generation has been attending his place.

MOHSEN: We need them to speak Arabic more than we need them to speak English. You are here. You're gonna speak English, like it or not.

LILA: But you need to understand.

MOHSEN: But our kids, we need them to speak Arabic.

SALLY: You need them to understand the Quran.

LILA: Yeah.

SALLY: I want to know how the mosque does fund-raising. Who organizes the events? What sort of events do you host?

LILA: OK. At the Islamic Institute, mostly we just have the dinners. We have fund-raising dinners twice a year, every six months. The Women's Society from the Islamic Institute gets all of that together.

MOHSEN: They do all the cooking.

LILA: The women do all the cooking and food preparation.

MOHSEN: Some of the butcher shops donate the meat. Because they, you know . . . it's business. You scratch my back, I scratch yours. So if you give and I announce your name, people will go to you and buy, and that's how it works in any religion. It doesn't have to be Islam. So, the vegetable places will donate the vegetables, and the butcher shops will donate the meat. The ladies will get together and cook. And the board members, everybody knows somebody . . . they give them tickets to sell, and people come.

LILA: And that's it. The board members hang around the *majma'*. Each one knows their position, what to do. Somebody will stand at the door and greet the people. Something that Mohsen and I started with them, is starting to involve people from outside the Islamic community. It was something that they never wanted to do before. I think it was out of fear as to how people were accepting of them.

MOHSEN: They wanted to stay within themselves. They didn't . . .

LILA: So, I told Mohsen, "You know, you are on the board. Why don't you tell them that we need to involve our people with outside." And actually, I'll blame Ismael for all of this. He got me involved with politics, him and Alan Amen [an American-born cousin of Mohsen's who was elected to the school board in Dearborn for several terms and is active in local democratic politics]. I swear. So, when I got involved with politics, I saw the power. There's a lot out there. And if we bring these political people in to us, and let them realize that we are human beings, they'll start to see us differently than what they see over at congressional meetings or things of that sort. Let them see the other guy, you know, the person that's living here.

MOHSEN: We started to invite them, like ACCESS does.

LILA: We did. We started to invite a couple of them, little-by-little. We started off small. We went from local, to state, to United States. And we've befriended many of them in more ways than one.

SALLY: So who has come?

LILA: Mostly we've had . . . United States Congressman John Dingell always comes. [United States Senator] Carl Levin has come once. [State Senator] George Hart and state Representative Agnes Dobronski come.

MOHSEN: Last year we had two thousand people.

SALLY: Where did you hold your last dinner?

MOHSEN: We bought a new building.

SALLY: You can seat two thousand people in your new building?

LILA: We had, well, we had about fifteen hundred at the dinner. There were other workers, too.

MOHSEN: No, we had a lot of people on the outside. A lot of people walked away because there was no more room.

LILA: Fifteen hundred were seated.

MOHSEN: We had fifteen hundred sitting down.

LILA: We bought the old Holiday Bowl on Schaefer. They gutted it out, and they revamped it totally. It's a beautiful building inside now. So we had the grand opening on the 15th of March,

1998. Congressman Dingell was there. George Hart was there. The mayor of Dearborn came, which is the first time he's attended. [State Representative] Agnes Dobronski, Governor Engler, Sheriff Ficano . . .

MOHSEN: We sent invitations to others, but they sent representatives. They were busy.

LILA: Engler was in, yeah. There was such a large scale. And, you know, I ask myself, "Do they know where this all began?" Not that you want the recognition, but it's something that they fought us over for the longest time. "We don't need these people. We don't need to have politics. We don't need. We don't need." Until finally now it's like, "Can you get these people to come?" When Congressman John Dingell walks up to Mohsen and gives him a hug, they look twice. It's like, "I guess he wasn't kidding." There is good out there. He's a human being and we are human beings. But we need to let him see us different from what is being portrayed.

SALLY: You should get Levin to come. That would be . . .

LILA: Levin did come last year.

MOHSEN: He came here one time, but somehow he feels uncomfortable.

[Chuckling]

SALLY: Well, gee, I can't imagine why.

[Laughter. Senator Levin is a staunch supporter of Israel. He is also Jewish.]

MOHSEN: Well, he comes to the ACCESS dinner. He does fine.

SALLY: Yeah, but there's a difference.

[ACCESS is a secular organization with strong ties to both the Democratic and Republican Parties.]

MOHSEN: Like it or not, he is our senator.

SALLY: Yes. I know he is.

MOHSEN: No. I'm saying for *him,* like it or not, he is *our* senator. We saw him in Washington.

SALLY: How about [United States Senator] Spencer Abraham? Has he ever attended?

[Senator Abraham is an Arab American of Lebanese descent. He is also an Orthodox Christian, a sect opposed to the Shia Muslims during the Lebanese civil war. His family immigrated to Michigan in the early 1900s, and he has no ties to Dearborn other than recently created political ones. He did, however, receive a large percentage of the Lebanese Shia vote in the 1994 election.]

LILA: No. He has never shown up. Isn't that funny? And I told Mohsen, "That should tell you something."

MOHSEN: He came to the Islamic Center of America, but not to the Islamic Institute. We have that, uh . . . [Mohsen tugs at an imaginary, full-grown beard; there is laughter all around] the beard reputation and all that stuff.

SALLY: I can picture him standing at the door, you know, surrounded by beards, wondering where he is.

[More laughter]

MOHSEN: I'd be glad if he came.

[He chuckles.]

LILA: That's a shame though, because it's true. They'll show up at the Islamic Center of America [the more Americanized mosque], but they won't show up for others.

SALLY: How much money does the mosque raise each year? Do you have any idea what the budget is?

MOHSEN: This year, because it was a grand opening and we just bought the place, which cost us almost two million dollars, people had to give extra. So we made about two hundred thousand dollars.

SALLY: Do you get any money from overseas?

MOHSEN: No.

SALLY: And who pays for the imam?

MOHSEN: Nobody. He does not get paid.

SALLY: He doesn't get paid?

LILA: He gets his money from the *khums* [a fifth of one's annual savings. Muslims are obligated to give this sum to the poor]. You know, when you pay the *zakat* [alms].

MOHSEN: He does not take any money from the money that people donate to the Islamic Institute. You heard of *zakat*? You have to give some of your money that you have extra over the year. Alms. Like, I save five thousand dollars from now to the end of the year. My next year starts five thousand dollars ahead. So I take 20 percent of that five thousand dollars and I give it to the imam. He takes part of it and gives it to the poor, the needy, and all of that. It goes into five parts.

SALLY: That's not part of the budget of the mosque? This is separate from the mosque?

LILA: No. This is separate from whatever people donate to the mosque. That's just for the mosque.

SALLY: And this *khums* you give directly to the sheikh and he distributes it?

MOHSEN: He distributes that to the poor. And he has a share, if he needs it. Not every time you give to him he takes that share. He takes as he needs. For instance, out of a month he takes the house payment from what the people pay him. He takes that share and he pays his rent. He pays his family expenses. The extra he puts right back in.

SALLY: But is there any accounting of that?

LILA: No. *bi Allah dimtu.* This is something that is on his soul, or between him and God.

MOHSEN: I have nothing to do with it, and you have nothing to do with it.

SALLY: When people give to a church, that is a tax write-off. When you give to the mosque, that's a tax write-off.

MOHSEN: Yes, that's right.

SALLY: But when you give this, it's not a tax write-off?

MOHSEN: No, it's not a tax write-off. That's the whole issue.

LILA: It is a tax write-off between you and God.

MOHSEN: This, and whatever my God asks me to do, is written in the Quran for me to do. I do that. And what the imam does with the money is between him and God. I have nothing to do with it.

SALLY: This is fascinating. I never knew this.

LILA: You know too, that when people go to *hajj,* that they have to pay so much money before they go for all the wrongs that they have done in their life.

MOHSEN: Like for drinks that you have drunk, or one time you went into an orchard and you saw an apple, and you took some and you pocketed some. You pay money for all of that.

LILA: You tell him everything that you have done in your lifetime. He actually figures out how much money you owe.

SALLY: This you pay to him, not to the mosque?

MOHSEN: You pay it to him so that he will distribute it to the poor.

SALLY: This is radically different from the way Christian organizations are structured in America. It seems so . . . This is fascinating.

LILA: But you see, churches get their monies from the outside. We don't. The community helps the building survive. And the imam survives by the community.

SALLY: But it's such a separation.

MOHSEN: He lives among us, between us, from us.

LILA: Doesn't he have to send his money to the *marj'a* [Shia religious authority] first?

MOHSEN: Yes. He gives the money we give him to the *marj'a,* because the *marj'a* sends money to Muslims all over the world. Wherever there are the needy, they send it to them.

SALLY: I wanted you to discuss how much money the mosques bring in each year. This should show how much power they have in the community and say something about the size and relative wealth of the community. But if there is no accounting of this . . .

MOHSEN: How many mosques do we have? Let's count them first. The Islamic Center. The Institute. The Masjid.

LILA: There are about eight. I can tell you offhand. Eight.

MOHSEN: No, I am talking about the ones in Dearborn.

LILA: In the immediate area, I am telling you, there's eight.

MOHSEN: Sheikh Mohammed Ali Berro, Abdel Latif Berry, Al Sayyed Qazwini, Sheikh Hicham, and Sheikh Elahi, those are the main six right around.

LILA: And the American Moslem Bekaa Center [a Sunni institution]. What, are you only talking about the Shia mosques?

MOHSEN: The Shia. Those are the main ones in the community here that have two dinners every year. Somehow we find out when they are having their dinner so we can have our dinner on a different week than they do. One time, the Islamic Center of America and the House of Wisdom had theirs one hour apart.

LILA: Which is *ayb* really, because it's like forcing the community to choose.

MOHSEN: Yeah. You can't divide the community to go to two places at the same time.

Lila: People want to support all their mosques. At our grand opening this year, there were fifteen hundred people. They pledged more than $280,000. This was a grand opening mind you. And these are pledges I am talking about, not actual donations. Only about three hundred families gave money. Before, when our dinner only had six hundred people, we used to make eighty thousand dollars, ninety thousand dollars maximum. Every six months, when money got low, we would have a banquet to cover the costs of the Institute.

Sally: That is much more money than ACCESS was making at the time from their annual telethon.

Lila: Again these are pledges. You only see a certain percentage of this money.

Mohsen: Some butcher shops give twenty thousand dollars. They give the meat. The guy's brother gives money. They add it up.

Lila: They factor in all the gifts to get that total. The thing is, when people come together and donate their money to a mosque, they feel better than they do spending it on whatever.

Sally: I want to know about the mosque's relationship with the larger society, not so much in the Arab community, but what sort of programs you do to bring in non-Arabs or non-Muslims. What sort of educational programs do you offer?

Lila: Well, lately, the kids have been only attending weekend classes and getting involved in youth groups that we have on Friday nights. There are several different youth groups at the Islamic Institute, the House of Wisdom, the Islamic Center of America, and the Islamic Mosque of America. We have begun trying to rotate the programs among mosques, so that the children can go to all the meetings and meet each other. There's nothing *haram* [forbidden] or *ayb* about everybody meeting the other guys, so to speak. And this would help to lower tensions between the groups. "As you attend so-and-so mosque, I can't be bothered with you." We are trying to deter that.

In most cases, as I see the young people, they appreciate themselves for what they are and the community they've been born into. However, we've had some difficulties in our community for the last five years, where Arab American kids have been targeting Arab families and robbing their homes of everything that they have ever saved in their lives. It's happened to me twice. They rob you when they know you are at the mosque. The sad part is that at least one of my kids has slowly but surely moved away from, not from her identity so much, because all my girls wear *hijab,* but moved away from what she always used to believe in. These were her "friends" who broke into our house, and she feels to blame. It's those kinds of things that we're seeing. These kids who aren't kept busy, and I can only blame—well—we can't really say we blame the parents, but what the parents have been doing is dropping their kids off at the door of a mosque and expecting that their child is going in. But if you are not right there with them, to learn and to comprehend what's happening around them, those kids go right back out on the street. Our adults choose to be at home watching TV, drinking coffee, having a *sahrah.* They are forgetting what they were taught back home, or here even for that matter, culturally, Islamically. I think today's lifestyle has become so selfish that they are forgetting they have children to raise and they need to teach them. America is not going to teach them the right roads: they are certainly not taking the right roads.

That's what's painful. We are trying to break this routine and get our younger generation involved. If they are fearful of coming into a mosque because of the strict Islamic code, then we've come in and started doing meetings on other issues that relate indirectly to Islam. We are trying to get more youth programs rolling that would interest the kids. We have weekend classes, like what I taught. My classes weren't just health programs. We talked about things of interest to you, yourself, as a child, things like sexually transmitted diseases. People were like, "What are you talking about? They shouldn't even be worried about that." I said, "Oh, yes they should! Do you think your daughters are not trying to kiss guys? Do you think your sons can keep their pants on?" And this is the mentality of some of the people in our culture. That boys can go out. It's OK. They are boys. What is that supposed to mean?

MOHSEN: We don't teach our kids, "if you have sex, do this." We teach our kids not to have sex. That's when we say "do not." They know the consequences if they have sex before marriage, what impact that will have on families, and what kind of treatment they will get from their parents. So they know all, and they take everything into consideration, and they abstain.

LILA: And the neat thing about it is that we've gotten the parents involved, not just in the mosques now, but in the schools. The schools have that Human Growth and Development Program that I'm sitting on a committee for and so is Suehaila. Suehaila was sitting on it since she was sixteen to give her opinion as a student. "How would you perceive this if it was taught to you this way?" She still sits on this committee today. We got the parents involved to stand forward for their right to determine what is taught to their children. Forget teaching them about condoms and things of that sort, because, even setting Islam aside, we are talking about human values. Value to yourself as a human being. Things aren't as they were twenty years ago. There is a lot of ugly garbage going on around here and we are not fully aware of what is happening and how it's happened. HIV, in technical situations, might not be detected for five years. But these kids don't care. They don't think about it. So our point now is to get the parents involved. They have come to the school board and demanded that there be no more teaching of "safe sex." They will now teach abstinence. And that's what's happening. It's actually happening!

SALLY: In the Dearborn Schools?

LILA: Yes.

SALLY: Isn't the Institute planning a school as well?

LILA: They are saying in two years.

MOHSEN: It depends on the flow of the money.

SALLY: And is the Islamic Center building a school, too?

LILA: They have a school on Ford Road, called the Muslim American Youth Academy.

SALLY: How many students do they have? Is it a five-days-a-week school?

LILA: It's a regular school. The only difference is they include Islamic instruction one hour a day, just like the other Islamic schools that have opened. The *majma'* also has a school, but its only prekindergarten through fifth grade. The one on Ford Road is also through fifth grade. Every year it will add a grade. Our intention at the *majma'* is to build a school on Schaefer, adjacent to our new building. It is supposed to be for pre-K to twelfth.

SALLY: Does the community really need two or three Islamic schools in Dearborn? This seems unrealistic to me. The community can't possibly support them financially.

MOHSEN: Right.

SALLY: Is there a move among the different mosques to combine their efforts?

MOHSEN: I'll tell you what. We will see how the Islamic Center of America does with their school. If it is successful, we don't have to build ours. But if we see we have the need for the community to have another school, then . . . Yes. Because a school supports itself. The Islamic Institute is different. There is activity going on all the time, different kinds of activity. Whereas a school, whoever wants a school will pay tuition. That will cover the cost of teachers. We hope the school will support itself.

SALLY: There is no private school in America that supports itself [from tuition alone].

MOHSEN: If the Islamic Center of America says they have five hundred kids, still, there are a lot more than five hundred kids on the street.

LILA: And people are paying up to thirty-five hundred dollars a year sending their kids out to the Islamic School in Canton Township.

MOHSEN: The thing I worry about . . . I have four kids. If I want to send four kids, we are talking about over twelve thousand dollars a year. That's a lot of money to pay.

SALLY: And Arab families are often bigger than American families.

LILA: Well, of course they give you better rates.

SALLY: I would like to hear the two of you describe the future of Islam in this community, as you see it. It is obvious from your lives, that the Islam you practice today was brought to America by the immigrant community. What is the future of the religion as immigration tapers off, or as your children assimilate? Will Islamic practice in Detroit continue to be strongest among immigrants, or is the community developing an Arab American, ethnic form of practice?

MOHSEN: We had a dinner with the Detroit President's Association the other day. Each member is the president of a local corporation or organization. They asked me the same question, "How do Muslims live here? How do you teach Islam?" Well, first you don't send in a teacher to spread Islam. We don't have a missionary. We spread Islam by contact. I am a Muslim. Wherever I go, I do my prayers. People ask me why I am doing that. I explain to them, "I am a Muslim. I do this. I pray five times a day. I have to wash up five times a day. So with the prayer comes cleanliness." Whatever they ask me, I tell them. I am not going to lie. I pray to God. So Islam is spread through contact. People see the way you look, the way you talk with people, the way you conduct yourself in front of them.

That is how you preach Islam. The sheikh is there. He has a higher knowledge than me. If I have a difficulty with something, then I go to him and ask about this area or that. He will explain the right path to me.

Some people think we pray to the moon, we pray to the sun. We don't. When you go deeper into the religion, a lot of Muslims don't even understand. I talk to a lot of people. I tell them, "My wife is a Muslim. She believes in it in one way. I believe in it another. I went to a certain person to teach me about spirituality and things like that. She learned from books. She has a feeling of one thing. I have a feeling of another."

Lila: She wants to know about the future for our kids. I will tell you. There are going to be more mosques. No one thought there would be eight today in the immediate area.

Sally: Well, I am actually asking about something else. There are many Arab Americans from your generation who are Muslim today in name only. Their kids don't speak Arabic and know almost nothing about the religion. You participated in the recent Islamic revival, or renaissance, in Dearborn, but what about your children and others in the community? Will this recent strengthening of Islam be enough to sustain it twenty or thirty years down the road?

Lila: I think Islam will be stronger on a reformed, conservative note rather than a radical note. In the very beginning, everybody went gung ho. I did too. All of us went through that in the early 1980s. I think it was more, "Yes. Yes. This is our identity." We went out on a radical note. It was a political statement. It was a statement of who we are and letting people know it. But now, little by little, we are being accepted. Everyone is mellowing out. Even Mohsen is mellowing out. He used to be at a point where he would say, "Don't listen to music."

Sally: You shook my hand today. You didn't used to. I didn't mean to offer it. It's a reflex with me, but I was surprised that you shook it. [Mohsen, like many conservative Muslims, believes that the bare contact involved in a handshake between a man and a woman is both sexually and ritually polluting. In his earlier, more radical days, he would not shake a woman's hand at all. Although rooted in notions of respect and modesty, many Americans find this practice to be offensive.]

Lila: See. He doesn't want to hurt people's feelings.

MOHSEN: I used to pull my hand away. I don't care who it was. Then I had to explain why I wasn't shaking hands. It became a burden to me.

LILA: People would be offended and not understand. But in turn, when you do explain to people what you are doing and why, they start to respect you more. They see what you are up against. Now he will shake someone's hand and then explain later. And if it happens again, so what. Nobody is going to die over it. We have learned that we were too strict in the beginning, even with the kids. I have to say that my daughters all wore the *hijab* on their own. People used to say that we were pushing them because we were so gung ho, but they decided this on their own. However, the things that we were doing at home, "no music, change that station," it was always things that they had to do. I worried that everything we were telling them not to do, they were turning around and trying it on their own. It got to the point where Mohsen would say, "Don't listen to music." And then he would get in the car and turn on the radio to make the kids happy. He had a double standard. We didn't want to lose the kids. We saw that we were starting to lose them.

MOHSEN: I was against weddings all the time. I saw animosity toward me and my wife from my kids because of weddings. Their friend is getting married. Their cousin is getting married. We go to the wedding and we eat and we leave [before the music and dancing start]. And everybody is still there. My aunt and my cousins are still there.

LILA: A lot of people leave, though, too.

MOHSEN: The kids would wonder, "Why can't we? Why can't we stay?" Then I gave in one time at their cousin's wedding.

SALLY: And they had too good a time . . .

MOHSEN: [Laughing] They had too, too good of a time. I said, "OK. This is it. Don't push me on the subject anymore." I understand. I want to do the same thing, but I can't.

LILA: We are starting to realize that, yes, Allah might say that you shouldn't do certain things. But then I started to think, would God really put you in Hell for this? Enjoy your life. Let your children enjoy their lives. You are still doing your obligations. You are still praying five times a day. You still did the *hajj.* I can't imagine that after completing your obligations, that you can't go and do the things you want to do.

MOHSEN: That's where me and my wife differ on things, to be honest. She thinks the big issue is about sin, big sin. A big sin is adultery, murder, lying, backbiting everyone. Those are the big sins. Then it comes to the small sins, which you heard us arguing about. But it's like they say. How did the mountains become mountains? From atoms. You put atoms together and it becomes a mountain [of sin].

SALLY: So you believe in setting an example with your whole life, whereas Lila is more willing to compromise. Maybe this has to do with where you were raised and how you think religion relates to your total way of life.

LILA: Yes, I think so too.

The interview ended here. We were all pressed for time, and I felt somewhat thwarted by my inability to draw Mohsen and Lila out on their vision of the future of the Muslim community in Dearborn. It is obvious, though, that they have divergent views. Mohsen, whose radical religious conversion has disposed him to believe in absolutes, is troubled by the compromises he is already making in his life. Lila, who retains the right to be outspoken and critical of her own political/religious movement, is an advocate of moderation and temperance. The constant tension between the assimilationist and the hard-liner is familiar to anyone who lives or works in Arab Detroit. It is a problem faced by every immigrant community, and by religious conservatives of every creed.

Lila, who was raised in an ethnic, assimilationist environment, sees the political and religious events that have overtaken the community during the last two decades as a positive, greatly needed corrective. In the 1980s, she was able to embrace and redefine a Lebanese/Islamic heritage that had been reduced to a set of family relationships and negative feelings about "Syrians." But her vision of the future harkens back to the era of accommodation in which she was raised. I suspect that Lila's "reformed, conservative" Islam is, in practice if not in theory, an Americanized Islam, and it appeals to her precisely because she is already so thoroughly American.

For Mohsen, compromise is a tempting, ever-present reality, and he can hardly be expected to see an attractive future in it. He believes that certain acts are morally wrong, no matter how simple and inoffensive they seemed during his youth. He wants to keep his children, and his community, away from dancing, drinking, gambling, dating, and other sinful pleasures. He is experiencing great difficulty in doing so. The emotional revival the Shia community experienced a decade ago has already cooled into more stable, less extreme forms. Mohsen's children, now young adults, are voicing their own ideas about right and wrong behavior. These ideas are not shaped solely by the youth programs they attend at local mosques. Instead, they are shaped by the larger American society in which the entire Amen family is utterly and unavoidably immersed. This American cultural landscape is more familiar to Lila than to her husband because, like her children, Lila grew up in it.

If I had pressed Mohsen further on the future he envisions for Islam in Detroit, I think he would have conceded the strength of Lila's prediction of an increasingly "reformed, conservative" Islam. He certainly would not have endorsed it. Whereas Lila embraces change and actively seeks it out, Mohsen is more aware of the losses change will bring. It will cause his children to view their own Muslim-Lebanese heritage as a small part of some bigger, vaguely defined, and obviously non-Muslim society. It will perhaps cost his grandchildren the ability to speak and understand Arabic. Mohsen and Lila are people of faith, walking the "straight path" charted by the Prophet. They both insist that "culture" and "religion" are different things, separable in thought and deed, and this assumption colors their attitudes toward change. Lila looks forward to a time when Islam in Dearborn will be more purely Islamic, when all Muslims, male and female, will know and respect the rights God has given them, when immigrant custom will give way to a more tolerant and enlightened approach. This progressive vision is as American as Lila Amen. It is filled with biases and assumptions every bit as "cultural" as those Mohsen brought with him to Dearborn from Lebanon. Lila's ideas are already producing, in Detroit, an Islam that speaks to the lives and needs of American-born Lebanese who can no longer confine their understanding of Islam to the attitudes of parents (and spouses) who grew up in villages on the other side of the world.

The integrity of Mohsen's convictions, and the value he places in upholding them, also plays a part in defining the future of Islam in America. He and thousands of Lebanese immigrants like him have returned to the Muslim community in Detroit a faith that is based on a close, literal reading of the Quran. Mohsen is firm in his beliefs yet generous and thoughtful in the ways he accommodates his differences with Lila. I wish him strength and wisdom as he struggles, day by day, to level the "mountain of sin" that accumulates with each innocent, seemingly inconsequential step he takes away from the Islam he so transformatively embraced in 1982.

Arab Detroit's "American" Mosque

Nabeel Abraham

One Friday in 1976 a group of Muslims gathered on the doorstep of the Dix mosque (officially known as the Moslem Mosque) in the Southend of Dearborn. Finding the door locked, they forced their way in and proceeded to do what Muslims all over the world do every Friday at midday: perform Jumaa communal prayers. For this group of mostly immigrant, mostly Yemeni and Palestinian worshipers, their dramatic entrance into the mosque symbolized its reclamation by "authentic" Muslims. The "inauthentic" Muslims from whom they reclaimed the mosque were not American converts. They were mostly the families of early Lebanese-Syrian immigrants, and their mosque was one of the oldest in America.

The nationalist Yemenis among whom I was conducting ethnographic fieldwork at the time were hardly devout. They found the actions of their zealous countrymen, whom they referred to as "*al-musalee'een*" (literally "those who pray") mildly amusing.[1] Yet even the avowed atheists among them understood the logic of the *musalee'een*'s action. The Lebanese and Palestinian immigrant population residing in the Southend of Dearborn in the late 1970s also readily comprehended the reasoning behind the *musalee'een*'s forced entry into the Dix mosque. Mosques in the Middle East, and elsewhere in the traditional world of Islam, are open on Fridays, their primary function being to serve as a place to hold the Friday communal prayer. That the Dix mosque was not open on Fridays was abnormal, even scandalous, in the eyes of the immigrant Muslim community. This fact was obscured in my mind by the rhetoric employed by my Yemeni informants, leftists as well as rightists, who considered the *musalee'een* to be political reactionaries and social neanderthals. With hindsight, it is clear to me that whatever the personal, social, and political attitudes of the *musalee'een*, the driving impulse behind their action that fateful Friday morning was as cultural as it was religious.

The "reclamation" of the Dix mosque that began in 1976 culminated two years later when the *musalee'een* wrested complete control of the mosque from its more assimilated Lebanese Sunni members following a bitter court battle. With the help of a Yemeni sheikh trained in Saudi Arabia, they instituted a series of seemingly radical measures. Whereas in the past the mosque was open once a week for communal prayers (mostly on Sundays), henceforth it would be open twenty-four-hours a day, seven days a week. The newcomers also did away with the historic division of the mosque into a prayer area on the main floor and a social area in the basement; thus they disallowed weddings and other social celebrations that were long the mainstay of the Dix mosque. "Henceforth," the *musalee'een*'s imam declared, "there will be no singing or dancing in this house of worship."[2]

In another departure from established practice, the new leaders placed restrictions on women entering the mosque. In the past, female members of the congregation were at liberty to enter the mosque as they pleased. After the takeover, they were required to wear head scarves, enter through a special side door, and restrict themselves to designated areas within the building. According to the former imam, Mike Karoub, who was unceremoniously ousted, the *musalee'een* felt that the women and children were defiling the mosque. Women were believed to be ritually "polluting" the mosque if they entered it while they were menstruating. This "danger" applied even to the parts of the building that had been considered social areas. In the view of the newcomers and their sheikh, the entire building was a "house of worship." Theological rationalizations about "ritual pollution" aside, the *musalee'een* sought to replicate in Dearborn the public forms of female segregation and subordination they were accustomed to in their countries of origin.

To outside observers, the new restrictions comported well with the image of "Islamic revivalism" and "fundamentalist Islam" taking shape in the wake of the Islamic revolution in Iran and elsewhere in the latter half of the 1970s. This was especially true of the injunctions applied to the women of the congregation. By the mid-1980s those images became the norm in much of Dearborn's Muslim community, the largest concentration of Arabic-speaking Muslims in North America. It is quite commonplace today, for example, to see Muslim women clad in head scarves, long sleeves, and ankle-length dresses even on the hottest summer days throughout Arab Detroit. The recent influx of Iraqi Shia refugees has brought with it the heretofore unfamiliar sight of the black *abayas* (cloaks) worn by women in southern Iraq. Such images, always perplexing to outsiders, including assimilated Arab American Muslims, fit neatly into American views of Islam and its attitudes toward women.

It is a simple matter today to point to the profusion of Islamic institutions and organizations in Metropolitan Detroit and conclude that an Islamic "revival" has indeed taken place. In Dearborn and its immediate environs alone, there are at least a dozen Islamic mosques, centers, schools, and bookstores that address the needs of Muslims, Shia, and Sunni alike. *Halal* (ritually slaughtered) meat markets and food abound. It is easy to forget that this profusion is a relatively recent phenomenon. In the early 1980s, Dearborn's large Muslim population was served by only two mosques—the mainly Sunni Dix mosque in the Southend and the predominately Lebanese Shia Islamic Center on Joy Road in nearby Detroit. Arguably, this profusion of Islamic dress, centers, schools, Muslim identity, and *halal* food derives its primary impulse from developments taking place in the Muslim world. The scale of this proliferation, however, obscures its prosaic nature. The prevalence of things *Islamica* in Dearborn has much to do with the influx of Muslim immigrants to the area in recent decades. They brought with them an Old World view of Islamic practice, partly energized by the Islamic revival, that contrasts sharply with the evolution of mosques and Muslims in the United States. The now-forgotten history of the Dix mosque reveals the impact recent immigration has had on Islamic practice in Dearborn.

An "American" Mosque: Lost and Found

Tucked away on Chase Street on Dearborn's east side in the heart of the new Lebanese immigrant community sits the American Moslem Bekaa Center. Operating out of a converted building, the Bekaa Center is the forgotten stepchild of the "reclaimed" Dix mosque; it is all but unrecognizable to those who attended its myriad religious and social functions through the four decades leading up to the dramatic events of 1976. The founders of the American Moslem Bekaa Center were the losers in the battle over the shape and tenor of Islamic practice in the Dix mosque. Their story is now buried beneath the rubble of the present. Paradoxically, the history of the Dix mosque provides both a deeper understanding of Islam in Arab Detroit today and a glimpse into its future.

By 1978 the Lebanese old guard at the Dix mosque found themselves on the losing end of a struggle to retain control of the mosque they had built. Those who were not physically ousted in the tumult of 1976 found themselves defeated and dejected after a bitter court battle that ended in 1978. Several years of dormancy followed. Eventually, the ousted group was able to reconstitute itself as a distinct congregation under the name of the American Bekaa Lebanese League, a name used decades earlier by a previous generation. The name reflects the group's regional roots in the Bekaa Valley of Lebanon. By 1983, some five years after its ouster, the group acquired the small building on Chase Street that it converted to a social hall and religious sanctuary. What made this resurrection especially noteworthy was that the effort was spearheaded by women, not men.[3]

The women had long maintained their own organization under the name of the American Moslem Women's Society, whose title and treasury they retained after the change in leadership at the Dix mosque. The Bekaa men, in contrast, found themselves "penniless" and in disarray, as the mosque's treasury, which they once controlled, fell into the hands of the newcomers. Thus, when it came time for the Bekaa League to secure a mortgage for its new building, the Women's Society stepped forward with the down payment on the mortgage. The women's financial leverage gave them an unprecedented voice not only in the Bekaa Center's administration but also in its overall direction. Half of the seats on the center's new board of directors went to women as well as to representatives of the youth organization, who were allied with them.

The new arrangement stood in sharp contrast to the one that once prevailed at the Dix mosque. In preschism days, the men officially dominated the affairs of the mosque and its activities, while the women were confined to secondary roles. After the takeover, the positions of men and women reversed, with the women enjoying unprecedented leadership in the day-to-day affairs of the Bekaa Center. The new arrangement between the sexes caught the notice of many observers, including one imam in another congregation who remarked with some alarm that the Bekaa "women want to control their men." In no other Muslim institution in the Dearborn area did women play a leadership role in the respective institutions. The fact that many of the Bekaa women worked outside the home probably accounts for their readiness to assert themselves into a leadership role in the reconstituted Bekaa Center.

Origins of the Women's Society

By the late 1920s, a large number of Lebanese Muslim immigrants had moved into the Southend of Dearborn to work at Henry Ford's sprawling River Rouge automobile plant. Many of the immigrants had relocated from Highland Park, the site of the original Ford operations and the home of the earliest Lebanese Muslim settlement in the Detroit area. At the time, Detroit's Lebanese Muslim community consisted of Sunnis from the Bekaa region of Lebanon and Shia from the southern region of the country.

In the 1930s the Lebanese in Dearborn established a Muslim congregation that was dominated by Sunnis. "A year or so after the establishment of this mosque," Linda Walbridge writes, "the Shi'a rented a hall only a few blocks away. They named it the Hashimite [*sic*] Hall, in honor of the family of the Prophet" (1997, 44).[4] By 1937 the Sunni congregation completed work on the ground floor of what would eventually become the Dix mosque. Meanwhile, the Shia congregation began efforts to purchase and convert a bank into the Hashemite Hall.

The rival mosque projects necessitated the mobilization of the still-nascent immigrant community's meager financial and human resources. This need appears to have been an important impetus behind the establishment of women's auxiliaries in each congregation. Novel developments in themselves, the auxiliaries are said to have played important roles in raising funds for the building projects, although documentation is nonexistent. It should be noted that the very idea of Muslims building and then financially supporting a mosque is itself novel, given that the construction and upkeep of mosques in the Middle East invariably is the responsibility of the state.

Although the precise role of the women's auxiliaries is not known, it is said that the Hashemite auxiliary was disbanded by the late 1940s, while its counterpart at the Dix mosque continued to function and even flourished. The exact cause, as well as the date, behind the demise of the Shia women's group is lost to us.[5] It is, nevertheless, worth speculating why one auxiliary survived into the present while the other did not. According to some informants, the Hashemite auxiliary disbanded around the time the mortgage on the Hashemite Hall was retired and no major projects that would tax the congregation's resources were on the agenda. In contrast to the single-phased project at the Hashemite Hall, the building project at the Dix mosque consisted of multiple phases in a long-term construction project. Construction of the Dix mosque continued into the late 1950s with plans for further expansion. During the second half of the 1950s and early 1960s, when my family was a member of the congregation, there was constant talk of building a school on a vacant lot adjacent to the mosque. The idea remained unfulfilled at the time of the takeover in the late 1970s.

By necessitating the mobilization of the community's resources and ingenuity, the building projects at the rival mosques enabled the greater involvement of Muslim women in the affairs of the mosques. The women were called upon to actively engage in fund-raising. They organized sales, parties, and picnics at which they sold baked goods, knitting, and other crafts. "Blessings" from the wives were needed so husbands could pledge portions of their take-home pay to the projects. Presumably, the women also needed to agree to their husbands spending scarce nonworking hours away from family supervising projects, raising money, and occasionally pitching in a hand in the actual construction or renovation of the buildings.

Overall, the women, individually and collectively, probably played key roles in the success of the community projects, even though their contribution was undoubtedly less recognized than the men's, and it may have been resented as well. According to a longtime female member of the Hashemite congregation, "the women were criticized all the time for being so organized and for being so aggressive. . . . The men felt the women should have stayed at home. They didn't like the idea of the women being so politically active." The exigencies of the communitywide mobilization necessitated a softening of the men's conservative social attitudes toward the participation of women in the public life of the mosques. The men were not altogether happy about the changes taking place as a result, but they faced a kind of Faustian bargain: to preserve their Lebanese Muslim cultural and religious identity they needed to build the mosques, but building the mosques entailed the participation of women in the public life of the community, a step that undermined the very cultural world they were seeking to preserve in the New World.

The early immigrants must have suffered from extreme cultural and social alienation in depression-era Dearborn. Their neighborhood, the Southend, was mostly populated by Italian, Romanian, and Polish immigrants. The Arabic-speaking residents were relatively few, as their immigration into the area did not peak until the periods 1927–33 and 1946–53 (S. Abraham, N. Abraham, and Aswad 1983, 166ff.). The mosque construction/acquisition projects helped them overcome their alienation and strengthen their communal solidarity, their Sunni-Shia sectarian rivalries notwithstanding. The projects gave them a special purpose—the advancement of Islam in an alien, Christian land. Those benefits probably outweighed the public activism of the women in the mental calculus of the men.

Men, Women, and Their Imams

The Sunni women's auxiliary, which was also known as the Women's Society, remained active throughout the 1950s, as the congregation moved to implement the second and third phases of the mosque construction project. Although the auxiliary continued to be largely dominated by women from the Bekaa region of Lebanon, membership expanded during the decade to encompass women from Palestine as well as other areas of Lebanon, a move that reflected the changing composition of the congregation during this time. In 1952 work on the important second phase was completed with the opening of the first-floor prayer area, the adjacent lecture hall, and the imam's office. The congregation soon made plans for the third phase—the construction of a large metal dome atop the mosque. The dome, adorned with a characteristic Islamic crescent, was finally erected in 1957.

Following the raising of the dome, the congregation's attention turned to internal matters, particularly to bringing a scholarly imam to head the now prosperous working-class congregation. The proposal ignited a conflict between the mosque's board of directors and the congregation's longtime spiritual head, Imam Hussein Karoub. Karoub had founded the congregation, but his lack of scholarly credentials, his surprising progressive views, and the taint of scandal associated with the first mosque in the Detroit area—in Highland Park—conspired to weaken his standing in the eyes of the Bekaa old-timers on the board of directors. Citing a news story that appeared in the *Detroit News* on July 29, 1927, Walbridge (1997, 43–44) recounts the controversy that followed Karoub from the original Highland Park mosque:

> The mosque was short-lived, though it apparently had support from a variety of Muslim countries. The article reports that there was a difference of opinion regarding the failure of the mosque. Karoub had brought a religious leader, a mufti, from Lebanon whose ideas were too progressive for the Muslims, who were far from being a homogeneous group . . . from Persia, Turkey, Spain, Morocco, Siberia, Arabia and Syria. Others, apparently, were not happy with Karoub's financing of the mosque. The greatest controversy came when a coffeehouse proprietor who had usurped Karoub's leadership and popularity was killed. While Karoub was acquitted of any wrongdoing, his name was tarnished.

By the late 1950s, the incident had been largely forgotten, but other controversies remained. Most pronounced was the fact that

Imam Karoub lacked any formal theological training. Being largely self-taught, his knowledge of Islamic theological and legal matters was considered dubious by some in the congregation. My mother's attitude was typical of some. A Palestinian immigrant who arrived in Detroit in 1955, she was quietly skeptical of Imam Karoub's religious knowledge. Seeing no alternative, she nevertheless continued to send her children to the mosque for religious and Arabic-language instruction.[6]

The erection of the dome signaled a change in attitude among a segment of the congregation. The completion of the building project conferred new confidence in the small congregation. Around the same time, Egypt's charismatic leader, Gamal Abdel Nasser, nationalized the Suez Canal, sparking Arab nationalist fervor throughout the Arab world, including the tiny Dix mosque congregation in far-off Dearborn. Egypt's ability to stave off a combined military attack by Britain, France, and Israel following nationalization of the Suez Canal further enhanced Arab nationalist sentiment in the mostly Arab Dix congregation. This glowing account by Elkholy (1966, 48) of the Arab nationalist fervor he found among Detroit's Muslims, though somewhat ecstatic, is nevertheless accurate:

> The Arab defeat in the Palestinian War [1948] aroused the anger of Moslems in America but discouraged them as well. The Egyptian Revolution and the rise of President Nasser to world prominence, however, aroused their sense of nationalism. To Moslems in America as well as in the Middle East, Nasser became the symbol of Arab nationalism. In almost every Moslem home in America there is more than one picture of Nasser. In their social and religious events, the Moslems receive enthusiastically and applaud strongly the songs about Nasser. As a prominent woman in Detroit put it to a Jordanian official accompanying King Hussein during his visit in 1959: "Whenever a party is opened in the name of the Prophet, no one is particularly moved. If it is opened in the name of God, no one cares either. But the name of Gamal Abdel-Nasser electrifies the hall."

A framed portrait of the Egyptian leader hung prominently in the social area of the mosque as late as the mid-1970s.[7]

This period was also marked by developments in parts of the Arab world that buoyed Arab nationalist sentiment, namely, the Algerian war of independence (1954–62), political union between Egypt and Syria (1958–61), the overthrow of the monarchy in Iraq (1958), pro-Nasserite disturbances in Lebanon (1958), and the overthrow of the imamate in Yemen (1962).

By the early 1960s, possibilities and alternatives that once seemed impossible began to pose themselves to leaders of the congregation. The most attractive was a proposal to invite a Muslim scholar, a sheikh, from Cairo's famed al-Azhar University to preside over theological and Arabic-language instruction at the Dix mosque. The proposal was deliberately left vague in deference to Imam Karoub.

Adding a sense of urgency to the congregation's deliberations was Karoub's approaching retirement. Of concern to some members of the congregation was his plan to pass the imamship to his son, Mohammad "Mike" Karoub. If some in the congregation harbored doubts about the authenticity of the imam's religious bona fides, they had even greater doubts about his American-born son's credentials. Mike Karoub received his religious schooling at his father's knee.[8] His command of classical Arabic, the sine qua non for establishing authority in a religion that holds up Arabic as the language in which God delivered his final message to mankind, was suspect. In all fairness to the imam's son, doubts about his facility in Arabic were probably due more to his American-accented Arabic rather than to his actual competency in the language. Perceptions, however, are important. That the very Americanized Mike Karoub was also married to a Lebanese Christian, whose conversion to Islam was not in dispute at the time (but would become so later), contributed to the skepticism about his capabilities to lead the congregation. Imam Karoub's intention to hand the mantle of leadership to his son was the unspoken issue in the debate over whether to invite a Muslim sheikh to the mosque. Beneath that concern, however, lay a much more profound issue: should the mosque continue as an "American" mosque or should it "Arabize," that is, revert to being an Arab-style mosque.[9]

According to a longtime member of the congregation, the controversy over who should succeed the elderly Karoub was couched in the following terms: The men demanded the "preservation" of (in actuality, a return to) "authentic" Islamic traditions, while the Women's Society insisted on maintaining the status quo. The men betrayed their true feelings when they complained that some of the women were "too aggressive," faulting Imam Karoub for failing to preserve "traditional Islamic doctrine," which they believed resulted in the women's assertiveness in congregational matters. As the head of the congregation, the men reasoned, Karoub could have used his influence and knowledge of "the traditions" (sacred texts) to curtail the demands and independence of the leaders of the women's auxiliary. This had not happened, according to the mosque's male leaders, because the imam lacked sufficient "authority" (i.e., his command of theological and legal matters was wanting) and because of the taint of scandal in his background.[10]

In Middle Eastern culture, men have ultimate authority in the family. By extension, the imam serves as the symbol of that authority in the congregation. Unlike traditional Christian clergy, Muslim sheikhs (imams) do not function as intermediaries between the faithful and the Almighty. Imams are theoretically "first among equals." Their standing and authority, therefore, are linked to their knowledge of the Quran, Hadith, and Sunna, as well as the Sharia (Islamic law). These alone, however, do not guarantee a following or convey stature. A holy man must win approval by demonstrating his knowledge, wisdom, and leadership abilities. He must also demonstrate piety in his daily conduct. In short, an imam may need to go beyond mere knowledge of the sacred and demonstrate other virtues in order to gain legitimacy, including, among others, winning peer recognition and exhibiting proper disposition and personality.[11]

Initially, Imam Karoub and his allies in the women's auxiliary sought to delay the hiring of a new sheikh, but the male-dominated board of directors ultimately prevailed and invited an Old World scholar to Detroit. Dr. Ahmed Mehanna, an Egyptian graduate from al-Azhar University, arrived in 1959. With a sheikh from the citadel of Sunni Islam, the men probably reasoned they would be able to reassert their authority over the congregation, putting the women's auxiliary in its "place," while simultaneously blocking Karoub's plan to install his son at the head of the congregation.[12]

Dr. Mehanna was popular with those who grew up in the Middle East and with some American-born Muslims like myself who longed for a "purer" form of Islam and Arabic culture than what was available in Detroit. His soft-spoken manner accentuated his scholarly credentials, while his Egyptian identity added to his standing in the eyes of those who felt Egypt was leading the Arab world into the modern era.

His presence, however, did not resonate with everyone in the congregation, and it even exacerbated tensions within it. Atif Wasfi, who conducted anthropological field work in the mosque in 1963, noted:

> Although hundreds of letters were sent to al-Azhar University, asking for a religious scholar to teach the descendants [of] Islam, very few people attend the meetings held by this scholar. While

> the Shi'ah boycott the religious services of this Sunni mosque, many Sunni do not participate in the religious activities because of personal quarrels among the families. In addition, this reluctance to attend religious services, especially Friday group prayer, may be due to the weakness of the sense of religiosity in the community. (1964, 132–33)

Wasfi didn't elaborate further, but the "weakness" he found might be better viewed as an adaptation to American culture and way of life rather than to a slacking "religiosity," a point to which we shall return.

It is significant that the women who supported the new sheikh tended to be mostly immigrants who still spoke Arabic and were for the most part not employed outside the home. My mother fit this category. In her eyes, the young sheikh represented a "modern and well-educated" class of clergy (*ulama*), more symbolic of the future than of the past and better able to transmit "correct" Islam to American Muslims than Karoub. The women who sided with Imam Karoub, in contrast, tended to be mostly American-born or American-raised, and many held jobs outside the home.[13]

The two camps squared off during the election of new officers for the Women's Society. The outcome had direct implications for the broader struggle over leadership in the congregation. The election pitted the most assimilated women, who supported Imam Karoub's daughter-in-law, Ida, against the foreign-born members. The victory of Ida Karoub and her slate prompted accusations of cheating, which resulted in a walkout by the opposing side. When the losing group sought to hold a meeting in the mosque, they found they had been locked out. Some of the disaffected, like my mother, began attending the Shia-dominated Hashemite Hall.

The bickering and infighting took its toll on Dr. Mehanna, who left his post in 1964 at the end of his five-year contract. His greatest disappointment appears to have been the reluctance of the congregation's Men's Club to back his bid for a position on the board of directors. It is said that the men feared the sheikh would use a position on the board to dominate the mosque as Imam Karoub had done. This explanation has plausibility. If the example of other congregations has any bearing, mosques tend to be dominated by the founding imam—the case of Imam Chirri, who founded the Islamic Center on Joy Road is a good example. But after declining health or death removes a founding imam from the scene, the mosque's board of directors asserts control and subsequent imams are usually denied a position on the board. Sheikhs who demand complete control usually establish a breakaway mosque.

End of an Era

In the wake of the Egyptian sheikh's departure, tensions continued to simmer between the Men's Club and the Women's Society at the Dix mosque. The conflict reached a stalemate, as indicated by the congregation's inability to make a decision on the vacant lot adjacent to the mosque. When I was attending Arabic school at the mosque in the early 1960s, there was persistent talk that the lot, on which stood a large commercial billboard, would someday be developed as the location of a full-fledged Arabic school on the model of the Armenian schools that some of my schoolmates attended on evenings and weekends. The Women's Society argued for launching the school construction project immediately, while the Men's Club, which essentially controlled the board of directors, hesitated for reasons that remain unclear.

It was about this time that the congregation began experiencing a loss of members, particularly of second- and third-generation offspring who began moving from the Southend to east Dearborn and to the more middle-class suburbs that better reflected their social and economic progress. Wasfi (1964, 136) captured this group's attitude, writing, "Many young Arab-Moslems do not dare take their American friends or American wives to the old-fashioned mosques [in the Southend] because of their location. Moreover, the mosques are the symbols of the sectarian differences."

Not only were the middle-class children of the Southend congregations defecting to the newer suburbs, a good number were beginning to attend the new "upscale" Islamic Center on Joy Road. The biggest loss appears to have been suffered by the Hashemite Hall congregation that like the new Islamic Center was predominately Shia. Wasfi (1964, 146–47) reported that whereas the Hashemite Hall congregation numbered 600 in 1958, by 1963 its numbers had dwindled to 150; even some of its leaders "moved to the Islamic Center and obtained offices there." Like its longtime rival, the Hashemite Hall, the Dix mosque was facing competition from the new Islamic Center and its dynamic, young leader Imam Chirri. Assimilated members of the Dix mosque congregation also defected to the Islamic Center, ignoring the Sunni-Shia divide in the process. That is precisely what my family did in the mid-1960s after a short stint at the Hashemite Hall.

Chirri held a full-time position as director and president of the Islamic Center, in contrast to the imams at the other mosques, who were denied similar positions. He also had the most schooling in religion, and therefore he had the greatest authority. Moreover, he spoke

English better than his rivals—with the exception of Mike Karoub who hadn't yet assumed the mantle of leadership at the Dix mosque. Chirri adopted an embracing attitude toward all Muslims, ignoring the Sunni-Shia cleavage that had long divided the Dix and Hashemite mosques. He also garnered support from two Sunni-dominated Arab governments: Nasser's Egypt as well as Jordan, which donated forty-four thousand dollars and seven thousand dollars respectively to help build the Islamic Center. "He collected other contributions from the community members themselves. In two dinner parties he collected $30,000" (Wasfi 1964, 136). In comparison, the financial situation at the Dix mosque was dismal, according to Wasfi (145), who found:

> Most of the members do not pay the subscription of one dollar per month. While there are more than 120 members (married and unmarried males and females), only 40 of them pay the subscription. These are old Sunnis. In order to get money to maintain the mosque, the association arranges dinner parties accompanied by Arabic songs and dances. Some Arab-Moslem girls perform belly dances to collect contributions. At a recent party, they collected about $700.

In the late 1960s, an influx of new immigrants from the Arab world began to change the complexion of the neighborhood and with it the makeup of the Dix congregation. The new arrivals were mostly Yemenis and Palestinians, the latter from the Israeli-occupied West Bank. The Dix mosque also began attracting worshipers, mostly men, from nearby areas of Detroit, recent immigrants from Jordan, Egypt, Pakistan, Afghanistan, and Lebanon, as well as African American converts to Islam. Most of the new Lebanese immigrants in the Southend at the time were Shias, who preferred to attend the predominately Shia mosques. This was not the case with the Zeidis, who are nominally Shia but preferred to attend the Dix mosque.[14]

The influx of new immigrants to the Southend not only brought new worshipers to the mosque, it brought a demand for a different kind of Islam—a more traditional Middle Eastern Islam. This type of Islam placed a strong emphasis on male-oriented public piety and worship and left no place for women except in the home. Initially, the mosque's old guard viewed the influx of new members as a sign of resurgence after years of declining attendance. The established leadership also saw in the new members a revival of "Islamic tradition" in the mosque. The members of the Women's Society viewed the matter differently—they saw the men recruiting the newcomers to their side as a way of cementing their control over the mosque.

Conflict soon erupted over a proposed revision in the mosque's bylaws. Imam Karoub and the leaders of the Women's Society argued for an amendment restricting membership in the mosque. They feared that the newcomers would eventually form a majority and come to dominate the mosque. They were naturally opposed by the newcomers who resented being shut out of the mosque's decision-making body, considering it "un-Islamic." The Men's Club opposed both the Women's Society and Mike Karoub, who had replaced his father in semiofficial capacity after the latter's death in 1973. Confident of their control of the mosque, the leaders of the Men's Club dismissed their opponents' warnings. Although the debate over the proposed bylaw change never came to a vote, it was a harbinger of things to come.

Following the forced entry of the *musalee'een* into the mosque in 1976, the *musalee'een* gained positions on the mosque's board of directors. Their leader, a Palestinian immigrant by the name of Hajj Fawzi, was a firebrand Islamicist, who vehemently opposed Mike Karoub and his followers. Not long afterward, a showdown occurred between the *musalee'een* and Mike Karoub and his wife and their supporters. "The police were summoned, but not before Karoub and his followers were physically assaulted and chairs flew. Karoub's wife triggered the melee because she had walked into the mosque wearing a large cross on her chest."[15]

At the urging of the *musalee'een,* the mosque's board of directors invited a young Yemeni sheikh to head the congregation. The Saudi-trained imam was extremely conservative, even anachronistic, by the standards of the congregation. He banned all social activities from the mosque, saying there would be no music or dancing in it. Women visiting the mosque were required to dress modestly by covering their hair, arms, and legs. The new imam ended coed Islamic classes, forcing boys and girls into separate classrooms. He also called on members of the congregation to withdraw their savings from interest-bearing bank accounts, in keeping with the Muslim injunction against charging or accepting interest on money. The imam further advised fellow Muslims to refrain from keeping dogs as pets, as they are traditionally considered ritually impure by Muslims.

When the women's auxiliary protested the imam's decrees, particularly his ban on the holding of social functions like weddings and fund-raising parties in the mosque basement, he sternly told them, "I am here to teach you the right way; you have gone astray." When they complained, he unceremoniously banned the women's group from the mosque.

By the standards of the Middle East, the new imam's attitudes were not altogether atypical, his Wahhabi-training notwithstanding.[16] Nor were his positions necessarily at variance with those expressed by several other imams at the time. Haddad and Lummis (1987, 100) interviewed several North American Muslims in autumn 1983 whose respective imams echo the Dearborn sheikh's position. One informant said, "The imam is always stressing that we ought not to take interest, it is *haram* [sinful]." Another notes, "The imam says that interest is forbidden." Unfortunately, the authors of the study do not reveal the specific identities or locales of their informants so it is impossible to know if there is an overlap with the Dix mosque. During my own fieldwork in the Dearborn Yemeni community (1976–77) informants reported compliance with the new imam's directive to withdraw their savings from the bank and keep their money at home. This resulted in at least one theft of a Yemeni worker's savings.

In their study of five mosques in the Midwest, upstate New York, and on the East Coast, Haddad and Lummis (1987, 120) found several imams who disapproved of music that inspired "love and sexual feeling" and at least two imams who banned music and dance from mosque buildings. They relayed the following stories, "Two mothers in their thirties, trying to interest young people in attending mosque functions, were reprimanded for trying to bring music and dance there. In one instance the mother was told she could not have any music in the mosque building, even for children to dance and sing." The mother relates the following incident, which resembles what happened at the Dix mosque, "Music was intoxication. . . . So you could not have music. It is against Islam to listen to music. At that time they said there will be no music downstairs (in the mosque basement) and I made the suggestion that I would hold the party in my house, and I would like to have music. The imam said no, I could not bring the boys and girls together and have them listen to music or dance as couples" (120). "In another mosque," report Haddad and Lummis, "a mother upset the mosque leaders greatly by inviting a belly dancer as entertainment for a community dinner. The event was canceled before the dancer had a chance to perform" (120).

Walbridge (1997, 111) recorded the reactions of recent Lebanese Shia immigrants to the past practice of holding wedding celebrations in mosques by Dearborn's assimilated Arab Muslims:

> In Lebanon, weddings do not occur at the mosques. "People went to the mosques for prayers and funerals, not for weddings and engagements like they do here," one woman told me. When the new

> immigrants arrived and saw weddings with dancing and music at the mosques, they were shocked. Very recent immigrants who never witnessed such things can hardly believe their ears when they are told that people actually danced in the mosques. One woman, a college student who is quite liberal in her dress and attitudes, was astounded when she learned of this and exclaimed, "That's terrible!" In the old country, weddings and engagements took place in halls, private homes, and gardens but not in mosques.

Although the board of directors of the Dix mosque liked the Yemeni sheikh's stress on upholding "Islamic tradition," they were uneasy about some of his actions. Ironically, the sheikh was forced to resign and return to Yemen because of allegations of impropriety. According to Yemenis I interviewed in the mid-1970s, the sheikh allegedly molested a twelve-year-old girl. After the girl's parents complained, he purportedly offered to marry her, but her family rejected the offer. I was never able to confirm the story, but the sheikh left the community shortly after the rumors began circulating in the Yemeni community.

The sheikh's brief tenure seems to have emboldened the newcomers. By 1978 they not only constituted a majority at the mosque, they also won a court battle with some of the old guard who challenged their interpretation of the mosque bylaws. The court decision, along with the loss of the mosque's treasury of forty thousand dollars, only deepened the humiliation of the Bekaai men who once controlled the mosque. In the eyes of other Bekaais, especially the women, the men had "lost" the mosque. The humiliation visited upon the Bekaa old-timers was compounded by the disdain the women harbored toward them for initially having allied themselves with the newcomers for the purpose of keeping the Women's Society "in its place." In a moment of lament, one former board member remarked, "We lost the mosque. We lost the treasury. And, now, we have lost our women."

An "American" Mosque in Arab Detroit

The passage of time allows us to put developments at the Dix mosque in perspective. What the newcomers who eventually took over the mosque found so scandalous and so "un-Islamic" at the Dix mosque in the mid-1970s was that it had become an American mosque, a kind of "Islamic Protestant church" that was run largely by and for Americanized Sunnis whose roots in the Bekaa region of Lebanon extended back two generations. The leadership was still mired in petty family quarrels, still stuck in Lebanese-style Sunni-Shia prejudices as well as other Old World impulses. But at its zenith in the 1960s, the congregation of mostly working-class families had acquired American social and cultural sensibilities and outlooks, irrespective of what some of the old-time male immigrants who ran the mosque thought or felt.

In 1963 Wasfi (1964) found an institution that would have been unrecognizable to any Middle Eastern Muslim. He observed that "An average of 12 persons attend the Friday group prayer" (132), which he mistakenly attributes to a "weakness of the sense of religiosity in the community" (133). In this he is echoing conclusions drawn by Abdo Elkholy (1966), who studied the congregation in 1959, where he found many second-generation and better-educated Arab Southenders lax in their observance of the Ramadan fast, in meeting their obligation to pray five times a day, in attending the Jumaa Friday prayer, and in their knowledge of the five basic pillars of Islam.[17] This decline in the congregation's "religiosity" is further bolstered by the finding, which alarms Wasfi, that there are "increasing" conversions to Christianity by Dearborn Muslims. Wasfi (141) is quick to add, however, that "their number is very small," not more than "two percent" of the community. In reality, the "converts" are a handful of Muslim women who married non-Muslim men.[18]

Wasfi, an Egyptian doctoral student, appeared surprised by other developments in the Dearborn Muslim community as well. To a Middle Easterner's mind in the early 1960s, these developments would have appeared alien and scandalous. Commenting on the fact that 82 percent of the families in his sample fit the nuclear family model, Wasfi (1964, 110–11) observed:

> The wife in this nuclear family insists on her American right of being equal to her husband. Even the wives who were brought up in the old country insist on this advantage. At the same time, the husbands of the first generation are not convinced of this right. Most of the quarrels between the husbands and their wives are related, directly or indirectly, to this claimed equality. Some of the unconvinced husbands beat their wives to ensure their superiority. But the wives who refuse to be beaten sometimes call the police, and the husbands are put in jail. Old men of the first generation, who are very upset, always say that America is for women and not for men. The American law gives the wife many privileges, such as the right of divorcing her husband, the right of taking the half [*sic*] of his wealth in case of divorce, and the right of being the only wife. She will never be a second or third wife. Consequently, all the

> decisions in the family are made by the wife and the husband. In fact, she has become the boss of the family, because the husband is always busy in [*sic*] making money. This conflict is almost nonexistent when both the couples [*sic*] are brought up in the United States.

Wasfi observed other social phenomena among Detroit's Arab Muslims that must have appeared outlandish to his Middle Eastern sensibilities and that bolstered his view that religiosity was waning in the Muslim community. "Some Arab girls," he notes, "performed belly dances to collect contributions" for an Arab American organization (1964, 151), and some members of the Islamic Youth Association "dance the 'Twist' and the Arabic 'Debka,' but they like the 'Twist' more" (153).

In light of Wasfi's observations on the Dix mosque and Detroit's Muslim community in general, we should not be surprised by the reaction of the *musalee'een* who followed him a decade later. Wasfi, after all, was highly educated and presumably sophisticated as well. The same cannot be said of many of the newcomers, who for the most part were semieducated laborers. Although they claimed to be more devout than their assimilated coreligionists, the source of their fervor was a Middle Eastern model of what a mosque should be. Everything they found at the Dix mosque (social parties, Nasser's portrait, the women's auxiliary, coed Sunday school classes, a preference for spoken English, Sunday as opposed to Friday communal prayer) was at variance with their entire life experience.[19] In this light, it is no small matter that the Women's Society used to run bingo games at the mosque, both as a source of entertainment and as a way of raising funds.

The irony is that the Dix mosque and similar "American" mosques seem to have—unwittingly, no doubt—reverted back to the model of the earliest type of mosque (*masjid*) in Islam. Following the work of Oleg Grabar (1969), Walbridge (1997, 98) reports that in the "very early history of the Islamic world . . . the masjid was basically an open space that served exclusively Muslim purposes such as prayer, collection of taxes, and military recruitment. There was no formal structure or well-defined purpose." To some extent one could argue that the Americanized Dix mosque (and others like it in Arab Detroit) represents a distant outpost of Islam, which by necessity serves multiple functions—as a community center, a school, a social venue, a place to hold weddings and funerals, a place for community solidarity and political expression, and as a house of worship.[20] These various purposes suited the needs of an immigrant community settling into a new cultural milieu, but the new forms may not have been recognizable to later immigrants (or recent converts) who held a model of the mosque prevalent in the contemporary Muslim world.[21]

The reaction of the newcomers to the Dix mosque in the late 1970s is entirely understandable—they either would have to "reclaim" the mosque for Islam as they understood and practiced it, or failing that, withdraw from the congregation and establish a new mosque. In this instance, they succeeded in wresting control of the mosque and forcing the founders group, the Bekaais, to leave and establish a new institution. In so doing, they were foreshadowing a conflict that has played out several times in the mosques of Dearborn (and presumably in mosques throughout North America), albeit in various ways and with different outcomes.

The Joy Road Mosque: Similar Conflict, Different Outcome

A similar struggle between the established (and generally Americanized) Muslims and a wave of immigrant newcomers subsequently took place within the larger Lebanese Shia community in Dearborn. It centered on the long-established Islamic Center. Unlike the Sunni-dominated Dix mosque, the struggle at the Islamic Center resulted in the old guard prevailing over those newcomers who sought to redefine the tenor and role of the mosque. The newcomers and their respective imams were forced to establish separate congregations only a few miles from the Islamic Center. This struggle has played out at least four consecutive times at the Islamic Center. Walbridge (1997, 112) documented three of those cycles, which occurred in the 1980s, and drew the following sweeping conclusion:

> In Dearborn, there is a new interpretation of the purpose of the mosque. It is actually part of a process that was started in the early part of this century. The mosque initially was used for all social events, many of which had nothing to do with religion. Then an earlier group of the new wave of immigrants came. Steeped in tradition, they tried to bring the mosque in line with what was done in Lebanon, so they moved weddings out of the [Islamic Center]. A slightly later group, strongly influenced by political changes in the Middle East, arrived, and once again the mosque (particularly the Majma' [Islamic Institute of Knowledge]) became

> a center for all types of occasions. But all of these occasions have been redefined as religious. For this latest group, the Shari'a minded [of the Islamic Council], there simply is no distinction between religion and nonreligion, between sacred and profane.

Of the many factors that conspire to determine the outcome of the struggle to control a mosque (personalities of key players, relative numbers of the opposing sides), leadership, particularly in the person of the "founding imam," seems to be the determining factor. As we have seen in the case of the Dix mosque, as long as Imam Karoub was running the affairs of the mosque, the board of directors were unable to reverse the Americanization of the mosque or curtail the activities of the women's auxiliary. As Imam Karoub prepared to retire, however, his grip weakened, allowing those who longed for a more Old World mosque to temporarily thwart the rise of the imam's son to the head of the congregation.

In the first confrontation, the younger Karoub and his allies in the women's auxiliary were able to retain control of the Women's Society and send the Egyptian sheikh packing. Even if the Egyptian sheikh had wanted to assert his influence on the mosque, he lacked a critical mass of potential supporters because the new immigrant segment of the congregation was still small at the time.

The Women's Society was emboldened by the support it received from Imam Karoub and his American-born and American-educated son. To the traditionally minded men in the Men's Club and on the board of directors, Imam Karoub was too Americanized. His unwillingness to impose a Middle Eastern behavioral code on the congregation (and thereby "curb" the women's auxiliary) made him suspect. But Karoub was also the founding imam who helped establish the mosque, and thus there was little the conservative men could do while he was alive, other than to stall his plan to have his son replace him as the mosque's part-time imam. He died in 1973, three years before the takeover of the mosque by the newcomers.

Consider, in comparison, developments at the Islamic Center on Joy Road, which since the early 1980s has found itself where the Dix mosque was in the 1970s. As long as Imam Chirri, the "founding sheikh," was in stable health, he was able to control the board of directors, oversee the hiring of a series of assistant imams from the Middle East, and maintain control in the face of a massive influx of new immigrants. Chirri was able to maintain his grip on the mosque while making essentially cosmetic concessions to the newcomers.

In the period before the late 1970s, when the recent wave of immigrants began arriving, Chirri was quite Americanized, having immigrated to the United States in the late 1940s. He wore a small white turban and a cloak over a Western-style business suit, and was more comfortable speaking English than Arabic to his largely Americanized mosque congregation. "A photograph of a children's class in 1965 shows a group of school-aged children dressed in their 'Sunday best.' The girls, sitting among the boys, wear crisp, frilly dresses and, except for one little girl in an 'Easter bonnet,' no head coverings at all," observes Walbridge (1997, 47). Social parties and wedding receptions were held at the Islamic Center just as at the Dix mosque. Services were held on Sunday, with Chirri giving the sermons in English with a little Arabic thrown in for emphasis. Although it is an exaggeration to claim, as one of Walbridge's informants did (47), that "the women used to wear curlers in their hair to the mosque!" it is quite true that no woman wore "Islamic dress" and few covered their heads. I once took a German American girl I was dating in high school to the Islamic Center for an ecumenical introduction to Islam. It was the mid-1960s and no one at the mosque thought it strange, least of all Sheikh Chirri, who always seemed to relish the prospect of a new convert.

With the influx of new immigrants from southern Lebanon in the 1980s, Chirri made stylistic accommodations, but otherwise made no substantial changes. Few people, I suspect, know that for many years a framed photograph of Imam Chirri shaking hands with President Nixon in the White House hung in his study at the Islamic Center. I remember scrutinizing the photo at length while listening to Chirri suggest to a group of Palestinian nationalists gathered for a lecture on Palestine that "half-a-loaf is better than no loaf." The reference was to the notion, then gaining currency, that Palestinians would be better off abandoning their maximalist goals and resigning themselves to live in peace with Israel in only part of their ancestral homeland. At the time, the idea was anathema to most Arabs, and those promoting it were suspected of being pro-American.

After the fall of the Shah of Iran in 1979, a large poster-sized photograph of Ayatollah Khomeini suddenly appeared in the foyer of the Islamic Center, where it stayed for several years. Nearby, hung a handwritten sign in Arabic and English requesting women entering the building to cover their hair. A box brimming with polyester scarves of assorted colors sat on an adjacent table. Soon, letters under Chirri's signature were being sent to the congregation celebrating the anniversary of the founding of the Islamic Republic of Iran, "whose establishment is the greatest gift to the Muslims and mankind at this time."[22]

Other curious missives emanated from the Islamic Center as well. One, dated May 20, 1989, notified Muslims that Imam Chirri would no longer "perform burial services at Roseland Park [the cemetery used for Muslim burials in the Detroit area for decades] because of the improper positioning of the plots." Apparently, someone noticed that the burial plots set aside for Muslims were not facing east as prescribed by Islamic precepts. An arrangement was reached with Roseland Park to reinter "loved ones" in another section of the cemetery "in accordance with Islamic requirement." My hunch is that one of the new imams discovered the "error," and in the process created undue emotional strain on Chirri and countless hapless American Muslims, who had long assumed their loved ones had received a proper Muslim burial.

Unlike the Dix mosque, the Islamic Center has, under Chirri's leadership, successfully weathered the strains created by the arrival of newcomers by simply holding the reins of power and not allowing control of the mosque to devolve to the congregation. Chirri was inadvertently aided by the very imams he had brought over from the Middle East who led the dissatisfied out of the Islamic Center and founded their own mosques. The population of Lebanese Shia Muslims in Dearborn has been sufficiently ample to sustain four spin-off congregations, all located within a ten-minute driving distance of the Islamic Center.

Following Chirri's death in the early 1990s, the old guard of established and Americanized families who helped found the Center has strengthened its own hold on the mosque. The board has refused to appoint any of the successor imams to the board or to the presidency of the center. Unlike the Dix mosque, the Islamic Center has never relaxed its opposition to elections—seats on the board of directors are filled by invitation only. That oligarchical policy may have ultimately saved the Islamic Center from the fate that befell the Bekaais at the Dix mosque.[23]

The largely Americanized board continues to make cosmetic accommodations to those in the congregation who yearn for an Old World–style mosque while it simultaneously pursues the long-established policy of adapting to the political and social realities of Dearborn and the wider American society. The Islamic Center is preparing to build a new complex on land purchased in Dearborn. The complex is projected to cost seven to eight million dollars, and will include a new mosque, social center, and Islamic school. The school is already operating out of an existing structure at the site. When asked if the social center would be a return to the days of "dancing and singing in the mosque," board member Ronald Amen said "no, that won't be the case." Confronted with the fact that having a social center where wedding parties will be held means "dancing and singing," Amen paused momentarily, before saying, "The social center will be in a separate building connected by a walkway to the mosque" (interview, May 6, 1998). Such are mosque politics in the 1990s.

Present and Future Mosques

Tell a typical Muslim in the Middle East that people sing and dance in the mosques of America, and you will surely scandalize him or her.[24] Yet for decades American Muslims in Detroit and elsewhere thought nothing of holding social and political functions at their local mosques and Islamic centers. They simply built their mosques in such a way that they could segregate the prayer area from the social area. It was an ingenious intellectual division not unlike what the early Muslims did when they built their mosques in the first flush of territorial expansion. For American Muslims, their model of the mosque was a necessary adaptation to the world in which they found themselves. It was an act of cultural survival.

Curiously, the cultural ingenuity of earlier generations of American Muslims is ridiculed by today's Muslims. Even American-born Muslims who attended Dearborn's "American" mosques have succumbed to the claims of the latest waves of immigrant Muslims that they, the newcomers, and only they, practice Islam properly; and it is they who have rid Islamic praxis of artificial cultural accretions and adaptations that corrupted and undermined it in Dearborn.

A 1993 article titled "Muslim Community Growing—and It Shows," published in the November 21 *Detroit Free Press*, counted twenty-five mosques in the Metro Detroit area. There are at least eight mosques in the Dearborn area alone. To be sure, Dearborn's Arab Muslims tend to eschew calling them "mosques," preferring more ambiguous and broader titles like the Islamic Center of America, Islamic Council of America, Institute of Knowledge, House of Wisdom, to name several. Nonetheless, technically they are mosques given that they are places where Muslims gather and perform the Friday communal prayer. In that sense, they cannot escape their primary raison d'être. But, like the Dix mosque of old, these Islamic "centers," "institutes," "councils," and "houses of wisdom," also perform other vital social functions as social gathering points, as quasi community centers, as schools for religious and language instruction, and as reservoirs of cultural and ethnic identity. It is precisely these functions that distinguish Dearborn's "mosques" from mosques in the Middle East rather than the lack of minarets and the other non-Middle Eastern forms in their architecture.[25]

The great irony is that Dearborn's new mosques have already taken a giant step toward becoming "American congregations," and thus are well on their way, once they abandon the outward displays of religiosity (beards and veils), to becoming as unrecognizable to future Middle Eastern immigrants as the Dix mosque had once been to the *musalee'een*. The absence of the *muezzen*'s daily five calls to prayer is but one obvious difference between Dearborn's mosques and those of the Middle East.[26] Other departures from the Middle Eastern model are equally apparent. Dearborn's mosques, both new and old, operate under the direction of (mostly elected) boards of directors, a major departure from the Middle Eastern model. These boards hire and fire imams ("founding imams" excepted) and busy themselves with fund-raising, a task essential to the survival of all mosques in the area. All of this is unheard of in the Middle East.

Imams play roles in Dearborn for which they feel unprepared and that were unimaginable when they entered the *madrasas* (seminaries) in their native lands. They must administer mosques that are for all intents and purposes community centers. Further afield, Dearborn's imams, even those steeped in notions of "pure, scholastic" Islam, are called upon regularly to provide marriage and family counseling, a task that, if done at all outside the kinship network in the Middle East, was best left to others. In lieu of Islamic courts, Dearborn's imams must also serve as experts on the fine points of Islamic law and serve as arbiters in disputes. Dearborn's sheikhs must also assume the role of school administrators, as nearly every Dearborn-area mosque operates or has plans to open an Islamic parochial school.[27]

Perhaps the greatest departure from the Middle Eastern mosque model is in the participation of women in the local mosques. That women attend mosques regularly in Dearborn (and elsewhere in the Metro Detroit area) in itself constitutes a radical departure from Middle Eastern practice. Mosques in the Middle East are mainly the preserves of men, places in which women almost never set foot. In even the most scripturally minded congregations in Dearborn, women (and children) attend communal prayers, if not on Fridays, then at least on Sundays. Sunday communal prayers are another American innovation, something unheard of in the Muslim world, where Sunday is usually the first day of the workweek. The presence of women and children in Dearborn's mosques is superseded only by women's participation in the life of the mosques, from teaching Sunday school to preparing communal and holiday meals at the mosques.[28] Even in the new mosques, where Middle Eastern sensibilities and norms are prevalent, women have formed auxiliaries. In at least two Dearborn mosques, women sit on the boards of directors. Can Saturday night bingo be far off?

Taken together, these developments demonstrate the extent to which Dearborn's new mosques have become, for lack of a better term, "American mosques." The histories of the Dix mosque and the Islamic Center provide a glimpse into the future. Each crop of new immigrants will attempt to wrest Dearborn's mosques from the myriad adaptations they have made in the New World. Some will succeed; others will fail.

Even before the flow of new immigrants turns into a trickle, it can be expected that the ardor of today's newcomers will eventually wane. Cultural accretions and accommodations will become normal to local Muslims. Gradually, women will assume greater roles in the mosques, just as the Bekaa women did two generations earlier in the Dix mosque. Today's Muslim women in Dearborn will be compelled by a need to transmit their religion and ethnic culture to their children. They will be driven by the fear, as one of the Bekaa women once put it, "of losing their kids and grandkids to another faith." Ultimately, today's women will demand that English be spoken in the mosques, that the Sunday school classes be given more than passing attention, that only sheikhs who have a solid command of English and an understanding of American culture be hired, that interdenominational marriages be tolerated, and that religious belief and practice be less outwardly devotional and more inwardly spiritual. If the past is any guide to the future, it will be these women and their daughters who will one day resist the demands of future immigrants for a return to a Middle Eastern form of Islam. For they will have discovered that "Islam" and "Islamic identity" are really code words for their respective Lebanese, Yemeni, Iraqi, and Palestinian cultural identities. When the Middle Eastern model of mosque has faded into a memory, and when people once again sing and dance in the mosque, it will be the women who will constitute the backbone of Islam in Dearborn. For the time being, however, they will be content to prepare the communal meals, teach Sunday school, and sit in the audience at mosque functions while the men dominate the podium.

Notes

I wish to thank Andrew Shryock and Sally Howell for their valuable comments on an earlier version of this study. Responsibility for any errors and omissions is entirely mine.

1. For a detailed look at the nationalist community see my *National and Local Politics: A Study of Political Conflict in a Yemeni Immigrant Community of Detroit, Michigan* (1978).
2. I shall use the terms "sheikh" and "imam" interchangeably; both refer to a Muslim cleric knowledgeable in the Quran, *Hadith* and *Sunna* (sayings and actions of the Prophet Muhammad), and some aspects of Islamic law.
3. Information on this period is gleaned from interviews with several informants while I served as a consultant to a study of five U.S. Muslim congregations conducted by Yvonne Haddad and Adair Lummis. The Haddad/Lummis study was published as *Islamic Values in the United States: A Comparative Study* (1987). I would like to thank Mohammad Okdie for the insights he provided while working as a field-worker on the project.
4. On this period, see also Elkholy (1966); Aswad (1974); S. Abraham, N. Abraham, Aswad (1983); and Naff (1985).
5. While conducting field work in Dearborn in 1963, Atif Wasfi (1964, 153) noted the existence of a women's organization affiliated with the Hashemite Hall. He says little else other than to observe that the women's group affiliated with the Dix mosque was "the most organized and has a President and a Secretary."
6. Elkholy (1966, 131) observed that the congregation "had no regular respectable religious leader." He added, "Their religious leader, not an imam, but a volunteer sheikh, had a limited degree of self-education, despite the weekly Arabic newspaper which he publishes in Detroit. All religious activities performed by him were on a voluntary basis. When he did not go to the mosque, because of sickness, out-of-town marriage or funeral ceremonies, the Friday noon prayer was suspended."
7. For many years, a framed picture of Nasser contemplating a chess move was displayed prominently on a lamp table in my family's living room. Nasser's popularity among Dearborn-area Arabs, which continued in the Southend after his death in September 1970, is described in detail in Wigle and S. Abraham (1974). The euphoria of the period should be contrasted with the embarrassment that existed before the 1956 Suez War, when many parents "tried to hide their origin. Some changed their Islamic names and others identified themselves with Italian or Armenian ethnic groups" (Wasfi 1964, 113). For a discussion of how Arab Americans coped with anti-Arab, anti-Muslim stereotypes, and hostility, see my studies on this and related topics (1989; 1992; and 1994).

8. Mike Karoub first visited the Middle East in 1974 at the age of fifty. He died in April 1998.
9. Elkholy (1966, 125) observes that, "Having searched a very long time for a scholarly religious leader, Detroit was offered the services" of a highly trained Yugoslav graduate of al-Azhar University but demurred. "He was rejected," Elkholy noted, "on the grounds of being non-Arab."
10. One outsider saw the situation differently. Elkholy (1966, 90) found that the older generation's "traditionalistic approach to religion" actually weakened religious practices in the congregation. "The mosque is still seen by the Detroit members as a place for men. Even in the rear ranks they do not tolerate participation by women. As a result, the youth associate the mosque with the aged and the backward." Elsewhere, Elkholy describes a development that might have been at the heart of the tensions dividing the men and women of the congregation. Elkholy discovered that many of the Dearborn Muslim women were marrying Christians and turning away from the faith. The women told Elkholy that they had "converted out of frustration, having been slighted by the Moslem men who left them to marry Americans." By marrying outside their community, they "found themselves rejected by their relatives and the entire community," in contrast to the Toledo congregation, also studied by Elkholy, which absorbed outsiders into the community.
11. Cf. Gilsenan (1982, 27–54 passim); Bates and Rassam (1983, 54ff.); Keddie (1972). See also the useful discussion on the subject of the Dearborn imams and their functions by Walbridge (1997, 113–26).
12. As previously noted, the congregation refused an offer from a non-Arab scholar (Elkholy 1966, 125). One member of the leadership explained to Elkholy, "the majority, and I am one of them, would rather have a sheikh from Cairo [i.e., an Arab] for reasons one of which is (Arab) nationalism."
13. Wasfi (1964, 105) found that 30 percent of the assimilated men in his sample (defined as those having grown up in the United States) had wives who worked outside the home, as opposed to only 8 percent of the wives of men who spent their formative years in Lebanon. Wasfi limited his study to Lebanese married men who were members of the Dix mosque.
14. The majority of Yemeni immigrants were probably Zeidis, one of several Shia sects worldwide and the majority in the northern part of Yemen. Yemeni Sunnis refer to themselves by the name of their "legal school," Shafei. The Shafei-Zeidi schism, while real in the home country, tends to be played down among immigrants. See Wenner (1967) for discussion of the Shafei-Zeidi split in Yemeni society.
15. Personal communication from Ronald Amen (May 6, 1998). My mother had heard an identical claim about Mike Karoub's wife and the large cross around her neck. Neither informant actually witnessed the altercation,

news of which had circulated widely in the Southend at the time. I am unable to locate any eyewitnesses who actually saw the cross. Personally, I doubt the veracity of the claim and believe it to be an after-the-fact distortion created to justify the physical expulsion of the Karoubs from the mosque by the *musalee'een.*

16. Wahhabism is arguably the most conservative and literal of all the Sunni sects. It calls for a return to "an unadulterated Islam of primitive simplicity—the Islam of the Prophet and the Qur'an." It is puritanical, disallowing all innovation in theology and practice. The Quran is consulted for direction regarding all economic and social problems of the day (Cragg 1975, 115–18).
17. Nevertheless, the group still identified themselves as Muslims, and significantly, as Wigle (1974, 162) found in the early 1970s, "religion [among Southend Arabs] appears to have taken on a political nature due to recent events in the Middle East. Being a Moslem is synonymous with being an Arab and there is a strong relationship between this fact and sympathies over the Middle East conflict."
18. Curiously, a quarter-century later Walbridge (1997) documented similar laxness in the maintenance of the monthlong Ramadan fast, simmering heretical beliefs, doubts about the existence of the afterlife, widespread belief in superstition, and malicious gossip at a time of extreme and overt religiosity (expansion of mosques, Islamic schools, mosque attendance, and widespread wearing of "Islamic dress" by women and girls) in the Lebanese Shia community. On the all-important issue of prayer, Walbridge (137) found: "Most Lebanese Shi'a in Dearborn will say that they pray, that is, perform salat, the obligatory prayer. However, they might be exaggerating. Salat takes time, not only for the prayers themselves but also for the ablutions that precede them. There is a strong tendency in this community to want to convince others of one's religious commitment. Religiosity is held in high esteem. Those who are lax in their religious obligations are the ones who are on the defensive these days."
19. The display of photos of political leaders, such as Nasser, in the mosque, albeit the social area, could be offensive to Muslims who take seriously the Islamic injunction against graven images. Moreover, the Egyptian president was known for his repression of Egypt's Muslim Brotherhood organization. Even in the heyday of Arab nationalism in the mid-1960s, Nasser was resented by politically active Islamists, who considered Arab nationalism antithetical to their goal of establishing an Islamic state.
20. In commenting on the various functions of the Dearborn mosques, Wigle and Abraham (1974, 294) note that in the wake of the June 1967 Arab-Israeli War, "Meetings were called in the [Dearborn] Mosque and the Islamic Center where funds were collected and sent to the defeated countries."

21. In the second stage of mosque development (between A.D. 650 and 750), Walbridge (1997, 98) notes, "Mosques were built so that they could be expanded or contracted according to the needs of the community. They were enclosed by walls and did not have exterior facades," a structure entirely befitting a religion on the move, as it were, expanding and contracting as its freshly won borders shifted. Again, a parallel of sorts can be drawn to the Muslim communities in America (and elsewhere) as distant ethnic-religious settlements on the far reaches of the Muslim "expansion." The contemporary model of the mosque in Arab Muslim society probably harkens back to the twelfth century, an era known for its monumental mosques. Most noteworthy from the standpoint of our discussion is that "the trend for the separation of secular buildings from the religious sanctuaries became more pronounced during this period" (99).
22. These commemorations were being held as late as 1989 (the date of the most recent announcement in my files), fully a decade after the founding of the Islamic Republic. Presumably, the celebrations continued thereafter.
23. Maintaining control was not always easy. The fourth and most recent spin-off was precipitated by a stormy confrontation between the board and Chirri's initial replacement, Imam Ilahi, in the early 1990s. Ilahi and his youthful supporters were "thrown out of the mosque," according to current board member Ronald Amen. The event has entered the lore of the Islamic Center as "black Sunday," the day when the Iranian-born Ilahi was accused of "bringing in his armed Iranian supporters" in a power grab—an inflammatory claim similar to the allegation that Ida Karoub wore a large cross to the Dix mosque. According to Amen, Imam Ilahi "challenged the authority of the old guard, and you don't do that. Had they been democratic they would have been voted out." Amen was speaking from firsthand experience. In the early 1970s he had been "invited" to sit on the board, only to find himself unceremoniously tossed off it several months later amid charges that he was a "commie" for helping to build ACCESS (Arab Community Center for Economic and Social Services). At the time ACCESS was viewed as an organizational interloper run by Arab American radicals and atheists. Amen accepted a seat on the Board again two decades later.
24. Most Levantine Arab Muslims seem to be utterly unaware that Sufi Muslims have been "singing and dancing" in praise of the Creator, the Prophet, and their faith for over a millennium. To be sure, Sufis periodically suffered grievously for their ardor at the hands of purists and literalists.
25. Dearborn's mosques have no architectural merit to speak of, being mostly converted stores, banks and other run-of-the-mill former commercial

buildings. Of Dearborn's "mosques" only the Islamic Center is adorned by a minaret. Located in a struggling neighborhood inhabited mostly by non-Muslim African-Americans, the minaret serves a decorative purpose, more of a reminder of the past than a functioning part of the present, as putting it to use would border on the surreal.

26. In the early 1980s, the *musalee'een* began broadcasting the daily calls to prayer over loudspeakers from the Dix mosque to the great annoyance of some residents of the Southend. The city of Dearborn attempted to prohibit the practice but failed when the courts considered the broadcasts the Muslim equivalent of church bells.
27. Some also have small businesses on the side with which to supplement their income. One owns a doughnut shop; another, an ice-cream parlor.
28. See Walbridge (1997, 195ff.) for a discussion of the developments of women's involvement in mosques.

References

Abraham, Nabeel. 1978. *National and Local Politics: A Study of Political Conflict in a Yemeni Immigrant Community of Detroit, Michigan.* Ann Arbor, Mich.: University Microfilms.

———. 1989. "Arab-American Marginality: Mythos and Praxis. In *Arab Americans: Continuity and Change,* edited by Baha Abu- Laban and Michael Suleiman. Belmont, Mass.: Association of Arab-American University Graduates.

———. 1992. The Gulf Crisis and Anti-Arab Racism in America. In *Collateral Damage: The "New World" Order at Home and Abroad,* edited by Cynthia Peters, 255–78. Boston: South End Press.

———. 1994. Anti-Arab Racism and Violence in the United States. In *The Development of Arab-American Identity,* edited by Ernest McCarus, 155–214. Ann Arbor: University of Michigan Press.

Abraham, Sameer, Nabeel Abraham, and Barbara Aswad. 1983. The Southend: An Arab Muslim Working-Class Community. In *Arabs in the New World: Studies on Arab-American Communities,* edited by Sameer Abraham and Nabeel Abraham, 164–81. Detroit: Center for Urban Studies, Wayne State University.

Aswad, Barbara. 1974. The Southeast Dearborn Arab Community Struggles for Survival against Urban "Renewal." In *Arabic Speaking Communities in American Cities,* edited by Barbara Aswad, 53–83. New York: Center for Migration Studies and the Association of Arab-American University Graduates.

Bates, Daniel, and Amal Rassam. 1983. *Peoples and Cultures of the Middle East.* Englewood Cliffs, N.J.: Prentice Hall.

Cragg, Kenneth. 1975. *The House of Islam.* Belmont, Calif.: Wadsworth.

Elkholy, Abdo A. 1966. *The Arab Moslems in the United States: Religion and Assimilation.* New Haven, Conn.: College and University Press.

Gilsenan, Michael. 1982. *Recognizing Islam.* New York: Pantheon.

Grabar, Oleg. 1969. The Architecture of the Middle Eastern City. In *Middle Eastern Cites,* edited by Ira M. Lapibas, 26–46. Berkeley: University of California Press.

Haddad, Yvonne, and Adair Lummis. 1987. *Islamic Values in the United States: A Comparative Study.* New York: Oxford University Press.

Keddie, Nikki. 1972. *Scholars, Saints and Sufis.* Berkeley and Los Angeles: University of California Press.

Naff, Alixa. 1985. *Becoming American: The Early Arab Immigrant Experience.* Carbondale: Southern Illinois University Press.

Walbridge, Linda. 1997. *Without Forgetting the Imam: Lebanese Shi'ism in an American Community.* Detroit: Wayne State University Press.

Wasfi, Atif. 1964. *Dearborn Arab-Moslem Community: A Study of Acculturation.* Ann Arbor, Mich.: University Microfilms.

Wenner, Manfred. 1967. *Modern Yemen: 1918–1966.* Baltimore: Johns Hopkins University Press.

Wigle, Laurel. 1974. An Arab Muslim Community in Michigan. In *Arabic Speaking Communities in American Cities,* edited by Barbara Aswad, 155–67. New York: Center for Migration Studies.

Wigle, Laurel, and Sameer Abraham. 1974. Arab Nationalism in America: The Dearborn Arab Community. In *Immigrants and Migrants: The Detroit Ethnic Experience,* edited by David W. Hartman, 279–302. Detroit: New University Thought Publishing.

Part 4

POLITICS

Fig. 13. Students protest the Gulf War at the University of Michigan, Dearborn, 1991. Photograph by Millard Berry.

Introduction

To a large degree, the Arab Detroit we see today owes its existence to a century of political conflicts and wars in the Middle East, most of them caused or prolonged by the interventionist policies of France, Britain, Russia, and the United States. In the second half of the twentieth century, the dominant foreign power in the region has indisputably been the United States. Washington's Middle East policies—its backing of Israeli territorial conquest, support for tyrannical Arab regimes, and opposition to the national aspirations of the region's indigenous peoples—have helped shape the composition of Arab Detroit.

The recent arrival of Iraqi Shia refugees offers a dramatic example of how U.S. foreign policy creates new communities locally. Arab Detroit's Iraqi Muslim population mushroomed overnight as Saudi Arabia closed POW and refugee camps set up to house thousands of Iraqis fleeing the death and destruction of the 1991 Gulf War and its bloody aftermath. After Washington abruptly halted its blitzkrieg on Baghdad, it called on Iraqis to topple Saddam Hussein then watched from the sidelines as Hussein's Republican Guard crushed the *intifada* (uprising) in southern Iraq. The ensuing massacres caused thousands of destitute Iraqis to swell the U.S.-sponsored refugee camps in Saudi Arabia, where the hapless refugees suffered further humiliation and torment at the hands of their reluctant Saudi hosts. The Saudis are among America's "friends and allies" in the Arab world, as was Saddam Hussein, before he sacked neighboring Kuwait.

Linda Walbridge and Talib Aziz document Arab Detroit's newest community, taking readers into a world virtually inaccessible to outsiders due to heightened political suspicions, not to mention cultural and linguistic barriers. "The Iraqis live in a world apart from the other citizens of Dearborn," observe Walbridge and Aziz. The

Iraqis present a classic example of isolationist immigrant politics. They see Dearborn as a holding tank, a place to wait for the fall of their nemesis, Saddam Hussein, so they can return home. Time is their biggest enemy as they settle into life in Detroit and begin a slow drift into the mainstream. As months turn into years, these Iraqis will likely coalesce into feuding political camps, quarrel over the future of Iraq, dream about an imagined homeland, and watch in amazement as their children slowly become Americans.

There is nothing exceptional in the parochial, inward-looking, isolationist politics of the Iraqi Shia. It is in the nature of marginal immigrant politics, which still flourish in Arab Detroit, to give priority to events in the home country, whether it is Palestine, Lebanon, Yemen, or Egypt. At the opposite end of the political spectrum one finds the mainstreaming, integrationist politics displayed in Sally Howell's interview with Maya Berry. This is the world of U.S. ethnic and identity politics, politics in *America* as opposed to politics about *Amreeka*. This is the kind of politics Americans comprehend—media sound bites, photo ops, national conventions, party politics, lobbying, droning banquet speeches, precinct elections, and foreign policy briefings. This is electoral politics writ large, redolent with optimism, brimming with insiders. Its connection to places like Arab Detroit is driven by the need for votes, voices, and dollars unified solidly behind an "Arab American" national agenda, a need that inspires the periodic voter registration drives, letter-writing campaigns, and the endless exhortations for financial contributions. The activists who control the Arab American political agenda seek to harness the populist energy of Arab Detroit by responding to crises and issues emanating from the home country: Israeli military aggression in southern Lebanon, demands for Palestinian statehood, lifting the travel ban on Lebanon, removing Syria from the U.S. list of states supporting terrorism, ending the economic sanctions on Iraq. In the language of realpolitik, this strategy is a way of garnering immigrant support for U.S. domestic issues, which means electing Arab Americans to public office. Integrationist/mainstreaming political agendas appeal to a growing cross section of Arab Detroit, especially to professionals and businesspeople. Mainstreaming politics also attracts "American-borns" who are attending college, since ethnic identity is one of the few avenues by which to enter campus political and (just as often) social life. Ethnic politics is to the 1990s what radical politics was to the 1960s, at once an attempt at self-definition and a secure foothold in the political discourse of the moment.

Between the isolationist immigrants and the ethnic integrationists lies the vast middle of Arab Detroit, which is loosely enmeshed in the overlapping politics of community organizations, Arab homelands, and local governments. Neither completely marginal nor comfortably mainstream, the everyday political agendas of Arab Detroit's center are ingenious, unpredictable, and tactically hybrid. The group most adept at negotiating this uneven terrain is ACCESS, whose history is briefly recounted by Karen Rignall in part 1 of this book. Because its primary function is to provide social services to immigrants in need, ACCESS must map out and operate in large swaths of political reality that lie outside the ambit of integrationist politics. For most of its history, ACCESS has been headed by a duo whose cultural backgrounds make them ideal for political work at the center of Arab Detroit. Ish Ahmed, executive director, born and raised in the U.S., is the organization's American face, its link to mainstream institutions. Hassan Jaber, deputy director, born and raised in Lebanon, is the organization's Arab face. The integrationist sensibility endorsed by Ahmed dovetails nicely with the views expressed by Maya Berry. Indeed, ACCESS is a training ground for young Arab American activists like Berry, who owe their political vision to the ideas and organizing strategies they learned from Ish and others at ACCESS. Though Hassan Jaber is by no means oblivious to American electoral politics, his attentions are focused elsewhere: namely, on mastering the political intricacies of Arabic-speaking Detroit by nurturing alliances with key behind-the-scenes players in the kinship system (and in the powerful social clubs and mosques) who ultimately determine whether a particular group will back an ACCESS project or support its claim to represent them.

As editors of this volume, we have discovered what activists like Hassan Jaber have known for years: politics in Arab Detroit is embedded in contexts that seldom correspond neatly to the theory, or even the practice, of American politics as usual. Michigan's Arab constituency materializes out of mosques, churches, villages clubs, clans, and the intricate networks of social obligation that bring them together and, just as often, tear them apart. As sites at which basic loyalties take shape, these settings generate the political energies "Arab American identity" is meant to fuse and transcend, but so often cannot. Our contributors, likewise, have seen how quickly big politics can succumb to the immediacy of personal experiences and attachments that, when measured on a geopolitical scale, seem utterly parochial. Several essays intended for this section eventually settled in other parts of the book. We supported these shifts in category and perspective, if only to disturb the popular tendency to treat Arabs as nothing more than a political issue. We trust, however, that the careful reader will find subtler forms of politics on every page of this volume.

For readers who equate "real politics" with the Arab-Israeli conflict, Islamic resurgence, U.S. foreign policy in the Middle East, anti-discrimination campaigns, and the consolidation of the Arab vote, we should stress that the most visible and effective political groups in Arab Detroit today are social service agencies (e.g., ACCESS and the Arab-American and Chaldean Council) and business associations (e.g., the American Arab Chamber of Commerce, Metro Detroit Service Stations, Associated Food Dealers, and the Michigan Food and Beverage Association). These groups attract and train young activists, represent the Arab community in the popular media and in local, state, and federal politics, and help new immigrants and refugees weather the transition to life in America. This nuts-and-bolts political work, carried out in settings as diverse as the Democratic and Republican Parties, the Islamic Mosque of America, the Detroit Institute of Arts, the Yemeni Benevolent Association, and the Dearborn Public Schools, has created an elaborate terrain on which unprecedented forms of Arab activism and cultural assertion, both marginal and mainstream, can now be sustained.

The vitality of Arab Detroit's political center is epitomized in the efforts of Hajja Aliya Hassan, to whom we dedicate this section of the book. Hajja Aliya led ACCESS through its fledgling years as a volunteer, grassroots organization. Were she alive to read it, Hajja Aliya could easily identify with the sentiment expressed in Amira Saad's poem that leaving one's country, only to become strange and stigmatized in a land "not our own," potentially turns all immigrants into refugees. As an Arab American, however, Aliya Hassan believed that new homelands could be established in Detroit—in America—and that a politics of engagement with the larger society, not a retreat from it, would make those new homelands possible.

Aliya Hassan

ALIYA HASSAN WAS one of Arab Detroit's most effective leaders. As executive director of ACCESS (1972–81), she built bridges between the first Arab immigrants to America, their children, and the new waves of refugees and immigrants that crashed into Detroit in the 1970s. Through her political and religious activism, Aliya shaped thousands of lives. Her power was based on her moral authority and nurturing spirit. In her later years, Aliya's friends and family called her Hajja, a title honoring her pilgrimage to Mecca. To the generation of activists she inspired, Aliya Hassan was the mother of the Arab American community in Detroit.

Aliya Hassan was born in Kadoka, South Dakota, in 1910. Her parents were among the first Lebanese Muslims to arrive in America. Aliya came to Detroit in 1925 to attend the Briggs Boarding School. Blessed with an independent, adventurous spirit, she moved to New York City in the 1950s, where she worked as a private investigator, civil defense director, and political organizer. Aliya was both a feminist and a lifelong advocate of Islam. In the 1960s she struggled to improve relations between orthodox Muslims and the Nation of Islam. Her friendship with Malcolm X grew out of her desire to unite all Muslims in adherence to an inclusive, egalitarian Islam. Aliya helped arrange Malcolm X's pilgrimage to Mecca, during which the Black Muslim leader embraced orthodox Islam. She also traveled several times to the Middle East to discuss the growth of Islam in America with Arab leaders.

In 1972 Aliya Hassan returned to Detroit and became active in local politics. She was a guiding force in the development of the Arab Community Center for Economic and Social Services (ACCESS). Aliya helped Yemeni, Palestinian, and Lebanese workers organize to secure basic social services from state and federal governments. Under Aliya's direction, ACCESS provided English classes, food, housing, and translation services to thousands of new immigrants. Twice she helped rebuild ACCESS after it was destroyed by fire. Aliya received dozens of awards and citations for her work, including the Jefferson Award for Public Service in 1981. Despite ailing health, she

Fig. 14. Aliya Hassan. Photograph by Millard Berry.

continued to advocate for Detroit's Arab and Muslim communities until her death in 1990.

Aliya Hassan led an unconventional life, and she was proud of the damage she did to the stereotype of the Arab Muslim woman. She grew up as an Arab homesteader in the American West, sleeping under buffalo robes and Indian blankets; she was an avid cardplayer who never lost her taste for gambling; she believed in nonviolence and studied the martial arts; she was married and divorced several times; she prayed in Arabic and journeyed to Mecca; she taught others how to wash the bodies of the Muslim dead yet chose, in defiance of custom, to be cremated when she died. For all her radical ways, Hajja Aliya never abandoned the basic values of her Arab American upbringing: faith in God, identification with the dispossessed, respect for tradition, and a willingness to fight for change. Today, her legacy survives in the work of ACCESS and in the vibrant growth of the Arab community she loved.

In the following poem, Saladin Ahmed tries to make sense of the heroic figure he knew only as a doting great-grandmother. As he remembers the Hajja, blending his private recollections with her public persona, he re-creates the spell she cast over Arab Detroit.

Important Things to an Eight Year Old

Saladin Ahmed

For Haji Aliya Hassan

Experience with matriarchs began with Haji

She was . . . an Arab
She was . . . a Woman
She was . . . a private detective!
circa 1950 New York

But no connections were drawn
by his Crunchberry-powered brain
as he sat on the edge of her bed thinking
"Dang! Cagney and Lacey are tough!"

She was . . . acquainted with Malcolm
She was . . . one of his guides to Mecca
She was . . . a jet-haired smoke screen, blinding FB's eye

But no connections were drawn
as his little chocolate peepers
were peekabooed by wrinkled yellow brown hands
that looked like old treasure maps.

Amid the mountains of social justice,
the oceans of personal achievement,
the plateaus of religious scholarship,
were hidden
the important things
to him
at the time

To him,
at the time
the greatest miracles she hid
in that crowded little green apartment on Central
were . . .
Sky blue Dutch girl pepper shakers
Mother-of-pearl turtle-shaped candy dishes
Non-*halal* steak and
juicy family legends
cut up just right

She was . . . at peace when cooking for him
She was . . . happy when telling stories
She was . . . very good at spoiling him

But no connections were made
on the day of her funeral,
as he stood
rubbing soap into his eyes,
figuring he was not crying hard enough.

As he stood, staring at her
white scarf and sewn lips,
at the age when he could
begin
to appreciate the awesome significance
of her public accomplishments,
wishing he
loved her for these things,
instead of
loving her for the
coffee
she had made him at eight years old . . .

He did not
understand
that these were
important things
to her
at the time

After Karbala

Iraqi Refugees in Detroit

Linda S. Walbridge and T. M. Aziz

What struck me was just the immensity of the human tragedy. Clearly the people I saw were in big trouble. They were desperate. I would have to say though that it wasn't immediately clear to us, having newly arrived there, that the refugees were fleeing Iraqi government attacks. We helped people initially because they frankly looked like civilians to us. Despite the feeling of human misery we inevitably felt, it was clear that we would be putting at risk our ability to provide adequate water and food for our own troops if we had tried to continue aiding the refugees rather than just directing them on down the road toward Basra. We would have arrived at highway 8 from central Kuwait, where we ended up at the close of the ground war, some time around the third week of March. But there was a heavy flow down the highway, moving northwest to southeast, for about two weeks.

No one spoke English especially well. Those that did just gave us basic intelligence. They were going toward Basra to escape government forces; that the Iraqis were killing everyone: women, children, etc. It was a purely revenge motivated operation. They were actually more concerned with immediate humanitarian needs: food, safe water, shoes if available. They were obviously suffering not only the exhaustion of their trek—difficult under the best of circumstances—but also the general deprivations from the war, in which the Iraqis had diverted food, etc. to the front-line troops.

I could see mortars firing (I even have pictures of smoke explosions which I am positive were from mortars.) I also watched Iraqi army mortars firing to the north and west, shelling outlying areas of An Nasiriyah. But the helicopters stayed back from the road, on the north side of Highway 8, to avoid enticing the Americans to shoot them down. We were appalled to see Iraqi helicopters at all,

> actually. We were somewhat dispirited by the evidence before us. It undermined any real sense of a complete Allied victory, despite the fall of Kuwait City and the tentative Iraqi laying down of arms. There was something very temporary and artificial in the feeling many of us had about the neatness of the 100 hour endpoint. (Maj. Brian McNerney, artillery commander of C Battery working in support of the 3rd Squadron of the 2nd Armored Cavalry Regiment (2ACR) west of the city of Ur, on the road between An Nasiriyah and Basrah in March 1991. [personal communication])

From Linda Walbridge's Field Notes

Talib and I interviewed refugees for several hours in May 1997, in Dearborn, Michigan. Many of them were from Najaf, some from Diwaniyya, and one from Karbala. One man had been in prison since 1987 and was freed by the fighters (the *mujahidin*) during the 1991 uprising—the *intifada*. But they were all forced to flee when the Allies, who had urged Iraqis to rise up against Saddam, pulled back and allowed Saddam's tanks and guns to turn on them. Some fled on foot, others in trucks. They weren't allowed to enter Saudi Arabia. They waited in the desert until the UN found them—men, women, and children without food, water, or shelter. The Saudis had to take them in; they set up a tent camp outside the city of Rafah. There, tens of thousands of refugees were surrounded by Saudi guards so that they could not leave the enclosed area.

The men told of drinking salty, rusty water from tanks, of eating nothing but rice, of being infiltrated by Saudi and Iraqi Baathist spies, of being hounded and beaten by Saudi police, of seeing their friends forced to cross the border back to Iraq. They talked about the wind (*khamsin*) that blew across the desert. They used water recycled from washing and cooking to build mud-brick walls to protect themselves from the wind and the nighttime cold. The Saudis tried to stop them by beating them, but the walls went up anyway because the refugees couldn't survive without protection. One man gave us pictures to prove what they had accomplished—pictures of men laying their handmade bricks and smiling out of pride over their industriousness and courage. They were also proud of how they recycled every scrap of paper and tin they received, how they eventually made a store for themselves, started a school for their children (writing their own books by hand), turned a tent into a mosque, and even established an art gallery. The "smuggler" gave us pictures of these things too.

There was the time when the Saudis threatened the women with rape. The refugees responded with an act of desperation. Having no weapons, they symbolized their willingness to sacrifice all rather than face an assault on their women and on their sense of peoplehood and honor. The children formed the front line in the protest. The women stood behind them and the men were in the rear. They squared off with Saudi tanks. Again, a smuggled photograph provides evidence of this uprising that successfully shamed the Saudis.

The men were easily drawn back to the memories of suffering. One man told us that his brother, driven to madness by conditions in the camp, crossed the border to Iraq, hitching a ride in a truck. He passed the army checkpoints by hiding under the truck's cargo—dead bodies. Another showed a picture of a friend from the camp who had been shot dead by the Saudis. Finally, their stories wound down, and the men, emotionally spent, urged me to go talk to the women.

A group of women had been called to meet with me in a home in Detroit. Wrapped in their black *abayas* (traditional long cloaks), they were driven to the meeting. The husband of one of the women had a job, and thus the family could afford to live alone—a husband and wife and four children—in a house, albeit a dilapidated one. We sat on the floor. There weren't enough of the thin mats to accommodate us. Children swarmed the house. One little boy hobbled on crutches. His mother explained that she had fallen in the camp while she was pregnant. Women sat and nursed their babies. One mother told me that her son was always sick. On the day I visited, her baby was not considered sick, but he did not appear to be well. The young girl who sat closely to me gave me a running commentary of overly precocious observations. "You will hardly find a healthy baby," she said when she noticed me watching the baby.

The women, too, had tales about the journey from Iraq to the refugee camps. They told me that some women had lost their babies while fleeing in panic. The babies, wrapped in their mother's *abayas,* had fallen from their mother's arms. They talked about their days in the desert and how they tried to catch the food airlifted to them by the Allies by holding out their *abayas* as if they were baskets. They remembered trying to cook in the tents on the kerosene burners provided by the Saudis. When the winds came, the tents would be blown down over the stoves.

Mostly, though, they wanted to talk about their lives in Michigan.

Introduction

The most recent Arabic-speaking group to have settled in Dearborn and on the Detroit/Dearborn border are Shiite (or Shii) Iraqis from the south of Iraq, refugees from the post–Gulf War uprising against Saddam Hussein's regime.

The refugees began to arrive here in 1992. They did not come directly from Iraq but from a refugee camp in Saudi Arabia near the town of Rafah, where they spent months or, more commonly, years, in a tent camp. Because of their recent arrival in the United States, their lack of English, and their isolation from the larger American society, little is known about this community. Even in the city of Dearborn, home of North America's largest concentration of people from the Arab Middle East, these people are considered an anomaly in many respects.

It should be noted that there is much ambivalence throughout the Arab world toward the Iraqi Shia. First, as Shia they are part of a minority sect that is generally associated with Iran. In parts of the Gulf, as in Iraq, they are marginalized or openly persecuted. Furthermore, while various Arab governments supported the Allied attack against the Iraqi regime during the Gulf War, it was an unpopular war in the Middle East since it was viewed as an imperialist attack against Arabs. Because they are seen as having collaborated with the Allied Forces against Saddam, the Iraqi Shia have not gained sympathy in the Arab world. While Iranians see them as coreligionists, they also see them as Arabs, with a different language and customs. They are thus not part of some larger umbrella community. Their isolation is complete.

This article reflects preliminary research among the refugees. What is very clear thus far is that the adjustment to their new surroundings has been fraught with problems. Rather than compare their migration to that of other groups in the last part of the twentieth century, it is more appropriate to draw comparisons with nineteenth-century refugees from pogroms and famines.

Background

Shia constitute about 53 percent of the population of Iraq (Batatu 1978).[1] Shiism has roots in southern Iraq. It was there that the first Imam of Shiism, Ali ibn Abi Talib was assassinated. Less than twenty years later, in 680, his son, Hussein, while staking his claim to leadership of the Muslims, was killed in battle along with most of his small retinue of followers. Southern Iraq is the home of the four most sacred shrines of Shiism. In fact, the cities in which these shrines are housed are referred to as the "shrine cities" since the shrines constitute the most important aspect of these places. To these cities, particularly to Najaf and Karbala, flow untold numbers of Shii pilgrims who mourn the deaths of their two greatest heroes, Imams Ali and Hussein. Over the centuries corpses have been transported from other lands, principally from neighboring Iran where the largest number of Shia reside, to be buried near the shrines (Nakash 1994).

Southern Iraq is largely a sedentary tribal society, though nomadic groups also live there. The tribes have, at least until the devastation of Iraq during the Gulf War, constituted a major and formidable force in Iraqi society and have been strongly resistant to central authority. The tribal sheikhs dominated the peasants of Iraq until the 1958 Iraqi revolution (Batatu 1978). Even after the overthrow of the monarchy, however, the tribal sheiks continued to be a powerful force. In the early 1970s, tribally organized villages rose up against the Baathist regime, attacking the railway that linked Baghdad and Basra. And after the brutal suppression of the Shia following the Gulf War, Saddam attempted to placate the Shii tribal leaders because he realized that he would need their cooperation (Bengio 1993).

Elizabeth Fernea's prerevolution ethnography of an Iraqi village provides a close-up view of life in a community owned by one of these tribal sheikhs. Her account reveals the traditional pattern of life found in the region and shows the deep cleft between the society of Baghdad and that of rural peoples in the south (see E. Fernea 1969 and R. Fernea 1970). Although the socialist regime that replaced the old society dramatically changed the power structure and economy of much of Iraqi society, social distances among regions of the country and various social groups continued. No matter how brutally the government retaliated against the tribes, tribal organization has survived.

While the cities of Najaf and Karbala have been the principal centers of religious scholarship in the Shii world since the mid-eighteenth century, according to Yitzhak Nakash the tribal peoples converted to Shiism only in the nineteenth century, as they began to settle down and take up agriculture. Nakash writes:

> The conversion of the tribes resulted in the establishment of a more unified religion and a more cohesive value system embracing the urban dwellers in the shrine cities and the tribesmen of their hinterlands. . . . The introduction of Shii Islam as a unifying religion was

essential to the maintenance of the various classes, ethnic groups, and tribal and urban elements that constituted the new society, as well as to the expansion of the Shii polity.

Thus, while occupational, ethnic, social class, and urban/rural divisions existed in southern Iraq, there was at least a common religious bond that provided some basis for a common identity. The tribal leaders came to the cities to pray at the shrines and to pay homage to the great *mujtahids*[2] of the religious schools, the *madrasas*, as did other Iraqi Shia (as well as Shia from all over the region, including Iran, India, Pakistan, Lebanon, and the Gulf).

Even the bond of religion among Iraqi Shia was damaged during the rise of the secular regimes that replaced the monarchy. Some of the religious leaders, fearing that their youth were turning to communism and atheism, began to actively recruit students back to religion by encouraging them to study at the *madrasas* in the shrine cities. The most prominent *mujtahid* to address the problems of modernity and religion and to turn the youth toward religion as a means to understand and solve the world's ills was Sayyid Muhammad Baqir al-Sadr (Aziz 1993; Mallat 1993; Wiley 1992). Breaking with the tradition of the *madrasas,* he wrote books and articles that addressed modern problems in contemporary terms. His books, *Our Philosophy (Falsafatuna)* and *Our Economics (Iqtisaduna)* have become classics for Muslims, Shii and Sunni, who are actively seeking Islamic solutions to global and societal problems.

During the Iranian revolution Saddam was fearful that Baqir al-Sadr would lead the Iraqi Shia in a rebellion against his government, and he had him executed along with his eloquent and devout sister, Bint al Huda. While persecution of the Shia by the Iraqi regime was all too familiar, the execution of these two influential religious leaders precipitated major protests, which in turn led to an increase in arrests, torture, and executions. Because Saddam saw religious revivalism among the Shia as a serious threat to his power, Iraqi Shia both inside and outside Iraq were hunted down and killed.

During the latter part of the 1970s, Iraqi Shia began moving to the West, many of them as students. They were both pulled by the attraction of educational opportunities and pushed by an oppressive regime. Some of the clergy also fled at this time. Students in secular studies formed an organization called The Muslim Group, a tightly knit group of university-educated Shia of Arab background who have largely settled into middle-class life in the United States and other Western countries. Inspired by the martyred Baqir al-Sadr, these

"Islamists" were truly modernists and rationalists; they believed in the importance of a secular as well as a religious education and promoted the immediate need for an improved status for women.

The United States had never seen a large wave of Iraqi Muslim immigration. It was not until the *intifada* in southern Iraq that large numbers of Iraqi Shia came to America. This group of people are always referred to by Iraqis as "the refugees," while Iraqis who came earlier, even those who fled from the tyranny of the Iraqi regime, are never included in this category. It is reserved for the people who fled at the time of the *intifada* and ended up in the Saudi camps.

Identifying the Refugees

The refugees are a cross section of Iraqi Shiite society. Saddam's tanks and mortars did not discern between rich and poor, educated and illiterate, old and young. The first city to be attacked was Najaf. The shrine of Imam Ali, supposedly a safe area for anyone seeking sanctuary, was stormed by Iraqi troops. Men, women, children, and babies were mowed down by the tanks that rolled into the holy shrine.[3] Najaf, though it is a city of religion, is also home to artisans, merchants, mechanics, bureaucrats, and schoolteachers. On the outskirts of the city, an area that did not escape attack, are peasant farmers. Survivors fled from Najaf and its environs. They headed south for protection, but there was none. The Allies who were supposed to assist them in their rebellion against Saddam pulled back. They had to continue their flight, picking up newcomers who streamed out of the villages and towns in panic. It was not just one class of people who fled; it was all.

One of the cities in southern Iraq, Samawa, which has a population of about fifty thousand, produced many refugees who ended up in the United States. Talib Aziz grew up in this market-town, where, during the busy harvest seasons, herds of goats and sheep would dominate the streets instead of cars and people. He frequently meets refugees who knew his father, a man who had gone from being a cloth merchant to a building contractor and then to a factory owner, changes that indicate his ability to adjust to new economic conditions. The oil boom of the 1970s was transforming the town from one of mud-brick houses and horses-and-buggies to an embryonic modern city. While the city boasted a hospital and a high school (and even a suspension bridge—the only one outside of Baghdad), illiteracy was still commonplace. Even though the Iraqis have a reputation for being "handy," occupational skills were often very basic. Travel outside of the town was unusual; even prosperous families were able to visit Baghdad perhaps once a year.

The refugees who are scattered throughout the Western countries are not of one class, one political persuasion, or one ideology. Yet, as usually happens, refugees lose everything when they become refugees. Therefore, even people who were making a middle-class living before they left, have come penniless and without documents such as diplomas. The overriding impression one has of the Iraqi refugees in Dearborn and Detroit is that they are desperately poor.

One important consideration in looking at the situation of the refugees is their relative lack of contact with the outside world prior to living in the refugee camps. Villages and small cities such as Samawa did not send migrant workers to foreign places—not within the Middle East and certainly not to Europe or America. This town and the entire region are remote from both the outside world and other parts of Iraq. The situation here is in sharp contrast to Lebanon, a nation long familiar with emigration, and where it is not uncommon for relatives working abroad to send home remittances to support those still living there. Along with these remittances come accounts of life in strange lands and lessons in how to negotiate life in these places. Not so with the Iraqis. They had no such education prior to their departure from the refugee camps.

Life in Dearborn for an Iraqi Refugee

There is a myth that circulates throughout the city of Dearborn, both among the "American" community in the west side of the city and the Lebanese Shii community that dominates the northeast section. The myth is that the Iraqi refugees are rich. Some say that they have money from Iraq—oil money. Others say that the United States government gave them each a grant of eight thousand dollars. The myth also has them living "on the dole." They get generous welfare benefits and food stamps and all their health needs are met. They are a privileged class.

This myth proves that myths have a life of their own and need no evidence of reality to sustain them. A visit to the homes of the refugees, to ACCESS (Arab Community Center for Economic and Social Services) to speak with social workers, or to the Karbala Center on Warren Avenue during a meeting would quickly dispel the myth. But it lives on because few people actually visit the homes, talk to the social workers, or visit the Karbala Center. The Iraqis live in a world apart from the other citizens of Dearborn.

Issues of Health and Welfare

ACCESS was established to assist with immigration matters and to address the basic social and health-care needs of the large Arabic-speaking community in Dearborn. Often it serves as a link to other providers of services for the community (Aswad and Gray 1996). ACCESS opened in the Southend of Dearborn, but when the Lebanese Shii community migrated to the northeast portion of the city, a new office opened in 1992 on Warren Avenue, the heart of what is referred to as east Dearborn. That same year the first Iraqi refugees began arriving in the area. At first there were about three hundred families. They had been assigned to Michigan by the UN.[4] However, Dearborn has a reputation nationally and internationally for being an Arabic-speaking enclave, a place where an Arab and, particularly a Muslim Arab, can feel at home (Walbridge 1997). Furthermore, east Dearborn is inhabited by other Arab Shia who have opened mosques and religious centers. It is natural that upon hearing news of relatives and friends in Dearborn, Iraqis assigned to other states often decide to join refugees in Dearborn. It is not just the restaurants, shops, and mosques that draw people here. In the Arab sections of Dearborn, Middle East notions of modesty and social/sexual propriety prevail. One does not find bars or other public places that would violate Islamic law and distract people from their religious and family duties. Thus Dearborn has both primary and secondary immigrants and has a larger concentration of refugees than other American cities.[5]

The first wave of Iraqi refugees to arrive in Dearborn—that is, the primary refugees—had sponsors who would offer them basic assistance for a three-month period when they first arrived. The secondary migrants, however, did not have these sponsors in Dearborn. Once they left their originally assigned city, they were completely on their own. According to Amni Darwish Talab, director of social services at the east Dearborn ACCESS center, "they [the refugees] would come to ACCESS for the basics: asking how to mail a letter, how to have electricity turned on in their homes, and to have their junk mail translated." The Iraqis who turn to ACCESS are mostly from village areas. The ACCESS staff suddenly found themselves doing work that they had previously not done and which was certainly not in their job descriptions. There was, for example, a man who needed surgery but did not know how to go about getting it. He had a wife and six small children (the oldest was nine-years-old) but no one else. An ACCESS employee took the man to the hospital and spent the night with him there. ACCESS employees report finding people, who are obviously disoriented by their new surroundings, wandering the streets. Initially, they would bring these people to ACCESS to try to assist them, but eventually the numbers grew too great and this sort of assistance became impossible.

One of the principal responsibilities of the ACCESS employees has been to help the refugees fill out forms so that they can receive eight months of government assistance. The eight months of assistance is for people who are single or married, with or without children. For some, this eight-month period was all that was needed to launch them into their new lives. But for most it was not. The obstacles to easy adjustment are many.

An obvious hurdle to integration into American society is a lack of English. The vast majority seeking help from ACCESS have no knowledge of English. Even the refugees with high school education and higher are not fluent in English. There would have been little opportunity in southern Iraq to practice English with native speakers. However, it is not just English skills that they lack. ACCESS regularly encounters people who are illiterate in Arabic as well, which reflects the fact that they have not been to school and have not learned the basic skills that come with even minimum schooling.

An overriding concern of both the Iraqis and the people in Dearborn who are attempting to assist them is health problems, both physical and mental. Dr. Adnan Hamad of ACCESS reported that about thirty of his patients are Iraqi refugees. Most of them have spent years in the refugee camps, where communicable diseases, particularly tuberculosis, are rampant. People with chronic health conditions such as diabetes and heart problems had not been receiving medical treatment while in the camp. A common problem cited repeatedly both at ACCESS and by the refugees was kidney failure. The refugees also talk about an increase in conditions, from eczema to asthma to cancer, that were once relatively rare in this population. These are a people who have been exposed repeatedly to possible chemical contamination during the Iran-Iraq War and the 1991 Gulf War. The people to whom we spoke were confident that their health conditions were connected to exposure to chemicals, and they compare their illnesses with those of Gulf War veterans among the Allied Forces.

Dr. Hamad reported that refugees have high levels of lead in their blood from drinking water from tanks in the camps. Babies regularly come to ACCESS with severe problems. Echoing the view expressed by the young girl at the meeting with the refugee women, Amni Darwish Talab said, "Women who were pregnant and had babies here—I don't know what it is but there is something, perhaps nutrition or something else—but these babies have a lot of things wrong with them. Kidney problems are a common problem."

Mental and emotional problems were repeatedly mentioned by ACCESS workers and by the Iraqi refugees, who know that they are psychologically damaged from their ordeals. They witnessed the bloodbath of the *intifada,* then endured years in a refugee camp. Some had been imprisoned and tortured in Iraqi prisons. Dr. Hamad spoke of a man who, whenever he saw the police, became immobilized. As the result of living in so much fear in Iraq, he simply froze with fright. This fear is carried over into American life because many people are convinced that Saddam Hussein continues to spy on them. These may not be unreasonable fears since Iraqis in opposition to Saddam have been assassinated while living in exile.

Expectations at Cross Purposes

The refugees interviewed claimed that the American delegation with whom they met in Saudi Arabia told them that they would be provided with financial assistance, adequate housing, and health and education benefits. They accepted the proposal to come to America, expecting to live respectable lives here.

They also expected to return home to Iraq when Saddam was overthrown. This was to be a temporary arrangement. They needed a safe haven, a place where their children could lead relatively normal lives until they could go home to their cities, towns, or villages. They have continued to live with the daily hope that tomorrow Saddam will be gone.[6] They did not come here expecting to establish roots. They do not wish for their children to become Americans. For many of them the United States is a holding tank until they can take back their lives.

Because the Iraqis are often compared to the Lebanese who settled in Dearborn earlier, it is important to understand the differences between the two groups. Many Lebanese also expected to go home after the end of the civil war in their country. Some of them, too, resisted any indication that the United States was a permanent residence. Yet the long experience of the Lebanese as entrepreneurs served them well. No matter where they go, they set up shops or restaurants or buy real estate. These are all businesses that can be easily liquidated so that, if they do go back, they can sell out. Alternatively, they can let relatives who desire to remain in the United States run the business.

The majority of Iraqis lack the history of migration, the entrepreneurial background for which the Lebanese are so famous, and the international networks that are an important component of entrepreneurship. Furthermore, the extended family is often scattered throughout the world due to UN placement policies. For some Iraqis who are exhausted by deprivation, a brutal war, and years of internment, the idea of working long hours for wages that will not sustain a family is a difficult choice to accept. The Iraqis thought that government assistance would get them through until they could return to Iraq.

Instead, the refugees found that at the end of the eight months, assistance virtually comes to an end. At that point they are expected to become self-supporting. Every person is supposed to show up for job training at MOST (Michigan Occupational Skills Training). It is one of the goals of ACCESS to enable people to become self-supporting. Other members of the Arabic community have largely succeeded in this. The ACCESS workers would like to see the Iraqis become independent as well, but they express reservations that are mostly linked to the problems discussed above. How, they ask, is someone who speaks no English, has no job skills, and suffers from physical and mental illness (often severe depression) able to work? They readily give examples of some of the cases with whom they are working, such as a twenty-two-year-old man with burns over 90 percent of his body. He has a cancerous tumor, tuberculosis, high blood pressure, and psychological problems. He is finally receiving social assistance, but it took a year and a half to get it approved. They also referred to a seventy-year-old man who had two sons, one with an amputated leg and another with a missing arm that had been blown off in warfare. They will help this family apply for SSI, but it will be a long, painful process. Until aid is approved, all family members should appear for job training. Another man, they said, could not function without an oxygen mask. Proving the need for this mask was evidently difficult, and in the meantime, he was being turned down for services.

People who are found eligible for SSI receive assistance for five years unless they become citizens. Gaining citizenship is particularly difficult for many of these refugees because of illiteracy and health problems that interfere with education.

Some of the men that ACCESS has worked with do find employment. Sometimes the Lebanese give them jobs at gas stations or stores where they usually receive minimum wage (some report receiving less). At the gathering of women described above, each woman brought her household's monthly bills. The bills always far exceeded the husband's wages. The bills never included food or other necessities. They were only for rent, electricity, heat, and sometimes a telephone. Many said they couldn't receive food stamps. All said that their husbands are supposed to work thirty-five hours a week and that they are supposed to work twenty hours in order to maintain medical and some other assistance such as food stamps.[7] "How can we work?" asked one woman, "We all have babies. Who is supposed to take care of them?"

These families each have between five and twelve children. In the villages and small towns of Iraq, a woman who gave birth and raised large numbers of children was valued. This was her one source of status in traditional life. While education was becoming more common throughout Iraq both for boys and girls, in southern Iraq sexual segregation was considered normal. Women simply did not play visible roles in society. They were expected to tend to the needs of home and family. With so many children, how could it be otherwise? Still, most women had family and close friends to visit and who visited them. Women might live a more secluded life than men, but it was not one of social isolation. Visiting with other women family members and close neighbors and friends was both a common occurrence and a great source of pleasure.

In the Detroit area, however, the women find such social intercourse difficult or impossible. First, they did not come here as extended families. Their family members may be scattered throughout the world, or they may be dead. Visiting relatives and friends who do live in the same city is still extremely difficult. For women who do not drive, who have not been accustomed to moving about in strange places and among strangers, who have large numbers of children to pack up and transport in an unfamiliar environment, life is very secluded indeed.

Iraqi women, in dismal flats and apartments, are finding themselves tied down to their large numbers of children, with few adults to turn to for consolation and assistance. They do not have to speak of their sadness and depression. It shows on their faces.

Relations with the City and the Neighbors

The size of the Iraqi family has itself been a major barrier to smoothing relations with other residents of Dearborn. As one Lebanese man said, "you rent to one Iraqi and twenty people show up." It is not uncommon for several families to rent a house or even an apartment. They were very quickly shut out of the east Dearborn rental market, which is largely controlled by Lebanese. Prices of homes have almost doubled since 1991. The Iraqis simply cannot afford to rent in east Dearborn; nor are they wanted as renters. There are complaints that they damage the houses, putting holes in what the Iraqis, accustomed to mud-brick houses, refer to as "cardboard" walls.

The housing problem has exacerbated other problems. Resentments have developed between the Lebanese and the Iraqis. The Lebanese are quick to say that the Iraqis are lazy and unwilling to work. They are obviously nervous about having an Arab group move into their community that lives up to America's negative stereotype of Arabs. The Lebanese were once accused of accommodating too many people in one home, of not taking proper care of property, and of having too many children. Many have worked hard to dispel these negative images, and now the Iraqis prove to be a great embarrassment and a reminder of their very recent condition.

Many Iraqis have had to move to more humble neighborhoods. They go either to the Southend, which is home to a large Yemeni population, or just over the border to Detroit. Iraqis we interviewed said they found the Yemenis more accommodating than the Lebanese, an interesting observation since the Lebanese are their coreligionists and the Yemenis are not.[8] The Yemeni immigrants, however, are used to living on the edge of society. They often work as wage laborers in factories or as farmhands, boarding in rooms or in small apartments (see N. Abraham 1977; S. Abraham and N. Abraham 1983).

Detroit is seen as a less-desirable solution to their problems, as they are fearful of the violence of the city. Yet, the price of housing and the desire to be away from the critical eyes and tongues of the Lebanese drive them to take housing there.

Other issues divide the Lebanese from the Iraqis. The Iraqi refugee women invariably wear the all-encompassing *abaya.* While some Lebanese women who have been strongly influenced by the Iranian revolution have opted to wear this garment, it is hardly the dress of choice for the majority. Lebanese women who want to live by Islamic law opt for light-colored scarves and modest, loose-fitting clothes. Many Lebanese women continue to go without any head covering at all. One Lebanese boy asked his mother why the Iraqi women cover themselves in black, saying that they "look like witches," a sentiment that has been echoed by some less-religiously observant

Lebanese adults. Hygiene is another topic that is regularly referred to by the Lebanese. Whatever people's bathing habits had been during life in southern Iraq (where in most places water would have been at a premium), life in a refugee camp would not have permitted good hygiene. If families are crowded into apartments and flats with limited bathing facilities, it is unlikely that they find it convenient to bathe regularly in Dearborn either. Aside from finding poor personal hygiene offensive for its own sake, the Lebanese are also concerned with the poor image that the Iraqis give Arabs in general.

The Iraqis, of course, also have to be concerned about non-Arabs, particularly the police. Like many immigrant groups before them, they see many U.S. laws as irrational and alien. Traffic laws, for example, are inexplicable. If there are no cars around, why stop at a red light? They do not know how certain laws could possibly pertain to them. After all, America is simply a safe haven until Saddam is gone. Then, they will return to their homes. This belief colors every aspect of their lives here, including their attitudes toward the law. Why, for example, should they pay taxes? They are not American citizens. Yet whenever they receive a paycheck, taxes have been subtracted. Better to find an employer who will pay cash "under the table," if possible.[9]

Iraqi customs in child rearing are often at odds with those of the larger society. For example, punishing a child by spanking or hitting is not considered abusive among Iraqis, but it is among Americans. At home, older children watched younger ones, and the refugees expected that this same behavior could continue here. In one case, parents allowed a child to sit on the curb of a busy street watching cars go by, while his very young sibling was left in a stroller on the sidewalk. The parents had difficulty understanding why the police felt it necessary to intervene.

The men with whom we spoke expressed concern about the case of an Iraqi Shii man in Lincoln, Nebraska, who was arrested for having married his young teenage daughters to Iraqi men in their late twenties, who were also jailed. These men were obviously grappling to understand the issue here. One said that he sees young girls, twelve or thirteen years old, who are pregnant but with no man coming forward to claim the child. Yet, no one goes to jail.[10]

The refugees share an attitude common among other Arabs in the area: do not bring the police into your disputes. Reportedly, they turn to a lawyer affiliated with ACCESS to settle some of their internal problems. Aside from being a lawyer, he is of Arab background, even though he is not part of their own community. He is neither completely inside nor completely outside of their world and thus they believe he is in a good position to mediate.

The Children

An article in the Dearborn *Press and Guide* discusses the challenges of trying to integrate the children from the refugee camps into the Dearborn school system (Slaughter 1997). Lowrey School, the story says, "has seen 70–80 children a year enroll who come from that situation. In fact, throughout the district, the number of Iraqi children has risen from 13 in 1992 to 836 this year [1997]." The article focused on finding ways to help children who had missed out on childhood—many of whom witnessed violence and killing and experienced sexual assault and other abuse—deal with post-traumatic stress and to bring order into their chaotic lives. Apparently, the children still do not feel safe. They "jump if a car backfires and a parade for a patriotic holiday is scary at first for them."

The *Free Press* quotes a social worker who said, "They never grew up. It's like they are fossilized." Children who have been subjected to trauma and who have not attended school previously are difficult to place in the public school system. One person at ACCESS complained that the schools sometimes placed children in "special needs" classes, those meant for children with learning disabilities or who are developmentally disabled. It is obvious that the Dearborn school district, in spite of its history of coping with a large influx of immigrants who fled the long and bloody civil war in Lebanon, is now facing its greatest challenge yet.

A young girl we interviewed said that she had learned a lot from everything she had been through. She was "not going to make the same mistake her parents made." When prodded, she said, "I will be prepared when I have to run away." She had a bag packed near her bed with basic necessities for her family. And, she added, "we will all stay together."

Efforts to Organize the Community

Throughout the Middle East people tend to identify themselves not in broad ways such as national identity, but as smaller groups—a clan, a village, a town. Thus, that the Iraqis are Arabs and Shia has generally not been sufficient grounds for a sense of unity between them and Lebanese (Arab) Shia. While Iraqis might have gone to

Fig. 15. Newly arrived refugee from Iraq plays with granddaughter. Photograph by Millard Berry.

the local Shii centers for prayers, the meetings held in these centers would not have seemed relevant to their own lives. The sermons most likely would not have addressed their concerns. The Dearborn Lebanese have largely tried to keep political speeches out of their centers' day-to-day activities so that the community did not rupture along ideological lines. The Shii community in Lebanon, after the civil war began, became fractious. They did not want their political divisions played out in the streets and mosques of Dearborn.

The Iraqi situation is different. While ideological differences are found among the Iraqis, they unanimously agree that Saddam must go and that they must return to their homeland and rebuild it. This is what they want to discuss in their religious centers. They link this struggle to take back their homeland with the suffering of Imam Hussein, their martyred seventh-century leader. The Iraqis have always commemorated the Imam Hussein's death during the month of Muharram in a dramatic fashion. But these days Muharram takes on an even greater poignancy; the ceremonies are far more frequent and more intense among the Iraqis than they are among the Dearborn Lebanese. Lebanese men tend to sit at the tables in their centers with bowed heads while listening to the tragedy of Karbala

(Walbridge 1997), where Iraqi men remove their shirts, pound their chests, and cry openly for the suffering of their beloved martyr. The women sob and strike their faces, actions far more dramatic than those of the Lebanese women. These differences underscored the fact that Iraqis arriving in Dearborn needed their own place of worship.

Thus, the Karbala Islamic Education Center (the Markaz Karbala) opened on west Warren Avenue with Sheikh Hisham Al-Husainy as director. This center was intended specifically for the refugees; it was the one place where they could gather. The Center ran into problems with the city when there were complaints about the number of people in the building at one time. The crowding problem was addressed—at least to some degree—by having the women's gatherings held in the afternoon, while the men met at night.

Like other Shii centers in Dearborn, the large main room is lined with formica tables and folding chairs with space reserved for ritual prayers behind the sheikh. The most striking difference between this center and the others in the city is the large poster board covered with pictures of Iraqi torture victims. The person removing his or her shoes at the door is greeted by this sight. It sets the tone for what is to follow. After prayers, people talk openly about their plight—the persecution they have suffered, their exile from their homeland and their sacred shrines, and the suffering they continue to endure in this country.

Sheikh Husainy is both praised and criticized for his efforts in the community. Some of those who have been critical formed a committee in April 1997 to draft bylaws for a new organization whose goal would be to help the Iraqi refugees cope with the problems they face in the United States. The organization, led by educated members of the community, is opening a center that plans to provide employment and placement service, a trade union for professionals, language education, and a women's education committee. Concerned about issues raised earlier in this paper such as physical punishment of children and arranged early marriages of daughters, they specifically want to address the refugees' lack of knowledge of U.S. civil laws. In other words, they intend to focus more on social needs rather than purely religious needs.

Conclusion

The Iraqi refugees who have settled in Dearborn and Detroit are unlike the other Arabic-speaking communities that have settled in this area. They suffer from chronic illnesses that may be a result of chemicals used in warfare and/or from deplorable conditions in the refugee camp where they lived for months or years after they rose up against Saddam Hussein at the end of the Gulf War. Having believed American promises that they would be assisted by the Allied Forces, but then abandoned, they carry with them bitterness at the betrayal by the American government as well as fear that Saddam will still retaliate against them.

Unemployment, underemployment, extremely poor living conditions, lack of proper medical care, even problems with obtaining food are only some of the difficulties that confront the refugees. Even those with advanced education and some knowledge of English are having difficulty finding adequate employment.

Children of the Iraqi refugee community are challenging teachers and the school system as never before. Reports coming out of schools are substantially different from those when the schools were trying to integrate Lebanese children. While Lebanese children had seen war and suffering and did pose problems, the trauma suffered by Iraqi children appears to have been of a far greater magnitude.

The conditions in which many of the refugees are living are reminiscent of those among immigrants at the turn of the century in major cities. In New York tenement houses, single flats were frequently divided into four sections to accommodate four families, yet sometimes even more people squeezed into these tiny places. Communicable illnesses such as tuberculosis spread easily, and infant mortality rates soared. People who found employment worked for pittances but were afraid to complain lest they lose even this work. These are the conditions in which social problems flourish.

Irving Howe in his comprehensive work on Jewish immigrants in the United States described the abominable living conditions of Eastern European Jews (who often worked for people of German Jewish background). He explains:

> That symptoms of social dislocation and even pathology should have appeared under the extreme circumstances in which the early Jewish immigrants lived, seems unavoidable. There was crime, there was wife desertion, and there were juvenile delinquency, gangsterism, and prostitution during the eighties and nineties, as well as during the early decades of the twentieth century—probably more than the records show or memorists tell. How could there not be? (Howe 1994)

Conditions for this immigrant population improved over time, of course. But it took great effort, not only on the part of the immigrants themselves, but on the part of more fortunate members of the larger community: volunteers, philanthropists, social workers, political and labor activists. Obviously, people whose lives are in such disorder and who have been left with so little can hardly be expected to survive without assistance. Nor can they be expected to avoid the social problems that other groups in their situation have experienced.

The Iraqis have the particular misfortune of having arrived just as government policies are undergoing radical retrenchment. They can no longer expect the assistance that they might have had if they arrived only a short time earlier. While individuals and groups might lobby the government to reverse these policies, it will not happen soon enough. It is apparent that grassroots efforts—within the Arab and non-Arab communities—will be needed to avoid an even greater deterioration in people's conditions.

Efforts are being made within the Iraqi community to provide a base of support through the Karbala Center and the center that is now being established. It will be up to the larger community—both Arab and non-Arab—to play a role in helping this community adjust to, or perhaps just survive in, its new environment.

Notes

1. Batatu provides a chart with a breakdown of religious and ethnic groups.
2. In Shiism, there is a hierarchy of religious scholars. At the top are the *mujtahids*. This is a more or less generic term for the high-ranking scholars. *Mujtahids* are graded among themselves, the ones at the top being referred to as *maraji' taqlid* (sources of emulation).
3. Journalist Michael Wood of London went into Iraq not long after the *intifada* and filmed the destruction of the area. The film is called *Saddam's Killing Fields*. Wood also had footage from a video made by an amateur producer. The actual attack against one of the shrines appears in this homemade video that Wood included in his film.
4. The UN has assigned refugees to various states in the United States and to European countries. If a person already had relatives in a particular country, he or she was encouraged to inform the UN representatives of this, so that they could meet with that country's delegation when visiting the camp in Saudi Arabia.
5. Chaldeans, who are from northern Iraq, migrated to the Detroit area earlier, primarily after 1965 and throughout the 1970s. But the Shiite Iraqis

and the Chaldeans are clearly distinct groups. Chaldeans are Christian and speak Aramaic as their first language (though most also spoke Arabic in Iraq and some spoke Kurdish). The Chaldeans have concentrated in Southfield, a suburb on the far side of Detroit. The two groups would have little, if any, contact (Sengstock 1980).

6. While conducting research at an Iraqi foundation in London, England, Linda Walbridge found that the people talked frequently about the overthrow of Saddam Hussein. They described telephone hoaxes in which Iraqis would call the foundation and report a revolution in the streets of Baghdad. This indicates both the desire to see their oppressor gone and the desire to be able to return to their homeland.
7. ACCESS workers report that when families do start to work their aid is often cut off or reduced substantially since they are viewed as self-sufficient and not in need of assistance.
8. The Yemenis are either Zeidis (a Shii sect) or Sunnis of the Shafei School.
9. A myth has been generated in Dearborn that the Iraqis are immune from paying taxes. Men were keen to let us know that indeed they paid taxes like anyone else in the United States.
10. There is much debate about the proper age at which a girl should marry in the traditional Iraqi community as well as in other areas of the Middle East. One member of the clerical establishment said that he did not think it was right for fourteen-year-old girls to be marrying men in their late twenties. In another clerical family living in the West, two of the daughters are completing a university education and have not yet married, while their elder sister married in her early teens. It is apparent that life in the West is affecting people's attitudes on this issue.

References

Abraham, Nabeel. 1977. Detroit's Yemeni Workers. *MERIP Reports.* (May 1977):3–9, 13.

Abraham, Sameer, and Nabeel Abraham, eds. 1983. *Arabs in the New World.* Detroit: Center for Urban Studies, Wayne State University.

Aswad, Barbara, and Nancy Adadow Gray. 1996. Challenges to the Arab-American Family and ACCESS. In *Family and Gender among American Muslims,* edited by Barbara Aswad and Barbara Bilgé, 223–40. Philadelphia: Temple University Press.

Aziz, T. M. 1993. The Role of Muhammad Baqir al-Sadr in Shi'i Political Activism in Iraq from 1958 to 1980. *International Journal of Middle East Studies* 25(2):207–22.

Batatu, Hanna. 1978. *The Old Social Classes and the Revolutionary Movements of Iraq*. Princeton: Princeton University Press.

Bengio, Ofra. 1993. Iraq's Shi'a and Kurdish Communities: From Resentment to Revolt. In *Iraq's Road to War*, edited by Amatzia Baram and Barry Rubins, 51–66. New York: St. Martin's Press.

Fernea, Elizabeth Warnock. 1969. *Guests of the Sheik*. New York: Doubleday Anchor.

Fernea, Robert A. 1970. *Shaykh and Effendi* Cambridge: Harvard University Press.

Howe, Irving. *World of Our Fathers*. New York: Galahad Books, 1994.

Mallat, Chibli. 1993. *The Renewal of Islamic Law*. Cambridge: Cambridge University Press.

Nakash, Yitzhak. 1994. *The Shi'is of Iraq*. Princeton: Princeton University Press.

Sengstock, Mary. 1980. Iraqi Christians in Detroit: An Analysis of an Ethnic Occupation. In *Arabic Speaking Communities in American Cities*, edited by Barbara Aswad, 21–38. New York: Center for Migration Studies.

Slaughter, Sally. 1997. Staff Helping Lowrey Students Overcome Turmoil of Years Spent in Refugee Camps. *Dearborn Press and Guide*. March 27.

Walbridge, Linda. 1997. *Without Forgetting the Imam*. Detroit: Wayne State University Press.

Wiley, Joyce N. 1992. *The Islamic Movement of Iraqi Shi'as*. Boulder, Colo.: Lynne Riemer Publications.

Politics, Pragmatism, and the "Arab Vote"

A Conversation with Maya Berry

Sally Howell

MAYA BERRY IMMIGRATED to Michigan in the early days of the Lebanese civil war, when she was eight years old. She grew up in east Dearborn, where her family was among the first Lebanese to settle. Today, slightly more than twenty years later, this part of town is overwhelmingly Lebanese. Maya attended the University of Michigan in Dearborn, where she became politically active for the first time. Since her college days, Maya's career in politics has taken her from voter-registration drives organized by the Arab Community Center for Economic and Social Services (ACCESS) to one-on-one meetings with members of the U.S. House and Senate. Maya is currently the director of government relations for the Arab American Institute (AAI) in Washington, D.C.

Maya Berry and I spoke on April 20, 1998, by telephone. I interviewed Maya because I was looking for an Arab Detroiter who was familiar with the two political constituencies I had encountered during my own years as cultural arts director at ACCESS (1987–95). The first is comprised largely of recently arrived immigrants who focus their political energy on influencing events in their countries of origin. In many cases, they resist involvement in American domestic politics, which seems alien and antagonistic to their interests. The second constituency is more likely to be American-born, middle-class, and college-educated. They focus their energies on the Arab dimension of local, state, and national issues. While events in the Middle East are still important to this group, they often seek to influence "foreign affairs" through American channels. American public opinion is important to them. These two constituencies, which Nabeel Abraham has labeled "isolationists" and "ethnic integrationists" respectively, are by no means mutually exclusive (1989, 22). Political activists move between them with varying degrees of ease, acceptance, and success. Maya Berry is an immigrant who, because she is a member of the politically influential Berry clan (Nabih Berri is currently the Speaker of the Lebanese Parliament), has numerous personal links to Lebanese in Dearborn whose political imaginations are firmly rooted in the homeland. But her own political career, especially her work at ACCESS and AAI, falls clearly within Abraham's "ethnic integrationist" category.

In our interview, Maya and I discussed her evolution as a political organizer: the issues, individuals, and campaigns that shaped her career and her values. She was eager to draw connections between her grassroots organizing activities in Dearborn and their repercussions for Arab Americans nationally. Maya resisted my efforts to have her describe the political life of the community in a dichotomized manner, arguing that, at least in her experience, isolationists and integrationists cooperate on a broad range of foreign and domestic issues. Maya advocates, instead, a pragmatic agenda in which Arab Americans, regardless of background, work together on issues of political expediency. Her examples include local gas-station owners seeking to affect state legislation on the cleanup of abandoned service stations in Detroit, community women organizing to fight police brutality against local youths in Dearborn, and Lebanese immigrants working to raise awareness of the many injustices created by the Israeli occupation and bombing of south Lebanon.

Participation in the American political system allows Arab Americans to influence "domestic" issues. Their effect on U.S. policy in the Middle East, however, has been insignificant. Integrationists are willing to see this reality as one that will change in the long run, through engagement in the American political system. New immigrants, for whom events in the Arab world have deep personal significance, are less willing to take this gradualist approach, and they are usually unwilling to engage in political dealings with the very government—that is, the U.S. government—that supports policies that endanger, dispossess, or kill their relatives in the homeland. When they try to influence events in their countries of origin, they do so outside (or in spite of) the American political system.

I arrived in Detroit shortly before Maya's political awakening and worked at ACCESS for almost a decade during a time when many events took place in the Middle East that warranted a strong political reaction from Arab Detroiters. During this period, local Palestinians spent most of their political energy supporting the *intifada*, the uprising against the Israeli occupation of the West

Bank and Gaza Strip. Palestinians in Detroit were divided in their responses to the 1993 peace treaty with Israel that led to the creation of the Palestinian National Authority and continued occupation. For the Iraqi Chaldean community, the most significant political event of this period was the Persian Gulf War. The war had a tremendous impact on Chaldeans in Iraq and in Michigan. Local Chaldeans continue to lobby the U.S. government to lift sanctions against Iraq. These sanctions are devastating for everyday citizens, and they have done little to weaken Saddam Hussein and his allies. In 1990, the countries of South and North Yemen unified under one flag, causing celebration and concern among Yemeni Detroiters. When civil war broke out in 1994, local Yemenis divided along existing political lines and sought to support their political allies back home. In Lebanon, the civil war ended. Many Lebanese Americans visited the country for the first time in decades. Their efforts have since focused on rebuilding the Lebanese economy and ending Israel's occupation of south Lebanon.

In each of these cases, the response of Arab Detroiters was to raise and send home millions of dollars in support of humanitarian, personal, and political causes. Dinners were held. Radio and television interviews were produced in the local Arabic media. Letters were written to the U.S. Congress and to political leaders back home. Sermons were preached in local churches and mosques. Envoy missions were sent to deliver medicines, find facts, or create goodwill. Nonprofit organizations were established. These responses were personal, intense, and varied. I was surprised, however, by the degree to which they were absent from my conversation with Maya Berry. These absences, more than anything else, reveal Maya's real location on the Arab American political spectrum. Had I interviewed an Arab American whose political efforts during the past decade had focused on influencing Middle Eastern events through Arab (as opposed to American) channels, it is highly unlikely that they would have discussed the U.S. electoral issues so important to Maya Berry.

In our interview, Maya did not deny the centrality of Arab world events to her own life or the lives of her Arab neighbors in Detroit. In fact, she displayed a remarkable ability to draw links between events in the Middle East and the evolution of an "ethnic American" political agenda. Maya is more comfortable with this ethnic agenda, which focuses on voter-registration drives, getting Arab Americans elected to political office, participating in Democratic and Republican Party primaries, and presenting Arab American perspectives and concerns to politicians on Capitol Hill. That Maya describes issues originating in the Middle East as foreign-policy issues is itself a semantic shift most new immigrants would find radical. For them, "foreign policy" is what happens in America. For Maya, and for her political colleagues, this is clearly not the case.

In a follow-up conversation, Maya told me of the frustration her parents feel over her active involvement in American domestic politics, an exertion of energy they see as futile. They were delighted, however, when she accompanied a congressional delegation to Lebanon earlier this year. They now have a picture of Maya standing beside Lebanon's president, which they proudly display on their living-room wall. For me, Maya's political career and the reactions of her family sum up the two political imaginations most common in Detroit. One is an immigrant perspective, reluctant to engage fully in a political system that is unfamiliar and often hostile. The other is an ethnic American perspective which pulls together disparate worlds, seeks connections between them, and tries to build a political identity that is insistently and unapologetically American.

Maya Berry, telephone interview, April 20, 1998

SALLY: Would you tell me, briefly, about your personal history, your family's immigration to the U.S., and a little background on yourself?

MAYA: I was born in Beirut, Lebanon, in 1968. I stayed there with my family until a year after the war broke out in Lebanon. The family moved here in 1976 to escape the strife that was happening at the time and fully intending to move back. We never moved back, obviously. I'm one of seven siblings; five girls and two boys. We left Lebanon at different times, primarily because of the conflict. My oldest brother was at the university and, given what was happening in the country, he was being pressured to become . . . actually involved in the conflict itself. So my parents got him on a plane and shipped him over here to the university. A few months after that, I and four other siblings came. And then, within a few weeks of that, my youngest sister and parents came over. When I first arrived, I spent a few weeks in a cousin's home in the Southend of Dearborn, and then we ended up purchasing a home in east Dearborn, which at the time had very few Arab Americans. My parents have lived there ever since. I am the second youngest of a family of seven kids, as I said.

Sally: East Dearborn at the time was not very Arab, or not as Arab as it is now. When you were growing up were there a lot of Arabs in the school?

Maya: I knew one other kid. I remember it only because he too was Muslim and we used to have these conversations with our American friends, explaining to them that we really did believe in God, too. We just called him "Allah" and it was OK. [Laughter] And that was the one other kid, and he changed his name . . . to something much more American.

Sally: Which school were you in?

Maya: I was at Woodworth Junior High School.

Sally: And when did you start to notice more Arabs in the classroom with you? Surely there were a lot more Arabs by the time you went to high school?

Maya: Oh yeah, actually that was huge for me, when I went to high school. Because it was, like, overwhelming. All of a sudden I went, "Oh wow, where did these kids come from?" And I was in a very precarious position—one I continue to be in. That is to say, I saw the Arabic kids speaking only Arabic to each other and often about other people in Arabic. And I pretty much resented it. And then I saw the American kids being incredibly prejudicial and racist in their views toward the Arabic kids, and, obviously, I was completely isolated and couldn't relate to that. So high school was a very interesting period for me, where I really didn't relate to either planet. I just said, "OK, I am going to get this over and done with quickly." But I would have to say that it really wasn't until high school that I met a lot of other Arabic kids. I remember just a few in junior high school.

Sally: Who did you hang out with in high school? Who were your friends?

Maya: They weren't American kids and they weren't Arab kids. Oddly enough, I didn't discover this until many years later. One friend was a Slovak girl whose father spoke broken English. One was a Greek girl whose mother spoke no English. We were all just immigrants. But we were never conscious of it at the time. Now, as adults, those are the only relationships I continue to have with people from high school. Our mothers are very similar people. They just happen not to have been from the Middle East, but rather immigrants.

SALLY: Tell me a little bit more about your family. I'd like to know how they made a living when they first got here. How involved were they in Arab American institutions, events, that sort of thing?

MAYA: My dad worked for an American [insurance] company in Lebanon, so I remember growing up we had a lot of American friends, a lot of parties where we would be entertaining Americans. My parents had visited Detroit on several occasions. It wasn't unusual. America was not a place we were unfamiliar with. I knew we had relatives here. And it was, actually, a very happy existence. I had a great time as a kid.

When we moved here, it was considerably different for both of my parents. My mother has been a homemaker for all of her life. But in Lebanon, I know that she had a world that involved others in a way that she doesn't here. Her contacts here tend to be immediate family and that's about it. On my father's side, he completely had to start a whole new career. And his English skills were not strong. His [experience] was obviously more difficult. It was very hard for him when we first got here. We were lucky enough to be in an economic position to make the move for all of us, and even purchase a home within the first few months we were here and start to begin a life. I'm realizing that there were a lot of people who weren't even in that position.

SALLY: Did you get help from anyone?

MAYA: Yes. We did what I think a lot of people did at the time, and that is that you come here and you visit the sort of patriarchs of the family or of the clan in the community. [For us] it was Mike Berry [an important player in the local Democratic Party and Berry clan patriarch.] I still remember Mike being over at the house and how helpful he was to a lot of people, and particularly to my dad, who he helped get a job at the airport at the time. That was very difficult for my father, and I don't think he ever adjusted. I don't think he was ever satisfied doing that, but that is what you do. You earn a living to support a family and get by the way that you can.

SALLY: Tell me a bit about your parents' participation in community organizations or political things when you were growing up.

MAYA: My parents did not participate, actually, in any of our social institutions or religious institutions here in the U.S. I know for a fact they were more active in Lebanon. It's very important to understand that when they moved here, there really was a major shift in their lives. Their lives were put on hold to raise the rest of the family, and I don't think they ever resumed living life fully. I struggle with knowing how much they had to give up for us to leave a war-torn area, but it's completely true.

Politics has always been a part of our lives. That's just the way it is. We talk about it at dinner. We yell about it over food. But I never knew my father was a labor organizer until looking at photo albums when I was older and seeing him behind this banner leading a labor demonstration. And when I asked him about it later, it was like, "Oh yeah, I did that." All of that came to a halt here. I'm not even certain, actually, as to why that would be the case. I just know that my father spent a few years a little bit more involved in the mosque and then stopped again.

Sally: What sources did you have in the home for news? If you were always talking about politics and things that were happening overseas, what were your sources for information?

Maya: "The Journal" on the Canadian news channel, and Faisal Arabo on Saturday evenings [a local Iraqi Chaldean TV news and information program]. We watched that religiously together at ten o'clock in the evening. I mean they got the typical news sources. They got, obviously, all of the Arabic publications. People talk about, "Are you involved in politics?" Well, you move to this country because of politics. You don't ever stop. . . . It's a whole part of your life. There are no divisions there so . . . They got the news because they had to get the news, and you couldn't imagine not keeping up. We were one of those families that bought a VCR when it first came out, for my mother, because she still doesn't know English and that was her outlet. She would watch videos and films (in Arabic) that way. As soon as there was a network available, where we could get Arabic channels, we were doing that. But it used to be Faisal Arabo and "The Journal" on Canadian television.

Sally: You are saying that politics was a part of the everyday fabric of your family life. Politics affected the way you communicated with each other, the issues you discussed, and even forced you to immigrate to America. And yet you are not political in the same way your parents were. You are actively engaged in American politics. Were there any specific events or individuals that influenced you to become so political in your own life?

Maya: A joke growing up for me, that my mother still tells, was that I would come home from school and ask for milk and the newspaper. I was really young. But I can't . . . identify a point where I started to say, "This is important." I remember when I got my citizenship, President Reagan was coming to the ceremony. The president of the United States was going to be at the ceremony where I was getting sworn in as a citizen. I went with my dad. At the time I loved taking pictures. I was this huge photographer. And I remember it was two years after Sabra and Shatila [the massacre of Palestinian refugees by Maronite soldiers under the gaze of Israeli forces during the 1982 Israeli invasion of Lebanon] and it was after comments the president had made, and . . . my little protest was not to take photographs that day—not to photograph the president. Now obviously this was not a very sophisticated move, to [draw a] direct relationship between not photographing the president and having that be a protest. But I had an awareness.

SALLY: I understand. You didn't want one of those "glam shots" of yourself with President Reagan on the wall. You didn't want to be associated with him.

MAYA: Yeah, and it was at a time when I used to write letters, I must say, but never send them. Yeah, that was always a thing, too. In terms of being politically active, my parents strongly discouraged me. When I went to college was the first time I met other Arab Americans like me—that is, Arab students who had interests in the politics of our region, but who also . . . who . . . It was just different. I can't identify why, but I related to them differently. We played on an intramural volleyball team and beat out all the little frats, but at the same time we were organizing around everything that was happening in the [Arab] region. And that to me was what I was about. It was a perfect match. That's really when I started to become . . . outwardly active.

SALLY: Did you organize your work with other students through some sort of group?

MAYA: Yes, I joined an Arab student organization for the first time in my life!

SALLY: What was it called?

MAYA: Actually, the Arab Student Association of the University of Michigan, Dearborn. I met wonderful people who had similar interests in terms of what they were learning, in terms of our work back home, and we also got together socially. And that was, for me, sort of the beginning. Because it was just an extension of the foreign-policy interests I had. The real beginning in terms of political work in *this* country and being rooted in that would actually have to go to ACCESS. When I showed up at the Center with an interest in registering voters, I met Ish [Ismael Ahmed, ACCESS executive director] for the first time and told him we were part of a group that wanted to do that, and I really sort of took off from there.

SALLY: You have so far said that the Arab Student Association was involved explicitly in foreign-policy issues. Now you are talking about domestic, internal American politics. Can you tell me which issues were important to you in college? Were they international, or local, or both?

MAYA: Local things meant very local. I mean you are in a university setting. You are very enclosed from the rest of the world. There was a big issue with, this is really silly now, but a group of young students organized on campus under the guise of the Young Socialists of America. The student government at that time voted them out illegally. I happened to be part of a small group of people who just thought that is not what you do on a university campus. And I was then, quite honestly, recruited to run for office, and did so, and ended up winning [the vice presidency]. I'm not sure, but I think I may have been the first Arab American elected at the University of Michigan, Dearborn.

The student government at the time was run by fraternities and sororities and a very right-wing political element who outlawed a group because of their political beliefs. They didn't happen to be Arab, and I certainly wasn't a member of the Young Socialists at the time, but I just didn't think that was the right thing to do. From that it spearheaded into the Young Democrats, who were on campus doing voter-registration drives. I remember thinking that I'd like to do this in the Arab community as well. And then I went to ACCESS to run a voter-registration drive in the Southend.

SALLY: What was the political scene like in the community when you first started doing voter-registration work?

MAYA: I had never even seen ACCESS before actually. It was a whole new world for me, because it really was the first time I started to . . . There's a difference between knowing something intellectually and doing it. When we did that first voter-registration effort in the Southend, that's when I took my principles and my beliefs and this desire to say "this is what we need to be doing," and actually did it for the first time.

SALLY: And what year was this? Which campaign was this?

MAYA: I don't think there was any particular campaign. It came more out of a desire to register voters. It had to be in the late 1980s, but I don't remember. I could think about that, but I know that I never left ACCESS.

SALLY: This is before you started working there?

MAYA: It was before, but . . . I definitely got sucked in. It went from [the voter-registration drive] to Ismael offering me a job there. Once I ended up at the Center, it was an incredible experience because then it was a total merging of all of my worlds. I mean, I was being paid to do a certain type of work. I continued my interests. I was obviously still in school, and at the same time I was able to do all the political stuff that I very much love to do.

SALLY: Well, why don't you tell me briefly about your job and the political issues you organized around.

MAYA: I was hired as coordinator for an emergency food and shelter program. It was a very hard job, as you can imagine, because I either saw people when they were hungry or were getting evicted. But it was a part of the ACCESS family, so as depressing as that job may have been, and as difficult as it was, I was very rewarded by the environment I was in. I just completely dove in. I got as involved as I could in all of our programs and learning about the Center and in doing everything that I could. I mean, I loved going to the Southend. I loved physically being there. It was an incredible learning experience. I probably went into ACCESS more idealistic than I can imagine, but left so much more pragmatic because of learning so much from Ish, quite honestly.

SALLY: [Laughing] I'm not sure that's such a good thing.

MAYA: Yeah, it's true. I learned so much from Ish, from our work there, from our campaigns and our experiences.

SALLY: You're still speaking in very general terms. Could you describe some of the issues that were important to you during your time at ACCESS?

MAYA: Our first big effort was to try to get precinct delegates elected [to the Democratic Party]. The folks I was working with had already been delegates to the national convention during the Jesse Jackson campaign. I just came into that, and again, it was textbook learning versus what they already knew. And we ran a campaign in 1990, where we identified maybe thirty people and developed these flyers where at the top of the ticket was Governor Blanchard and Senator Levin and Congressman John Dingell, and then [State Representatives] Agnes Dobronski, George Hart, and us. I still have my flyer where, you know, I am at the bottom of the ticket, but actually it was a real campaign in that your name appeared on the ballot. We did this in a bunch of different precincts, where we identified Arab Americans to run. And I have to say that for a campaign it was very successful, because these were things where you ran unopposed. These precinct delegate seats were generally empty. No one had filled those positions. And, for some reason, I became engaged in the Democratic Party locally. I would go to their meetings, and they had identified the fact that west Dearborn would have these precincts that would be full and then east Dearborn had precincts that were just wide open. And we proceeded to fill them.

SALLY: Did you have an agenda behind this other than getting Arab Americans elected and filling the seats? What specific issues were you pushing?

MAYA: Yes. The agenda was entirely local. We were dealing with local city politics and dynamics relating to city operations and the education system. In 1991 the bond issue was happening. If you remember, the bond issue in 1990 was defeated. This is when [the city of Dearborn] asked for, I think, over one hundred million dollars for the schools, which were hurting primarily in the east side where they were bursting at the seams. [The school board] was thinking about potential growth [in the size of Dearborn's school-age population] in ten to twenty years and saying, "My god, we have to do something." And typically in Dearborn, where even a simple bond election like that in 1990 was perceived as being a sort of ethnically rooted issue, it was voted down. They said "Our schools are fine. It's just that side [that has the problems]."

SALLY: "That side" being the Arab side of town.

MAYA: Yes, which at this point had grown considerably beyond the Southend. I mean we are talking about the east side of Dearborn. And we put together our first real campaign. You know, you identify precincts. You target them. You phone bank. You get voting records. You deal with voter turnout. You drive people to the polls. The first real campaign was in 1991, when the second bond came up for election. And we won by maybe five hundred votes. This is out of like twenty thousand or something, so we were definitely the margin of victory in that. It was a huge success for us. Because folks in Dearborn are notorious for saying, "Yeah, the Arab vote, the Arab vote . . . Yeah. I'll wait until I see it." Well, in that campaign you actually saw it.

SALLY: Who is the "we" you keep referring to? I'm interested in hearing who the other players were in this drive.

MAYA: At that time the Arab American Institute had sent Peg McCormick, a woman who was doing their political consulting work, and Ish, Joe Borrajo, Zena Maaki, Maryanne Maguire, all sorts of people. Mike Awad and Zena, at that time, were doing part of the campaign work for the Institute.

SALLY: So the political leadership on this domestic issue was coming out of people around ACCESS who had very much of a leftist political agenda, and a track record of being very successful at accomplishing their political ends. I'm interested in hearing about the issues that were engaging people who weren't involved in the American side of things. Was there a type of person who would be more involved in American domestic issues and another type of a person who would be involved in international issues?

MAYA: My experience so merged both that I don't know that I can speak to that. We registered voters at the mosque. People who did door-to-door work were certainly far beyond the ACCESS family. We were part of the agenda at local meetings the same way a hospital in the south of Lebanon or a bond issue would have been. My experience may have been unique in this way, but it was a merging of both [sets of issues]. Whether a meeting was at the mosque or Arab American folks organized around school issues, like PTA groups, we just asserted our agenda in all of those different things.

SALLY: So you just showed up wherever you could?

MAYA: Yes. And it wasn't unusual. It wasn't an unusual match. These are concerns for all of us. We are dealing with this [the bond issue] here, and you obviously cared about [humanitarian and political causes in the Arab world], so you dealt with that as well.

SALLY: Then what happened? You helped organize the voter-registration campaign and then the Gulf War broke out?

MAYA: Yes. And that was very interesting. The Gulf War was very troubling for me on numerous levels. I was fairly quiet, I would say, before I ran for student government. I just participated in what I was interested in, and I didn't see the university setting for what it could be. After running for student government and becoming involved, I had my first real enlightenment. We did a program at the university about liberation struggles and self-determination movements, and the student government had a panel that featured both South Africa and Palestine. I happened to be one vice president. The other vice president happened to be an African American. We both put it together as part of a university program that received wide attention. Much to my surprise . . . I was so naive . . . our particular panel drew enough attention that the university felt it needed to pull its sponsorship. The panel went on without university sponsorship. A professor complained that this was an inappropriate area for a university to be involved in. Because I was a member of the student government, I was an extension of the university and so was my colleague. That was the only time when I was on campus that I said "Oh wow! Maybe I am not as much a part of this as I thought I was." Because all of the sudden what were very simple intellectual pursuits became political issues that warranted the university pulling its sponsorship.

My second enlightenment came during the Gulf War, where the entire world was sort of turned on its head. You know, you had fellow students who were, like, yelling at you to go back where you came from. It's a cliché, but it's really true. I actually heard that because I was a part of a campus effort to say that war was not a good alternative and there were other venues for us to take. Oddly enough, I would love to talk to those people [now] because almost a decade later we can honestly see that it continues to be a flawed policy. I was primarily organizing around opposition to the war and the need to have at least a debate on the subject.

SALLY: Your work on this issue was mostly done within the university community?

MAYA: Entirely.

SALLY: Were you aware of efforts that were going on outside the university within the Arab community?

MAYA: I was a part of that, too, oddly enough. I was in a meeting with Congressman Dingell on the day we started bombing. Congressman Dingell was one of the few Democrats who had voted in support of Bush's resolution to take military action. He realized that would be a concern to our community, and he took it upon himself to say, "I would like to meet with you and talk to you about my vote." We were sitting in a restaurant on Michigan Avenue [in Dearborn] having this meeting, and the television was on. They announced that they had started bombing. I remember getting up to leave, and Ish saying, "No. It's important that the congressman hear what you have to say." To this day I will never forgive him for that [Maya laughs.] But you are young and you have very heated, passionate views about things. I don't know if I would call it a tirade, but I remember certainly expressing to the congressman my discontent with his vote . . . and leaving. And I thank God to this day that Dingell doesn't hold that against me, because we have a very good relationship. But the focus of my activity, honestly, was around the university stuff. But as I said, I was a part of . . .

SALLY: . . . a community coalition. I'm interested in hearing more about the specifics of the community response to the war. I'm familiar with the things that were happening around ACCESS, trying to have Bush negotiate instead of bombing. I know we had the media all around. You couldn't breathe without the media asking a hundred questions.

MAYA: The media and the FBI.

SALLY: And the FBI. You might talk about that issue as well. That was very critical for several months. But I am also interested in hearing, if you can talk about it, about the internal community reactions to this. Can you address that at all?

MAYA: I only know it through people like Ish and Ali Dagher, Jessica Daher, Zena Maaki, and those types of folks. I think it would be best if you talked with them about the internal community stuff. But I understand it in the context of this total media attention suddenly microscoped [on the Arab community]. They're not interested in you until there's a crisis where they can say your loyalty is being called into question. Then the headlines read, "Arab American Loyalties Called into Question." That was the tenor and tone of most of what happened in Dearborn, because, as you know, any time there was a crisis, that is what they came to Dearborn for.

And the second component came with the FBI. They sent out a press release saying they were going to be investigating a couple of hundred community leaders, including people like elected city councilwoman, Suzanne Sareini. They interviewed elected officials, leaders like Ish. It was an attempt to get information that would be useful in "protecting us," is how they phrased it. And in the same press release they were forthright enough to say, "and also gather information about possible illegal activity." To me that was one of the most amazing things. Few people doubt that the various [federal] agencies have programs—and I hope this doesn't sound like a crazy conspiracy—that do things a lot of us don't like to think about. [We think these programs are] rare. It is quite telling in terms of how the Arab community is viewed and the nature of our political power that a government agency can put out a press release announcing this program.

Sally: Yes, but they rescinded it pretty quickly. They apologized officially.

Maya: Well, I don't know that I would say pretty quickly. It only came when there were editorials in newspapers across the country and people were indignant about it. Congressional members sent out materials saying, "What are you doing?" Congressional offices inquired about it. I think it is one of those telling cases where the FBI thought they could do it and not have a problem. We had to create a problem for them, in order for it to stop.

Sally: This is important, but you seem to want to talk about all these mainstream things. I am interested in drawing a contrast between the types of events that are internal to the community and the mainstream, democratic events that you participated in. You mentioned a hospital fund-raiser for Lebanon. Are there other specific issues that you were aware of people organizing around that had to do with the situation back home? How do people organize? What issues and appeals motivate them? What exactly do people do? Do they have demonstrations, fund-raisers, meetings? Do they produce things for sale?

Maya: It's not that I don't want to talk. We did programs on the anniversary of Sabra and Shatila each year. The way in which we did them happened to focus on public education. If I had to sit back and think about it, I would say that a lot of it was preaching to the converted.

Sally: And who was "we"?

Maya: Most of the Sabra and Shatila activity was on campus. Groups outside the university participated, either recent university graduates, other Arab students, Arab American students, or community activists. If there was a speaker coming, you would schedule things, and there would be these forums held. The point being that there is no debate on these issues. There is no discourse on the Arab-Israeli conflict, including Lebanon, Palestine, and all of the other areas. So our simple task was to provide an alternative viewpoint on all of this. That is pretty much what we did. We would show a documentary that you couldn't get on PBS at the Dearborn Public Library and try to draw an audience there. A lot of [our work] was that type of activity. I'm certain that local mosques would have been more involved in direct-assistance work that would have gone to both Lebanon and Palestine. But I was not involved in that. [This work] came around the crisis of the day. If there was a particular air raid, or a particular massacre, or a particular proposal, or this thing in Iraq, or the peace process, or . . . They came as needed. Whatever happened [in the Arab world], we found ourselves needing to react to it here.

SALLY: So it was very reactionary in that sense. You would react to public events, usually military events where Israel was the aggressor?

MAYA: Yes, almost exclusively. We didn't do much public relations work that way. A lot of our effort was in public education. In the few cases where it was particularly . . . and I hate to imply that there is a hierarchy of abuse . . . but in the few cases when it was a particularly bad incident, there were demonstrations. And the community would organize demonstrations where a couple of thousand people would march on Dearborn city hall.

SALLY: I remember marching with you one time.

MAYA: That's right.

SALLY: I'd like you to talk about that event, specifically. How effectively do you think those events reached a non-Arab audience? I wonder what the purpose of those marches was. Was the purpose to galvanize sentiment within the community, or to reach a larger, non-Arab audience? Which of those did it accomplish? Did it accomplish something more?

MAYA: I hope my point of view doesn't offend, because I'm going to be very frank. Those demonstrations, to me, were measures of an almost powerless community. I qualify that by saying I recognize how incredible it is that without any organized faction, or fax broadcast, or e-mail networks, or anything, that someone decides on a Thursday that there is a demonstration tomorrow and three thousand people show up. That is exactly what happened. That is a powerful statement about both the unity of the community and the commitment and deep level of concern about these issues.

So for that reason, you can call them a resounding success. We came together and, even though we had divergent views within our communities, we were all one to say that this was an affront to humanity. I don't mean to use such glorified language, but it was . . .

SALLY: This was when Israel was bombing civilian targets in the south of Lebanon.

MAYA: Yes. [These types of demonstrations] are not effective in promoting our concerns, or educating non-Arabs, or those who don't sympathize with us about our concerns. I know what you are talking about. I remember whining about the signs we had, because I felt they were politically inappropriate. Perhaps they were factually accurate in some cases, but they were not the right message.

SALLY: Can you give a few examples?

MAYA: For the most part, I remember them drawing similarities to the Holocaust. My position has always been that we don't need to have competing wounds with regard to any of this. The Holocaust [and] the current occupation were and are horrific periods. But, we don't need to make comparisons. I am of the opinion that the Holocaust was a fairly unique period in history. But my point is that these issues could be part of an intellectual discussion between two people. But carrying a sign like that at a demonstration is entirely different. You can disagree about the substance of that statement, but when you hold that up [on a placard], you are not helping. You are doing a disservice to your cause. You actually alienate others who may agree with you.

And then [she adds, laughing] the simple fact that we blocked traffic. I remember thinking, "Yeah, these guys are just beeping their horns. They are ignoring us, trying to get home from work, and they are not going to relate." But again, that is uniquely my perspective. I don't mean to be negative. And I participated. I participated because I thought it was important to do so.

SALLY: Do you see there being separate political communities in Arab Detroit?

MAYA: I think there are in some ways. It is the same thing we would see nationally. More recent immigrant communities work on issues relating more directly to what has happened overseas, "back home issues." The conditions in the south of Lebanon, or conditions in the Occupied Territories, or in Iraq, the plight of the people postwar. Then you have a segment of the community that is either second generation or third generation and has been established here for much longer time periods. Their involvement tends to be in domestic politics first, with some ties to the "back home issues." The reason I am so grateful for my experiences in Dearborn is that I've worked with people who did both of those things. That is really my experience. I have not worked solely on issues related to the region or solely on party politics with different groups of people. For me those groups are intertwined and they tend to be the same folks.

When we did, for example, the precinct delegate work, we were recruiting from organizations and institutions that were not as actively involved in the electoral process or civic responsibility types of issues yet. We would enter the door talking about larger issues, and then hone in and get them focused on what another part of their agenda needs to be, and that is the Arab American community's concerns and our work here in this country.

SALLY: I wanted to ask if you see a crossover between these two audiences, and you have already begun to address that. Can you give an example of a type of issue or event that might have led people whose political focus might ordinarily lie overseas to focus on the local, or vice versa?

MAYA: Yes. For people like Ali Jawad and Ali Berry [Lebanese immigrants who are partners in a highly successful gas distribution company] who work with the Lebanese American Club and who are prominent, the crisis leading up to and after Qana was important. They hosted daily meetings at the club.

SALLY: This is a specifically immigrant club.

MAYA: Yeah. Yeah. It's where we have our weddings and our meetings and cultural events, and it's very important. I think it plays an important role both socially and politically in our community. And while it is associated with immigrants and we think that the Qana protest is a logical extension of their work, it's also important to realize that Ali Jawad and Ali Berry happen to be part of the Service Station Dealers Association. Another logical extension of their work revolves around issues of environmental cleanup relating to gas stations and the disposal of certain wastes. [When Governor John Engler began drafting legislation that directly affected the ownership and management of gas stations in the mid-1990s, the Service Station Dealers Association, a largely Arab American organization, began actively lobbying the state for assistance with meeting environmental cleanup costs.] That purely state-politics concern played a major part in getting them active with the governor and with the state legislature.

SALLY: Has that involvement continued?

MAYA: Oh, very much so. There was a time when it was a big deal for an Arab American committee to be set up in support of a particular candidate. It was a big deal for candidates to meet with the Arab American community. Now, I am happy to say, particularly in Dearborn, it doesn't even warrant special attention. I know Congressman Dingell recently attended a special anniversary program on Qana held at the Islamic Institute of Knowledge [a mosque often characterized as pro-Hizballah.] [This organization is the topic of my interview with Lila and Mohsen Amen in part 3 of this volume.] And this is the dean of the U.S. House of Representatives, the congressman from that district. We are at a point now where it is logical that he should attend such an event. These are his constituents and among their concerns are health care, which he champions, and other issues, and this particular concern as well. So I think we've come a long way.

SALLY: You mentioned a second example as well.

MAYA: [In 1996] Israel had been bombing south Lebanon for several days, and folks went to the UN base at Qana for protection, basically. Israel then proceeded to bomb the UN base. It resulted in over one hundred people dead. I think it was 103. Two of the kids who died were from Dearborn. So it was a very personal event for a lot of people. They chartered planes, they organized, and they came down here for a demonstration/rally in front of the White House. I have been to these things both at home and in Washington, and the uniqueness of this event was that it drew an incredible mix of folks: the National Arab American Business Association, the Arab American Chamber of Commerce people, the hajji [grandma] who is pretty much behind the scenes making the food at the *jamaa* [the Islamic Center of America in Dearborn] each evening. One of the photographs and newspaper clippings I saved [from this event] is of a woman, who looks just like my mom. She had come to the demonstration in front of Lafayette Park, right in front of the White House. She was carrying a sign about needing to resolve this conflict peacefully.

So it was a significant event for our community that way. But even more interesting, when they went back to Michigan and they continued to do their work, a group of women organized to do voter registration. I remember getting a call from them. They wanted some help in terms of the best mechanisms or methods to do this, very basic, simple stuff. One woman told me she was going to fax me something, if I would just add my input. At the time I thought to myself, this is great. This is exactly what we want. The extension of this type of work is to realize that they need to be more politically active and organized. And I was expecting this fax to be information about Qana and the number of people killed, the statistics about Israeli occupation of the south, that sort of thing. What she sent me was this wonderfully done flyer that said, "Did you know how many Arab Americans live in Dearborn? 'X' amount are in our schools. 'X' amount are here. But we only have four police officers. And we only have one city council member." It was very basic—just city and local politics.

It was an incredible sign for me because that's the way I've worked in the past. [ACCESS, the Arab American Institute, and I] have had to drive these linkages. This time we didn't need to. People organized around the issue of Qana because it was an incredibly horrible event, and that's what brought them together. But they saw the direct link between needing to do that and, at the same time, get to the other stuff. And that meant getting to members of Congress and looking at conditions here as they relate politically to issues there. Things are just so different in even the short time that I have been working in community politics.

SALLY: Well, I would partly agree. If you wanted to compare the two protests that we have talked about, the one that took place in Dearborn and the one that took place in Washington, they were the same group of people. I am always impressed at protests in Dearborn by the number of baby strollers you see at them. They are not just a bunch of college kids out there wearing shorts. It's the whole community. It's a very representative cross section of the Lebanese community. I agree that both events were ineffective at reaching a larger audience. But you are making a different point. You were encouraged by the event in Washington because people went home and thought about what they had participated in and then took other steps. They became active on the local level, perhaps, because they realized that was the only way they could have any power.

MAYA: Right. It was incredible. The festival, the [1996 east Dearborn] Arab Festival that ACCESS sponsored, included, as a result of the work on Qana, and the petition drive that came later, a voter-registration drive. Two different groups were doing them. These women were going door-to-door, at one point.

SALLY: So you see involvement in international issues leading to local participation. That's how you get access to power, so for you that is very positive.

MAYA: Absolutely. Absolutely. And the reverse is true as well. Our community came to Michigan because Henry Ford said, "Five dollars a day!" It's a very pragmatic reason. I think you'll find, just as among the service-station dealers, party persuasion is determined by very pragmatic business interests. I'm saying that [this pragmatism] is much more central to our work in this community than people give it credit for being. You know, we are very strategic in some ways, in the decisions we make. Because there are different interests at the table, people say our community is all over the place, or that we are disorganized. Well, no, actually, I think that there are people in our community who have different interests. That's what you see more and more in Michigan.

SALLY: Well, I want to ask two other sets of questions. One, I wanted to give you a little bit of a chance to talk about AAI and AAI's political agenda and your participation in it. Why have you made this move? What is satisfying to you about your new experiences?

MAYA: Well, when I was first offered the job, I thought, "No way!" And then I got excited at the prospect of doing what I did part-time in Dearborn full-time on the national scene. And that is what I did for my first two years here. I worked to organize our community across the country. Instead of just organizing a bond election in Dearborn, I would work on a city council race in New Jersey, or the state party platform in California. It was very exciting work which was entirely electorally based. It involved either Arab Americans who were running for office, or candidates that Arab Americans supported on very local—state, city, county—kinds of issues. To me, this grassroots work is what makes AAI different. I'm pleased to be doing it. This organization merges two very different aspects of our community; the third- and fourth-generation folks who are judges . . . elected officials . . . the Senate majority leader, and the newer immigrant community who are struggling to get a city council person elected in New Jersey. And we work with both of those communities. To me, that was a perfect match. I am even happier now, actually, in terms of what I am doing because about a year ago we started a new government-relations project, and that is what I am doing now. I work with members of Congress, the Administration, and the State Department. I address our concerns to this community. At the same time, I take officials from the Hill, the Administration, and Washington back to our community. I work to give our community a better understanding of the way things happen up here and why, and to have the policymakers up here get a better understanding of the important issues to Arab Americans.

SALLY: Allow me to segue into another question. I would like to know if you have experienced difficulty organizing in the community because of who you are, either as a Muslim or a woman or as someone from Dearborn? How does your place within the community affect your reputation and your ability to work within and among Arab Americans? And then address the flip side of the issue. How does being an Arab American color the work you do outside the community? How are you perceived and received outside the community?

MAYA: In Dearborn, at least in Michigan, at home, I didn't feel that I encountered any barriers within our community. I was of the community. My family is large enough that this is not a problem. I can honestly say that on the national scene there are some folks I've encountered who have made certain assumptions about me because of my name.

SALLY: And what are those assumptions?

MAYA: You know, I don't want to speak to that other than to . . . [long pause]

SALLY: I am interested because Detroit has a reputation among Arab Americans elsewhere.

MAYA: Detroit does have a reputation, and when I talk with people and I tell them where I am from, they know that and they even know ACCESS. There is an association with Dearborn and with what that means. And for the most part, I think people, especially the people we work with at AAI, tend to be very open and respectful of my past community organizing work. I can't say that in other circles there isn't perhaps an immediate association, you know, Shia Muslim woman, [Maya laughs a bit] and that's what first comes to mind. If that's the case, well, I'm sorry for them. That would be their problem. I can't say I haven't had experiences like that.

Sally: I want to draw you out just a little further and have you tell me what it means to them for you to be a Shia Muslim woman. What are the associations that other Arabs have about Dearborn and about the Shia community?

Maya: They want to distance themselves from it in a way that surprises me. Part of my work was to set up Arab American support committees for both the Democratic and Republican nominees for president. There have been occasions when I have called someone and talked to them about their interest in serving on such a support committee, and when I told them who I am, there is a conversation. They ask questions. When I answer those questions, I can't say that I haven't heard the surprise of some that I was doing such benign political work. Perhaps there's an expectation that I should be doing something different. But, my point is, that's their problem. That's their hang-up and it's not something that I've ever allowed to affect my work.

Sally: Would you say that any doors have been closed to you because of it?

Maya: No. But that's . . .

Sally: Because of who you are.

Maya: Yep. Without saying it that way, yes. Because . . . for example, I was the only Muslim at the Institute until about a month ago.

Sally: Wow.

Maya: So would it be fair to say I am the only Shia Muslim doing this type of work? Absolutely. Would it be fair to say the State Department folks don't get someone like me calling to speak with them about the technicalities of updating the status of the PLO, so that waiver laws allowing for U.S. contact are no longer required? Yes. But I don't even think about it in that way until you ask me about it in that way. And I don't think they do either.

Sally: Well, you don't foreground that part of your identity in those contexts.

Maya: Right. But it doesn't take long when Arab Americans ask me who my relatives are, and if I am related to . . . you know.

Sally: Yes. I know how people try to situate you within the community. It is very important. It's the first thing people do when they talk.

Maya: Right.

SALLY: Well, tell me about how Arabs are perceived outside the community. How has being an Arab affected the way you have been received in mainstream political circles.

MAYA: Because I have been doing this for such a short time, I feel I am privileged to ride the coattails of some people who have done a great job before me. I have read about the times when trying to set up a Middle East Studies program at a university was considered controversial and had its support pulled. I know about Arab money being returned to its donors. In fact, calling it "Arab Money" is in itself an offensive term. I'm familiar with all of that. I was actually a delegate to the 1992 convention, when the Democrats turned us away and said, "You need to access this party differently." So I am familiar with how bad it can be. It's not necessarily my being an Arab American that would be a problem, but rather my political views. And now, in this day and age, it's being a Muslim that's a problem. Today Muslims are where, I think, Arab Americans were two decades ago. That is very troubling to me. The same way that Jim Zogby [president of the Arab American Institute] was blacklisted in the early 1980s when a couple of pro-Israel organizations were after him, is how Abdurahman Alamoudi, the president of the American Muslim Council, is treated now. And that is very troubling. But, again, it's not so much because I am an Arab as . . .

SALLY: . . . your being Muslim.

MAYA: Right . . . or both.

SALLY: Can you briefly give your analysis of how and why this transfer between Arabs and Muslims occurred?

MAYA: To me it is very similar to the way that it used to be considered safer to be Lebanese than Palestinian, politically. There were Palestinians who tried to identify as Lebanese because it was politically more expedient. Now, I think, Arab Americans have made certain inroads [as Arab Americans] that you have not seen yet in the Muslim community. It's also tied to regional politics, you know, the "green scare" [green being symbolic of Islam], the need to replace our cold war hostilities. I don't need to get into that, but the point is that this [green baiting] has been real. AAI submitted a report to the Department of Justice on civil-rights concerns in our community. The INS, FBI, and FAA are each targeting Arab Americans, but more specifically American Muslims, in the same way these same agencies were targeting primarily Arab Americans in the early and late 1980s.

Sally: Is this because Muslims are more identifiable than Arabs were, physically? Can they be picked out of a crowd because Muslim women often cover their hair, or things like that?

Maya: When it comes to this profiling stuff, it is incredible the cases you see. Often it is Muslim grandparents returning from a trip, and at the same time it's Ed Gabriel [a Lebanese American] who is now the ambassador to Morocco. When he told us this story, he blamed the profiling on his semitic nose. This is a man who has now been sworn in as ambassador to Morocco and he was profiled, so profiling is one of those very interesting issues because it has bridged everybody. It has touched people who were born here, or whose grandparents were born here, and the more recent immigrants. This is one of those issues that can provide cohesion for our community because it reminds you that, no matter how assimilated or accepted you think you are, something like this can happen to you simply because of your last name or your "semitic nose."

Sally: Are there issues that we haven't touched on that you would like to discuss?

Maya: I may be naive, but the one point I want to emphasize is that in the late 1960s, when Arab Americans organized in the Southend of Dearborn because the city sought to eliminate the residential area they lived in, they were defending themselves against an aggressive move by a government entity to take them on as a community. They had to respond. And after that, Alan Amen ran for office. After that, Helen Atwell might have. Didn't ACCESS get started as a result of that? We can talk about which issues came first, foreign or domestic, the old chicken/egg thing. But in Dearborn they are very directly intertwined. My reason for getting involved in politics was not to be a Democratic Party activist. It just wasn't. I would be lying if I said it was. It was about concerns I had relating to a country I had left because of war, and the injustices which continue to happen there. But it didn't take me long to figure out, now that I am here, that there are all these different injustices here. And for me that is what drives my agenda. So that is why I am engaged on the immigration issue, and I am engaged on campaign finance–reform issues. They are going to target legal permanent residents on their way to becoming citizens and deny them the right to make political contributions. And I don't have to switch brains in order to think about foreign aid going to Israel to continue building its settlements, or to relocate the U.S. Embassy to Jerusalem. It is the same thing. These are justice issues and some have more of a domestic focus because we are dealing with them here. But the others are my concerns as an American as well. It is my tax dollars that are going to rebuild the embassy in Jerusalem if we move it. So they are not these polar sides. It's not a dichotomy. And that is why, when you ask me to talk as though there are two separate sets of issues that motivate Arab Americans, I respond that my experience is the diffusion of the two all the way through. I never did it any other way.

SALLY: I think the point you are making is that your sense of community is larger than that of many Americans. Your sense of community extends over to Lebanon and into Palestine, and it is focused specifically on the immigrant community you came out of and the issues that are affecting the people you know.

MAYA: I am also concerned with what the U.S. has or has not done in Bosnia, and with NAFTA in Central America. I understand that the [U.S. government] was set up as an incredible system. But it only works if we actually participate in it. That's a cliché, but its true. I happen to focus on the [Arab world as a] region and on domestic stuff. Other people do other things.

SALLY: Do you envision any directions for the Arab community's political future?

MAYA: I envision a future of ethnic America. As Arab Americans, we are an important ethnic constituency. We have an advantage that our community needs to understand. Even though our numbers are only 2.5 to 3 million across the country, we happen to be concentrated in key electoral states. We are swing voters, whether people like it or not. The more we organize, the more influence we can apply with regards to all of our concerns.

Jim [Zogby] likes to give this example. You know how the media swarm around when something happens [in the Middle East] and raise all the dual loyalty and other issues that get reported on. That stuff is always happening to us. But in 1996 the *New York Times* went to Dearborn to talk about the Arab community in terms of its ethnic voters. It was during the 1996 campaign. Michigan was one of the key swing electorates. They talked about Asian Americans in California, and Mexican Americans in the Southwest, and Arab Americans in Dearborn. And Jim says that for him this was among the highlights of his career. All this time he has been arguing that we are a genuine force, and for the first time he got a call from a *New York Times* reporter saying, "Hey. I want to talk about this electoral group in Michigan." This is a significant change.

As a political system, the U.S. is not perfect. It has numerous flaws and can be unjust. I hate to sound like a poster girl for pragmatism, but I only hope that our community can understand that it is a gradual process. It is a slow process. We have come a long way and we are unique in that most of what we do, even in the most benign stuff, our basic political involvement is considered to be a threat by some people. The fact that we are organized politically has been considered a very dangerous thing for certain members of the Jewish community. That is why we have been blacklisted and why we have been targeted and these problems continue to exist. So our desire to play a more holistic role in this country has to come with a knowledge of this reality. We need to understand why the president's position on the Middle East is not ideal. The president's position has to be put in a certain context. He is the president and we have to come to terms with what that means in terms of our work and our agenda and how we pursue it. That's the whole point of politics. If I could live in an ideal world, I wouldn't have to do what I do.

SALLY: You wouldn't need to be in politics at all. So your point is that if Arab Americans want to make a difference, they have to be ethnic Americans, they need to participate, and you see that happening increasingly, and on a broader range of issues.

MAYA: I do see that happening, like in other ethnic constituencies and communities of color. That's the point.

We are unique. For example, when Italian Americans organize they don't encounter another side saying, "How could you let Italian Americans into your campaign?" Ten years ago in our community you would hear things like, "We are not going to support you because you have a campaign worker of Arab American background." Things really are much better now in Michigan. But the point is, that was a part of what we used to be up against. The reality of our having been a threat by simply working on a campaign, or hosting a fund-raiser for a political candidate, or participating in some other benign type of political activity has in some ways affected the taste of our community for American politics. That's something we need to be aware of as we tag along. Our work is like that of any other ethnic constituency, and it doesn't need to be any different. We have interests that relate to our domestic concerns and interests that relate to our foreign-policy concerns. It is very important that we not be defined differently just because of the political climate in the United States.

[We conclude. As Maya and I prepare to say good-bye, she wants to add one last point.]

MAYA: I want this interview to reflect something else. Even now when I go up to the Hill and I am doing what I am doing, there really is a receptive audience for that. [Arab Americans] consider it to be such a hostile environment because of the type of high profile work that they do about the region, in terms of some of the "Dear colleagues" letters which circulate in Congress. But I have found that there are some very receptive people, audiences that would be friendly, who will tell you very directly, because this is a political process, "If you were just better organized, or if you just had more voters, or if you had more PACs [Political Action Committees] out there making more contributions, that it would provide me with the cover I need in order to take your positions," which they tend to find appropriate and consistent with what is in the best interests of the United States. I wanted to add that part because I think the perception out there is that it's a lost cause and there is nothing we can do. I don't think that's true at all.

SALLY: Well, the thing is, in a sense they are right about it being a lost cause, because Arab Americans don't have more numbers, and aren't better organized, and don't make contributions. What does it mean if they agree with Arab causes morally and in terms of U.S. interests, and yet still vote against them? I am also interested in how Arabs participate politically in terms of their financial contributions.

MAYA: That's the one area where we have a great deal to learn, in my opinion. Because we give a ton of money, but we give it as individuals instead of bundling it as a community or giving it in PACs. But I also think that, that is getting better. I'm a little more removed from it now than I was, but I used to call up a list of people and ask a certain list of people for money, and they end up getting tapped numerous times because we are doing it as individuals instead of as a cohesive constituency. The truth is that it's a very catch-22 situation for us, because I strongly believe that we need campaign finance–reform, and there need to be things fixed with the current system. One only need look at the example of AIPAC [the American-Israel Political Action Committee] and the hundreds of PACs out there that don't have Middle East in their title at all, but that give contributions strictly based on pro-Israel positions. It's hard to be in that position, but the point is that until the system is better, until the system is fixed and operates in a more representative way, we have to be realistic enough to know that we have got to participate, and that is to set up our PACs and to give to candidates that way, and we have done that. You see it on the national scene, in terms of PACs set up to give to federal candidates, and you certainly see it in Dearborn with Arab Americans for Good Government and numerous other titles. I just saw something the other day about a new PAC that was announced in Detroit. So it is, again, another way in which we are approaching this process in a more sophisticated way.

REFERENCE

Abraham, Nabeel. 1989. Arab-American Marginality: Mythos and Praxis. *Arab Studies Quarterly* 11:17–43.

Status

Refugee

Amira Saad

Not when we packed our dreams in luggage—
Nor when we wished we had just another day—
Not when a plane as big as our dreams—and just as
ghastly—
Carried us to a land that was not our own—
Not when we heard our parents talking of the point of no
return—
Nor when excitement mingled with fear—
Did the revelation occur.
Oh, no, not then!
Our status—as refugees—was confirmed
with years of packaged dreams
and longings for another day
When our names were mispronounced
over, and over, and over again.
When we learned that our region of the world
harbored criminals, guerillas, and other deviants.
When our language became
outdated, irrelevant, and useless.
When our customs and our culture
were neglected and negotiated.
When we had nothing left . . .
But what this new world offered.
Then, and only then, were we confirmed refugees.

Part 5

LIFE JOURNEYS

Fig. 16. Senior graduation at Fordson High School in Dearborn, 1994. Photograph by Millard Berry.

Introduction

An undercurrent of disquiet runs through the memoirs that follow. Much of the disquiet emanates from the struggle to reconcile, negotiate, and otherwise transcend the margin/mainstream distinction that casts a shadow over the lives of Arab Detroit. In everyday discourse this struggle is manifest in a nagging discomfort with self-referential categories. To wit, "Am I an Arab or an American, or something in between?" "Does a hyphen separate me, and Us, from Them?" Or, "if I can be Arab and American at the same time, why does the hyphen still exist?" These loaded categories, and the definitions of self and Other embedded within them, are foisted upon the (unsuspecting) inhabitants of Arab Detroit in overlapping areas of life: family, religion, work, school, and neighborhood. These worlds, categories, and definitions intersect in unpredictable ways, often with unforeseen results. Most vexing are the categories handed down within the secure confines of the family, which are taken to heart then carried out into the world. Their problematic quality is always contextual. What does it mean to be a Yemeni Muslim, a Lebanese Shia Muslim, a Palestinian Christian, or an American-Irish-German-Lebanese in late-twentieth-century America?

The memoirs offered here resurrect the personal dimensions of familiar social categories (Yemeni, Muslim, Arab woman, Lebanese, Palestinian American, Ramallah Palestinian, American of Lebanese background), pumping life into them, attaching names and faces to them. On one level, these memoirs serve as evocative portraits of the individuals whose life experiences they recount. The memoirs cannot substitute for abstractions and social categories, but they can illuminate them in ways statistical data never will, while simultaneously revealing the limitations and imprecisions of such data.

The six essays collected here move along a continuum from margin to mainstream. At one end is Shams Alwujude, a first-generation Yemeni Muslim woman; at the other, Marilynn Rashid, a third-generation American of Lebanese, Irish-Protestant, German-Catholic ancestry. Marilynn is not so sure about who she is and what her name represents; Shams is so certain of her identity that she has prudently decided to use a pseudonym. In between lie the essays of four individuals who are at various points along the margin/mainstream continuum. Lara Hamza and Hayan Charara share a similar age and Lebanese Muslim background but reveal divergent life experiences due partly to differences in gender. Lara, the only foreign-born among the four, resents her Lebanese identity and favors her American side until she reaches college, where she begins to embrace her Arab heritage. Hayan straddles the line between margin and mainstream the way a young boy might straddle a neighbor's fence, using the advantage of height to see his world from a new perspective.

Nabeel Abraham and Jeffrey Ghannam trace their roots to two nearby towns on the West Bank in Palestine, but they wrestle with their Palestinian identity in radically different ways. They are a generation older than Hayan, Lara, and Shams, which adds another dimension to their perspectives. Jeff approaches his ethnic side from a position squarely in the mainstream. Like Marilynn Rashid, he must reach back to find his ethnic past, but unlike Marilynn, his roots in Ramallah are semiaccessible, however distant and remote the town of Ramallah might seem to him now. Consciously or unconsciously, Jeff accepts his place in the American mainstream. Not so Nabeel, who at an early age rejects the mainstream in which he finds himself immersed. In college, Nabeel consciously embraces his ethnic identity and struggles to reconcile it with his mainstream existence. He must undergo the "sweat lodge" of experience to discover his place in the world.

The subversive aspect of these memoirs should not be overlooked. Their power (and that of similar essays scattered throughout this volume) lies in their ability to undermine established Arab-as-Other categories. By highlighting the particular and the individual at the expense of standard representations of Arab Otherness, the memoirs transcend Otherness altogether, reaffirming Ralph Waldo Emerson's observation that what is most personal is most universal. The power of these memoirs also lies in their ability to dislodge and subvert self-referential categories: Lebanese, Yemeni, Palestinian, Muslim, Christian, Arab man, Arab woman, and even the all-purpose "Arab American" label. These categories and others like them are found across the entire spectrum of Arab Detroit. Like the Arab-as-

Other categories, they are equally freighted with meaning, stereotype, prejudice, and imprecision. They obviously serve a purpose or they would not continue to exist. By their very nature, however, such categories and labels invariably flatten individual differences for the sake of abstract brevity.

Personal reflections do not come easily. A measure of detachment from one's familiar habits of thought is a prerequisite for the excavation of one's own life. The process is haphazard, running in fits and starts, and one is never quite sure what one is looking for. Like trying to recall a vanishing dream, fragments surface: an image here, an embarrassing moment there. Secrets long hidden from oneself come mysteriously to mind. Some discoveries are too painful to bear: an inability to visit the grave of a parent, a dislike of oneself, embarrassment and fatigue from being ethnic, a sense of disconnectedness from family and community. If the process is pursued honestly, the excavator will periodically be confused and overwhelmed. She will be tempted to digress or revert to the standard categories and accepted stories underpinning them. The road is arduous. One contributor confessed that she kept sending signals about her lack of progress hoping we would tell her to quit. Two would-be contributors, recent arrivals in Detroit, initially agreed to try their hand at self-reflection, but after several unpromising starts, abandoned the effort. Those who made it to the finish line came in tardy. Usually a draft was run by a trusted sibling. Invariably, there were disapproving reactions. In Shams Alwujude's case, a brother's silence told her all she needed to know. She asked us to apply the pseudonym she had previously thought unnecessary. In another case, a sibling who heard about the project half-jokingly threatened to sue the writer if he revealed embarrassing family secrets.

In their desire to overcome the fear and sensitivity that so often prevent complex representations of Arab communities and selves, the authors presented here are *a*typical of Arab Detroit. The reader will notice a subtle rebelliousness toward inherited and imposed categories running through the memoirs. This rebelliousness is usually combined with a sense of justice and outrage at life's inequalities. Often a significant person is present (a parent or teacher) who promotes education or sacrifice and offers guidance at a critical juncture. Yet when all is said and done, these voices belong to Arab Detroit.

Daughter of America

Shams Alwujude

My parents grew up in the same village in Yemen. My father fell in love with my mother after watching her from a distance while she did her chores. He, being the handsomest young man in the village, married who he thought was the most beautiful girl. My soon-to-be mother moved into his family home and shortly thereafter they started a family.

My parents both came from peasant farming families. What food they had to eat came from what dairy products they could get from the cow they owned and from whatever crops they were able to harvest, if it rained and the crops grew. Because my parents had a difficult existence, my father had to leave the country to find a decent job. He worked for a while in the Persian Gulf island nation of Bahrain. Eventually, my father looked to America, the land of tremendous opportunity for those who seek it, where he had a cousin who worked at a factory and earned a decent living. This cousin was the man who helped my father find work in the United States, and the same man who would later convince my father not to allow my sister and me to immigrate to America with the family.

I sometimes think about the difficulties my father must have had when he decided to go to America—to leave a culture that was his own, the country where his ancestors were buried; to go to a new land with another language, a land where people dress, look, act, and believe differently than would a Yemeni farmer's son. The one thing that my father had in common with other Americans, he believed, was that he sought a better way of life, just as the earlier immigrants to America did. He felt that because it was a country founded by and made up of immigrants, he would only naturally blend in.

He told me about how, after he arrived in Detroit and was met by his cousin, he was immediately sent on a Greyhound bus that took him to California, where he would work picking grapes and asparagus stalks as a migrant farmworker. I asked him how he communicated, because I knew that he did not speak any English. My father explained that he did not speak to anyone, and that when he had left his cousin in Detroit, his cousin gave him a piece of paper with the word "chicken" written on it. His cousin advised him to follow the crowd on the bus and do whatever they did. If they stopped off at a place to eat, he was to show them the piece of paper. He eventually got to the camp where he lived and worked with other Yemenis and sent whatever money he earned to Yemen to support his growing family, his parents, and his siblings.

After working a while in America my father would travel back to Yemen to be with his family, and then he would go back to America to work. When I was born my father was in Yemen. When it was announced that my mother had given birth to a girl, my father wore his *meshedeh* (turbanlike head covering) loosely to show his disappointment. He was hoping for another son because boys traditionally earn money and help support the family, whereas girls are just more mouths to feed and do not contribute to the financial well-being of the family. Little did he know that I would capture his heart with my cleverness as a child and that he would announce to the family that I was his favorite.

My family immigrated to the Southend of Dearborn in the summer of 1972, a year after I was born. My father had a well-paying job working on the assembly line in the Ford Rouge Plant and was able to have us brought close to him. We rented a flat in a house owned by my father's cousin, the same man who always insisted that females should not immigrate to America. In fact, when we did finally come here so that we could live with my father, we left my sister behind. We immigrated to the United States without her. My father also wanted to leave me behind, but my mother would not allow it because I was only a baby.

My sister was eight years old when she was left behind. She was told that we would be back in a year or two and that she should take care of our grandparents until we got back. This was my father and his cousin's idea. They felt that girls should not be raised in the United States, that they were better off in the old country where they could be protected from any and all evils that might be found in the new country's foreign culture and ideas. My mother, when leaving my sister behind, honestly thought that we would be going back to Yemen. Life's circumstances, such as my father losing his job, led to our not being able to go back to Yemen. My mother remained separated from my sister for nine agonizingly long years. It had not been her choice to leave her.

My earliest memory of being aware of my identity is when I was five years old. We had moved to a neighborhood in Detroit that year, out of the safety of the Arab culture of the Southend. We moved into a neighborhood where we were one of only two Arab families. One of our next door neighbors did not appreciate that we had bought the house next to theirs. They made sure to let us know this at every opportunity.

One day, when I was five, I was sitting on the front sidewalk playing with some rocks—an innocent child not knowing what kind of hatred lurked in the world. The teenage girl who lived next door approached me and started calling me a camel jockey. Not only did she call me this, she started cheering, like a cheerleader does, about my being a camel jockey. The cheer she used was a popular cheer called "Firecracker." For the word "firecracker," she substituted the words "camel jockey." I remember sitting on the sidewalk staring at her in awe, not really understanding what she was talking about, but realizing that when she said "camel jockey," she was saying it at me and that it was a very negative word. I also remember sensing her disdain when she looked at me.

I sometimes wonder about bigoted people like our neighbors who believe they are superior to others and have the right to hate immigrants. Do they know that they live in America? Do people have to keep reminding them what that means? Are some people just so stupid that they think immigrants traveled to their exclusive homeland to live, and not to America? This country is only about two hundred years old. It is a baby. The only people who have a right to be angered at immigrants being here are Native Americans.

Sometimes I feel that I might be discriminated against because I dress differently than the average American and that it threatens people. But when I was five, and I was sitting on the sidewalk being called a camel jockey, I did not dress differently than any other five-year-old kid in this country. So I, with my assimilated clothing and English-speaking capabilities, had not warranted my neighbors' angry looks.

After my neighbor finished her camel jockey cheer, and I got her message that I was a camel jockey, I asked her what she was. Looking down her nose at me she answered, "I'm Polish." I ran into my house to find my mother. I knew that I was not this bad "camel jockey" word, so I asked my mother what I was. She said that I was an Arab. That sounded right to me. I told my mother what that girl had said. My mother, not knowing how to speak any English, and also being afraid of those people, told me to stay in the house and play. I was not even allowed to go to kindergarten that year because my mother was worried that something might happen to me. I remember vividly that one of the males who was not appreciative of our ethnicity once threatened me, a five year old, with a switchblade. It was very soon after this that we moved back to the Southend of Dearborn. The night after we moved, the house in Detroit was burned down. My parents suspected the neighbors did it.

My family bought a house in the Southend because many of the people there had the same culture we did. My mother had new neighbors that she could communicate with. We felt embraced by other Arab families who had the same concerns that we did about being in a different culture. Like us, they wanted to be a part of it, but they did not want to give up their own identities. Since this is a free country, there was always the sense that if we did not want to give up some of our traditional Yemeni customs, we did not have to. So my parents sent us into the schools, and I got to go to school because my mother felt it was safe.

The older my brothers and I got, the more we became aware of our dual cultures. One culture was that of television, which, more importantly, we also found in our school. The other culture was that of our home.

When we were in school six to seven hours a day, we were exposed to a curriculum that catered to Christians of European descent. I remember how absurd it was when we Arab Muslim children would sing in the Christmas concert that was done every year (the school was made up of mostly Muslim Arab children) and that the teachers would say "Merry Christmas" to us when we did not even celebrate the holiday. The teachers didn't even ask us if we celebrated it or not. I wondered if they assumed that we did or if they did not care whether we did. Needless to say, it was a very awkward situation where two cultures met and assumed not to notice the differences they had.

After the long days with our teachers who were all, as I recall, ethnically European Christian people, the same kind of people who belonged to the culture that we watched on TV, we went back home. As soon as we walked over the threshold into our house, we walked into Yemen. We would immediately be met by the mother whom we spoke to in Arabic. We would be in a home decorated with pictures of Muslim holy places and handwoven Yemeni *debegs* used to serve Yemeni breads. My mother would use authentically Yemeni exclamations such as *jinnie bezeha eishih!*, which means "may the *jinn* (spirits that Muslims, especially Yemenis, believe exist) take this life away!" whenever we children did not do what we were supposed to, which was often. We would be allowed to play outside at night. My mother would yell at us if we counted the stars, warning us, probably as her mother warned her, that if we counted the stars we would get the same amount of dark blemishes on our faces. I would of course laugh thinking how silly that was and purposely count more stars than were actually in the night sky. Now, however, considering my face and the constellations of beauty marks popping up, I wonder if she was right. My mother would also remind us of our religion when prayer time came (five times a day). She would do her ritual washing before the obligatory prayer, then spread the neatly folded prayer rug toward Mecca and start praying where we could see her.

In this Yemeni world, I had a certain role to play based on my gender. I was very protected and worried about. Every day before I went off to school, my mother would remind me not to play with boys because they were very bad and had nothing better to do than take advantage of girls and ruin their reputations. I believed her and stayed away from boys. I have never had a male friend in my life, and I am not sure that I could have one, or that I would even want one. I was also often reminded to keep my virginity. I had to be a virgin when I got married or else I might be killed. I took this threat very seriously and became resentful of the opposite sex for having so much power and say over my life and my death.

Besides being a virgin when I got married, I also had to be a good cook and housekeeper. My mother often told me that if I did not learn how to cook and keep house, my husband would divorce me. Because she was sincerely worried that I would be of no use as a wife without these skills, she began training me when I was ten years old, so that by the time I became a teenager, and was old enough to marry, I would be able to cook for my husband and for any amount of guests he might want to entertain, and therefore be a good wife. She taught me to cook traditional Yemeni food and how to serve and clean up by making me serve my brothers. My brothers, being the evil boys they were, would call me "slave" and taunt me for my having to serve them.

As I got older, my mother started asking me to wear the *hijab*, the head scarf that Muslim women wear. When I started wearing it, it was easy since all of the Yemeni women I knew wore it. When I asked what it was about, my mother said that we wear it because we are Muslims, that it is part of our religion. That was as good an explanation as I needed at the time. Later in my life when I was faced with a crisis and was looking for help from God, I had a profound religious experience during which I realized the significance of wearing the *hijab.* I understood my identity as a Muslim woman, and that the *hijab* identified me as one of "the believing women" the Holy Quran talks about. I realized that my ethnic heritage is significant and legitimate and cannot be ignored. It is significant to the extent that those who hate Muslims hate me because I am one, even though they have never met me. I knew and loved who I was historically and became able to see how beautiful people of other cultures were. My recognition of my Yemeni history helps me to know which way I should be heading in my life. I choose to dress like a Muslim so that I may honor my religious beliefs and my identity. I wear my *hijab* and also my *jilbab* (a long robelike dress) in order to feel sacred and in touch with God.

I learned to believe in God and that He would be the only One that I would submit to. In so believing, I had embraced my cultural and ethnic heritage and rejected the Western idea that the less a woman wears the freer she is. I had found true freedom when I found God, and when I found Him I was fully dressed—there is absolutely no greater freedom that can be known (and people who have known God will attest to this) than the freedom one knows when one submits to God and is encompassed by Him. I felt, at the same time, that because I lived in a free country and the Bill of Rights guaranteed my religious freedom, that I was blessed to even make such a decision. I felt that I must be the ideal American. I am a Muslim Yemeni woman who espouses her identity wholeheartedly, but who also cherishes the ideals of freedom. By my very existence in this country, I prove that this is truly a free country because I can be who I am, not who the conformists want me to be. If I am made to submit by assimilation into the dominant culture, then how could this country be called "free"? Certainly many of my beliefs are Muslim, but I also sincerely believe in the ideals that this country was founded on, in the Constitution and in the Bill of Rights, and I do consider myself an American who would fight for the cause of freedom.

When I was a girl, like all other Muslim girls in this world, living in free countries or not, I received proposals of marriage. I remember the first time that I knew someone was proposing to my family. I was about twelve years old. I walked into the house after I had been playing outside. I don't remember why I went inside, but I found my mother on the telephone talking about me. She was saying things like "Yes, I understand, but she is too young"; "I know your family, you are very well respected, you come from an excellent family." My jaw dropped when I heard her say these things. I was petrified. I interrupted her, saying that I was only a child, that I could not get married yet, I had to go to junior high. After my mother finished talking on the phone, she explained to me that it was a man from Ohio who wanted me to become engaged to his son, and that he had no intention of my marrying him right away. My mother kindly said no to him, that I was too young.

A year later, however, my mother gave me a proposal of her own. She had gone to Yemen that year and after she came back, she showed me a picture of her nephew and said that he wanted to be engaged to me. She said that I would not have to marry him until I finished high school. I agreed to the engagement mostly because it meant that I was "taken," it was a guarantee that I could finish high school without worrying about marriage proposals. At age thirteen, I became engaged to my eighteen-year-old cousin whom I had never met or spoken to. We were engaged for four years. When I was seventeen, his mother died after giving birth to one too many babies. Because my fiancé was the oldest son and his mother had left behind a house full of children who needed someone to take care of them, he and his father looked to me to fill her role, but I had other plans. I had not finished high school as was the agreement, and besides that, at this point in my life I did not look at marrying a cousin as something that I wanted to do. Neither was I capable of going to Yemen and instantly becoming the mother of a house full of children or becoming a wife. We broke off the engagement, which then opened the door for others to propose.

Many proposals came. Some were from cousins who wanted to marry me so that I might bring them into the country; others were just from young men who wanted to get married to start a family. I eventually accepted a proposal and got married when I was twenty years old, in 1991. At the time, I was considered an older bride. Most of the weddings then had brides who were still teenagers. I had graduated high school, which was very important to me. I had known girls who were married at young ages and consequently stopped attending school because they had started families. I did not want to do that. I knew that it was important for me to get an education. Marriage could wait, at least until I finished high school.

I remember when I first heard of the man I would later marry. I was preparing my sister's new house for my high school graduation party. My sister's husband told me that there was a man who was interested in marrying me and asked me if I would marry the man. I looked at my brother-in-law wanting to say, "Are you crazy?!" like I always wanted to say to him, but I tried to keep calm and asked him to tell me what the man's name was. He told me and then asked me again if I would marry him. I again kept calm and asked him to tell me more about this man. He said that he drove a taxicab in Detroit and that he also lived there. This information did not satisfy me. I could not make a decision to marry or not, so I asked my brother-in-law to find out more about him.

Eventually, this man who wanted to propose marriage paid a visit to our house and proposed in person. He did not propose to me, he proposed to my family. My family did not see any reason not to like him. After an investigation into his family and their roots, and his reputation, he was deemed an acceptable marriage partner. After he passed my family's tests, it was up to me to decide whether I would marry him or not. I agreed to marry him. I agreed to the marriage for several reasons. I was out of high school. I was tired of living at home and could not leave home unless I got married. I thought that marriage and family life would be much more fulfilling than going to college.

During our engagement of one year, we spoke on the phone about three times, but we never sat together or went out anywhere—not that I wanted to. I wanted to stay away from him as long as possible. I was surprised that I was even allowed to speak to him on the phone. We eventually had the wedding party, which was quickly followed by the wedding night. That was the night my whole life depended on, so I had been brought up to believe. Right before my wedding night, a close female friend of the family had a "chat" with me that I didn't expect to hear. My mother had also tried to "chat" with me, but I ended that "chat" by telling her that I already knew about the birds and bees (I was twenty years old, for heaven's sake!). Anyway, this woman, whose identity I will never reveal, told me that I should keep some frozen chicken's blood with me on my wedding night just in case I wasn't a virgin, and that if I wasn't a virgin, I could use this blood to save the family's honor. I could not believe what I heard. I had no idea people did that.

The wedding night came and went. Nine months after we were married, our son was born. I had never felt such blessing and love than when he was born. God had smiled down upon me and gave me this child who would be a light in my life. My marriage was not a marriage. I tried to "make it work" but it never did. My husband and I separated, then eventually divorced. Afterward, I decided to go back to school so that I could earn a degree that I could use to get a decent, secure job. I found myself having to support myself and my child; I could no longer look to a man to support me.

Even though I was engaged and married in a very Yemeni way, I took to the marriage some beliefs that were American in influence, which might have contributed to my eventual divorce. Because I grew up in America, even though where I grew up was made up of ethnic immigrants, I was influenced by American ideas that belonged to mainstream American culture. I am reminded of this American influence by Yemeni people who call their children who grow up in America, *'eyal imreeka,* which means "children of America."

Older Yemeni women sometimes compare themselves and their former difficult lives in Yemen with the "easy" lives that their daughters have in this country. This makes our existence even more difficult because we do not have it easy. It is not easy to be an identifiable ethnic immigrant. It is not easy to be a Muslim woman who wants to wear the *hijab* and has to deal with people who think of her as being oppressed by it—a piece of fabric. These people never really understand that what truly oppresses Muslim women is that which oppresses all women. It is also not easy to be a Muslim Arab immigrant in this country, because America occasionally makes immigrants feel unwelcome. Besides the pressures of mainstream American culture, *'eyal imreeka* are pressured by the guilt sometimes put on them by their elders, who had to live a more difficult existence—so difficult an existence that one might lose his mind—as happened to my father.

I have not mentioned my father very much in my story. In the fall of 1987, when I was sixteen years old, my father had a nervous breakdown. He had been having trouble finding work after he was laid off from Ford Motor Company, and he had other problems that my parents were excellent at keeping away from us children. We did not expect what was about to happen to us. Our father went insane before our very eyes. I had never felt so absolutely devastated. I felt like the world was pulled from under my feet. All that I had believed in was an illusion. The strongest most influential man in my life had instantly disappeared and was replaced by a man who inhabits his body and mumbles to himself.

I remember hiding in my room not wanting to look when the police handcuffed him and took him away. He was sent to a hospital for mental patients in Northville, Michigan. He had become suddenly violent toward my mother. He hallucinated that she was plotting against him with some of our family friends. I remember coming home from school and seeing my mother looking very distraught.

My father had never laid a hand on her before. They were a very happy couple who, when in front of us, would often flirt and play with each other. I remember that when my mother was feeling ill, my father would have no problem cooking for us and cleaning the house. My mother often told me stories of how, after arriving from America to visit the family in Yemen, my father would hide presents for her so that his mother and sisters would not know and would not be jealous. He made sure that she wore the latest Yemeni fashions and that she had everything that she wanted.

Oftentimes I think about how my father struggled, how his life was totally devoted to us. He lived his whole life to bring his children to freedom and opportunity. He didn't even have the chance to get an education. From a very early age, before he was a teenager, he had to leave the village to find work because he was the oldest son and was therefore obligated to support his parents and siblings, who stayed on the farm. As soon as he became older, but was still a teenager, he married my mother and started a family, as was the custom. My mother brags that we were the first family in the village to wear shoes. My father worked abroad and sent enough money so we could buy them. The demands of his growing family kept him working very hard to provide the necessities of life. When he wasn't able to provide for us anymore, due to forces beyond his control, he slipped away from the rational world into a dreamworld of his own.

I feel that it is absolutely necessary for me to succeed in my life in this country. If I don't, all my parents did would have been in vain, even though they had the intention of seeing my brothers succeeding in this country, while all I was supposed to do was get married. Times change, and then so do expectations. God willing, I will remind my son of our story when he is a grown man. It's a shame that people forget what immigrants go through to try to grow roots in a new land. I hope my son will not forget what we went through and that he will use our story as fuel to drive him so that he might fulfill the hopes of his immigrant parents.

Coming Home

Lara Hamza

There is more day to dawn. The sun is but a morning star.

HENRY DAVID THOREAU

Yet knowing how way leads on to way,
I doubted if I should ever come back.

ROBERT FROST

WHEN MY FAMILY immigrated to the United States from Lebanon in 1979, I was only five years old. We were forced to abandon our lavish high-rise apartment complex in Beirut because of the escalating war. Economically we were fine, but emotionally my parents were desolate. The first sign of this devastation appeared to me as I watched my mother pack the last of our suitcases on her bed the night before our departure. At the time, I could not understand why she was crying instead of rejoicing like my brothers and me. We were, after all, moving to a new country, and we were eager to meet old friends and relatives who had moved before us. Little did I know the reasons behind her worries and fears. She knew then what has taken me eighteen difficult years to discover. Now, as I continue struggling to find a balance between Arab and American culture, I not only have a deeper understanding of the pain my parents felt, I realize that the notion of assimilation is as false as the possibility of maintaining a pure cultural heritage.

After briefly residing in Dearborn, Michigan, within one of the largest Arab communities in the United States, and living comfortably among relatives and schoolmates like myself, my father decided to open a business in Hollywood, in southern Florida. Only when we moved to Florida did I become conscious of my differences. I never thought of myself as a "foreigner" in Dearborn because of the prominent Arab community into which we naturally blended.

Unlike Dearborn, however, Hollywood was not a welcoming home away from home; it was a harsh city in which my family struggled to survive. What may seem the simplest of habits, such as eating or worshiping, turned into tremendous ordeals, as they do for many Muslim Arabs who do not live in large ethnic communities like Dearborn. My father opened a restaurant, and, after realizing the significance the sale of alcohol had on profits, he began to sell liquor. This, as far as my mother was concerned, began our "fall" into American culture.

Not only was it impractical for our parents to teach us values they were no longer practicing, it was almost impossible for us, as children, to fully comprehend the clashing differences. Although I grew up in an Arab home, learned Arab customs, spoke the Lebanese dialect, and was vaguely conscious of my Muslim religion, I received no reinforcement of my heritage outside the home. The only times I experienced our "ethnicity" was when my dad took me to work with him. I was fascinated by our restaurant, especially by the mysterious music flowing from the band and by the provocative moves of the belly dancers on stage. This was hardly the proper setting for a child to learn anything substantial about her heritage. Though ostensibly an Arab restaurant, it was Arabic only in that its sensual setting pandered to stereotypical perceptions.

Despite my parents' attempts to maintain our religion in an area that was predominantly Jewish and Catholic, they had limited resources since not a single mosque existed in our neighborhood. I vividly recall the time my younger brother bought my mom what he considered a "pretty necklace" from the school fund-raising sale. Although this gift was shimmering with gold, it instantly brought her to tears the moment she unwrapped it, because dangling from it was a crucifix. To my mother, the gift symbolized our growing detachment from our roots; to my brothers and me, it symbolized our growing confusion since we hardly knew what our "roots" were.

My emerging divided identity troubled and confused me. My family life increasingly appeared "foreign" to me, and I longed to fit in with the majority, to fully assimilate into the American lifestyle. This displaced loyalty made me resent not only my Arab heritage but, much to my later misfortune, my family life as well. In 1984, after four years of detachment from our cultural roots, and after losing all our wealth in a restaurant wrongly named Beirut, we returned to Dearborn. By then I was ten and already plagued with misconceptions, stereotypes, and ignorance about my Arab identity. Once more I felt awkward and displaced in school; only this time, I believed I had the upper hand. I spoke much better English than my classmates and it made me feel good knowing that I wasn't like *them*. I felt empowered when replying to my relatives in English instead of Arabic; I was proud rather than ashamed when they asked: "Have you forgotten your native tongue?" Even my looks helped set me apart from the rest. With my light brown hair and light complexion, I felt good when people told me: "You don't look Arabic." Such negative feelings about my heritage made adolescence all the harder to endure.

By the time I was thirteen I had accumulated considerable negativity toward my Arab ancestry. These feelings stemmed from not only the media and the movies I absorbed, but, oddly enough, from the shared ignorance prevalent among my Arab peers. The first time I became conscious of my divided political identity was after studying the Vietnam War in high school. I was fascinated by that era and infuriated by the government's ability to practically wipe out an entire generation of young Americans. One evening my mother asked what I was studying and I replied: "The Vietnam War, the war we lost." She smiled at my use of the word "we," and I instantly

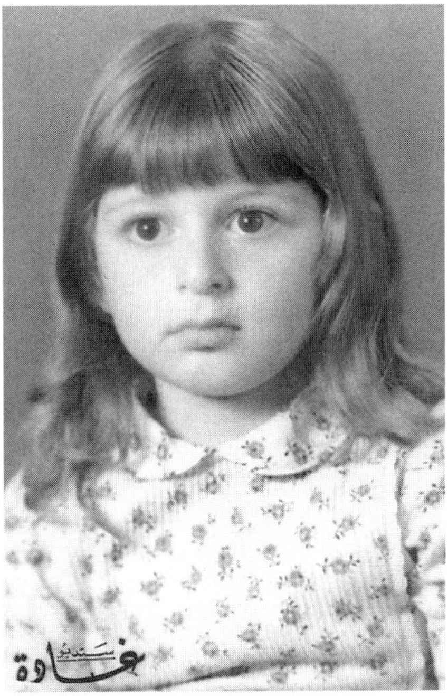

Fig. 17. Lara Hamza as a child. Courtesy of Lara Hamza.

felt a sense of disloyalty. A few months later the Gulf War started. I understood then why she smiled so sadly at me. The day after the United States invaded, I could feel the commotion pulsating through Fordson High School's walls. I was surprised when I heard many of my Arab peers expressing relief that it was a war against the Iraqis, not the Lebanese, Syrians, or Yemenis. What shocked me even more, though, were the jokes I heard from Arabs about Arabs, jokes that seemed to surface in reaction to the confusion, insensitivity, and ignorance of the time. I recall Mr. Todd's marketing class in particular that day. Students kept asking: "Mr. Todd, are they going to throw us in concentration camps?" Everyone got a good chuckle out of that; even I joined in the laughter, not realizing the horrifying possibility of it.

Our perceptions of gender roles were as confused as our political identities. Along with many of my Arab female friends, who also felt burdened and trapped by the conservative expectations of their families, I began to manifest serious feelings of resentment. The hostility I nurtured kept me blind to the reality before me. It kept me from accurately assessing my own family structure and realizing that contrary to what I longed to free myself from, my mother, *all of our mothers,* actually held more power and stronger positions than we gave them credit for. They were not the stereotypically submissive women we thoughtlessly rebelled against. Sadly, however, I did not see this back then and my bubbling pessimism toward my "cultural subordination" kept me on edge.

Like the Arab girls, Arab boys failed to clearly evaluate the truth they lived. They proudly boasted their "cultural chauvinism" and enjoyed mimicking the misconceptions they blindly accepted. They failed to see that the majority of our homes were not dominated by a male authority who simply provided monetary support while the female provided the rest. They did not acknowledge the reality that the Arab family unit is extended rather than nuclear and that within this intricate extension thrives a cooperative relationship in which mothers and fathers share household and family responsibilities. Thinking back on all the parent-teacher conferences I took my parents to (acting as their guide to our classrooms), I vividly recall the hallways full of other Arab couples—both mothers *and* fathers. Even those who spoke no English were accompanied by their children, who would translate. I believe this is the type of avid cooperation that sets the Arab family apart. Despite all the false ideas we fostered, our experiences at home did, in fact, point away from the horrible stereotypes that plagued us.

I especially despised attending weddings during my teenage years because of my jaded perception of Arab marriages. Memories of my mother shooting angry looks at me across banquet tables make me laugh now. I often displayed sharp disapproval during any type of gathering, whether it was a wedding, a New Year's eve party, or even a holiday celebration at a mosque. In my foolish rebellion, I viewed all these social functions as nothing more than female auctions in disguise. The notion of "arranged marriages" repulsed me even though I knew my parents were adamantly against it as was much of the community. Still, I assumed the worst and whenever I heard of a couple getting engaged I felt sorry rather than happy for them.

Now I see that while marrying for love is very important, it should not be the sole basis of a wise decision. Other crucial factors are taken into account to ensure lasting unions among Arabs. The opinions and advice of parents, aunts, and uncles are often highly regarded, because unlike many Americans, most Arabs do not just marry a mate, most marry a family. I had difficulty seeing the good in this "communal" philosophy because I grew up in an American culture that emphasizes individualism. Reevaluating my views, however, allowed me to see the strength of the Arab social structure. I feel that it is one of the best systems in which to raise children because of the tremendous value it places on the unit as a whole, rather than the selfish, "one-dimensional" approach people carelessly seek in society today. But at the time, of course, I could not imagine myself thinking this.

My resentment toward my family was furthered by my abuse of dangerous, mood-altering diet pills. In the Arab world it is desirable to be healthy and full-figured, whereas among Americans it is desirable to be painfully thin. Although I was the proper weight for my height as a teenager, I developed this culturally driven obsession to become thinner—popping four to five different amphetamines for lunch and dinner, even though the boxes specifically warned against more than *one* every six hours. If I did eat anything, I quickly threw it up to avoid gaining weight. Once when my mother came in to kiss me goodnight she hugged me tightly and said: "Why are you disappearing like this Lara? . . . You're all skin and bones." My self-image was so distorted that it shocked me to hear her say this, but rather than being worried by her comment, I was *thrilled.* It was too late—I had already assimilated the American conception of beauty that would haunt me for years to come.

The mood was quite tense among many Arab families when I was still in junior high. They heard rumors of drug and alcohol abuse at parties and worried about the fast-paced environment we were growing up in. The news of the day was about an Arab father who shot his seventeen-year-old daughter after suspecting her of dating. Disturbing stories like these kept tensions high, especially between Arab adolescents, who simply wanted to enjoy the freedoms their friends did, and their parents, who dreaded any form of hurt or shame descending upon their families. I became friends with people who lived by a drastically different moral code than my family's, and I increasingly saw my family's unity as a repressive chain from which I had to break free.

My father used to ride around with a custom plate on his car made just for me. The words "I" and "Lara" were written in red against a pure white background and joined by a small red heart in the center. One night when my cousin dropped me off at home, after I had escaped to a late-night party my parents knew nothing about, my father met me out on the street. He looked as I'd never seen him look before: worried, tired, and *furious.* Rather than striking or reprimanding me, he walked up to that plate, forced it off with his bare hands, and smashed it into the pavement. He knew how badly that would hurt me; I knew exactly how deeply I had hurt him. As I approached the front door of my home, I was in shock. Since no one knew my whereabouts, the house was cramped with relatives, and in the corner of the living room, amidst all the noise and commotion and smoke, my mother sat hunched over in agony. For a moment she stared at me in disbelief. Then she jumped up, dragged me into the kitchen away from the hearing distance of others, and whispered, "Were you hurt?" I looked deep into her exhausted eyes, saw my distorted reflection in those sunken pools, and in that split second I registered her anguish: "I'm fine Mom . . . please stop crying . . . I just hung out with my friends . . . nothing bad happened . . . I'm fine, really I am," and she hugged me so tightly I thought my ribs would cave in.

Shortly after, my mother was diagnosed with cancer. My parents made sure to keep us in the dark about it. One evening as I tried to focus on my geometry homework, I heard my father weeping in the background. He was on the phone with my mother's older brother in Florida. As I strained to listen, I heard him repeat the words her doctor said: she had only six months to live. Oddly enough, I totally dismissed this and returned to studying as though my life depended on it. I also tried to ignore the events that followed, such as her rapid weight loss, hair loss, and numerous hospital visits. Once, when my father could no longer take time off from work, he asked me to take her in for a "checkup." I knew he meant chemotherapy. As I sat in that depressing waiting room, I felt suffocated by the sterile stench of death that surrounded me. I found it difficult to meet her eyes after the session; she no longer resembled the beautiful mother I knew, but a diminishing shadow that I just could not grasp. I think what hurt me the most was her lack of honesty with me. I think what finally saved her was her refusal to accept death.

Four years ago I took her in for a routine exam. Since her regular doctor was on vacation at the time, she saw his colleague—a woman who knew nothing of the cultural sensitivity that my mother's physician eventually learned to understand. While glancing over her chart, her eyebrows shot up and in an annoying, high-pitched voice she shouted, "Wow! A six-year survivor . . . that's amazing!" My mother was horrified by the doctor's callous indifference to her presence. My mom understood every word and I instantly saw the change in her expression. Afterward she explained to me how her regular physician learned never to say such hurtful words. In her own way, she taught him the important roles faith and positive thinking play in people's lives. In the Arab world, doctors never tell their patients, especially to their faces, that they only have "six months to live." Instead they say: *"Ittikil 'ala Allah"* (Have faith in God). This contrasts greatly to the insensitive pessimism often found in American medicine. Even though a doctor may have good intentions in being forthright, I believe a patient's well-being ultimately lies in the interpretation of the illness. *Al-Humdullilah* (thank God), ten years later my mother is still living proof of the power of faith.

The alienation I felt from my Arab heritage slowly tapered off as I got older. The year before I transferred to the University of Michigan, Ann Arbor, from Henry Ford Community College, I had a long talk with Dr. Michael Daher, one of my dearest English professors, about my mixed emotions. I was concerned about living on my own, away from my friends and family, even though Ann Arbor was only a forty-minute drive away. He advised me to seek out Arab American groups on campus and to be active in a cause I felt passionate about. Not only would I make new friends and find comfort, he said, I would probably derive personal satisfaction from my involvement. Although I listened intently to his suggestions, I couldn't help thinking, "I'm moving away to school, away from the Arab community I lived in all my life, in order to discover *myself*, not to remain within that same circle of people I already know." I took his advice but with quite a bit of reservation. Yet, the first night I called home from school, I was barely able to utter the words: "Hi Mom." Leaving is always hard . . . especially when you come from a loving home.

Ironically, I found myself drawn to my professor's advice once I arrived at the university. I was driven to take courses about Arab culture and even to learn the Arabic language—something that my parents tried for years to get me to do. I found that the more knowledge I gained about the culture I tried so desperately to evade during my youth, the more I hungered for clues and insights into my heritage. I even have closer Arab friends now than I ever had in the past. Only after separating from my home did I discover the importance of affirming my Arab identity. Struggling to find a balance has made me find strengths in both of my cultures that I never knew existed.

I am fortunate that my parents gave me the chance to begin this precious journey toward self-discovery. Although I was excited once they agreed to let me transfer away to the University of Michigan, their decision did not surprise me. My father learned the hard way that without an education in America you were doomed to a life of hardship. He gave up his successful career as an architect and worked menial jobs in America to secure better opportunities for us than existed in war-torn Lebanon. This is why he encouraged my desire to further my studies—even if it meant parting with me. By giving me independence, my parents enriched my academic experience, but, more importantly, they enabled me to move closer to self-realization. Thankfully, they did not permit social pressures to hinder my opportunities.

I am reminded of one of the saddest lines in modern drama that still holds true for many women today. In Henrik Ibsen's *A Doll's House,* once Nora discovers she has lived her whole life as a "doll"—first as her father's, then her husband's, and later her children's—without ever becoming a "human being," her world crumbles. Just before she tragically slams the door on her family, Nora tells her husband: "[F]rom Father's hands I passed into yours. . . . You and Father have done me great wrong. You've prevented me from becoming a real person." Such is the plight that many women—both Arab and non-Arab—still face. I am grateful that my parents had the insight and courage to allow me to become "a real person" by loosening their protective hold. They understood the importance of letting go, and this has enabled me to find my way back on my own. Their continual sacrifices have come to signify my Arab American experience.

At school I live in a cozy eleventh-floor apartment overlooking central campus. Because my room faces west, I am blessed with a spectacular view of the sunset. Sometimes, when I'm lucky enough to catch those few flickering moments before darkness sets in, my room becomes engulfed in the richest of hues. Soft yellows, deep reds, vibrant pinks, and the most amazing gleams of orange flood through my window, and I cannot help but marvel at the awesome intensity of the horizon before me. Glancing down at the building across from mine, I often notice it submerged in darkness—too low to catch any of those fiery rays, too cold and distant from the warm glow I sense towering above—and I am filled with sadness for those who do not share my experience.

Many Arab Americans remain suspended in the shade—existing without evaluating, living without contemplating—and all the while, whether consciously or subconsciously, they continue to accept the negativity that so viciously degrades them. I believe strength can come only from the struggle. My mother once said: "How can we forget the East when the sun rises in the east?" In translation, her sentiments may sound awkward, but in Arabic her words jab at the core of anyone longing for their homelands in the East. My mother still looks to the east and I to the west, but all the while we are drawn to the center, continually pulled into compromise. We don't have to forget . . . we can find great solace in those sunsets.

I can only imagine the anguish my parents felt eighteen years ago when they were forced to abandon their home in Lebanon. They weren't simply leaving behind friends and family, but a beautiful culture in a country brutally ravished by war. Although they ache for the day they can go home again, they know that America is now our home. It took my family a long time to accept this, but I think the only way for us to ultimately gain control of our lives and find comfort is by acknowledging that we belong to America just as much as America belongs to us. Like many Arabs here, my family continues struggling to strike that difficult balance between the two cultures. We continue to believe in our progress in America, despite the difficulties we faced searching for a place to call "home."

Becoming the Center of Mystery

Hayan Charara

Salt

I learned how to recite the Fatihah, the opening prayer of the Quran, before I memorized the words to the Star-Spangled Banner. In the basement of the house on Carlin Street, eight houses from the border between the Motor City and the hometown of Henry Ford, I sat beside my mother on a Borden's milk crate while she gutted and scaled fish from neighboring Canada. She reminded me that Detroit was north of Canada and that the salt mines were the greatest in the world. She explained that in her village in Lebanon, if you breathed long enough, you could inhale God in the salt air that drifted eastward from the Mediterranean. I asked why God turned Lot's wife Sarah into a pillar of salt. She had sent me to a parochial preschool and eventually, despite being born into Islam, I attended the schools of the Saints Barbara and Alphonsus. There I learned the bitterness of salt, the taste of it down the back of the throat, how the truth could be compressed into the space of a molecule. When she asked how I knew the story of Sodom and Gomorrah, a reference I had heard made about Detroit from the fathers of the black families on the street, I explained that the nun in school lectured on the wrath of God, the God of the Bible and showed Lot and his wife as an example of what happened to those without belief. Knife in hand, scales of fish in the sink, she recited the Quran's first words, over and over again until they would never leave my thoughts: In the name of God, Most Gracious, Most merciful. Praise be to God, the Cherisher and Sustainer of the Worlds; Most Gracious, Most Merciful; Master of the Day of Judgment. You we worship, and Your aid we seek. Show us the straight path, the way of those on whom You have bestowed Your Grace, those whose portion is not wrath and who do not go astray.

Reprinted from *Forkroads* 1 (winter 1996), 4–15.

How could an American city be north of Canada, why were the mines of the old French town of Antoine de la Mothe Cadillac unlike the rest of the world, and would I turn into the mineral filling the Morton Salt containers if I did not believe? I prayed to Allah in the basement kitchen, ate fish at the breakfast table and watched my father's blood pressure rise as he lifted the salt shaker, stood without a slouch before the cross in Sister Antoinette's classroom, the father, the son, and the holy spirit gazing down at me, and all the hierarchies of angels waiting for the moment I would turn in disbelief and be cast into stone.

Work

Hughes & Hatchers kept my father from the route of life most immigrants took when arriving to Detroit—the factories. He refused the late shift, the Ford steel plant at River Rouge, the furnaces at Dodge and the assembly lines at General Motors. An uncle ruined his back at the Buick plant in the Polish neighborhood of Hamtramck, another retired after thirty-odd years to receive a plaque engraved with the smokestacks of the colossal Rouge and cancer in his lungs, and yet still another rises at the break of day to listen to the pounding of presses and the cutting of glass at Chrysler.

My father is the oldest of the brothers that left southern Lebanon for the great paychecks of the carmakers. After Hughes & Hatchers he borrowed money to build a beer & wine, the prison he claims he made for himself. He reminds his brothers and anyone with ears to listen that he has had a gun pressed into his back three times, that the third ended with a man explaining that after he robbed him, he would shoot. He lay flat on his stomach in the bottle room of Charara Beer & Wine and examined the cracks of the tile floor and how desperate a man could be to steal as many packs of cigarettes the pockets of a pair of jeans could fit, enough money to get him home perhaps, and then to kill. He could not make excuses for him. I have not taken a day off in thirteen years, he says with authority. He will hold up photographs of himself with sideburns, standing beside a GTO, to display how work has made him age. He has failed miserably he believes, and this, in the city of cars, is what it means to be a man. Out of respect, because his brothers are in his house, they agree and nod their heads. When they leave, the vivas for those who have failed will sound throughout the entire night as their wives and children sit at the table in the kitchen or in front of the television, realizing this could last forever and begging for more sleep than they could ask for.

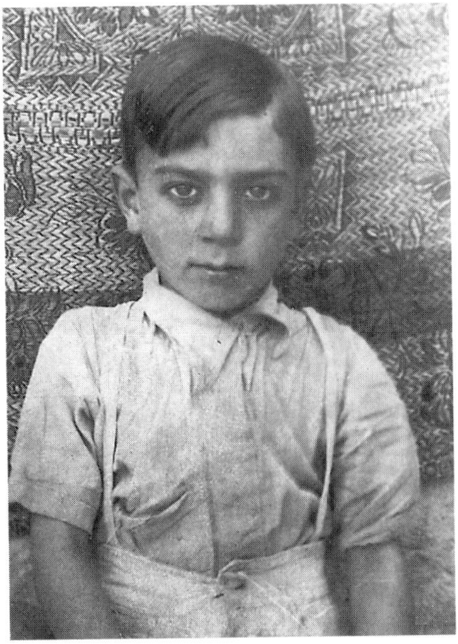

Fig. 18. Charara's father in Bint Jubail, south Lebanon. Courtesy of Hayan Charara.

Sand Nigger and Camel Jockey

The first time I heard "sand nigger" was in the hometown of the great carmaker. I cried and beat up the kid with the big mouth.

On a drive to the supermarket with my father, waiting at a stop sign, a young man crossing the street noticed the color of our skin and begged of us to go back home.

At the factories my uncles argued that "sand nigger" was reserved for the soul brothers from the Middle East. Uncle Khalil, Charlie at Chrysler Glass, explained that the black assembly line workers said they were all immigrants, that when he arrived in Detroit on a plane from Beirut, they arrived to the city on buses and trains from Alabama, and that both were "niggers." But only they could call each other that. Charlie, the factory rats would warn, never let anyone call you a camel jockey.

In the fifth grade after lunch, in the parking lot of the parish rectory, a classmate insisted I was a camel jockey. I slammed my fist into his cheeks until he nearly passed out. I had a bloody nose, and in the principal's office, ended up with penance, writing five hundred times, I will not punch my classmates in the face. After school, I was

Fig. 19. Charara's mother with his grandfather and uncle in Bint Jubail. Courtesy of Hayan Charara.

punished at home, told never to do this again. I cannot remember if I was told that sometimes right equals wrong, and vice versa, but when I was no longer grounded, I walked to a local park in Dearborn, Hemlock Park, where trains passed behind a hillock, climbed the fence and began placing rocks, pebbles, rusted muffler parts and beer bottles on the railroad tracks, and hid behind the trees, waiting for the trains to pass, the pile unnoticed by the conductor, so I could witness the trains derail. Then I'd be able to sleep and never be bothered by the sound of those two words. When the train sounded its horn, I breathed and breathed, and in disbelief, watched the pile break apart and the train continue to somewhere I would never see.

Despite the defeat at the hands of the train conductor, I was certain that wherever the boxcars went, someone would notice the slight dents and scratches on the train and I would be recognized. It was my warning, reminding any passerby that I was somehow different, a slightly lighter-skinned nigger from the city on the strait and they had better keep it to themselves. For years, this much was mine.

Joe & Ed's

Almost every neighborhood has its Joe & Ed's. Call it the Sunny Fruit Market, or Deli Delights, it is the place of meeting. To be Lebanese in Detroit during the 1970s and mid-1980s is to be between cities, between the hometown of Henry Ford and the hometown of his factories, Dearborn and Detroit. In the east end of Dearborn, where the city hall stands on Michigan Avenue, pigeons pecking at Mayor Hubbard's statue, and down the avenue where the local civic center has checkerboards for the senior citizens and a roller rink for the children, Arabs occupied most of the houses and apartment buildings. As a resident of the neighboring city, I found myself studying at the school in Dearborn named after the protector saint of theologians, Alphonsus. And when a double feature was playing, the car never headed further into Detroit, but south to the Camelot Theater, a theater so packed with little Arab children, punks and hoodlums referred to it as the "Camel's Lot." My mother bought groceries from the Lebanon Fruit Market across the street from the medieval film venue—all within the city limits of Dearborn. And despite the Pink Pussy Cat at the end of the block, my father paid many visits to Joe & Ed's. There was, of course, the Turkish coffeehouse on Warren Avenue, near the Camelot and the Lebanon Fruit market, closer to the house and the Beer & Wine, but the

Fig. 20. The author in Detroit, 1978. Courtesy of Hayan Charara.

coffeehouse had billiard tables and dice games and rumors of hashish in the stock room.

If you must know, there is no Joe or Ed. Those buying pickled grape leaves or loaves of pita bread from the market, those who did not know the family that operated the store, still called the man behind the counter Ed and most figured Joe was his father. To place their real names in plastic letters on the side wall of the store seemed, at the least, inappropriate. Even my mother agreed Yousef & Adnan's sounded peculiar.

I could say it was the fact that Yousef's father respected my grandfather, or that his house in the village of Bint Jubail in Lebanon was beside my grandfather's, and that is why my father spent his days at Joe & Ed's, until he opened his own store and work made him forget where he used to sit for hours. Fingering worry beads and waiting for the tea kettle to boil, Joe and Ed, and anyone else who wanted to sit on milk crates beside bags of rice or stacks of beer bottles, would argue over the price of fruit, how and when Israel should leave the south of Lebanon, should Syria continue to bomb, was Saddam Hussein a hero or insane, and every once in a while, when a customer complained about the cost of eggs or cigarettes, each would take turns cursing the boat or plane that brought them to this country. I could say that in Joe & Ed's they believed that despite the cars and trucks outside at a standstill in traffic and the newspapers near the door written from right to left, they were in another place, a place where because they were all immigrants, none of them were different, where they could curse and praise God in the same breath, a place that resembled something lost but not forgotten, and where they practiced the life they had and the life they intended on getting back with calm and ease.

Joe and Ed might admit to all this, or they might change the subject, ask about the score between the Detroit Tigers and the Baltimore Orioles, ask a customer whether Reagan screwed America more than Bush, or even remind a stranger to the market to read the sign near the cash register that read "In God we trust, all others pay cash."

I could say that every neighborhood in Detroit has a Joe & Ed's, but somehow, that would seem wrong. Joe and Ed would not want it that way.

Sundays

Behind the garage, from where if you had the aim of David and the strength of Goliath, you could hit a train passing on the railroad tracks with a rock, there was a vegetable garden—rows of tomatoes held up with yard sticks and metal rods, yellow summer squash, cucumbers, peppers and a fig tree sent from Lebanon years ago as a seedling. Mint leaves and oregano lined the edge of the garage, and at the fence separating the house from a neighbor no one in the family knew, bunches of onions.

Every Sunday, with my father home until noon (the liquor license at the Beer & Wine prohibited the sale of alcohol before 12:00 P.M. on the Day of the Lord, so he kept the doors locked until then), and my mother off from the local elementary school, the family ate breakfast together. My friends from St. Alphonsus joined us, in spit-shined shoes, ties and tight-collared shirts, skipping the twelve o'clock mass (but stopping by the church for the weekly parish bulletin as proof for their parents that they attended).

Standing above the kitchen sink, peering out through the window across the street at the old Muslim ladies paying a neighborhood kid five dollars to cut the grass or to take the garbage from the backyard to the curbside, my mother rinsed the vegetables under the faucet in a tray she had since her first trip to Niagara Falls in the early 1970s—on the wood tray were painted the Canadian side of the falls, the Lady of the Mist, and a portrait of a mounted police officer and his horse. She carefully peeled the curved, bumpy cucumbers with a knife, sprinkled salt over them and set them onto a plate. Then, diced the tomatoes, still green. In one hand, she held the bunches of green onions and with the other, chopped them, and the same with the mint leaves, which she used in almost everything. She cut up the squash and in a frying pan, cracked an egg over them. In another pan, she boiled eggs slightly, so that the yolks were not solid when the eggs were peeled and eaten. Chick peas, dried yogurt, and goat cheese were added to the table. There was never ham or bacon, toast and jelly. And when breakfast was over, each of us cleared our plates. No one ever said grace or thanked God. If anything, my friends and I were reminded that breakfast came from the backyard. Leftovers were wrapped in foil—lunch for my father at work. There were no rules, no table manners to speak of, except perhaps the obvious. We ate, chatted about this and that, and when it was over, we did whatever came next (baseball in the park, a visit to an aunt or uncle, television, the newspapers, work), but always one thing was certain, we'd do it all again the following Sunday, like clockwork, like religion.

Baseball

At the end of the block in the Detroit neighborhood I first lived in, beside an old automobile junkyard, against the back wall of a

Truan's candy store, the kids of Carlin Street replayed major league TV moments. Then it was the Tigers of '84, World Series champs for the first time since 1968. A strike out box was spray painted on the wall of the store, fifteen paces were made from the wall to the pitcher's mound, a piece of cardboard from a household appliance box. And the fence of the junkyard, the edge of the field. Hitting the baseball over the fence meant a home run, and the end of the game. Dobermans kept close watch over the mufflers and tires littering the lot, and the ball was their price for security.

I don't ever think a clutch moment occurred, except perhaps when one of the neighborhood kids lost at "paper, scissors, rocks" and had to climb the barbed wire fence to bring back the baseball that would extend the game. Sure, a few pitches that reminded us of Willie Hernandez were thrown, but that was, without a doubt, childish imagination. I hit the baseball as hard as my hero, Kirk Gibson, I think, once, and that did not end in a rounding of the bases, which were made of emptied egg cartons. That incident ended in an emptied parking lot, kids fleeing into the alleyway, hiding behind the bushes, from the neighbor whose side-door window was broken by the fly ball. Nothing mattered as much as baseball. Stomachs growling only upset or worried parents. The sudden darkness above the treetops only slightly ruined our vision. As long as we could still make out the blur of leather and stitching, we played. Black, Arab, Puerto Rican, it didn't matter. The Great American Pastime was ours. I don't suppose history was ever made; in fact, it seemed to ignore the three-block-long street of Carlin in Detroit. When the Tigers won the World Series in 1984, Michigan Avenue burned and Carlin remained silent. When Kirk Gibson retired from Motor City baseball the second time, the sandlot had become part of the past, the players years separated from the wall and fence of our private Wrigley or Fenway. At least once a day, after school in winter, at the break of day from June to August, we were glad not to be a part of history. There were no race riots to speak of while the gloves were oiled and padded, no one was killed when the Louisville Slugger was swung, and when one side was beat, there were no down-trodden faces, no collapsing neighborhoods, no unemployment. You lost, but tomorrow there was another baseball game, another impossible to predict outcome. Witnessing the unwritten screenplay to the 1988 World Series assured us nothing was impossible, no one could not be a hero, and anyone could play and this, despite what our parents thought or what we would believe in the years to follow, was pure Americana, and people could argue the fact, but despite the growls of dogs, the curses of neighbors, the makeshift field, baseball was perfect and we were Americans.

Becoming the Center of Mystery

Bob, the old black man whose garage housed pigeons, would line up the neighborhood kids on the sidewalk every Sunday and let them enter his backyard to see the city birds; rats with wings is how we referred to them years later. After a fight with snow one winter in front of his house, he stopped us by yelling, "You kids got good folks, why do you want to ruin their names like this?" He made us shovel the sidewalk and after we finished, told us to go back to our houses and that we should be ashamed of ourselves. In 1986, when the pigeons stopped nesting in his garage, Bob sold the house and moved to Alabama.

The Howards lived several houses down on the same side of the street. Although my family did not celebrate the birth of Christ, my mother would buy toys for the Howard kids so that we could trade with them the day after the 25th of December. Before high school, the Howards moved to Flatrock, a factory town like Detroit but smaller.

Across the street, the Saad family, another Lebanese house. After Fadi's mother was raped in the middle of the day under a pulley clothesline, his father packed their clothes and pots and dishes and furniture and moved out.

Next to Fadi's house, Little Jimmy and I would sit on the porch and imitate the actors we watched at the Camelot Theater. Kung Fu and Creature Features were Little Jimmy's favorite. The first time Little Jimmy stepped into our house, we ate plums in the basement and spoke of girls. When I first peered into his house, he led me to Big Jimmy's bedroom and we stared for hours at the stacks of dirty pictorials hidden behind several pairs of work shoes piled up in the closet. Little Jimmy grew to be bigger than his father and bought a car when he was sixteen, and was happier than anyone on the block. I'm staying here forever, he'd say, and almost did, until he showed up at our Beer & Wine, a man with a job and a family, to say he finally was packing up and heading out.

Little Jimmy talked of wanting to take Karen, a girl whose brothers were in a gang, to the Camelot for "Godzilla" and "Enter the Dragon." Because I was young and a classmate of Karen's, her brothers kept an eye out for me and didn't allow the other punks on the street to call me a camel jockey, reminding them I was "all right."

Her brothers argued over whether Aretha Franklin sounded better than Diana Ross while Karen and I talked about Sister this and Saint that. Karen moved and left Saint Barbara's, and I never saw her again.

Cicadas resonated throughout the night, above our heads in the three-story trees that kept us dark. As children we'd hear them and run to our houses, afraid they'd turn into demons, angels that fell from heaven under the weight of huge buzzard wings, and sweep us off the streets, a tale told to us by the old man whose house we believed was haunted. His name we didn't know, and when he died in the house and was found days later, the stink unbearable, to make sure we'd never forget, my bald uncle Ahmed retold the stories. He'd rub his bald head and describe how the factory angels fell from the skies and the pigeons were their feasts, their spirits would leave the birds, whose little hearts had stakes driven through them, in search of boys and girls asleep at night.

In the houses in Detroit, we learned about shame and respect, about loss and change, about the agony of puberty and the power of imagination, the dead and the living, those hovering somewhere in between, and when the moving trucks finally pulled into the driveway and lifted the cardboard boxes out of our house, I knew I would take each face, each voice with me, each terrible incident and the beliefs that seemed impossible yet real. I would take them to a new neighborhood, use them until they became the stuff of remembrance, the stuff of the unexplainable and of imagination. Standing beside the old Buick Riviera, waving good-bye to Little Jimmy, the cold air of winter allowing me to pretend to smoke a cigarette, I realized I'd never live here again, and all that came with it would be part of the past, but somehow, for some reason, I did not cry, but smiled and as though for the first time understood the old man whose best friends were pigeons, the man whose house became a grave, the uncle whose lack of fear made him the center of mystery, and driving away, the street in the rear-view mirror, I began to laugh.

Reasons

We climbed fences because they were there, feared dogs because they strutted the alleyways and we were tiny and helpless and did not want shots in our bellies, the only relief from the disease our parents warned us about, the disease acquired through the snarling bite of a four-footed master of the backstreets. Our garage was racked with rakes and shovels and empty Coke bottles, and on the second floor, where we never climbed, dead pigeons turned into dust before our eyes. These, my bald uncle described as victims of fallen angels. Like Moses, we doubted, and needed to see to believe.

There was a plum tree in the backyard of a family we called "hillbillies" (their necks were red and they relocated north from Tennessee, and using what we learned as children, we understood that all white people from the South were redneck hillbillies). Near the edge of our backyard, a raspberry bush grew tall beside the fence separating the house from the alley, a neighbor picked grapes off the vine along the side of his house near the driveway, but nowhere except in this neighbor's yard were there plums. We wanted what we didn't have, so we climbed the fence and stole the fruit, unashamed, tucking them in our shirts and into our pockets.

Any day we could be killed. I watched the limp bodies of Palestinian children bulldozed into make-shift trenches. Karen's brothers spray-painted their names on the walls of the supermarkets in the area. When one of her brothers found his name circled, he left the house at night, his clothes in a shopping bag, worried he would be followed by other gang members should he leave during the day. Helicopters interrupted sleep with bright beams of light, and the next day, we'd read in the newspapers of an escaped prisoner, armed and dangerous. Two boys from the old country, engineers at the university in Detroit, were killed in a house that exploded, the gas pilots loosened an entire day, and when they turned the key given to them earlier, oxygen robbed them of life, their bones found at the door steps of the porch.

I never used the word "nigger" because I witnessed Little Jimmy cry and then punch the kid that called him that. In grade school, when "nigger" was hyphenated with "sand," I did the same.

Each day, a pack of cigarettes inhaled into my lungs. In 1986, I left my Detroit neighborhood for the first time without my parents. Two boys from Saint Barbara's pulled up on bikes, and we rode into Dearborn. At a park behind the Edison Power Plant, we smoked Marlboro cigarettes and poured whiskey down the backs of our throats, thinking both tasted like poison. When we returned to Carlin Street, my father pulled up in his '76 Buick, walked me up to the second floor bathroom and belted me hard enough for the other kids waiting outside the house to hear. He asked why I did it, I replied I wanted to be a man. He explained the failure of work and the loss of dignity and the rewards of time, then belted me again. I still blame work for nearly everything, the early gray hairs and the heart attack warnings of my father, the reason I'd write poetry, the death of my mother, whose hands and back and mind ached for years until she could no longer bear it and she collapsed in the morning, drinking coffee and smoking a cigarette, her body refusing life.

I pray to God the Father and Allah the Merciful. Both one and the same, are they not? Don't ask me. When the school bell rang, I stood up, back straight, palms at my chest, gazing at the crucifix, Jesus nailed to the wall just below the clock. In bed, before I'd sleep, I would recite the *Fatihah* and ask God, Allah, all the saints and angels, and anyone or anything that would listen to offer a moment's peace. This, because my parents are Muslims and my teachers Roman Catholic.

I am dark-skinned and have a look to kill—I am an Arab and from Detroit. I am ill-tempered and sorrowful, gentle and filled with life, stubborn but eager to listen, patient yet always in a hurry—I am an Arab and from Detroit. I praise death and hail Henry Ford as a genius, I cursed God the day my mother died and rejoiced when I saw smoke on the horizon and believed it to be the Rouge Plant smokestacks burning down. I will explain the unexplainable by saying, It was written, but I wouldn't bet a nickel on Fate. I speak Arabic, able to tell a visitor, Welcome to my house, in two languages, but I have been heard yelling, Get the hell off my porch you motherfuckers!

Saddam

In the old neighborhood of Carlin Street, I made my first decision concerning the leader of Iraq. At the time he was not an enemy of the United States, nor a target of some special military force. He was an ally, driving his people into hunger, death and oblivion with war against Iran, a battle supported by my country, and as I would understand later, my money.

I did not respect Saddam. This wasn't solely because he was behind the killing of people he did not see face to face. There were other reasons.

When I was a child I refused to kill even an ant, respecting the fact that if I were to lift the equivalent of nearly a thousand times my body weight, as they did with pieces of dropped leftovers on their backs, I'd be crushed to death. Also, the fact that stepping on an ant might cause it to rain, a myth enjoyed by the kids of St. Barbara's and of Carlin. If it rains, no baseball, no playing outside. Let the ants live.

Saddam was no ant, he was more like a dog. He could eat his own shit. He'd maul my new school shoes if he had the chance.

He'd bite my sister's hand if she pet him while he ate supper. Saddam carried rabies in his blood.

The Revlon representative whose Saturday route included 8090 Carlin, the eighth house from the border between Dearborn and Detroit, the house I lived in, stopped by one summer afternoon to sell us more than lipstick or eye shadow. She had a litter box, crowded with German Shepherd-Huskie mixed dogs, all black and able to fit in the palm of her hand. Before she left for the next family, one of those four-footed mutts was mine.

What's his name, the children who gathered at the steps to the porch would ask? I didn't know. The first dog I had was named Tom, after the cat of my mother's favorite cartoon character. I asked for suggestions—I got the usual names: Blackie, Butch, Benji, even Doggie. None of these seemed appropriate. My father overheard the conversation, and noticed my uncle, who lived across the street, washing his car, a sticker of the flag of the Republic of Iraq on his bumper. He told me to walk over to him, check both ways as I crossed the street, keep the dog tight on the leash and ask my uncle Ibrahim, the self-professed Communist and political enemy of my father, if he thought Saddam was a good name for the animal.

I thought it was funny, in fact, a good idea. I knew Saddam through the late night arguments in the television room of our house, how each man would bring up names and dates I did not recognize or hear before. I knew two facts, my uncle praised Saddam, and my father hailed the Ayatollah. Uncle Ibrahim might be flattered.

I'm going to name my dog Saddam, I told Uncle Ibrahim.

He hesitated, peered through the windshield of his car at my father. Then he smiled, a sign of approval I thought, and replied, You'd be better off naming him Abdul Karim.

Disappointed and angry, I left him to his Buick and strutted across the street, defiant. How could Saddam be worse than my father? Make no mistake, I made this dog out to be as good as any person I'd met. I recalled the old saying that if a man has the reputation of a dog, he is a saint; but still I understood his breath was ranker than mine, he could kill, and before the knowledge of AIDS and other human diseases, I thought only dogs could make people sick enough to die. How could Abdul Karim, my father, be a more fitting namesake than that of a man who did not care whether or not he ruined the day, or the lives, of thousands of people, his own for that matter?

I decided Saddam was less than a dog. This blue-eyed mutt did not deserve the title of "killer." I would not be that cruel. I named him after the purple prehistoric canine belonging to the Flintstones, Dino. He would make mistakes, shit in the house, run away twice, nearly tear off my sister's thumb, but he'd never turn boys into dust, cities into graveyards, he'd never make me shrug in disgust. Growling in the backyard, when his black lips curled back to expose his white fangs, I'd still inch toward Dino with open hands, knowing this creature of the back alleys and trash cans, born and sold out of an empty fruit box, could never hurt me the way a man my uncle loved could, the man on the television and newspapers whose face grinned at the sight of footprints in the sand where feet once were, a man who'd sleep better knowing he put another body in the ground, torn apart, dust-covered, forever.

Camp Dearborn

If you've never heard of Camp Dearborn, don't ask me. Not because I don't want to talk about it, just that you'll get sick and tired of hearing about the place. Either you want to visit, or have it burned to the ground.

Camp Dearborn is neither a camp nor in Dearborn. Forty miles west of the city, a piece of land was purchased, man-made lakes filled and an admission price charged to enter through its gates.

On Sundays, a smart thief will rob every house owned by an Arab in Dearborn. He'll walk away a richer man, with enough televisions and VCRs to start a small appliance business. Why? The Middle Eastern residents are at the camp operated by the City of Dearborn nearly an hour away in the township of Milford.

This is where I learned to swim. That or drown—an uncle had me straddle his back and in a matter of fifteen strokes, we were in the middle of Lake 3. Then, he shoved me off and demanded the ability to tread water. In the backroads of the Camp, I learned to drive a car. My parents took a stroll around the lake and when they disappeared around a hill, I stole the keys to the Sunbird and pressed down on the gas pedal.

We'd rise at the break of day, pack the cooler and our clothes into the trunk of the car, and begin the ride out. Halfway there, we'd stop to use the bathroom and pick up breakfast, usually at a small-town McDonald's. Once inside the limits of Camp Dearborn, we'd find a place to park the car, unload, and while my parents set up the barbecue grill and the radio, I'd head down to the beach, which I learned years later, while paying the Camp a visit in mid-December, was drained for the winter. Huge tubes ran under the bottom of the lake and into a water system, which pumped life back into the lake once the weather warmed up. This explained the brownish color of the lake, even at six in the morning when kids and adults had not kicked up the sand off its floor.

At the outskirts of the Camp, a dam dropped seaweed and water nearly thirty feet into a stream leading to the waste dump of a local lumber company. Those who dared, climbed the fence around the dam area and jumped off the side, disappearing under water and ending up down-stream. I had the courage—coupled with the insight of an idiot—to let myself drop down the side of the dam. I might have done it again if not for the dead body of a boy pulled out of the stream, his feet caught in the steel rafters at the bottom of the dam. He drowned, unnoticed, and when another boy landed on him, his feet loosened and he drifted close to the shore, his bloated stomach and purple face putting fear and hesitation in the eyes of those waiting to jump.

When the sun began to fade, we'd sit and watch my father drain the cooler, my mother would collect the trash and throw it into the Keep Dearborn Clean waste cans. Before reaching Dearborn, we'd be asleep in the backseat, the drone of the wheels against asphalt and the humming of air through the car windows casting us into a spell.

If anyone claims that Camp Dearborn is an oasis, they're telling a lie. By any standard, it's a failed attempt at nature. Shit from gulls on the beach, children pissing in the lakes, and the stink of the Camp's bathrooms so heinous, I'd hold whatever urge I had to use the restrooms until we reached our house, that or the McDonald's halfway. Today, it is no longer the same; the city, fed up with maintenance, sold most of the land to the people of Milford, and they turned that into a private Golf Course. Despite all that, Camp Dearborn was a getaway, a place where the rules did not apply. I could wander the entire camp, never worrying about drifting into a bad neighborhood. I drove a car at thirteen, doubled the speed limit (15 mph) and was not taken to jail or sent to a school for juvenile delinquents. Camp Dearborn was a dump, but somehow I could not fall asleep the night before going there. It did the job every time. For all I cared, that piece of land (its lakes operated not by the rhythms of nature, but by hydraulic pumps, tiptoeing around its urinals when I could not stand the pain that resulted from drinking too much water) was as close as it came to being away from it all. And that was all any of us needed at the time.

Halal

"Kosher" for Muslims. I'd see the signs that read "Halal Meats" in the butcher shops of the Southend of Dearborn, the part of the city where Arab immigrants settled into after arriving from Lebanon, Yemen, Jordan and Iraq. Until Arabs became as visible as the Model T in the 1930s, the Southend was the only place a Muslim could buy lamb, beef or poultry slaughtered with the breath of Allah on the animal's throat.

We'd leave our Detroit neighborhood for Berry & Sons, the first Arab Butcher in Dearborn. Berry's sons would open another shop in east Dearborn, and in a matter of five years, both the east and south ends of Henry Ford's town would be crowded with Halal Meat stores. As far as I know, the west end of the city has not yet established such a business, being reserved for the houses of Ford Executives, outdoor swimming pools, and Golf Courses.

Arab residents would never purchase steaks or chicken breasts at the local Kroger supermarket or at Farmer Jack's—since most of the Arabs in Detroit and Dearborn would bend their knees facing Mecca, which is also in the direction of the colossal Ford Rouge Plant and the River, allowing the butcher at the supermarket to wrap your purchase in white paper would be a crime against God. Besides, Filet Mignon cost nearly ten dollars a pound at Kroger's, while Berry and his children sold it for less than half of that. I'd walk into the freezer of Berry & Sons and flinch in horror at the sight of cows hanging from steel hooks, their eyes still in the sockets, some not yet removed of their skin. This I was reminded proved the meat was more fresh at the Arab butcher markets than that at the end of the canned food isles of the supermarkets.

On a field trip to Hemlock Park, while in the fifth grade at Saint Barbara's, the school cooks prepared hot dogs and pizza for the grade-schoolers, served with watered-down Kool-Aid and slices of watermelon. A cousin whose family lived on the same street as my own, with whom we shared the ride to school, and whose father did not allow a single word of English spoken in his house, asked me if I brought my own lunch to Hemlock. I said no, almost in disbelief. Why bring a lunch in a paper bag when there was pizza and hot dogs? How did I know, she wondered, if the food was halal. The fact is I didn't, and the truth is I didn't care.

I went into one of my tirades about God and the rules that came with it. Even as a ten year old, I had doubts and questions which were hardly answered or simply given up to faith. Halal was only the beginning, what if the hot dogs and pepperoni on the slices were pork? I'd be violating God's command concerning the dirty nature of swine, an animal that bathes in its own filth. I'd start with a logical approach. Did you eat Twinkies? Of course she did. What about Hostess Fruit Pies? Any civilized child ate those. Well, I demanded, those are made with lard, and the ingredients clearly state "lard, made from various animal fats." Wasn't it possible that pigs fit the description of animal fats? Then, incorporating Christianity with Islam, I'd ask if she ever disobeyed her parents, pointing to the incidents when her father scolded us for saying "school" or "homework" in his house, and the countless times we "swore to God" something was the truth? You're breaking the Ten Commandments, numbers 3 and 5. Why all the attention to pigs or a prayer before you cut off a cow's head, I'd yell. And then an explanation of reason: Arabs didn't know how to clean a pig in those days, that's why it's dirty, and if you hate your parents and insult God, you think He cares if you eat a hot dog that isn't blessed. Here, I'd demonstrate, I'll bless this frankfurter for you. And I'd wave my hands over the prepackaged lunch and say something to the extent of "God made you and thinks you're all right." It's O.K., and then I'd bite into the bun and smile. She was always horrified. And when, driving back to Detroit, my mother behind the wheel, my cousin would tell all, how I pretended to be the All-Mighty himself, baptizing pizza and frankfurter alike, my mother would turn and ask if I did so. I'd shrug in the backseat and reply, I was just joking, besides when no one was looking, I spit the lunch out and ate what you made.

Rule #9, You shall not bear false witness against your neighbor.

Things Could Be Better

Dirt poor? No, but poor. I didn't know it growing up on Carlin Street. Three cars were parked in front of our house. Not at the same time, but nevertheless, others drove an automobile until it refused to move, whenever and wherever that might be. First, it was the '76 Buick Riviera, then my mother's Pontiac Sunbird, and finally, the big time, the Lincoln Mark V, the longest car on the block.

When my father bought the Buick, an uncle worked for that carmaker and got it under a worker's plan, and the Sunbird was simply cheap, price and quality, and the Lincoln belonged to a woman whose husband no longer wanted the car in his garage after his wife died. He knew my father from the Beer & Wine and sold it for enough to cover the payments.

The house we lived in sold for enough to make a down payment for the house in Dearborn, which we moved into after a neighbor was raped, and our house was broken into twice. The third time, my mother figured, she'd be in the basement or watching television and that was a chance she did not want to take.

Poor might still seem like the wrong word, or at the very least, inappropriate. We lived day by day, on the edge so to speak. Had my mother lost her job as a bilingual teacher, we would have lost everything. For sixteen years, she worked at the public schools, and tutored after her shift to make extra money, enough to put me in a parochial school, and for the last two years she attended night classes at Henry Ford Community College so that she'd earn a degree and bring home a better paycheck. For nearly all that time, my father aged in the Beer & Wine, which failed miserably, and all he had and all that he had borrowed to put into the business never showed a return when he sold the store the year I graduated college.

Money did not come as easily as it went. But that American Dream persisted, and after years of hand-me-down clothes, shoes that would have to last an extra winter, junk cars and living in a neighborhood that collapsed before our eyes, it began to pay off. Although he made almost no profit, the selling of the Beer & Wine gave my parents enough money to pay off the house and finally return for a vacation together to the village of their birth, a place each had only seen once since they left back in the late 1960s. The loans to help pay for a parochial education ended up in a full scholarship to Wayne State University in Detroit, from where I'd graduate with the hope of a better life attached to the diploma.

The Pontiac caught fire one block from our house, the Riviera rusting somewhere in an automobile graveyard, and the Lincoln, still parked in front of the house was my mother's new car. Just when bills became easier to pay, the children out of college, the store out of the picture, and an easier life ahead, my mother died.

Every man and woman has their own hell, often without anyone having to give it to them. In Detroit, like so many other industrial cities, hell doesn't need a war or crime or drugs to find its way into a house. It comes out of nowhere. My parents often referred to it as work. They'd see it in a day that might last forever. They felt it in their aching feet and tired hands. And now, we sense it in the emptied bed my father sleeps in, in the Lincoln that does not have a driver, in the faces of schoolchildren who ask, Where is Mrs. Charara? Hell is fashioning these lines seven hundred miles from the cemetery my mother is buried in, in admitting I have never seen her headstone.

A person doesn't need more than a mind and the thoughts it creates to make the moment's stillness tick like water in a tin kettle, at first slow, persistent, and then almost suddenly, an unbearable scream. Enough is enough.

We were poor but not as poor as some of our neighbors. Our family was not trapped into welfare, neither my father nor my mother ever had to beg for food or spare change, no one starved to death or slept over a steaming manhole to keep warm. We didn't need that, no one does. Detroit too often gave us all we needed to curse it in the first breath and bless it in the next. When somebody asks why does an Arab from Detroit keep quiet when he sees a woman cry over a car that wouldn't start, rusted at the doors, a car she hated that burned to the ground, or why he chooses to keep his business in his house, or why he doesn't weep in front of his father when his mother is mentioned and how her death made every possibility of living better impossible, he might want to say that he'd rather keep his sorrow to himself, that passing it on might ruin the day of another person, and one is enough. He might say this, but he'll probably nod and agree with whatever it is you like, just to change the subject, so that you'll sleep better, and when he goes home and confronts the silence of his house or apartment, he'll ask God why and won't get an answer and will tell himself, reluctantly, half-believing it, Things could get better, they might someday get better.

Long Distance

A seven hour time difference between Detroit and Lebanon made for late-night phone calls to our aunts, uncles and grandparents in Bint Jubail, a village east of the Mediterranean and ten miles north of the Israeli border.

You want to speak with a friend or relative living in New York, Michigan City, or Washington D.C., you lift the receiver, dial the number and wait for an answer. Not quite as easy dialing Lebanon. First, the alarm clock goes off at 3 A.M., which makes it ten o'clock in the morning Bint Jubail time. Then, a conversation with a long-distance operator, repeating "Bint Jubail" several times, then spelling it and giving the international calling code. The line is connected with a central phone office, which is not an office like any in the States. It is the house or grocery store of a Lebanese that happens to have a phone. Someone picks up, the operator says "Call from Detroit, from the United States." The person on the other side asks for a name.

You tell them. Then, the operator hangs up, you do the same and wait. For what? For the person who answered the phone to leave the marketplace and find your uncle or grandfather and have him return to the office to wait for the second call. All this if you get through—with air raids, failing electrical generators and a tired or lazy office clerk, the call might not get through.

Give it fifteen minutes, a half hour to be safe. Dial again. And speak.

Only call during emergencies. Remember to keep it short, the bill is shared by both, the side that called and the side that answered. Long distance overseas to Lebanon costs anywhere from $3 to $5 per minute.

Shout into the receiver. In the late 1970s and early 1980s, communication across the Atlantic was less than perfect and, although today it sounds as if you're next door, the yelling has become customary.

Say "Alo" not "Hello."

Ask the person how their health is and tell them you miss them, and that, God willing, you will visit in the summer.

The children are okay, work is fine, the house hasn't burned down. Then, why the call? Emergencies only, remember.

Usually, we'd call to make sure no one died in a raid over south Lebanon by the Israeli air force, that or to see if an uncle was taken prisoner for questioning following a bomb attack on a pharmacy or the marketplace by Hizballah. Hajj Ali, my mother's father, ran a restaurant in the marketplace and his shop was always in the center of chaos.

Only once did someone die—a cousin whose face was ripped apart from a rifle bullet. An uncle, who escaped to New York and is selling t-shirts and socks on the streets of Queens, was arrested and vanished for three days. After several calls to people running border check-points, he was released.

In 1986 my family called to make sure cousins arrived safely. They flew into Tel Aviv (flights into Beirut International Airport from the U.S. were prohibited), took a taxi cab north, were harassed at the border, but let through anyway.

You never call just to see how someone is doing. Those sort of conversations are left to letters, which are sent with travelers, realizing that if you were to postmark an envelope "Bint Jubail, the house beside the olive grove around the hill from the reservoir," it might get stuck in the Dead Letter Office.

My father called Lebanon in March of 1996. Not really an

emergency, but more like the end of one. He told Hajj Ali and his wife, my grandmother Mariam, that their first born, my mother, collapsed while drinking coffee with her sister's children. Before the ambulance reached the hospital, the intern told my father that she was already dead. Although phone calls are nearly impossible to make, news seems to travel easily across the ocean. They heard rumors and we set them straight. When my father explained he decided to bury my mother outside of Detroit, my grandmother could not speak. She had not seen her daughter in almost two decades.

The last time I called was several weeks after the funeral. My grandmother had a stroke, and was still in disbelief. When doctors asked her where she was or said her name, she closed her eyes and went to sleep.

I got my uncle on the line. Tell her she'll be better, I said, that I miss her, and God willing, one day I'll see where my mother was born.

The Vow of Poverty

In the fifth grade, after a football game in the parish parking lot of Saint Barbara's, Sister Richard asked me to stay at my desk after school, so that we could talk. The school bell rang, a prayer was made, and I waited.

Weeks earlier, Sister Richard had my mother meet her at lunchtime and made me demonstrate how I wrote the number five on the blackboard. I took the chalk, and carefully etched a "5." I stepped back to find Sister Richard nodding, head swaying back and forth and then, looking to my mother, asked if she could take the chalk and show her how I really wrote my fives. Beside the five I wrote, she drew a line separating black from black on the board, then drew the following: S.

The truth is my five hardly ever resembled the fifth digit on the number scale, but was more like Sister Richard's rendition, more like the 19th letter of the alphabet. Being a schoolteacher, my mother didn't mind taking an hour off during her lunch break to discuss the intricacies of cursive and handwriting. I promised to straighten out the curves and write more legibly.

What did I do wrong this time? For the most part, I wasn't the type of student who required parent-teacher conferences, or after-school talks with the teacher or principal. I memorized the fifty states and their capitals, the multiplication table was a breeze, and even received a "21 Crayon Salute" for Art. Sister Richard pulled up her seat and sat before me, face to face, then looked down at my shoes.

They're dirty, she said.

I was playing football during recess, and since the parking lot was covered with hard asphalt, the end zone was the grass at its edges, grass that had turned to mud because of the late spring rains.

Ask your parents to buy you new shoes, these aren't right for school.

I kept quiet on the drive back to the house. When I changed clothes, replacing the tight-collared long-sleeve shirt and the tie with a Tigers t-shirt, the polyester uniform trousers with jeans, and the dirty shoes with sneakers, I rummaged through a box my father kept under the stairs to the basement for an old rag. I took shoe polish to the school shoes and rubbed. Almost instantly, the mud cleared off and the shoes looked new. Still, that night, without giving any reason, I begged for a new pair. And the next day, a Saturday, my mother took me to a Payless Shoe Store and we bought new size 5½ shoes. The old pair, I hid behind the box stuffed with rags and shoe polish. I was embarrassed. Now and then, I'd pull out the old pair and stare at them, nodding the way sister Richard did at my "5" and telling myself, over and over again, these look okay.

The following week, when Sister Richard saw me in the new shoes, she smiled in agreement. I felt defeated, as though she had won some battle against my parents, that she was correct in her assumption that they needed a woman vowed to poverty to remind them that their children did not deserve to live that way. She was wrong, but succeeded in this act of humility, intentional or not.

I'd remember the stories my father told of how he would have to wear the same pair of shoes until his toes stuck out of them, how when a pair of pants ripped at his crotch or behind, his father stitched them up and begged for another month of durability. In an old photograph when he was about the age I was in the fifth grade, he is dressed in tattered clothing, soiled at every wrinkle and tear. That is why, I still believe, he'd grow up to become a tailor.

I'd run into the nun seven years later, outside the rectory of Saint Alphonsus High School, a parish one mile down the road from St. Barbara's, where most of the students in Sister Richard's class ended up. I was helping the volunteers at the church pack boxes of canned soup and perishable goods for a local food drive. She did not recognize me until I reminded her who I was. I was dressed in the school uniform, but slightly out of code: the polyester slacks required by the Dean's Office were replaced with pleated wool trousers, and the white shirt was 100 percent cotton, button-down, and the tie, silk, designer. And the shoes, soft brown leather, loafers. Indeed, Sister Richard was impressed, enough, I flattered myself, to break her vow of celibacy to jump the bones of a hormone-crazed, exquisitely dressed 17 year old. And for a brief moment, I felt gratified. That is, until she patted me on the shoulder, looking me over from shoes to haircut and said, You turned out all right.

To Palestine and Back

Quest for Place

Nabeel Abraham

> Mother, if I've never really been Jewish, and I'm not actually American anymore, and I'm not English or European, then who am I?
>
> TESS, *THE SISTERS ROSENWEIG*, WENDY WASSERSTEIN

FROM MY VANTAGE point under a fig tree in the hills overlooking the Jordan Valley, I watched two Israeli military jets circle above, two silver triangles glistening against the pale summer sky. If they suddenly decided to swoop down on the Palestinian camp I was visiting, my life would be over. Having just turned nineteen, the absurdity of dying so young suddenly dawned on me. I thought about the futility of hiding under the fig tree. When the bombs and fiery napalm fell, I might as well have been hiding under the black umbrella I had left back home in Detroit. The bombs eventually fell. Fortunately for me and the fifty or so other men huddled in the fig orchard that day, their target was a Jordanian army position down in the valley, just across the river from the town of Jericho. The ground shook slightly, and the morning air rumbled with the thud of bombs falling in the distance. When the "all clear" sounded, I peered over the rocks into the valley below, silently watching the black plumage rise over the valley.

As I tried to imagine the death and destruction wrought by the marauding planes, the people of the camp gradually resumed their business. It was an odd place for a nineteen-year-old American kid to be. This was my first trip outside the United States. My facility in Arabic amounted to a handful of words, "kitchen Arabic," which I retained from childhood. In my mind, however, I was *not* out of place, for I *too* was a Palestinian and an Arab. Had I not traveled a long way to get here—by plane from Detroit via New York, Istanbul, Beirut, and then overland through Damascus to Amman and this camp? Had I not sold my British sports car to pay for the trip? And, hadn't I taken several odd factory jobs at the end of my freshman year in college to scrape together enough money to fulfill my childhood dream? I was even prepared to die right there and then for Palestine.

Little did I realize on that steamy night in July 1969 that I had already traveled a long way in the *other* direction when I took my seat on that Turkish Air charter from JFK airport to Istanbul. Everything seemed so clear back then. You were on one side or the other. You were on the side of the revolution or opposed to it; you were on the side of the people or you oppressed them. The late sixties was a heady time in my life and in the lives of those in my generation. The superficially placid world of the fifties had cracked and crumbled like parched clay before our eyes. First came the assassination of John F. Kennedy and then in succession the assassinations of Malcolm X, Martin Luther King Jr., and Robert F. Kennedy. During my childhood, the Civil Rights movement surged forward and backward like an incoming tide. By the late sixties, the movement had given way to the exuberance of youth and political revolution. As a college freshman in 1968, I found it difficult—if not impossible—to avoid getting caught up in the excitement of the times—whether in the counterculture or antiwar movements, in the Black Power and women's liberation movements, or in the Third World liberation movements. In these respects, I was indistinguishable from others of my generation. The journey, however, that took me to the hills overlooking the River Jordan on that fateful summer day had begun long before the ferment of the 1960s.

Parents

I was born to Arab parents from Palestine. My father had immigrated to the United States sometime before World War I, probably 1910. The son of the village *mukhtar* (headman) of Beit Hanina in Ottoman-ruled Palestine, he never knew the exact date of his birth, nor could he recall the exact date of his arrival in the United States. My brothers and I once calculated that he was born around 1896. He thought he might have been between twelve and fourteen when he left the village and made his way to New York City. His father put him on a steamer to the United States so he could avoid conscription in the Ottoman Turkish army. Like so much in my father's life, the story of his voyage went with him to the grave.

Mother came from a well-to-do Jerusalem Muslim family—the Aweidahs. At twenty-five, she was half Father's age when they married. Under normal circumstances their marriage would have never happened; Father's peasant background would have precluded marriage to the daughter of an upper-middle-class urban family. Palestinian society in the late 1940s, however, was anything but normal. The establishment of the state of Israel uprooted over seven hundred thousand Palestinian Arabs, my mother and her immediate family among them. They lost their home in the affluent Baqaa section of Jerusalem to the new Jewish state.

The loss of the house was merely the coup de grace, the final slide to financial ruin for Mother's wing of the Aweidah family. Their fall began in the 1930s as the growing Arab resistance to British Mandatory rule erupted into strikes and armed rebellion that culminated in the 1936 Arab revolt. The revolt was savagely suppressed by the British with the tacit support of the Zionists, combined with betrayal and divisions on the Arab side. Amidst the turmoil, the main family business—Aweidah Brothers & Co. Tourist & Travel Agency—founded in the early 1800s by Mother's great-grandfather, Aref, profited from the burgeoning Holy Land tourist trade. Great-grandfather Aref served as one of Jerusalem's leading notables and the local agent of the Thomas Cook Company of London. The business remained on Mother's side of the family until her father's (Fahmey) premature death in the early 1940s, when ownership, including lucrative franchises to major airlines like Pan Am, TWA, KLM, Egypt Air, BOAC, shifted to another branch of the family through a series of machinations orchestrated by Mother's paternal aunt, Bahia. The loss of the business sent Mother's immediate family on a downward financial spiral. Heeding bad advice, grandmother Sarah invested what remained of the family fortune in Bank al-Umma. The bank's Palestinian owners embezzled the assets during the chaos leading up to the dismemberment of British Mandate Palestine. After the fall of West Jerusalem to Israeli forces in 1948, Mother, her mother, and two siblings found themselves refugees in neighboring Amman, Jordan, "with their mouths open to the wind," as Mother was wont to say, employing a Palestinian expression.

Against the chaos and destitution of the late 1940s, my father, Younis Abraham, returned to visit his kin in Beit Hanina, a village lying on the northern approaches to Jerusalem. During his four decades in America, spent mostly in New York City, Younis had worked as a peddler and store owner. After his eldest brother, Issa, who was also an immigrant, had died in a Pennsylvania factory fire, Younis had "married" his brother's wife, Amina, following an ancient Levantine custom (the Levirate) and assumed the role of provider for her and her children. Being purely symbolic, the marriage was never consummated.

Younis's long years in America changed him in ways he could barely comprehend. He had married twice, each time to an American woman, each marriage ending in divorce. His first wife, Grace, the sister of a Lutheran minister, bore him a son, Richard, whom Younis and his relatives called by his Arabic name, Tawfik. The marriage lasted seventeen years. Younis was always proud of his son Richard, who had fought in World War II and worked as an engineer in Reading, Pennsylvania. Younis's second marriage was to a woman named Ethel. The childless marriage lasted four years. Along the way, Younis dropped his original surname, Abdallah, which remains until this day the name of a prominent lineage in the village, and adopted his father's given name, Ibrahim, which he anglicized to Abraham. I once asked him how it came to pass that we carried the Anglo-sounding surname Abraham rather than the original Arabic Ibrahim. Father explained that he had adopted the more Jewish-sounding Abraham when he lived and transacted business in New York City to escape prejudice from Jewish businessmen, who even pressured him to donate to the Zionist cause during the time he owned stores on Madison and Fifth Avenues in the 1930s. That's when I learned that our last name was really Abdallah. In one of life's great ironies, the hospital rabbi at Bellevue in New York City, where Father died, mistook him for a Jew. A nurse chanced upon the rabbi praying over my father's body and promptly informed him that Mr. Abraham was a Muslim, not a Jew. According to the nurse who related the incident to my mother, the rabbi turned pale at the news, then recited some incantations before hurriedly departing.

Younis's agenda on that fateful trip to Palestine in 1949 was to search for a bride. Why he didn't settle for a village girl is anyone's guess. He certainly could have had his pick, as my brother Sameer discovered when he ambled into Beit Hanina unannounced some twenty years later and was told by an elder relative that he could choose from among the score of village girls who had come out to see Younis's son from America. Younis had everything going for him: he was from a respected lineage in the village, he owned land that he had inherited and added to over the years, he was a prosperous and successful businessman, he lived in America, and, although he was in his early fifties by then, he was still strong and handsome.

Three decades of living abroad and two marriages to American women had doubtlessly altered Younis's tastes in women to the point where the thought of marrying an uneducated village girl might have been unattractive to him. An astute businessman imbued with the cosmopolitan view of a New Yorker, Younis undoubtedly knew that there were "bargains" to be had among the Palestinian urban upper classes, his social betters. The old social order of Arab Palestine was in tatters, as many upper-class families, including my mother's (Khadijeh Aweidah), had fallen on hard times and were thus grudgingly prepared to entertain the idea of marrying down socially. Even so, entrenched social attitudes in Palestine, as elsewhere, do not bend easily to reality, even after financial ruin. Younis's offers of marriage were rejected by several families before he arrived at the doorstep of Fahmey Aweidah's recently dispossessed family. A "deal" was struck whereby the Aweidahs would consent to Khadijeh's marriage to Younis if he would sponsor her immediate family's migration to America and help other family members financially. After much bickering and pressure, Khadijeh agreed to marry the "old peasant," regretting the many suitors she had turned down over the years and hating her aunt and uncles for having blocked still other suitors (doctors, lawyers, diplomats) from approaching the family with offers of marriage under the ruse that "Khadijeh has been promised to her first cousin."

From this inauspicious beginning, Younis and Khadijeh settled first in Charlotte, North Carolina, where I was born, and then in Erie, Pennsylvania, where Younis started yet another Oriental rug and linen business and another family. I was the first of five sons born to the couple. Social tensions and contradictions brought from Palestine colored the marriage from the outset, haunting it until Father's sudden death in 1969. Khadijeh made sure that none of her children spoke his peasant dialect, that none went out peddling on the streets like other boys from Beit Hanina, and that none married in their teens like the people from Father's village. The emphasis at home would be on education and on gaining entry into the professions—engineering, law, or medicine. Khadijeh had brought with her the Palestinian (and Arab) upper-middle-class social values and occupational aspirations of the period. Money was important but not at the cost of one's character development and social standing. Adhering to a matrilineal focus, unconventional for Arabs, she never tired of reminding her sons that they descended from solid urban stock, from a respectable family of "high social standing." All of this ran counter to the American egalitarian values and sensibilities inculcated in her sons at public school.

Detroit: A Place Called Home

In the first years of my life, we lived in a flat behind my father's Oriental rug store on French Street in downtown Erie. My younger brother Sameer and I played alone as there were no other children living on the street. At home, only Arabic was spoken. When I turned five, Father sold his successful business and moved the family to Detroit, against Mother's objections. He contended that business would be even better in the Motor City; Mother claimed that his real intention was to be closer to his nephew's family and others from Beit Hanina. Whatever the truth of the matter, the move was a major turning point in my life. The year was 1955.

In Detroit, my formerly placid world erupted into four confusing and contradictory worlds of home, school, neighborhood, and the Arab community of Dix (so called because of the main road of the same name that bisected Dearborn's Southend). Television entered our house the same year, adding a fifth dimension to our lives. Reflecting on this period, I now realize that Mother attempted to preserve a Palestinian Arab Muslim identity at home, while my brothers and I found ourselves increasingly pulled into other worlds, each demanding unconditional conformity. I subconsciously spent the better part of the next three decades trying to keep a strict separation between my home and these other worlds. To my chagrin and embarrassment, one world would inevitably collide with another, home with school, neighborhood with home. In the beginning, and for many years thereafter, moving among these worlds filled me with trepidation and anxiety, often resulting in terrible bouts of stress and self-doubt. My brothers and I managed to balance and occasionally integrate these conflicting worlds, each of us confronting the task in his own way.

Food was a daily reminder that home was a distinct world unto itself. As Muslims, we did not eat pork, of course. And, as far as I know, none of my brothers ever betrayed a burning desire to try the forbidden white meat while growing up. Well into adulthood, I broke the taboo and found smoked ham rather appetizing. But I and those of my brothers who developed an occasional yen for a slice of holiday ham keep this secret from Mother even today. She suspects

Fig. 21. Brothers Abraham, ca. 1960. *Left to right:* Malik, Zeiyad, Nazeeh, Sameer. Standing is Nabeel. Courtesy of Nabeel Abraham.

our transgression just the same. Growing up, *halal* merely meant abstaining from eating pork products. There was none of the ritual Islamic slaughtering of animals that one finds today in Dearborn and other parts of Metropolitan Detroit. To be a good Muslim in conscience and in deed, it was enough merely to keep pork and its by-products from touching one's lips. A dilemma arose, however, when we learned through the Muslim network that JELL-O, a favorite dessert in our house, contained pig bone marrow. The JELL-O ban subsided when Mother's sweet tooth gave way to a craving for the tainted product. In early adolescence, I tried fasting during the month of Ramadan. The longest I went was about two weeks one year, since I found it difficult to attend school without eating breakfast and lunch or drinking water. Sometimes I would break my fast before sunset, unable to contain my hunger. I would feel guilty about it, vowing to make up the day later in the year. My feelings of remorse would disappear as I joined my brothers in front of the television, snack in hand. Although Mother piously fasted, she thought the fast would be too hard on her young boys, so she didn't insist we join her and she excused us when we broke our fast prematurely. "God," she used to say, "was more angry with those who broke their fast, than with those who didn't fast at all."

As children, my brothers and I stuffed the pockets of homemade pita bread with feta cheese and other strange foods like hummus, as well as less exotic foods like strawberry jam and peanut butter. From our parents, we learned to soak Arabic bread in a plate of olive oil and then dip it again in an adjacent plate of *zatar* (thyme mixed with spices). At a certain point, I can't recall when exactly, I realized that the food we ate at home was different from what people around us ate. The other kids devoured sandwiches made of store-bought white bread, just like the stuff advertised on television. Our sandwiches were folded into what is called pita bread today but what we called *khubaz arabee* (Arabic bread).

Being different was hard to accept, especially as we moved into adolescence and the other kids would ask about our sandwiches with a look of disgust. Soon my brothers and I yearned for sandwiches made with white bread so that we could blend in with the neighborhood kids. Mother argued that her bread was better than store-bought bread, but her words fell on deaf ears. We were embarrassed by her irregular loaves of thick oven-baked bread. No longer able to abide our incessant cries, Mother one day relented and brought home a loaf of Wonder Bread. We were joy-struck at the sight of the white plastic wrapping decorated with red and blue balloons. At last we could be like everyone else. My brothers and I quickly made sandwiches with the new bread, all the while anticipating its delights. I took my first bite and waited for a taste sensation. Nothing happened. A second bite and still nothing. Brother exchanged glances with brother. We chewed in silence.

We never admitted to ourselves, let alone to Mother, that the much-heralded Wonder Bread failed to meet our expectations. We ate it and learned to love it just the same. We had to, as Mother used the occasion to cease baking bread altogether. In the days before bread-making machines, dough had to be kneaded by hand and flattened with a rolling pin. With five boys spaced over seven years to look after, Mother happily relinquished the task of bread making to the Wonder Bread Company.

Life was like Wonder Bread—great expectations followed by sudden disappointment, like the time Father brought home an armload of blue jeans from a trip to North Carolina, fulfilling an old wish that Mother had refused us. Running my hand on the stiff dark fabric, I thought to myself, "At last I can dress like everyone else." Mother, like many people in the 1950s, viewed blue jeans as a class emblem. "Jeans are for working people and hoodlums, and, besides, you can't wear them to school," she would intone. As I admiringly unfolded my pair of jeans, my eyes opened in disbelief. The zipper ran along the side.

"These are girls' jeans!" I muttered. A quick check around the room confirmed that each of my brothers was holding a pair of girls' jeans.

"There's no difference," Father said sheepishly, having boasted minutes before to Mother about the bargain he had obtained on them. "Boys' and girls' jeans are the same," Father clarified in his best salesman pitch. We knew better.

School: A Place Far from Home

Long before my brothers and I began clamoring for white bread, just arranging to stay in school for lunch required negotiating the conflicting demands of our two primary worlds—home and school. One day when I was barely in the first grade and Sameer was in kindergarten, my parents had to be away at the hour we normally returned home for lunch. School policy required pupils to produce a signed note from parents requesting that they be allowed to eat lunch in school. When I explained this to my disbelieving parents, they dismissed the idea of writing a note. Off we went, lunch in hand, trepidation in our hearts.

On the way to school, I instructed Sameer to meet me at the lunchroom at the sound of the lunch bell and to slip in behind me in the lunch line. We would pose as "regulars" and hope no one would notice. Someone did, and we were promptly whisked off to the principal's office. Calls to the house failed to elicit a response. Fearful, and not knowing what was coming next, I ordered Sameer in Arabic to make a run for it. A teacher's hand landed on my shoulder as I shouted to Sameer "*Urked, wala, urked!*" ("Run, kid, run!"), while another teacher chased him around a worktable near the staff mailboxes. He was caught in short order. The encounter ended with the two of us seated in the principal's office, two bottles of milk placed before us. As I chewed my lunch in silence, I resolved that my parents should understand the importance of parental notes in the school system. Eventually, my brothers and I would learn to write the notes ourselves and have Mother sign them.

Although my parents were hopelessly out of touch with the world of school, my brothers and I took it seriously. We had to. Mother carefully instilled in us an abiding respect for our teachers and the institution. This respect was underscored by her unswerving expectation that her sons would excel in school or face her wrath at home. In the fourth grade, I received a "D" in homeroom from a teacher who disliked me for no apparent reason. Seeing the handwritten "D," Mother ignored all my attempts to point out the incongruity of the "D" against a raft of "A's" for every other subject. In a fit of rage, she beat me on the buttocks with the most readily available object—a toy machine gun.

From Mother's upper-class Palestinian perspective, education promised to be the salvation of Palestine's Arabs. But we also came to appreciate the window school gave us to the world beyond our predominately working-class neighborhood in southwest Detroit. Although this opinion was never consciously expressed, school quickly came to embody the middle-class values that we saw played out on television every evening. Intuitively, we drew the connection between the lifestyles modeled on television and doing well in school. School was a ticket out of the neighborhood and away from the nearby Arab community in the Southend of Dearborn.

From the very first moment I set a tentative foot in Harms Elementary School, I felt myself in an alien world. I didn't speak a word of English and the only children I had played with up to that point were my brothers. By today's standards, these deficits alone would have rendered me wholly unprepared to enter kindergarten. My family compounded matters by moving to Detroit in early October, thereby forcing me to adjust to a school that was already a month or so into the academic year. Father needlessly raised my hopes by attempting to strike a "two for one" deal with the school whereby Sameer (who was only four years old then) would be allowed to enroll and keep me company in kindergarten. I overheard Mother arguing with Father, telling him his gambit would never work. Her remark dampened my hopes, but I continued to wish for a miracle. I didn't want to be left alone at school. The next morning I found myself sitting quietly behind a long table in Harms Elementary watching my father negotiate with the kindergarten teacher, Sameer standing beside him. Unable to follow the conversation in English, I could nevertheless comprehend its intent from the teacher's gestures. The realization that I would be left alone among strangers in an unfamiliar place sent tears streaming down my cheeks. The next day, I refused to return to school, so Father had to forcibly take me kicking and screaming, drawing his trouser belt for emphasis along the way. It was an unhappy beginning.

Somehow I adjusted and miraculously started speaking English. It wasn't long before my brothers were using me as their own window onto Harms Elementary. I emerged a star pupil. By junior high school, I would be so popular I would become class president. Yet the sense of alienation, of being different, which I experienced during this period, never completely dissipated. Much of it had to do with not considering myself American. I refused to learn all the words to the "Star-Spangled Banner" and the Pledge of Allegiance. I still don't know them. In music class, I sat in the back of the room, which was unlike me, and feigned participation. As a second grader, I despised the idyllic "See Spot Run" stories, which had no connection with my life. In the third grade I closed my mind to the penmanship lessons, something I now regret. Well into high school, I didn't feel that English was *my* language even though I thoroughly loved the literature classes. Ironically, my command of Arabic by that time amounted to a handful of words. At some deep unconscious level I must have sensed that internalizing the English language, singing children's songs, reciting the Pledge of Allegiance, and performing school rituals was the *way* people became American, like the way one became a *non*-Muslim by eating pork. My attitude was not shared by my brothers.

To get around having to recite the morning Pledge of Allegiance, I volunteered in the fourth or fifth grade to be the "radio man" for this ritual. My job was to pull the school radio from a storage closet and set it on a chair next to the flag stand. After plugging the radio in, I carefully adjusted the large brown knobs protruding from the shiny wood cabinet. Precisely at 8:00 A.M. the national anthem would come over the air from the broadcast studios of the Detroit Public Schools in downtown Detroit. Two classrooms of kindergartners would stand before the radio, the flag, and me, with their tiny right hands placed firmly on their chests and engage in this patriotic ritual, while I stood by relishing the fact I did not have to sing or pledge allegiance to the flag. On at least one occasion, the kindergarten teacher gestured to me to participate along with the others.

Harms Elementary was a traditional school run mostly by gray-haired women who were dedicated to an unstated mission: to impart middle-class values, along with the requisite hygienic and dietary habits, in their working-class charges. These women were the closest thing to secular nuns; most of them were in fact devout Catholics of German origin. That several of them never smiled augmented the seriousness with which they undertook their mission. To their credit, the school garnered several national awards. As adults, my brothers and I have come to appreciate the education and discipline we received at Harms, a school whose namesake, Fred Harms, would plant tulips around the school.

The doyenne of the school gray-hairs was Mrs. Mulkern. She taught "auditorium." Her classes did, in fact, meet in the school auditorium. The varnished walnut seats combined with the room's high ceiling and dark drapes lent the place a cathedral-like aura. On Tuesdays, several classrooms of noisy children were regimentally led into the room for a movie feature. There never appeared to be an overriding theme to the movies—on one Tuesday the feature was on the life of a boy in Africa, while on another a talking cartoon character instructed us on proper telephone etiquette. From time to time, Mrs. Mulkern would conduct "inspection"—hands would be displayed before her discerning eye as she would walk up and down a line of students waiting to enter her classroom. Careful never to touch the tiny fingers and hands stretched before her, Mrs. Mulkern would quietly make her observations, softly complimenting a clean pair of hands or, conversely, pointing out a set of dirty or chewed finger nails. Mrs. Mulkern's auditorium class was a unique blend of geography, economics, classical music, etiquette, personal hygiene, and nutritional instruction, with some citizenship thrown in for good measure. Following one of her frequent discussions on the importance of eating a balanced diet, I volunteered to describe the previous evening's repast at my home, hoping she would approve. After an enthusiastic description of Mother's dish of spinach, lamb, and rice, Mrs. Mulkern slowly nodded a tentative approval while simultaneously muffling her disgust.

Christmas was marked in Mrs. Mulkern's class by the annual Christmas play. In an era before sensitivity training, the play always posed a cultural/religious dilemma for me and my brothers. We avoided volunteering for a role in the play, even though as Muslims we believed that Jesus was one of God's prophets. The most painful part of Mrs. Mulkern's auditorium class (as well as Harms Elementary as a whole), however, was the return from Christmas recess, when students were encouraged to show and tell what Santa Claus had brought them. During my seven years at Harms, the resumption of classes after the Christmas break was the most dreaded time of the year for me.

Mother strictly opposed the introduction of Christmas gift-giving in our house. Her objections were both ideological and practical. "It isn't our holiday, and, anyway, I can't afford to spend money on presents for all of you," she would lament year after year. This meant my brothers and I had to console ourselves on being left out of the biggest event of the year for children. Compounding our dejection was seeing on television all the wonderful toys we knew we would never find on Christmas morning. One of the most coveted toys for boys in my time was a Lionel train set. By any measure, this was an expensive toy, making it doubly impossible for me to ever receive it. I fantasized about owning the train set anyway, since no one could stop me from dreaming. On one particular postholiday show and tell, the dream became a reality of sorts, as I impulsively stood before Mrs. Mulkern's class and claimed to have received a Lionel train set for Christmas, quickly adding, to make it sound plausible, that the gift was just a starter set. Mrs. Mulkern acted surprised and incredulous, noting that she was under the impression that Muslims didn't celebrate Christmas. Her remark left me feeling ashamed and remorseful for a long time, not only because I had lied but also because her remark indicated that even though I hadn't accepted my being different, she had.

Mother acquiesced to Christmas gift-giving one year when my brothers and I simply took our own savings—garnered ironically from selling Christmas cards door-to-door—and bought presents for her, Father, and ourselves. She (and Father) drew the line, however, at allowing a Christmas tree in the house, which she saw as a symbol of complete capitulation to Christianity and American culture.

It was in Mrs. Mulkern's auditorium that I was reminded of the necessity of keeping apart the two worlds I inhabited. I was in the fourth grade at the time and seated along the aisle in the back of the auditorium waiting for the Tuesday movie to begin. A teacher approached and bent forward to ask me about the extended absence of one of my younger brothers, who was a pupil in her kindergarten class. For reasons I have never understood, this brother had not been circumcised in infancy as the rest of us had been. At the age of five he was pulled out of school and circumcised at Detroit Memorial Hospital. Although my parents had informed the school he would be absent for a week or two, the teacher wanted to know why my brother wasn't in school. When I said that he had been in the hospital for some surgery, she grew concerned.

"For what?" she inquired.

Frustrated by my inability to come up with the right word in English, I said, "I don't know how to translate it into English." A pause followed. "It's called *tutheer* in Arabic," I added, hoping to satisfy her curiosity.

"What's that?" she said with a puzzled look. At a complete

loss for words, I raised my right hand slightly off my lap, pointed my extended index finger toward my lap, and made a slow circular motion. The teacher, who must have been in her late thirties, muffled a gasp with her right hand and hurried away.

Embarrassed by her reaction, I sat perfectly still, staring silently at the big white screen in the front of the auditorium. From the corner of my eye I noticed the teacher whispering to another female teacher, both of them laughing uncontrollably. I pretended not to see them. It seemed like an eternity before the lights went out and the film projector started turning. At the time, I didn't comprehend what had happened. I had recently attended a circumcision party for two Beit Hanina boys living in the Southend. I understood circumcision was an "Arab" custom, but the fact that men and women celebrated together and treated the event as a joyous occasion led me to conclude that there was no particular shame or embarrassment associated with the mention of this practice to a non-Arab woman. Mother later told me the teacher reacted the way she did because Americans must be like Palestinian Christians who do not circumcise their boys. The incident taught me to be circumspect about my family's private world or risk stinging embarrassment.

Our Private World

Our household brimmed with things we never dared share with outsiders. One of Mother's firmest rules was a ban on walking outdoors (or anywhere) eating anything, especially bread. "Why not? Everyone else does it." I used to plead, demanding to hear the reasons behind her edict. Mother argued it was *ayib* (shameful or, in this context, bad manners) to eat in front of others who are not eating. "It just isn't done. Moreover, you will drop bread crumbs on the ground which is *haram* [taboo, sinful] in the eyes of God," she would explain in reverential tones. We also were strictly forbidden to accept food from any of our friends for fear we might unknowingly eat pork. To accept the offer of a meal at a friend's house was also taboo, as this would obligate Mother to reciprocate in kind, something she wasn't always in a position to do. When we insisted that our friends didn't expect her to reciprocate, she grew visibly angry at our "ignorance."

Our house consisted of two flats. My family lived on the first floor and rented out the upstairs flat. For a while, my maternal grandmother, uncle, and aunt lived upstairs. A ghoul lived in the basement. The ghoul made any descent downstairs a precarious undertaking for the brothers Abraham. To venture downstairs after nightfall to fetch some laundry or a needed tool entailed wading into the darkness and groping for the silver chain to the light switch. It had to be pulled quickly so its protective light would bathe the venturer before the ghoul emerged from his hiding place and gobbled up his victim. The ghoul was a constant presence in our basement, even though we only saw and felt him in our mind's eye. A cultural artifact of Mother's childhood in Jerusalem, the ghoul always took his leave when outsiders visited the basement.

Mother brought other superstitions and taboos with her from Jerusalem. As a child I learned that it is bad luck to use scissors on Fridays. That meant Mother did no mending on the Muslim day of rest. It is also bad luck to leave a pair of scissors with the blades open on any day of the week. It is an affront to God to point the soles of footwear in the heavenly direction. I still find myself impulsively flipping over shoes and sandals whose soles are facing upward, my learned rationalism inexplicably giving way to superstitions acquired in childhood. I still feel a sense of alarm when I see a person stepping over someone lying in a supine position. This is a bad omen which could result in harm visiting the lounger, up to and including being cut in half. Other superstitions have long ago lost their potency, like the taboo against letting a child sit in the laundry basket (he will get lost) and eating cheese without an accompanying piece of bread (one will get a tapeworm).

Certain superstitions seem to have come to light only after I reached adulthood, leading me to wonder if Mother has been secretly adding to her repertoire over the years through her contact with local Arabs and other ethnics. Not many years ago I learned that to pour boiling water down a kitchen drain without uttering the Fatiha (the opening verse of the Quran) could provoke an angry response from the *Jinn* (genies) dwelling in the pipe below the sink. In retaliation for being scalded, the *Jinn* might slap the offender silly, literally driving him mad. As it turns out, this superstition is widely held in southern Lebanon and, I suspect, throughout the Levant as well.

During my childhood, my mother and grandmother spent their mornings divining how the day might turn out according to whose visage they saw first. To count, the person should not be residing in the household, so the unwitting visage usually belonged to a neighbor, milkman, or some stranger who happened to be passing by. When no outsiders were available, the face of a family member would be unwittingly enlisted in the divination. Certain faces were associated in my grandmother and mother's minds with good days, others with bad days. Occasionally, the two would disagree over which side of the ledger a particular face properly belonged on.

The moon held special properties in Mother's eyes. The light of a new moon shining on a youthful face worked as a beauty enhancer. Mother and Grandmother would each take a handful of moonbeam and rub the face of whichever hapless brother was standing nearby. After a while my brothers and I could sense a facial rub coming, and we prudently put some distance between ourselves and the moonbeam gatherers. Mother and Grandmother and Aunt would have to call out our names, beckoning us to hurry before the moonbeam in their cupped hands evanesced. This often took place in Patton Park, making it doubly embarrassing. Trips to the park often included the harvesting of *babounij* (chamomile), another "Old World" act I feared neighbors or, worse, schoolmates might see us engaged in. The *babounij*, dried and boiled as tea, was used to ease menstrual cramps. Along with moonbeam collecting, came moon-gazing—the sport of admiring the beauty of a full moon—a kind of poetry in motion, which ironically I have come to appreciate in adulthood.

Like moonbeam gathering and visage reading, divining the future in our house was the province of women. Mother, Grandmother, and Aunt daily studied the insides of their demitasse cups. After savoring an afternoon cup of Turkish coffee, they would ceremoniously swirl the grounds that settled at the bottom of the cup and with the flip of a deft wrist empty the grounds onto a saucer. The cup would be carefully tilted on its saucer and placed on the side of the sink to dry. After a while, the inside of the cup would be covered with a delicate brown pattern resembling an ancient Rorschach test. During a moment of relaxation, the women would "read" their cups, catching glimpses of the future. I once asked Mother to teach me to read my coffee cup. After several frustrating attempts at discerning meaning from the shapes of tiny swirls, I concluded that the entire endeavor was arbitrary. For example, Mother found a "camel" in my trial cup. According to her, this was a sign that I was about to embark on a journey. To where exactly was anyone's guess. My desire to travel was so intense that I badly wanted to believe her. At the same time, my mind-set and schooling predisposed me to doubt any connections between the swirls of coffee grounds and the future. School had rendered me skeptical and even arrogant about home ways and beliefs.

The divination of coffee grounds went hand in hand with easy conversation in the kitchen and the living room. The premier sitting area, however, was—weather permitting—the front porch. Mother and Grandmother often conversed there while conducting chores like sifting through trays of orange or brown lentils. Our porch was an extension of the living room, but that was true of many of our non-Arab neighbors as well. Admittedly, not every house on our block put its front porch to active use, but all houses had one. It wasn't until I reached high school and spent time in solidly middle-class neighborhoods on the east side of Detroit that I discovered houses without front porches. These neighborhoods seemed quieter and somewhat stuffier than my neighborhood but were appealing just the same.

Mother and Grandmother spent considerable time praying and performing ritual ablutions. They prayed separately, in a private corner of their respective bedrooms. When not in formal prayer, standing barefoot on a prayer rug, head alternately raised to the Almighty or lowered in humble submission, they reclined in an armchair and ran a string of worry beads called a *masbaha* through their fingers, keeping count of the devotional recitation of the ninety-nine names of Allah in Arabic and similar incantations. Every time they climbed into a car, Mother and Grandmother would *howwit*—recite Quranic verses—worry beads in the left hand, right hand extended upward moving in a circular motion to protect the car and its passengers. Their drone never failed to dampen the spirits of the other riders, raising everyone's anxiety level. My father politely tolerated the drone, even though it was obvious that he had no use for it. Uncle Zack, mother's brother, felt no compunction to be polite and demanded that Grandmother and Mother stop the ritual lest the drone lead him to crash the car. After a while, the *howwit* ritual faded into oblivion.

Neighborhood: A Place to Get Away From

I grew up on Casper Street in a largely white neighborhood in southwest Detroit, about a mile from Dearborn's Southend. Southwest Detroit shares the Southend's working-class character but lacks the latter's Arab ethnic character. In the 1950s, there were three other Arab families, all from Beit Hanina, in our neighborhood. They were related to my father but had little contact with us, given their antagonism toward my mother.

Nearly a dozen ethnic backgrounds were represented on our street alone: Armenian, French Canadian, German Catholic, German Protestant, Greek, Hungarian, Irish Catholic, Mexican, Maltese,

Macedonian, Polish, and Serbian as well as white southerners from Kentucky and Tennessee. Mother viewed the outside world in ethnoracial categories. Americans with readily identifiable names or ethnic backgrounds were considered to have a pedigree. Southern whites and whites with no discernible ethnic background were in Mother's parlance, "hillibillee." (The same categories were in use by Dearborn's Arabs.) Each ethnic group was believed to be endowed with an attendant social character and ranked accordingly. On the upper end were Southern Europeans, particularly Macedonians, Greeks, and Albanians (especially Muslim Albanians) with whom Mother shared a similar outlook on what was proper and improper social behavior. Mexicans, Poles, and Irishmen ranked lower on her social scale. They were potentially violent and exhibited dubious social morality. Their children weren't academically inclined, and the Poles and Irish were believed to dislike Arabs and other dark-skinned peoples. Near the bottom were the "hillibillee." They lacked a moral compass in Mother's estimation: the women smoked, drank, and had a promiscuous air about them. At the very bottom were the "*Zout-wa-Nowwar*" (lowlifes and vagabonds). This was the ultimate slur. Any person or family, regardless of ethnic affiliation (including Arabs), could qualify for this designation if they demonstrated certain qualities—low moral behavior, public drinking, aggressive and violent behavior, litigiousness, laziness, untrustworthiness, sexual promiscuity, and general lack of breeding. *Zout-wa-Nowwar* were to be avoided at all costs. Their potential for violence often struck fear in us, like the young tough who, completely unprovoked, lobbed a glob of spittle on my head one day as my brothers and I walked from the Dix mosque to a coffeehouse to rendezvous with my dad. We were four to their two, yet we silently walked on pretending nothing had happened.

Against this ethnic hierarchy, my brothers and I were constantly reminded that we descended from a family of rank and standing and were expected to conduct ourselves accordingly. The neighborhood kids provided us with an intimate view of mainstream American society, at least that segment of it they represented—the urban, white working class. From *their* standpoint, we probably were not noticeably different from anyone else, our peculiarities notwithstanding. But our ethnic idiosyncrasies weighed heavily on us as we attempted to lead normal childhoods playing in the streets and attending school. Our olive skin, Arabic names, knowledge of Arabic, Muslim religion, Arab ethnicity, awareness of Palestinian history, and skeptical attitude toward U.S. politics all conspired to reinforce an awareness that we were different. Having close relatives living upstairs (unusual on our street) and having parents who openly spoke to us in an unfamiliar language added to our sense of difference.

That our parents didn't take us to the typical places—Edgewater Park, Cedar Point, and that American mecca, the dream of every child, Disneyland—also bespoke our separateness. Similarly, our Otherness was reinforced when the Southend kids, whom we met at Arabic school, boasted of spending their summers at Camp Dearborn (a city-owned park and campground open only to Dearborn residents). My brothers and I felt left out in both worlds. Admittedly, our marginality stemmed in part from the personal idiosyncrasies of our parents. My father was old-fashioned and not very much into family outings; my mother was excessively protective, fearing the assimilationist tendencies of American society, although she complained of being married to a nonfamily man. So there were some things like traveling and visiting local amusement parks that other Arab parents might have done but that our parents couldn't or wouldn't do.

In an era when the majority of mothers worked as full-time housewives, a family's standing in the neighborhood rode on the father's job and vocation. In a neighborhood where the typical father worked in a factory either on the assembly line or in the skilled trades or drove a delivery van or interstate freight hauler, Father's work defied easy recognition. Unlike the other fathers, Dad didn't return home every evening. Instead he spent many months of the year on the road, peddling Oriental rugs and fine European linens to an affluent clientele. And when he was home, he seemed to be around all the time. Outdoors, he wore gray suits and a matching fedora with a black band around the base that closed in a faux bow. Even around the house, he wore neatly pressed white shirts. He smoked cigars and spoke English with a slight New York accent. Because Father was some twenty-five years older than Mother, strangers often mistook him for our grandfather. All of this required explaining. Our Otherness burdened us, often to the point of driving us to be like everyone else—eat white-bread sandwiches, celebrate Christmas, attend Muslim religious service on Sunday mornings, go on family outings. As a child I was immensely proud of my father and his business acumen and savvy, yet the families I saw on television in the 1950s and early 1960s often made me wish that my own family would blend into the mainstream.

In summertime when the windows of our house were open night and day, the odors of Arabic food preparation—fried cauliflower, boiled cabbage, sauteed onions and garlic, along with the aromas of allspice, cumin, turmeric—would waft onto Casper Street, along with the melodious sounds of Arabic music playing on the hi-fi. Mother's limited selection of LPs, works by Abdel Halim Hafez and Farid al-Atrash, her two favorites, played over and over again to the ears of passersby. In later years, after Mother "got religion," she would often embarrass my brothers and me by calling us from the front door of the house wearing her homemade Islamic prayer garb—a white billowing dress with matching head shawl. Our playmates would ask if Mother was a nun. Father added to our Otherness by occasionally taking out the garbage wearing only white boxer shorts and an old dress shirt. Father's forays to the alley behind the house sent Mother into fits of "what will the neighbors say?" His pat response was that his boxers were technically "shorts" and thus wholly permitted outdoors. Father also scandalized Mother when she saw photos of him lounging in his pajamas while staying as a guest of her relatives in Jerusalem one year.

For twenty of the twenty-three years Mother resided on Casper Street, the elderly couple next door, Mr. and Mrs. Detroiter (their real name) snubbed us. Only after my youngest brother entered college did Mrs. Detroiter and Mother strike up a civil, if limited, relationship. As a child, I often wondered what it was about us that caused the Detroiters not to acknowledge our existence. Perhaps it was merely the presence of five boisterous boys living next door that sent their noses skyward. Typical of working-class neighborhoods, the houses on Casper Street were crowded together so that a heated conversation at our kitchen table ricocheted in the Detroiter house ten feet away. I couldn't help wondering, nevertheless, what role our olive skin, exotic-sounding names, and Arab ethnic identity played in the Detroiters' attitude toward us.

The 1950s and 1960s were thick with racial tension. From time to time, rumor circulated on the street that "the Coloreds" were looking to buy a house in the neighborhood. Quarrels among neighbors often ended with one side threatening to sell their house to "the Coloreds." No one ever made good on the threat while we lived on Casper Street. Racial bigotry infected everyone, even the Arab kids at the Dix mosque in Dearborn's Southend, the irony that they were called "sand niggers" by the rest of Dearborn escaping them.

One of my first memories of Harms Elementary is a wall mural of paper cutouts depicting a jungle scene in which little black Sambo is being chased by a ferocious tiger. The only black person at the school, aside from the assistant janitor, was Erma Colding, the school science teacher. A tall, dignified, handsome woman, Mrs.

Colding was unfailingly proper with everyone she encountered. Her poise radiated an inner beauty and self-confidence rarely found in any of the other teachers. She recalled vignettes from a childhood shaped by racial discrimination and poverty as a way of reminding us how much better off we were. They were cautionary tales about not squandering opportunities. She was admired and loved by the children in her classes. Yet once in a while I would hear that some kid, usually a boy, rejected her kindness and unexpectedly hurled the word "nigger" at her in the middle of class. On one occasion, one of my brothers reported that Mrs. Colding abruptly left the room. After a while a burly male teacher by the name of Mr. Miller entered the room and took the young miscreant off to the principal's office. As far as I could tell, such outbursts didn't happen often, but they always left me wondering about my own place in the neighborhood and in America as a whole.

Mother and Mrs. Colding were friends, and Mrs. Colding would occasionally pay Mother a visit. On one occasion, she brought her son Frankie along. While Frankie and two of my brothers were playing down the street, a neighbor poked his head out the front door, asking, "Is that little nigger your brother?" Too stunned to respond, my brothers stood mute. The man quickly ordered them to get "the nigger out of here before I shoot you and your little brother." Alarmed, my brothers quickly ran home where they interrupted Mother and Mrs. Colding with news of what had happened. The incident touched off a tirade on "racist Americans" by Mother. Mrs. Colding, in contrast, reacted with the air of someone who had heard and seen worse things in her life. Frankie withdrew in silence. Feelings of loneliness and vulnerability came over me as I tried to imagine the face of the neighbor, which until this day I have never been able to conjure up in my mind.

By the time I entered Cass Technical, Detroit's premier all-city high school, I was largely alienated from the neighborhood I grew up in and relieved that I wouldn't have to attend Western High School, my local high school. Cass Tech served for me—and my brothers—as a window looking out upon a broader Detroit and its middle and upper-middle classes. For it was there that we met, befriended, and dated people from all parts of the city; a significant development because Detroit, as in urban America generally, geography is largely synonymous with social class. With the exception of one student with the unlikely name of Jim Ray, there were, to my knowledge, no other ethnic Arabs in the school, which numbered five thousand students. It should be remembered that this was a time—the mid-1960s—before ethnic consciousness had swept the country. In all probability there were other Jim Rays at the school—ethnic Syrians and Lebanese washed and bleached to the point of invisibility. Even Jim was invisible until the day I stopped by his house (which ironically was in southwest Detroit) and met his mother. Her utterances of a few Arabic words surprised me. Jim surprised me, too. One day he pulled up to the store where I worked wearing a towel on his head and a trouser belt wrapped around it. My coworkers thought him mildly amusing, whereas I found his "mock Arab" look demeaning, occurring as it did so soon after the Arab defeat in the June 1967 war. Long after we graduated and parted ways, Jim came up in conversation with an old stalwart of Arab American political activism in Detroit, Dr. Katherine Nagher. Nagher, who was active in a number of Syrian Orthodox and Arab American ethnic organizations during the time Jim and I were growing up, turned out to be Jim's aunt. Jim's mother had apparently dissociated herself from the local Syrian community, while Katherine (and her brother) chose to affiliate with the ethnic church and community of their immigrant parents.

Community: A Place Called Dix

Through my father's extended family, we gained a window on the Palestinian immigrants from Beit Hanina, many of whom resided in or near Dearborn's Southend at the time. Through our mother, we gained access to several mosques and the wider Arab Muslim community in the Southend and beyond. This community consisted primarily of people from the Bekaa region of Lebanon, Sunni Muslims like ourselves who coalesced around the Dix mosque. At the Hashemite Hall around the corner from the Dix mosque and the newer Islamic Center on Joy Road in Detroit, two mainly Lebanese Shia Muslim institutions, we learned about the Lebanese Americans who made up the majority of the Dearborn Arab community. What mattered to us was that they were Arabs and Muslims, even though to them we were outsiders.

As a result of my father's family connections, we attended several Beit Hanina weddings in the basement of the Dix mosque. The celebrations invariably took place on hot, humid summer nights with the celebrants dancing the *dabkah* and tossing dollar bills in the path of the lead dancer. The head dancer usually twirled a handkerchief in his right hand, while a solo dancer sliced the air with a gleaming saber. The festivities took place under the stern gaze of Gamal Abdel

Nasser, the Egyptian president whose portrait hung prominently to one side of the small stage next to a large wall clock bathed in a halo of neon green. Community at this level was confined to the village, a world in which my brothers and I felt uneasy and alien.

Through my father we also learned about another alien Southend institution—the coffeehouse—*al-Ahwa* in Palestinian dialect. Father spent an inordinate amount of time seated at card games in smoke-filled coffeehouses tucked away behind gray, nondescript storefronts. When I cast my mind back to the Southend of my youth, I associate the place with the Dix mosque, the Hashemite Hall, and these smoke-filled, dingy coffeehouses. My fondest memories, however, are of the vegetable gardens that graced the houses around the Dix mosque and the quiet road that coursed around Woodmere Cemetery. The gardens, the cemetery, and the asphalt road running between them exuded a placid, semirural air that contrasted sharply with the tense gambling in the coffeehouses and the towering smokestacks of the nearby Ford Rouge Plant to the west.

While Father spent most of his free time in the coffeehouses, my brothers and I spent ours in the Dix mosque or the mosque above the Hashemite Hall. Like soldiers carrying out some vital military mission, we often made the mile-long trek from Casper Street to the Dix mosque on foot through winter cold and snow and summer heat and rain to attend Arabic language school. Arabic school in the Southend amounted to a series of frustrating fits and starts: after the textbooks were imported (from Syria or Lebanon), an Arab student from Wayne State University enlisted to teach the class ("no experience necessary"), the initial monthly tuition collected (five dollars per head), the Saturday morning lessons would lurch forward like some carnival Ferris wheel. After a month or two the monthly tuition payments would decline, interest would wane and many students would drop out, and then the instructor would quit because he hadn't been paid. Mother would complain about the lack of scholastic interest and the miserliness of the Southend Arabs who failed to keep their end of the bargain.

With the exception of some of our Beit Hanina relatives, most of the other students were Lebanese (Sunnis as well as Shia) who attended Dearborn public schools. They formed their own cliques and seemed to me indistinguishable from the non-Arab kids attending my own school in Detroit. Beyond using Arabic nicknames like Hamoudy and She-she, they evinced little interest in learning Arabic or preserving their ethnic heritage. To my dismay, some of the Dearborn kids supported the Democratic Party, largely (as I deduced many years later) because kinsmen—the Berrys and Shamies—had built a patronage system around it. My parents tended to support the Republicans, whom they believed favored Israel less. Father also identified with the Republican Party's image as the defender of business interests and the upper classes. Not surprisingly, I developed only one serious friendship in the Southend. It was with a boy named Rida Simon, who, in later years as Dr. Robert Simon, gained notice for his work in providing medical relief to war-torn Afghanistan and other distressed countries. My brothers developed no close or long-lasting friendships at Arabic school.

Following a dispute in the woman's auxiliary at the Dix mosque, Mother switched allegiances to the Hashemite Hall mosque around the corner. Both mosques maintained the prayer area on the upper floor, retaining the ground level for social functions—Arabic classes, meetings, wedding parties. Of the two buildings, the Dix mosque was slightly cheerier and cleaner. The linoleum floor of the downstairs hall was polished and the thick cinder block walls were painted a bright color. In winter, when only a small area was used for Saturday Arabic classes, the hall felt drafty and cold. The Hashemite Hall, in contrast, was unfailingly depressing, as even the uncurtained upstairs windows refused to admit the light of day due to the thick coating of industrial dirt and grime. Arabic language and religious classes were held in rooms adjoining the ritual ablution and prayer areas. Mother insisted that we conduct our ritual ablution at home instead of at the Hall. I saw the wisdom of her advice, as the ablution room at the Hashemite Hall was cold, drafty, and of dubious hygienic standards. When the political winds shifted and Mother felt welcome again at the Dix mosque, my brothers and I were relieved. And when the Hashemite Hall burned down in 1974, more than a decade after we last attended Arabic and Islamic classes there, I felt little regret.

Arab Nationalism: Real Arabs Don't Live Here

Growing up, I felt distant from the Arab community in the Southend much as I had from my neighborhood in southwest Detroit. Mother's biases became mine: Dearborn's Arabs weren't real Arabs. Real Arabs spoke Arabic and lived in the Arab world, in places like Nasser's Egypt, which was standing up to Israel and the Western powers. Real Arabs didn't take the American political system seriously and certainly didn't join the Democratic Party. Real Arabs were, like Nasser's Egypt, engaged in the building of a modern society as epitomized by the Aswan High Dam. Coffeehouses, pool halls, and American political parties were not the haunts of real Arabs.

Mother often talked of packing us up and moving to Egypt so we could grow up in an Arab country. Father, in contrast, occasionally talked of returning to Beit Hanina, which was then part of the Hashemite Kingdom of Jordan. I dreamed of living in al-Ouds, the place my mother, aunt, and grandmother so often reminisced about in the stories they told and retold sitting around the kitchen table or on the front porch. I imagined al-Ouds to be a quiet, friendly, carefree residential quarter of large stone houses tucked behind leafy meandering streets. The al-Ouds of my childhood was the place where my family and I could find acceptance and belonging. As I reflect on this imaginary place now, it seems like a cross between small-town America and a verdant English country lane set in the Middle East.

As a child, I wasn't quite sure where or what *al-Ouds* was—other than somewhere in the heart of Palestine. Exactly why my mother, grandmother, and aunt kept talking about this place instead of the Jerusalem they were from puzzled me. Their conversations seemed too personal and private for me to join. And, anyway, this was "women's talk"—no place for a boy, I told myself. Through a process of deduction, I concluded on my own that al-Ouds must be the quarter of Jerusalem where Mother grew up. It wasn't until I reached college and enrolled in Arabic language classes, ironically taught by American and Israeli Jews, that I realized that al-Ouds ("al-Quds" in classical Arabic) was, in fact, the Arabic name for Jerusalem.

Every time my parents talked about returning to the Middle East, I mentally began to pack my bags and disconnect from the world around me. (I recently learned that my brothers never shared my attitude.) These imaginary preparations were inevitably met with disappointment. One particular spring my parents appeared to be in full agreement—at long last we were "going back" to Palestine. I was nine or ten years old at the time. Convinced of the solidity of my parent's decision, I rushed to tell my teachers and schoolmates that I wouldn't be returning to school in the fall. In the interim, my parents quarreled and nothing more was said about moving to Palestine. When fall arrived, I quietly took my place in school.

Years later, in the wake of my own failed attempt to find a place for myself in the Arab world, I asked Mother why the much-heralded move of my childhood never happened. Staring off in the distance, Mother admitted that as much as she had wanted to raise us in an Arab country, she opposed the move out of fear that Father's relatives would have prevailed upon him to divorce her.

Nasser was a hero in our household. The fact that he was not liked by the United States, Britain, and France made him even more appealing. It was naive hero worship born out of the helplessness we Palestinians felt in the decade following the dismemberment of British Mandate Palestine and the loss of our country. We were looking for a savior, someone who would liberate our villages and towns and return our homes to us. The time when we would learn about Nasser's draconian rule, his inept generals, and his manipulation of public opinion was still distant. From our vantage point in far-off Detroit, Nasser epitomized the Arab hope for the future. So strong was my father's enthusiasm for Egypt's political union with Syria in 1958 that he sent the Egyptian leader five hundred dollars. He did this without consulting Mother, while on a trip to Beit Hanina.

On Sunday evenings, Mother would take us to the Arabic-language movies at the ornate Detroit Institute of Arts theater. On the big screen flashed syrupy Egyptian romances starring Farid al-Atrash, Abdel Halim Hafez, and Muhammad 'Abd al-Wahhab and several female stars whose names I never learned. My brothers—like the other kids who ran around the theater in a state of pandemonium—found these films vapid and boring. The biggest turn-off were the "*bizzer* eaters," who spent the evening consuming dried watermelon and sunflower seeds and dropping the shells on the floor. I forced myself to sit through the movies naively hoping to broaden my comprehension of Arabic, all the while avidly scanning the screen for signs of Nasser's Egypt—modern buildings, roads, and factories. Soon, even my determination to derive a positive benefit from these insipid movies waned, and I added my voice to that of my brothers in protesting going to the Arabic movies, demanding instead to be allowed to stay home and watch Sunday night television.

When the June 1967 Arab-Israeli War broke out, I was a typical American high school sophomore: disillusioned with school, alienated from family, hopelessly stuck in an adolescent romance, laboring under a consumer fetish—in my case a fetish for British sports cars. The news media's suspense-filled buildup in May reawakened a dormant Arab nationalism in me. As the child of Palestinian immigrants, my hopes and dreams for Palestine and the Arabs were pinned on Nasser's Egypt in spring 1967. The showdown between the Arabs and Israel was the moment my family had been waiting for. My heart was filled with anxiety and anticipation. The news media depicted the conflict in deceptively simplistic terms: the tiny Jewish state was facing annihilation from vastly superior Arab armies. Reality, as I learned many years later, was radically different. Israel's leaders entered a war of their own making with only one major unanswered question—how many days would it take to defeat the Arab armies? Israel's massive and swift defeat of the Egyptian and other Arab armies hit like a bombshell, turning initial disbelief to demoralization and dejection. Curiously, I can recall only two or three fleeting memories from this period—the mental anguish and humiliation of the Arab defeat having been so great. The Arabs seemed finished, and I emotionally disassociated myself from them.

I entered my senior year less a conscious Arab than ever. Yet I still felt the sting of the Arab defeat and was called on to make sense of it to my friends and coworkers at my part-time job in a duty-free liquor store on the U.S.-Canada border. My alienation from home, school, and neighborhood ran so deep that I gave serious thought to joining the merchant marines and leaving everyone—my family, friends, and Detroit—behind me. The thought of Mother throwing a fit stopped me.

One spring day in 1968, my brother Nazeeh asked if I had heard the news that Arab guerrillas had beaten back an Israeli military assault in Jordan at a place called Karameh, which means "dignity" in Arabic. Having lost all faith in the Arabs, I refused to read the copy of the *Christian Science Monitor* he tried to hand me. Television images of the Vietcong's Tet Offensive were still fresh in mind. Tet had shaken America. Here was a *real* war, I thought, where one side stands up to the other.

Alienated from my Arab identity, I squandered my savings—earned through years of delivering newspapers, mowing neighbors' lawns, clearing snowy sidewalks—on a five-year-old red convertible MGB sports car. Along with the car came a new girlfriend, a sunny girl named Laura Robb. Like her parents, Laura was politically active. One day Laura dragged me to a campaign rally for Robert Kennedy in downtown Detroit, not far from Cass Tech. I felt uneasy being at the rally, partly because it was my first and partly because of my family's antipathy toward U.S. politics and especially the Democratic Party. After Kennedy had finished his stump speech, he waded into the crowd at the point where I was standing. I instinctively shook his outstretched hand, but later felt guilty over attending the rally.

Later that spring, Laura insisted that we walk in the Poor People's March that coursed its way through downtown Detroit behind Martin Luther King Jr. I was beginning to find a place for myself in American society. That summer my circle of acquaintances widened to include liberal Jews, antiwar protesters, and supporters of Eugene McCarthy's propeace candidacy for the Democratic presidential nomination. But they were also sympathetic to Israel. This made me feel awkward and uneasy. One summer evening, Laura invited some friends and me to a screening of a new movie, the proceeds of which would benefit the Black Panther Party. She assured me that I would find the movie of personal interest since it was about the Arab resistance to French colonial rule in Algeria.

Algeria had played a small but important role in raising my ethnic consciousness. The country had gained its independence when I was twelve. What little I knew about the war came from fleeting television images on the evening news and my father's commentary on it. Those images had raised my ethnic self-esteem and confirmed my marginality at the same time. Here were Arabs waging a heroic campaign against French colonialism, yet no one in my immediate world (school, neighborhood) knew or cared about Algeria. Thus when Laura took me to see *The Battle of Algiers,* I was suspicious of her assurances that this was not some Hollywood makeover of history.

The opening scene of Gillo Pontecorvo's critically acclaimed film devastated me. I couldn't follow any of the Algerian Arabic, but the cries of "Allah Akbar" by the FLN prisoner on his way to the guillotine sent a chill through my body. I released Laura's hand and drew inward. Tears welled up in my eyes. Here, at last, I thought to myself, is a true depiction of the suffering of "my people." I felt Arab again. Reeling with emotion, I couldn't even begin to imagine that in a year I would be sitting under a fig tree in Jordan.

Being and Becoming Arab

As a freshman at Wayne State University in fall 1968, I found myself increasingly drawn to left-radical circles—antiwar protesters, militant black nationalists, leftists, socialists, and Marxists. Mother worried about my growing radicalism, which she confounded with the hippie/drug culture sweeping the country. She raised it with Mrs. Colding, who sent word back to me that I should steer clear of socialists and other leftists. Mother prodded me to mix with the Arab students at the university, whom she believed would temper and rechannel my exuberance. She suggested that I raise funds for the charities operated by the burgeoning Palestinian resistance movement that she had heard about through her networks in the Arab community. Reluctantly, I agreed to contact the Arab student organization while holding out little hope of being favorably impressed by the group. The image of Arabs I carried in my head was of largely incompetent people, incapable of organizing a real people's resistance, the Algerian revolution notwithstanding. Against the revolutionary successes of the Vietnamese, Cubans, and Chinese, the Arabs came up pathetically short.

I responded to an invitation from the Organization of Arab Students (OAS) chapter to attend a general meeting. It was a beautiful autumn Sunday, sunny and warm. I resisted the temptation to spend the day relaxing in a park somewhere with Laura. She argued that I should attend the meeting and offered to accompany me. The meeting was already under way when we arrived at the Arab Clubhouse at 4600 Cass Avenue on the south side of the Wayne State University campus. Dressed in green army fatigues, Laura and I waded into a room packed end to end with about forty older-looking men seated in a semicircle on chairs, sofas, and the floor. I later learned that all were foreign-born. What struck me as highly unusual was that an Arab woman was chairing the meeting. Even more incredible was that she was a Saudi woman, whom I came to admire for her courage and intelligence. A graduate student in comparative literature, Soraya spoke fluent if slightly accented English and projected a no-nonsense demeanor, nothing like the image of weak and not terribly bright Arab females—*kitkoutas*, sweet and brittle like a Kit Kat bar—I had seen in Egyptian movies. Perhaps Mother was onto something; perhaps the Arabs, too, were undergoing a revolution of their own.

Gradually, I became active in the OAS and deeply involved with an Arab group in support of the Palestinian cause. Falling in love with Arabs and their culture, I strove to be Arab in every way possible. I enrolled in Arabic language courses at the university, studied Arabic in Cairo, developed an extensive network of Arab friends. My circle of non-Arab friends quickly shrank, and by Christmas of that year Laura and I broke up. The next ten years of my life, which broadly encompassed my undergraduate and graduate years, were organized around my decision to live and work in the Arab world. I saw myself as part of a wider movement to build a new Arab society. It was an unabashed utopian vision. Everything was built around my decision, even my switch in major from philosophy and history to anthropology. Here, at long last, I had found my place in the topsy-turvy world that was late 1960s America.

When I completed my graduate studies at the University of Michigan in early 1978 and left for Algeria, my intention was to live and work permanently in the Arab world. I taught at the University of Algiers with the rank of assistant professor in the Arabic section, which meant I lectured in Arabic, an arduous task under the best of conditions. This was to be a temporary assignment, a way station of sorts, arranged by my close friend, Mahfoud Bennoune, an Algerian and fellow graduate student, until I could figure out where I wanted to settle permanently. My preference was Beirut, but I was willing to accept meaningful work in several countries of the Arab East.

Algeria proved decisive in ways that I couldn't have foreseen. It was there that my personal plans, hopes, and dreams—worked out over the comfort of the previous decade—collided with reality. In the bureaucratic nightmare that is postcolonial Algeria, I realized just how efficient the U.S. government bureaucracy actually is. I discovered that my friendships with people across the Arab world often snagged on selfishly guarded national borders, residency rights, and kinship obligations. Although I found Algerians extremely hospitable toward Palestinians, much more so than the Arab countries which harbor large numbers of Palestinians, I remained an outsider.

Language posed one of the biggest obstacles, not only because Arabs as a whole are unaccustomed to hearing Arabic spoken

Fig. 22. Nabeel Abraham with fellow Arabic-language student in Egypt, 1971. Courtesy of Nabeel Abraham.

by a non-native speaker or in a dialect they cannot easily classify. Algerian Arabic is virtually incomprehensible to the untrained ear of speakers of eastern Arabic dialects. Compounding matters was the unstated fact that, although the country's language was officially Arabic, the elites, educated classes, and the government bureaucrats conducted business in French, the former colonial language. It was Algiers that convinced me that English, not Arabic, was my native language, as even the local Palestinians made me feel like a kind of "defective Arab" because of my unfamiliar Arabic (a pastiche of several dialects) and occasional gaffes in grammar and pronunciation. The ultimate frustration was to be considered an "American" by fellow Palestinians.

Two other developments forced me to abandon my plans to relocate to the Arab East. The first was the collapse of a long-distance romance with an Arab woman that paradoxically had been able to bloom in the United States but ruptured once the specter of confronting her tightly knit family and social connections became imminent. The other was my growing discomfort with the prospect of working closely with institutions aligned with the Palestine national movement, as I learned of the widespread corruption and cynicism within them. Both developments, combined with my experiences in Algeria, considerably dampened my utopian enthusiasm for settling permanently in the Arab world. Turning down two job offers, a professorship at Kuwait University and a research position at the Institute for Palestine Studies in Beirut, I packed my bags and headed home.

At Home in Arab America

Back in Detroit, I tried to salvage a ten-year-long quest that had shipwrecked on the rocky shoals of two failed romances—one with a nation, the other with a woman. Algeria had driven home the blunt realization that I wasn't an Arab. But what was I? An American? Intuition told me I was something in between, an "Arab American" perhaps? As I was wrestling with these issues, international events were gathering like storm clouds in a summer sky. Israel invaded southern Lebanon in May 1978 in an attempt to crush the PLO's presence in the country. More fighting was predicted for the region. A year later, an Islamic revolution toppled the Shah of Iran. Prices at the gasoline pump spiked upward. The American hostage crisis followed in Iran. Americans were treated to manifold images of billionaire oil sheikhs, armed Muslim clerics, Arab terrorists. Being "Arab" in America, in the best of times problematic, suddenly emerged as a daily dilemma for thousands of visible Arabs, Muslims, and native-born Americans like me who identified with them.

In the 1980s, in this climate, I found my place as an Arab American intellectual and activist, first as the director of the nationally based Association of Arab-American University Graduates and later as a special consultant to the American-Arab Anti-Discrimination Committee (ADC) in Detroit. Much of my time was spent explaining the Arabs, Islam, and the politics and culture of the Middle East to American audiences and the news media. I began to grow comfortable with a semimarginal place in American society as a hyphenated American, as an "Arab-American." I settled into a rewarding teaching job at Henry Ford Community College, married a wonderful woman, the daughter of a Canadian and an Egyptian. Paradoxically, Noula's father was relieved to have left Nasser's Egypt at a time when the country was a source of hope and pride for me and my family. Working with ADC during the 1980s, I, along with a small group of dedicated activists, attempted to organize the disparate Arabic-speaking communities behind a single national agenda under an Arab American umbrella. We partially succeeded in the first goal (organizing an effective chapter), but largely failed in the second (transcending parochial agendas). The "Arab American" agenda appealed to a very limited constituency—mostly educated, middle class, and "Americanized" individuals—and had little attraction for the new immigrant population, the strongly church- and mosque-oriented communities.

By the decade's end, I found myself increasingly marginalized in the Arab community of Detroit. I felt out of place as one of its spokesmen to the outside world. My alienation reached full force after the Gulf crisis and war that ensued in early 1991. I found myself sandwiched between the many Arabs and Arab Americans who sided with Iraq and the many Americans who supported the U.S.-led military assault on Iraq. In early autumn 1990, during the U.S. military buildup, I received a cool reception when I condemned Iraq's conquest and annexation of Kuwait in a speech to a gathering of Palestinians from Beit Sahour in Flint, Michigan. Likewise, I encountered similar cool receptions from Americans when I argued for a *negotiated* settlement of the crisis over a military solution. I had grown increasingly weary of Palestinian and Arab nationalist rhetoric and formulaic ways of thinking. I found myself preferring to advocate universal human rights and justice. I found myself more comfortable speaking as an anthropologist, an academic, and a politically conscious American, and very uncomfortable speaking as an Arab or Palestinian nationalist. To be sure, the Arab community had also changed enormously from the days of my childhood. It had even changed markedly since I conducted ethnographic fieldwork as a graduate student among the Yemeni community in the 1970s. By the mid-1980s the "community" that I knew (professionals more comfortable speaking English than Arabic, or those who had no facility in Arabic whatsoever) was itself marginal to the burgeoning population of new arrivals from south Lebanon, Palestine, Jordan, Iraq, Yemen, and Egypt.

Back to Palestine

In the immediate aftermath of the Gulf War, I found myself marginalized from the Arab community that I had once studied, lectured, and written about, and for a brief time served as an unofficial spokesman for. I felt more comfortable with like-minded academics and intellectuals—Americans, Jews, Arabs, Israelis, marginalized people who identified less with nation and ethnic group and more with universal principles. Against this background, I undertook my first trip to Palestine in 1993. It was a seminal journey in many ways. I had circled Israel/Palestine figuratively and geographically in my travels to the region since that fateful journey to Jordan in 1969. In the interim, I had visited Lebanon, Syria, Jordan, Egypt, Algeria, Tunisia, Yemen, Kuwait, Bahrain, Qatar, the United Arab Emirates, and Turkey, but never Palestine. Now, I was going to the epicenter of where it all began for me—the primary reason behind my search for place.

The visit was as anticlimactic as only visits of this nature can be. The Palestinians I met were weary and tired after thirty years of Israeli military occupation. The embers of the *intifada* in its seventh year were cooling. No one seemed happy, not the Palestinians, not their Israeli tormentors. The harsh human terrain matched the harshness of the rocky hills of the West Bank and the garbage-strewn sandy flatlands of Gaza. This was not the land of dreams, certainly not of mine.

On a return visit two years later, my mother and I visited an old olive grove in Beit Hanina that my father had left us as part of a larger estate in Beit Hanina. Since the June 1967 Arab-Israeli War, the estate has been whittled away by the occupying Israeli authorities in several land confiscations in the name of "security" and other pretexts. Our guide estimated the age of the trees at over three hundred years, possibly five hundred years. At dusk, shafts of light created a placid pattern of shadow and light in the grove. For a moment, I dreamed of leaving everything behind, of pitching a tent right there and then to work the land of my forefathers. I was dreaming about Palestine again; this time "Palestine" was confined to my father's old olive grove. As I looked up to the nearby hilltop in the southwest, my dream shattered against the imposing ramparts of the sprawling Jewish settlement of Ramot. To the east stood two more settlements—Pisgat Ze'ev and Neveh Ya'akov. Father's olive grove could only offer a harvest of nightmares now.

A Place outside the Old City

Mother and I are walking from Damascus Gate toward the Rockefeller Museum outside the Old Walled City of Jerusalem. Quite nonchalantly, Mother tells me that she walked past this place as a schoolgirl. I imagine her as a young girl against the backdrop of the giant blocks of yellow limestone. She is dwarfed by the wall. I feel close to her, closer than I have ever felt in my life. I try to imagine my grandmother and my uncle walking separately in the shadow of the Old City wall. Then I imagine my father as a village boy passing by this place. My eyes scan the sidewalk to determine how old it is.

Suha, one of Mother's distant relations, guides us to Bab az-Zahra graveyard above Salah-ed-Din Street, the main Arab business street outside the Old City. The place is overgrown with weeds, slate tombs poking out here and there through the overgrowth. It looks abandoned. Suha complains about Waqf, the Islamic society responsible for maintaining cemeteries, buildings, and other religious endowments. Silently, I'm unable to recall any well-maintained graveyards in all the Arab countries I've visited. At the far end we arrive at the place where Mother's father and other Aweidahs of his generation are buried. I help my mother clear the tombstone. Mother is distressed to find that the remains of her despised paternal Aunt Bahia have been buried in her father's tomb. Placing some hastily gathered wildflowers on the tomb, Mother laments in a soft voice, "She latched onto her brother in life and now in death."

Mother tells me that her grandparents and great-grandparents, along with her forefathers, are buried in Mamilla Cemetery located in the section of city that fell to Israel in 1948. I ask Suha to show us the Baqaa neighborhood where my mother grew up so I can

Fig. 23. Nabeel Abraham standing with his mother near Damascus Gate, Jerusalem, 1995. Courtesy of Nabeel Abraham.

see if her house is still standing. Mother had taken two of my brothers there on her first visit back in 1972. During my 1993 trip, her cousin had showed me what he thought was her house but Mother said that the picture I had was of another house. Suha says that the Baqaa neighborhood is far, deep in the Jewish part of town unfamiliar to her. Another of Mother's relatives, a young man, promises to take us there in his car but fails to show up for the rendezvous. The opportunity is lost, perhaps never to return.

Alone in Jerusalem

The Jerusalem I found was nothing like the al-Quds of my childhood imagination. Far from being placid and peaceful, it is a tense and anxiety-ridden place. Arabs are loath to cross into the Jewish side, Jews apprehensive about visiting the Arab side. Muslims live in fear that fanatical Jews will try to blow up the sacred Haram es-Sharif to make way for the rebuilding of Solomon's Temple. Jews, secular and religious, fear the bombs of angry Palestinians. Average Palestinians suffer incalculable humiliation, harassment, encroachment, arbitrary arrest and deportation at the hands of ideologically driven government authorities. Arab Christians lament their rapidly dwindling numbers. Religious bigotry and extremism abound on all sides. The racial housing patterns of Metropolitan Detroit and other American cities barely prepare one for the apartheid-like ethnic segregation that is contemporary Jerusalem.

As I walked down King George V Street in West Jerusalem, I thought of Suha's remark that the white baseball cap I was wearing for protection from the summer sun made me look like an Israeli Jew. Mother admonished me to be careful not to tell anyone on the Jewish side of town that I was an Arab. Such are the tensions in the City of Peace. After running an errand on Jaffa Street, I was on my way to the Israel National Museum before heading to the apartment of my friend, Israel Shahak, scholar, anti-Zionist, and human rights activist. I was in unfamiliar territory. A Palestinian suicide bomber had blown up a bus in this area not many months before. All eyes seemed to be on me and the brown handbag slung over my shoulder. I felt self-conscious of my own breathing, my gait, my feigned nonchalance. Would I be mistaken for a terrorist?

Dressed like an American in white Levis, and walking like one, too (Arabs and Jews each claim they can discern the gait of the other), I felt out of place. Suha was probably right: to Arabs I must have looked like an American Jew. But would the Israeli Jews on King George V Street draw the same conclusion? My limbs felt disjointed and out of step with the rest of my body. I was also playing a dangerous game. If a bomb went off, would I have time to explain who I was to the lynch mob? Who was I anyway? My emergency plan was to wave my dark-blue U.S. passport and holler, "I'm an American!" My head swirled with conflicting thoughts as I marched down King George V Street. To Israeli Jews, I am an Arab regardless of my passport, as I discovered at the airport when I was separated from other Americans and sent to the "Arab room" to be interrogated. My name had given me away. To my mother's relatives, I am Khadijeh's son; to my father's people, I'm Younis's son, even to those who were too young to have ever known him. To nonrelations among Palestinians, I am the American son of Palestinians; to Algerians, I'm a Palestinian; to the Jerusalem Islamic Court, I am a Muslim; to the U.S. Consulate in Jerusalem, I am an American.

Journey's End

I leaned backward on the wooden bench, surveying the great open oval at my feet, reveling in the warmth of the autumn day. Below, the University of Michigan Wolverines were battling the visiting Baylor College football team. Above, a clear sky yawned against a brilliant noonday sun. Seated between two friends, Bill Secrest and Jim Burke, I silently reflected on the ironies of the moment. Thirty years ago, the infamous Six Day War began, and with it my active quest to discover a place for myself. That quest, ironically, had steered me away from the very place where I was seated. I had spent five years as a graduate student at Michigan, never once attending a football game of the fabled Big Ten team. Yet, thirty years after the great Arab debacle that profoundly touched the lives of me and millions of others throughout the Arab world and Arab America, I journeyed to this stadium that had always been within reach.

Other ironies came to mind as I watched Michigan and Baylor spar on the oval playing field. I had declined an invitation to attend a three-day conference in honor of Edward Said, the celebrated Palestinian American academic and literary critic, taking place at that very moment in neighboring Windsor, Ontario, an hour's drive away. I felt uneasy about not attending since Said has been a friend for many years. Out of respect for him, I thought, I should be in attendance. I justified my absence by telling myself I would hear him speak in Ann Arbor the following Monday. What really kept me away from the conference, however, was its stated agenda—to discuss and debate the future of Palestinians in light of the 1995 Oslo Peace Accords. Thirty years of being and becoming an Arab, of "working" for Palestine, of traveling to and from the Arab world, of watching the slow withering of the revolutionary promises had left me feeling utterly detached from the conference's agenda. It's not that I no longer cared about the fate of Palestine and its people, both Arab and Jew. It's that I could no longer in good conscience hew to a narrow nationalist agenda.

I tried sharing these ironies with Jim but quickly realized that they would be too complicated to encapsulate in a few words. It would require too much explaining, and anyway he was engrossed in the game. Jim was himself another irony in this day of paradoxes. A year younger than me, he had been a physical anthropology student in the same Department of Anthropology at Michigan but then, seeing a future filled with poor job prospects, shifted to the business school and became a successful accountant. We only met through Bill many years later. Jim and Bill had met as undergraduates in college thirty years ago, their friendship blossoming and maturing during the years I was searching for the stability of place in my life. We were what anthropologists call "age-mates," and ironically our lives, at least superficially, intersected on many levels. In our own ways, we had protested the Vietnam War, experienced the joys and sorrows of repeated romances, traveled to faraway places, espoused liberal causes. We were truly children of the sixties and of our generation. On a deeper level, however, I couldn't help feeling that my journey over these past three decades was at once burdened and enriched by a history and cultural inheritance far bigger than the cities I lived in and the schools I attended, bigger than America itself, in fact.

I thanked Jim and Bill for the invitation to the game, telling them how much I had enjoyed myself. Out of earshot of Jim, Bill asked if I would attend another football game. "Probably not," I whispered. "Me neither," Bill whispered back, not wanting Jim, the avid football fan, to overhear us. I smiled.

Hope, Figs, and a Place Called Home

Jeffrey Ghannam

In the backyard of my grandparents' home, my family planted a fig tree.

Each spring for more than thirty years, the bush would grow fleshy leaves and buds that left my family praying for nothing short of a miracle.

And yet by fall, the buds would have barely grown.

Almost ritually, its branches would be bundled and brought close to the ground before the first frost in the hope that it would return the following year when its branches would finally weigh heavy with fruit.

Much later in my life, during my first trip to Ramallah, I visited my grandparents' former home there. Outside that three-room stone structure stands an enormous fig tree, flourishing.

My mother also took pains to raise exotic flora, a lemon tree she grew from seed. It, too, never bore fruit or grew more than four feet tall in the pot placed in our kitchen. But its leaves were special. She and her friends would pluck a leaf to rub between their fingers for its essence.

That tree transported my mother back, for a moment, into the scene of a small photo she liked to show us. It pictured her and her younger sister in the citrus groves their family once owned near the Mediterranean coast. It was land my grandfather bought with money he earned as a successful peddler. He died in a plane crash en route to do more peddling in the United States, a month before the war that changed so many lives in 1948. The land he bought was lost in the partition of Palestine. The family home nestled in the groves of orange and lemon trees stands in ruins, pockmarked and riddled with graffiti.

In Michigan the fig and lemon trees would ultimately succumb to the northern climate. But the will to grow them year after year speaks to my family's determination to recapture a sense of the lives they left in Ramallah and Palestine as they settled for good in suburban Detroit.

For me, that sense of the past is always present.

Metro Detroit has the largest concentration of Ramallah descendants; more live here than remain in the town itself. Once a resort known for its cool sea breezes, fine arak and relatively liberal values, Ramallah has since grown into a commercial and political center bursting at the seams under the Palestinian National Authority (PNA). The town is the dateline of countless news stories that describe the latest street battles or the meetings between foreign dignitaries and PNA officials.

Ramallah figures prominently in the headlong rush toward nation building. But lost in the name of progress is what distinguished the town. Red-tile-roofed shops and homes have been cleared away for boxy, concrete mini-malls and other less-than-artful architecture. Over the years, the graceful lines and intimate feel of the town have slowly vanished in the building boom. New restaurants and hotels have revived Ramallah's nightlife, making it once again an entertainment spot.

That alone is a far cry from the mid-1980s when Ramallah was a virtual ghost town at night.

But will it lead to the lasting change Palestinians need? When will civil rights protect the average citizen from the flagrant abuses of the PNA? Several human rights agencies accuse the PNA of torturing prisoners, of using secret trials, of intimidating political opponents, and of censoring media. Not the harbingers of a democracy, just repression in self-rule clothing.

Taking the place of this formerly sleepy town where languid afternoons were once easily passed in outdoor plaza restaurants, is the hustle and bustle of Cairo or Amman. Soon, if it has not already happened, Ramallah will have American fast-food franchises that erase the authenticity we, its American children, seek.

But my views would probably be dismissed. My family left Ramallah, as did many others. In the opinion of some of those who stayed or took refuge there from the coastal cities in 1948, we abandoned the town.

On my trip in 1994, a friend half-jokingly introduced me to a businessman in Ramallah as belonging to one of the town's original families *illee sharadou*, that is, which fled.

But when my parents came to the United States with their families they had no idea they would never return to live.

Those Palestinians who deride us as escaping to easier lives in the United States overlook the costs we would pay for our freedom. We have lost count of the loved ones murdered over the years in liquor store, bakery, or restaurant robberies.

We see our families on special occasions, or sad ones, scattered as we are across the fifty states.

As Holy Land Christians, we may assimilate relatively easily, but we run the risk of blending ourselves into extinction as Americans.

Still, we are unappreciated as descendants of some of the world's *first* Christians in a largely Christian United States.

"Do you celebrate Christmas?" goes the refrain each year from acquaintances and others.

"We invented Christmas," some of my cousins like to respond.

What is lost in the chasm that separates those of us here and those in Ramallah is that our experiences are just another chapter in our shared and variously tragic history.

Many in my parents' and grandparents' generations carry with them a sense of sadness and loss that is palpable. Like a lot of their contemporaries who emigrated from war-torn lands or repressive regimes, they left the lives they knew as youths or adults in their prime and never quite embraced American culture, or were not welcomed, wholeheartedly. Those of us born in the United States have mastered the complexities of living in two cultures. Unlike our parents, we have lived, worked, and traveled in the region. We are as comfortable in Cairo as we are in Chicago.

In addition to Detroit, Ramallah communities thrive in metropolitan areas around San Francisco, Chicago, Jacksonville, Cleveland, Houston, New York City, Washington, D.C., Knoxville, and Birmingham.

At the turn of the century, a handful of families made up Detroit's Ramallah community. Its numbers swelled after the establishment of Israel. The community grew larger after the 1967 war when Ramallah was occupied by the Israeli military. Today, Metro Detroit is home to between five thousand and six thousand Ramallah descendants of some thirty thousand nationally.

As the years unfolded, so did our roots in this land. What survived the journey halfway around the world were our kinships, our traditions, and our peasant dialect.

In the late 1940s, as families like my own settled into owning grocery and liquor stores, had Sunday picnics on Belle Isle, and bought homes in leafy west-side neighborhoods, we possessed a longing for what was left behind—a yearning that was complicated by the political uncertainty there and the opportunity here. We accepted, reluctantly, that we would never go "home."

Filling that sense of loss were the stories, the photographs, and the weddings that further knitted the community. In July 1997, the American Federation of Ramallah, Palestine, held its thirty-ninth annual convention in Michigan and drew more than thirty-two hundred people from all over the United States and Ramallah.

A Ramallah Web site, www.afrp.org, includes messages from folks who have some link, virtual or otherwise, to the town. The Web site even includes photos of Ramallah's main street, and its schools and churches, to the amazement of my parents, who had not visited since they arrived in the United States as teenagers more than fifty years ago. They finally traveled to Ramallah in early 1999.

Unlike Palestinians from other towns and villages, the elders from Ramallah do not return to build homes or visit in equal numbers. With few close relatives remaining in Ramallah, many don't consider returning for anything longer than an extended visit now and then. Many others say that to confront what was left years ago is overwhelming. In some ways, the hope to return *someday* is more sustaining than an actual visit to confront the ghosts that remain in the shuttered family home and the unfamiliarity in the faces that now inhabit it.

Out of our recollections comes a new Ramallah, one built on the present but linked to the past. From coast to coast, Ramallah families find something that makes them feel at home. In Metro Detroit, it's the size of the community where some Ramallah families are neighbors; in San Diego it's the weather, bright and dry, and in Birmingham, it's the green rolling hills. In subdivisions everywhere, their homes are the ones built with ochre brick or stone, with arched windows or raised brick verandas, elements that echo the look and feel of the family home in Ramallah.

So much of what defines us as a community is how our lives span the New World and the old country, a worldliness that was thrust upon us in the aftermath of World War II. But if we are at home everywhere, can we ever be truly at home?

My parents' recollections over the years turned the small town into one of mythic proportions.

Growing up in Michigan's interminable winters, stories of Ramallah conjured up images of an almost mystical and impossibly distant place drenched in warm, bright light. For me, the stories were a source of comfort. They made me feel that I belonged to some other more vibrant place.

In the early 1970s, my grandparents traveled to the town, their first visit since my grandmother emigrated to Detroit in 1946. My grandfather had come over much earlier, like a lot of men of his generation. He served as a private in the U.S Army during World War II.

At about age ten, I found a photo from their trip preserved beneath a sheet of glass atop my grandfather's chest of drawers. I recall gazing at the photo, almost spellbound by the cluster of olive trees amid large stones that were used to terrace the hillside. The scene was so unlike my own backyard. Foreign but strangely familiar.

I envied them and other relatives who would travel to spend the summer and return tan, rested, and at peace. They spoke Arabic elegantly, not some thick combination of Arabic and English.

I had not known it then, but I lived vicariously through my relatives' travels. They regaled us with stories of the sweet figs, the grapes the size of small light bulbs, and the afternoons spent at the Dead Sea.

The photograph I found planted a seed of longing for a place that I had never visited.

More than twenty years later, I picked up a lost thread of family history. I returned to Ramallah for the third time. This trip, like the others, had been inspired by so many of the stories I had listened to and photographs I pored over. But this time, I returned to live and work like the men whose stories infused my own life, to take part in the annual olive harvest in the West Bank. I worked at my family's former olive press and helped produce the river of oil that pours forth in villages and towns across the region.

My great-grandfather brought with him Ramallah's first mechanized press on his return from the United States nearly a century earlier. It rumbled to life each autumn and drew farmers who carried sacks of olives on their shoulders and peasant women who carried them on their heads. The oil is central to their lives, and I rediscovered my family's role in such a significant aspect of Palestinian life, one the world rarely gets to see. For a few short weeks in the fall of 1994, I reclaimed my family's contributions. I stained my hands and clothes with the green oil and nearly broke my back wrestling with sacks of olives the way my forefathers had done.

The press had been sold to another family in the 1950s, and they too were eager to make their mark in business with more efficient production. The following fall, the old press was replaced with an automated Italian machine that takes in olives on one end and spits out oil on the other. Lost are the crackling sounds of olives as they get crushed by two large stones the size of wheels on a pickup truck that spun around inside a large vat. Instead of a rumble and chug-chug-chug of the old press, there is a high-pitched whir.

Ramallah is where I go to reconnect with my history. I have visited three times since 1985 and consider it "home" in the sense that it gives me what I cannot find in metropolitan America, a sense of connection to the town's narrow streets and neighborhoods named after some of my ancestors. It's where I rejoin friends and relatives who graciously welcome me back, making it seem like days not years have passed since my last visit.

At the press and my great-grandfather's adjoining home, which has since been demolished so stores could be built in its place, I found an eerie sense of belonging. I also found my share of ghosts

Fig. 24. Children gather outside the door to the Ramallah olive oil press once owned by a great-grandfather and other relatives of Jeffrey Ghannam. Courtesy of Jeffrey Ghannam.

and a near-constant reconciliation of what was, is, and could have been, had my family stayed.

My trips assuage my longing, as if I have found a long-lost friend. Thousands of miles away, I often reconnect, as on the days in Michigan when the sunlight turns crystalline, when the Michigan wind is cool like a sea breeze that washes over Ramallah's hills, and when in a gathering of family and friends.

Ramallah is impossibly faraway, the way I have always known it to be, but it's also close at hand. It is welcoming in its embrace and often unforgiving in its reality.

It is the hope we have for the fig tree year after year after year, the joy we get from the leaf of a lemon tree, and the longing that stirs within us unexpectedly.

Ramallah is wherever we are.

What's Not in a Name

Marilynn Rashid

Arab American

Although I am married, I call myself Marilynn Rashid, "to keep my own name," I say. But, of course, it's only my father's name, so this partly defeats the purpose—the patriarchy can't be broken this way. It's small solace, a partial solution, no solution. So I should add my mother's name, Philipson (son of Philip?). But, of course, that wasn't her mother's name either, just her father's. So I should use Manders, my grandmother's name. But I know that name carries the same half-weight. Marilynn Manders Philipson Rashid. What's in a name? A lot, but somehow not enough.

These names hearken back to Lebanon, Ireland, Luxembourg, places of origin of people lost to me, places with which I have little or no connection, places that were distant shadows even for the ones who held the names and passed them on. I am a piece of the cultural entropy of the age, forever falling away from many centers.

If we truly knew who we were, our names would not be such a problem. It is difficult to find one's way in a world divided not only by war and racism, but by freeways, television, and the technological projects of so-called progress. If we could, in fact, go back where we came from, as some would like us to do, we would still not find ourselves, for those places are changed or destroyed or occupied or part of the same industrial grid we find ourselves in here. And too, some of us, many of us, would have to cut ourselves in twos and threes and ship pieces all over the globe. And surely that wouldn't help our sense of fragmentation.

An abbreviated version of this essay appeared in *Food for Our Grandmothers* (Boston: Southend Press, 1994), 197–203.

So we stay where we are, at least for now, and we know it as home. We stick with the names we've been given and we ask a lot of questions of the old people, if there are any left. And we listen carefully so that we can tell others. And we ask that others listen, too. The details are important.

Names limit meaning and delete important details. Yet the naming often comes from a need to make links and find common ground, to facilitate communication. And this is how the term "Arab American" came into being. Yet I must admit that I have rarely called myself an Arab American. Such a weighty term speaks for large abstractions, and I am uneasy in its presence.

When I think concretely of the word "Arab," I think of Arabic, the language that is, in my mind, one obvious thing that links most Arabs. Having studied English and several Romance languages, I know well the importance of language to a genuine understanding of a culture. But, except for a few wonderfully scatological and off-color words my Uncle Frederick taught my sisters and brothers and me, except for the names of certain Arabic dishes and a few endearing terms my *siti* (grandmother) used with us, and except for the sayings my father forever repeated to us, regrettably, I do not speak the language of my father's family. And I feel somewhat awkward calling myself Arab or Arabic.

Instead of Arab and American I'd rather deal with words of smaller places or regions you can see and smell, places you can imagine or actually get around in. Michigan, or Michigami, as the original inhabitants called it, the imprint of the hand of the Great Spirit; and Lebanon, *the* Lebanon, Marjayoun, J'daidit; and Detroit, the strait. We can see why these places were named the way they were. We know of the hills, the valley, and the mountain. We can see the river.

I am most comfortable, I suppose, defining myself as a Detroiter, since this is where I was born and where I've spent most of my life. In spite of its many social problems, or perhaps even because of them, I am proud to have survived here, to have made real connections with others. I am proud to have, in small ways, spoken out against racism and ecological destruction and for community here. Place, after all, is crucial to our understanding of who we are, and I must acknowledge that this fractured urban landscape has had much to do with my sense of the world and my place in it.

I am highly conscious of the fact that I have grown up in a place that is known throughout the country and perhaps the world as a violent, dangerous, and now quite impoverished city. I'm aware, too, that Lebanon, the homeland of my grandparents, is also known to the world as a place plagued by violence, torn by civil strife, a fractured land. My grandparents' former home is in occupied territory. It isn't Lebanon anymore. It is a place whose new name has an uncanny Orwellian ring to it; it is a "security zone." The nightly news tags people and places, and it functions by simplifying and sensationalizing. But sound bites and news clips cannot explain me or my world; I am not a product of violence. Violence has not created you or me or our families or the places we came from. We exist, all of us, in spite of the violence.

I am also hesitant to call myself an American or to identify myself as a citizen of a nation-state that claims this continent's name as its own. I am not at all proud to be an American; with its military power and cloak of legitimacy, "America" selectively condemns and fosters violence at home and in other places. I wave neither yellow ribbons nor flags because these speak for the blind forces of empire and its institutionalized violence. It is through slavery, plunder, and murder on this continent and abroad that "America" has become the most powerful nation in the world. How can we rediscover a toponymy that leaves the symbols of empire behind, a naming rooted in nature, one that helps to link us intrinsically to the places where we were born and the places where we live?

Semites and Anti-Semites

Identifying himself as "Lebanese" was problematic for my father early on because when my *djido* and *siti* came to the United States at the turn of the century, the region they had come from, called "the Lebanon," was considered part of Syria. It had also been occupied by Egypt for a time, controlled by France, and invaded by the Turks. In fact, it was to avoid conscription in the Ottoman Army that my grandfather came to this country. With such a history, I imagine that the concept of national identity was somewhat peculiar and arbitrary for my grandparents' generation. My *siti* occasionally forgot about the state of Lebanon and would sometimes give her nationality as Syrian, since that's the way things seemed when she left.

When we were children, my father told my brothers and sisters and me that we were not only Lebanese or Syrian, but also Semitic, and he told us stories about the Semites and Phoenicians who traveled the seas all over the world trading their wares. He was proud of these names and histories, and it seems to me now, looking back, that he told us these things to help us find our way in a world so far from the places that shaped his parents' families and their lives. And we could make small links to tales from faraway and long ago. He explained that Arabic, the language he and his family spoke, is a Semitic language, and that the Phoenicians were merchants like him. For my father, being a merchant was a skill, handed down through generations from long ago.

The word "Semitic" captivated me so much that for a time I incorporated it into my sense of self. I remember once in grade school I filled in the "other" blank on a form requesting race or nationality with the word "half-Semitic." I had passed up the boxes marked "Caucasian" and "black" and had filled in my own special race. When someone later told me that I could check the box marked "Caucasian," I was very disappointed.

My first year in college I met a young man named Paul in an English class. We went for coffee a few times after class and seemed to have a lot to talk about. One afternoon he told me he'd spent the summer on a kibbutz in Israel. He became very animated as he explained the details of his daily routine there, the camaraderie, and the cooperative spirit that fed the survival of each kibbutz.

At nineteen I was not very worldly or politically aware, and at first I was genuinely impressed. But then he told me about one of the rotated duties to which he had occasionally been assigned, that of keeping watch at night with a rifle at the perimeters of the kibbutz. He said that "Arabs" would occasionally try to get in. They posed a threat to the peaceful existence of the kibbutz, he told me, and, he added, they were "anti-Semitic." Confused, I asked him what he would have done if an Arab had approached his guard post. "I'd have blown his head off," he announced with pride and conviction. I then asked him if he knew that I was half-Lebanese, half-Arabic. I wish I had said "half-Semitic," but I had long since dropped that term from my self-description. An awkward, embarrassed pause followed. He changed the subject. We parted quickly and he never really spoke to me again, always avoiding situations in which we might have to look at each other.

There is something terrifying and yet utterly enlightening in the experience of being recognized on the street by a familiar face in a split second and then immediately, mechanically rejected, when the head shifts angles fast, pulling the eyes hard to avert your persistent gaze. It is the smooth, cold gesture of denial, a small but clear admission of disavowal or hatred, a bold repudiation of past human connection. If such experiences don't break you or occur too frequently to harden you to similar hatred, they can serve at least to jolt you from complacency, to make you question and help you understand your place in the world. They also alert you to similar and more extreme actions exhibited against others around you, and you begin at least to consider the world in ways you never did before.

Initially Paul's use of the word "anti-Semitic" disturbed me most because it tugged at, twisted, and forked some trail, some vague path not only to my past and my father's past, but to my faith in his words and stories. How could Arabs, who are Semitic, be anti-Semitic? But ultimately, more than the confusion over terms, what plagued me was the realization of the need that many people have to hate and to feed and cultivate that hate, to hold it tightly close to their hearts, to defend it, to brick it in, to count on it, to sleep with it, to dream of it, to weave it with their breath carefully, methodically, intricately until it captures the open gaze they had when they were children.

I came to understand that when a nation-state seizes land, it confiscates identity. Just as the United States conquered, colonized, so many words in "America," so Israel had annexed, appropriated the term "Semitic." But this is not so according to everyone, of course; Semitic is one thing, anti-Semitic is something else. I had to remind myself, before I became too deeply immersed in the argument, that language is not always logical and that words do limit meaning, often leaving gaping holes in their echo.

I was, after all, horrified and outraged by the massive torture, brutalization, and genocide of the Jews in Europe. I asked myself, then, if I am opposed to both subtle and blatant acts of racism against all peoples, why should I mind if the term "anti-Semitic" helps to expose hatred against the Jews even if it absents the Arabs?

While struggling with these ideas, I met Fredy Perlman,

a man who not only had lived through the consequences of one of history's most terrifying campaigns of institutionally imposed racism, but had thought about it a lot and become acutely aware of the insidious and pervasive character of many forms of oppression of many peoples. Fredy was a writer and a teacher and a printer. He was also a friend, who taught me and others not only to think and think deeply, but to be very careful with our ideas.

One of his essays titled "Anti-Semitism and the Beirut Pogrom" was crucial to my growing understanding of racism and, in many ways, inspired me to grapple with similar questions in the context of my own life through my writing. The essay, prompted by the Israeli bombing of Beirut in 1982, is essentially a personal, autobiographical statement against racism and oppression in the Middle East, Europe, and the New World.

Its fundamental message is simple and cogent: people who are victimized often become victimizers, using their victimization as a tool and a rationalization for the hatred, torment, and oppression of others. Reading the essay for the first time, I sensed a strong and urgent imperative addressed to the reader, to humankind, to break the cycle of this deeply ingrained psychological tyranny. Fredy was not only referring to flagrant atrocities committed against different peoples throughout history, but also to those smaller daily acts of racism, to the routine that bolsters an entire political or economic system; and he used the experience of people in his own family to exemplify it.

A month before the Nazis arrived in his native Czechoslovakia, Fredy's immediate family and several relatives escaped to Bolivia. The rest of his extended family died in concentration camps. He recalls that as a child living in Bolivia, he observed one of his relatives cheating the Quechua Indians and speaking disdainfully of them. This relative later became a promoter of the state of Israel and turned her hatred against the Palestinians, a people she had never met and about whom she knew little or nothing.

When I read about Fredy's family, I thought of my father's family. In the small Illinois town in which they settled, my grandparents and their children were often singled out and ridiculed as dirty foreigners who didn't speak English. The experience did not make them more understanding of other cultures. On the contrary, after moving to Detroit, several uncles became vehement racists who moved their families to various white suburbs as soon as they could afford it and then refused to come into the city to visit us, for fear, they said, of the blacks.

In discussions and in his writings, Fredy explained how the force of nationalist fervor had created exiled refugees, like the Central European Jews, in places all over the globe, and he made links between the oppression of indigenous populations in the Americas and in Israel. Fredy was the first person I heard who turned the term "anti-Semitic" on its head; he used it to describe the actions of the state of Israel against the Palestinians, stating that the ancient Hebrews, Arabs, Akkadians, Phoenicians, and Ethiopians were all Semitic because they came from the land of Shem, the Arabian Peninsula, and had spoken the language of Shem.

Though we might know that words are consciously chosen and language deliberately manipulated for political and ideological purposes by those in power, we rarely realize the inevitable deleterious effects they have on our own consciousness, our own self-conception. One would hope that in their linked origins and histories of oppression, a sense of kinship and understanding would arise among Semites and descendants of Semites. This will not happen through the bureaucratic processes of nation-states, but it can happen between individuals who have learned to value and respect each other and each other's pasts, their visions, and their hopes for the reemergence of community. We rediscover the openness that once guided our gaze when we were children and so affirm the Other, the refugee, the exile, the immigrant in each other and in ourselves. This may be an unremarkable statement, but it says something about who we are and who we must become.

Relating the Unnamed Half

It may seem peculiar, but it was through my Irish-German American mother that I came to understand and respect my father's family and to appreciate the trials they endured adjusting to life in this new country. I am not speaking of a blanket acceptance of a woman who leaves her home, muffles her own identity, and takes on the customs and concerns of her husband's family. My mother has always been too strong and independent to take on such a role, and her ties to her own family and her own remarkable past were as solid and fixed as was her desire to love and create a life and a home with my father.

My mother grew up on a farm in Indiana. Out of economic necessity, she left her parents' home at the age of eighteen and came to Detroit to work and study. She first worked as a live-in nanny while attending university classes and later was a secretary for a trucking firm. When she met my father, she had a demanding position as a medical technician in a Detroit clinic. By that time, she has told us, she had decided that she just might never marry and that she just might be quite content living as a single career woman. It still surprises her to think that she could have fallen in love with the Arab grocer down the street.

There were, of course, numerous problems and conflicts that resulted from the union of two such different individuals. Almost immediately, my mother found herself in a painful struggle with her mother-in-law, my *siti,* the matriarch, who both loved and manipulated her children and who, after years of almost daily contact, only grudgingly accepted her eldest son's non-Lebanese wife. In spite of the clashes, or perhaps because of them, over time my mother has developed a healthy identification with the Lebanese and other Arabic peoples, and this in a society that still feeds on ignorance and is ever-eager to find a people to hate.

Perhaps this willingness to understand and accept other peoples and their cultures came to her from her Irish Protestant mother and her German Catholic father, who also had cultural and religious differences to contend with, and who, together, grew to appreciate the native peoples in northwest Nevada. In 1920, these two farmer schoolteachers left their farm and their jobs in Indiana and headed west with their five children to work for the government on an Indian reservation. They had illusions, I am sure, of doing good work, of helping the unfortunate and the uneducated. They went to teach English and farming techniques, but they learned much more than they were capable of teaching, and those were painful, real-life lessons.

My grandparents soon found that the government agency was not formed to help but rather to control the people they were learning to love and respect, and that, despite their diligent efforts to make beneficial changes, the local white farmers and businesspeople would continue to cheat and trick the Indians. My grandfather became an advocate with no real power. The family was moved from one reservation to another, probably to keep them from forming too strong a loyalty, too solid an allegiance. After seven years, my grandparents resigned their positions and moved their family back to the farm in Indiana. The depression years would bring financial ruin and the eventual loss of the farm.

My mother was an infant when the family first arrived in Nevada, and while my grandmother taught English and other subjects to the Indian children in the one-room schoolhouse on the reservation, a Paiute woman named Suzy cared for my mother. It was Suzy, and not her teacher-parents, who taught my mother her first words. And those words were Paiute, not English. Although she cannot recall the words, she has a strong sense-memory of Suzy and of her first seven years of life in that dry, expansive country, where she learned from and played with Paiute, Shoshone, and Washu children.

I am not certain, but looking at my grandparents' correspondence from those years and talking with my mother about their recollections, I suspect my grandparents considered or sometimes considered the Nevada adventure a failed experiment, another period of loss in what was overall a difficult and impoverished life. My mother remembers her father pacing through the farmhouse at night, wringing his hands and asking himself, or fate, or some absent god, "Will I ever breathe a free breath?" But I am quite certain of one thing: my grandparents and Suzy gave my mother something that has enriched her life and mine and the lives of my sisters and brothers. The only words I can come up with to describe that gift are openness, acceptance, something akin to wisdom.

Part 6

ETHNIC FUTURES

Fig. 25. A Yemeni dance troupe performs at the Dix Festival, 1979. Photograph by Millard Berry.

Introduction

WE BEGAN THIS book by suggesting that Arab American identity is something made in public spaces. Although scholars repeatedly try to explain this identity by examining what is Arab about it, we think more is accomplished by focusing on the American contexts that create it. What is American about Arab identity in Detroit? First, it is portrayed as a kind of ethnic identity. Arab Detroit is not thought to be representative of American society at large, even though, as Schopmeyer's essay on community demography in part 1 shows, Arab Detroit is indistinguishable from the larger population in many ways. Second, Arab identity in Detroit is framed in relation to American culture. Whatever this book is about, it is not about the Arab experience in Mexico, Cuba, El Salvador, or Canada. Yet most Arab American readers will not perceive our narrow focus as a slight to Arab immigrant communities in other countries. This is because most Arab Americans are interested in a history that connects them, and by extension Lebanon, Yemen, Palestine, or Iraq, to the United States. Finally, Arab American identity is a product of the English language, the medium in which it flourishes. Arabs who speak only Arabic, and the thousands of Arabs in the New World and Europe who speak only Spanish or French, belong to Arab communities of a different kind altogether.

These points come together in the case of Janet, an Iraqi Chaldean born and raised in Detroit. Janet speaks only English, and she is a proud member of the Arab American community. Janet has several cousins whose parents migrated to Mexico in the same year Janet's father came to Detroit. Except for a handful of Chaldean greetings, these cousins speak only Spanish. Janet does not consider them to be Chaldean, much less Arab: "They think they are Chaldean, but really they are just Mexicans. They dress like Mexicans. They walk like Mexicans. They eat Mexican food. They even have Spanish names. I wouldn't call them Chaldean at all." Janet seems entirely unaware that her Mexican cousins see her as an American who "just thinks" she is Chaldean/Arab. Janet speaks English, dresses and eats like an American, presumably walks like one, and even has an English name. That Janet and her Mexican cousins are all convinced that they are good Chaldean/Arabs shows the extent to which their ethnic identity is shaped by the larger society—Mexico in one case, the United States in the other—and not by models of identity prevalent in the homeland, Iraq.

More ironic, still, is the fact that Janet and her cousins, when pressed to define and represent their Chaldean/Arab identity to others, would do so in virtually identical ways. They would prepare certain foods, highlight distinctive kinds of music and dance, display certain handicrafts, and perhaps trace the family histories and kinship ties that brought them to the New World and that simultaneously root them in their ancestral village, Telkaif. These symbols and traditions encapsulate ethnic identity not because they carry the "essence" of Chaldeanness, or Koreanness, or Italianness, but rather because they can all be displayed, bought and sold, and reproduced in new languages (when ancestral ones are forgotten) and public formats (when the private life of the community is no longer rich enough to sustain the imagination of its members). In fact, this new brand of ethnic identity has its greatest appeal among people whose links to the "old country" are intellectual, nostalgic, disgruntled, vexed, or merely ideological. For Arabs born and raised in Detroit, these imaginative links are often cultivated as a way of escaping the close quarters of immigrant family life, where "the homeland" is someone else's memory, and *Amreeka*, a morally suspect zone, is consistently off limits.

The essays in this section deal with the sometimes subtle, sometimes radical transformations that occur as "Arab immigrant cultures" become "ethnic American cultures." These transformations take place in the medium of public life, on the open market, and (most important of all) in the English language. Sally Howell's essay on ethnic arts-programming in Detroit shows how Arab American expressive culture is framed by categories that originated outside the Arab community, is legitimized by mainstream academics and scholars, and is supported financially by government and private endowments whose funding agendas are set in cooperation with community-based agencies (like ACCESS) that represent politically significant interest groups. Anne Rasmussen, analyzing the private sector, explores the growing market in Arab musical sounds—tapes, videos, live performances—and the development of a wedding industry that caters specifically to Detroit's Arab community. Whereas musical tastes in the Arab World are eclectic and slanted noticeably toward North America and Europe, the musical scene in Detroit is heavily invested in its Arabness, in its connections to the homeland. Market forces are combining effectively with nostalgia and ethnicity to produce audiences and performers who define themselves as Arab American. William and Yvonne Lockwood examine the evolution of "Arabic food" in Detroit, linking its emergence to market forces and the numerical and culinary superiority of the Lebanese community. They go far beyond this focus, however, by juxtaposing "Arabic food" as a restaurant commodity to "Arab food" as a family tradition confined almost entirely to private, domestic space. Andrew Shryock moves even further into private worlds through his study of kinship in Arab Detroit. He argues that the intimate realm of family life is, for most Arabs in Detroit, the ultimate locus of ethnic identity formation. It is the site at which Arabs first and most consistently perceive their own difference from mainstream society. For this reason, patterns of kinship and marriage are often the most psychologically formative aspects of Arab American identity and the patterns most likely to be hidden from public view.

We realize that our insistence on a distinction between "Arab immigrant culture" and "American ethnic culture," one rooted in Arabic and the other in English, will strike many readers, especially Arabs on the English-speaking side of the line, as an artificial boundary. Yet one example shows rather starkly how intermeshed but separate these worlds can be. Arabs in Detroit often refer to themselves as *al-jalia al-arabiyya*. This phrase is emblazoned on banners at community dinners, on the masthead of newsletters and journals, and on the graphics for locally produced TV shows. Most Arab Americans will tell you the word *jalia* means "community," and for thousands of English-speaking Arabs in Detroit this is all the word has ever meant. But in Arabic, the word *jalia* actually denotes something akin to "colony of foreigners," "ghetto," "ethnic enclave," or "delegation from abroad." It is a label applied to people who have settled far from their place of origin, do not mix with the local population, and have every intention of returning to the homeland. The two meanings (community and colony) are far from synonymous, but they pass by each other without a hint of friction. Newly arrived immigrants typically think of Detroit as a *jalia*, a place far from their "real" home. Arabs who have grown up in Detroit and do not speak Arabic well, or speak it as a house language, tend also to think of Arab Detroit as a *jalia*, a "community" solidly attached to American society in just the way Latino, Asian, and other special communities are. A semantic watershed has been passed without the slightest notice.

For Arab Americans in Detroit, building a cohesive *jalia* is a ticket to the ethnic mainstream, and they have the foods, folk arts, music, and family ties to prove they belong there. In America, proof of this sort can go a long way. The future of Arab Detroit, for the entire length of its complex history, has been (and probably will continue to be) ethnic. One could just as easily conclude, however, that Arab Detroit has always been (and will probably continue to be) fertile ground for Arab immigrant cultures. Negotiations across this cultural and linguistic border are more intense today than ever before, and the authors of the essays that follow, for all their analytical detachment, cannot pretend to be neutral observers. Their goal is to shed light on the process of negotiation itself, to encourage and prolong it, and to catalog a few of its more remarkable creations. The truly distinctive *jalia*, they seem to suggest, lies somewhere between Arabic and English meanings in the ongoing negotiations that are (and will probably continue to be) at the center of life in Arab Detroit.

The Art and Artistry of Arab Detroit

Changing Traditions in a New World

Sally Howell

In 1994 Nadim Dlaikan received the Michigan Heritage Award, an honor bestowed on the state's outstanding folk artists by the Michigan State University Museum. Nadim was the first artist from Arab Detroit to receive such recognition from the mainstream. Like other Arab immigrant artists, Dlaikan is engaged in a constant negotiation between his own artistic vision and the expectations of highly diverse Arab American audiences. This conflict, which is both limiting and challenging, is colored further by Nadim's traditional musical education, the goals and styles of his peers, and the place he has found for himself among mainstream Detroit audiences. His story, which I will explore in some detail, contains all the major themes of this essay.

From Community Performer to Mainstream Folk Artist

Nadim was born in 1941 in Alai, Lebanon, a village not far from Beirut. At an early age he became interested in playing the *nay*, a reed flute common throughout the Middle East. His family discouraged his interest in music, however, telling him that only ignorant shepherds play the flute. His parents expected him to get an education. In response, Nadim went out and made his own instrument, copying the details of another flute using local reeds. He then taught himself the rudiments of the *nay*.

When television first arrived in Alai, Nadim was delighted to see Naim Bitar, Lebanon's leading *nay* virtuoso, playing for a national audience. His family conceded that there might indeed be a future in music for someone with Nadim's commitment. His sister began taking him daily to the Lebanese Conservatory in Beirut to study with Bitar. There, Nadim strengthened his skills, repertoire, and opportunities. When he graduated from the conservatory and from high school, he moved to Beirut and worked as a professional musician. He traveled throughout the Middle East as a member of Lebanon's best-known folk troupe. In this way, he was exposed to the musical diversity of the Arab World and met many of its leading musicians.

Nadim was encouraged to move to the United States in 1969, when a member of the U.S. diplomatic corps heard him play at an embassy party. He told Nadim he had never heard the *nay* played in the United States. Nadim was excited at the thought of being America's only *nay* performer, and he traveled to New York with Samira Tawfiq, a popular Lebanese singer, at his first chance. He worked as a musician in New York for a few years and traveled around the country. Eventually he settled in Detroit, where he easily found gigs in the Lebanese community. After he married, Nadim took a day job. He continues, though, to place his career as a musician above his other professional interests, and his performance schedule keeps him traveling throughout the United States and abroad. He is a highly sought after musician, locally and nationally.

The milieu in which Nadim performs is filled with Arab musicians from different national backgrounds, whose families came to America at different times. In Dearborn, these performers must be fluent in the music of their own national group as well as that of others. An Arab ensemble might, for instance, contain a self-taught Palestinian American, a recently arrived Lebanese who was trained by an uncle in his village, an Iraqi Chaldean who picked up his love of music in a garage band, and a Turk who is struggling to learn Arabic and can barely keep up with what the others are saying. These men perform together in Arab night clubs, as backup for traveling singers from the Middle East, at ethnic festivals, and most often (usually two or three times a week) at weddings.

At Palestinian weddings, the band must play Palestinian *dabkah* (a type of folk song and line dance popular in the Levant), nationalistic songs, and a variety of Lebanese and Egyptian love ballads. At a Lebanese wedding, the crowd wants a faster *dabkah* and the love ballads of Fairuz and Umm Kulthum. At Yemeni weddings, one band will serve up the latest Arab pop, while another plays the regional Yemeni music essential to the occasion. Older classical and folk genres are favored by more assimilated Arab audiences, whose musical tastes were shaped by parents and grandparents who immigrated a generation ago or more. This part of the Arab community relates poorly to Dearborn's synergetic sound. They want to hear what they consider "the classics," which means generous helpings of Egyptian greats Ismahan, Umm Kulthum, and Muhammad 'Abd al-Wahhab. As Dearborn's hybrid sound gains larger audiences, live performances of the older classical and folk genres become increasingly rare and treasured.

In this dynamic musical community, Nadim Dlaikan is respected as a talented defender of traditional genres. His training at the Lebanese Conservatory and his collaboration with respected musicians such as Naim Bitar, Samira Tawfiq, Simon Shaheen, and Ali Jihad Racy place him securely within a prestigious line of artists. This gives Nadim the admiration of his colleagues and the ability to lead and work freely among the first tier of local Arab musicians. He is frequently invited to pull together classical ensembles for concerts at the Detroit Institute of Arts, to provide folkloric ensembles for ethnic festivals, and to present traditional Arab music to new audiences all over Michigan.

There is a side to Nadim's performance career that sets him apart from other musicians of his generation. His commitment to bringing Arab music to new audiences has led him to explore ways in which Lebanese folk music can fit into contemporary musical trends such as world beat. Typically, Arab musicians do not want to play for non-Arab audiences; they assume that non-Arabs would not enjoy or be interested in their music. Arab music in Detroit is heard almost exclusively at Arab gatherings. Long ago, Nadim realized the special power of music to transcend cultural boundaries. He enthusiastically supports local efforts to introduce Arab music to audiences outside the community. In fact, Nadim has discovered that not only do non-Arab audiences pay well, they are often fascinated by the music. In most cases, they are more attentive (and more appreciative) than revelers at an Arab wedding. Nadim is encouraging his colleagues to expand their musical vision. In his role as "culture broker" he joined the Earth Island Orchestra in the early 1990s, a band that featured artists from African, Asian, and Latin backgrounds. His involvement in the project enabled Arab musicians to shape the sound of the band. Nadim wrote and arranged *Farha,* an original piece commissioned by the band.

Nadim Dlaikan is also dedicated to teaching the *nay.* He has taught in apprenticeship programs at the Arab Community Center for Economic and Social Services[1] (ACCESS) and the Michigan State University Museum (MSUM). He also takes part, alongside several of the community's leading performers, in an Arab Summer Music Institute held biannually at ACCESS and funded by the National Endowment for the Arts (NEA). Despite all this outside intervention and support, Nadim has a hard time finding serious students. The *nay* is a difficult instrument to master, and local Arab audiences no longer seem to notice when the *nay* is missing from a wedding ensemble. A *nay* player is further handicapped by his need for at least a dozen different flutes. Each *nay* is capable of only one key, and Arab music, with its many quarter and half tones, contains more keys than Western music. The dearth of good *nay* performers in America concerns Nadim. He fears the instrument is losing out to keyboards and electric guitars, in Detroit as well as the Arab world.

Since his arrival in the United States, Nadim has been the only *nay* maker in North America. He grows bamboo reeds in his backyard, dries them, and uses them to make a variety of Arab flutes (figure 26). Musicians from around the country order handcrafted flutes from Nadim and send him damaged flutes for repair and tuning. His instruments are also in great demand among Arab Americans who want to display decorative *nays* and *mijwizs* (double reed flutes) in their homes. Nadim would like to teach others how to make these flutes, but he has found no student with the patience needed to master the craft.

Nadim's story is not a simple tale of successful adaptation to a new world of ethnic music in America. In many ways, Nadim is extremely frustrated by his Arab American audiences. In a 1997

Fig. 26. Nadim Dlaikan burns finger holes into a *nay* in his garage workshop. Photograph by Sally Howell.

interview, I asked him to describe the biggest challenges he faces in his performance career. He responded with a five-minute harangue detailing the ignorance of local audiences.

"They don't know or care about the music," he said. "If you make a mistake, they don't even notice. They still pay me the same thing today they paid me in 1969."

When I asked Nadim why he continues to perform, given the high levels of aggravation, he said, "I do it for the money, man."

In fact, Nadim has found a new source of motivation in American ethnic performance contexts. In part to appease me, and in part to conclude the interview on an upbeat, Nadim spent another five minutes discussing the support and encouragement he receives from non-Arab, American audiences. These audiences attend performances that are most often funded by federal and state art agencies and hosted by mainstream (or mainstreaming) institutions like ACCESS, MSUM, the Detroit Institute of Arts, and various university and college musicology programs. These audiences are prepped for Nadim's performances by anthropologists, folklorists, and ethnomusicologists who interpret his music in the familiar context of "appreciating other cultures" and "celebrating the American immigrant experience." The significance of this outside support is not lost on Nadim. Since he won his Michigan Heritage Award, Nadim has turned to the growing number of journalists and scholars who work with him for the patronage and encouragement he once received solely from local Arab audiences.

Nadim Dlaikan's experiences parallel those of other successful Arab folk artists in Detroit: (1) he is an immigrant; (2) the art forms he practices, Lebanese traditional music and instrument making, are considered folkloric even in the Middle East; (3) he learned music in apprenticeship to a master artist and now seeks to pass on his knowledge as a mentor; (4) he has identified a traditional audience for his work in America, an audience that does and does not resemble the ones he played for in Lebanon; and (5) he frequently performs for audiences outside the Arab community as a representative of Arab Detroit's musical and cultural heritage. Because Nadim is a musician, his career is flourishing in Detroit. Arab immigrants seldom marry without an Arab band at their wedding, and musicians are a common sight at baptism celebrations, graduation and engagement parties, ethnic festivals, and other private and public events throughout the city. The creative niches in which other Arab traditional artists work, however, are more narrowly defined. Their audiences are often limited to immigrants from their own country, or even their own home village. Nonetheless, several art forms (needlework, doll making, calligraphy) play a special role in creating and maintaining Arab identity in the United States. In the larger arena of American identity politics, traditional arts like Palestinian needlework and Lebanese *dabkah* have come to represent the Arab community as a whole. This representational link is part of a radical transformation, and I will try to explain why so few of us sense exactly how radical it is.

My Involvement in Arab Detroit

In 1987 I was hired by Ismael "Ish" Ahmed to create a cultural arts program for ACCESS. The program would be modeled on the work of the International Institute in downtown Detroit, which had a large hall filled with ethnic displays from around the world. ACCESS had received state funding in the 1970s to support *dabkah* lessons, an exhibition of Palestinian needlework, and a performance series featuring *dabkah* and local Lebanese musical traditions. Ish sent me in search of similar grants. As a newcomer both to Arab Detroit and to grantsmanship, I was discouraged to find so few options open to us. Arab music and dance, for instance, did not qualify for funding from the music and dance programs of the Michigan Council for the Arts and Cultural Affairs[2] (MCACA) or the NEA. These agencies were intended to support Western, mostly classical, music and dance, and ACCESS was not yet familiar with Arab American artists whose work might qualify for grants in literature, visual arts, or theater.

In 1987 as I explored dozens of funding options, I was repeatedly channeled toward programs that supported ethnic, traditional, and non-Western arts. These programs—sponsored by the NEA, the MCA (now the MCACA), the Ruth Mott Fund, and several other agencies—all bore the label "folk arts." The American folk arts establishment, it turned out, was eager to add Arabs to the roster of ethnic communities whose traditions it explored, nurtured, preserved, and displayed. From 1987 to the present, these agencies have awarded over two million dollars of funding to ACCESS, which has used this support to build the Museum of Arab Culture, support concerts, readings, exhibitions, festivals, research, apprenticeships, and a wide range of related projects.

The special nature of government, corporate, and private funding has profoundly affected the Cultural Arts Program at ACCESS, as it has the artists, traditional and otherwise, whose work we celebrate and present. The current NEA guidelines define "the folk and traditional arts" as: "those that are learned as part of the cultural life of a community whose members share a common ethnic heritage, language, religion, occupation, or geographic region. These traditions are shaped by the aesthetics and values of a shared culture and are passed on from generation to generation, most often within family and community through observation, conversation, and practice" (1999 application guidelines, 32). While many of the art forms practiced in Arab Detroit spill messily beyond the boundaries of this description, an equal number, often those practiced by Arab immigrants, fall neatly within it. It is the traditional art forms, however, that are most often used to represent Arab Detroit as an ethnic American community.

Identifying Traditional Artists

In 1995–97, after a decade of arts programming, ACCESS decided to conduct a traditional arts survey (sponsored by the NEA and the MCACA) to reassess our work and give new staff members a deeper understanding of the artists and art forms we present. We were already familiar with hundreds of traditional and nontraditional artists, but we wanted to make sure we were not overlooking new talent. We wanted to be sure we were not playing favorites, working only with traditions familiar to us, or supporting only the artists who were popular with audiences and organizers (or who were otherwise easy to collaborate with). We did not want to miss the recent waves of immigrants, the Iraqi Shia and the newly arrived wives and children of Yemeni workers in particular, who were perhaps bringing to Detroit forms of art and artistry no one had yet noticed. What we found in this research was and was not what we expected.

In the course of the project, we interviewed several artists for the first time. Henniya Shawine, for example, is a Chaldean doll maker. One of her dolls was donated to ACCESS by Athir Shayota in 1995 and was on display in our *New Arab World* exhibition. We had never spoken with Henniya directly, however, and this was our first chance to document her work. Henniya learned the skills essential to doll making, mostly needlework, as a young girl in Telkaif, a Catholic village in northern Iraq. She spent many of her spare hours stitching practical and decorative items for her home and family. Henniya knew that the local nuns made and sold dolls dressed in local Chaldean wedding costumes, but she never made these dolls herself when she lived in Iraq. They were simply a popular way for nuns to raise money for their convents. Wedding dolls were given to relatives or bought by friends of the family, partly to help the nuns and partly to display in homes.[3] As traditional clothing styles began to disappear in the 1950s, the dolls, dressed in the jewelry and finery of Chaldean brides, remained the same. For Henniya, these dolls came to represent a Chaldean identity temporally removed from the everyday world.

Henniya began making dolls when she immigrated to the United States in 1969. She could no longer buy them from Iraqi nuns; moreover, she had adopted American clothing and wanted a tangible reminder of the places, people, and clothing she had left behind in Telkaif. For Henniya, making dolls was, from the start, a self-conscious expression of her new ethnic identity. For her, the dolls stand for a Chaldeanness that is geographically as well as a temporally distant from the world she encounters in Detroit.

"This is what our clothes were like," she told me. "*Hay labisna kanit.*"

When Henniya makes dolls in Detroit, she begins by purchasing large plastic dolls, which she dresses in handmade clothing

Fig. 27. Chaldean dolls made by Henniya Shawine. Photograph by Mary Whalen, courtesy of the Michigan State University Museum.

resembling the traditional, formal dresses worn by Chaldean brides at the turn of the century (figure 27). These dolls are not made for children to play with; instead, they are given to new brides and expectant mothers. They are also displayed as a sign of ethnic and national pride. The first doll Henniya ever made was given to the Southfield Manor, a Chaldean social club, where it was displayed in the lobby for over a decade. Chaldean store owners sometimes exhibit a doll on a shelf behind the cash register, along with images of the Sacred Heart and the Hanging Gardens of Babylon. A delegation of Chaldean Democrats gave another of Henniya's dolls to Bill Clinton during the 1996 presidential campaign. When searching for a gift that would encapsulate their identity as Chaldeans, they turned to Henniya Shawine. Now in her sixties, Henniya continues to tour the Arab shops in Dearborn and Southfield, searching for materials to use on her meticulously crafted dolls. She strives to reproduce as accurately as possible the dresses Chaldean women wore in her youth. In her efforts to express the particular, Henniya is fully aware of the larger statements her dolls can make.

No one finds it odd, or essentializing, that a group of Chaldean millionaires would offer a presidential candidate a doll so clearly disconnected from the world of high finance in which these businessmen operate. They were, after all, giving money to Clinton's campaign because they thought it would persuade him to lift economic sanctions against Iraq. Henniya's doll established an artifactual link between Iraqi Americans and their relatives languishing in the poverty-stricken villages around Telkaif. For Clinton, who had no intention, then or now, of lifting the sanctions, the doll could be read as something else entirely. It could be read as a proud assertion of Iraqi Americanness.

Our collaboration with Henniya was rewarding. In other parts of the Arab community, however, we met with little success. The new Iraqi Shia refugees we approached were too shell-shocked to be of help. They had weathered the prying, disorienting questions of far too many people already, and they find it hard to trust anyone. They cannot imagine (nor do they even want) a place for themselves on the landscape of American immigrant and ethnic identities. In Iraq, their regional, tribal, and religious identities were something they had learned to play down in recent years, not celebrate. The one artist we did manage to speak with was a calligrapher. He had worked in a calligraphy unit for the Iraqi army, stenciling information on tanks and buildings. Having lost a wife and several children in the war, he had little desire to work now as a calligrapher or to teach calligraphy in Detroit. He finds the Arab Americans a shock and a disappointment.

"They aren't really Arabs at all," he told me. "They don't speak Arabic. What do they care about calligraphy?"

In the Yemeni community, we hoped to document an active henna scene, where young women stain each other's hands, feet, and legs with intricate patterns using the dried, crushed leaves of the henna bush, water, and a little lime juice. We had seen evidence of, and been told about, the henna parties so popular among young girls and women. Yet, despite continuous efforts, we could not land an invitation to such a party. Our primary Yemeni informant married a man who lived out-of-state and moved away during the survey. She had described a scene in which certain young women become highly adept at applying henna. Yemeni girls, she told us, are constantly rifling through books and magazines, even inspecting each other's limbs, to come up with ideas for newer, more complex henna designs. Over the years, I have seen dozens of ornate and simple designs on the hands of Yemeni staff at ACCESS (figure 28). The custom is not a

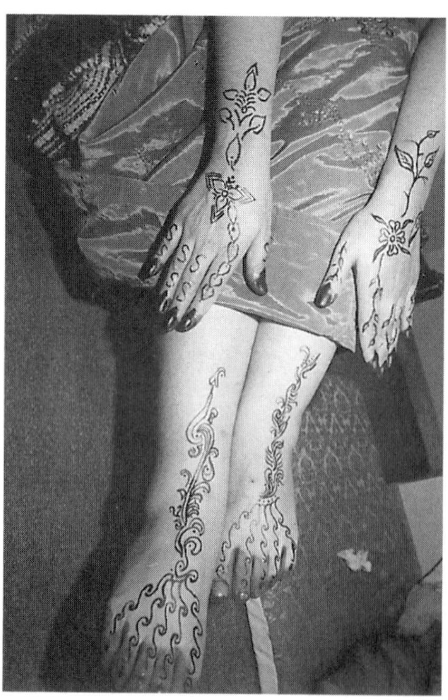

Fig. 28. Henna designs on the hands and feet of a young Dearborn woman. Photograph by Hajer Mitchell.

deep, dark secret. When it came time to document it, however, and put it on the public record, with or without photographs, we could not find anyone to work with. The application of henna is a private tradition shared by young women, usually before a wedding or the birth of a baby, or before a potential groom arrives for a visit from the old country. The finesse needed to intrude on such scenes was beyond us. We learned that our goal of finding young women who would be willing to teach this tradition at ACCESS, do public demonstrations at workshops or festivals, or have their work photographed and displayed in a museum was clearly unrealistic. The henna tradition does not represent the kind of public face Yemenis in Detroit would deem appropriate or respectable. Instead, it presents, as a canvas, something that should never be open to public view: the bodies of young, usually unmarried, women.

Our research made other things clear as well. The village community of Beit Hanina, for example—long our most reliable source of Palestinian needleworkers—has moved almost entirely out of Dearborn's Southend. The lure of grocery and gas station markets that are relatively free of Lebanese and Chaldean competition has drawn Beit Hanina en masse to Cleveland, while others have moved back to Palestine or to Detroit's middle-class suburbs. For ACCESS this migration has meant a sharp reduction in the number of women we can draw on to teach embroidery classes and provide demonstrations for public events. When I set out to interview needleworkers in 1995, I could find only three Beit Hanina women who were still embroidering dresses. Only five years earlier, I could have found well over a dozen.

Defining the Arab American Traditional Arts

The successes and failures of the ACCESS survey raised important questions about what folklore means and how traditional art forms endure, change, and are made public in American immigrant and ethnic contexts. Specifically, I was impelled by the research to take a closer look at the motives of individual artists, what they seek to express, who they imagine their audience to be, and how their work is received within and beyond their communities.

Among Arab Americans, the traditional arts are different from more contemporary or Western art forms in that the people who practice them are not usually considered "artists" at all. Their professional identity comes from some other occupation. Embroiderers are homemakers or store owners. Musicians are schoolteachers or truck drivers. Calligraphers are engineers, sign and awning manufacturers, or grocers. Even if a musician, for example, is recognized in the community as a skilled performer, the contexts in which he performs are often devalued. Only those musicians who perform in concert halls, or occasionally at prestigious nightclubs, are deemed worthy of the title *fannan* (artist). Others are quickly dismissed by statements intended to make their work seem small: "Oh, he only plays weddings."

The problem with weddings, as a venue, is that the Arab wedding audience does not sit still and focus its attention on the performance. Instead, people dance, talk, and move around the hall freely. Most Arab musicians in Detroit would agree that "artists" perform in concert halls where audience members cannot move from their seats, where they focus their attention on the music being played, and even if they sing along and talk freely (by the standards of Western classical concertgoers), their attention is focused on the creative expression of the "artists" on stage.[4] For local musicians who performed on radio and television before they immigrated, or on stages with all the trappings, this attitude can be especially vexing, and it is not limited to musical circles. In general, "artist" is not a title Arabs apply to sign makers and peasants who embroider dresses. "Artists" hang their paintings in the Detroit Institute of Arts and show their dresses on runways in Paris and Beirut.

In Arab Detroit the individuals known as traditional artists are almost without exception immigrants. I did not fully realize this until I was going over a set of videotapes produced for *A Community between Two Worlds,* an exhibition ACCESS and MSUM mounted together in 1998. As curators of the exhibition, Yvonne Lockwood and I brought together the work of several Arab American traditional artists with an earlier photographic exhibition ACCESS had created with the National Museum of American History.[5] The folk art exhibition featured video loops of interviews with the artists. As I was studying these videos to determine where subtitling might be needed, I noticed that none of the artists spoke English as a first language. Despite my long familiarity with these artists, I had never consciously separated them into an immigrant category. When I think about it now, I realize that all but one of the more than one hundred traditional artists we have worked with at ACCESS since 1987 speak English as a second language. Several speak no English at all. I must admit to being surprised by this realization. We work with an equally large pool of American-born Arab artists, but they produce art in another vein entirely. They are poets, novelists, painters, sculptors.

By contrast, "the traditional artists," the musicians and craftspeople, were *all* born overseas. To further emphasize this point, as I looked over the list of historical objects included in *A Community between Two Worlds,* I noticed that not one of these objects was made by a person born in the United States.

What is it about the label "folk arts" that, when applied to Arab Americans, reduces the community to its immigrant population? I have two answers to this question: (1) the meaning of the term "folklore" is intuitively understood by most people, Arab immigrants included, to mean "traditional" and "authentically of a place or people," and (2) objects that can be categorized in this way are especially valuable to national governments, who use them as symbols of unity, a shared heritage, and national belonging. For these reasons, the artists and art forms included in ACCESS folk arts programming are predominantly village traditions that are also considered folkloric in the Middle East, where they are likewise sponsored by government agencies (or nationalist movements) whose purpose is to cultivate these art forms on behalf of Jordan, or Palestine, or the Arab people as a whole.

Halimah AbdelFattah, a Palestinian needleworker, is a good representative of this type of folkloric tradition. Halimah hand-embroiders a full-length dress called a *thob* in Arabic. She is from the village of Beit Hanina, and her relatives and neighbors from this village are the primary audience for her work. The Beit Hanina community also makes up Halimah's social world. The wedding, engagement, birth, and graduation parties she attends in Detroit and Cleveland are the highlights of her year. A majority of the women over forty who attend these events do so wearing handmade *thob*s and headdresses adorned in row after row of gold coins. Many women now purchase their dresses from Palestinian refugees, or have machine-couched dresses made for them instead. Those who still make their own dresses are proud holdouts in a community whose recent economic success is driving the commodification and mass production of this art form. Halimah's status within Beit Hanina is enhanced by the diligence and artistry she exhibits in her dresses, which are made completely by hand.

The *thob* is no longer just a village tradition, however. It has become an internationally recognized symbol of the Palestinian nation, especially of its rural, peasant, landowning classes. George E. Bisharat notes the significance of this symbolism for Palestinian refugees living in the West Bank, for whom "the predominant idiom for articulating this urge to return [to their land within Israel] was the sentiment of 'localism' " (1997, 213). He describes the strong attachments Palestinian refugees feel to their home villages and towns, and the degree to which residents of specific communities were "often identifiable by distinct speech patterns and intonation, women by the patterns of embroidery on their dresses":

> The intense focus of diaspora Palestinians on the intimate, sensual details of their remembered landscapes reflected in their literature and elsewhere was not the same as the unstudied, spontaneous attachments to home that preceded exile. Rather it represented an early step in the construction of a more self-conscious relationship to place and an attempt to reconcretize a connection to the land that had been violently sundered. (1997, 217)

Palestinian dresses have been codified according to village and region, historic time period, and numerous other criteria. They have been described in hundreds of books (see Weir 1989, Weir and Shahid 1988, Rajab 1989, Kawar and Nasir 1992), assembled in several major collections, and presented in national and international exhibitions at leading museums in almost every Western country except the United States.[6] No Palestinian who stitches such a dress today is unaware of the nationalist assertions of her work.

Halimah, like many women in the Palestinian Occupied Territories and Jordan in the early 1980s, even began incorporating explicitly nationalist symbols in her already national costumes. First,

Fig. 29. A Palestinian *thob* stitched by Halimah AbdelFattah. Design features include the Dome of the Rock, the Palestinian flag, olives and grapes, and the words, "Palestine, the victory is ours." Photograph by Mary Whalen, courtesy of the Michigan State University Museum.

she began stitching the colors of the Palestinian flag into dresses of otherwise traditional design. When I asked what inspired her to do this, she said, "I am a Palestinian. I am proud of my flag!" Halimah eventually made a dress that featured the Palestinian flag itself, the Dome of the Rock (the principal Islamic site in the old city of Jerusalem), and the slogan "Palestine, the victory is ours" in a repeating pattern (figure 29). This innovation is significant. Much of Beit Hanina has been confiscated by the Israeli government and turned over to Jewish settlers. The rest has been illegally annexed and is now within Jerusalem city limits. Little remains for Halimah and her relatives to return to. Her dresses, almost in response to this truncation, now display a larger "national" Palestinian identity. The response to Halimah's "flag" dress has been enthusiastic among her Beit Hanina relatives. She proudly tells of the reactions of several shocked and envious competitors when they first saw the dress, which she had labored on in secret to increase the surprise and impact of her stylistic bravado.

The majority of traditional artists ACCESS has worked with over the years come, as Halimah does, from Arab villages. Their work as instrument makers, doll makers, calligraphers, and needleworkers falls clearly into the category of "folklore," even in their home countries. In museums throughout the Arab world, samples of work similar to that on display at ACCESS or in *A Community between Two Worlds* are used to document and represent a traditional culture that is being preserved, as of the past, to promote specifically nationalist agendas of the present. The strength of the folk traditions discussed in this paper is their ability to remain relevant to the everyday lives of millions of people. They are adapting, sometimes even thriving in a climate of rapid socioeconomic change in the Middle East, and, to a much lesser extent, in the immigrant communities of Arab Detroit.

There are exceptions to this village/folkloric pattern, the ambiguities of which are nicely illustrated in the work of Rifaat Zaghloul. In the Middle East, Rifaat would not be considered a folk artist at all. Raised in Kuwait, he is a trained master of a venerable calligraphic tradition that is centuries old. Rifaat has become a folk artist only in the United States, where his work finds its primary audience in an ethnic context far removed from the classical and mainstream contexts he knew in Jordan and Kuwait. Rifaat is a computer engineer who works for an engineering firm in Southfield. He is also a devout, carefully observant Muslim. His early reputation as a calligrapher in America was made in Toledo, where he attended college. Rifaat built his social life around friends from the Toledo Mosque, for which he became a sign maker, creating posters and banners for mosque events and Muslim student gatherings on campus. Much of this he did as a religious obligation. He described for me the work of a famous Syrian calligrapher who is still producing facsimiles of the Quran.

"Each time we read it, he gets a blessing," Rifaat said. "This is what I believe."

Rifaat is proud to practice an art form so old, beautiful, and laden with meaning. Each banner he makes to welcome home pilgrims from the *hajj* and each clock he ornaments with Quranic verses and arabesque motifs, is attached, in his mind, to the earliest days of Islam when the Arabic scripts were developed, codified, and used in the production of religious and political texts intended to spread the faith. Rifaat is also an innovator. He does not simply print Quranic texts on paper, with a pen. Instead, he scans hand-drawn images into his computer, cleans them with the most current computer-imaging techniques, and then either sandblasts the images onto glass or cuts them out of vinyl.

Fig. 30. A pair of champagne glasses created by Rifaat Zaghloul. Photograph by Bruce Harkness, courtesy of the ACCESS Museum of Arab Culture.

In addition to being a traditional calligrapher, a Muslim, and an engineer, Rifaat is an entrepreneur. He has invested heavily in sandblasting and computer technologies that he uses to make mirrors, doors, and decorative panels for local bakeries and restaurants. He makes decorative pieces for the home, using Arabic poetry and proverbs. He makes tombstones for local Muslims. And he makes champagne glasses (which he assures me should be used with sparkling cider) embellished with the names of the bride and groom or with wedding greetings (figure 30). The other sign makers in Dearborn have tried to buy his technological know-how, which he carefully guards. His equipment has been stolen three times in two years. The audience for Rifaat's work, as he is well aware, is Arabic-speaking and largely Muslim. His customers are attracted to the harmonic balance of his hand-drawn texts, and to the practical, mass-produced materials he uses. They recognize that his work is simultaneously more and less traditional than that of his rivals, who use computer fonts instead of handwritten texts and print them on mundane surfaces.

Objects of Everyday Life, and More

In 1997 Yvonne Lockwood and I reviewed the artifacts collected by Alixa Naff for the Naff Arab American Collection at the Smithsonian Institution so that we could determine which to include in the *Community between Two Worlds* exhibition. These historic artifacts are different in nature from the contemporary objects, and they are far less ambiguous. Many were produced for sale by peddlers and their families, mostly in the period between 1890 and the First World War. They were in no way self-conscious representations of Arabness. Instead, they were table runners, laces, doilies, handkerchiefs, and other items that could be produced at home, carried with peddlers on the road, and sold for profit. Some items, like a specially framed photograph of the Ghantous family in Lebanon, served as a reminder of loved ones and a way of life left behind. Some of these artifacts were produced to keep Arab traditions alive in America, but always in a domestic and private context. Faris Naff made his wife a bread paddle so she could continue to bake Arabic bread. The Coury family bought their daughter an *'ud* (Arab lute) so she could learn to play Arabic music. Mary Agemy made small *hijab*s, or talismans, to protect her children from the evil eye. John Koury made small crosses out of the palm fronds given to worshipers in his church on Palm Sunday. He placed these around the house to bless his home and family.[7]

These artifacts were once the objects of everyday life. Their significance today, as objects worthy of museum exhibition, comes from the meanings attached to them by the people who inherited them. By the time Alixa Naff began collecting these artifacts in the 1960s, they had come to stand not just for Mom and Dad, but for the Syria or Lebanon from which Mom and Dad came. These items came to symbolize an immigrant past rooted in the Arab world. Many were treasured and saved because they were links to a past that was Syrian and a present that was discernibly something else.

The contemporary objects Yvonne Lockwood and I selected for the exhibition have already participated in a similar semantic journey. They are far more than everyday objects. Rifaat's champagne flutes are made to mark weddings and graduations. His banners, hung on front porches, celebrate and announce the homecoming of Muslim pilgrims. Halimah's dresses are worn to *haflat* (parties) and other special occasions. Nadim's handmade musical instruments are played at critical moments in the lives of Arab Americans. Henniya's dolls are given as gifts when a couple marries or welcomes home a new baby, or even when presidential candidates are courting the Chaldean vote. These contemporary objects were produced, at least in part, as self-conscious assertions and celebrations of Arabness in Detroit.

This is not to deny that contemporary artifacts, like their historic counterparts, have multiple meanings. Arab American traditional artists, like all artists, are expressing a whole range of aesthetic, personal, and community concerns in their work. They are individuals; when being creative, they are expressing themselves. But they are not rootless; their selves are grounded in many identities at once. Irene and Reema Harb, for example, produce needlework for their home and the homes of their immediate kin. Irene, in particular, a widow with an abundance of free time, makes dozens of pillowcases and wall hangings in a year. The homes of her sons are all adorned with a copy of the Lord's Prayer in Arabic, an English language "Welcome to our home" or "God bless this home," and a wealth of pillows, tablecloths, and wall hangings in traditional Palestinian designs. Some of the patterns Irene reproduces come from books of traditional Palestinian design; some are religious motifs she borrows from relatives back home or from friends in Detroit. Some are in the red and black on white colors of Ramallah, while others are in colors that accent a certain rug or couch. Lately, Irene has made a dozen pillows that depict a *dabkah* line of men and women wearing *sherwal*s and *thob*s (figure 31). With every item Irene makes, a different aspect of the Harb

Fig. 31. A pillow stitched by Irene Harb featuring a line of Palestinian *dabkah* dancers. Photograph by Bruce Harkness, courtesy of the ACCESS Museum of Arab Culture.

family's multifaceted identity is being asserted: Palestinian, Arabic and English-speaking, Christian, suburban American, Ramallawi.

Irene and Reema are also making statements about themselves in the things they do not make. For example, they do not make or wear the Palestinian *thob*. Irene and Reema, unlike Halimah, are not peasants. They are (by the local standards of the West Bank) elite Christians. Their religious and class origins place them several steps closer to the American mainstream than their conationals from Beit Hanina. In fact, their family came to America a decade before Ramallah was occupied by the Israelis in 1967. They are not refugees. But Irene and Reema do not cross-stitch samplers from their local craft store, either. Their "God bless this home" pieces are trimmed with patterns like the star of Bethlehem and the cypress tree. Both women are careful in the motifs they choose to reproduce and display. Their identities are complex but specific; transnational but exceedingly local.

The audience for this work is not just the Harb family alone. It is also the Detroit Ramallah community, with whom the Harbs spend most of their social time, and the hundreds of friends, colleagues, and neighbors who round out this network. This audience also includes future generations. Reema described for me, in detail, the pieces of embroidery she inherited from her mother. She has divided these pieces, along with many she and Irene have made, into a collection for each of her three children, to be presented to them upon marriage. They are emblems and assertions of her children's Palestinian American heritage.

Transmitting Art and Culture

Traditional artists, perhaps more than other artists, carry forward art forms and cultural means of expression that channel individual creativity through either the local, private hierarchies of family life or through master/apprentice relationships designed to pass along a tradition whose authority is rooted in the accurate reproduction of the past, not free innovation and self-expression in the present. Palestinian needleworkers I have spoken to remember adolescent years in which they sat for hours with mothers, aunts, and cousins, working together on dresses and objects of practical use in the home. Halimah AbdelFattah describes many tearful episodes from her childhood when she wanted to play with friends but her mother forced her, sometimes physically, to continue her needlework. The clothing they made together had a use; it was needed. Dresses were made for crucial events and had to be finished on time. For the women of Ramallah, where the items being made were for the home, the pressures were not so great, but the social atmosphere was much the same.

The women I spoke with ranged in age from forty to seventy. All learned needlework when they were young by watching and working with others. Nadim Dlaikan learned to make instruments in a similar fashion—by observation, trial, and error. Producing his own reed flutes was the only way he could become a musician. Rifaat Zaghloul became a calligrapher through six years of active study with master calligraphers. He spent one year on each of the six major Arabic scripts. These pedagogical contexts, if they survive at all in Arab Detroit, do so in a radically altered fashion. If traditional artists are to succeed in Detroit or the Arab world, they must have traditional audiences for their work. They must also take an active role in creating their audience and turning it into a market that can sustain both their work and their traditions.

John Sarweh, for example, makes and repairs *qanuns*. His interest in instrument making began in Damascus in the late 1940s, when he commissioned Syria's leading instrument maker to produce a new instrument for him and was told he would have to wait three years and pay an astronomical fee. Instead, John began watching this artisan at work, attempting all the while to reproduce the process in his own home. Eventually, he traveled to Egypt, where he apprenticed himself to Gaby Tutunigy in Cairo. Tutunigy was considered the Arab world's finest *qanun* maker, and he produced instruments for all of the region's leading artists. Tutunigy fine-tuned John's technique, so to speak, and the two worked together on many instruments over the years. When John came to Canada in the late 1960s, he brought his instrument-making tools with him to keep his own *qanuns* in shape. As he grows older and becomes less eager to travel, John takes on more students, whom he teaches to play the *qanun*. These students make up his primary market for *qanuns*. Often, they commission one after their first year of lessons. John also repairs instruments for Arab and other Middle Eastern immigrants throughout North America.

American Audiences, Arab American Art Forms

Increasingly, village and national communities are not the only audience for Arab Detroit's traditional art forms. ACCESS, MSUM, and other organizations are presenting Arab artists to ethnically mixed and entirely non-Arab audiences in and out of Detroit. In these new environments, handcrafted objects are likely to lose their most familiar meanings. Typically, they take on new meanings altogether.

In 1992 I accompanied Halimah AbdelFattah to "An American Reunion on the Mall," a national folk arts exhibition hosted by the Smithsonian Institution as part of the Clinton inauguration. Halimah was invited to represent the traditional artists of Arab Detroit. She brought eight to ten dresses and several pillowcases with her to Washington, where she displayed them in a small booth, taking her place between an African American quilter and a Hmong needleworker. Halimah sat quietly and worked on a new dress as thousands of people streamed by, exploring this cornucopia of American exoticism.

Many people stopped to chat, especially older women who were greatly impressed by Halimah's work, by the sheer expenditure of time each dress takes, by their fabulous oddity. Our conversations were friendly, and Halimah enjoyed the attention, but not as much as she enjoyed the occasional "friend of Israel" whose suspicions were aroused by the sign over Halimah's head that identified her as a "Palestinian Needleworker." These suspicions were confirmed when the wary observer got closer to Halimah's booth and saw her trademark flag dress. Several viewers absolutely lost their cool. I doubt that any of them could read the Arabic slogan "Palestine, the victory is ours." But they recognized the Palestinian flag, the

Dome of the Rock, and the word "Palestinian" in Halimah's sign. This was an affront to them. They insisted the offensive dress be removed, stating that such a political statement had no place in a folk arts exhibition. Event organizers and guards quickly became deft at identifying these disgruntled viewers and handling their criticisms. Several were escorted away by Smithsonian guards. A smaller number of "friends of Palestine" also commented on the dress throughout the day. They were delighted and shocked to see their own political perspective represented in such an unlikely place. Both the support and the criticism delighted Halimah. Her dress had provoked, among new audiences, precisely the reactions intended.

I have also seen Halimah's dresses provoke responses that would not interest her. In 1997 ACCESS organized a meeting of Arab American arts presenters from around the country, hoping to pull them together into a national network. Farida and Sari Yusif (pseudonyms), who have assembled a large collection of Palestinian costumes in the United States, attended the meeting. The discussion had focused on the folk arts all morning. The Lila Wallace-Reader's Digest Fund was interested in supporting a national touring folk arts project among Arab Americans. I was having a somewhat difficult time explaining the value of a folk arts agenda to the network partners, many of whom believed that the immigrant, village, and peasant associations of the folk arts ran counter to the modern, professional image of Arabs they hope to project in America.

I brought out several of the artifacts that were slated for inclusion in the *Community between Two Worlds* exhibition to illustrate the rich and surprising local arts scene. I thought the Yusifs would be interested in purchasing an example or two of Halimah's work, since she represents the latest (and most American) version of the village costumes they so carefully collect, preserve, and exhibit. To my chagrin, they found Halimah's work inauthentic. They commented negatively on the fabric, the size of the stitches, the color choices, and even the nationalist images. Obviously, their aesthetic, while equally Palestinian, was different from that of Halimah and her peers from Beit Hanina. I found this exchange fascinating. The Yusifs could not see the value of Halimah's dresses because her work had migrated too far in both time and space from the dresses that filled their own collection, most of which were produced a generation or more before Halimah's.

The Yusifs' connoisseurship is itself a product of other times and places, and the high standards they seek to preserve can seem predictably snobbish to American folklorists. With growing frequency, Halimah AbdelFattah's dresses are being presented to American audiences for whom Beit Hanina represents, if anything, an unknown, faraway place. The fact that her dresses are made in America by an immigrant turned citizen is what makes them relevant to American identity politics. ACCESS, through its growing ethnic festival, its expanded summer apprenticeship programs, and the *Community between Two Worlds* exhibition, is using Palestinian embroidery and other traditional arts to represent Arab Detroit as a whole. People are meant to walk away from these programs with a clear understanding that what they have just seen is American and uniquely Arab American. This mainstreaming, Americanizing project can seem simultaneously artificial and authentic. It is artificial to immigrants, who often think of themselves not as Arab Americans, but as Chaldeans, Haninis, or Bazzis, but it is authentic to Americans and Arab Americans who have grown accustomed to, and can now speak, the language of the American immigrant experience.

Arabs in the United States are part of American society even if the extent to which they identify as Americans varies greatly within the community. The art forms Arab immigrants bring to Detroit become American—to the presenters and mainstream funding sources that support them—as soon as they are practiced on U.S. soil. The acquisitiveness of this nationalizing process mirrors the way in which colonial regimes of the past collected far-flung traditional objects and recast them as symbols of the size, diversity, and power of their empires. For better and for worse, the presentation of Arab traditional art forms to public audiences beyond the Arab community has the capacity to transform it, at least momentarily, into a standard, recognizable entity: an ethnic American community.

The long-standing relationship between the ACCESS Cultural Arts Program and state and federal governments has created an ambitious and self-conscious formula for the public representation of Arab American identity. This formula is now being used across the country in films, museum exhibits, curriculum materials for schools, concert tours, and academic publications like this one. This success is ironic for many reasons. Detroit includes immigrant communities from almost every Arab country and every wave of immigration, a mix of Christians and Muslims from all the Arab sects found in America, and a full range of professionals, entrepreneurs, and workers. It is quite natural that it would be considered representative. But in Arab American communities that are wealthier and more professional than Detroit—and less representative for that reason—Arab Detroit stands for something altogether unpleasant. It stands for peasants, the recently arrived, the poorly educated; in short, it stands for a "traditionalism" of precisely the sort embodied in the folk arts.

Yet to make a place for themselves in multicultural America, Arabs often find themselves compelled to assert "authentic" identities with which they are not entirely comfortable. In New York City, the cosmopolitan and professional capital of Arab America, an annual event called *Mahrajan al-Fan:* Festival of Arab World Culture was organized in 1994. It received the majority of its financial support from folk arts agencies (the NEA and the Ruth Mott Fund) and professional assistance from the Ethnic Folk Arts Center. Like ACCESS, the *Mahrajan* foregrounds the folk and traditional arts. Unlike ACCESS, however, its organizers are largely Arabs from Christian, urban, and elite backgrounds. They are trying to incorporate more prestigious, modern art forms in the festival. Yet in order to fund the *Mahrajan,* find a public location for it, build an audience, and receive technical assistance, its producers must assert their most folkloric selves. This reliance on traditional arts is all that enables even wealthy, urban Arabs to reach an American mainstream to which, in so many other respects, they already belong.

Conclusion

American public culture provides an obvious means of celebrating immigrant artistic traditions, and this process influences both immigrant artists and the traditions they practice. It is mundane and welcome, strange and threatening. When Arab artists arrive in the United States, the traditions they practice are deeply rooted in the specific communities and places they leave behind. Often these places are at odds with the U.S. government, and the individuals who arrive have no interest in becoming "American." They already have identities. They do not need new ones. Their artistic traditions already hold enough significance. And yet, the power of American cultural politics lies in the following condition: as immigrant traditions take on American meanings, they can and do retain Arab ones. Even as hand-embroidered Palestinian dresses come to represent the Arab community of Detroit and are absorbed into a vast, multiethnic landscape, they are still dresses made by women like Halimah AbdelFattah to be worn to a neighbor's graduation party; they still represent the aesthetics and values of Beit Hanina. This constant but never total overlap of seemingly separate worlds contains all the ambiguities of the American ethnic experience.

These ambiguities are a source of pride and inspiration to traditional artists who, in the day-to-day practice of their work, are gradually discovering that they are, in fact, cultural innovators. When Nadim Dlaikan won the Michigan Heritage Award in 1994, it made him aware of something he already knew: the diversity of his audiences—immigrants, assimilated Arab Americans, non-Arabs, or any combination thereof—keeps his creative energy flowing. Nadim performs the latest Arab pop, the oldest village songs, the most respected classical repertoire, and the hippest jazz and world beat. When he takes the stage, he is no longer a Beiruti immigrant performing for other Lebanese immigrants; instead, he is an artist with the power to represent and create communities as parochial and cosmopolitan, as open and intimate, as the many worlds in which he lives.

ACKNOWLEDGMENTS: The traditional arts survey mentioned in this paper was supported by grants from the National Endowment for the Arts and the Michigan Council for the Arts and Cultural Affairs. Interviews I conducted for the *Community between Two Worlds* exhibition were additionally funded by the Ruth Mott Fund and the Lila Wallace-Reader's Digest Community Folklife Program administered by the Fund for Folk Culture. This paper was first presented at a National Endowment for the Humanities-sponsored conference titled *An Arab America Century,* hosted by ACCESS, MSUM, and the Detroit Historical Museum. I would like to thank the many artists from Detroit with whom I have worked over the last decade. Their encouragement, support, friendship, artistry, and example made my job at ACCESS a possibility and a pleasure. In particular, I thank the artists mentioned in this paper and their families. Careful readings of this paper were provided by Andrew Shryock and Nabeel Abraham, who shaped my conclusions in significant ways. The errors and ideas embedded in this work remain my own.

NOTES

1. Established in 1971, ACCESS is a nonprofit, human-service organization that provides social, economic, health, employment, educational, mental health, and cultural services within and beyond the Arab community of Detroit. ACCESS established a Cultural Arts Program in 1987, of which I

served as director until 1995. I continue to work for the arts program as an adviser and consultant.

2. The Michigan Council for the Arts and Cultural Affairs was, at the time, known as the Michigan Council for the Arts. Their name and responsibilities shifted in 1992, when Governor John Engler led a campaign to reduce or eliminate public arts funding in Michigan.
3. Athir Shayota provided me with background information on the doll-making tradition of Chaldean nuns in Iraq.
4. Some better-known Arab artists are beginning to resist audience participation in any form. Marcel Khalife, for example, who is known as a political, revolutionary folk artist, is trying to establish himself as a classical artist now that the Lebanese civil war has ended. During his 1996 American tour, he insisted that event organizers direct audiences before each performance not to sing along, not to shout out requests, to remain seated during the performance, and to clap only in applause at the end of each piece. Audiences are deciding for themselves which manifestation of Khalife's career they appreciate. Attendance for his more recent tours is dropping steadily.
5. This earlier photographic exhibition was titled *Arab Americans in Greater Detroit: A Community between Two Worlds*. It was curated by Alixa Naff, Andrew Shryock, and myself and was displayed at the Smithsonian Institution's National Museum of American History in the fall and winter of 1995–96.
6. Several curators and collectors of Palestinian costume have cited the close relationship between the United States and Israel as a reason Palestinian exhibitions are kept out of mainstream art and textile museums in major American metropolitan centers. Museum curators are wary of offending Jewish donors whose sympathies lie with Israel.
7. Information concerning these historical artifacts and their makers was taken from field notes Alixa Naff made when she was collecting artifacts for the Smithsonian Institution's Naff Arab American Collection. These notes and the objects they refer to are held at the National Archive Center of the National Museum of American History in Washington, D.C.

References

Bisharat, George E. 1997. Exile to Compatriot: Transformations in the Social Identity of Palestinian Refugees in the West Bank. In *Culture, Power, Place: Explorations in Critical Anthropology*, edited by Akhil Gupta and James Ferguson, 203–33. Durham: Duke University Press.

Kawar, Widad Kamel, and Tania Tamari Nasir. 1992. *Palestinian Embroidery: Traditional "Fallahi" Cross-Stich.* Munich: State Museum of Ethnography.
Rajab, Jehan. 1989. *Palestinian Costume.* London: Kegan Paul.
Weir, Shelagh. 1989. *Palestinian Costume.* London: British Museum Press.
Weir, Shelagh, and Serene Shadid. 1988. *Palestinian Embroidery.* London: British Museum Press.

Continuity and Adaptation in Arab American Foodways

William G. Lockwood and Yvonne R. Lockwood

The process by which immigrants become ethnic is long, gradual, and very complex. One can think of this process as ethnogenesis, or the creation of a new social group. Along with the development of a new ethnic group is a parallel development of a new subculture that both symbolizes the group's uniqueness to its members and marks off its social boundaries. The new subculture is created in the American context, altered to a greater or lesser degree from what was known in the homeland. Lebanese Americans are not the same as Lebanese in Lebanon, and Lebanese American culture is different from the culture(s) found in Lebanon. Neither do Lebanese Americans belong to a culture somewhere between American and Lebanese cultures, as might be surmised from the overly simple models of acculturation that have so far dominated thinking on the subject. Ethnicity exists only in specific contexts where one sort of people (Us) is brought into regular and intimate contact with people of other sorts (Them) (Barth 1969). In what follows, we are concerned with the cultural expressions that grow out of such contact, especially with regard to Arab American food and foodways and how these came to be the way they are.

The process by which immigrants become ethnic begins as soon as they board the boats and planes that carry them to the New World. Selective processes are already at work. No group of emigrants from any country represent a cross section of that country's population. They are always drawn from some regions more than others, some social strata more than others, and some communities more than others. Since each of these groups possesses a recognizable subculture (including distinctive foods and foodways), it is logical that immigrant communities cannot replicate exactly their old national culture in the New World.

Out of immigrant culture develops an ethnic culture that differs from it in significant ways. There are several primary sources on which this developing subculture draws. The first is the culture of the homeland. One aspect of the process is an amalgamation of the local, regional, and class-related subcultures that are represented in the immigrant community. A second source in the creation of an ethnic culture is the culture of mainstream America, such as it is experienced by immigrants and ethnics. The third source—too often overlooked—are the cultures of other immigrant and ethnic groups encountered in America. Most often, immigrants settle in neighborhoods and work in occupations associated with earlier immigrant groups. Yemeni immigrants in Detroit, for example, moved into houses vacated by Poles, Romanians, and Lebanese who were ready to move uptown or to the suburbs. An immigrant worker's foreman at the auto plant is likely to have been hired from a previous wave of immigrants. The creation of ethnic culture from these various sources takes place within the particular constraints of minority life: the homesickness, the prejudice, the sense of being different, the urge to assimilate or to resist assimilation, the need to recreate the Old World in the New or reject all possible reminders of the life that was. All shape the specific form taken by the new culture. Many anthropologists and folklorists refer to this cultural process as "creolization" (Abrahams 1980, 376–77) after the term for a similar linguistic process.

One can observe creolization in any aspect of ethnic culture, but it is particularly significant in food and foodways.[1] There are numerous reasons for this. First, cooking and eating are expressive behavior, relatively easy to observe, and heavily laden with symbolic meaning. Because cuisine is especially responsive to new environments, where some ingredients are unavailable, and because new social settings bring new ways of eating and cooking, foodways are especially quick to adapt and change. At the same time, however, perhaps no aspect of culture is so resistant to change, so tenaciously held. Generations after the loss of their mother tongue, ethnic Americans are still likely to be cooking and eating some version of the family's "mother cuisine."

In this essay we argue that in the creolization of Arab food and foodways (and quite possibly other aspects of culture) there are clear distinctions between the public, or commercial, and the private, or familial, spheres of behavior. For non-Arabs, it is invariably the public sphere that shapes the conceptualization of Arab American cuisine.

Food and Foodways in the Public Sector

The first Arab restaurant in Michigan was located in downtown Detroit in what was then the Maronite community (Ahdab-Yehia 1983). Sometime after the First World War, Fadel Ganem, a Maronite immigrant from Lebanon (then part of Greater Syria), opened a small restaurant to serve his countrymen. At that time, the Maronite community still included a large number of single men, and Ganem's restaurant, like restaurants serving the earliest waves of other immigrant groups, provided familiar, inexpensive food. The restaurant had no name, only a small sign in the window that announced, in Arabic, "Arab Food." Nevertheless, non-Arabs would occasionally wander in for a meal. Ganem was forced to close during the Great Depression and remained closed through most of World War II. Then, in 1944, he reopened across the street from his original restaurant. This time he put up an English sign, "The Sheik: Syrian Food." At first he worked alone; customers would go to the kitchen to serve themselves. Later, as his restaurant became more popular, he hired a waiter and then a woman to help out in the kitchen. His children would come in after school to wash dishes. In 1956, Ganem received an "Outstanding Immigrant of the Year" award by Michigan's governor, G. Mennen Williams for, according to one version of family legend, "having introduced Arab food to the public in Detroit." When Ganem died, The Sheik was taken over by his oldest daughter's husband, who had started working at the restaurant as a waiter. When he died, his widow and one of her sisters ran the restaurant for many years. The restaurant closed in 1987. For many older Detroiters, The Sheik was the place where their conception of Arab food was created.

According to our best sources, the first Middle Eastern import grocery was established in 1954 by another Lebanese Maronite, Gabriel Wadia. The site, across the street from the Eastern Market, had been previously occupied by an American-style grocery owned by a Lebanese Muslim. Wadia established the first Middle Eastern import market in Michigan, renaming his store Gabriel's. Gabriel's has changed hands several times since, but it still carries on a Middle East import business in the same location under the same name. Today, it is owned by a Greek from Lebanon, and his customers are mostly Yugoslavs, Albanians, and other non-Arabs, but many older Arab Americans remember when Gabriel's was the only source for many of their culinary necessities.

In Detroit, the earliest shops served the Christian (especially Maronite) community from Greater Syria, who constituted the majority of early Middle Eastern immigrants. These businesses were located in downtown Detroit, where the first Syrian/Lebanese neighborhood emerged. By 1900 they had formed a small community around Congress Street just east of downtown Detroit. Many of these immigrants worked as peddlers. Others were day laborers in Eastern Market wholesale businesses. Once they secured their economic footing, many used their savings to open small retail businesses. It was decades, however, before stores serving the specific needs of the community were established. By the time The Sheik closed in 1987, there was little left of the original Maronite neighborhood. As early as 1920–25, Maronites and other Syrian/Lebanese Christians were moving to the eastern fringe of Detroit and to Grosse Pointe, St. Clair Shores, and Roseville. Today, they are a highly assimilated, middle- and upper-class community, dispersed among German Americans, Italian Americans, and others. Many attend the nearest Catholic Church rather than a Maronite Rite congregation.

There is no Arab American commercial district within this community, though there are a number of Lebanese markets and restaurants scattered throughout the area. Food tends to be excellent, but it reflects the acculturation of older Syrian/Lebanese families. Typical is Steve's Backroom, which was founded as a bakery and Middle Eastern import grocer and later opened a restaurant in the back room. The store now specializes in Middle Eastern products and gourmet foods (Celestial Seasonings teas, flavored coffee beans, fancy bottled salad dressings). The restaurant decor is chic and decidedly non-Arab: Monet prints on the wall, lemon slices in the water glasses, flowers on the table, and cookies with the bill. The menu includes all the Lebanese standards, but also "Greek" salad, Armenian *lahmajoun* ("Armenian-style open-face meat pie," topped with cheese at an extra price), pasta primavera, cheesecake, lots of vegetarian variants, and some Americanized versions of traditional foods such as *kibbeh* sandwiches and baked apricots with butter pistachio paste.

There were also a few Lebanese Muslims who immigrated at the end of the nineteenth century. They included both Sunni and Shia, though the difference was not as important in Detroit as it had been in Syria. The largest group settled in an ethnically mixed community of auto workers near the original Ford plant in Highland Park. In 1919 they established one of the first mosques in America. When Henry Ford moved his operations to Dearborn in the 1920s, the autoworker community moved also, and the neighborhood known as the Southend was established adjacent to Ford's River Rouge Plant. Until the 1970s this neighborhood housed a mixture of Lebanese Muslims and central and southern Europeans. During and after World War II, migrants from Appalachia were added. Over the years, Lebanese immigrants continued to arrive, as did a growing number of Palestinian refugees and Yemeni sojourners. This flow increased substantially after the reform of U.S. immigration laws in 1965 and with political troubles in the Middle East. Meanwhile, central and southern Europeans were moving elsewhere, and the Southend became increasingly Arab, reaching a majority by the late 1960s. Today, the Southend has the densest Arab population in America. The commercial district at its core is wholly Arab-owned and very Middle Eastern in character. The Southend is still probably the best known of Metropolitan Detroit's Arab neighborhoods, but relatively few non-Arabs patronize its stores.

Throughout the 1970s, problems developed between the Southend's more acculturated Lebanese and Palestinians and its more conservative, rapidly growing population of Yemenis. By the time a Yemeni cleric was hired in 1976 at the Southend mosque (built by Lebanese Muslims in 1934), many Lebanese and Palestinians had left the Southend for the more affluent neighborhoods of east Dearborn, nearer the Joy Road mosque, which was established during the 1960s.[2] This new community is served by a large, ever-expanding commercial district located east, west, and south of the intersection of Warren and Schaefer Avenues, which is quickly becoming the new epicenter.

A third Middle Eastern business district lies along Seven Mile Road, east of Woodward Avenue. It serves what was once the core of Detroit's large Chaldean community.[3] As the Chaldean community prospered financially in the 1970s and 1980s, the majority reestablished themselves in Detroit's affluent northern suburbs, especially Southfield, Birmingham, Oak Park, Bloomfield Hills, and Troy, where they live interspersed among the area's large Jewish population. Scattered restaurants and stores serve this suburban community, but many Chaldeans return to Seven Mile for their weekly shopping. Moreover, the Seven Mile neighborhood continues to serve as a "reception neighborhood" for newly arrived Chaldean immigrants (Agócs 1981, 135–36).

Thus there are three major commercial districts serving the Middle Eastern community of Greater Detroit: the Southend, now mostly Yemeni; Warren-Schaefer Avenues, entirely Levantine (mostly Muslim Lebanese with some Palestinians); and Seven Mile, entirely Chaldean. There is, in addition, one small cluster of businesses on south Joseph Campeau in the Yemeni enclave that developed along the Hamtramck-Detroit border near the old Dodge Main plant, and another small cluster in Livonia, in an area of Palestinian settlement. These districts, together with other businesses in Metropolitan Detroit and in the suburbs, constitute an infrastructure of the national communities they serve and of the Arab American community as a whole. Virtually anything one might want is available in the districts: appliance repair shops, Arabic-language bookstores, tuxedo rentals, doctors, lawyers, accountants, realtors. Here, community members can easily conduct all their business completely in Arabic. Of particular importance in this infrastructure are a variety of food-related businesses, including grocers, *halal* butchers, juice bars, fruit and vegetable stands, coffeehouses, bakeries, pastry shops, and, of course, restaurants.

Ethnic Markets and National Boundaries

Each of the three major Arab business districts has a distinctive feel. The Southend, with its prominent mosque, covered women, and arabesque architecture appears the most "Middle Eastern." Warren Avenue, a busy thoroughfare, has the most hustle and bustle. Seven Mile, set in an economically depressed area and subject to a constant siphoning off of more financially secure residents, is a bit rundown by comparison. But inside the stores and restaurants, at least to an uninformed outsider, the products offered appear much the same. On closer examination, of course, there are differences. This is most obvious in the Chaldean markets because Chaldean food, which reflects both the Iraqi regional cuisine of which it is part and specific Chaldean characteristics, is quite distinctive. Moreover, the Chaldean community tends to be composed (unlike the Yemeni—though this is gradually changing) of families with women there to cook, and the large Chaldean middle class can afford pricier imports when necessary.

A market serving a Chaldean clientele will almost always include *toorshi* (see glossary) along with the usual bulk olives and pickled vegetables, dried shallots used to season homemade toorshi, large jars of pickled mangos (from India but with labels printed partly in Arabic), frozen quail (a Chaldean delicacy), dates (four or five varieties, inevitably including the best available in Detroit, several brands of date syrup, date vinegar, and date confections), specific spice mixtures, and certain breads not seen elsewhere. By contrast, in Yemeni markets serving a clientele that is made up of a disproportionate number of males without families, is less financially secure, and is saving money to send home to Yemen instead of spending it on fancy foods, there is little difference from Levantine stores, except for less variety. This is so even though Yemeni food is as different from Levantine food as is Chaldean. In Yemen, for example, there is a large variety of regional breads (Alford and Duguid 1995, 24–25), yet none of these has ever been bought and sold in the Detroit market.

Similarly, there are certain items specific to Lebanese markets. Most Lebanese markets with Lebanese clientele will stock *yerba maté*, a tea imported from Argentina whose use was established in parts of Lebanon and Syria after immigrants returned from South America accustomed to its use.[4] Any larger Lebanese market will carry *faraykee* (smoke-dried green wheat), a local specialty of the Bekaa Valley. Neither *yerba maté* nor *faraykee* would be found in a Chaldean or Yemeni market. There is amalgamation at work here as Lebanese from other regions at least become aware of these local specialties after encountering them in Detroit markets. We have no indication, however, that there has been any diffusion of *yerba maté* or *faraykee* to the local Palestinian, Yemeni, or Chaldean communities.

In nearly all respects, the stock of Palestinian markets cannot be distinguished from that of Lebanese markets even though they are sometimes marked by a distinctive name such as "Palestinian Food Market" or "Jerusalem Market." This is to be expected, since both groups are part of a larger Levantine culture area and share the same foodstuffs, if not always the same specific dishes. Much of what makes a cuisine distinctive has to do with recipes, techniques, and interpretations, even when this involves the same raw ingredients. This is especially true in the immigrant community, where a certain leveling takes place. Different national groups often make the same culinary accommodations. For some common ingredients, cooks from different backgrounds learn to make the same substitutions. The same item need not be imported from three different homelands. *Bulghur* is *bulghur,* after all. In fact, there may be an American producer of *bulghur;* no matter that he is an Armenian from California.

Not surprisingly, considerable amounts of shopping are done across national boundaries in Arab Detroit, the overriding objective being the acquisition of ingredients essential to home cuisine. Although patronizing a countryman may sometimes be a consideration, many others also determine where people shop, including proximity, convenience, service, and price. Arab markets serve a clientele far larger than the Arab American community. Many Greeks, Yugoslavs, Albanians, Romanians, Pakistanis, Indians, Jews, and especially Armenians find at least part of what they need to maintain their own culinary traditions in Arab markets. In fact, the failure to develop Armenian markets in greater Detroit, despite its large Armenian population, is probably a consequence of the excellent markets already available in the Arab community. A newly opened Armenian bakery, Arax Bakery in Warren, markets its products in Lebanese stores in the Southend and Chaldean stores in the suburbs, both of which are convenient to the principal Armenian residential areas.

Another reason for the similarity of stores in different neighborhoods is the strong emphasis on entrepreneurship in Levantine culture, coupled with the numerical and historical dominance of the Lebanese in Detroit. Nearly half the businesses in the Yemeni Southend, and these include all the larger markets, are owned by Lebanese. Markets in the small Yemeni neighborhood along the Hamtramck-Detroit border are also Lebanese.[5] This tendency in Yemeni neighborhoods has been reinforced by the perspective of many Yemenis who consider themselves sojourners who should make money quickly and send it back to Yemen, rather than invest it in stores in Detroit. But one also finds Lebanese markets in the Chaldean suburban neighborhoods (though not on Seven Mile, with one exception), where the stock includes all the Chaldean specifics found in Chaldean markets. This same entrepreneurial spirit can sometimes result in differentiation as well. Proprietors of stores will stock what they think their customers will purchase, whether these customers are of their own culture or not. One Lebanese baker in the Southend learned to make Yemeni specialties *samboosa* and *sabaya* for the Yemenis who form the majority of this community. When this same baker opened a second store uptown in Dearborn, where he hoped to attract non-Arab customers, he began to make broccoli pies, *halal* pepperoni rolls, and *zatar*-flavored croissants. Suburban Chaldean markets near Jewish residential areas make a point of stocking Israeli imports and certain foodstuffs of special interest to a Jewish clientele. Before Jewish holidays, they have special sales.

Before the proliferation of *halal* butchers in Detroit, some area Muslims used to purchase kosher meat. Now there are numerous *halal* butchers, with some in each of the three Arab commercial districts, including several wholesalers located near Eastern Market. All are more or less identical, with the same stock (including *basturma* and *soujouk*) and Middle Eastern-style butchering (cutting meat to order from carcasses rather than selling precut meat from cases). Chaldean butchers, being Christian, could sell pork. Yet patterns established in Iraq, where pork was not available, continue in Detroit, and pork is handled only by special order. Or, as one Chaldean butcher told us, "they buy their pork at Krogers." In fact, much of the meat sold by these Christian Chaldean butchers is *halal,* since they purchase at least some of their stock from fellow Arabs, the *halal* wholesalers.

Pastry shops are a special case. With just one exception, every Middle Eastern pastry shop in the Detroit area is Lebanese. Pastry making represents a Lebanese hegemony within the Middle Eastern community, just as Chaldean supermarkets and Lebanese gas stations constitute ethnic hegemonies (Hannerz 1975, 48–54). Lebanese pastry is held in extremely high esteem throughout the Middle Eastern community, and non-Lebanese find it very difficult to compete. In the Southend, a small pastry shop opened recently; the owner was Yemeni, but his products were purchased from a Lebanese producer. Along Seven Mile, there is only one establishment not owned by a Chaldean; it is a Lebanese pastry maker. The repute of Lebanese pastries is such that he, despite being surrounded by Chaldeans, calls his shop Beirut Pastries.

The one pastry shop that is *not* Lebanese, Fabulous Masri Sweets, is an interesting exception and provides a useful example of cultural standardization in food commerce. The owner of Masri's is a Palestinian, Kader Masri, whose paternal grandfather founded a pastry shop in the West Bank town of Nablus, in 1902. Kader's father took over the business in 1936 and added a second shop just outside Jerusalem. Both shops are still open, owned and operated by one of Kader's five brothers. All of them grew up in the business, and their father insisted that they learn to make pastry before they went on to their chosen professions. Kader came to the United States in 1974 to study accounting at the University of Detroit. After graduating he worked as an accountant for eleven years, mostly in Arizona. He then returned to the Detroit area, in large part because he missed the large and lively Arab American community, and he opened a pastry shop in east Dearborn outside both the Arab commercial districts. Although his shop has no economic relationship with the family business, it bears the same name, uses the same recipes, and has a picture of "the founder," his grandfather, prominently displayed on the wall.

Kader's shop differs in significant ways, however, from the family shops in Palestine. Lebanese pastry shops, reflecting the long history of French political and cultural influence in Lebanon, always include one case of French pastries in addition to phyllo-based and other Middle Eastern-style sweets. The Masri shops in Palestine have a more limited stock; they specialize in *kanafa,* a specialty of Nablus, and also carry a line of phyllo-based Middle Eastern pastries, but no French-style pastries. Nevertheless, Kader felt obliged to offer them here because all his (Lebanese) competitors offer them. He took a couple of seminars in French pastry but learned mostly from a cousin trained in Germany and Greece, who now works as a pastry chef in Los Angeles. He worked with his cousin for several weeks and learned fast. "Once you have knowledge of baking, it's just tricks and recipes," he commented. When Kader first opened, he hired specialists to do his French pastry. Now he can tell *them* what to do. Similarly, there are several Middle Eastern-style sweets, such as fried sweets and farina cake, that in the Middle East are sold only at specialty shops. In Dearborn, however, Kader had to add them because his Lebanese competitors already offered them. In the same manner, all Lebanese pastry shops in Detroit now feel obliged to offer *kanafa,* Masri's specialty. As a consequence, every pastry shop in the area, including Fabulous Masri Sweets and all the Lebanese shops, tend to have the same stock differing only in some specific variations of the same dishes.

Restaurants

The context in which non-Arabs most often encounter Arab foodways is the restaurant. And restaurants in Detroit, even more than grocers and pastry shops, demonstrate the amalgamation of different Arab national culinary traditions. Menus of nearly all Arab American restaurants, no matter what national group they serve or are owned by, have a core of Lebanese dishes. These include all those dishes Americans have come to think of as Arab food, including *tabbouli, fattoush, kibbeh* (in several of its many forms), *hummus,* and *baba ghannouj.* There are several reasons for this, but most important is the fact that the Lebanese were the first to open Arab restaurants in the United States and for many years had a monopoly on them. Thus, it was Lebanese restaurateurs who developed and standardized the Arab American menu, establishing a set of fairly standard expectations.[6] Both an upscale Chaldean restaurant in the suburbs and a working-class Yemeni restaurant in the Southend arrange a few of their respective national dishes around a Lebanese core. The only exception to this pattern are the Chaldean restaurants along and near Seven Mile Road, which cater to new arrivals. Even these places invariably serve Lebanese-made pocket bread (pita) instead of the variety of fine Chaldean breads available just a few doors away.

The acceptance of Lebanese menus by Yemeni and Chaldean restaurants was made easier by the fact that Lebanese food is known and respected throughout the Middle East. The Lebanese are cited by

Roden (1988, 3) as one of only two Middle Eastern societies—the other is Turkey—to have developed a restaurant culture. Detroit Chaldeans speak of having eaten in Lebanese restaurants in Iraq. In Detroit, many dishes considered by all to be Lebanese were already known elsewhere, at least by more sophisticated urbanites, as Lebanese. An Iraqi cookbook, for example, includes a recipe for *tabbouli,* noting that it is "originally Lebanese, but is popular in Baghdad" (Ing 1976, 28).

Pocket bread, which is widely known as pita or (in Detroit) as Arab bread and historically as Syrian bread, can now be bought in nearly every American supermarket. It is common in Levantine cities but is not known in Yemen and is only rarely eaten by Chaldeans in Iraq. Both the Yemenis and Chaldeans have a rich variety of other breads in their homelands. Yet every Yemeni and Chaldean restaurant serves pocket bread, with the exception of an upscale Chaldean restaurant in the suburbs, where they bake their own Chaldean rolls.

The diffusion of cuisine has not been one-way. All Lebanese restaurants in Detroit include one dish of Yemeni origin on their menu, *galaba.* The origins of this dish can be traced to the early period of Yemeni immigration to the Southend, before the development of Yemeni restaurants. Yemeni immigrants are said to have taught a Lebanese restaurant cook how to prepare their national dish. Once one Lebanese restaurant had it on the menu, it was only a matter of time before all Lebanese restaurants would have it, whether they had Yemeni customers or not. Similarly, a Lebanese restaurant, recently opened in the suburbs near a substantial Chaldean population, has several Chaldean specialties on the menu. Time will tell whether these dishes too will spread to other Lebanese restaurants.

The pattern, then, is one of considerable amalgamation of national cuisines in the public sector. While differences remain between restaurants, markets, and other food-related businesses associated with the different Arabic-speaking groups, and especially between Chaldean and all others, a general coalescence is obvious. The reasons behind the trend are numerous; they include Lebanese preeminence in Detroit, the vitality of Lebanese entrepreneurship, the sojourner status of Yemenis, specific cases of diffusion, and shared adaptations to American foods and foodways. The end result, albeit still incomplete, is the development of a new ethnic cuisine that is produced, consumed, and marketed in public contexts as Arab food. This New World cuisine is not the same as the national cuisines of Lebanon, Yemen, Iraq, Palestine, and other Arab homelands. As the next section will show, public versions of Arab American food are also unlike the foods Arab Americans eat at home in Detroit.

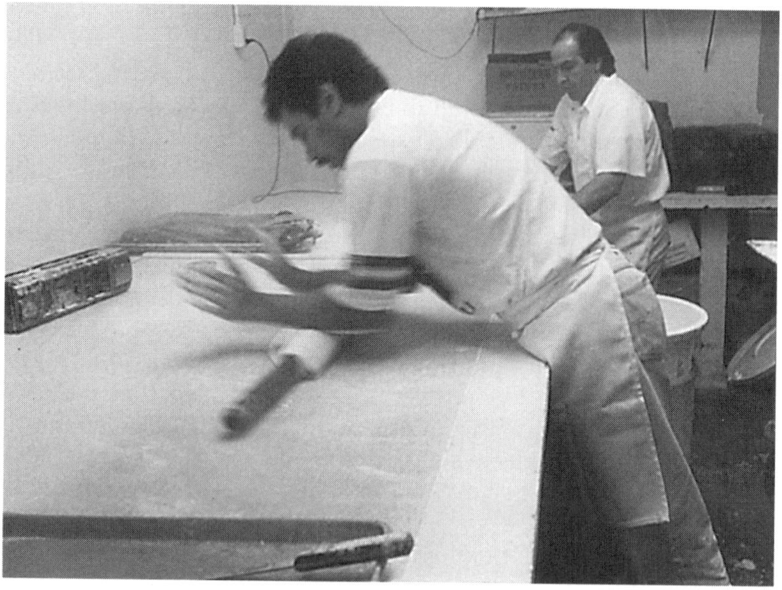

Fig. 32. Making phyllo at Fabulous Masri Sweets, Dearborn. Photograph by Hajer Mitchell.

Fig. 33. Crowds of shoppers purchase pastries during Ramadan at Shatila Bakery, Dearborn. Photograph by Bruce Harkness.

Fig. 34. The Sheik, ca. 1950. Proprietor Fadel Ganem is seated at the table. Courtesy of the ACCESS Museum of Arab Culture.

Fig. 35. Filling dinner orders at al-Ameer restaurant, Dearborn. Photograph by Bruce Harkness.

Fig. 36. Warren Avenue *halal* meat market, Dearborn. Photograph by Millard Berry.

Food and Foodways in the Private Sector

One should start at the beginning (of the meal, that is) with *mezzeh*, and so, too, *mezzeh* is an appropriate place to begin a discussion of Arab foodways in the home. *Mezzeh*, a varied selection of hot and cold appetizers, includes some of the best-known Arab foods. It is part of the culinary repertoire throughout the Levant, but it has been especially refined by the Lebanese. Some *mezzeh* dishes, but not *mezzeh* culture—that is, the body of ideas and practices surrounding *mezzeh*—have been adopted in the cuisine of most Arabic-speaking countries.

Mezzeh is consumed in both Arab American restaurants and homes. In the former context, it is more or less codified; in the latter, it is ever-changing and adaptive. As a system, *mezzeh* and the *mezzeh* culture are a legacy of the Ottoman Turks (*meze* is Turkish, meaning tidbit). As a culinary tradition, *mezzeh* extends beyond the Arab world as far west as the former Yugoslavia, where its function, structure, and practice are similar to the *mezzeh* of the Arab countries. Anyone buying a drink in Greece, for example, is automatically served a plate with something to nibble on as part of their order.[7]

Including in its very structure any number of small plates of varying foods, a *mezzeh* table often represents amalgamation and acculturation, as it contains foods from other regions or nations, a chef's invention, or adaptations of traditional foods. *Mezzeh* may be as simple as Arab bread and olives. For special occasions, it can feature dozens of dishes, including cheese, pickles, salads, savory pastries, stuffed vegetables, dips, and meats. Several *mezzeh* dishes, however, are regarded as Lebanese national foods, and their presence is almost mandatory except in the simplest *mezzeh. Tabbouli,* characterized by one Lebanese American as "the queen of the table," the ubiquitous *hummus, baba ghannouj,* and *kibbeh nayee* are all standardized *mezzeh* fare. They are available in Arab restaurants and are part of every Lebanese home cook's repertoire.

With its great variety of dishes, *mezzeh* invites new additions and easily lends itself to change. Women often add a platter of American-style raw vegetables and dip to the *mezzeh* table when they entertain. Consequently new combinations occur, such as when celery is dipped into *hummus* and *kibbeh* into mayonnaise-based dips. While cheeses and crackers are not strangers to an Arab American *mezzeh,* at one event, blue cheese mixed with *labneh* was such a success that it now appears on *mezzeh* tables throughout southeast Michigan. Cookbook writer Mary Laird Hamady (1987, 72) encourages readers to use their imaginations. "If we have Arabic bread," she writes of herself and her Lebanese American husband, "we could convert ordinary leftovers of any national origin into a respectable *mezzeh.*" One Lebanese woman in Detroit occasionally includes Chinese egg rolls on her *mezzeh* table.

Today, the *mezzeh* served in Arab American restaurants and that served in homes can differ in its relationship to the rest of the meal. In restaurants one can eat *mezzeh* by itself, but when an entree is served, removing *mezzeh* from the table, leaving only the main dish, is a traditional pattern. In many homes, however, *mezzeh* consists of a limited number of dishes and is served along with other foods as side dishes. Other differences can be attributed to the distinctive Lebanese *mezzeh* culture. First, according to some Lebanese Detroiters, one cannot fully partake in *mezzeh* without *arak* or alcohol of some kind. Whether Muslim or Christian, Lebanese distinguish themselves from other Arabs by drinking alcohol with *mezzeh.*[8] Second, an elaborate *mezzeh,* consisting of a wide assortment of dishes, is more often served at holidays and to guests. It is used to create a social time during which diners eat, drink, and converse.[9] It is not everyday fare.

It is popularly thought by strangers to the Middle East that wine and alcohol are taboo and do not figure in the food cultures of the area. This is not entirely true. Prohibition came to be associated with Muslims, but drinking alcohol is common in much of Arab society, though it is done more discretely among Muslims. Alcohol has always been part of urban settings, and in sophisticated, literate, and prosperous circles, elaborate cultures and etiquettes grew up around drink (Zubaida and Tapper 1994, 15; Tapper 1994, 219). With or without alcohol, *mezzeh,* with its variations in content and performance, is a durable component of Arab American culture and cuisine.

Unlike *mezzeh,* in which amalgamation and acculturation occur and are even celebrated, overt signs of amalgamation in *kibbeh* are not. Although one may speak loosely of national cuisines, in reality, each locality and community within national boundaries has its own distinctive food styles, including dishes that are described in a common vocabulary but that differ from each other in definable ways. The same word for foods may cross numerous linguistic and political boundaries. The *kofte/kibbeh* category is one such example. *Kibbeh* exists in many *bulghur*-based versions throughout Lebanon, Syria, and Palestine, and in parts of Iraq, with *bulghur* and with rice (Zubaida 1994a, 35). Lebanese claim *kibbeh* as their dish, stating that each village makes a distinctive version and each cook has her special recipe, only a few of which seem to exist in Michigan. In most Arabic restaurants, the *kibbeh* menu is limited, offering at best baked, raw, and fried versions. In homes, there may be an amalgamation of types found in Lebanon, but there is still considerable variety.

Kibbeh takes many shapes. The stuffing can be placed between two layers of meat, filled into oblong shapes of meat, or mixed directly with the meat and *bulghur* and shaped into balls. It is served raw, baked, fried, simmered in yogurt, in broth, or in a tomato base. There also are variations with rice or potato. It can be simply spiced or it can use a special blend of many spices such as the mix from south Lebanon that includes (among other ingredients) rose petals. Another Lebanese variant includes pomegranate juice. This hardly exhausts all possibilities, but it does account for more versions than are found in restaurants. *Kibbeh* is one of those foods for which there are as many versions as there are cooks, and each prefers her own to that of others. For the time being, the amalgamation of even the Lebanese *kibbeh*s (not to mention the Palestinian and Chaldean versions) seems unlikely in such an atmosphere of pride. Changes are taking place, nonetheless. The tradition of pounding lamb has given way to grinding it, a change that may have started in the old country, and lamb is being replaced by beef.

The widespread use of rice in the Middle East is relatively recent (Zubaida 1994b, 93). Except in a few rice-producing areas, rice was a luxury food for the tables of the wealthy and for special occasions. Today, the cultures of the region share similar methods of preparing rice. "Arab rice," a term denoting certain ingredients and preparations, is one example of a pan-Arab dish. In Greater Detroit, most Arab Americans refer to rice by equating it with their nationality—Lebanese Americans, for example, call it Lebanese rice. Yet Arab rice (whether it is called Lebanese or Palestinian) is essentially the same; it can be cooked simply with butter or elaborately with nuts, butter, spices, and lamb. Of course, many Lebanese Americans proclaim Lebanese rice to be the best. Every culture is ethnocentric about its food. Expressions of pride and boastfulness almost always focus on the basics, what Sidney Mintz (1989, 118) refers to as the core of a people's diet: the starchy center of a cuisine that must be eaten with every meal in order to feel as though one has eaten. Arab rice and bread are examples. An Arabic saying asks, "what do people in Paradise eat?" The answer is, "Rice and butter" (Zubaida 1994b, 93). Lebanese American ethnocentrism is not unusual, according to Mintz, but it does imply a lack of contact and experience with the rice of other Arab Americans in Detroit.

In the Middle East, rice was a staple only in limited rice-growing areas, the Nile delta, the Caspian provinces of Iran, and the southern marshlands of Iraq (Zubaida 1994b, 93). It was imported into other areas, where locally grown wheat was the primary staple. Rice is not served, for example, at every meal in the Middle East, but bread is, even when rice is also served. However, rice is a valued and important ingredient for celebrations in the Middle East. As in many other cultures, with affluence and availability, prestigious foods such as rice often become more everyday. *Bulghur,* though, when cooked as a pilav, is regarded by most Arabs as an inferior substitute for rice. This sentiment contrasts with that of the Chaldeans, who take great pride in the *bulghur* produced in northern Iraq and various dishes made with it.

While *bulghur* is not always regarded negatively in Greater Detroit, rice is held in high regard. In Dearborn, the first dish Lebanese grandmothers teach their granddaughters to cook is Lebanese rice.[10] For Thanksgiving, Lebanese rice with butter, nuts, spices, and meat is always present, sometimes as turkey stuffing, sometimes as a side dish. Lebanese rice is so central to the diet of one woman we interviewed that she eats it with almost everything, including Chinese food. An Arab American firefighter told us he is proud of having taught his fellow firefighters to cook Arab foods, especially Lebanese rice.

Sharing Arab Foods and Foodways

Every culture is proud of its food traditions and tends to be ambivalent about (or even contemptuous of) others. Others may eat foods similar to ours, but they do not cook them half as well, they use too much or too little spice, the fats are greasy, the oils smell, and so on. However, under conditions of social stability and harmony, people are curious about the foods of others and experiment with them. Within and between ethnic groups in Greater Detroit there exist formal and informal means of food exchange that contrast sharply with the formal distribution systems found in restaurants. The stability of Arab ethnic cuisines may be greatly affected by the nature of these nonmarket exchanges with non-Arabs and Arabs of other national backgrounds.

The foods traded over the backyard fence, at the workplace, and over coffee are regarded as "foreign" foods by the people who receive them, even when they can successfully reproduce them in their own kitchens. In Dearborn, neighbors frequently exchange gifts of cooked food and try each other's recipes. As a token of their friendship and hospitality, for example, Yemeni women give gifts of *sabaya* to their female neighbors. As in Yemen, offering this layered flaky pastry, lavished with clarified butter and honey, is a way of honoring a person (Maclagan 1994, 161). The women who receive this dish may not always understand the deeper meaning of the gesture. Nonetheless, a pattern of neighborly exchange and a sense of obligation are established through this gift of food.[11]

In one such demonstration of friendship, Fatme Boomrad, a Lebanese woman, reciprocated a Yemeni woman's gift of *sabaya* with a gift of spinach and meat pies. Failing miserably when she tried to make *sabaya* herself, Fatme and her neighbor agreed to continue exchanging Lebanese pies for Yemeni *sabaya*. In another exchange, Samiha Abusalah, a Palestinian woman, picked grape leaves from her Yemeni neighbor's fence and in return taught her to make stuffed grape leaves, a food unknown to the neighbor before she arrived in Dearborn. In exchange, the Yemeni woman occasionally sends *sabaya* to Samiha. An Italian/Polish American has built a close friendship with her Lebanese neighbor over coffee and Lebanese pastries during mid-morning visits. On occasion Samiha also makes Lebanese hot potatoes that a Lebanese coworker taught her. Similarly, Hana

Khraizat, a Lebanese woman, learned to make apple pie from her Hungarian American neighbor.

When sharing special foods with other groups, one usually tries to maintain a balance—sometimes a delicate one—between what is distinctive and what is familiar enough to appeal. *Aseed,* an interesting Yemeni dish similar to several West African dishes, is a case in point. Flour is stirred in simmering water until it is very stiff. It is then turned out onto a platter and around it is poured *maraq,* a robust lamb broth. *Aseed* is eaten by tearing off a piece with the fingers and dipping it into the broth. Whereas it is normal for immigrant foods to change, the change in *aseed* in Michigan has been strictly ideological. In Yemen, *aseed* is considered poor food; in Detroit, it has acquired new meaning as an ethnic marker.[12] Yemenis do not make gifts of *aseed* as readily as they do *sabaya,* perhaps because they have realized the taste for *aseed* is acquired. In one case, a third-generation Lebanese American who received a gift of *aseed* and *maraq* liked the *maraq* very much but not the *aseed.* Now she makes *maraq* herself and prepares American-style dumplings with it instead of *aseed.*

Muslim women of the Southend also offer informal hospitality to their neighbors with mid-morning coffee and snacks. After chores are finished, women casually visit each other. The talk often comes back to the topic of food: "what are you cooking today?" Children present listen closely. If they don't like what is being cooked at home, they know they can eat with the neighbors instead. They just appear and are welcome. This open-door policy extends to one's married children as well, especially when the daughter works and has little time to cook properly for her husband and herself. They eat their main meal with her mother, or his.

Foods from the Homeland

Although almost everything needed to cook and eat Arab food is readily available in Greater Detroit, some food items are just better in the homeland, and Arab Detroiters look to their kin back home for products they are accustomed to. Sumac, though available in the United States, is neither as strong nor as flavorful as that obtained from a trusted merchant back home. *Kishik* available in Detroit is generally not acceptable. Some families make their own, but the best is made from goat's-milk yogurt. *Kamuni* is a special combination of spices and rose petals added to the kinds of *kibbeh* made in south Lebanon, and the best *kamuni* originates in this region.[13] Two grades of *faraykee* are available in some Dearborn markets, but only one is regarded by south Lebanese women as the real thing. It should be greenish-brown and smoky, the result of being roasted over an open fire in the field. And only *faraykee* roasted by one's family will do. Women visiting relatives in the old country bring these essential foods back to the States in amounts sufficient to share with kin and neighbors. Relatives also mail seasonal packages when these valued foods are freshly prepared.

Until recently only dried and frozen *molokiyeh* (mucilaginous green leaf) were available in local markets. Not satisfied with its cleanliness, some women continued to bring from the old country *molokiyeh* dried by family members. At first grown only by a few, *molokiyeh* is now being grown in yards and gardens throughout Greater Detroit and shared with neighbors across the fence. It is beginning to appear in markets as well, although the seeds for this much-loved green are still not available commercially. This culinary link with people back home facilitates informal food exchanges that reinforce family ties and increase the stability of ethnic foods in Greater Detroit.

Innovation and Change

Ethnic foodways are more than surviving relics or inferior versions of old country cuisine. Foods are constantly changing. By altering a dish, instead of refusing to make it for lack of proper ingredients, women demonstrate both their commitment to a food tradition and their creativity. Cuisines in the old country change too. Women often return from visits to the Middle East with new recipes they have learned from kin or with new ways to cook familiar foods. One of the first, almost imperceptible changes in ethnic food occurs as "substitution," a process about which there is very little ethnographic study (Mintz 1989, 119). Without access to traditional foodstuffs, cooks make substitutions. However, lack of ingredients is not the only reason for substitution. Today, despite the availability of raw materials, cooks are increasingly likely to substitute "foreign" ingredients for traditional ones. Ricotta or mozzarella are used in *kanafa,* lamb is replaced by beef, Mazola oil is substituted for clarified butter, pancake syrup for date syrup, Crisco or peanut butter for *tahini,* and pinto and navy beans for small fava beans. Some innovations are said to improve Old World recipes. Mayonnaise is added to *hummus* to make it creamier. Lamb is basted with soy sauce to enhance its color. Dried onion soup mix is combined with meat for Lebanese pies. In areas without Detroit's Middle Eastern culinary resources and overall ethnic infrastructure, much more substitution is necessary.

Children are the quickest to adapt to American culture and change the way their families eat. Through their school experiences, many kids come to like American food better than Arabic. Some women accommodate their children by cooking American food whenever they request it. Ehsan Mroui, for example, no longer prepares lamb brains, lamb stomach, stuffed casings, or green beans with lamb. Instead, she cooks mashed potatoes, gravy, hamburgers, hot dogs, and french fries for the children, and Arab food for the adults.

On the other hand, American experiences can strengthen Arab traditions. At home in Lebanon, Fatme Boomrad recalled how much she disliked *mujaddara.* The lentils were never cleaned well enough. In the United States, however, she found lentils to be grit free, and now she loves this dish. For some, traditional foods become a priority because of their nostalgic associations. Julia Najor speaks for many when she says, "We eat these old dishes more in America than we did at home—lentils, *bulghur,* wheat berries, barley. [They] bring memories. When you are poor, you want what you can't afford. When you can afford [what you had wanted], you want those dishes you ate when you were poor."[14]

Clearly, cultural heritage and identity are factors contributing to the perpetuation of some foods. Several Lebanese Detroiters (one of whom is a third-generation American) still make *dehen,* or *qawahrma,* a confit-like preserved meat. Before refrigeration, Lebanese village women preserved lamb by boiling pieces in the fat from the tail of sheep until the meat was dry. It was then placed in pottery jugs and covered with fat, which sealed out air and preserved the meat. Lamb prepared in this way has a distinctive flavor much loved by older people who grew up eating it. Today, Detroit women make *dehen* not to preserve the meat, but because it is a distinctive food with a special flavor and is part of their diet.[15] It is used in pies and with fried eggs. Many women make their own *maftool,* despite its availability in markets. Fatme Boomrad continues to make *khubuz markook* (mountain thin bread), baking it on a steel dome (*sajj*) brought from Lebanon, even though it also is available in nearby Arab bakeries.[16] In all these examples, the individuals are motivated by a desire to keep a tradition that consciously links them to their Lebanese American identity.

New Traditions and Old: Foodways at the Holidays

Ethnic religious observances and holidays are also closely linked to heritage. The greatest stability in Arab American foods is seen in these contexts. Women who do not have time to cook Arab food every day gather with other family members and cook it for holidays. The dishes tend to be traditional, distinctive of one ethnicity, and have symbolic meaning. Christmas, for example, is the most significant Chaldean holy season and is widely celebrated with feasting and visiting. A special and very popular Chaldean Christmas dish is *pacha,* a great favorite among Chaldean Americans of all ages, who feel united spiritually by the knowledge that all Chaldeans are eating it at the same time.[17]

Among Muslims, Ramadan is the most holy observance. Although this is the month of fasting, it is also a time of communal feasting. The breaking of the fast, *fatur,* functions for Muslims as does *pacha* among Chaldeans. Symbolically, Muslims are united by the very act of breaking the fast according to the same proscriptions. Between sunrise and sunset there is total abstinence from food and drink. Breaking fast is done in a number of ways; the traditions vary from culture to culture, sometimes from family to family. At sunset, people might eat a date, drink water, coffee, or an apricot drink (made from apricot "leather"), or take a taste of salt, after which they pray and then eat a meal. Extended families gather to break the fast together. Except for specific sweets made for Ramadan, the meal does not necessarily consist of special foods (but the foods are usually traditional and ethnic); there is just more of everything and every attempt is made to prepare the food well. Women prepare many different dishes to ensure that everyone will find enough of what they like to eat. Soup is often served at the *fatur.* At the Lebanese Muslim Mroui household, for example, the table was covered with dishes containing *fattoush, baba ghannouj,* south Lebanese *kibbeh nayee* and radishes, Lebanese rice, barbecued lamb, fried sardines with *tahini* sauce (*tarator*), pocket bread fried in the same oil as the sardines, roasted chicken, french fries, Pepsi, punch, and water.[18] Among the homemade sweets were *mamoul,* rice pudding, and *katayef.* Other sweets had been purchased at bakeries.

By contrast, at the first-generation Yemeni American Al-Mawri home, the menu had been prepared from familiar Middle Eastern ingredients, but the results were quite unlike Levantine fare. The *fatur* included the following: *shafoot* (a creamy souplike dish of yogurt, pieces of Arab bread, garlic, hot peppers, cilantro, cumin, salt, and liquid smoke), *samboosa* (fried triangles of Chinese egg roll dough filled with ground lamb, onion, parsley, garlic, cilantro, black pepper, green hot pepper, cumin, and salt), *aseed* and *maraq, fatoot* (Arabic bread, dribbled with hot clarified butter and a little liquid smoke and covered with meat broth), *ma'soub* (flour and water mixed to the consistency of thick cake batter, cooked on the stove until firm like bread, then broken up, mixed with hot clarified butter and honey, and eaten with fingers), *bagiah* (a falafel-like dish made from a "special bean," cilantro, onions, parsley, and deep fried as patties and eaten with bread and *sahawig*, a sauce with cumin and hot pepper), *zurbian* (rice with lamb, potatoes, yogurt, black pepper, cinnamon, cardamom, and garlic), *sabayah* (layers of paper-thin dough made from flour, water, eggs, milk, and black cumin seeds), *salata* (head lettuce, onions, tomatoes, cucumbers, radishes, carrots dressed with lemon juice, salt, and pepper), several types of Arab breads, fruits, and sweets (*mahalabiah*, a custard with fruit; *labanieh*, fruit custard served on cake; *kalaj*, cream-filled thin dough fried and covered with sugar syrup); sweet *samboosa* filled with dates, coconut, or raisins fried and dribbled with sugar syrup. Of this large menu, only *kalaj* was not Yemeni and, according to the family, is not known in Yemen. Rather, they learned it from Lebanese Americans after settling in Detroit. There is otherwise little indication of amalgamation in this Yemeni menu, a factor that may reflect limited contact with non-Yemenis.

Easter among Christian Arabs is also a time for feasting. Sylvia Freij and Yasmine Harb, first-generation Palestinian Americans from Ramallah, served their extended family a large Easter meal consisting of fourteen *mezzeh* dishes followed by meats, Arab rice, yogurt, and salad. The only break with Palestinian traditional cuisine was the inclusion of cheddar cheese as *mezzeh*.[19] In Ramallah, it is customary at Easter to have a whole roasted lamb stuffed with rice, and a salad. In Detroit, people are too busy to cook Arab food every day, and cooking an entire lamb is no longer convenient, even on special occasions. Therefore, instead of preparing a whole lamb for Easter, the extended family gets together to share an array of their favorite traditional Ramallah dishes. What used to be ordinary food in the home village has become, in Greater Detroit, the holiday food on which these Palestinians feast together.

One should consider, by way of contrast, the holiday dinner served by the Christian, extended family of Olivia and Lafi Khalil and Mary David. Family members include first- as well as fourth-generation Americans, great-grandparents as well as great-grandchildren, all of whom trace their ancestry to Syria, Palestine, or Lebanon. Their Christmas dinner reflects this mix of generations, decades of changes in the United States, and the periodic reinvigoration of old country food traditions by newly arrived family members. Appetizers were mainstream American (sliced cheese and crackers, nuts, sausages, and nachos). The main course, the same each year, was a conscious selection of traditional Levantine dishes, including traditional *mezzeh* served as side dishes. The menu consisted of baked *kibbeh, tabbouli* (served with head lettuce), grape leaves stuffed with rice and meat, yogurt, *hummus,* and *mansef.* Other dishes included sliced roasted turkey, mixed pickles, and Arab bread. *Mansef,* traditionally served at weddings and other celebratory events, was the centerpiece. Dessert included Arab pastries, American pies, cookies, and fruit. Covered with Levantine and ethnic American fare, this holiday table reflected the identities of all the celebrants gathered around it.

Thanksgiving

Thanksgiving, the all-American holiday, is eagerly adopted by immigrants as a way of participating in American culture and demonstrating their Americanness. Most ethnic groups participate in this day by intermingling holiday foods from their own cultures with symbolic American foods. In the process, however, the history, symbolism, and mythology of the day, as most Americans understand them, often do not transfer. What does carry over is the universally understood practice of feasting. The traditional Arab-style show of abundance at table coincidentally communicates a bountiful Thanksgiving meal.

The requisite turkey is always present. Its size a symbol of bounty, the Thanksgiving turkey would be appropriate for an Arab feast as well. Often, Arab American tables include one or two other large pieces of meat, such as a leg of lamb or beef roast, increasing the sense of boundless plenty. Arab rice is perhaps as essential as turkey; it may stuff the turkey (in the same way it stuffs a whole lamb), or it may be cooked separately. Among the symbolic Thanksgiving foods, Arabs in Detroit rarely eat cranberry sauce, most admit to disliking pumpkin pie, and many do not particularly like turkey. The Thanksgiving menu of Fatme Boomrad's multigenerational Lebanese Muslim family, for instance, includes the essential Arab dishes and illustrates their idea of what an American feast should be: "Lebanese" rice; turkey without stuffing; Lebanese rice with meat, spices, and nuts; yogurt; canned cranberries; corn; mashed potatoes; gravy; green and fruit salads (canned peaches on lettuce with cottage cheese). Desserts included homemade apple pie and Sara Lee pumpkin pies and cheesecake.

For a first-generation Yemeni family, the Thanksgiving meal also represents Arab and American cultures. Having once been married to an American, the head of the Hamdani household instructed his new Yemeni wife on how to prepare a Thanksgiving meal. She roasted a turkey with Stove-Top dressing and made potato salad, white rice, and salad with creamy French dressing. The husband purchased several JELL-O salads from a delicatessen. Served with this was a Yemeni lamb and vegetable stew with Arab bread. The turkey, stuffing, and JELL-O salads are appropriate foods for a Thanksgiving feast, which was consumed in the traditional Yemeni way. The male guests, who ate separately from the women and children, sat on the floor around a tablecloth laden with food. Each had a plate and tableware but soon dispensed with these and finished the American meal in traditional Yemeni village style, with bread and fingers.

The third-generation Palestinian/Lebanese Christian family of Frank and Sylvia Sophiea in the vicinity of Flint, celebrate their Thanksgiving in a consciously ethnic manner, evoking their heritage on this all-American occasion. The grandmother was introduced to Thanksgiving by an American friend soon after she arrived in the United States. The friend's turkey recipe is still the basis of this family's Thanksgiving meal, which, in 1995, consisted of turkey with American-style dressing, accompanied by Cornish hens stuffed with Arab rice and a salad of tomatoes, cucumbers, parsley, and lettuce. This was preceded by *mezzeh—hummus* and *baba ghannouj,* Arab bread, and sliced fresh vegetables. The meal concluded with fresh fruit followed by *harissa.* This celebration repeats a pattern seen among other ethnic groups. The turkey, as the center of the meal, is surrounded by ethnic dishes. On holidays, families several generations removed from the immigrants often go back to traditional ethnic foods; at Thanksgiving, these are the foods they want to eat.

Thanksgiving in Arab American homes does not differ radically from other American homes. The difference is in the meaning of the event more than its content. Arab Americans have taken up the turkey as a symbol of this American holiday and surrounded it with their traditional ethnic foods. However, Arab American Thanksgivings do not embody the Pilgrim mythology known to most other Americans. Consuming turkey, stuffing, cranberries, and JELL-O salads in itself symbolically demonstrates Americanness, but by including Arab foods at Thanksgiving, the families discussed here mesh two cultures, demonstrating their Arab Americanness. Thanksgiving is an American family holiday rooted and observed according to family tradition. Consequently, it is unlikely that Arab American celebrations of Thanksgiving will amalgamate to become a kind of pan-Arab tradition. Rather, Arab Americans, like all Americans, will observe discrete family or ethnic Thanksgiving traditions that have been maintained across successive generations.

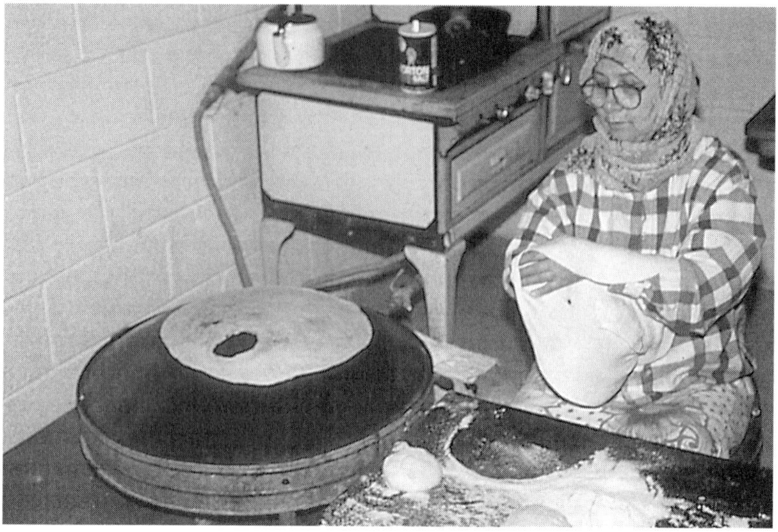

Fig. 37. After almost fifty years in Michigan, Fatme Boomrad still makes her own mountain bread because it tastes best. Photograph by William G. Lockwood.

Fig. 38. Fatme Boomrad fills *fatayer* (pies) with meat, spinach, and *dehen*. Photograph by William G. Lockwood.

Fig. 39. Making *kibbeh nayee* for the 1996 annual fund-raising dinner at the American Bekaa Center, Dearborn. Photograph by Yvonne R. Lockwood.

Fig. 40. An evening meal at the Mroui home during Ramadan. Photograph by Bruce Harkness.

Conclusion

The foregoing has been a demonstration of ethnic cultural processes, specifically the evolution of Arab American food and foodways in both the public and private sectors. Within this context, it is possible to identify several specific types of culture change. Considerable debate has ensued in the past over the meaning of "acculturation." Here we will reserve the term for the simple meaning of one subordinate group adopting the culture traits of a dominant group. Ample example of this exists in both the private and public spheres of Detroit's Arab American community, from grocery stores selling Cheez Whiz and Cool Whip amidst the *tahini* and olive oil, to mothers preparing hot dogs for their kids. In some cases, the cultural exchange is accompanied by a change in meaning. The recently arrived Yemeni family gathered for the first time around a Thanksgiving turkey do not invest it with the symbolic load of the Pilgrims, Native Americans, and giving thanks but, rather, with the meaning "Now we are Americans."

Another common process is the diffusion of culinary traits from other ethnic groups. A Palestinian who makes tacos and burritos after eating them in a Mexican restaurant, a Lebanese woman who learns southern cooking from her Appalachian migrant husband and then passes recipes to her sister, a Lebanese cook who adds Chinese egg rolls to her *mezzeh* table: all are examples of diffusion at work. This process is not limited to the private sphere. One Arab-owned restaurant advertises "Arab, American and Italian Food." When asked "why Italian?" the owner's only answer was that there are many Italians in Dearborn. A newly remodeled Lebanese bakery-delicatessen on Warren Avenue has "welcome" written on the wall in Arabic, English, and Italian, presumably for the same reason. Yemenis who purchased a previously established pizza restaurant added *halal* pizza (though they have not listed it on the menu). Similar diffusion of foods occurs between different national groups, principally the Lebanese, Yemenis, and Palestinians, who most commonly are neighbors or work together.[20] They seem to regard foods from other Arabs much as they do foods received from non-Arabs: as exotic treats. In some cases, women incorporate such dishes into their own repertoire. But just as often, they do not try, or, if they do try, they are unsuccessful. In such cases, enduring trade partnerships are often established for continued exchange of "foreign" treats.

The process of amalgamation of culinary traditions has been of particular interest to us. In other words, to what degree have original differences between national cuisines decreased? Just how much diffusion has there been between them? To what extent is there a generalized Arab American cuisine? It is impossible to quantify such changes, but it seems that far greater amalgamation of food traditions has occurred in the public or commercial sector than in Arab American homes. Driven especially by commercialism and the need to keep up with competitors, an Arab American cuisine is emerging in most restaurants. Markets and butcher shops have more or less identical stock. There is a near monopoly of pastry shops by members of one national group, who supply the same pastry to all others.

Although some cultural exchange happens between national groups, each can be seen to constitute a separate but parallel process of creolization. Thus, to some extent, separate Lebanese American, Yemeni American, Palestinian American, and Chaldean American cuisines have developed. It is not surprising that Arab American amalgamation and national group distinctiveness can coexist at different levels of cultural integration. It is the cultural manifestation of the phenomenon called "nesting." Ethnic groups are almost never mutually exclusive. More often, one identity is nested within another more encompassing one, which sometimes lies within another more inclusive identity. Thus, to be Lebanese American or Yemeni American does not mean one is any less Arab American or vice versa. Individuals are free to chose their identifying label situationally, based on strategic considerations, from any number of such identities, including both nested ethnic identities and others based on occupation, class, region of origin, gender.[21] Each of these identities is associated with a particular subculture. It seems to us that a model of ethnic change based on parallel processes of creolization is much more in line with a view of America as a multicultural society, just as the acculturation model was more appropriate for the image of America as a melting pot or, predating that, as an Anglo-conforming society (Gordon 1964).

It must be emphasized that the cultural processes we have discussed above are ongoing, resulting in an ever-evolving situation. Even as we write, a new community of Iraqi Shia is taking shape in the Detroit area, new restaurants with new menus are opening, and a new group of immigrant homemakers are adapting their cooking to new and unfamiliar circumstances. Iraqi Shia will soon make their own contributions to ever-changing Arab American food and foodways in Greater Detroit.

Acknowledgments: This work draws in part from informal contact with Metropolitan Detroit's Arab American community, particularly its public sector food and foodways, since our arrival in Michigan in

1969. More formal field research was conducted in 1988 and 1994–96 with the support of the National Endowment for the Humanities, National Endowment for the Arts, Michigan Council for Arts and Cultural Affairs, and Michigan Traditional Arts Program (Michigan State University Museum). We wish to acknowledge field-workers Barbara George Gallagher, Sally Howell, Haajar Mitchell, Rosina Hassoun, and Dawn Ramey, whose reports and discussions about food and celebration contributed to this paper. And last but not least, we thank the many community businesses and men and women who shared information and food with us.

Notes

1. See Sidney Mintz (1989) for a particularly eloquent statement of why anthropologists should study food and foodways.
2. This is an extremely abbreviated account of a complex series of events. For a more complete history, see Abraham, Abraham, and Aswad (1983, 171–75).
3. For further history and ethnography of Detroit's Chaldeans, see Sengstock (1982) and (1983).
4. For further data regarding the diffusion of *yerba maté* to Lebanon, see Luxner (1995).
5. In contrast, an entrepreneurial subculture is alive and well in some other migrant Yemeni communities, especially those in South Arabia, East Africa, and Southwest Asia (Nabeel Abraham, personal conversation, ca. 1998).
6. We have been amazed over the years at how fast and how thoroughly menus in ethnic restaurants become standardized in America. There is a strong tendency for all restaurants of any ethnic group to offer the same selection of dishes from what is inevitably a much larger repertoire. Afghani Americans provide a good example, one easier to document since the entire population came all at once relatively recently. Within just a couple of years, Afghani restaurants were opened up across America by people who had never previously owned a restaurant and with menus of the same ten to twelve dishes.
7. For the history and development of Arab foods, see Goody (1982, 127–33), Roden (1972, 1–29), and Zubaida and Tapper (1994, 1–17).
8. Our informant was a sophisticated, educated, urban, nonobservant Muslim. Her opinion, though shared by many, is denied by observant Muslims. Consumption of alcohol by Lebanese Americans dropped signifi-

cantly after the Iranian revolution in 1979, which led to increased awareness and politicization of Islam in Detroit and Lebanon.

9. Some restaurants in Lebanon are known for *mezzeh* tables of over a hundred dishes. Only one upscale Lebanese restaurant in southeast Michigan offers a large and varied *mezzeh.*
10. With few exceptions, women we interviewed attributed their first cooking lessons to mothers-in-law, neighbors, and extended kin after they married. As unmarried teenagers their mothers regarded schooling and studies most important and discouraged their presence in the kitchen. Although education is still highly valued, we found a number of grandmothers in greater Detroit who insisted their granddaughters learn the basics of cooking while still living at home.
11. *Sabaya* is generically an old dish. The invention of layered pastries, such as baklava and *sabaya,* is attributed to the Turks. Nomadic Turks were making layered dough products as early as the eleventh century. Paper-thin layers of dough are thought to be the invention of the royal kitchens at the Topkapi Sarayi (Perry 1994, 87).
12. See Halpern (1958, 57) regarding a similar shift in Serbia with corn bread and wheat bread.
13. The "all spice" of the Lebanese and Palestinians and the "curry powder" of the Chaldeans are other mixtures of a variety of spices, up to seven spices for the all spice, and as many as thirteen for the curry powder. These are available in markets, premixed or mixed to order.
14. First-generation Chaldean woman, interview by authors, 1995.
15. The example of corned beef in the United States is analogous to this Lebanese preserved meat in that it is prepared for its taste long after the need for preservation is gone.
16. Talal's, an upscale Lebanese restaurant, employs a recently arrived immigrant woman, dressed in her village apparel, to make this bread in full view of customers.
17. Athir Shayota, a Chaldean artist, personal conversation, 1996.
18. One of the family said, "Our food goes best with Pepsi."
19. *Mezzeh* included: open-faced meat pies, ravioli-shaped meat pies, spinach pies, *kibbeh* meatballs, lamb stew, stuffed grape leaves, stuffed squash, *tabbouli, hummus,* raw vegetables, pickles, olives, Syrian white cheese, cheddar cheese, and leavened Arab bread. Entrees were lamb shoulder larded with garlic; chicken roasted with all spice and garlic; rice with pine nuts, lamb, and all spice; yogurt; and salad of lettuce, tomatoes, cucumbers, green onions, and mint, dressed with lemon and oil. Among the sweets were *mamoul* and date-filled cookies.
20. The first Chaldean immigrants settled among the Christian Lebanese, who were then still located in downtown Detroit. We assume that this same sort of culinary exchange prevailed between them at that time.

21. For further discussion of situational ethnicity, see Nagata (1974) and Okamura (1981).

Glossary

Culinary terms may vary according to regional dialect. The practice of transliterating Arabic in different ways also gives rise to variation in the spelling of food terms. The following terms appear here as they have been spelled in the text.

arak: anise-flavored distilled alcohol

aseed: stiff water and flour dough eaten with special, highly flavorful sauces and soups

baba ghannouj: a dip made from grilled eggplant mixed with *tahini* and lemon and eaten with Arabic pita bread

bagiah: Yemeni dish of falafel-like patties eaten with bread and special sauce

basturma: beef preserved with a coating of mixed spices, usually served in paper-thin slices as *mezzeh*

bulghur: cracked wheat available in fine, medium, and coarse grain

dehen (also *qawahrma*): pieces of lamb, sometimes beef, traditionally cooked and preserved in the fat from sheep tails in the manner of confit

faraykee: green wheat kernels roasted over an open fire making them greenish brown in color and smoky in flavor

fatoot: Arabic bread dribbled with clarified butter and liquid smoke and covered with meat broth

fattoush: originally a village salad mixed with baked or fried Arabic pita-bread pieces

galaba: pieces of meat, usually lamb, sauteed with vegetables, originally Yemeni but now widespread in the Detroit area

halal: term applied to meat slaughtered according to Islamic law

harissa: baked semolina, butter, and milk soaked with a syrup of sugar, honey, and water

hummus: a dip of mashed chick peas with *tahini* and lemon eaten with Arabic pita bread

kalaj: cream-filled thin dough fried and covered with sugar syrup

kamuni: a special combination of spices and rose petals

kanafa: a cheese and semolina confection served warm with rose-flavored syrup

katayef: crepe filled with cheese or nuts and fried

khubuz markook: mountain thin bread

kibbeh: pounded or finely ground meat, traditionally lamb, mixed with bulghur
kibbeh nayee: raw lamb
kishik: yogurt, wheat, and milk fermented and dried in cones
kofte: ground meat, traditionally lamb, mixed with onions, spices, and parsley for grilling
labanieh: custard with fruit
labneh: drained yogurt with consistency of sour cream
lahmajoun: Middle Eastern type of pizza, best known in America as its Armenian variant of the same name
maftool: a grainlike pasta resembling couscous
mahalabiah: custard with fruit
mamoul: molded semolina cookies filled with nuts or dates
mansef: a celebratory dish of rice topped with chunks of lamb cooked in *kishik*, nuts, and moistened with broth
maraq: robust lamb broth often eaten with *aseed*
ma'soub: baked flour and water dough eaten by dipping pieces into hot clarified butter and honey
molokiyeh: mucilaginous green leaf in the mallow family, usually associated with Egyptian cuisine
mujaddara: lentils with rice and onions
pacha: individual-sized "pockets" of tripe filled with rice and spices, Chaldean holiday food
pita: also called Syrian bread, Arab bread, or pocket bread
qawahrma (also *dehen*): lamb traditionally preserved in the fat from sheep tails in the manner of confit
sabaya: multilayered flaky pastry lavished with clarified butter and honey
sahawig: sauce with cumin and hot pepper
sajj: convex metal dome used for baking flat bread
samboosa: fried triangles of thin dough wrapped around mixture of ground lamb and spices or dates, coconut, and raisins
shafoot: souplike dish of yogurt with garlic, hot peppers, cilantro, cumin, liquid smoke, and pieces of Arabic bread
soujouk: Middle Eastern sausage
tabbouli: salad made of tomatoes, mint, parsley, cracked wheat (*bulghur*), and other vegetables
tahini: sesame-seed paste
tarator: sauce made with *tahini*, lemon, and garlic
toorshi: pickled vegetables with turmeric
yerba maté: a bitter, slightly smoky tealike drink made from the leaves of a small evergreen tree grown only in the semitropical lowlands of Brazil, Paraguay, and Argentina

zatar: thyme, or a spice mixture that includes thyme
zurbian: rice with lamb, potatoes, yogurt, garlic, and spices

References

Abraham, Sameer, Nabeel Abraham, and Barbara Aswad. 1983. The Southend: An Arab Muslim Working-Class Community. In *Arabs in the New World: Studies on Arab-American Communities,* edited by Sameer Abraham and Nabeel Abraham, 164–81.

Abraham, Sameer, and Nabeel Abraham. 1983. *Arabs in the New World: Studies on Arab-American Communities.* Detroit: Center for Urban Studies, Wayne State University.

Abrahams, Roger D. 1980. Folklore. *Harvard Encyclopedia of American Ethnic Groups,* edited by Stephen Thernstrom. Cambridge: Harvard University Press.

Agócs, Carol. 1981. Ethnic Settlement in a Metropolitan Area: A Typology of Communities. *Ethnicity* 8:127–48.

Ahdab-Yehia, May. 1983. The Lebanese Maronites: Patterns of Continuity and Change. In *Arabs in the New World: Studies on Arab-American Communities,* edited by Sameer Abraham and Nabeel Abraham, 148–62.

Alford, Jeffrey, and Naomi Duguid. 1995. On the Flatbread Trail. *Aramco World* 46 (5):16–25.

Barth, Fredrik. 1969. *Ethnic Groups and Interethnic Relations.* Oslo: Universitetsforlaget.

Goody, Jack. 1982. *Cooking, Cuisine and Class. A Study in Comparative Sociology.* Cambridge: Cambridge University Press.

Gordon, Milton M. 1964. *Assimilation in American Life: The Role of Race, Religion and National Origins.* New York: Oxford University Press.

Halpern, Joel M. 1958. *A Serbian Village.* New York: Columbia University Press.

Hamady, Mary Laird. 1987. *Lebanese Mountain Cookery.* Boston: David R. Godine.

Hannerz, Ulf. 1975. Ethnicity and Opportunity in Urban America. In *Urban Ethnicity,* edited by Abner Cohen, 37–76. London: Routledge.

Ing, Daisy. 1976. *The Best of Baghdad Cooking, With Treats from Teheran.* New York: Saturday Review Press and E. P. Dutton.

Luxner, Larry. 1995. The South American Leaf. *Aramco World* 46 (6):28–29.

Maclagan, Ianthe. 1994. Food and Gender in a Yemeni Community. In *Culinary Cultures of the Middle East,* edited by Sami Zubaida and Richard Tapper, 159–72.

Mintz, Sidney W. 1989. Food and Culture: An Anthropological View. In *Completing the Food Chain*, edited by P. M. Hirschoff and N. G. Kotler, 114–20. Washington, D.C.: Smithsonian Institution Press.

Moerman, Michael. 1965. Ethnic Identification in a Complex Society: Who Are Lue? *American Anthropologist* 67:1215–30.

Nagata, Judith A. 1974. What Is a Malay? Situational Selection of Ethnic Identity in a Plural Society. *American Ethnologist* 1:331–50.

Okamura, Jonathan Y. 1981. Situational Ethnicity. *Ethnic and Racial Studies* 4:452–65.

Perry, Charles. 1994. The Taste for Layered Bread among the Nomadic Turks and the Central Asian Origins of Baklava. In *Culinary Cultures of the Middle East*, edited by Sami Zubaida and Richard Tapper, 87–91.

Roden, Claudia. 1972. *Book of Middle Eastern Food*. New York: Alfred A. Knopf.

———. 1988. Middle Eastern Cooking: The Legacy. *Aramco World* 39 (2):2–3.

Sengstock, Mary. 1982. *Chaldean-Americans: Changing Conceptions of Ethnic Identity*. New York: Center for Migration Studies.

———. 1983. Detroit's Iraqi-Chaldeans: A Conflicting Conception of Identity. In *Arabs in the New World: Studies on Arab-American Communities*, edited by Sameer Abraham and Nabeel Abraham, 136–46.

Staub, Shalom. 1989. *Yemenis in New York City: The Folklore of Ethnicity*. Philadelphia: Balch Institute Press.

Tapper, Richard. 1994. Blood, Wine and Water: Social and Symbolic Aspects of Drinks and Drinking in the Islamic Middle East. In *Culinary Cultures of the Middle East*, edited by Sami Zubaida and Richard Tapper, 215–31.

Zubaida, Sami. 1994a. National, Communal and Global Dimensions in Middle Eastern Food Cultures. In *Culinary Cultures of the Middle East*, edited by Sami Zubaida and Richard Tapper, 33–45.

———. 1994b. Rice in the Culinary Cultures of the Middle East. In *Culinary Cultures of the Middle East*, edited by Sami Zubaida and Richard Tapper, 93–104.

Zubaida, Sami, and Richard Tapper, eds. 1994. *Culinary Cultures of the Middle East*. London: I. B. Tauris.

The Sound of Culture, The Structure of Tradition

Musicians' Work in Arab Detroit

Anne Rasmussen

WITH THEIR LOUD sound systems and lively dance tunes, Arab American musicians bring to community gatherings an all-encompassing sonic environment that replaces the host culture with the home culture. Night after night, performance after performance, they supply "the language of Diaspora" (Clifford 1994). While I have framed musicians as "curators of culture" and their activity as "art," they have continuously referred to the same as "work" (Rasmussen 1989, 1991). Their work, as they have told me time and again, is audience driven, and they are surprisingly compliant with the sometimes abrupt demands of their clientele. Although this way of performing cannot be reduced to a simple formula, several patterns are apparent in the careers of Arab American musicians that help explain why they tend to discuss their "art" as "work,"[1] and these patterns have been in place for much of the twentieth century.

In this essay, I offer a historical synopsis of the rise of musical professionalism and the development of music patronage in the Arab American community. I then profile the ways in which professional musicians supply the "sounds of culture" by discussing prevalent lyrical themes and musical styles and the ways in which these are transmitted in live performance and through transnational media networks. Finally, I explore the ways in which musicians, particularly those of Arab Detroit, involve their audience and community in the "structure of tradition" by presenting examples of their work in the context of wedding celebrations.

Parts of this work were originally presented at a 1995 conference titled "Sounding the Difference: Music and the Politics of Identity in America and Beyond," hosted by the Department of Ethnic Studies at the University of California, Berkeley.

Arab American Musicians and Musical Patronage

During my original field research, I came to know a group of professional musicians who played a dominant role in establishing the musical life of Arab America (Rasmussen 1991).[2] These musicians, who are now elderly or deceased, were part of a community made up largely of Syrian and Lebanese Maronite, Melkite, or Orthodox Christians. They immigrated to the United States at the beginning of the twentieth century, before immigration quotas, enacted in 1923, slowed Arab immigration to a trickle. By the 1950s and 1960s the immigrant population and their American-born offspring were relatively stable and assimilated. With the eradication of strict immigration quotas in 1965, a new wave of large-scale immigration from the Arab World began. Today, at the end of the 1990s, the flow of human traffic and the exchange of media between the Arab countries and the United States is no longer a one-way (or even two-way) street. Instead, it is a continuous, transnational movement comparable to a rotary highway with multiple exits. This shift in the nature of culture flow is having a tremendous impact on the climate in which Detroit's Arab musicians work.

During the early years of the twentieth century, the musical amateur was responsible for informal music making in the newly formed Arab immigrant community. By the mid-1940s, however, it was more common for a professional contingent of touring musicians to entertain during formal events. The shift in status from amateur to professional came to define two important groups: (1) musicians who could be hired for their services; and (2) patrons who would organize events, hire musicians, and generate audiences. Due to the bittersweet nature of musical values in Arab culture—where singers and dancers are cherished and stigmatized, often at the same time—the evolution of the professional musician and the public performance was not always easy or natural.

One performer's wife told me that when her husband began to sing professionally, around 1930, audiences were sensitive to the difference between a common entertainer and a polished, professional artist. She emphasized her husband's concern for being involved in properly organized and respectable performances. Evoking similar themes, Virginia Soloman, wife of a noted Lebanese American violinist active from the 1940s through the 1970s, recalled that community members were critical of her marriage to a musician: "In some instances Arabic male musicians, they didn't have too good of a reputation, you know. In those days the prototype musician was fast type of living and drugs and all that and some of the people here, they thought: 'You know you're marrying a little below when you're marrying a musician.' What a great mistake that was on their part, yes it was, because there was never anything like that. My husband was a perfect gentleman" (personal communication, 1987). In spite of traditional attitudes about entertainers, musicians began to fashion full and part-time careers with their artistic abilities. They performed at large community parties, called *haflat,* arranged by philanthropic Arab American organizations with the goal of fund-raising for the community. When Arab musicians assumed the role of "professional entertainer," they also, by way of organizing the musical life of their era, became artistic and social leaders, commanding positions of respect within the community. As Americans, their self-image may have been bolstered (or tarnished) by their status as popular entertainers. As Arabs, they were no doubt encouraged by the rising-star system in the Middle East epitomized by such figures as Umm Kulthum, Muhammad 'Abd al-Wahhab, and others who performed live in concert settings, made numerous recordings, and assumed principal roles in the burgeoning motion picture industry in Egypt.

From the 1950s through the 1970s, musical professionalism was further institutionalized among Arab Americans by a contingent of commercially oriented musicians from the nightclub scene who performed in *public* for *profit.* Today, these professionals include musicians who work both in nightclubs and for community weddings and private parties. Some are second- and third-generation offspring of early immigrants, while others arrived and continue to arrive in the post-1965 wave of Arab immigrants. Older musicians can look back across a landscape of musical history that encompasses both the early era of professionalism, when philanthropic, community sponsored *haflat* were the order of the day, and more recent times, when family-based partying and celebration are at a premium. They echo one another in their descriptions of how their work as musicians has changed over time. They often claim that their artistic license was lost as contexts for musical performance began to diversify, and especially when modern, eclectic styles and audience dancing came into vogue. Musicians sometimes speak of their patrons and audiences with ambivalence and derision. One respected musician, composer, and music teacher explained that it was a musician's job to play everything, to please people, be they Iraqi, Lebanese, or Egyptian. He explained that every three or four months he played for an audience "who liked to listen to music." The rest of the time, he said, "we play for the dance, for the *dabkah.*" Judging from comments like these,

Fig. 41. Sana Kadaj mesmerizes the crowd at a Detroit nightclub in the 1950s. Courtesy of the ACCESS Museum of Arab Culture.

Fig. 42. Detroit crooner Amer Kadaj sings for a party at Club La Macarena, 1955. Courtesy of the ACCESS Museum of Arab Culture.

it would seem that Arab musicians define themselves as "workers" providing a service, doing a job.

Whether their performance is considered "art" or "work," musicians in Arab Detroit are highly valued as culture brokers. They bring to community events a bouquet of sounds associated with homeland (place), tradition (history), and ethnicity (origin), and this sonic patchwork allows Arab Americans to experience their collective past and present in distinctive ways. The musician's "job description," if you will, also includes the delicate skills of the ritual specialist. In addition to playing music, musicians structure time and space by directing audience participation at weddings, engagement parties, baptisms and circumcisions, high school and college graduation parties, and a host of other celebratory events.

The Sound of Culture

With the lyrics of their songs and the styles of their music, performers crystallize community sentiment. Sorrow and separation have been common themes of Arabic songs performed and recorded throughout the century, as exemplified by titles such as "The Hoot of the Steamship," "The Return of the Immigrants," and the following song, "Standing on the Seashore," recorded by the Lebanese-born, New York singer, Hanan Harouni.[3] During our conversations, Hanan remarked that whether she sang this song for Arab audiences in the United States, Canada, South America, or Lebanon, there was *never* a dry eye in the house.

"Waqef 'ala Shat al Baher" ("Standing on the Seashore"), composed by Zaghlul al-Damnour, was originally recorded as a 78 rpm on the Arab American Cleopatra label (819 A&B) with Arab American musicians Joe Bedway on *'ud,* Yacoub Ghannim playing *qanun,* and Hakki Obadia and Naim Karakand on violins. The lyrics, which Hanan and I translated together at her home in Brooklyn, New York, read approximately as follows:

> From the minute I stood on the sand
> They could tell I was a stranger
> Now that I am alone, I do not sleep; the stars spend the night with me
> And I'm so afraid to go back without my loved one
> Whether I go back or ahead, danger awaits

Every hour apart [away from my country] is longer than a
year
We were together, but now the heart, from parting, burns
and what is between us is only paper and ink

I curse the first boat [that ever took the emigrants] to sink
Every time my old country comes to mind
I wish it would sink

My eyes cannot see any sailboats
The only thing I see is the fog coming from afar
The fog comes down to take from my eyes the tears
that fall, with every hour, like driving rain

Themes of separation, unrequited love, and longing for reunification are certainly not unique to the poetic discourse of immigrants. In Middle Eastern poetry, particularly Sufi verse, separation from and reunion with a lover, or God, has been a literary trope for centuries. "Standing on the Sea Shore," however, sings specifically to the immigrant experience. This song's portrayal of distance and ambivalent longings for the homeland is summarized by the song's lyric "whether I go back [to the old country] or ahead [to the New World] danger awaits." These words comprise an explicit narrative of place that, if not shared by all immigrants, can at least be imagined. The mere mention of a village or city name or simply the physical features of the homeland can also serve as powerful symbols of collective experience. "The music event," Stokes reminds us, "from collective dances to the act of putting a cassette or CD into a machine, evokes and organizes collective memories and present experiences of place with an intensity, power and simplicity unmatched by any other social activity (1994, 3; see also Rasmussen 1997a, 75).

When on stage, Arab singers encourage audience members to identify their village or city of origin so that songs may be chosen and lyrics tailored appropriately. Contemporary singers are challenged by the tall order of keeping songs from several Arab countries and regions in their repertoire to please their mixed and sometimes very demanding audiences. I am reminded of a winter evening in January 1991 that I spent in a Cleveland nightclub, where a few musicians from Detroit were playing. At one point, a man on the dance floor requested a song about Basra, Iraq. The events of the impending Gulf War dominated the news. As the song unfolded, people danced. Then the host of the club approached the singer mid-song with a request from another patron. Using a piece of tape, he stuck a one-hundred-dollar bill on the singer's microphone and conveyed the patron's request for a song from Lebanon. The musicians quickly complied, aborting the first song and beginning another extolling the virtues of Lebanon. Having myself performed for several years as a jazz singer and pianist in venues where the "customer is always right," I cringed at the demanding and ostentatious display of artistic control made by the customers in the club. Yet I marveled at the musicians' ability to switch gears mid-song and deliver the product requested by the most powerful—and obviously the highest paying—patron in the establishment.

The power of music to convey notions of place and time lies not only in its lyrical content, but also, and perhaps more comprehensively, in its style. Most second- and third-generation Arab Americans, for example, do not understand the Arabic lyrics or regional dialect of songs; they respond to musical sounds. Genre, instrumentation, form, rhythm, mode, melody, and intonation are immediately suggestive of history, modernity, region, religion, emotion, and context. Whether fabricated on the synthesizer or offered on traditional instruments, musical style can stand for ethnicity and identity in very specific ways. For example, the opening phrases of a traditional improvisation, or *taqasim,* on the *'ud,* an eleven-string fretless lute—perhaps the oldest and most widespread of Arab instruments—can evoke the weight and staying power of *turath,* or traditional art music. The sound of the *nay*—the plaintive, breathy, bamboo flute—or the *mijwiz*—the double piped, reedy wind instrument Levantine folk musicians use for *dabkah*—might bring to mind images of village life and rural landscapes. Audiences recognize and enthusiastically react to certain musical modes (*maqamat*), which are characterized by specific scales and intonations heard only in Arab music; they also are alert to rhythmic patterns used for regional dances.

In searching for the signature sound of Arab Detroit, it is important to recognize the musical influence of the Lebanese, who have created a kind of musical hegemony in the Midwest. The unique contribution of Lebanese music to Arab America is the urbanized folk music-and-dance complex of nonmetric improvised poetry and lively, robust music for the *dabkah,* a traditional line dance. The appeal of rural folk music and dance genres among even the wealthiest and most sophisticated Arab Americans is testimony, perhaps, to the power of the sounds and symbols of village society to convey a sense of rootedness that is not yet corrupted by war or possessed by capitalism.

Lebanese musical discourse is part and parcel of a larger language shared by Syrians, Jordanians, Palestinians, and Egyptians. This music shares a set of rhythmic patterns, musical modes, traditional instruments (*'ud, nay, qanun,* violin, *daff,* and *darabukkah*), and the powerful sound of the synthesizer, an instrument programmed to reproduce the particular scales, rhythms, and instrumental colors of Arab music. While Lebanese musical styles have been at the forefront in Arab Detroit, there are two other schools that are quite distinct from this central Arab idiom: the Iraqi Chaldean and the Yemeni. Each has different rhythms, distinctive repertoires, various instruments, and unlike dialects of Arabic. Furthermore, Iraqi music features many songs in Aramaic, a different language altogether. It should be noted that, even today, North African music is not a significant part of the Detroit soundscape. Although cassettes of North African singers are available, and some of their songs are "covered" during local performances, world beat genres such as *Rai*—which can be heard on Detroit's public radio station, WDET—are hardly known in Arab Detroit.

Musicians are aware of the emotional tools available to them—text, style, rhythm, mode, intonation, and instrumentation—and how these elicit powerful responses of nostalgia, pride, homesickness, remembrance, and imagination for individual listeners. A shared history of separation, or "deterritorialization," may invest music with a sense of yearning for the homeland even among Arab Americans whose families have been in the United States for generations. "Deterritorialization," writes Appadurai (1990, 11–12), "creates new markets for film companies, art impresarios and travel agencies, who thrive on the need of the deterritorialized population for contact with its homeland. Naturally, these invented homelands, that constitute the mediascapes of deterritorialized groups, can often become sufficiently fantastic and one-sided that they provide the material for new ideoscapes in which ethnic conflicts can begin to erupt." Although political rivalries (such as those demonstrated in the nightclub in Cleveland) may be an emergent quality of live performance, songs that *collect* the community, highlighting positive or humorous aspects of Arab America, are equally abundant. There is no place in America, and perhaps no place in the world, that better approximates the ideological notion of the "Arab World United" than Detroit and its adjacent suburb, Dearborn. While Yemeni, Palestinian, Lebanese, and Iraqi populations remain relatively endogamous in their private and professional lives, they *do* come into contact through various public institutions in Detroit and Dearborn, most notably the school system. Annual events like the Arab World Festival, during which the community attempts to represent itself as a whole, also put the people of Arab Detroit in touch with each other.

It is not uncommon at such events to honor notions of unity and diversity in song by adapting the lyrics of popular tunes to recognize the many homelands of the Arab Detroit audience. For example, one singer, a popular performer at the Arab World Festival, altered the lyrics of "Ya Saree Saree Layl," a Jordanian song about the happiness of the wedding night, to welcome each subset of the Arab community. Different sections of the crowd cheered and waved in the hot afternoon sun of downtown Detroit as they heard the singer belt out the name of their country and its capital city.

> Lubnan baladna, wa Beirut 'asimitna
> Filistiin baladna, wa
> l-Quds 'asimitna
> Al-Urdun baladna, wa 'Amaan 'asimitna
> Al-Yaman baladna, wa Sana'a 'asimitna
> 'Iraq baladna, wa Baghdad 'asimitna

> Lebanon is our country, and Beirut is our capital
> Palestine is our country, and Jerusalem is our capital
> Jordan is our country, and Amman is our capital
> Yemen is our country, and Sana'a is our capital
> Iraq is our country, and Baghdad is our capital

To exemplify the flip side of deterritorialization, I bring your attention to a case of musical *re*territorialization in Arab Detroit, as executed by Rana and Naim Homaidan, musicians who work together and reside in Dearborn. In Dearborn the Homaidans are surrounded by friends and extended family; their social life in the New World is similar in many ways to that which they knew in "the old country."

"Dearborn is almost more Lebanese than Lebanon," Rana explained to me. To illustrate her satisfaction with American life, Rana stressed her pleasure in being able to "bring up my daughter with good education in a safe place." In the summer of 1995, when the couple was asked to perform at a Dearborn street festival, Rana's husband and partner, Naim, composed a peppy song to mark the event. The music was in the most Western sounding of modes, *maqam Ajam,* which is similar to the major scale; the lyrics, a combination of Arabic and English, run as follows:

> Dearborn, Dearborn, Dearborn, we love you
> Dearborn, Dearborn, Dearborn, our heart with you
> *Inti al-yom biladna* [Today you are our homeland]
> *Narabbi fiik awladna* [In you we raise our children]
> God bless you.
> Dearborn! Dearborn!
> God bless you.
> *Allah yahmiiki, Ya Dearborn,* [God protects you, O Dearborn!]
> *Allah khaliiki, Ya Dearborn* [God keep you, O Dearborn!]

Josef, a family friend, offered his own interpretation of this and another verse.

> Dearborn you are now our country.
> We raise our kids in Dearborn so this is like our home
> We protect you with our hearts.
> You are our whole days.
> We are happy because you made us happy.
> We left our old country a long time ago.

"You know, *most* of the Arabs are here," Josef went on to explain. "There are 120,000 Arabs in Dearborn only."

Melody, Rana and Naim's fifteen-year-old daughter, joined the discussion.

"Yeah!" she said. "In my classroom, the teacher calls 'Ali and fifteen kids stand up. We have to give them all [the 'Alis] special nicknames!"

Through the words and melodies of their songs, Arab musicians in Detroit invent for their audience new ways to share familiar notions of home and homeland. Whether they make reference to the faraway land of their ancestors, the contemporary Arab world diaspora, or the new Arab America, musicians cater to audience demand with their special combinations of lyrical content and musical form.[4]

Transmission: Music and Media among Arab Americans

How do musicians learn and perpetuate these sounds of culture? When they are summoned by their community to supply the musical "language of Diaspora," what keeps their language contemporary, yet rooted in tradition? It is primarily through the transnational flow of music media that immigrant musicians connect audiences to the homeland by keeping their music fresh and up-to-date.[5]

Anderson (1983) argues that the advent of "print capitalism" in the fifteenth century served to connect and collect people into the "imagined communities" we now call nation-states. Novels and newspapers, he suggests, accommodated the modern phenomenon of nationalism because they linked people conceptually by providing them with news and events that could be shared among compatriots who shared little else. Certainly, novels and newspapers can facilitate an "image of communion" for diaspora communities struggling to maintain links with the homeland. I would suggest, however, that for much of the twentieth century, the global spread of Arab sounds has been equally (if not more) important in collapsing distance and shaping notions of nation, culture, and identity in Arab Detroit.

Arab Americans have always used media technology—from the 78 rpm in the early 1900s, to the CD today—to import sounds from the Old World and redistribute them in the New. Professional musicians "straight off the boat," like Moses Cohen, Naim Karakand, and Constantine Souse, recorded their repertoire for *Victor* and *His Masters Voice* during the early 1920s. In the 1940s musicians and producers created their own record companies: Maksoud, Ma'arouf, Star of the East, and Cleopatra. Today, singers market their cassettes, videos, and compact discs in their own neighborhoods and throughout the Arab diaspora. Through their work in the music business, these professionals made and continue to make aesthetic choices for their communities. Throughout the century, Arab American musicians have kept the Old World and the New contemporaneous by learning the latest hits from home and performing them for their de- and reterritorialized audiences.

Using whatever technological means available, musicians have been engaged in maintaining what Clifford (employing Said's musical metaphor) has referred to as "contrapuntal modernity." "Diasporist discourses," writes Clifford (1994, 311), "reflect the sense of being part of an ongoing transnational network that includes the homeland, not as something simply left behind, but as a place of attachment in a contrapuntal modernity." Here I offer only one example of the myriad ways in which musicians act as middlemen in the transnational flow of culture. George Musally, a Rhode Island keyboard player I have known for many years, revealed his particular version of "contrapuntal modernity" during a conversation we had in

1995. George told me that in addition to the authentic and syncretic sounds available on his keyboard, he copies various patches from synthesizer players who visit from abroad.

"I just bring a formatted disc to the *haflah* [party]," he said, "and ask if I can copy their string or horn sound. They [the Lebanese musicians] do it a little better over there."

Like George, the young keyboard players of Arab Detroit strive to sound like their homeland brothers, often by using the exact model of instrument imported from the Middle East. For young Arab American musicians, it is the precise imitation of a Lebanese keyboard player through the medium of the computer disc, or an Egyptian band through use of the same synthesizer imported from Kuwait—rather than, say, learning to play a traditional instrument such as the *'ud*—that satisfies their desire for an authentic sound from the homeland.

The Structure of Tradition

The work of musicians involves more than bringing the right songs and musical styles to an event. They also manage time and space in the celebration of festivals and rituals. Here I will foreground the structural aspects of three festive rituals, all of them weddings held in Arab Detroit. While weddings are the quintessential performance event among Arab Americans, musicians commonly manage the "acting out" of tradition in many other ritual contexts, from office parties to circumcision rites.

The Wedding Prototype

In Detroit, Arab weddings are rich intersections of food, music, religion, ritual, dance, socializing, and business exchange. The wedding is a social gesture of unmatched importance in the community. As hosts, the families of bride and groom do their best to accommodate and impress their guests. The guests in turn play their part as enthusiastic participants. Both families and guests depend on the musicians they hire to produce a ritual that divides the evening into multiple segments, organizes the celebrants spatially, and directs their activities. Discrete beads of meaningful action are strung together with music, connecting one part of the ceremony to the next and lending coherent grace to an evening that should (if all goes well) proceed from the subdued to the exuberant. Furthermore, by organizing procession and dance, musicians ensure the personal

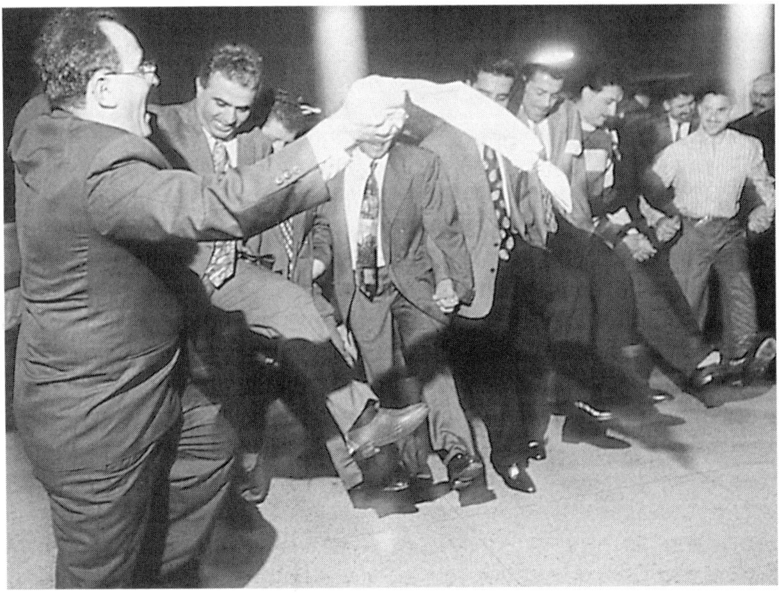

Fig. 43. An energetic *dabkah* line at a community celebration, 1995. Photograph by Millard Berry.

involvement of every celebrant present. During a wedding, or any music event for that matter, passive vocabularies become active and "cultural narratives become personal narratives" that can then be used to construct and activate a sense of community (Bruner 1984, 6).

The summer wedding season is busy in Detroit. Although every wedding is unique, Arab American weddings share numerous features. In addition to bride, groom, family, and friends, the "cast" of an Arab American wedding includes an essential crew from the local Arab wedding industry, including:

1. One or two bands of 3–8 people, one of which may also provide a disc jockey
2. A dancer or two hired just for the *zaffah* procession, or for the *zaffah* and a "show" later in the evening
3. Photographers and videographers (1–7 in number)
4. Caterers and servers
5. Bridal clothing experts from local boutiques
6. Florists (who also provide balloons and rent special chairs called *samdi* for the bride and groom to sit on)

Fig. 44. Abdul Karim Badr, master of the *'ud,* takes a break during rehearsal, 1994. Photograph by Millard Berry.

7. Printers (for invitations/matchbooks, etc.)
8. Banquet Halls and Caterers

Various people from within the party may fulfill other roles such as:

1. Master of ceremonies—announcer of events and dances
2. Poet—someone who has composed a special poem for the bride and groom

Members of the "wedding industry" follow the wedding party from start to finish. The videographers and photographers, for example, stage and capture every important moment, from the time the bride is "taken from the house," to the cutting of the cake, to the departure of limousines. Unlike an ethnographic videographer, who might just turn the camera on and let it roll, professional wedding video people can often be seen telling the participants where to go, how to stand, and what to do next. When I visited Nazih Video, one of several companies specializing in making videos of weddings, they explained, without hesitation, all the important elements that must be in a video.

1. The bride alone with her parents in their house
2. The groom's house
3. The limousine going to the bride's house to fetch her
4. The wedding party at a park posing for photographs
5. The parents at the hall welcoming the guests in a receiving line
6. The entrance of the bride and groom
7. The *zaffah* procession
8. Dancing
9. Dinner
10. The cutting of the cake
11. Dancing
12. *Dabkah* dancing at the end of the wedding
13. Optional *zaffah* at the end of the wedding

The wedding videos produced by these professional videographers circulate widely among family and friends and are even sent to family members in the "old country." One woman told me that she knew all her family in Lebanon (and vice versa) because they saw each other regularly on the party videos they exchanged.[6]

The Zaffah

An essential component of the wedding party, the *zaffah* is a procession during which the bride and groom are literally danced into the public space of the community.[7] Combining ritual, music, and dance, the *zaffah* shows off all the key players in a wedding. A family might have a very good idea of how they want to do the *zaffah,* but for all *zaffah*s, the wedding party is dependent on the musicians and dancers to organize the crowd outside the hall and bring the family in with the pomp and circumstance required. Singer Rana explained her role in the *zaffah:*

> Weddings? Oh, God . . . thousands. I meet the bride beforehand or I talk to her on the phone. I tell her what I want to do [for the *zaffah*] . . . and they accept it. They like my show. Some brides, they feel happy, they are close [to me]. Some are scared. I sing from my heart. This is my job, my work. If they are not happy, I make

> them happy. This is really from our heart, me and Naim, not just for money. We make it like our wedding, or like my daughter's wedding.

Rana imitates the announcement that brings her and Naim into the wedding hall, " 'And now will the beautiful bride and groom enter; they're going to do the *zaffah* with Rana and Naim' I begin to sing a *mawwal.* First come the family and the men, then the father of the bride, then the bridesmaids." Rana and Naim's *zaffah* is a sight to behold. She and Naim work with remote mikes, somehow communicating tempos and transitions through the dense crowd to the rest of the band members who remain on stage. As Rana escorts the couple down a sinuous, imaginary path, she sings, claps, and dances with the handsome (but naturally shy) couple. Naim performs crowd management while playing *'ud* standing up. Money is tossed into the air, collected, and counted. Once there is a critical mass on the dance floor and all key players of the wedding party are dancing, Rana and Naim "work the tables," greeting in song the guests who did not make it to the front. Perhaps twenty or twenty-five minutes after the onset of the procession, Rana has woven her way through all the tables, and the majority of the celebrants are clapping, crowding around the path of the *zaffah* toward the dance floor. Videographers capture it all. Rana and Naim then join the newlyweds on a special, tiered stage where they sit on thronelike chairs with their "court" of about a dozen young bridesmaids. Rana and Naim wave to the crowd before they leave the couple alone, the center of attention. The musicians exit by the same path taken to bring in the bride and groom. There is a break in the action, but their work for the evening is hardly over.

Throughout a wedding party, musicians facilitate kin group dancing by offering special songs for the bride's family, the groom's family, all the male friends of the groom, a special ladies' dance, and so on. In some traditions, musicians are required to present a structured sequence of dances during which each family group present at the wedding is announced and called up in turn.[8] As they express their joy publicly though dance, these discrete groups of family or friends throw money into the air, which, once collected, serves as the young couple's "start-up package." The band may also provide a commercially recorded American slow song for a "bridal dance" (usually the only American tune of the evening) and perhaps recordings of American music for the cutting of the cake. Segmented ritual activity eventually gives way to *dabkah* dancing for the entire crowd. If present, special musicians, such as players of the *tabl baladi,* the *mazhar,* and the *mizmar,* will parade through the crowd, infecting it with the spirit of celebration. These instruments, the large double-headed bass drum (the *tabl baladi*), the loud and large tambourine (the *mazhar*), and the sharp, loud double reed oboe (the *mizmar*) have been associated with weddings and celebration since the time of the Prophet Muhammad. And today, if the real thing isn't available, the sounds of these drums and aerophones will be approximated on the synthesizer.

The Work of Musicians

Like the hundreds of Iraqi-owned party stores in Detroit, or the ribbon of Lebanese gas stations that winds through Dearborn, music is yet another Arab American "ethnic occupation." Family groups are as common in the music business as in any other. Musical ensembles are comprised of brothers and sisters, husbands and wives, nephews and uncles, fathers and sons. Musicians are part of a service industry that is essential to the lifeblood of this huge community, and for the most part they see their work as just that: work. As contractors or curators of Arab culture, Arab musicians are in a position comparable to Arab immigrant women, who bear more of the anti-assimilation burden than men when it comes to rearing children and running a household in the ways of the old country (Cainkar 1994). The desire to "keep our culture alive" provides a strong patronage system for musicians, whose skills as "ritual specialists" and cultural caterers are very much in demand. While it is healthy patronage that supports so many musicians, the thriving culture industry of Arab Detroit also functions as a deterrent to musicians who might otherwise engage in American popular music, Western art music, or other crossover and fusion projects.

Rana's altruistic attitude toward her work may be the exception; many musicians seem to regard their wedding duties as a tedious and boring job, especially when they play the same songs night after night on summer weekends. One musician who is often hired just to play *mizmar* for the *zaffah* procession summed up his role by saying: "It's an easy gig; they just want it to look good for the video—they just want to make a nice video." One smiling *tabl* player confided to me: "It's all show."

While our academic grandmothers and grandfathers were concerned with documenting authentic, original musical cultures, contemporary scholars of expressive culture, especially those working at home in the United States, are challenged with interpreting how cultural authenticity is identified, selected, reworked, and interpreted in new environments, with new technologies, in musical ways. Appadurai, in his provocative discussion of the global cultural economy, suggests that "the world we live in today is characterized by a new role for the imagination in social life" (1990, 4). My research suggests that the role of imagination in social life is nothing new and that music, whether recorded or live, continues to inspire Arab Americans in their creation of culture in the diaspora.

Memory and imagination are fueled by musical style, textual references, and regional repertoires. Listening to Arab music invites a multisensory reception because of the association of recorded music with live performance and, by extension, because of the "creative tension," the physical/verbal interaction, between performers and audiences at live music events (Nelson 1985, xvi). An evening at an Arab wedding party is by anyone's account, insider or outsider, an overwhelming experience. The wedding party is a social ritual, a rite of intensification. As the music and dance unfold, intimate cultural languages abound in particular kinds of hand clapping, the twirling of worry beads, the bodily and vocal gestures that indicate musical appreciation, the trilling of tongues (*zagharit*), and the rhythmic shouts of men as they dance and fraternize. This is a time and a space that not only reflects but also projects Arab, and more specifically Arab American, culture.

Scholars, myself included, are intrigued by expressive culture in diaspora communities. I am only now beginning to sort out the relationship between the Arab musician's work and how it is experienced by individuals, perceived by scholars, and represented in academic writings and everyday lives. Clifford refers to the "language of Diaspora" as something invoked by displaced communities who "feel (maintain, revive, invent) a connection with a prior home" (1994, 311). When does Arab music and culture stop being romantically imagined and magically invoked and begin to be an indigenous feature of American culture, or of the American workplace? When, in my ethnographic writing, will Arab Detroit's music scene receive the residence permit that polka music has in Wisconsin, salsa in New York, or conjunto in Texas? Certainly many Arab immigrants yearn for return—a recognized feature of diaspora life—but no matter how many do return, there will remain a thriving and burgeoning

Arab America that cannot abandon the unique cultural, social, and economic institutions it has created. And every weekend in Detroit, musicians will continue their work, serving their audiences a multi-course, tailor-made menu of expressive culture from the homeland.

NOTES

1. I analyze early Arab American musicians' practices and their special ways of working in an earlier article (Rasmussen 1989). See Abu-Lughod (1993) for a provocative discussion of how ethnographers make systems of knowledge and culture out of the pastiche of their collected experiences.
2. I began fieldwork in the Detroit area in 1988 and have returned nearly every year out of professional interest and social obligation. I am deeply indebted to the musicians whose work, with permission, I represent here.
3. These translated titles are from 78 rpm discs from Arab American family collections.
4. I deal extensively with musical style in my dissertation (Rasmussen 1991) and other publications (Rasmussen 1992, 1996).
5. Sound media—records, radio, and television—may actually be a more effective medium for the transmission of the Arabic language. The transfer of Arabic through print media can be problematic, especially for second- and third-generation Arab Americans. Although they sometimes learn Arabic at home, if they do not receive formal instruction in Arabic, they will probably not learn to read and write standard Arabic (in Arabic script). In fact, one of the early Arab American newspapers published during the first half of the twentieth century experimented with a format in which spoken Arabic was transliterated into the English alphabet, which Arabs born and educated in America could read.
6. At Christian weddings, a church service, usually held in the morning or afternoon, is also part of the event. The videographers will attend this service. Sometimes, an engagement party is thrown some weeks or months before the wedding. It too is videotaped and photographed, with music, food, and dance.
7. See Kent (1989) for a dancer's account of *zaffah* processions in Egypt and in the Los Angeles Arab American community.
8. In some Arab countries, the singer/announcer is known as *sayyah,* literally "shouter." It is his job to announce every guest who arrives and the gifts they bring to the wedding. I am indebted to Dwight Reynolds for pointing out this connection.

Glossary

INSTRUMENTS

darabukkah: also called *tabli* or *derbekkee;* ceramic, vase-shaped drum, one head

mazhar: large heavy tambourine with heavy jingles, of Egyptian origin, always used for weddings. The song *"Duq il-Mazahir"* (Play the mazhars) is played at all weddings

mijwiz: single-reed double-piped "clarinet" associated with folk music

mizmar: double-reed "oboe" associated with folk music

nay: reed flute; to play all modes, several sizes are used

qanun: trapezoid-shaped zither with seventy-two strings in triple courses. Strings are tuned with pegs; tuning is refined with levers called *mandal*s or *urab*s

riqq: also called *daff;* tambourine of ten–eleven inches with heavy brass cymbals

tabl baladi: literally, "country drum." A double-headed drum played on one head with a beater and on the other with a thin willow branch or stick. One head is thicker than the other, giving the drum two distinct pitches. The drum is suspended from the neck of the player, who is free to roam around the floor and play directly to the dancers. Often paired with the *mizmar,* the dynamic performance style of *tabl* players gives dancers a tremendous jolt of energy

'ud: fretless lute with rounded belly, bent neck, and eleven strings, five of them in double courses

violin: same as a Western violin or fiddle. Tuned bottom to top: G-D- g-d-

OTHER TERMS

dabkah: line dance of rural origin. Variations exist throughout Lebanon, Syria, Jordan, and Palestine. Iraqis also do line dances distinct from the Levantine style in rhythm, feel, and step

haflah: formal music party

mawwal: vocal song or introduction, rendered nonmetrically by the singer

raqs ('arabi): dance known in the United States as belly dancing. It also might be referred to as *raqs al-sharqi,* or Oriental dance. A nonprofessional form of this style of dancing occurs at nearly every wedding and party. People dance alone (i.e., not touching or in a line) with their hands held shoulder-height or higher. Curvy arm, hand, and hip gestures are typical of the style. People dance in couples or groups. It is common for groups of women to dance together or for men to dance together. *Dabkah* (line) dancing and *raqs 'arabi* often occur together (during the same musical performance) although there are distinct musical styles appropriate for each. Little children, especially girls, can usually be seen learning to dance in this style at weddings and parties *zaffah:* procession during which the bride and groom are danced into the public space of the wedding party

zagharit (in English, *ululation;* in Arabic, *zaghlouta):* A high trilling sound performed mostly by women but also sometimes by men as an expression of joy. Synthesizer players often have a sample of *zagharit*—thus you now hear this very human sound both live and "canned" at weddings and parties

References

Abu-Lughod. 1993. *Writing Women's Worlds: Bedouin Stories.* Berkeley and Los Angeles: University of California Press.

Anderson, Benedict. 1983. *Imagined Communities.* London: Verso.

Appadurai, Arjun. 1990. Disjuncture and Difference in the Global Cultural Economy. *Public Culture* 2 (2):1–24.

Bruner, Edward M. 1984. *Text, Play, and Story: The Construction and Reconstruction of Self and Society.* Prospect Heights, Ill.: Waveland Press.

Cainkar, Louise. 1994. Palestinian Women in American Society: The Interaction of Social Class, Culture, and Politics. In *The Development of Arab-American Identity,* edited by Ernest McCarus.

Clifford, James. 1994. Diasporas. *Cultural Anthropology* 9 (3):302–38.

Coplan, David. 1982. The Urbanisation of African Music: Some Theoretical Observations. *Popular Music 2: Theory and Method.* 112–29.

Haddad, Yvonne Yazbeck. 1994. Maintaining the Faith of the Fathers: Dilemmas of Religious Identity in the Christian and Muslim Arab-American Communities. In *The Development of Arab-American Identity,* edited by Ernest McCarus, 61–84.

Kent, Carolee. 1989. Arab-American Zaffat-Al 'Arusah Procession, *UCLA Journal of Dance Ethnology* 13:23–28.

McCarus, Ernest, ed. 1994. *The Development of Arab-American Identity.* Ann Arbor: University of Michigan Press.

Musally, George. 1995. Interview with the author. Foxboro, Mass.

Naficy, Hamid. 1991. The Politics and Practice of Iranian Nostalgia in Exile. *Diaspora* 1 (3): 285–302.

Nelson, Kristina. 1985. *The Art of Reciting the Qur'an.* Austin: University of Texas Press.

Rasmussen, Anne. 1997a. The Music of Arab Detroit: A Musical Mecca in the Midwest. *Musics of Multicultural America: A Study of Twelve Musical Communities,* edited by Kip Lornell and Anne Rasmussen. New York: Schirmer.

———. 1997b. *The Music of Arab Americans: A Retrospective Collection*. Compact disc recording with documentary notes, photographs, and text. Rounder, CD1122.

———. 1996. Theory and Practice at the Arabic Org: Digital Practice in Contemporary Music Performance. *Popular Music* 15 (3).

———. 1992. An Evening in the Orient: The Middle Eastern Nightclub in America. *Asian Music* 23 (2).

———. 1991. Individuality and Musical Change in the Music of Arab Americans. Ph.D. Diss. University of California, Los Angeles.

———. 1989. The Music of Arab Americans: Performance Contexts and Musical Transformation. *The Pacific Review of Ethnomusicology* 5:15–33.

Stokes, Martin. 1994. Introduction: Ethnicity, Identity and Music. In *Ethnicity, Identity and Music: the Musical Construction of Space*, edited by Martin Stokes, 1–28. Providence: Berg Publishers.

Family Resemblances

Kinship and Community in Arab Detroit

Andrew Shryock

Kinship Ex Nihilo: (Re)Building a Family from the Ground Up

In 1982 Husayn's[1] family was killed by an Israeli bomb. It leveled the Beirut apartment building where they were spending their last anxious days in Lebanon. Husayn's father, mother, aunt, three sisters, and two brothers had recently fled their village in the south—ironically, to escape Israeli shelling—and were making arrangements to emigrate to America. They would join Husayn in Dearborn, where he had been living for seven years. Husayn was a success in America. He owned two gas stations in Detroit, and he was making big money without the help of a big family. Among the Lebanese, Husayn was odd in that way. When he heard about the bomb, he realized he would go on being odd.

Husayn lived without kin, but he never lacked friends. When I met him in 1986, he was especially close to Imad and Saeed, fellow immigrants he had known since he first arrived in Detroit. Like Husayn, they were Shia from south Lebanon; neither had family in Detroit. In the old days, Husayn, Imad, and Saeed lived in the same house, worked in the same gas stations, wore the same clothes, and spent almost all their free time together. They were like brothers. In 1987 Bilal, Husayn's real (and only surviving) brother came to Detroit. Bilal had just divorced his wife, and, unaccustomed to being single, he was desperate to remarry. Husayn arranged for Bilal to marry Hayya, his accountant. I attended that wedding, and over the last few years I have watched as Husayn's friends, Saeed and Imad, have married two of Hayya's five sisters. In 1990 Husayn married Hayya's cousin, Batool, giving her U.S. citizenship and setting in motion the steady relocation of her family to Detroit. What began as a circle of friends living without kin has evolved, in less than a decade, into a close-knit group of in-laws. The children of these marriages—eleven so far—are first and second cousins, some paternal, some maternal, some both.

When I told Husayn how unusual this evolution might appear to most Americans, he gave me a puzzled look, then said: "Friends, in-laws, and kin [*habayib, wa nasayib, wa arayib*]. These are the only people you can live with. What's so strange about it?"

Kinship as Community Infrastructure: Or, What's (Not) So Strange about Husayn's Family

Since the arrival of the first Syrian immigrants over a century ago, Arab Detroit has been dominated by networks of kin and, whenever blood relations are lacking, by networks of friends who treat each other as if they were kin. As an anthropologist at work in Detroit, I have been exploring these networks for twelve years. The communities they lead me to are marked, always, by a strong "family resemblance"; or, to put it another way, they share a resemblance based on strong families. This strength is not a by-product of "family values" or the idea that "kinship is important," vague notions to which most Americans subscribe. What sets Arab Detroit apart from the larger society is the extent to which Arab immigrants use kinship to accomplish things, and the extent to which things cannot be accomplished—cars and houses cannot be bought, businesses cannot be run, mosques cannot be established, political coalitions cannot be held together—without resort to kinship ties.

Ernest Hebert captures this distinction perfectly when he differentiates between "kin" and groups that see themselves, quite explicitly, as "a kinship":

> Kinship groups are strong and pervasive throughout American life. Members of kinships can be rich or poor, or anywhere in between. They can hold political views and values of every stripe. What binds the members of a kinship has little to do with money or politics. *As long as the members of an extended family are caught in the grip of a loyalty above immediate family, nation and society, the group can grow into a kinship.* (1993, 18; emphasis added)

American immigrant communities are fertile ground for the growth of kinships, for exactly the reasons Hebert suggests: the immigrant's "immediate family," transplanted from its homeland (or left behind there), can seem hopelessly small; the "nation," new and still alien, is often construed as little more than a legal fiction; and the "society," a juggernaut of customs, beliefs, and attitudes very different from one's own, can seem hostile and unattractive. Whether Nigerian, Cambodian, or Arab, newly arrived immigrants are irresistibly drawn to kinships, and Arabs, like so many new immigrants, come from a postcolonial region in which nation-states are new, families are big, and kinships are strong.

The importance of family life in Arab Detroit is a general feature of the American immigrant experience. The patterns I discuss in this essay would be intelligible, for instance, to members of Detroit's Italian and Greek communities. Nonetheless, there is something intensely particular and recognizably Arab about the networks of loved ones and relatives that enable men like Husayn, Imad, and Saeed to live comfortably in a world that is not yet American and no longer Lebanese. The qualities Arab immigrants use to distinguish themselves from each other (nationality, religion, village of origin, clan affiliation) do almost nothing to weaken the basic likeness, the "family resemblance," of Arab kinships. As I will argue in this essay, the power of kinship in Arab Detroit originates in particular assumptions about gender, parenthood, relatedness, marriage, and the politics of family life. These assumptions, when combined with (and arrayed against) mainstream American alternatives, create the vast "in betweenness," the transcultural space in which thousands of Arabs negotiate their own passage through the identity maze of ethnic Detroit.

Arab Families as Global Communities: Or, Families before and beyond the State

In the United States, people think of the family as a small thing. We use terms like "nuclear" and "immediate" to describe what are, in daily life, its largest forms. As a social institution, the family exists in our living rooms, in the blue glow of the TV set, on national holidays, after work, and after school. We say family is important to us, but we also suspect that the American family is falling apart, and conservative politicians have built impressive careers on this chronic sense of domestic instability. The scenario is older than most of us think. "For at least 150 years," historian Linda Gordon writes, "there have been periods of fear that 'the family'—meaning a popular image of what families were supposed to be like, by no means a correct recollection of any actual 'traditional' family—was in decline; and these fears have tended to escalate in periods of social stress" (1988, 3). In the Arab world, where the family plays a dominant role in both public and private life, one finds an opposite fear: namely, that the family is too big, too controlling, too influential in the affairs of society. In fact, there is no general agreement on where the family stops and society begins. Arab social critics will assert, without much equivocation, that the Arab family is "a society in miniature" and that Arab society is a "family writ large." According to Halim Barakat:

> kinship loyalties may conflict with national loyalty and undermine national consciousness, [but] much of the legitimacy of political orders and rulers derives from the family and its values. Political socialization takes place in the home, resulting in the congruency of political orientations among members of the family. Also, rulers and political leaders are cast in the image of the father, while citizens are cast in the image of children. God, the father, and the ruler thus have many characteristics in common. (1993, 116–17)

Hisham Sharabi bases his entire critique of contemporary Arab political culture on the notion of "neopatriarchy," which he depicts as a malign, psychosocial blend of modernity and male dominance whose defining characteristic

> is the dominance of the father (patriarch), the center around which the national as well as the natural family is organized. Thus between ruler and ruled, between father and child, there exist only vertical relations: in both settings the paternal will is the absolute will, mediated in both the society and the family by a forced consensus based on ritual and coercion. (1988, 7)

The case is overstated, but it is hardly "wrong." It corresponds to something real in the world it describes. Clearly, a nation-state is not a kin group; a bureaucracy is not a family. But not all people would be equally offended if the converse were true. There are places in the Arab world—Libya, for instance (Davis 1987)—where the nation-state is officially described as a kin group. In the Gulf states, national identity is assigned on the basis of tribal affiliation and genealogical pedigree. Half the Arabic-speaking states are ruled, officially, by hereditary monarchs, while others, like Syria and Iraq, are said to be ruled by the president "and his relatives." In Jordan many people believe bureaucratic structures "work" only insofar as family and familylike networks of favoritism (*wasta*) are contained within them (Cunningham and Sarayrah 1993). Oil states like Kuwait and Saudi

Arabia are, in practice, the world's largest family-owned, family-run businesses.

Indeed, the entire political economy of the Arab world is shot through with family ties, and those ties extend beyond the region to influence the way global business networks, military alliances, and diplomatic elites operate. The same family networks, operating at lower levels of power and prestige, facilitate the global spread of Arabic-speaking peoples: the flow of immigrant labor from Algeria to France; the "brain drain" from Egypt to the United States; the relocation of Arab Christians to the West and Arab Jews to Israel; the systematic displacement of Palestinians from Israeli-controlled territories to the Americas and Europe. The largest Arabic-speaking communities in Detroit are part of this global expansion. They have come to America in streams, or "chain migrations," of kin. The Lebanese families in Dearborn are mostly from Tibneen, Bint Jubail, and other villages near the Israeli border. Chaldeans trace their origin to Telkaif, a village in northern Iraq. Many of Detroit's Palestinians have a family connection to Ramallah (if they are Christian) or Beit Hanina (if they are Muslim); and the majority of Yemeni immigrants come from a handful of villages in the central region of the former North Yemen.

Despite its tremendous size, Arab Detroit consists almost entirely of people from four rather small areas of the Arab world, and these people belong to "kinships"—to families (*'aylat*), houses (*buyut*), tribes (*gabayil*), clans (*hamayil*), religious sects, and ethnic minorities—that predate the entities known today as Lebanon, or Yemen, or the United States. I once asked a Lebanese friend what he did during his monthlong visit to the homeland. I was surprised when he said he spent the whole time in his parents' house, visiting with relatives, drinking tea and being fed, exchanging gifts, and fending off marriage proposals. I discovered, in dozens of similar conversations, that this was an altogether ordinary way to spend a return visit. The "homeland" might be located in a nation-state called Yemen, in a geopolitical region called the Arab world; but one's practical attachments to Yemen are concentrated in a particular family from a particular city or village. These places and family names existed long before the Yemen Arab Republic was created (in 1962), and because of global chain migrations, they exist far beyond Yemen as well.

Images and Icons: Or, a Gallery of Arab Family Portraits, Some More Conventional than Others

For Amni Taleb, this overlay of old and new, local and global identities is visible in one of her dearest possessions: a panoramic photograph of Qaraoun, her native village in Lebanon. Figure 45 shows Amni standing beside the picture, which she has had enlarged and framed and which she now proudly displays on her office wall in Dearborn. It is an icon that combines notions of family, place, and nation; and it combines these things effectively only for Lebanese from Qaraoun.

"My husband makes fun of me," Amni said when we talked about her photograph. "He says, 'Why do you get so excited about this place? It's just a village.' And I tell him, 'I just can't help it. Qaraoun is in my blood. It's my origins.' "

The way Amni describes her connection to Qaraoun is the way Arab immigrants tend to think about the family: not as a mother, father, and children but as a community of shared blood (*damm*) and origins (*usul*), a community that can be as small as a single family, or as big as an entire nation, depending on the context.

In both America and the Arab world, the prevailing symbol of kinship is the family tree. The "tree of relationship" (*shajarat nasab*), as it is called in Arabic, is an attempt to map, in scrupulous detail, the links through which the blood of community flows, links that lead, ideally, to a single ancestor. Yusif Barakat's pedigree, inscribed on the leaves of an olive tree (figure 46), was crafted by a professional genealogist in Palestine, probably in the 1930s. The tree links Yusif

Fig. 45. Amni Taleb and her portrait of Qaraoun. Photograph by Millard Berry.

Fig. 46. Yussif Barakat's family tree. Courtesy of the ACCESS Museum of Arab Culture.

and thousands of his kin to a man named Sa'dullah. When Yusif came to America in the 1940s, he brought this tree, and the blood of Sa'dullah, with him. Yusif's tree differs from most American family trees in that it records only the names of men and only men on the father's side. A community of blood and origin is created in sexual collaboration with women, but it is publicly controlled by men and passed down in the male line. Arab immigrants bring to Detroit a patrilineal, patriarchal model of kinship groups. Yusif's tree is part of the same genealogical tradition that produced the lists of begetting and begotten that fill the Book of Genesis, the daunting pedigrees of Jesus found in the Gospels, and the elaborate genealogies of the Prophet Muhammad and his family that are still being compiled in the Muslim world today.

Most Americans can name only two generations of ancestors in their father's line. When I did research among tribal groups in Jordan, my hosts thought it odd (pitiful, actually) that I did not know the name of my own paternal great-grandfather. In fact, some of them assumed I was concealing his name; perhaps he had been a criminal, a derelict, a gypsy, or even a bastard. I pointed out that Americans generally cannot recite their pedigrees and—with the notable exception of gray-haired genealogy buffs—feel no desire to do so. My admission was taken as further proof (for Jordanians who needed it) that American society was rootless, ill-bred, and morally suspect. Without genealogical knowledge, how can you tell what people are like, who the best and worst people are, how they are related, what their loyalties are?

These concerns are crucial in a social system that uses kinship to accomplish things that Americans, for the most part, leave to government, the job market, our "invisible" class structure, and chance. If I tell you my name is Andrew Shryock, you know almost nothing about me. Even if you knew the complete genealogical history of my family, you probably would not feel free to make assumptions about me personally. The opposite is true in the Arab world, and in Arab Detroit. If a Detroiter tells me his name is Muhammad Hasan Berri, I can make the following guesses about him, and most of them will be correct: he is Lebanese; his family is probably from the village of Tibneen; he is probably a Muslim, a Shii Muslim; he probably prays at the Islamic Institute on Schaefer or the Islamic Center on Joy Road but not at the Dix Mosque; he is probably sympathetic to Hizb al-Amal or Hizbullah (Lebanese political parties) or is related to people who are; he probably lives in Dearborn; he probably graduated from Fordson High School; and so on. This information is reliably conveyed by his name, and it is worth keeping track of ancestral names like Berri only if they contain useful information of this sort. The exact information may differ in Tibneen, Beirut, and Detroit, but it will always be based on the assumption that Berris share certain qualities and life experiences because they are Berris; because they are "a kinship."

Each of the major national groups that make up Arab Detroit is divided into several large kinships like the Berris. Immigrants from Ramallah, a Christian village in Palestine, are a striking example. Ramallah has its own social club in Livonia, where the community is concentrated. This club is one branch of a national immigrant organization called the American Federation of Ramallah, Palestine. The organization has its own Web site on the Internet, and this foothold in cyberspace is symptomatic of Ramallah's increasingly delocalized existence: it has become, quite literally, a global village. There are now more Ramallawis living in America than in Ramallah, and the branches of the Ramallah family tree are held together by satellite phone links and fiber-optic cables. What it means to be Ramallawi, however, is not determined by advanced information technologies. According to Roy Freij, a computer graphics designer and former president of the Ramallah Club (1994–95), a person can belong to the club "if he or she descends from one of the five brothers who founded the village" many generations ago. The club itself, like all the families within it, is still a community of blood and origin.

It is difficult, however, to maintain the "purity" of kin-based communities in an immigrant diaspora, especially when a group is small. The Ramallah Club, which serves as a marriage pool for the children of its members, is already letting the descendants of females into the club. That is how Roy Freij became a member. In fact, marriage outside the family, sect, and national group is changing the face of Arab America. It is also reducing the amount of reliable information carried in a name, since the stereotypical characters and complexions of people like the Ramallawis and Berris have been reinforced by many generations of related families marrying disproportionately among themselves.

Joe Zainea, owner of the Majestic Café, a popular nightclub in Detroit, proudly announces to his patrons that he is a "thoroughbred" Syrian with deep roots in Damascus. Behind the bar Joe keeps a studio portrait of his grandfather's family, taken in Syria in 1897, just before Joe's uncle began the chain migration that brought the Zaineas to Michigan (figure 47). The men in the picture wear tarbooshes, a conical hat fashionable at the time. The women, dressed in fin de siècle dresses, look equally exotic. In fact, the Otherness of this photograph is exactly what Joe, born and raised in Detroit, finds so irresistible about it. To intensify its power as an unusual artifact, Joe also shows his customers a group shot of the 1990 Zainea family reunion (figure 48). Many of the people in this portrait are lineal descendants of Abdullah Zainea. A century separates them from the old, tarboosh-wearing brass engraver from Damascus, and Joe consciously plays up the sharp contrast between the pictures. During my first look at the reunion shot, Joe directed my gaze to the light-skinned children sitting on the front row. These, he explained, are the sons and daughters of Zaineas married to non-Syrians. As I studied the photograph, I noticed that, among third- and fourth-generation Zaineas, blond hair and blue eyes were common.

Some people in the Detroit Arab community would say these children are Zaineas but not Arabs; many of the people in the picture would agree that they are not Arabs but only Zaineas. Even the full-blooded, fourth-generation Syrians at the Zainea reunion would feel out of place in Damascus today. For Joe, this radical transformation is a success story. Becoming American is a process he understands intuitively; the process itself is part of mainstream American culture. Our popular media and public schools equip us, from an early age, to

Fig. 47. The Zainea ancestors in Damascus, 1897. Courtesy of the ACCESS Museum of Arab Culture.

Fig. 48. A section of the Zainea family reunion, 1990. Courtesy of the ACCESS Museum of Arab Culture.

experience and talk about "becoming American." But how do people experience and talk about becoming "less" Arab? Why is it so obvious that lessenings of this sort occur but so hard to explain what they mean? What happens as a huge family like the Zaineas moves, over a span of decades, from Ottoman Syria to postindustrial Detroit?

Contact Zones: Or, How Detroit Turns Normal Arab Families into Abnormal Ones

The belief that immigrants will assimilate, that they or their children will eventually "become American," is still our national creed, and new Arab immigrants have even more reason to believe it than Zaineas do. My Italian landlord in Dearborn complained that the Lebanese family next door would never be good Americans; the Lebanese next door complained that their children would never be good Lebanese. Narratives of "Arab American identity" evolve in the space between these opposing critiques. They are told in hopes of attaining, postponing, or fending off an inevitably American future. Tales of Arab American family life fixate on qualities that are not yet generically American. For this reason, Arab Americans often imagine their families to be unique—just as Syrian cuisine, Yemeni dance, and Palestinian embroidery are unique—when in fact the Otherness of Arab domestic cultures is shaped by the American mainstream against which new immigrants struggle to define themselves.

Immigrants from the Arab world must contend with the abnormalization of things that, in Lebanon, Yemen, or Iraq, seemed perfectly normal. In particular, there are four aspects of Middle Eastern cultures that clash with (or are simply inconsistent with) patterns dominant in American society. These very quickly become battlegrounds on which family members decide how American and Arab they will be; what it means to be American and Arab comes to be defined precisely by these four areas of conflict.

Gender/Sexuality

Throughout the Arab world, gender segregation in public is the norm. Men and women pray separately at mosques and churches; in most countries, they study in different schools or on different sides of the same classroom; they celebrate weddings and funerals in different quarters (and in different ways); they rarely mix at sporting events or political rallies; even on buses and trains, unrelated men and women try to sit apart from each other; if this is not possible, cross-sex interactions are kept to a polite minimum. Women spend most of their time in spaces defined as domestic, interior, and protected. Friendships are made with members of one's own sex. These divisions break down only in the privacy of the home, among close neighbors, and in the congested, anonymous spaces found only in cities.

In Detroit old habits of gender segregation fade quickly. American public space is not designed to accommodate them. Still, among all newly arrived immigrant groups, cross-sex socializing is encouraged only among close kin. Dating remains taboo (unless it is followed quickly by a marriage proposal), and family-arranged marriages are common. If the bride and groom dated before their engagement, they often pretend they did not. To do otherwise would draw suspicion on themselves or their families. Virginity is taken very seriously for girls—hardly at all for boys—and anything that hints of sexual impropriety among females is potentially damaging to a family's reputation.

Given the notions of "sexual impropriety" that prevail among new Arab immigrants, simply attending an American public school is an ominous experience. In American schools, the immigrant parent sees unrelated boys and girls actually being encouraged to date, touch, and dance together (i.e., the prom); hand-holding and kissing are tolerated in the hallways (i.e., high school sweethearts); boys and girls are encouraged to socialize together after school, and even after dark (i.e., in clubs); girls are allowed to display themselves, wet and virtually naked, before crowds of unrelated men (i.e., the swim team); and the most popular girls are those who, dressed in revealing uniforms, jump, dance, and kick before crowds of unrelated men (i.e., cheerleading). Odder still, all these bizarre activities are taken, matter-of-factly, to be *good;* they are said to "build character" in young boys and girls. Perhaps no institution is more immediately offensive to traditional Arab notions of gender and sexuality than the American high school.

Social Life

In 1994 I taught a class on anthropological fieldwork methods at the University of Michigan in Dearborn. One of my students decided to take part in and analyze a Lebanese wedding. The wedding was called off, but the student was captivated by other aspects of family life along Warren Avenue. Many of the patterns she recognized had become ordinary to me, but they struck her (and strike most

Americans who have the rare chance to observe them) as strange. In her oral report to the class, she noted that

> They had family in and out of the house constantly; there were always aunts and uncles and cousins down in the basement. They didn't seem to use any other part of their house; everyone was always in the basement.

The Lebanese basement, I told the class, is now a staple of Dearborn vernacular architecture; its appeal as a living space is based on its lack of interior walls, which allows many people to socialize within eye- and earshot of each other. Its lack of windows, which gives the basement a private, closed-in feeling, also makes it desirable. In summer Lebanese families go aboveground—eating, socializing, and watching TV in their garages, another space without interior walls. Meanwhile, their first-floor living rooms, the wall-to-wall carpet meticulously vacuumed and the plush furniture cloaked in plastic, await the appearance of special guests:

> They loved to be together, obviously. They fought and yelled a lot, but they seem to enjoy that, and they made me feel like a queen. The mother stopped everything and prepared a meal whenever I came by to visit. For me, to be honest, it was overwhelming. I always thought Polish families were close. But we're nothing next to the Lebanese.

Americans are routinely amazed by the high decibel level of Arab homes, where loud, animated conversation is made louder by the need to talk over the ambient noise of TVs and stereos, which are rarely turned off in front of guests. Impressive, too, is the aplomb with which Arab families entertain their frequent visitors. A respectable Arab family is a well-oiled hospitality machine, eager (and prepared at a moment's notice) to present meals to friends and relatives. Sharkey Haddad, a Chaldean community leader, told me that Iraqi housewives like to keep two large, fully stocked freezers in the basement, each full of *kibbeh,* grape leaves, *kafta,* and other delicacies suitable for company.

My student continued her oral report, returning time and again to themes of sociability and connectedness:

> They were on the phone twenty-four hours a day. They had a line upstairs, a line downstairs, and a cellular phone that the brothers were always fighting over. They would gossip about their next-door

> neighbors here in Dearborn by calling their village in Lebanon and getting information from their in-laws, who I guess were married into the same family. I only call my mom once or twice a week, and we live in the same city.

Long-distance telephone companies, like AT&T and MCI, are well aware of this pattern; they advertise heavily in Arab Detroit, in both Arabic and English, and lend corporate sponsorship to community events. Paula Dababishi, a Palestinian pharmacist, told me that managers at Perry Drugs (now Rite Aid) had noticed that Arab employees made and received family calls at work at a dramatically higher rate than non-Arab employees; pharmacists were asked to reduce such calls, but the connectedness of Arab families demands that people "check in" with each other frequently. Paula shared this information with me over dinner. When we returned to Paula's house after the meal, having been gone for only two hours, seven messages had accumulated on her answering machine: five from members of her immediate family, two from her husband's family.

When middle-class Americans first encounter Arab domestic space, they are impressed by exactly those qualities middle-class American families lack: high-density living, more or less constant togetherness, and a heavy schedule of interfamilial hosting and visiting. My student described these qualities warmly, even nostalgically, as if Lebanese home life pointed back to a more human, family-oriented past that she, and all Americans, had lost. I have come to realize, however, that middle-class Americans quickly tire of high-intensity family life; too much of it too soon and they yearn for escape. A Chaldean friend told me about bringing her fiancé ("a totally American white guy") to celebrate Thanksgiving with her family for the first time. She promised him it would be a small gathering of just her immediate family. When they arrived, there were already fifty guests, and eventually there were eighty. After the traditional turkey dinner, the family retired to the basement, where they danced the *dabkah* (an Iraqi line dance) all afternoon. A technically inclined uncle captured the proceedings on a handheld video camera. The fiancé enjoyed himself, but he thought it was exhausting and "too much of a good thing." His Chaldean sweetheart was surprised by his reaction.

"Don't all American families do this on Thanksgiving?" she asked.

Patriarchy

Most Arab immigrants accept as a fact of life that a man should be head of the house, even if "the mother is the neck that moves the head." The Arab fathers I know are treated (in public at least) with scrupulous respect by their wives and children. Mama is typically a source of lenient affection, but Baba is the embodiment of domestic authority and power, and it is quite common for Arab men to complain that they never felt close to their father. Women, in my experience, are apt to describe their fathers differently. Layla Mahinna Beckley, teacher in a Detroit-area public school, described to me her "authentic Lebanese dad," a man who demands of his children (and their mother) a delicate mix of awe, respect, and unreserved adoration.

> When our father came home, the whole house changed. We'd stop talking; we'd sit up straight in his presence. If he said something, we did it. Really, we were kind of afraid of him. We all respected him. He was king. Mama unlaced his shoes when he came home from work. She'd actually heat up the water and scrub his back for him when he took a bath. Do you believe it? We lined up to serve him; I mean, we fought for the privilege. Even now, my parents hate the way my [teenage] daughters play with Robert [Layla's American husband], rubbing his head and teasing him. They're loud in front of him. They talk back. My mother says it's not respectful, and I kind of feel ashamed for Robert when I hear this. Robert doesn't care, though, 'cause he doesn't know this is their way of saying he's not a real man.

Layla is trying to explain the superior moral position of a specific man in a particular family. Unlacing Baba's shoes and scrubbing his back are certainly not universal habits in Arab homes, but the theme of preferential treatment and respect for males underlying Layla's account would be familiar to most Arab readers. In the Arab world, it is generally not thought proper for women to have authority over adult men. Men are supposed to be the protectors of women, the managers of their affairs. In return, women are expected to show men the appropriate respect, and this is taught from the earliest age. The brother/sister relationship is the training ground for skills and attitudes that will eventually be expressed in husband/wife, mother/son, father/daughter, and other intimate, cross-gender relationships. Maha Hamadi captures the emotional strength of this apprenticeship in the following anecdote.

> We Palestinians prefer the boys. It's true. When I was little, I remember we used to sleep on the floor: my sister and my two brothers. On mattresses. But when we came to America, our cousins here all had beds, so my father bought one, just one at first, and my brothers

> slept on it, and my sister and I slept on the floor beside it. And we would make the bed for them [her brothers] every morning, and put out their clothes and shoes for them. And I remember we used to love doing this for my brothers. It never occurred to us that it was sexist, until we got older. I still don't feel, in my heart, that it was wrong. It was a sign of respect. I took care of my brothers like that until they got married and moved out. They married American girls, and I don't think those girls take care of them at all. I just don't see the same respect. To this day, I'm convinced that my sister and I love them more than their own wives do.

Interdependence/Cohesiveness

Arab immigrant families are gregarious; family members see and talk to each other often. This cohesiveness is not something middle-class Americans could reproduce if only, as a teacher at a cultural diversity workshop told me, "we chose to value our families more." The cohesiveness of Arab immigrant families derives, instead, from a worldview in which human society beyond the realm of kinship, filled as it is with nonrelatives, strangers, and unreliable institutions, is construed as amoral and fundamentally dangerous, as a domain in which one's resources and affections are drained away from the "loved ones, in-laws, and kin" (*habayib, wa nasayib, wa garayib*) who truly deserve them. Arab immigrant families are designed to protect their members from this larger world and to help them engage with it successfully; that is, with the backing of a group.

Family solidarity is established at a tremendous psychological price. The desire for independence—the desire to pursue one's own interests, question authority, break away, think one's own thoughts—must be discouraged. This is done in numerous ways. First, children are taught that they cannot survive outside the family; that no one in the larger society will love or assist them; that they cannot attain happiness on their own, apart from kin. In the American middle class, by contrast, children are taught that they must eventually leave the family, and they are trained for independent living from earliest childhood. Among Arab immigrants, living alone is not generally desired or encouraged. In Lebanon, Palestine, Iraq, and Yemen, most people, male and female, live in their parents' home until they marry; and if they divorce, women are apt to move home again. There is intense pressure to socialize and form close friendships with kin. Friendships with non-kin can provoke feelings of jealousy and suspicion within the family.

The power of these sentiments became clear to me when I interviewed Clarise, a Chaldean painter who is constantly on the lookout for a full-time teaching job in Detroit. I asked her why she refuses to apply for positions outside the Detroit area. Clarise was not surprised by my question; her American friends ask her this all the time. I was surprised, however, by her answer.

"If I don't live close to my cousins," Clarise said, "who will my children play with?"

Clarise was not married, or even engaged, when I interviewed her. Nonetheless, she had constructed a future in which she and her first cousins lived side by side in an exclusive cul-de-sac in Bloomfield Hills. For me, Clarise's vision was parochial, even suffocating; for Clarise, it was liberating. A community of shared blood and origin was the only world in which her children could be genuinely happy.

"They Fuck You Up, Your Mum and Dad": Or, Diagnosing the Mutual Neuroses of Arab and American Families

All these values and traditions, which are commonplace in the Arab world, become problematic in American society, which gives official support to individualism, romantic love, the gap between generations, the erasure of gender differences, and relatively open (though not always enlightened) attitudes toward sex. Everywhere Arab immigrant families turn, they see these values encouraged at the expense of their own. Their collectivist sensibilities, their ideas of male and female, their ways of marrying and raising children are consistently portrayed as backward and immoral. The result, for newly arrived immigrants, is a classic double bind: "the family traditions that make us superior to the Americans are exactly the ones Americans use to stigmatize us."

The public school system is the incubator in which this double bind is hatched and brought to maturity. As a consultant to Detroit-area schools, I have learned that counselors and teachers (inculcators of our national psyche) tend to think of Arab immigrant homes (Christian and Muslim) as unhealthy child-rearing environments. These homes are not perceived to be moral communities drawn along different lines, as Mennonite, Mormon, or Orthodox Jewish households typically are. Rather, they are assumed to be intrinsically flawed: sexist, patriarchal, controlling. The children who grow up in these families, counselors tell me, develop self-images that are morally ambiguous and full of contradictions. In the psychologizing rhetoric of American individualism, personalities of this sort are easily cast as sick. Words like "burdened," "stressed," "trapped," and "compromised" are invoked, like mantras, to account for them. When teachers in Dearborn and Detroit ask me to "explain" the Arab family, as if it were a syndrome or a social problem, the best of them are looking for ways to help Arab students cope. I always insist, however, that the largest problem facing Arab immigrant kids is not the morality of their own family, which made sufficient sense in Yemen or Iraq, but the immense power of the American public school to revalue that morality, turning it into a source of confusion and shame.

At the same time, however, this revaluation of domestic morality is an indispensable aspect of "becoming American," since personalities vexed in this way—that is, personalities shaped by the struggle to gain independence from parents—are commonplace in our society. When Americans talk about family, tales of love, caring, and support are not the only (or even the most common) topics of discussion. Just as often, Americans describe family as a source of stress, an obstacle, as emotional baggage, a financial liability, or a context one must get out of to be happy, successful, and well-adjusted. The self-help industry is fueled by an insatiable national desire to escape the consequences of a dysfunctional childhood that included (depending on the latest fad): satanic child abuse, incest (remembered or repressed), parental negativity, emotional blackmail, alcoholism, drug abuse, too much pressure to succeed, not enough pressure to succeed, and countless bad attitudes about food, sex, work, religion, race, gender, and body fat.

I have begun to suspect that images of "messed up" first-generation Arab Americans are the result of Americans projecting their own ambivalent feelings about family life onto individuals whose family relationships are even more "oppressive" than their own but who are not yet able or willing to loosen kinship ties. Their "psychological ties to their parents' tradition," Jon Swanson writes of the children of immigrants,

> often remain strong. This can be a source of considerable role stress for, in contrast to their parents who were enculturated in only one cultural tradition, they are brought up simultaneously in two markedly different worlds. On one hand they are socialized according to the norms and expectations of their parents, and on the other they are enculturated to the expectations of a wider cultural context, represented by their peers, teachers, and the media. (1996, 243)

Arab Detroit, like other immigrant/ethnic communities, is located "in between" moral spaces. On one side are newly arrived families from Lebanon, Yemen, Iraq, and Palestine; on the other is "a wider cultural context." If immigrants linger too long in the borderland between family and mainstream society, they become "abominations"—the ominous Old Testament label for creatures that confound categories—and borderland selves are quickly recast as borderline personalities.

At a deep ideological level, the American family and the immigrant family are linked in their common opposition to the autonomous, free-standing individual: the ideal citizen of the state. Just as the loosening of family ties is part of becoming a healthy American adult, so the creation of moral distance between child and parent is part of becoming a healthy Arab American. Indeed, one way Arab Americans learn to (re)interpret their Arabness in American terms is to problematize their family life (especially relationships with parents). The search for individual identity—Who am I? Why am I like this?—leads Arab Americans progressively inward (to ponder the complexities of a childhood perceived, somehow, to be different) and backward (to explore the branches of family trees rooted ultimately in other nations). The result, visible in the pages of this book and in ethnic studies generally, is the prominence of the memoir, the family history, the puzzled reflection on returning "home."

One needs only to read the voluminous literature on Chinese, Italian, Latino, and Irish Americans to realize that Arab immigrants are not alone when they learn to criticize, then come to terms with, and finally appreciate—from a safe cultural distance—the "patriarchy," "traditional gender roles," "inwardness," and "dependency" that distinguish their families from those in the larger society. Being able to talk and write about family in this way is proof that a boundary has been crossed; it is proof that a kind of emotional assimilation is taking place. Not only are these accounts written in English, but they are written for an American audience whose opinion of the author counts more than the opinion of an Arabic-speaking audience: thus, the necessary betrayals that fill these narratives—the tales of secret dating, a father's attempts to control, a mother's attempts to manipulate, the stigma of a wife's former divorce, the father's financial failures, private contempt for one's relatives, descents into madness—few of which would be included in an account written in Arabic for Arab readers. Despite the heartfelt sensitivity that pervades these memoirs, they tend only to reinforce dominant American images of Arab family life. They do so because, contrary to what their authors think, they are part of America's mainstream "culture of ethnicity," a culture that insists on narratives of self-discovery in which heroic individuals assert their uniqueness as x-Americans by differentiating themselves from what they consider—and, more precisely, are now *capable* of considering—the Otherness of immigrant family life. The narrators who tell these tales must present themselves as successful escape artists, perhaps proud of getting away, perhaps ridden with guilt and gratitude, but always decisively beyond the familial worlds they recall.

Ordinary People: Or, Four Brief Encounters with Arab/American Lives

As an outsider whose art is entering, not escaping, I can tell stories of a different sort; stories that people would not ordinarily write or publish; stories about people who are still "in between" Detroit and some other place; and, most importantly, stories that are not stereotypically Arab, American, or even Arab American. These stories reflect *my* experience in Arab Detroit, which has brought me into contact with hundreds of families, almost all of which strike me as functional (if occasionally contentious and controlling) frameworks in which to live. Dysfunctional Arab families exist, certainly—domestic violence is a problem in the community, as are "teen" issues like drugs and sexuality—but their peculiar dynamics should not overshadow the ordinary and adaptive quality of Arab immigrant family life. The people I discuss below are interesting to me because, like most individuals, they are peculiar in ordinary ways; their problems are common to Arab Detroit, and their solutions tend to work there, if nowhere else.

Jonas

Jonas is forty-two years old. He is a Chaldean from Telkaif in Iraq. He came to America in 1979 to study and, as he forthrightly puts it, "to get rich." Jonas worked in his uncle's liquor store while he attended Wayne State University in Detroit. His uncle looked out for him, fed him, and clothed him. He never paid him much, but Jonas secretly saved the money he and his cousins made by fencing stolen goods.

> It was a rough neighborhood. These black guys would bring in TVs and stereos and air conditioners, you know, and we'd give them cartons of cigarettes in exchange, or booze. Then we'd sell the stuff to friends. We made good money that way. In the beginning, I didn't

> even know the stuff was stolen. But my cousins made me promise not to tell their dad, so I figured it was probably illegal. They said they got the idea from the Lebanese guys who worked in the gas stations around there, and they all made money like that on the side.

As soon as Jonas got his degree in computer graphics, he found a job in a print shop owned by the husband of one of his cousins. With his knowledge of desktop publishing technology, Jonas soon doubled the owner's profits and made him totally dependent on his expertise. In 1987 Jonas returned to Iraq for a visit, got married, and brought his bride, Rose, to Detroit. Using some family money he smuggled out of Iraq—"in the heels of Rose's shoes"—he bought the print shop from his cousin's husband, inheriting a workforce of relatives from Telkaif, in-laws from Baghdad, and a Yemeni janitor. He appointed Rose as his business manager. She worked without pay, and she loved her job. Unlike her sister, who got pregnant during the first month of marriage, Rose and Jonas were waiting, and they made big profits.

One-by-one, Jonas's immediate family came to Detroit, including his father and stepmother. He was responsible for them; he found them work and lodging. For three years, there were always newly arrived kin living in his two-bedroom house near Seven Mile, in Detroit. I have never heard Jonas complain about what, to me, often looked like sponging. It was his honor and (more to the point) his duty to support his family. Jonas's father was sixty-seven years old when he came to Detroit, but he had a young wife and three children. He expected Jonas to provide for them financially. He also expected Jonas to produce grandchildren who would carry on the family name. Rose fed her in-laws and entertained their guests, but the demands of office and home gradually began to wear her down.

"I felt it was not my house," she told me. "I thought we were living under Jonas's father and his wife. I don't think they appreciated all Jonas was doing for them. They complained that he wasn't doing more! They still do."

When Jonas and Rose had their first child in 1989, there were eight people living under the same roof. To pacify Rose—who, in a bout of postpartum depression, cursed Jonas's stepmother and threatened to return to her family in Iraq—Jonas bought his father a house in Southfield and a new car. He and Rose bought a house farther down the same street, had another child, then another. Today, Jonas owns two print shops, three video stores, and brings in a (high) six-digit income. Last year, he bought a beautiful house in Bloomfield Hills, but by Chaldean standards, he leads a relatively modest lifestyle. His largest investment is his family—his father and brothers are all on his company payroll, though only one of them actually works—and his ability to keep them in new cars and houses brings Jonas prestige in the Chaldean community, where much of his business is conducted.

Jonas speaks Chaldean with his parents and Arabic with his wife. His children, however, are already speaking English to each other and to him. This makes Jonas proud, but it worries him as well.

"I look at them," he told me, "and I see American kids. I didn't think my kids would ever be American like the neighbors' kids. But they're growing up Americanized. They like American TV. They make Rose cook American food like what they eat in school. The other day in the mall, they told Rose not to speak Arabic in front of other people. I asked my priest about it, and he tells me to keep them in church or it will only get worse."

Jonas may dread Americanization and he may discourage his children from playing "too much" with the American kids next door, but he has no desire to return to Iraq. He wants his son to go to the University of Michigan and become "a doctor or a lawyer," and he wants his daughters to marry Chaldeans from good families, "maybe someone from Telkaif." He doesn't want them to date Americans, since the American moral system, he says, "is not good for women, who should be treated with respect." Jonas finds it hard to believe that he originally came to America to get away from his family: "In my heart, I used to be afraid my family would catch up with me." Now he is firmly in their grasp, and he is pleased and reasonably content. As long as his business is strong, Jonas can build his own world in Detroit, and he is convinced that he can hold his family together using the social glue that holds so many big Chaldean families together, "a lot of respect and a lot of money."

Nasreen

Nasreen is from Bint Jubail, a village in the south of Lebanon, but she has lived in Detroit since she was nine years old. She works as a secretary in an accounting firm. One day, a carpenter named Imbarak was hired to install new cabinets in the office. He was Lebanese, but he was not from Bint Jubail. He was also what Nasreen disparagingly refers to as "a boater," a newly arrived immigrant: "You know, the ones that talk and think like peasants." Nasreen was oblivious to him. Imbarak, however, thought Nasreen was beautiful. He sent a message through his sister, who knew a friend whose cousin was Nasreen's sister-in-law. The message was simple: "I would like to sit with you during your coffee break and talk." Nasreen refused twice, but after Imbarak's third request, she accepted. They sat together and talked during her coffee breaks. They realized that they were attracted to each other, and the carpentry project, which Imbarak said he could finish in a week, stretched on for a month.

Imbarak knew he had to take action. He could not date Nasreen: she was a proper Muslim girl. He couldn't call her at home because her father answered the phone. So he got his courage up, went to Nasreen's house accompanied by an uncle and a cousin, and proposed marriage. The family was startled, but they agreed, and Nasreen and Imbarak were formally engaged. They drew up the traditional prenuptial contract, which specified the amount of gold jewelry and furnishings Imbarak would provide Nasreen, and the amount he would have to pay her if they ever decided to divorce. The first amount was eighteen thousand dollars; the second thirty-five thousand dollars. Once they agreed to this contract in the presence of an imam (a Muslim cleric), they were married by Islamic law, and they were allowed to go out on dates with other engaged couples.

"This would have caused a scandal back home," Nasreen told me, "but in Dearborn it's sort of OK."

They also snuck off on a few dates alone, she confided, "but no one ever found out."

After an engagement of six months, Nasreen and Imbarak had their official wedding ceremony and moved into their own house, which they purchased with a down payment from the eighteen thousand dollars Imbarak and his family pledged at the engagement. Nasreen and Imbarak know their marriage was not arranged in the traditional way. They knew each other beforehand, they socialized in public, they dated in groups and on the sly, and their parents played a very small role in getting them together. Still, Imbarak and Nasreen are convinced that their wedding was a proper mix of Muslim, American, and Lebanese traditions. They spend little time worrying about what those labels mean, however. In Dearborn Nasreen and Imbarak can pray at the mosque, take their kids to Chuck E. Cheese for pizza, drive the family minivan to soccer practice, and attend a wedding party for the latest "arranged" marriage; and they can do these things in the company of fellow Arab immigrants. For Nasreen and Imbarak, everyday Detroit is a very Muslim, very Lebanese place. Only when they take their son and daughter on a summer visit to Lebanon—something they have been talking about doing for ten years—only then will they realize just how American they have become.

Daris

Daris was born in Dearborn in 1970. His parents are Yemeni immigrants; neither speaks much English. His dad is a retired autoworker. His mother, one of the first Yemeni women to come to Detroit, has never worked outside the house. Daris is married with five children, and he works in a sausage factory. He describes himself as a Yemeni American.

"Most of the folks down here in the Southend," he told me, "are 100 percent Yemeni, even if they've lived in America all their life. I'm not like that. I think we have to accept the fact that we live in America now; we won't succeed unless we do."

When Daris was a teenager, he went through a wild phase: "did some drugs, got caught drinkin.'" His dad sent him back to Yemen, where he was persuaded to marry his first cousin, who was then thirteen years old. Daris did not want to do this, but he felt he could not say no to his father.

"I still can't contradict him," he told me. "Most Yemeni guys are scared to death of their fathers. But my dad is a good man. He's very strict. I respect him."

In fact, Daris's father controlled every aspect of his life.

"When my wife and I tried to get our own apartment on another street, my dad said she was trying to break up the family and control my paycheck. He broke our contract. He threatened to kill the landlord if he gave the apartment to us—called him up at night and said he'd shoot him. So the landlord said forget it. That's my old man."

When Daris and his wife had their fourth child, his father let them move into their own place. With Daris out of the house, his younger brother started misbehaving. He was doing drugs, staying out late, dating "Puerto Rican girls from Vernor" (a street that runs into Detroit), and he was repeatedly sent home for fighting at school.

> He would get in trouble at school and lie to my dad about it. He'd say the teachers hate Yemenis. They framed me. And my dad would just believe it. He'd go down to the school and cuss the teachers out. I knew this was all bullshit, 'cause I'd been in trouble like that myself. So I says to my dad that the school doesn't make that kind of thing up. I went down there myself and took care of it and got my father to cooperate with the school and keep my brother in line. Pretty soon, all my relatives expected me to solve their problems with the school, or with the boss, or the utilities. Man, I'm like a street lawyer

> for the Yemenis. I'm a one man ACCESS. Always doin' what I can to serve the community.

Daris is slowly modifying the nature of patriarchy in his neighborhood. He respects his father and accepts his domineering habits, but Daris has effectively taken over his father's role as spokesman to the outside world. Daris's knowledge of how Americans and American institutions work is a new source of power that allows him to change his family and help it adapt to life in the American working class.

Vicky

Vicky is a Palestinian from Ramallah. She is thirty-two years old and still single. Needless to say, her mother, Eva, is not pleased. Vicky's life has been a relentless tug of war with Eva, who has been trying to fix Vicky up with "a good Christian man from Ramallah" since she graduated from high school. She even convinced Vicky's father to allow his oldest daughter to go to college at the University of Michigan in Ann Arbor, where she could attract a husband with a professional degree. Preferably a doctor or lawyer.

Vicky ignored her mother's nuptial strategies. Rebellious by nature, settling down was the last thing on her mind. Vicky got a degree in art history ("because my mother said I shouldn't"); hung out with Americans ("they were so totally not Ramallah"); and, largely to shock her mother, she moved in with Doug, a non-Arab law student ("Mother always wanted me to get involved with a professional"). Eva was horrified, but Vicky had her over a barrel. Eva couldn't complain to her friends—that would simply destroy the family's reputation—nor could she tell her husband, since it was Eva's idea to send Vicky off to Ann Arbor in the first place. So Eva became a silent partner in Vicky's secret life, even though it meant paying rent for the student apartment Vicky claimed she was still living in.

Vicky's mother was hurt by all this, and she was frightened, but she never gave up hope. She firmly believed that a man like Doug would not marry a girl he could sleep with without so much as an engagement ring; surely it was only a matter of time before Doug would dump Vicky. Meanwhile, Vicky had fallen deeply in love, and Doug, who felt rejected by Vicky and her family (whom he was never allowed to meet), had no intentions of proposing marriage. Five years went by, then six and seven, and everyone held their breath.

Vicky waited for a proposal that never came; Eva foresaw "breakups" in her coffee grounds; Doug pursued his law degree, then his own practice, largely taking Vicky (and her mysterious family life) for granted. Vicky watched as her girlfriends from Ramallah married into good families, moved into good neighborhoods, and had good children. Despite her rebellious posturing, these were things Vicky desperately wanted.

After eight years, Vicky split up with Doug. Her mother cooked a whole lamb to celebrate the occasion, and her father pretended not to know that Eva was now winning the war he had decided, long ago, to ignore. Now Vicky and her mother have formed a temporary alliance. They are trying to attract some attention from available Palestinian men, and Vicky has moved back home.

"It's better not to be living on your own if you're not married," she told me. "There are a lot of guys who would get the wrong idea."

Like her mother, Vicky bends the rules to her own advantage. After a decade of professing her faith in love, feminism, and independence to her American friends—while denying everything to her friends from Ramallah—she now says she wants a man who respects her and does not ask questions. He has to be Christian. He has to be Arab.

"And he's got to be able to provide for me. I won't pretend. I want a comfortable life. I want the huge wedding, I want the gifts, and I want a diamond ring to go with it. If you're from Ramallah, these things are very important."

"Is it important that you love each other?" I asked her.

"No. I've been the love slave. My mother was right about all that. If he loves me—which would be nice—I want him to love me ten times more than I love him, so he won't be able to string me along, like Doug did."

Vicky is not unlike many single women who have rejected a more traditional life only to hear the clock ticking as they approach their mid-thirties. Her story is very American, as is her use of Arab tradition, which (with her mother's help) will finally bring Vicky the things she really wants in life. Vicky is opting now for the more conservative route; she has cut herself off from her American friends; she is trying to erase all evidence of her long, sexual relationship with Doug; and she insists that this is her choice. Vicky is caught now in a web of denial, deceit, and potential betrayal, but she is spinning the web with Eva's help, and it would be hard, perhaps even foolish, to portray Vicky as oppressed by the traditions (or the mother) she now so avidly embraces.

In from the Margins: Or, How Immigrant Families Make Ethnic Arabs

These four examples offer a glimpse into Arab American family life, which is more diverse than most people would ever imagine. The people I have just described are Muslim, Christian, Chaldean, Lebanese, Yemeni, Palestinian, upper class, lower class, urban, suburban, merchants, laborers, and professionals. They have in common only the family resemblances that mark their kinships as "Arab," and these they share only in relation to the statistical norms of North American domestic life. This lack of fit between their household culture and the culture of the larger society has shaped the most important aspects of their lives. What impresses me most about Vicky, Daris, Jonas, and Nasreen is their ability to create an identity that seriously challenges, but never quite rejects, the moral world of their parents. They are constantly moving in and out of that world, just as they move in and out of the Arabic language. Their mobility depends on intricate patterns of concealment, reinterpretation, surrender, and willing conversion to mainstream culture; yet for all their relentless shape shifting, they cannot foresee a time when they will be "just like the non-Arabs."

But the Zainea family reunion, with its front row of deracinated Syrians, offers strong evidence to the contrary. The children of Daris, Jonas, and Nasreen will challenge their parents in new and even more radical ways. If their families stay in America, few of these kids will speak Arabic or Chaldean well, if at all; none of them will know the homeland as a place they once lived in; some of them will marry non-Muslims or non-Christians; some will marry non-Arabs; and some of them will live far from home. In all of these "deviations," they will have the support of the larger society, which will all but compel them to change. The era of optionless assimilation, however, is over and gone. In the 1940s, there were probably two hundred thousand people of Arab descent in the entire United States. Today, there are two hundred thousand in Metro Detroit alone. With a population of this size, new kinds of family life (and ethnic identity) become possible, and even members of the old Syrian and Lebanese families have taken up the difficult task of reimagining themselves and their kinships, as Arab.

Fig. 49. Don Unis at work. Photograph by Millard Berry.

Don Unis is a second-generation Arab Detroiter and a captain in the Dearborn Fire Department (figure 49). His father came to America from Ottoman Syria in 1917. Don grew up in the Southend of Dearborn in the 1940s and 1950s, when it was a multiethnic neighborhood. It was a time when Arabs were still Syrians and Lebanese; when men changed their names to get jobs; when parents forbade their children to speak Arabic in public; when "everyone wanted to fit into that American ideal." Don has three sisters, two of whom married men of Arab descent. Of his four brothers, only one married within the community. Don's wife, Nancy, is Polish. They eloped in 1963 and were remarried in the Catholic Church in 1967, even though Don was nominally a Muslim. It is hard now for Don to articulate how he thought and felt about being Arab in those days, because he was not "Arab" in those days. Like so many sons and grandsons of the early Syrian immigrants, he was moving into the mainstream. As historian Alixa Naff would put it, Don was about to "assimilate himself out of existence."

But 1967 marked a turning point in Don's life. The Six Day War made him realize that most Americans saw him, and his entire people, as the enemy. Like tens of thousands of old-line immigrants, Don began to identify as an Arab. This was an act of will, a conversion of sorts. Not everyone in his family adopted this new account of who they were. Today, the Unis clan is a mix of people who do and do not identify with the Arab community. Being Arab, for Don, is a matter of choice. He must actively cultivate, explore, and assert his Arabness because, in so many other respects, Don Unis is indisputably American. He has mixed feelings about newly arrived immigrants, who seem alien to him, but he has made strenuous efforts to learn about their culture, which he now considers somehow his own; he has studied up on Islam and Arabic; he has traveled to the Middle East; and he is currently planning to return for the first time to his father's home village in Lebanon, video camera in tow.

There is something very American, and very ethnic, about Don's image of himself. His ability to reconnect with Arab things is limited by the distance he has already traveled into American culture and history. Newly arrived immigrants face the same limitation as they attempt to appropriate American things, and their adaptations, like Don's, manage somehow to leave much of their domestic culture intact. Don's return to Arabness has changed his politics, but it has not made his family more patriarchal (Nancy does not unlace Don's shoes, call him "Lord," or ask his permission to leave the house); it has not changed his ideas about gender and sexuality (all of his daughters dated openly); it has not increased the intensity of his family life or the level of interdependence between him and other members of the Unis family (if anything, Don's political involvements have kept him away from home more). For Don, being Arab has very little to do with Middle Eastern family structures. Instead, it is a matter of ancestry, political commitment, and personal identification with the global Arab community.

Identity Marriage: Or, Closing the Gap between Immigrant and Ethnic Worlds

Increasingly, Arab identity in Detroit is answerable not to shared blood and common origin, but to the choices people make—sometimes freely, sometimes by default—as members of a self-conscious kinship. One of those choices—marriage—is a powerful statement about boundaries, about where one belongs and where one is headed. In Detroit the desire to overcome cultural differences at the level of everyday family life leads to a practice people call, variously, "marrying back into the culture," "marrying an American-born," or "marrying a real Arab." Despite the confusion of labels, both partners in marriages of this sort are of Arab descent.

Consider the family of Warren and Amal David (figure 50). Amal is a Palestinian from the city of Nazareth, in Israel. She came to America to attend college in the early 1970s. Warren is a third-generation Lebanese American. In his family he is the only person in his generation (twenty-six cousins in all) to marry an Arab. Warren and Amal have two girls, and Amal's parents have now retired to Metro Detroit. They represent a kind of marital blend that is becoming more and more common in Detroit: one spouse is culturally Arab (often an immigrant), the other is American-born or American-educated. Warren and Amal bridge the gap between two worlds every day of their lives. Their children, who are sensitized to Arab and American ways, reap immense benefits, socially and emotionally. Amal, a feminist, is pleased that her daughters have an Arab father who, in her words, "loves them but does not try to control and dominate them." Warren is pleased to have a wife who can give his daughters an intimate connection to the music, food, family life, language, and Orthodox Christianity he finds so beautiful and came so close to losing. What Warren and Amal are accomplishing in

Fig. 50. The Davids bless their Sunday meal. Photograph by Millard Berry.

their relationship is a practical resolution of the four conflict areas that define the borderlands of Arab and American identities. By wedding himself to Amal and her family, Warren is increasing the intensity and cohesiveness of his family life; by wedding herself to an Americanized man and his family, Amal is decreasing the amount of patriarchy and gender segregation in her family life. Each party wants something different, and so far, both Warren and Amal have realized their goals.

All the bicultural couples I know—and I know dozens—talk frankly about how marriages of this sort keep people close to two cultures at once. Albert Harp, a teacher in the Dearborn public schools, was born in the Lebanese village of Kufr Houna in the 1950s, but his father, Rossette Harp, was an American citizen who had gone back and forth between Lebanon and the United States since 1938. Albert's grandfather, Haj Abdullah, was also an American citizen. The Haj came to America for the first time in the 1890s and, after nine return visits, eventually retired to Kufr Houna in the 1940s. Albert Harp spent much of his early childhood in America (he was naturalized at age six). He spent his adolescence in Lebanon and has lived most of his adult life in Dearborn. He is fluent in both Arabic and English; he is a devout Shia Muslim, a community activist, and a man generally averse to the isolationist tendencies of the newly arrived Lebanese immigrants who fill his mosque and school.

Albert knows he straddles two worlds. It is a Harp family tradition (figure 51). His grandfather, he told me, was much more Americanized than his grandmother, who never left Kufr Houna; Albert's father was "more American" than Albert's mother, who was born in Lebanon; and Albert, in his own view, is more American than his wife, who is also from the home village of Kufr Houna. For three generations, the Harps have been traveling in and out of Arab and American space, without much difficulty, and bicultural marriages are part of their traveling ethos. Albert sees no reason to believe this transnational cycle will soon come to an end. At the moment, his sons do not speak Arabic well, but their grandfather, Rossette, has retired to Lebanon, and Albert expects the family to spend more time there in the future. Perhaps his sons will marry village girls. As Albert would say when confronted by a future not his to control, "God knows best."

A Moment of Ambivalence: Or, Can We Do without All the Blood and Origins?

It would be wrong to imply that kinship is always the solution and never the problem. When grafted onto political agendas, the warm,

Fig. 51. Three generations of Harps: Haj Abdullah (standing), Rossette (seated), and young Albert, 1957. Courtesy of the ACCESS Museum of Arab Culture.

inclusive image of "the family" is often transformed into a concept that marks, with alarming precision, zones of stigma, isolation, and even violence. A tendency to perceive kinship—or, more exactly, the kinship of others—as a potentially threatening force, is common among humans. It is an effective weapon to use against immigrants (the ultimate Them), and it is a ready weapon for Arab immigrants to use against each other. In America, laws against nepotism are part of a cultural package that includes, in a place like Dearborn, stereotyped (and entirely predictable) criticism of big Arab families: the two-bedroom rental "with fifteen Lebs crammed into it"; the high school brawl in which "one white kid gets jumped by Hamoodi and all his cousins"; the liquor store where "they only hire their relatives." With the recent influx of Gulf War refugees, I have heard similar criticism unleashed against Iraqi Shia, only now the critics are Yemenis who cannot help but savor their new position one notch from the bottom of Dearborn's totem pole of (stigmatized) immigrant and ethnic groups.

Arabs often blame kinship for this sense of alienation from the larger society and each other. Communities of blood and origin,

I am told repeatedly, are jealous of each other, exclusive, and highly competitive, a fact Arab religious and political leaders have criticized (and capitalized on) for centuries. The great philosopher of history, Ibn Khaldun (1332–1406 A.D.), called this jealous respect for kinship ties *'asabiya*, a term often translated as "group feeling" or "solidarity" but also as "clannishness" and "factionalism." *'Asabiya*, Ibn Khaldun wrote, "produces the ability to defend oneself, to offer opposition, to protect oneself, and to press one's claims. Whoever loses it is too weak to do any of these things" (1967, 111). Ernest Hebert, writing six hundred years after Ibn Khaldun, analyzes the American (and now Arab American) fear of large, cohesive kin groups in terms the Arab philosopher would have immediately recognized:

> What we fear in such families is not their family affiliations but an x-factor that may threaten us; this x-factor is the power of kinship, a power that rises up from the inside and which serves not us but the members of the kinship. Not all families develop into kinships, and it's more than blood ties that make up a kinship. It's culture and class as well as clan; it's a selfish attitude that the group has about itself. (1993, 18–19)

Contemporary American society is replete with selfish groups of this sort, as are all complex, highly stratified societies. But these groups congregate in some areas of our national landscape more than others. In Arab Detroit, the x-factor is especially prominent, since:

1. The power of Arab governments to suppress it (through appeals to national unity) cannot be effectively exercised in Detroit.
2. Creation of inclusive Arab American identities is difficult among newly arrived immigrants who do not yet identify with pluralistic forms of American nationalism.
3. Second- and third-generation ethnic Arabs, who tend to identify neither with new immigrants nor with the regimes that today rule the "Old Country," find their Arabness in domestic, family culture or in American identity politics, which fosters clannishness of a not-so-different sort.

Under these conditions, the "x-factor" of shared blood and origin asserts itself with a vengeance. Business associations divide along Lebanese and Chaldean lines; mosques divide along national, sect, party, and village lines; social service agencies divide along Muslim and Christian lines; public access TV programs divide along all these lines. On either side of this multitude of dividing lines stand critics who complain that organizations are "run by," "controlled by," and "dominated by" cliques whose unity is rooted in shared blood and origin.

Some Arab readers will wonder why I have written so positively about an institution (family) and a social force (kinship) that clearly must change if such relentless divisiveness and parochialism are to be overcome. It would be fairly easy for me to endorse these criticisms. I have seen far too many community initiatives destroyed by clannishness and mindless factionalism. Far too many talented individuals are hemmed in and slowly suffocated by their kin. But the reality of family life is not reducible to a single story with a single moral. I have been trying to coax out of this essay a slightly different but equally important idea: namely, that the unmarked areas that exist between, across, and in spite of cultural boundaries are not simply areas of contest and exclusion; they are also areas of innovation, creativity, and progressive change. These hybrid zones are exactly the areas in which Detroit, as a new Arab world, is flourishing: in the arts, in politics and business, in religion, in the intellectual life of the community, and certainly in the lives of Arab American families.

(In)Conclusion: Or, A Parting Reflection on Borders, Lives, and Probable Futures

Whenever I doubt this upbeat conclusion, I think of Mujan SeifAzzou, the three-year-old daughter of Nader Seif and Wegdan Azzou (figure 52). The child of an interfaith, international, multicultural marriage, Mujan embodies several worlds at once. Her father is a Palestinian Muslim from Jordan; her mother is a Chaldean Catholic from Iraq. Nader and Wegdan are both American citizens, but their childhood memories, their first languages, and a large part of their psyche will always be rooted in Zarqa or Baghdad. Mujan's roots, by contrast, attach her to Arab Detroit. She was born there and she will probably grow up there. She will speak English and, as time goes by, less and less Arabic. She will have to combine the Muslim and Catholic beliefs of her parents and grandparents, or she will discard them and create new beliefs of her own. She will probably think of herself as a Palestinian and a Chaldean, but she will definitely be taught that she is an Arab, and as long as Nader and Wegdan live in Metro Detroit, Mujan's home will be filled with Arab faces, Arab food, and Arab music.

Fig. 52. Mujan SeifAzzou with her parents, Nader Seif and Wegdan Azzou. Photograph by Millard Berry.

Nader and Wegdan agree with most of these predictions, but my forecast for Mujan includes possibilities they find threatening. I suspect that Mujan, like other Americans, will go through a phase when she rejects her parents' values. This will mean rejecting things her parents (and the society around her) define as Arab. Although Mujan sings and dances and squeals with excitement when Nader plays her favorite Abd al-Halim Hafez records, she might learn to hate Arab music. Certainly, she will come to realize that her parents are not like other Americans, and this will puzzle her and, at times, confuse and embarrass her. As Mujan matures into adulthood and learns how to be "ethnic," the values and practices she rejected in adolescence will begin to please her and make her proud, but by that time she will be more American than her parents ever thought possible.

Nader insists that this will not happen—that it need not happen—and he is doing all he can to ensure that Mujan's connection to Arab culture remains strong. He watches Arabic TV with Mujan (and tries to keep her from watching too many English programs); he and Wegdan speak and read to her in Arabic (and try not to read her too many English books); and even though Nader and Wegdan are not especially religious, they occasionally talk about sending Mujan to an Islamic school, "Not for the religion. For the language." I occasionally suggest to Nader that these attempts to "keep America out of the house" all but guarantee that Mujan will someday rebel—indeed, they give her a well-defined regimen to rebel against—but I also tell them not to worry, since "She'll learn to appreciate the Arab heritage in her own way."

But then I realize that Nader and I are no longer talking about a real three-year-old girl named Mujan. We are building a model of her, then insisting that this model conform to the future as we see it and to "Arab" and "American" as we understand those terms. It is far too soon for that. I do not really know what lies ahead for Mujan. At the tender age of three, she is already derailing our plans for her. I remember the genuine shock on Nader's face when Mujan sang "The Itsy Bitsy Spider" to my wife, Sally, in English, complete with hand gestures. Apparently, she had learned it in day care. I, on the other hand, am constantly amazed by Mujan's ability to keep home and society separate. She knows that Sally and I are not Arabs, and she will not speak Arabic with us, even when we speak it to her. Mujan seems very comfortable with the idea that inside and outside are mutually exclusive. Why do I assume she will not be able to maintain that neat conceptual distinction into adulthood? Why do I insist that her two worlds will inevitably collide and that Mujan, as a person, will be fundamentally changed by the collision?

I insist because, as a "social scientist," I know the odds. I also know that, at the level of discrete individuals, historical patterns and social forms dissolve into a messy soup of aberrations, exceptions, and improvisations. I cannot pretend that Mujan is a statistical average; she is a real person. Like other people in her predicament—Nasreen, Jonas, Vicky, Daris—she will piece her life together from the patterns of tradition and change that are spread out before her by her Arab parents and the larger American society. What pieces go together, what parts of the pattern need to be altered to fit her unique personality: these are things Mujan SeifAzzou, sooner or later, will have to decide for herself.

ACKNOWLEDGMENTS: This essay has benefited greatly from the careful attention of Nabeel Abraham, Sally Howell, and Lara Hamza, each of whom offered insightful criticism of my method and the conclusions

I draw. Other readers, no less helpful, asked to remain anonymous. I have presented shorter versions of this paper to several audiences in Arab Detroit. I thank them for their (often emotional) responses, which have been worked into the final version in countless ways. Research for this paper was funded by the National Endowment for the Humanities as part of "Creating a New Arab World: A Century in the Life of the Arab American Community in Detroit," a public lecture, research, and exhibit project sponsored by ACCESS in 1994–95.

Note

1. Most of the people described in this essay are referred to by pseudonyms. In Arab Detroit, however, a pseudonym is no guarantee of anonymity. The community is close-knit, and clever readers can always figure out who "John Doe" really is. To avoid this problem, I have resorted to a method I call "scrambling," which entails mixing national labels (Lebanese, Iraqi, Yemeni, Palestinian) and/or personal details (place of residence, time of arrival in United States, occupation) from several real lives and applying them to one real person. The result is not a composite character—it is based on a real person—but neither is it one (legally) identifiable person. In some cases, the people I describe are perfectly real. For the sake of convenience, I will list the people in this essay who are not "scrambled" (in order of appearance): Amni Taleb, Yusif Barakat, Roy Freij, Joe Zainea, Sharkey Haddad, Don Unis, Warren David, Amal David, Albert Harp, Nader Seif, Wegdan Azzou, and Mujan SeifAzzou. Other characters might be exactly who you think they are; then again, they might not.

References

Barakat, Halim. 1993. *The Arab World: Society, Culture, and State.* Berkeley: University of California Press.

Cunningham, Robert, and Yasin Sarayrah. 1993. *Wasta: The Hidden Structure in Middle Eastern Society.* New York: Praeger.

Davis, Jon. 1987. *Libyan Politics.* Berkeley: University of California Press.

Gordon, Linda. 1988. *Heroes of Their Own Lives.* New York: Viking Press.

Hebert, Ernest. 1993. *The Kinship.* Hanover, N.H.: University Press of New England.
Ibn Khaldun. 1967. *The Muqaddimah.* Translated by Franz Rosenthal. Edited by N. J. Dawood. Princeton: Princeton University Press.
Sharabi, Hisham. 1988. *Neopatriarchy.* New York: Oxford University Press.
Swanson, Jon. 1996. Ethnicity, Marriage, and Role Conflict: The Dilemma of a Second-Generation Arab-American. In *Family and Gender among American Muslims: Issues Facing Middle Eastern Immigrants and Their Descendants,* edited by Barbara Aswad and Barbara Bilgé, 241–49. Philadelphia: Temple University Press.

Steps

Naomi Shihab Nye

A man letters the sign for his grocery in Arabic and English.
Paint dries more quickly in English.
The thick swoops and curls of Arabic letters stay moist
and glistening till tomorrow when the children show up
jingling their dimes.

They have learned the currency of the new world,
carrying wishes for gum and candies shaped like fish.
They float through the streets of Dearborn,
diving deep to the bottom, nosing rich layers of crusted
shell.

One of these children will tell a story that keeps her people
alive. We don't know yet which one she is.
Girl in the red sweater dangling a book bag,
sister with eyes pinned to the barrel of pumpkin seeds.
They are lettering the sidewalk with their steps.

They are separate and together and a little bit late.
Carrying a creased note, "Don't forget."
Who wrote it? They've already forgotten.
The purple fish sticks to the back of the throat.
Their long laughs are boats they will ride and ride,
making the shadows that cross each other's smiles.

Reprinted by permission of the author from *Fuel* (Rochester, N.Y.: BOA Editions, 1998), 79.

Index

Titles in the Great Lakes Books Series

Freshwater Fury: Yarns and Reminiscences of the Greatest Storm in Inland Navigation, by Frank Barcus, 1986 (reprint)

Call It North Country: The Story of Upper Michigan, by John Bartlow Martin, 1986 (reprint)

The Land of the Crooked Tree, by U. P. Hedrick, 1986 (reprint)

Michigan Place Names, by Walter Romig, 1986 (reprint)

Luke Karamazov, by Conrad Hilberry, 1987

The Late, Great Lakes: An Environmental History, by William Ashworth, 1987 (reprint)

Great Pages of Michigan History from the Detroit Free Press, 1987

Waiting for the Morning Train: An American Boyhood, by Bruce Catton, 1987 (reprint)

Michigan Voices: Our State's History in the Words of the People Who Lived It, compiled and edited by Joe Grimm, 1987

Danny and the Boys, Being Some Legends of Hungry Hollow, by Robert Traver, 1987 (reprint)

Hanging On, or How to Get through a Depression and Enjoy Life, by Edmund G. Love, 1987 (reprint)

The Situation in Flushing, by Edmund G. Love, 1987 (reprint)

A Small Bequest, by Edmund G. Love, 1987 (reprint)

The Saginaw Paul Bunyan, by James Stevens, 1987 (reprint)

The Ambassador Bridge: A Monument to Progress, by Philip P. Mason, 1988

Let the Drum Beat: A History of the Detroit Light Guard, by Stanley D. Solvick, 1988

An Afternoon in Waterloo Park, by Gerald Dumas, 1988 (reprint)

Contemporary Michigan Poetry: Poems from the Third Coast, edited by Michael Delp, Conrad Hilberry and Herbert Scott, 1988

Over the Graves of Horses, by Michael Delp, 1988

Wolf in Sheep's Clothing: The Search for a Child Killer, by Tommy McIntyre, 1988

Copper-Toed Boots, by Marguerite de Angeli, 1989 (reprint)

Detroit Images: Photographs of the Renaissance City, edited by John J. Bukowczyk and Douglas Aikenhead, with Peter Slavcheff, 1989

Hangdog Reef: Poems Sailing the Great Lakes, by Stephen Tudor, 1989

Detroit: City of Race and Class Violence, revised edition, by B. J. Widick, 1989

Deep Woods Frontier: A History of Logging in Northern Michigan, by Theodore J. Karamanski, 1989

Orvie, The Dictator of Dearborn, by David L. Good, 1989

Seasons of Grace: A History of the Catholic Archdiocese of Detroit, by Leslie Woodcock Tentler, 1990

The Pottery of John Foster: Form and Meaning, by Gordon and Elizabeth Orear, 1990

The Diary of Bishop Frederic Baraga: First Bishop of Marquette, Michigan, edited by Regis M. Walling and Rev. N. Daniel Rupp, 1990

Walnut Pickles and Watermelon Cake: A Century of Michigan Cooking, by Larry B. Massie and Priscilla Massie, 1990

The Making of Michigan, 1820–1860: A Pioneer Anthology, edited by Justin L. Kestenbaum, 1990

America's Favorite Homes: A Guide to Popular Early Twentieth-Century Homes, by Robert Schweitzer and Michael W. R. Davis, 1990

Beyond the Model T: The Other Ventures of Henry Ford, by Ford R. Bryan, 1990

Life after the Line, by Josie Kearns, 1990

Michigan Lumbertowns: Lumbermen and Laborers in Saginaw, Bay City, and Muskegon, 1870–1905, by Jeremy W. Kilar, 1990

Detroit Kids Catalog: The Hometown Tourist by Ellyce Field, 1990

Waiting for the News, by Leo Litwak, 1990 (reprint)

Detroit Perspectives, edited by Wilma Wood Henrickson, 1991

Life on the Great Lakes: A Wheelsman's Story, by Fred W. Dutton, edited by William Donohue Ellis, 1991

Copper Country Journal: The Diary of Schoolmaster Henry Hobart, 1863–1864, by Henry Hobart, edited by Philip P. Mason, 1991

John Jacob Astor: Business and Finance in the Early Republic, by John Denis Haeger, 1991

Survival and Regeneration: Detroit's American Indian Community, by Edmund J. Danziger, Jr., 1991

Steamboats and Sailors of the Great Lakes, by Mark L. Thompson, 1991

Cobb Would Have Caught It: The Golden Age of Baseball in Detroit, by Richard Bak, 1991

Michigan in Literature, by Clarence Andrews, 1992

Under the Influence of Water: Poems, Essays, and Stories, by Michael Delp, 1992

The Country Kitchen, by Della T. Lutes, 1992 (reprint)

The Making of a Mining District: Keweenaw Native Copper 1500–1870, by David J. Krause, 1992

Kids Catalog of Michigan Adventures, by Ellyce Field, 1993

Henry's Lieutenants, by Ford R. Bryan, 1993

Historic Highway Bridges of Michigan, by Charles K. Hyde, 1993

Lake Erie and Lake St. Clair Handbook, by Stanley J. Bolsenga and Charles E. Herndendorf, 1993

Queen of the Lakes, by Mark Thompson, 1994

Iron Fleet: The Great Lakes in World War II, by George J. Joachim, 1994

Turkey Stearnes and the Detroit Stars: The Negro Leagues in Detroit, 1919–1933, by Richard Bak, 1994

Pontiac and the Indian Uprising, by Howard H. Peckham, 1994 (reprint)

Charting the Inland Seas: A History of the U.S. Lake Survey, by Arthur M. Woodford, 1994 (reprint)

Ojibwa Narratives of Charles and Charlotte Kawbawgam and Jacques LePique, 1893–1895. Recorded with Notes by Homer H. Kidder, edited by Arthur P. Bourgeois, 1994, co-published with the Marquette County Historical Society

Strangers and Sojourners: A History of Michigan's Keweenaw Peninsula, by Arthur W. Thurner, 1994

Win Some, Lose Some: G. Mennen Williams and the New Democrats, by Helen Washburn Berthelot, 1995

Sarkis, by Gordon and Elizabeth Orear, 1995

The Northern Lights: Lighthouses of the Upper Great Lakes, by Charles K. Hyde, 1995 (reprint)

Kids Catalog of Michigan Adventures, second edition, by Ellyce Field, 1995

Rumrunning and the Roaring Twenties: Prohibition on the Michigan-Ontario Waterway, by Philip P. Mason, 1995

In the Wilderness with the Red Indians, by E. R. Baierlein, translated by Anita Z. Boldt, edited by Harold W. Moll, 1996

Elmwood Endures: History of a Detroit Cemetery, by Michael Franck, 1996

Master of Precision: Henry M. Leland, by Mrs. Wilfred C. Leland with Minnie Dubbs Millbrook, 1996 (reprint)

Haul-Out: New and Selected Poems, by Stephen Tudor, 1996

Kids Catalog of Michigan Adventures, third edition, by Ellyce Field, 1997

Beyond the Model T: The Other Ventures of Henry Ford, revised edition, by Ford R. Bryan, 1997

Young Henry Ford: A Picture History of the First Forty Years, by Sidney Olson, 1997 (reprint)

The Coast of Nowhere: Meditations on Rivers, Lakes and Streams, by Michael Delp, 1997

From Saginaw Valley to Tin Pan Alley: Saginaw's Contribution to American Popular Music, 1890–1955, by R. Grant Smith, 1998

The Long Winter Ends, by Newton G. Thomas, 1998 (reprint)

Bridging the River of Hatred: The Pioneering Efforts of Detroit Police Commissioner George Edwards, 1962–1963, by Mary M. Stolberg, 1998

Toast of the Town: The Life and Times of Sunnie Wilson, by Sunnie Wilson with John Cohassey, 1998

These Men Have Seen Hard Service: The First Michigan Sharpshooters in the Civil War, by Raymond J. Herek, 1998

A Place for Summer: One Hundred Years at Michigan and Trumbull, by Richard Bak, 1998

Early Midwestern Travel Narratives: An Annotated Bibliography, 1634–1850, by Robert R. Hubach, 1998 (reprint)

All-American Anarchist: Joseph A. Labadie and the Labor Movement, by Carlotta R. Anderson, 1998

Michigan in the Novel, 1816–1996: An Annotated Bibliography, by Robert Beasecker, 1998

"Time by Moments Steals Away": The 1848 Journal of Ruth Douglass, by Robert L. Root, Jr., 1998

The Detroit Tigers: A Pictorial Celebration of the Greatest Players and Moments in Tigers' History, updated edition, by William M. Anderson, 1999

Father Abraham's Children: Michigan Episodes in the Civil War, by Frank B. Woodford, 1999 (reprint)

Letter from Washington, 1863–1865, by Lois Bryan Adams, edited and with an introduction by Evelyn Leasher, 1999

Wonderful Power: The Story of Ancient Copper Working in the Lake Superior Basin, by Susan R. Martin, 1999

A Sailor's Logbook: A Season aboard Great Lakes Freighters, by Mark L. Thompson, 1999

Huron: The Seasons of a Great Lake, by Napier Shelton, 1999

Tin Stackers: The History of the Pittsburgh Steamship Company, by Al Miller, 1999

Art in Detroit Public Places, revised edition, text by Dennis Nawrocki, photographs by David Clements, 1999

Brewed in Detroit: Breweries and Beers Since 1830, by Peter H. Blum, 1999

Enterprising Images: The Goodridge Brothers, African American Photographers, 1847–1922, by John Vincent Jezierski, 1999

Detroit Kids Catalog II: The Hometown Tourist, by Ellyce Field, 2000

The Sandstone Architecture of the Lake Superior Region, by Kathryn Bishop Eckert, 2000

"Expanding the Frontiers of Civil Rights": Michigan, 1948–1968, by Sidney Fine, 2000

Graveyard of the Lakes, by Mark L. Thompson, 2000

Arab Detroit: From Margin to Mainstream, edited by Nabeel Abraham and Andrew Shryock, 2000.

For an updated listing of books in this series, please visit our Web site at http://wsupress.wayne.edu